A History of Political Thought

Once again, and always, for Gary and Georgia

A History of Political Thought

From Ancient Greece to Early Christianity

Janet Coleman
London School of Economics and Political Science

BLACKWELL
Publishers

First published 2000

2 4 6 8 10 9 7 5 3 1

Blackwell Publishers Ltd
108 Cowley Road
Oxford OX4 1JF
UK

Blackwell Publishers Inc.
350 Main Street
Malden, Massachusetts 02148
USA

British Library Cataloguing in Publication Data

A CIP catalogue record for this book is available from the British Library.

Library of Congress Cataloging-in-Publication Data has been applied for

ISBN 0–631–21821–1 (hbk)
ISBN 0–631–21822–X (pbk)

Typeset in 10½ on 12 pt Bembo
by Ace Filmsetting Ltd, Frome, Somerset
Printed in Great Britain by MPG Books Ltd, Bodmin, Cornwall

This book is printed on acid-free paper.

Contents

4 Aristotle   115

5 Cicero's Rome and Cicero's Republic   229

6 St Augustine   292

Preface

I have greatly enjoyed writing *A History of Political Thought*, especially because so many of the issues raised and for which I have tried to provide some explanations, are the result of discussions with generations of remarkable undergraduate and postgraduate students at the London School of Economics and Political Science. Coming from a wide variety of departments in the School, and individually from a range of international backgrounds, they have approached the thinkers of a long-distant past with energetic idealism and critical astuteness. This is all the more remarkable since the new managerialism and vocational functionalism dominating today's universities would lead us to believe that what an ancient Greek or a medieval Christian had to say about living a successful human life in a structured community in which they played active roles in contributing to collective governance, would have no interest for today's students. But in addition to the small number of Government Department students for whom an introduction to the history of Western political theorizing is a requirement of their degree, at the LSE the course is also taken as an open option by hundreds of students specializing in a variety of other social science subjects. And both more advanced undergraduates and our post-graduate political theorists choose to follow up the introductory course by focusing in depth on some of the thinkers discussed in these volumes. If we are meant to treat students as consumers who vote with their feet then I am delighted to inform the more sceptical among us that the history of political thought is alive and well, and this because students quickly see that the ideas to be studied here mattered and continue to matter.

At times I have had the impression that students are frankly relieved to be given the opportunity to look at world views that emerged from within historical, intellectual and social settings that are different from their own. And it has given some of them a space in which to reflect on their own, previously unexamined, but cherished views on what politics is for. It has also astonished them to see how much their own cultures are more or less reliant on certain strands of these earlier epistemologies, moral philosophies and theories of the 'state'. They have been both delighted and appalled. And everyone discovers a favourite thinker and (at least) one they most love to hate.

Because my students are asked to read set texts themselves and then to read as much historical background to get a sense of the 'theatrical backdrop' to these differing philosophical and political perspectives, as well as a selection of secondary analytical commentaries on these works, I am aware that I overload them in what is already an overloaded university curriculum. My aim in *A History of Political Thought* has been to provide as much of a historical and cultural setting as would make the texts they are asked to read look full of plausible and important arguments, given the dilemmas and circumstances their authors sought to address. Students cannot help asking themselves whether there are ideas here which just might be applicable to the present, and there is much shouting about whether or not past whole theories can be brought into a different and modern world. They are helped to make up their minds by seeing what specialist commentaries can tell them.

But academic disciplines have become increasingly specialized over the years and it is now virtually impossible to cover the results of international research undertaken by classicists who specialize in philosophy or history, to say nothing of the enormous amount of fascinating research on the early years of Christianity, the early Middle Ages, the political history, philosophy and theology of the high Middle Ages and the explosion of texts, written and printed, during the Renaissance. While I have tried to reflect a variety of current academic preoccupations in all these different fields of expertise – and here I have benefited tremendously from having edited the journal *History of Political Thought* from the beginning, when Iain Hampsher-Monk and I founded it in 1980 – I have also provided, as a consequence of my own years of research, some original and possibly controversial perspectives on some of these thinkers.

Had I been asked to write a textbook on these thinkers, say, twenty years ago, it would have looked more like a reasoned synthesis of other specialists' views and the footnotes would probably have been longer than the already over-long text. But at this stage in the game, I fear I know too much about how current perspectives penetrate the reading and interpretation of past texts that are none the less held to have something to say to us. All these years down the road I have come to realize, as I had not when a student, how there have been interpretative trends, often dominated by contemporary ideological preoccupations, which have closed off alternative readings. If nothing else, I have realized that certain utterances by past political theorists get differentially high-lighted in different generations. I have tried to indicate where I think certain current orthodoxies distort what an old text could have been taken to be saying by a past audi-ence for whom it was originally written. In believing this to be the least I could do, I have undoubtedly put my own imprint on a variety of texts despite the enormously generous guidance given me by Dr Paul Cartledge of Clare College, Cambridge for the Greeks; Dr Andrew Lintott of Worcester College, Oxford for the Romans; Professor Robert Markus, formerly of Nottingham University, for St Augustine; and Professor Nicolai Rubinstein of the Warburg Institute for Machiavelli and Renaissance Florence. I also owe a considerable debt to Professor Antony Black of the University of Dundee and Professor Brian Tierney of Cornell University, who offered their judicious com-ments especially on volume two concerning medieval and Renaissance political thought. I can only hope that where they do not agree with my interpretations or emphases, they will at least allow me to acknowledge with heartfelt thanks that I could not have come even to these views without their help. It is also to the numerous writings and friendship of two distinguished medievalists, Professor Dr Jürgen Miethke of Heidelberg Univer-sity and Professeur Jean-Philippe Genet of the University of Paris, that I owe a continu-ing debt of gratitude because they have kept me actively in touch, through off-prints and their invitations to conferences, with research done in Germany, France and other European centres, where approaches to the texts studied here adopt perspectives that often differ from those current in British and American universities.

It is not clear to me that there is any longer the institutional will to train students, as I was trained, in the languages, histories and philosophies that enable one to approach the texts of classical, medieval and Renaissance intellectual history. Today, a student who is drawn to a study of pre-modern ideas and historical settings will be asked why on earth such an irrelevant subject matter should attract any interest or indeed, funding. The student will probably require independent means and if persuasive, might be able to become enrolled in several university departments at once and for at least five years at postgraduate level in each. In Politics and Government Departments there has been a tendency to keep alive small pockets of normative theorists who have neither interest in nor knowledge of the history of their own discipline or of the languages they use with such confidence. This is to say nothing of what appears to be the sad fact that one department's agenda and methodology is now increasingly seen as incommensurable with that of another, so that specialists no longer seem to have either time or inclination to read each other's work. But the history of political thought is above all an interdisciplinary endeavour and that is by far one of its chief fascinations for staff and students alike. Of all the courses a student is likely to take at university, this is the one students tell me prepares them for being a serious tourist, and I have a stash of postcards going back over twenty-odd years sent from Athens, Rome, Paris, Avignon, Munich, Florence, Padua, Cordoba with statements like: 'it's seeing this landscape daily and the possibility of working in these buildings, and the quality of this strange light everywhere that made me realize why Aristotle or Marsilius or Machiavelli could say what he said the way he said it'. Furthermore, there is a sheer pleasure, physical and intellectual, which comes from a serious confrontation with the plausibility of alternative views on the living of a successful life. It is also a privilege to be able to read the musings of great thinkers, even if one is also aware that it is no longer quite possible to grasp wholly what they meant and why it so mattered to them – especially if one thinks them wrong. To try to listen to plausible, coherent and 'other' perspectives on human nature and its socio-political organization develops patience and tolerance, but more than that, a kind of reverence for the extraordinary creatures humans have shown themselves to be over the centuries. In defending their truths with such eloquence and energy they give us the courage to challenge that mentality which always seems to have been in our midst and which has sought to manage the creativity of individual and collective agency, not least by labelling people with critical ideas 'the chattering classes' and by pretending that a successful life lived in common is reducible to the 'social inclusion' that is supposedly achieved through market economics.

Several years ago I was astonished to read in Blackwell Publishers' current list of new publications that my long-awaited *History of Political Thought* was to appear imminently. I am thoroughly embarrassed at how long I have kept them waiting and I am grateful for their long-standing (and discreet) encouragement. It was meant to appear as the precursor to Iain Hampsher-Monk's excellent *A History of Modern Political Thought* (1992). Through the efforts of Jill Landeryou at Blackwell Publishers my 'long awaited' history of political thought now appears in two volumes: volume 1 *From Ancient Greece to Early Christianity* and volume 2 *From the Middle Ages to the Renaissance*. I am immensely grateful for her enthusiasm, advocacy and patience. But textbooks, no matter how original, are not highly regarded in intellectually ambitious centres like the London School of Economics, not least because national Research Assessment Exercises have financial consequences for departments and universities that seek to retain their high-flyer research-orientated status. Hence, during the years I had hoped to complete this history of political thought I was otherwise engaged in writing and publishing the work that was meant to matter. I have, however, been able to draw on this research material in these books and I hope that more advanced students and colleagues will find it useful, stimulating and contentious. In so far as the scholarly research has shaped the contents of what is meant to be a more introductory text, I can only hope that what I have done here gives students a view of how at least one academic sees the ancient, medieval and Renaissance worlds of political discourse as having sustained certain continuities and fictitiously constructed others. The primary hope is that it will get students to go back to the original texts and argue about them, thereby countering the tabloid scepticism about politics which has come to sound so loudly in all our ears.

Janet Coleman

Introduction

The two volumes of *A History of Political Thought* treat those political theorists who are most frequently discussed in university courses dealing with the history of Western political thought from the ancient Greeks to the sixteenth-century Renaissance. They aim to give students – beginners and the more advanced – a historical and a philosophical way of reading the set texts that are normally prescribed: Plato's *Apology* and *Republic*, Aristotle's *Nicomachean Ethics* and *Politics*, Cicero's *On Duties* and the *De re publica*, Augustine's *City of God*, selections from Aquinas's *Summa Theologiae* and other writings where he deals specifically with ethics and politics, and Machiavelli's *The Prince* and *Discourses on Livy*. Because there is usually a leap from the medieval Thomas Aquinas to the Renaissance Machiavelli, I have also included a range of political theorists (John of Paris, Marsilius of Padua and William of Ockham) who wrote during the fourteenth century and whose writings have been translated into English, and I have said something about fourteenth- and fifteenth-century conciliarism in order to give students some idea of the legacy of the Middle Ages to the Renaissance.

Canonical Difficulties

The writers listed above are *traditionally* considered to have contributed most influentially to political debate on the principles and practices of good government across the centuries, and therefore are taken to be the key figures in the history of European political thought.

This may look like an uncontentious statement, but it is not. Just how we evaluate who contributed most and how we determine which authors and which of their works ought to be included on the list of 'great political theorists and theories' are hotly debated questions, not least by those who teach courses called 'the history of political thought' in European and North American universities. This debate over the 'canon' consists in asking: how has the tradition become what we have taken it to be, and why have certain thinkers been traditionally included while others have not? Why, for instance, have there been no women?[1] Why, until very recently, are most of the 'great

---

1   See the various responses to this question in, for instance, M. L. Shanley and C. Pateman, eds, *Feminist Interpretations and Political Theory* (Oxford, 1991); C. Pateman, *The Sexual Contract* (Cambridge, 1988); D. Coole, *Women in Political Theory: from ancient mysogyny to contemporary feminism* (Hemel Hempstead, 1988); E. Kennedy and S. Mendus,

names' in this constructed tradition of an intellectual elite mainly dead, 'white' and male?

There has been considerable irritation expressed over the fact that even in recently published histories of Western political thought, the history of feminism has been relegated to footnotes. But a good deal of writing on the political tradition of dead, white males has precisely made the point that whatever else the history of much of Western political theorizing is, it is, and was meant to be, a male and white enterprise. Women's voices, black voices, colonial and immigrant voices, non-Christian voices other than those of the pagan ancient Greeks and Romans are, for the most part, absent. We should not thereby assume that dead, white males were the only distinguished theorists who existed in the past. But it was the seminal male-authored political theories that led first to a focus on sexual difference, to the extent that the early 'state' became an exclusive preserve of men, and more recently, to the contemporary modern liberal state with its persistent denial of difference and implicitly, its favouring of men as universal models of citizen rationality and behaviour. A history of 'our' political thought, that is, the varieties of political theorizing that have dominated and structured the West's 'state', is a history of narratives that either have edited out alternative discourses or have subsumed other voices within the dominant (male, white and Christian) discourses. No matter how eloquent the women or any other marginalized group of the past, they were not taken explicitly to have helped to construct the modern state and it is precisely for this reason that contemporary feminisms have challenged dominant male-stream political theories of all kinds. The reconstruction of a history, say, of feminisms in order to liberate women's voices from the past is, therefore, a different enterprise from the one that seeks to uncover and reconstruct what has been called the European, patriarchal state and its political theories. I shall try to explain, below, why I believe this to be the case.

Nor is the canon of 'great political theorists' as stable as some may think. It does not always include the same thinkers, nor give the same thinkers similar weight. This becomes clear when we go beyond the Anglo-American university and consider what different Continental European traditions take to be the 'great thinkers' on the principles and practices of good government. But in general, it remains true that when we select those names that appear on all lists, we confront what have only quite recently been shown to have been cultural prejudices concerning race, gender and religion. And it is these prejudices which have, through complex processes of exclusion and selection, determined which voices were, in fact, taken seriously in the past. There is no doubt that for specialists in any period, certain authors who are relatively or virtually unknown today appear at the time to have been much read and influential. Specialist historians wonder why their names and texts gradually disappeared in the references of subsequent generations and they try to provide some answers. Especially when we study the political theory produced from the period of the ancient Greeks to the sixteenth-century Renaissance, we can see this exclusion and selection process operating in the testimonies

---

eds, *Women in Western Political Philosophy* (Brighton, 1987); A. Saxonhouse, *Women in the History of Political Thought: Ancient Greece to Machiavelli* (New York, 1985); J. B. Elshtain, *Public Man Private Woman: women in social and political thought* (Princeton, NJ, 1981); G. Lloyd, *The Man of Reason: 'male' and 'female' in western philosophy*, 2nd edn (London, 1993); S. M. Okin, *Women in Western Political Thought* (Princeton, NJ, 1978); S. Rowbotham, *Women, Resistance and Revolution* (Harmondsworth, 1972).

of those who wished to make explicit to contemporary and future readers of their works which authors *they* believed to have influenced them. As a consequence, and retrospectively, the *traditional* canon of thinkers *is* surprisingly small and relatively stable and it goes back a long way.

Most of us would, however, agree *where* the history of Western political theorizing begins for us: in ancient Greece followed by ancient Rome. Today, however, we need to explain why this is so, because students come to read translations of Greek and Latin political and philosophical texts without any background in the culture or language of classical antiquity. This is a relatively new phenomenon. As recently as the first quarter of the twentieth century it was thought that a training in Greek and Latin was the prerequisite for being considered an educated person, even if we are under no illusions about the degree of fluency in either 'dead' language that was acquired by a nineteenth- and early twentieth-century elite of students. Furthermore, today's students often learn about the history of political thought in university departments which focus more directly on modern political and social sciences, where the historical and cultural contexts in which these theories were first generated are not necessarily discussed or even thought to be relevant to an understanding of these texts. Today, as never before, we need to ask and answer the question: why should we think the ancient Greeks followed by the ancient Romans, and thereafter, Christian medieval and Renaissance thinkers who selectively absorbed 'Greek' and 'Roman' lessons and adapted these to a Judaeo-Christian biblical world view, to be worthy of study, either in their own right or as relevant to our current concerns?

It seems to me that there are at least three interrelated reasons for beginning a study of the history of political thought with the ancient Greeks. The first two are so generally accepted as to be thought (wrongly, I believe) to require little further discussion. They concern (1) what we take 'the language of politics' itself to be and the range of its application ('language' is used here in its generic sense to include the many distinct discourses that developed over time). Related to this is (2) the belief that philosophy has a history within which political theorizing has played a determining role. Most people who are somewhat familiar with what is often referred to as 'the classical heritage' would agree that in some sense we owe to the Greeks our very willingness to accept that there is a distinctive 'language of politics' as well as the belief that what we think of as the discipline of philosophy began with them. But I would suggest that the reason we accept that there *is* a language of politics *and* a history of philosophy owes rather a lot to the third reason we begin with the ancient Greeks, and this is not often discussed by historians of political thought. I want to argue here that we begin with the Greeks because of the way in which a European (Euro-American, in fact) identity has come to be constructed over the centuries.[2] It is this constructed identity which has determined the significance to us of (1) the language of politics and (2) the history of philosophy in the first place. And it is also this process of constructing an identity which has ensured the exclusion of other voices from the traditional canon. Let us begin, then, with the third reason for starting with the ancient Greeks.

---

2   See, for instance, C. J. Richard, *The Founders and the Classics: Greece, Rome and the American Enlightenment* (Cambridge, MA, 1994); W. Haase and M. Reinhold, eds, *The Classical Tradition and the Americas* (Berlin and New York, 1994).

The Construction of a European Identity

European cultural identity came to be intimately tied to its purported foundations in ancient Greek culture and values not only during the Middle Ages but even more so during the sixteenth and seventeenth centuries. During this period the ancient world was intensely re-investigated as the inspirational source of a number of key contemporary issues. Perhaps the most prominent of these concerned how emergent national states understood the possible range of *legitimate* constitutions and their respective relations to citizens and subjects. Scholars declared Greece to have initiated something peculiarly European: a tradition of 'legitimate' government. Consequently, they separated ancient Greece from its actual cultural ties to its geographical neighbours in the semitic Middle East and Asia Minor. But they were not the first to insist that Greece stood out as different from those supposed 'non-European' traditions of autocratic, indeed often tyrannous government, despite their awareness that there had been Greek tyrants too.[3] Learned men during the medieval and Renaissance periods of Western European history also acknowledged the Greeks, and their heirs, the Romans, as superior to other civilizations. They lamented the loss of the traditions of Greco-Roman culture in their own times and nostalgically sought to revive and pass on the traditions of their illustrious forebears, however inadequately.

Important recent but controversial studies have emphasized, however, that ancient Greek cities displayed more affinities with the contractual trading republics of the oriental societies of the Levant and Mesopotamia and with the cities of the medieval and modern oriental (Arab) world which are their heirs than with anything that developed in Western Europe.[4] It is beyond doubt that European political institutions were, in fact, derived far *less* from ancient Greek *practices* than from Roman law and Canon (Church) law supplemented by an extensive knowledge of the Old and New Testaments, and from an indigenously developed feudalism and a common law that was based on immunities from monarchical powers during the European Middle Ages. Ancient Greece contributed little to these practices. Indeed, certain ancient Greek practices, like direct democracy, for which they are honoured today, were subject to severe criticism (by the Greek philosophers Plato and Aristotle), if not to 'editing' early on (for instance, by the historian Polybius in the second century BC, by the Roman Cicero in the first century BC and by Plutarch in the first and second centuries AD), as the legacy of ancient Greece was reconstructed by later self-proclaimed heirs who wished to favour a society based on differential rank rather than one based on the ancient Athenian acknowledgement of the equal potential of all free men to take turns in ruling and being ruled. During the Middle Ages, northern European nation-states did not see themselves as the legitimate heirs of the *historical* ancient Greek *polis*/city-state of which they knew little, but of that ancient *polis* reinterpreted by moral and political philosophers like Plato and Aristotle and thereafter, the Roman Cicero and other Roman historians, by the fifth-century AD Christian

---

3   J. F. McGlew, *Tyranny and Political Culture in Ancient Greece* (Ithaca, NY, 1993); G. Giorgini, *La Città e il Tiranno, il concetto di tirannide nella grecia del vii–iv secolo a.c.* (Milan, 1993).
4   M. Bernal, *Black Athena, the Afroasiatic Roots of Classical Civilization*, vol. 1 (London, 1987); P. Springborg, *Royal Persons, Patriarchal Monarchy and the Feminine Principle* (London, 1990) and P. Springborg, 'The Contractual State: reflections on orientalism and despotism', *History of Political Thought 8* (1987) pp. 395–434.

theologian St Augustine and the thirteenth-century medieval scholastic theologian St
Thomas Aquinas. Furthermore, even if some of the most distinctive features of Plato's
and Aristotle's preferences for monarchical or aristocratic constitutions can be shown to
reveal 'eastern' influences,[5] the eastern sources, none the less, came to be ignored early
on, indeed much earlier than during the early-modern period and for important reasons.
The point is that although some have argued for examples of democracy prior to the
Greeks (for instance, the tribal democracies of early Mesopotamia), their impact as well
as the impact of actual Athenian direct democracy on later European society was to be
virtually null.[6] If ancient Athenian democracy was itself to play virtually no role in the
forging of Roman, medieval, Renaissance and early-modern political institutions, a history of political thought must try to explain why this was so. What was the reason for
the most distinctive of ancient Athenian *practices*, a practice of direct democracy or rule
by the *dēmos* or mass, not surviving into later periods while ancient political *theories* did
survive?

There is no doubt that the 'idea of ancient Greece' was exploited – in what today
we may regard as historically inaccurate ways – to serve medieval, Renaissance and
early-modern Europeans' prejudices about themselves and others. None the less, ancient Greek culture *was* at the heart of a constructed European identity and this identity was in the process of being formulated well before the sixteenth and seventeenth
centuries. Through the descriptions, often critical, of the workings of its political institutions, and even more so through the doctrines of its various schools of philosophy,
through its sciences including medicine, its drama, architecture and sculpture, and its
tradition of historical writing concerned with narrating events in Greek history and
explaining why they happened as they did, ancient Greece played a foundational role
in the development of the Roman and Christian civilizations which chronologically
succeeded it. Even when the writings of the Greeks were later misread, awkwardly
translated into other languages or deliberately misconstrued in order to serve prejudices and beliefs the Greeks could not or would not have shared (and they had
plenty of their own, as we shall see), educated men took them to have set the agenda
for the ongoing debates in almost all fields of intellectual endeavour, not least concerning the principles and practices of good government and government's service to men
of principled behaviour. Ancient Greece educated ancient Rome in a selective way, or
rather, the Romans took the lessons they 'chose' and with the development of Christianity, both theologically and institutionally, the Greek legacy as it came to be construed by various Church Fathers with the Bible dominating their thoughts, was not
forgotten.

Instead of calling the ancient Greeks the first Europeans we could say that educated
Europeans have thought of themselves as having inherited a range of values and a variety
of institutions from ancient Greece. But it is even more accurate to say that educated
Europeans have thought of themselves as having inherited *ways of thinking about and
discussing values and institutions* from that extraordinary culture that flourished in several
centres in the Aegean, on the western shores of modern-day Turkey and in southern
Italy, most notably during the sixth to fourth centuries BC. The Romans and then various 'schools' of Christian thinkers interpreted Greek values and institutions in a variety

5   Springborg, *Royal Persons*, p. 405.
6   M. Finley, *Democracy, Ancient and Modern* (London, 1973).

of ways and then applied these interpretations to their own historical experiences during subsequent centuries.[7]

Furthermore, Plato and Aristotle, who more than any other ancient Greeks set the norms for the subsequent tradition of *political philosophy*, often tell their audience that they mean to criticize and provide a hostile commentary on some of the most revered values and practices of the city in which they lived – Athens. But when we read these philosophers and recognize that at times they are hostile witnesses, we cannot be certain that they are telling us how institutions actually operated nor what *ordinary* people thought of the values and systems of rules by which they lived their daily lives. Indeed, the history of political thought comprises the voices of a selection of men who, in their own times, were anything but ordinary themselves, nor (more importantly) were they considered such by future readers of their works. They were taken to be 'simply' the *best* of their age. Therefore, we can examine to what extent Plato and Aristotle appear to have shared or rejected their contemporaries' values by reading what they tell us are the opposing positions to their own. From these accounts we *try* to build up a picture of what it must have been like to be an ancient Greek and participate in their discussions. But we must be careful not to assume that we arrive at certainty in these matters, for the following reasons. The voices from the page are today presumed to give accounts that, on the one hand, are taken to be *normative* for their societies and, on the other, stand out as *atypical* in being perhaps more reflective, synthetic or critical than would be those of many of their ordinary contemporaries, were the latters' views preserved for us to examine. Only through a comparative examination of all surviving voices could we come to some view on the degree to which Plato or Aristotle, for instance, were representative of ancient Greek attitudes on a range of issues. But in the construction of a European intellectual tradition, representativeness of the 'ordinary' lived life of the culture from which these philosophers came was not seen to be an issue because it was *assumed* that their voices were exemplary of the *best* of their tradition and therefore, the ones worthy of being heard.

It is also important for us to realize that what we can uncover to have been ancient Greek attitudes *in general* – to slaves, to women, to non-Greeks, to honour, birth, leisure, to politics and society, even to democracy, freedom and equality (whether they were attitudes that were rejected or modified by contemporary political philosophers or were apparently accepted by them and even justified philosophically and logically) – were attitudes with which we now may have no sympathy. Furthermore, the *meaning* of Athenian values in their ancient contexts did not survive unchanged in later periods of history and in different cultures that, none the less, *can* trace their intellectual roots to ancient Greece. For instance, in translating from Greek to Latin, Romans often referred to what they took to be the same virtues in Greek society as in their own, but it can be established that they often meant rather different things by 'the virtues' than the Greeks appear to have meant. Nor did the philosophies of Plato and Aristotle, massively influential though they were on later European culture, survive unscathed in subsequent interpretations. Later thinkers believed themselves to be followers of Plato or Aristotle but, in the process of writing commentaries on these works and making these philoso-

---

7   See Andrew Sherratt's review of Alain Schnapp, *La Conquête du passé, aux origines de l'archéologie* (Paris, 1994), *Times Literary Supplement*, 21 October 1994, p. 6.

phers' theories their own, they changed them. It has been noted to be the fate of great persons who have put their mark on the ages that commentary very soon comes between their work and posterity. The commentary qualitatively goes beyond the works upon which it is commentary. 'More seriously yet: it becomes autonomous and generates a superimposed tradition which, driven by its own logic, obliterates the work from which it has issued, masks it, distorts it, and makes it disappear.'[8] A study of the history of political thought can show us that the *historical contexts* in which certain ideas became dominant, the dominant ideas themselves changing through commentaries and reinterpretations undertaken in different contexts, can answer some of the questions that philosophy cannot.

In general, then, we shall need to come to some decision concerning the degree to which the Greek legacy – *ways of thinking about and discussing values and institutions* – is affected by specific historical and cultural milieux: ours, theirs, and those cultures intervening between them and us.

Furthermore, we must try to assess whether we can apply any of the values argued for in earlier political theory to our own situations, or to the world as we think it is. This can be decided only after we have come to some decision about whether we believe that there is a possibility of our understanding what earlier political theorists meant at all, given that they lived in conditions that are not those of Western post-industrial modern society and we, of course, do not live in societies that are like theirs. To what extent do we have, as it were, other things on our minds of which the Greeks, indeed any earlier political theorists, had not the slightest conception? And to what extent did they similarly have things on their minds with which we may have no sympathy and, worse, no comprehension at all? To say that Europeans have constructed their histories and their identities, taking the Greeks as their beginnings, does not at first help us to understand how we can be certain that when *we* read their texts, we grasp what *they* meant. Is there a method by which we can read the political theory of past authors without imposing our current agenda on them, without confusing our interests with theirs?

Interpretative Difficulties

To raise this as a problem of understanding is to raise an issue that was *not* one during earlier centuries in which Europeans were in the process of forging their identity with the Greeks at the beginning. For centuries it had been thought that one could read the writings of, say, Greeks and Romans, and see there portrayed behaviour that was thought to be admirable in any age. The past was read about for no other reason than that it was thought to be exemplary and capable of being imitated.[9] It was reckoned to be a useful past. Hence, a fourteenth-century thinker like Petrarch, the Italian poet who was enamoured of what he took to be the personality and values of the first-century BC pagan Roman, Cicero, could imagine having an unproblematic conversation with Cicero in Latin. Petrarchan 'speaking' with someone from the ancient Roman world did not involve considering that the ancient might not understand him for the reason that each

---

8   J.-F. Durvernoy, *La Pensée de Machiavel* (Paris,1974), p. 3.
9   See J.Coleman, *Ancient and Medieval Memories: studies in the reconstruction of the past* (Cambridge, 1992).

came from such different worlds of experience and value that their words might refer to different things, Cicero's words conveying resonances that had been lost over the centuries to a Christian, late medieval, Italian user of Latin. Petrarch and other medieval and Renaissance users of Latin were aware that language *use* had changed over the centuries, indeed they increasingly damned the deviation of medieval church Latin from ancient Roman styles and tried to revive the latter. But while they acknowledged that Latin had changed over the centuries, indeed, according to them had declined as a means of eloquent expression, they did not believe that *values* had changed or that different social experiences might have led good men in different cultural milieux not only to exalt different virtues but build political systems that reflected these different values. Therefore, it was relatively unproblematic for earlier Europeans to converse with those whom they admired in the past and thus, to build up a picture of their chosen ancestors as being very much like themselves. For them there was an undoubted continuity between good and virtuous men throughout history. It was the construction of this continuity, the construction of a continuous European cultural identity with the Greeks at the beginning, that enabled medieval and Renaissance thinkers to raise to prominence the first two reasons I proposed for our beginning the history of political thought with the Greeks: the language of politics and the history of philosophy, that is, the language of 'our' politics and the history of 'our' philosophy.

The Language of Politics

If we turn to the language of politics as a reason for beginning the history of political thought with the ancient Greeks, we see that it is not only that certain contemporary words for specific types of constitution like democracy and monarchy derive from the Greek; indeed, our current political vocabulary (even the word politics itself) derives from the Greek. It is also that the Greeks came to speak about 'the political' in a systematic way within a detailed and unified world view and this is what makes them the beginning of a tradition of political discourse where 'the political' is somehow privileged and in which we share. By believing it possible to give a human account of the social world and then asking what role, if any, the gods, or good and bad luck might play in this account, the ancient Greeks fashioned a range of explanations which are still recognizable ways of speaking, for instance, about the motivation behind men's actions within social structures, and whether or not these structures should be viewed as having developed naturally or by convention. By enquiring into the nature of social reality they discussed the roles played in that reality by human consciousness and agency. Through observation, description and commentary on their own activities of reaching decisions in public and then obeying collective judgement, they came to formulate political theories that argued for the *principles* on which well-run societies must be based. In this way, they defined reasonable principles to guide human behaviour, on the one hand, and to justify a variety of social and political structures according to which they operated, on the other. Today, when we speak about a systematic and rational understanding of nature, of human psychology, of principles of human conduct and the relation, for example, between self-interest and morality, that is, one's own good and its relation to the good of others with whom one lives in community, we may not all come to the same conclusions on these matters any more than did the Greeks, but we are giving an account of 'the political' in a language that was developed to a high degree in ancient Greece.

In privileging 'the political' as an exclusive realm in which certain values such as freedom, equality and justice can be realized through rational debate followed by consistent behaviour (even if what we mean by these values in liberal democratic societies is not quite what the Greeks meant when they spoke of freedom, equality and justice), Greek discourse ensured that later generations would associate notions of participation, rights and freedoms with a distinct sphere of 'civilized' human living, the political realm that was, in the Greek world, confined to male soldier-citizens of the *polis*. Rationalizing activity carried on within a distinct and exclusive sphere of collective life has thereafter been taken, for good or ill, to be characteristic of a peculiarly Western understanding of the purpose of social institutions and their relation to free individuals who make choices about the ways they live their lives.[10]

The privileging of 'the political' was related to and perhaps dependent on another characteristic of Greek thought. It has often been noted, not least by the Greeks themselves, that there emerged a tendency in the Greek world to develop different methods for investigating distinct but interconnected subjects of study. The natural world, morality and ethics, logic and language, human psychology and theories of knowledge, human history and explanations of why things had happened in the ways they had, although related to one another, were also distinguished as discrete areas in which expertise and understanding could be acquired. In this way, those Greeks who specialized in one or more of these varied subjects of enquiry with distinct methods of proceeding, helped to set the agenda for what would become the education curriculum in the West, most notably the liberal arts as they were taught in medieval European universities and which survived well into the seventeenth and eighteenth centuries, and in some cases beyond. The specification of what subjects constituted the arts and sciences in the early-modern period and debates concerning what methods of investigation were appropriate to each go back to the Greek division, and especially to Aristotle's systematic version of the division of subjects, each with its own methodology and vocabulary.

The History of Philosophy: From the Pre-Socratic Naturalists to Moral Philosophy

This division of subject matter to be investigated follows the development of Greek speculation itself. The history of philosophy is thought to begin with what are known as the pre-Socratic naturalists (seventh to fifth century BC) who were concerned with enquiring into the nature and origins of the universe (*kosmos*).[11] It gradually shifts to those engaged in a more critical philosophy (fifth to fourth century BC), concerned with the foundations of morality and knowledge. Because we still take these kinds of concerns to be central to many contemporary major philosophical concepts, the beginnings of Greek

---

10   See the feminist debates on the gendered political realm alluded to in n. 1 above.

11   See M. Gagarin and P. Woodruff, eds, *Early Greek Political Thought from Homer to the Sophists* (Cambridge, 1995), pp. ix–xxxi and texts in translation; G. S. Kirk and J. E. Raven, *The Presocratic Philosophers* (Cambridge, 1957) and revised editions with M. Schofield; A. P. D. Mourelatos, ed., *The Pre-Socratics* (New York, 1974).

philosophical discussions are considered to be inextricably involved in the historical origins of philosophy as it is still practised. Most notably, the vocabulary of reflective and critical thought in ancient Greek has contributed key terms to our own philosophical vocabulary (*physis* – nature; *aletheia* – truth; *logos* – discourse, account, reason). How, when and from what origins Greek philosophy arose are questions which have been controversially answered from the time of Aristotle onwards. In general, however, Greek philosophy is said to have begun from a view of the world or *kosmos* as a well-ordered totality of concrete and relatively discrete things governed by uniform periodicity, a balance of cosmic opposites that are proportionately and symmetrically structured. The cosmic structure was taken to conform to an intelligible formula and this is the tradition from which the philosophical rationalism of Plato and Aristotle would emerge.[12] Indeed, Aristotle took the naturalists to be the first philosophers, concerned as they were with law and regularity, change and stability in the universe. Not only was nature viewed by some of them as an all-inclusive system, ordered by immanent law. The natural world was somehow the result of reason which, for some thinkers, was not itself part of nature but sovereign over it. A normative, necessary, rationalistic explanation of all that is, and which assumes a well-ordered universe, sometimes conflicted with an assumption that men can argue *from* reason and appearance *to* justified conclusions about objective reality. But in all cases, the pre-Socratic naturalists did not defend their arguments by appealing to the evidence of observation alone.[13] Rather, they relied on *principles* which were not derived from observation. They framed their scientific theories so that the use of observation relied on and indeed, confirmed, the theoretical principles of the sort they discovered. Hence, prior to observation for them was the assumption that natural processes conform to general laws and such laws are not known from authority or tradition but by *logos*, that is, by reason, by giving an account or an argument.

The shift from the focus on how the 'world' came into existence and to be as it is, to the question 'what do I have to know and then do in order to live a worthwhile human life which is what I desire above all else?' is the shift in focus that marks off the beginning of our subject, moral and political philosophy, from other philosophies in the ancient world. So the history of political thought in one sense, as a part of a history of philosophy, is thought to have begun in ancient Greece with the kind of distinct philosophical investigation which, as systematic reasoning, was consciously brought into the communal life. There it asked ordinary men to consider questions of virtue and vice, good and evil, justice and injustice, and the respective roles played by *nature* and *convention* in the constitution of a good society and the understanding of man's role within it and its institutions. Once this occurred, we confront discussions of human awareness and activity in a universe whose reality is governed by laws which somehow circumscribe human freedom, enabling men to distinguish between their capacities to cause 'events' and actions or to be caused or determined by them. As we shall see, aspects of these discussions have a peculiar, even discordant ring to contemporary liberal democratic ears.

---

12   D. Furley, *The Greek Cosmologists* (Cambridge, 1987); D. Furley and R. E. Allen, eds, *Studies in Presocratic Philosophy*, 2 vols (London, 1970–5); Mourelatos, *The Presocratics;* W. K. C. Guthrie, *A History of Greek Philosophy*, vol.1: *The Earlier Presocratics and the Pythagoreans* (Cambridge, 1962); vol. 2: *The Presocratic Tradition from Parmenides to Democritus* (Cambridge, 1965).

13   G. E. R. Lloyd, *Magic, Reason and Experience: studies in the origins and development of Greek science* (Cambridge, 1979).

To ask questions about the limits of human autonomy, about the extent to which humans can be the architects of their lives, individually and collectively, given their place in the natural and customary schemes of things, *however* one understands these to be arranged, is to ask not only about humans in general, but about the nature of the reality in which they are situated and within which and because of which they behave in what are taken to be peculiarly human ways. To ask these kinds of questions and also to try to find some answers is to engage in a kind of thinking that is meant to transcend time and one's own culture. It is meant to 'raise' the discussion to levels of abstraction that would allow people from a variety of different cultures to move beyond opinions prominent in their own society in order to discover the truth about such issues. On this view, the logic of certain kinds of arguments should be able to transcend people's opinions that tie their views to the historical times and conditions in which the argument may have first been made.

Certain Greeks thought it possible to enquire comprehensively, systematically and according to general laws and principles in order to disclose what they took to be evident or apparent regularities in the natural environment and in human cultures as responses to it. And instead of appealing only to traditional authorities, whether gods or ancestors, they insisted that a *logos*, a reason, argument, an account could be sought and found to enable them better to understand their collective social myths as well as those assumptions they already accepted when they said they understood common-sense reality. The discovery and account of what the basic laws of human nature are should explain not only how each and every society came into being but why they have the histories they have.

For some Greek thinkers, the *logos* discovers an objective and evident order in appearances. For others, the *logos* discovers a hidden order that is inaccessible to common sense, so that reality is to be sharply distinguished from appearance. Still others argued that human nature does not follow objective and independent laws at all, but rather, results from arbitrary human customs and conventions and therefore, our definition of human nature depends on culture and the processes of acculturation. On this view, there is no reason to prefer one moral outlook or one account of reality to another. Instead of there being a knowable and fixed truth about reality, how things are is a measure of convention; how things are is how they appear to any perceiver or thinker in a certain milieu in which he experiences what he experiences. These kinds of discussions and the debates concerning how humans evaluate reality and discover not only their moral convictions but the standards they use in judging or criticizing conventional norms, laws, structures of organized power, in their own society and in that of others, were central to Greek political philosophy, that is, to their systematic accounts of the social world. Variations on all these views still exist in our own world.

Here, however, we must pause. There is no Greek philosophy or social discourse which presupposes or aspires to the idea that man is self-made, an autonomous thinking 'I' whose cognition is culture-free. No Greek claimed what Descartes in the seventeenth century was later to claim: that there was only one clear and distinct idea to which man is inwardly compelled: *cogito ergo sum* (I think, therefore, I am), the existence of the thinking, conscious self, an idea which is established autonomously, privately, without any extraneous aid, and which transcends culture and its prejudices.[14] Culture

---

14   E. Gellner, *Reason and Culture: the historical role of rationality and rationalism* (Oxford, 1992).

for the Greeks was either natural (for instance, divinely established or simply the result of natural impulse), or conventionally established, but man was not usually conceived of as being capable of thinking without it. How humans classify and handle the things to be known was discussed by the Greeks in terms of an order that inheres in the culturally instilled manner of holding shared conceptualizations, and these came about through society. Greeks were prepared to admit that shared conceptualizations varied from one society to another and that the content of concepts was socially guided. But the boundaries of shared conceptualizations were understood to be acquired only by being part of a community, be that community a naturally or a conventionally established one and it is this which defined man for them, as distinguished from beasts. A hypothetical man who lived outside the social was, by definition, not a man at all but either a beast or a god. Man, for the Greeks, was rational in the large sense, meaning that generically, men think in circumscribed, shared concepts that arise in them by means of controlled and collective social habituation, be that acculturation process a consequence of nature or of convention (*physis* or *nomos*). Society, however it came about, through force, or through fear, or through a kind of pragmatic utilitarianism, or as the consequence of divine intervention, and however it was arranged, was sacred to them because it was the context in which 'man' could be defined. 'Man' could not be defined without it. This context was comprised of a shared history, rituals, myths, religions, customs and norms. In considering man's ability to reason, they situated him within a context where reason either lived side by side with Greek religion and myth or had to confirm religion and myth. Although some, namely the leading philosophers, came to depersonalize their conceptions of nature and they increasingly accounted for cosmic history without continual references to gods with human-like motives, they none the less did not separate nature from religion. They may have considered sense experience and human knowledge to be limited but they were not sceptical about the general orderly structure of the world or about the separate existence of gods and their general relation to humans.[15] Reasoned explanations were, for them, the means of rephrasing rather than replacing myth. This is a rationalism that is not the rationalism of modern analytic philosophy which begins, more or less, with Descartes, although elements of it can be found in Hobbes.[16]

What is often taken to be the modern notion of reason[17] assumes the existence of a generic faculty that is identically present in each human mind, capable of categorizing and calculating, and it assumes a general criterion of truth applied to all cases, impartially and universally, without being tied to local circumstances. When the emphasis is placed on the general criterion of truth applied to all cases, this modern reason's method of discovering it is said to be detached, procedural, a rule-following logic that is meant to liberate from a specific culture each self-sufficient and autonomous mind that operates

---

15   E. Hussey, 'The Beginnings of Epistemology: from Homer to Philolaus' in S. Everson, ed., *Companions to Ancient Thought, 1: Epistemology* (Cambridge, 1990), pp. 11–38.
16   J. Cottingham, *A Descartes Dictionary* (Oxford, 1993), p. 5 on the slippery concept of modernity and Descartes as the 'father of modern philosophy'.
17   See the co-authored introductory essay in R. Rorty, J. Schneewind and Q. Skinner, eds, *Philosophy in History* (Cambridge, 1984); K. Popper, *The Poverty of Historicism* (London, 1957); K. Popper, *Objective Knowledge: an evolutionary approach*, revd edn (Oxford, 1979); E. Gellner, *Reason and Culture*; J. Rawls, *A Theory of Justice* (Oxford, 1972).

on its own. Indeed, this kind of reason is meant to transcend the natural in the sense that it requires that explanations be subject to tests which are not under the control either of a prevailing system of ideas, an orthodoxy, or a culturally induced vision of the world. No world vision is allowed to dictate the rules of evidence. The truth this modern reason is said to establish is unified and systematic, external to and independent of any society's social requirements. Furthermore, and of great importance, a modern account of the truth is not meant to be stable; it is open to change and is ever revised. No stage in its progress is ever regarded as final, so that the past and its truth is always viewed as provisional. Modern truth is therefore cognitively unstable. But the means to its achievement is methodologically orderly and fixed. Through its logic of proceeding it is said to owe nothing to community, or to one society or another, when it gives all and sundry *the* valid view of reality, a reality that is thought to be immune from the dominance of any collective 'illusion'.

This modern reason is not ancient Greek (Roman or medieval and Renaissance) reason in certain fundamental ways. For Plato, notably, the truth is not open to change and revision. It is not progressive. For Plato, the truth is cognitively stable and access to it is methodologically orderly. This is because of his assumptions about cosmic orderliness and his belief that human reason may obtain access to it in the here and now. Aristotle, too, provides a version of this cognitive and methodological stability. There is similarly a range of prior assumptions which need to be uncovered before we can assess the cogency of the arguments of many other political theorists in the tradition of Western political theorizing.

How Should We Study the History of Political Thought?

The preceding paragraphs may appear rather abstract. But it is important that we consider the difference between 'ancient' and this type of 'modern' reason before we look at the writings of earlier political theorists. The purpose of trying to draw a distinction between ancient and modern reason is to elucidate some of the consequences of studying the history of political thought in one way as opposed to another. Modern philosophers and political theorists have increasingly displayed an interest in ancient philosophy and have applied modern logical analysis to ancient Greek texts, thereby seeking to attract contemporary students back to the classics.[18] They tell us that they are not engaged in reconstructing the past ideas of political history and therefore are not interested 'simply' in what the ancient Greeks believed and why.[19] They confirm instead that their interest in the history of thought requires a selection of past beliefs and arguments which are of philosophical interest to *them*. Such a selection of interesting philosophical ideas is not largely concerned with those ideas which *in fact* influenced social organization and behaviour in the past. Rather, modern philosophy is interested in the beliefs expressed in ancient philosophy for which a certain kind of rational argument has been provided and such rational arguments can then be assessed or evaluated *now* according to what *we* take to be the logical criteria of coherence and the cogency of inferences drawn,

---

18   S. Everson, 'Introduction' in S. Everson, ed., *Companions to Ancient Thought, 1: Epistemology*, pp. 1–10.
19   See the introductory essay in Rorty, Schneewind and Skinner, *Philosophy in History*.

assuming that the logical criteria of coherence are themselves timeless and the only criteria to be invoked in judging an argument. This philosophical approach has produced some stunning analyses which will be drawn on to help explain distinctive features of certain political theories of the past.

But let us consider the possibility that an ancient, medieval, Renaissance or early-modern philosopher held the views he did because of *non*-philosophical or indemonstrable beliefs that were sustained in his religion, society and culture, that is, let us consider that his philosophical discourse and its logic actually begin in unexamined premises that are held not to be open to logical proof or philosophical scrutiny. These views sustained by indemonstrable premises can be open to a kind of *historical* scrutiny of a tradition of enquiry and discourse, and this leads to another kind of investigation alongside the philosophical. This would not be, as some historians of philosophy seem to think, an investigation which 'merely' and uncritically reproduces arguments and conclusions as found in the original sources.[20] A 'mere' reproduction of original arguments is virtually impossible for us to achieve because a 'faultless reproduction' could only come about by doing no more than citing the text itself in its original language. And it would also require a 'perfect reader' who would have to be more 'perfectly receptive' than simply a contemporary of the author with whom the author intended to communicate, assuming the author knew how to achieve this.

Furthermore, students of the history of political thought today read ancient Greek and Latin texts in translation, and every translation is an interpretation. Indeed, every reading of a text is an interpretation. Once one re-presents an ancient, medieval or Renaissance argument cogently in *our* language, we require that an explanation be given concerning not only what we take to be the 'logic' of its argument, but why this kind of argument might have appeared plausible and sustainable to its original audience even if, and perhaps especially if, not to us. In other words, we would want to know what question these arguments were meant to answer in order to judge an argument both logically coherent and plausible *in given circumstances*. Only if we insist on the modern rationalist criteria by which we assess *all* past philosophical arguments for validity and universal truth claims achieved by a very specific (and narrow) understanding of reasoning can we dismiss certain past philosophical arguments as 'obviously fallacious',[21] and therefore take no further interest in them. In doing this we certainly extend our modern philosophical brief, but we lose in the process our historical sense and see the Greeks or anyone else as interesting only in so far as we can make them at home in *our* world, always assuming that our world is 'the world', explained according to culture-free criteria of truth.

Hence, a history of political thought ought not to limit itself to setting past political theories in a philosophical context of other contemporary theories (e.g. Plato surrounded by Sophists who were his opponents) and thereafter 'simply' assess them in terms of a universal, logical coherence and cogency appropriate to an autonomous mind operating on its own and divorced from local circumstances. The aim should be to examine the theories proffered against cultural norms and explicitly expressed, often theological or

---

20   This is asserted in the introduction to Rorty, Schneewind and Skinner, *Philosophy in History* and similarly by the 'Introduction' in Everson, *Epistemology*, p. 2.

21   Everson argues, in contrast, that 'Some of the arguments proferred by even great philosophers are too obviously fallacious to warrant our attention': *Epistemology*, p. 2.

metaphysical premises which have not necessarily survived as our premises. In doing this, the Greeks no less than the Romans and the medievals can be shown to have argued logically and coherently where they did so, given that we have grasped the questions *they* thought it important to answer. They can also be shown in important ways that were essential to their identity, not to have been like us and necessarily so. A balance between trying to understand the cogency of ancient arguments on the one hand, and an elucidation of why Greeks, Romans, medieval and Renaissance thinkers, respectively, thought the ways they did (and why we often think differently) on the other, is central to a *history* of political theorizing. It is, in other words, a history of sameness and difference.[22] In providing what I take to be the necessary socio-historical context from within which different political theories were generated, as well as often lengthy philosophical analyses of theorists' positions, I have attempted to satisfy some of the demands of modern philosophy without ignoring the claims of historians.

I hold to the view that we cannot always assume that the problems of political philosophy are eternal or subject to true solutions. To say this is not, however, to adopt the relativist position of the sort where anyone who happened to express a view can be defended across time. Nor is it the kind of historicism which thinks that human thoughts and beliefs are 'caged' by the context in which they were thought, so that they perish with the leaving behind of the historical time in which they came to light. It is simply to observe that the political theorists we study in the history of political thought were not all answering the same universal questions. Their activities are, for us, arranged in a continuum of changing problems in which the very questions that were asked changed over the course of time and culture. Therefore, we should not think that Hobbes's 'state' was his answer to Plato's question about the Greek political ideal, the *polis*.[23] From our point of view as readers of past texts who are interested in the evolution of political theorizing as an activity, ethical and political questions and their answers are transitory and historical rather than permanent. But some of the questions and answers still appear to be alive for us because they have entered our thought in an evolved state, a reconstructed state, having already been taken up, re-thought and reinterpreted by earlier thinkers who thought it important to keep *their* interpretation of the thought of 'their fathers' alive. The old questions and answers are part of our tradition of re-thinking, of making intelligible, in different intellectual and social contexts, these wide-ranging matters. In this way, the past necessarily penetrates our present lives. But ideas from the past are not universal or transhistorical; they have a history but not on their own. Their history is due to their having been re-thought, reconsidered and rendered intelligible by historically situated thinkers and we are the latest in the queue.

Today, what seems to hold this tradition of evolving thought together for us is our assumption that there is a universal logic of thinking as an activity. This is not a new idea by any means; Aristotle, in particular, works with this assumption. A thinking mind is assumed to have a nature that is expressed in the ways it functions as mind in general, and also as a particular mind with its dispositions and faculties which it exercises in

---

22   'The artefacts of the ancient world stumble upon different meanings in new locations.' James Davidson, 'To the Crows!', review of Bernard Knox, *The Oldest Dead White European Males and other reflections on the classics* (London, 1993), *London Review of Books*, 27 January 1994, p. 20.

23   Compare R. G.Collingwood, *The Idea of History* (Oxford, 1946), p. 229; G. W. F. Hegel, *Lectures on the Philosophy of World History*, trans. H. B. Nisbet (Cambridge, 1975), first draft, p. 21.

contingent, historical circumstances to express its individual thoughts. But this does not mean that mind's activities lead, in specific past and future moments, to the same, unalterable, universally applicable conclusions, so that how humans will think and act in the future may be fixed forever by laws that are determined on the basis of how minds have thought and men have acted in the past. Some of the thinkers we study in the history of political thought did, however, believe this to be the case. I have already noted that it was quite common for past European thinkers to assume that men of antiquity were just like them and that is why they believed they could imitate past actions by uncovering universal laws of human behaviour that operated in all circumstances.[24] Today, we assume something a bit different.

Today, psychologists and neuroscientists seem to assume that humans do share a general procedure in thinking, that mind is recognizably structured and it happens to function in ways determined by its structure. But what individual minds happen to think is not simply dependent on their functional capacities, but rather on function related to the determinate situations they are in. Such determinate, contingent situations are not repeatable over long tracts of time. *Types* of human behaviour may seem to recur when thinking humans are taken to be in the same kinds of situations, but when, with hindsight, we observe that the social structures and certain of men's values have changed, then the types of behaviour also change and men think and act in ways that respond to the collective and individual, historically transient circumstances they are in. We recognize this when we say not only that ancient Athenian and Spartan societies were different from the societies of fourteenth-century Italian city-states and, in turn, all of these were different from our own society, but also that each society left evidence of substantively different behaviour and activity. This seems to be a relatively modern observation and one that matters to us today. But it is a perspective on the past that was not shared by medieval and Renaissance thinkers when they recorded their reflections on what they took to be the *essential similarity* between ancient Greek and Roman societies and their own.[25] For them, the basic situation between persons where virtue and vice were exposed remained always the same with every deed arising from this basis. The recurring occasions which gave rise to appropriate alternatives in human behaviour – courage or cowardice, truth or mendacity, moderation or excess – were considered the primordial conditions which were never superseded, so that moral behaviour could be viewed as typical, and hence, it conformed to precedent. But for us, what might be considered acts of courage and cowardice, moderation or excess, even rational or irrational behaviour, are not taken to be essentially the same in all cultures, nor across time.

Therefore, the continuity between, say, Plato's thinking and ours has to be *established* by our thinking in a new context, ours, what he tells us in his texts he took to be, for instance, the components of the unchanging ideal of political life. But our understanding of it is as a Greek ideal and not as one of ours. The common ground we share with Plato is not, of course, context. Nor is it enough to say that we all share an ability to understand the logic of coherent expression so that we grasp Plato's meaning by doing no more than

---

24   This is further discussed at length in J. Coleman, *Ancient and Medieval Memories.*
25   J. Coleman, *Ancient and Medieval Memories,* and J. Coleman, 'The Uses of the Past (14th–16th Centuries): the invention of a collective history and its implications for cultural participation', in A. Rigney and D. Fokkema, eds, *Cultural Participation: trends since the Middle Ages,* Utrecht Publications in General and Comparative Literature 31 (Amsterdam, 1993), pp. 21–37.

read his texts (in translation). To take Plato or any other past political theorist seriously we need, in addition, to situate Plato and attempt to recognize the range of his meanings, a range that is in part determined by his ancient Greek context and his ancient Greek language, so that we are aware, at least to some degree, of how this context places a limit on what he could *not* have said or meant.[26] This does not leave us without access to the logic of his communication. But the logic is insufficient to convey his meaning or the way in which his views were received when he communicated to his contemporaries.

We cannot, of course, crawl into Plato's psychology, but we can and do respond to the ahistorical logic of his various positions which speak beyond the text and beyond his age, and we also try to reconstruct his cultural premises in order to place this logic within a context of the underlying presuppositions and accepted principles he never argued for. In this way, we modify our own ways of thinking *and* the thought of the author we read without ever eliminating our modern overview. We achieve an awareness that past thinking and activity are both similar to and also different from present thinking and activity. We are unable to conceive of past political thinking as wholly alien and different from the present because if we did so conceive of it, we would have no means of making any sense of it. Some ways of thinking may no longer be current but they cannot be completely lost to us or we would have no access to them. But this does not mean that texts from the past do no more than present us with mirror images of ourselves. The history of political theorizing is a history of changing but related ideals of personal conduct as well as of ideals of social organization. And we make sense of these changing ideals by attempting to grasp something about what people of a certain time and culture believed about the nature of their world even if, or perhaps especially if, it is not what we believe about the nature of our world.

We can never re-present the past or past thinking in a pure form. These are always mediated through our present perspectives and orientations.[27] This was no less true of Romans reflecting on Greece, or of medieval churchmen reflecting on Rome. And this is precisely why in our reconstruction of past arguments we need to engage *both* a philosophical and a historical sense. Doing this we can assess a philosophical proposition in terms of what we take to be its logical cogency, *which is, in practice, how we first read any text*. But we must then go back and look at the argument as a historical phenomenon, as a local utterance, and try to place it in terms of the circumstances in which it emerged and to reconstruct plausible reasons for which it was enunciated in a particular language. We must examine a text within the context of an author's contemporary world of meaning and distinguish, where we can, its differentness from ours, in order to show, at least minimally, what an author might have meant as well as what he could not possibly have meant. This language, as a social product, rather than as the author's private code, cannot but have been used by the author to argue his position with his contemporaries.[28] But social codes or discourses, ways of speaking and using words, indeed, the concepts

---

26   See P. King, ed., *The History of Ideas: an introduction to method* (London, 1983), especially King's contribution, pp. 3–65; Q. Skinner, Parts II and IV in J. Tully, ed., *Meaning and Context: Quentin Skinner and his critics* (Oxford, 1988).

27   See H.-G. Gadamer, *Truth and Method*, 2nd revd edn, trans. J. Weinsheimer and D. G. Marshall (London, 1989), part II, i.1: 'Elements of a theory of hermeneutic experience'.

28   See R. Ashcraft, *Revolutionary Politics and Locke's Two Treatises of Government* (Princeton, NJ, 1986), especially the introduction; J. G. A. Pocock, 'The Concept of Language and the *Métier d'historien*: some considerations on practice', in A. Pagden, ed., *The Languages of Political Theory in Early-Modern Europe* (Cambridge, 1987), pp. 19–40; D. Boucher, *Texts in Context: revisionist methods for studying the history of political thought* (Dordrecht, 1985).

expressed by the words spoken, all have histories that are developed by the social groups that use these languages and who, inadvertently or consciously, change the previously accepted meanings of terms.[29] There are linguistic histories that are then situated in non-linguistic, socio-economic and political contexts which also have histories. Ideas, languages and customary non-linguistic behaviour all have histories, they all change, but not necessarily at the same rate.

We all need a 'crib' when we read Shakespeare today because we no longer speak that historically 'local' kind of English that was current in the sixteenth century. But with a bit of help with sixteenth-century definitions and information on how the constraints of sixteenth-century literary genres operated, along with information on the social and political life of his times and how this was discussed by the author and his contemporaries, we grasp a meaning that is coherent although it still will not be precisely a sixteenth-century meaning. We may not agree with the views expressed or we may even find some of them implausible. Some positions may appear very strange to us and we may not be able to sustain them in our own world with its current discourses. And yet some positions appear to have been sustained in languages other than the author's own. It is here, in the reconstructed *uses* made of earlier political theories by later generations and societies in different historical contexts, that we can observe how and why political theories are open to a kind of survival as intelligible, where practices as enshrined in particular institutions often are not.

With this in mind, we can point to a distinctive feature of the social context in which Greek political philosophy's discourse developed. Their systematic accounts of the social world became a kind of critical reflection on moral and political questions that was not confined to speculatively trained small groups of men. It was engaged in more widely, especially in fifth- and fourth-century BC Athens, where questions and arguments concerning whether ethical values exist by nature or by convention were raised both for and against the prevailing democratic order. Indeed, the very conditions of Athenian democracy appear to have created a unique and fruitful, unresolved tension between social elites and the mass of people, a tension which seems to have been the very source of much of the Greek literature that Europeans take to have been foundational for their own intellectual identity. The democratic order allowed traditional elites and the ambitiously competitive within the society the scope for criticism and a valid place to express their values and their dissent from democracy. It has plausibly been argued[30] that the educated elites were cast in the role of critics by Athenian democratic practice itself, which not only allowed forms of dissent but often actively provoked it from all quarters. Precisely because the critical reflection on moral and political questions was not limited to debates between philosophers, the history of political thought in general and its beginnings in ancient Greek culture in particular, pays attention to more than the writings of political philosophers in order to grasp the discursive context in which such

---

29   See the explanatory method of *Begriffsgeschichte* in R. Koselleck, *Futures Past: on the semantics of historical time*, trans. K. Tribe (Cambridge, MA, 1985); M. Richter, *The History of Political and Social Concepts: a critical introduction* (Oxford, 1995); and the various contributions to H. Lehmann and M. Richter, eds, *The Meaning of Historical Terms and Concepts: new studies on Begriffsgeschichte*, German Historical Institute occasional paper, 15 (Washington, DC, 1996); see J. G. Gunnell, 'Time and Interpretation: understanding concepts and conceptual change', *History of Political Thought* 19 (1998) pp. 641–58.

30   J. Ober, *Mass and Elite in Democratic Athens: rhetoric, ideology and the power of the people* (Princeton, NJ, 1989).

philosophers said what they said. It takes into account other kinds of evidence such as contemporary drama, historical writings, or political speeches and legislation in order to assess what the surviving sources reveal about the business of conducting political affairs, especially in Athens.

The historian Herodotus (c. 484–425 BC), for instance, not only provides a comparative description of Greek and non-Greek political systems, but he also appeals (as did the pre-Socratic naturalists) to general laws which allow him to evaluate how people with certain customs and in distinctive environments may be expected to act in given circumstances. He explains the collective actions of Athenians and Spartans and attributes their respective success to their collectively held moral and political outlooks. For him, types of societies and specific social and political institutions produce expected effects on men's actions. Hence, history is, for Herodotus, a kind of enquiry, a methodological investigation of the relation between men and their environments which must be carried out *before* one composes one's narrative account of what happened, when, where and why. In explaining Athenian success he refers not only to the actions and decisions of aristocratic individuals but also to the collective behaviour of the people, the *dēmos*, in the growing democracy, which resulted in a greater sense of individual responsibility for the *polis* and its well being. Democratic Athens was not, for Herodotus, some happy accident; it was caused and the historian could assert the consequent effects. Herodotus did not collect his empirical evidence uncritically. But his is an additional 'voice' to that of the philosophers Plato and Aristotle on the principles and practices of Athenian democracy.

So too, the 'voice' of the historian Thucydides (c. 460–400 BC) must be added to that of the philosophers. His account of the Peloponnesian War (431–404 BC) was meant to illustrate how the basic *laws of human nature in collectivities*, once known, can explain social and historical processes and predict men's behaviour, especially in times of war and revolution. In the seventeenth century, Hobbes would provide the first English translation from the Greek and develop Thucydides' argument that a study of human nature in the conditions of peace and war leads to the conclusions that men are motivated to observe justice out of a more basic concern for their own power and from a fear of loss of security.[31] Those who believe that men are motivated by moral considerations over and above a concern for power and fear are, according to Thucydides, deceiving others if not themselves as well. His views on the evolution of the democracy under Perikles, in mid-fifth-century Athens, provide a critical evaluation of the subsequent democratic populism (to 411 BC) when politics was no longer in the hands of his hero, Perikles, Athens' first citizen. Of course, Thucydides' laws of human nature are influenced by his political views and these colour his analysis of the events he narrates. But like Herodotus, he provides us with his version of the cultural ideal so that we can also add his 'voice' to that of the philosophers on the principles and practices of Athenian democracy.

Some of the thinkers who are most well known to historians of political thought, like Plato and Aristotle, and whose orientation was more or less anti-democratic in

---

31 Thucydides, *History of the Pelopponesian War*, 4 vols, trans. C. F. Smith (Loeb Classical Library) (London, 1965), III.82. 1–2, 84.2. See also E. Hussey, 'Thucydidean History and Democritean Theory', in P. Cartledge and F. D. Harvey, eds, *Crux: essays presented to G. E. M de Ste. Croix on his 75th birthday*; also in *History of Political Thought* 6 (1985), pp. 118–38.

democratic Athens, persisted in their concentration on moral philosophy even to the extent of creating, as in Plato's case, a theoretical city that was in crucial ways the *opposite* of the classical, Athenian *polis*. Committed democrats, on the other hand, often responded to their attack simply by going about the business of conducting political affairs according to their own notions and established traditions without writing theoretical treatises. If this means for us that we lack contemporary writing of the kind *we* might call 'political science', we do, none the less, know something of the range of political ideals and behaviour 'on the ground'. In so far as accounts of the ancient Greek practice of politics survived, along with the justifications for the developments of customs, laws and constitutions, in the writings of dramatists or in the works of historians like Herodotus and even more so, Thucydides, or in the accounts of those who made political speeches in the Athenian Assembly (e.g. Demosthenes), along with the more strictly political analysis provided by the 'Aristotelian' *Athenian Constitution* (*c.* 320 BC),[32] the form of political organization that evolved in Athens over the course of the sixth to fourth centuries BC has come to be better known. Indeed, from these additional sources a model of democratic political behaviour and institutional practice became available to later, especially post-Renaissance generations, to supplement if not to balance the accounts offered by Plato and Aristotle in their philosophical works. That later political theorists still remained more impressed by the ancient political theory of the philosophers than by ancient political practice tells us something about the later historical culture and its perceived requirements. But from our point of view, which is concerned to situate Plato's and Aristotle's theories in the context that helped to generate them, we need to examine these other sources. If we can construct a picture of what Athenian democracy was like it will help to provide a background against which Plato's philosophical dialogues and Aristotle's ethical and political philosophy can be set. It was, after all, to their contemporaries that these philosophers addressed their works in the first instance, Plato establishing a school known as the Academy where Aristotle himself studied before he later came to set up his Lyceum.

---

32 See P. J. Rhodes trans. and ed. the Aristotelian *Constitution of the Athenians* (Harmondsworth, 1984) and Rhodes, *A Commentary on the Aristotelian Athenaion Politeia with Addenda* (Oxford, 1993).

1

Ancient Athenian Democracy

Two Hundred Years of Greek Democracy

The Greeks were not Greek. They called themselves Hellenes by the seventh century BC and before that, Achaeans or Argives or Danai. In the fifth century BC the historian Herodotus, himself probably not of purely Hellenic origins and a subject of the Persian Empire, tried to define what it meant to be self-consciously Greek (*to Hellēnikon*) in terms of common blood, language, religion and customs.[1] Herodotus also tells his readers that an early form of *dēmokratia* can be traced back to the early fifth century BC in a variety of Greek cities in which popular rule was adopted to replace tyrannies. If *dēmokratia* was not an Athenian invention it was said to be of Greek origin, although we have noted that some have argued for even earlier tribal democracies. Democracy was even more self-consciously elaborated and introduced into Athens by Kleisthenes in 508/7 BC[2] and developed through numerous reforms to culminate in the period of Demosthenes' speeches in 355–322 BC and Aristotle's description of democracy in general and Athenian democracy in particular *c.* 330 BC.

Etymologically *dēmokratia* means power or rule (*kratos*) by the people (*dēmos*). Some scholars have made much of the fact that the evolution of democratic institutions and ideals most notably occurred during a period of nearly two hundred years in which Athens engaged in warfare: resistance to two Persian invasions of Greece (490, 480) with Athens (and allies) victorious; the Peloponnesian war against a coalition headed by Sparta (431–404) with Athens defeated and her empire dissolved; wars against Philip of Macedon ending with the Battle of Khaeronea (338).[3] The democratic *polis* has been seen as one successful arrangement for collective action against regular, outside threats. In the ancient world, then, democracy was an evolving political system as well as a set of

---

1   See P. Cartledge, *The Greeks* (Oxford, 1993), p. 11 who argues that although the Greeks were not unique in dividing humanity into ideological polarizations, Us and Them, Greeks and non-Greeks/barbarians, they showed a more developed ideological habit of polarization that Cartledge thinks was a hallmark characteristic of their mentality.

2   Herodotus, *The Histories*, trans. A. de Sélincourt, revd A. R. Burn (Harmondsworth, 1972), 5.66, 69, 78; 6.131.

3   See A. Lintott, *Violence, Civil Strife and Revolution in the Classical City* (London, 1982); D. Cohen, *Law, Violence and Community in Classical Athens* (Cambridge, 1995) discusses the courts as competitive arenas where conflicts continued to be played out in what was a feuding society; C. Meier, *Die Rolle des Krieges im klassischen Athen* (Munich, 1991) – without war, no democracy – following the insights of Max Weber, *Economy and Society* [*Wirtschaft und Gesellschaft*], 2 vols, ed. and trans. G. Roth and C. Wittich (Berkeley, 1978).

ideals, both of which were effectively destroyed at Athens after Philip of Macedon's heir, Alexander the Great, had died. This means it lasted for about two hundred years. It also means that ancient democracy was brought to an end not through internal failure but by external intervention.[4]

Between *c.* 300 BC and *c.* AD 1800 democracies were only momentary realities: some have suggested twelfth to thirteenth-century Iceland, some Swiss cantons from the thirteenth century, possibly Florence during brief periods in the mid-thirteenth and later fourteenth centuries. A 'radical republic' is the more accurate term for the Florentine constitution.[5] Until the later eighteenth century the Western world preferred to listen to those political philosophers who normally favoured 'mixed constitutions', republics with a princely element or constitutionally limited monarchies, because these corresponded more closely to their ideals of contemporary European regimes based on rank than did ancient democracy. Before the nineteenth century a direct democracy of the sort that flourished in Athens in the fifth to fourth centuries BC was regarded with disdain, if not fear. Eighteenth-century commentators frequently pointed to the failings of Athenian democracy, by which was meant its apparent lack of any mechanism for 'harmonizing the various ranks of men' of which it was believed any nation must consist.[6] Greek democracy in particular was said to have been in constant turmoil because of the idle 'poorer many' who considered themselves free from serving the propertied few, not only because it was thought that in ancient society slaves did all the work but also because the poor, free citizens received state payment for performing their public duties. It was believed that this was a society without the economic mutual dependence between ranks which alone, for eighteenth-century thinkers, could lead to a 'common national interest'. When, in the nineteenth century, direct democracy was taken to be no more than a historical concept, the word *democracy* came to be used in a more favourable way, but now to mean the government of the whole people *by a majority, themselves represented.* Hence, there is not an unbroken tradition of democracy from ancient to modern times.[7]

Ancient Athenian Democracy in General During the Fifth and Fourth Centuries BC

Because Athenian democracy inscribed its state documents on stone (most regularly from *c.* 460 onwards) and Athenians (and non-Athenians who lived in Athens) produced a great deal of literature in the fifth and fourth centuries, we have more information

---

4 On the extinction of democracy see G. E. M. de Ste Croix, *The Class Struggle in the Ancient World* (London, 1981), Appendix IV, and chapter 5, this volume. J. M. Bryant, *Moral Codes and Social Structure in Ancient Greece: a sociology of Greek ethics from Homer to the Epicureans and Stoics* (Albany, NY, 1996), ch. 5 ('Fourth-century Greece and the Decline of the Polis') argues for the combined external Macedonian pressure with internal conflicts between rich and poor in a fragmenting civic order. For an overview based on his previous prolific and distinguished studies see M. H. Hansen, *Athenian Democracy in the Age of Demosthenes: structure, principles and ideology* (Oxford, 1991).
5 See *A History of Political Thought*, volume 2, ch. 6.
6 E. M. Wood, *Peasant–Citizen and Slave: the foundations of Athenian democracy* (London, 1988), pp. 14–15.
7 See, for instance, M. H. Hansen, *The Athenian Assembly in the Age of Demosthenes* (Oxford, 1987), pp. 5–6; J. T. Roberts, *Athens on Trial: the antidemocratic tradition in western thought* (Princeton, 1994). The classic is M. I. Finley, *Democracy Ancient and Modern* (London, 1973); see also M. H. Hansen, 'Was Athens a Democracy? Popular rule, liberty and equality in ancient and modern political thought', *Historisk-filosofiske Meddelelser* 59 (Copenhagen, 1989), pp. 3–47.

about Athens than about any other classical Greek *polis*.[8] These documents show that as a political system and as a set of ideals ancient Athenian democracy was not representative. Unlike indirect democracies which centre on elections of representatives, Athenian democracy as a political system was direct rule by the citizens in Assembly (*Ekklēsia*) and Courts (*Dikastēria*). In the Assembly, the decisions concerning major communal issues were taken in public by a simple majority, usually by a show of hands, after open debate between all citizens who wished to participate. Nor was there any state bureaucracy to speak of beyond a few public slaves who acted as officials to keep copies of treaties, laws and lists of taxpayers.

But classical Athenian society was segregated by sex and status, determined by the opposition between free and enslaved. A citizen was defined as male, aged eighteen and over, and of free birth, itself eventually defined (451 BC) as having both parents as citizens without regard to wealth or rank. Citizenship therefore excluded all women: they were responsible for maintaining the household (*oikos*), that is, they were not only crucial to bearing and raising children but they supervised the household economy and the work of slaves. And there is ample evidence that many women worked in the fields, sold produce in the market, were nurses and midwives.[9] Their work was the *sine qua non* which provided their men access to the wider life of the *polis*. Citizenship also excluded many other inhabitants, notably slaves (see below, p. 25) and metics – those non-Athenian Greeks and other free aliens who were legally required to have a citizen protector or patron (*prostates*) and were liable to taxation and military service.[10] Athens could confer citizenship on such men as a mark of favour but they had no right to it as residents. It has been estimated that during the fifth and fourth centuries the numbers of citizens fluctuated between 20,000–40,000 amid the 200,000 or more inhabitants of Attica.[11]

If the vast majority of Greeks were not entitled to participate in political life, that is, they were excluded from what went on in the law courts, the Council (*Boulē*), the Assembly (*Ekklēsia*), theatre, *agora* (civic centre and market-place) and battlefield, ancient Greek sources of all kinds nevertheless insisted that politics and the political life of citizens were privileged above the private and personal life. Citizens were regarded as equals in the sense that each could claim the right of private free speech (*parrhesia*) in general, and equality of public speech (*isēgoria*) in the Assembly, without regard to aristocratic lineage or wealth. The *polis*, then, was a society of citizens (not inhabitants) concerned with communal matters.

Committees and annual offices were filled by lot and this meant that a considerable proportion of Athenian citizens had direct experience in government, even if many of their duties were of a limited and routine character.[12] Their political education was on the job. Rotation of offices and limited tenure encouraged the involvement of large numbers of citizens in political–judicial activities. Selection of most office holders by lot

---

8   See Hansen, *Athenian Democracy*, ch. 2, pp. 4–26 on the ancient evidence, what has survived and the gaps in our knowledge.
9   In general on attitudes to women see S. Pomeroy, *Goddesses, Whores, Wives and Slaves* (New York, 1975).
10   Hansen, *Athenian Assembly*, pp. 34ff. and n. 232, pp. 149–50.
11   In general see Cartledge, *The Greeks*, and R. K Sinclair, *Democracy and Participation in Athens* (Cambridge, 1988), p. 114.
12   Aristotle, *Athenaion Politeia* [AP] 51 gives examples.

was meant to limit the possibilities of the emergence of one powerful individual or faction. Before taking up office each citizen underwent a preliminary scrutiny (*dokimasia*) before a jury court to determine his citizen ancestry, *deme* membership (see below, p. 26), whether he treated his parents well, paid his taxes, served on military expeditions, and fulfilled his religious responsibilities: 'they ask whether he has an ancestral Apollo and a household Zeus and where their sanctuaries are'.[13] After his year in office the official publicly had to account for his conduct (*euthynai*), submitting financial accounts to auditors and advocates who were appointed by lot from the whole citizenry. 'There is nothing in the city that is exempt from accounting, investigation and examination.'[14] Serious offences in office or a failure to render proper accounts resulted in prosecutions, private and public suits[15] and impeachment (*eisangelia*).

Certain military officials who commanded the army and navy, most notably the ten *stratēgoi* or generals were, however, elected by the Assembly rather than put in office by lot and these men could be re-elected and build up experience and influence. In a society geared to warfare this was seen as a necessity.[16] But the making of policy and administrative decisions in the Assembly, which all citizens were entitled to attend and for which they were paid from the 390s, characterized the exercise of democracy.

Athens had been given a first code of laws by Drako (621) and a second by Solon (594/3). Until the end of the fifth century further laws were enacted and the Assembly made decrees which were 'published', that is, inscribed on stone pillars and erected on the Acropolis and in the Agora for all to see. At the end of the fifth century the laws were republished and a revised code was completed.[17] This means that the Assembly acted under the rule of law. Where changes to the law were proposed, the Assembly could initiate the change only after due consideration.[18] The fundamental laws and institutions (*nomoi*) of the *polis* were not easily disregarded by, for instance, votes to alter them by a decree in a single Assembly.[19] Indeed, every year in the Assembly, after *c*. 400, there was a vote of confidence in the laws. Justice according to the laws was dispensed by citizen juries, members of which were chosen by lot and paid for daily attendance. These laws (*nomoi*) were not simply Athens' 'legal system'. The *nomoi* did not differentiate legal from moral concepts and therefore they encompassed customs and 'a way of life' as well as actionable misdeeds which were, at the same time, moral misdeeds. Included here was religious non-conformity.[20]

In this agrarian society (Attica) with an urban centre (Athens), the incorporation of the peasant farmer and the urban craftsman as full members of the political community appears to have been an ideal peculiar to classical antiquity (and rarely repeated). The problem for modern scholarship has been to assess the degree to which this ideal was realized in practice.

---

13   Aristotle, AP 55.3.
14   Aeschines, *Against Ktesiphon*, 3.20–2.
15   Aristotle, AP 54.2.
16   Pseudo-Xenophon, *On the Constitution of Athens*, I.2–3.
17   Decree and Law (403) quoted by Andocides, *On the Mysteries*, 83–4, 87 in P. J. Rhodes, *The Greek City-States: a source book* (London, 1986), p. 124.
18   Sinclair, *Democracy and Participation*, p. 221.
19   M. H. Hansen, *The Sovereignty of the People's Court in the Fourth Century* BC *and the Public Action Against Constitutional Proposals* (Odense, 1974); and M. H. Hansen, *Eisangelia* (Odense, 1975), pp. 161–206.
20   See Bryant, *Moral Codes and Social Structure*, especially ch. 4.

The Attic countryside in classical times comprised numerous small properties owned and worked by peasants and their families. Some would be able to afford a slave or two whose main work was in the house but who would also help in the fields, especially at harvest time. These slaves, mostly non-Greeks, were acquired as chattel, by capture or purchase. The relatively few large estates owned by wealthy citizens were supervised either directly by the landowner or by estate managers who oversaw their stock of farm labourers comprising slaves and casual hired labour. The latter consisted of propertyless citizens or small farmers whose own properties were insufficient to support their families. Apart from the large numbers of slaves who worked in the silver mines at Laureion (whose silver deposits enabled the expansion of the Athenian navy but temporarily went out of production in the final years of the Peloponnesian war), the bulk of Athenian slaves worked as domestic labourers or in the lower echelons of the civil service as policemen, recorders of laws and treaties, in 'white collar' services as business agents, clerks or scribes, bank employees, magistrates' assistants and craftsmen.[21] Slaves were undoubtedly essential to Athenian life.

But it is now thought to be too much of an oversimplification to describe the Athenian economy as 'simply' based on 'the slave mode of production'.[22] Rather, it should be seen as centring on the Athenian citizen who was both the 'productive base' and the focus of the political system.[23] The independence of citizens as free men, whether labourers in agriculture, in crafts, in business ventures or as small owners, an independence from bonds to the wealthier, typified *polis* life with its distinctive form of property relations and labour organization[24] and its recognition of these men as entitled to political participation. There is little doubt, however, that the availability of slave labour allowed even moderately poor citizens the leisure sufficient to participate in the 'affairs of state'. Eighteenth-century European commentators were distressed by the possibility of such men being admitted to deliberations on 'matters of state'. As we shall see, Plato and Aristotle also argued against the engagement in political deliberation by these sorts of unleisured amateur; for the political philosophers, statesmanship was a skill that could only be perfected either by a small group of naturally talented and highly trained men (Plato) or by those with sufficient leisure to enable them to have experiences beyond those of private economic survival so that they could then develop the kind of habitual behaviour that was considered suitable to men engaged in political deliberation on the *common good* (Aristotle).

21   Wood, *Peasant–Citizen and Slave*, p. 45; Sinclair, *Democracy and Participation*, pp. 197–8; Bryant, *Moral Codes and Social Structure*, ch. 4 on the inappropriate modern analogy, already signalled in Marx and Weber, between this society based on landed property, agriculture and growing seaborne trade interdependence, and later capitalism with its polarization of town and country. The political economy of *polis* society was not orientated towards maximal utilization of productive forces but towards the civic existence of the citizen.

22   Modifying the positions of G. E. M. de Ste Croix, *The Class Struggle* and P. Anderson, *Passages from Antiquity to Feudalism* (London, 1974).

23   Hansen, *Athenian Assembly*, pp. 32ff. and Wood, *Peasant–Citizen and Slave, passim*. Max Weber, *Economy and Society*, ch. 16 argued for the peasant–citizen as the bearer of ancient democracy. In contrast, Bryant, *Moral Codes and Social Structure*, pp. 137–8 argues that the peasant's political ascent from bondage fostered the emergence of a slave mode of production, the *polis* ideal of free and independent self-governing citizens being intimately linked to chattel slavery.

24   Wood, *Peasant–Citizen and Slave*, pp. 88–9; M. Austin and P. Vidal-Naquet, *Economic and Social History of Ancient Greece* (London, 1977), p. 15.

Citizens: The Historical Emergence of the Athenian Democratic Constitution

The Athenian citizen came about as the consequence of a number of now famous attempts first to solve conflicts between rich landowning aristocrats and poor peasant farmers and then to unify separate human groups divided by social, familial, territorial and religious customs. From the early sixth-century populist reforms of the poet–legislator Solon (650–561), when debts and debt bondage (loans on the security of the debtor's person) were cancelled (594/3), obligations in the form of produce, rent or tribute owed by a dependent peasant to a landlord disappeared.[25] Solon seems to have ended the status of peasant dependence as well as to have cancelled their debts. From then onwards, Athenian agriculture was free from relations of juridical dependence and the 'cause of the common people' was furthered, as the Aristotelian Constitution of Athens puts it.[26] Solon also created a new Council (*Boulē*) of 400 to perform 'advance deliberations' on topics before the meeting of the Assembly of citizens. And he extended to any person the right to take legal action on behalf of an injured party, thereby allowing any citizen to contribute to the enforcement of the laws. Plutarch[27] recounts that when Solon was asked which is the best-run city, he answered that it is the one in which wrongdoers are prosecuted and punished no less by those who have not been wronged than by those who have. The determination of what actions violated the laws and were, therefore, detrimental to the well-being of the *polis* was no longer the preserve of the upper classes. The people (*dēmos*) became the court of last resort and from this the later popular sovereignty of Athens was to develop.[28]

Between the times of Solon and Kleisthenes, an urban *dēmos* appeared and a city-dwelling group of wealthy business families with it. An urban–rural continuum was established when Kleisthenes, in part seeking to acquire power for himself and his own family and friends against the dominant dynastic faction in the late sixth century, devised a system to neutralize aristocratic, dynastic rivalries and to ensure that the power of the people could at least counterbalance that of the upper classes in the making of political decisions (508/7).[29] As part of a new political order he reorganized the citizens into ten new tribes. He also introduced new regional units, *demes,* largely based on existing villages, as the smallest political entities by which citizens were to be identified. *Demes* not only enjoyed local self-government but also acted as constituencies and contributed a quota to those 'elected' in the Council (*Boulē*), now a body of 500, which set the agenda for the Assembly. Through his *deme* a man became a citizen and his *deme* identity followed him despite changes of abode. *Deme* identity became more important than the name of one's father or ancestor (patronymic), so that political identity was linked to a group that had resulted from an artificial mixing of geographical and social origins. Anyone who was registered in a *deme* acquired the name of the *deme,* however humble his origins. The ten new tribes, and the allotment of parts of *demes* to

---

25 Lintott, *Violence*, pp. 43–8; M. Ostwald, *From Popular Sovereignty to the Sovereignty of Law: law, society and politics in fifth-century Athens* (Berkeley, 1986); Bryant, *Moral Codes and Social Structure*, pp. 68–73 on Solon's reallocation of civic rights on the basis of wealth rather than birth.
26 AP 9.1.
27 *Solon,* 18. vii.
28 Ostwald, *Popular Sovereignty,* p. 15.
29 Lintott, *Violence*, pp. 54–5, 125–6; Herodotus, V. 62.2–63.1; Aristotle, AP 19.3–4.

each, meant that each tribe had a share in all the regions.[30] These *demes* were created to break up a range of traditional allegiances including important religious cults that had previously been dominated by aristocratic dynasties.[31] Kleisthenes also created ten generals (*stratēgoi*), one from each tribe, to command Athens' armed forces. At the height of Athens' military power in the fifth century, these generals became the political leaders of Athens as well.[32]

Then, in 462/1 Ephialtes transferred to more representative bodies those politically important powers that had been exercised by the council of the Areopagus, whose members had been appointed on the basis of their good birth and wealth. From this time onwards, Athens was self-consciously democratic.

Until the death of Perikles in 429 BC, there remained property qualifications for eligibility to high office so that birth and wealth were still preconditions for political leadership in Athens.[33] But in most cases the people as a whole, in Assembly, elected these men to offices. Indeed, the leadership of the armed forces was determined by popular vote although those *originally* 'permitted' to fight voluntarily under a general's leadership were *hoplites,* that is, members of the top three property classes. This signals that although major decisions or legislation could not be made or implemented without the approval of the Assembly of all citizens,[34] and the common people had the right to elect their magistrates, a full voice and participation in *polis* activities were *initially* only secured by those of *hoplite* status. By the mid 450s, however, and during the leadership of Perikles, himself the grand-nephew of Kleisthenes, the democracy was further opened out to ordinary citizens, not least by his institution of pay for jury service. Normally, it was up to individual citizens to prosecute someone even on 'public' charges. Some saw this as a major Athenian vice. Aristophanes' comedies (e.g. *Acharnians, Knights*) blame Perikles for turning Athenians into wage-earners (an observation paralleled in Plato's *Gorgias,*515e, 5–7), resulting in a breed of sycophants who flattered the *dēmos* and took care of their stomachs by getting the rich brought to court, thereby securing the confiscation of their money which then went into the 'state' coffers to pay the wages of jurors! But justice was now to be dispensed by paid amateur magistrates or, in more important cases, by large juries made up of citizens over thirty years old. These magistrates and juries were concerned as much with the merits of the litigants making their case before them and with what they took to be the 'best interests' of the *polis,* as with the strict application of the laws. Litigants were required to plead their own cases within an allotted amount of time, although they could hire someone to help them in writing their speech. By instituting pay for jury service and by increasing his focus on the Athenian people in Assembly who required convincing of the soundness of his proposals, Perikles further opened out the democracy to wider public participation.

---

30   Aristotle, AP 21, ii, iii, iv, vi; the citizens were mixed together, overriding kinship and regional distinctions in favour of collective self-governance.

31   J.-P. Vernant, *Mythe et pensée chez les Grecs, études de psychologie historique,* vol. 1 (Paris, 1981), p. 211 speaks of Kleisthenes as the founder of a new religion–politics.

32   See O. Murray, *Early Greece* (London, 1980), ch. 15; D. Whitehead, *The Demes of Attica* (Princeton, 1986).

33   Ostwald, *Popular Sovereignty,* pp. 15–23.

34   Ibid., p. 26.

Equality: Of What and of Whom?

Isegoria, equality of public speech, was intimately tied to democracy as a unique kind of civic life, especially in contrast to tyrannies. *Isegoria*, as Herodotus speaks of it, was that unique characteristic of democracy that allowed each citizen to express his equal membership of the community and in this way he achieved 'his very self' through and in community.[35] This *isēgoria*, introduced by Kleisthenes in 508/7 BC, was closely linked with the notion of equality of opportunity to participate in the public sphere of collective decision-making. It has often been asked whether ordinary citizens availed themselves of such opportunities. Did they engage in debate prior to collective decisions being taken?[36] We are so used to an apathetic citizenry that Athenian *ideals* appear to be no more than that.

It seems clear that no one expected that everyone of those citizens who attended a meeting of the Assembly could or would address his fellow citizens. There were numerous 'quiet Athenians',[37] not least because to address the Assembly one needed some skill and experience in public speaking and some familiarity with the debated issues. Furthermore, to draw up a proposal in writing was a specialist skill. But as an ideal, public speaking was also a possibility, there for anyone who cared to put his views before the Assembly and so demonstrate his own excellence on the basis of which he would be publicly acknowledged and rewarded. As a regular procedure, a herald issued an invitation to all at the Assembly by asking 'who wishes to speak?'

This conception of equal consideration for each citizen where each had the opportunity to realize equality by being entitled to public speech, seems to have formed the basis of the uncoerced and informed allegiance to the democratic constitution where all citizens were made to feel they had a stake in the *polis,* obeying the laws and co-operating. It did not, however, mean that all men were considered the same in their capacities to convert whatever personal and private resources they had into worthwhile or satisfying public activity. Athenians were aware that different individual contexts served to alter, to some degree, an individual's personal ideals of what he wanted for himself and his kin as well as his means to achieving them. But collectively, the ideal of public participation and the admiration for those who chose, in suitable contexts, to serve the community, were upheld. As we shall see, Aristotle was intensely interested in those aspects of life which prevented some men from realizing their collective and individual ideals.

For the later fifth century BC, these ideals were famously put into the mouth of Perikles by the historian Thucydides (2.37) when he said that in Athens, 'rule is not by the few but by the majority. In private disputes all are equal before the law, whereas in public affairs appointments are according to merit and personal reputation. What matters is not rotation [of office] but ability. Poverty does not debar a man from recognition if only he can be of value to the *polis*'. He added that in their private lives Athenians were free and tolerant and in public affairs they kept to the law because it commanded their deep respect.[38]

---

35   Herodotus, 5.78.

36   B. Campbell, 'Paradigms Lost: classical Athenian politics in modern myth', *History of Political Thought* X (1989), pp. 189–213; R. Osborne, *Dēmos: the Discovery of Classical Attica* (Cambridge, 1985), pp. 64ff.

37   See L. B. Carter, *The Quiet Athenian* (Oxford, 1986).

38   See M. I. Finley, 'Leaders and Followers' in his *Democracy Ancient and Modern*, ch. 1; but see also N. Loraux, *The Invention of Athens: the funeral oration in the classical city* (Cambridge, MA, 1986).

In the fourth century, the ideal of public participation was expressed by Aeschines,[39] who noted that

> in oligarchies [where the rich rule] it is not he who wishes but he who is in authority that addresses the people [in Assembly]; whereas in democracies he speaks who chooses and whenever it seems to him good. And the fact that a man speaks only at intervals marks him as a man who takes part in politics because of the call of the hour and for the common good; whereas to leave no day without its speech is the mark of a man who is making a trade of it and talking for pay.

The types of people with a variety of personal talents and from a variety of backgrounds who sought power and influence in the Assembly changed during the two centuries of expanding democracy. If in the sixth century Athenian public life was dominated by aristocrats, greater account was taken of the ordinary citizens of the *dēmos* during the fifth century, some of whom increasingly participated in debates and voted in the Assembly. The constitutional reforms of Ephialtes, beginning in 462/1 BC, brought into being what some were to regard as the full democracy, so that Perikles could thereafter argue that democratic principles relied on the fact that the conduct of Athenian affairs was entrusted to many.[40] For the more ambitious, instruction was offered by Sophists (see below, pp. 45–9) in the art of getting on in life through persuasive public speaking. Those who could afford their fees or could pay for the services of a professional speech-writer to help them speak on their own behalf in court, prospered in their public ambitions. At the end of the fifth century some of these ambitious men may have lacked traditional aristocratic birth but they had acquired sufficient wealth, often in manufacturing enterprises. Such men became increasingly influential with the *dēmos* so that by the fourth century hardly any political leader was of aristocratic descent. This meant that the ordinary citizens, collectively, enjoyed the last word in major decisions, whereas an ordinary man on his own and as an amateur could not realistically hope to compete with those whose acquired rhetorical skills and expertise, owing much to their fortunate economic circumstances, brought them to prominence. Therefore, in the Athenian *polis* in which political initiative was stimulated by ambition (*philotimia*) and competition (*hamilla*), the equality that was seen to matter was that of opportunity among peers.

Isonomia on the other hand, or equality through the law, or, as Thucydides says (2.37.1) equality before the law, ensured that men of differing wealth, power, social status, cleverness and eloquence were to be treated equally by the laws and by judges or state-paid jurors in the courtroom who were responsible for the administration of justice. Aristotle would refer to this kind of justice as corrective or rectificatory. He said:

> It makes no difference whether a good man has defrauded a bad one or vice versa, nor whether a good man or a bad man has committed adultery; all that the law considers is the difference caused by the injury; and it treats the parties as equals, only asking whether one has committed and the other suffered an injustice, or whether one has inflicted and the other suffered a hurt.[41]

---

39   *Against Ktesiphon*, 3.22.
40   Thucydides, 2.37.1.
41   *N. Ethics*, V, iv, 1132a2–7; see ch. 4, this volume.

What seems *not* to have been argued in democratic Athens was that all men were equal by nature in the sense that all men were the same. Satisfied with political arrangements that secured legal equality, and ever-concerned with political stability, Athenians for the most part accepted economic inequality. No one *deserved* to be poor but some had the ill luck to be so. They also accepted an inequality of talents and temperament,[42] as is clear from Perikles' reference to merit. The latter was often fostered by what was clearly a differential in the kind of wealth that could sustain more than average leisure for political engagement on the part of the ambitious who sought leadership and prominence through debate in the Assembly. Observing retrospectively the behaviour of those who chose to exercise their freedom to speak in Assembly, democrats were willing to reward those who deployed their leisure in such a way as obviously to give more valuable advice than others. To speak in the Assembly was acknowledged to require more than mere leisure; it required either natural talent or training and the will to put these to public use. As Demosthenes insisted in the fourth century,[43] Athenian democratic freedom was preserved by the competition of virtuous men for public honours. It was only anti-democrats who stressed that democracy meant a belief in the equality of nature in the sense of an equality of talent, intellect and ambition,[44] giving the impression that democrats had no interest in recognizing that some men had proven themselves to be more worthy of public recognition than others.

Sparta

Those who had little admiration for Athenian democratic 'freedoms' looked to the other large and powerful city-state of the time, Sparta, for inspiration. Indeed, the Athenian oligarch Kritias, the leader of the Thirty Tyrants imposed on Athens by Sparta in 404/3, and an associate of Socrates and relative of Plato, argued against the Thucydidean Perikles. He claimed that the most free of free Greeks were not Athenians but Spartans. We have very few contemporary documents from Sparta, but during the fifth century BC this city-state came to be seen by anti-democrats as an ideal oligarchy of a very distinctive kind.[45] Both Herodotus and Thucydides describe Spartan history and organization, although they are not always in agreement. Other information comes from the Spartan admirer Xenophon,[46] from Plato,[47] from Aristotle, who is often critical,[48] and from the later Plutarch[49] among others.

Full citizen Spartiates (also called Lacedaemonians) were members of an Assembly

---

42   J. K. Davies, *Wealth and Power of Wealth in Classical Athens* (New York, 1981), pp. 15–37; P. Millett, 'Patronage and its Avoidance in Classical Athens', in A. Wallace-Hadrill, ed., *Patronage in Ancient Society* (London, 1989), pp. 15–47; P. Cartledge, 'Comparatively Equal' in J. Ober and C. Hedrick, eds, *Demokratia: a conversation on democracies, ancient and modern* (Princeton, NJ, 1996), pp. 175–85.

43   *Against the Law of Leptines.*

44   For instance, Isocrates, *Areopagiticus*, discussed in Millett, 'Patronage', pp. 28ff.

45   E. N. Tigerstedt, *The Legend of Sparta in Classical Antiquity* 3 vols (Stockholm and Uppsala, 1965–78); P. Cartledge, *Agesilaus and the Crisis of Sparta* (London, 1987).

46   *Spartan Constitution, Hellenika.*

47   *Republic*, VIII, 548; *Laws.*

48   *Politics* II and IV.

49   *Lives* of Lykourgos and Agesilaus.

where they had some power of decision-making in running their city-state, but not as much as citizens in the Athenian Assembly. Spartan citizens were a small minority of the overall population that included *helots*, a subjugated, often volatile, indigenous people who were bound to the land and left with a degree of freedom, including the capacity to own goods so long as they produced enough to support the dominant Spartiates. *Helots* could be liberated by the state as a reward for fighting well for Sparta in war. But they could also be killed with impunity and there was an annual state declaration of war against them! The population of Lakonia also included *perioikoi* (dwellers around), free men who lived in cities other than Sparta, ran their own communities, engaged in commerce and crafts, and served as military auxiliaries, but they were not full citizens and in greater matters were subject to Spartiates. Spartiates cultivated austerity in a way that set them apart from all other Greeks. They devoted themselves to a near full-time military life in order to maintain their conquests and were forbidden by law to own silver and gold or to engage in commerce and crafts.

The Spartan constitution (the *nomoi* which included rules, customs and practices), established probably early in the seventh century BC, was held to have been granted by a legendary lawgiver, Lykourgos. His institutions lasted, with modifications, until the third century BC.[50] According to Plutarch, Lykourgos had originally persuaded all Spartiates to pool their lands and redistribute them afresh, equally, so that each citizen had an allotment that secured his livelihood, worked for him by *helots*, and permitted him to devote his time to being a full-time Spartan. Thereafter, Spartiates 'sought primacy through virtue in the belief that there was no difference or inequality between one man and another, except that defined by reproach for shameful actions and praise for good'.[51] Spartan virtue was equated with a disdain for personal luxury and wealth and a love of military valour in the service of the city-state's military demands.

Lykourgos was also said to have provided for two hereditary kings, originally said to have descended from Herakles (Hercules), who served both as religious heads of state and as commanders of the army. They were answerable to the citizens when they returned from campaigns. The two kings sat with twenty-eight men over sixty years of age, elected for life and by popular acclaim from a privileged circle of aristocratic families, to constitute the *Gerousia*. This council of elders acted as a lawcourt to try important cases and not only discussed initial proposals for foreign policy and legislation before these were presented to the Assembly (*Ekklēsia*) of Spartiate citizens, but could reject 'crooked decisions' made by the Assembly. Aristotle says they were not required to render an account of their office holding and hence, were subject to bribery.[52] Lastly, there was a group of five *Ephors* (overseers) who were the civilian heads of state, responsible for day to day affairs, elected for one year from the whole body of male adult Spartiates. Xenophon said the *Ephors* could, like tyrants, prevent a man from completing his term of office if they detected him to be in breach of the law and they could punish him on the spot. *Ephors* received the reports of outgoing officials, decided lawsuits concerning contracts and generally supervised the system of Spartiate military life.

To Lykourgos was also attributed the distinctive Spartan system of military training by

50 See D. M. MacDowell, *Spartan Law* (Edinburgh, 1986).
51 Plutarch, *Lykourgos* 8, i–viii.
52 *Politics* II 1270b 35–1271a 6, 1271a 9–12.

age-classes. Spartan fathers did not have the right to decide to rear their offspring. Their infant was inspected by elders and if the child was 'ill born or deformed' it was sent to 'a place with pits by Mount Taygetus' and exposed to die.[53] If 'well-built and robust', however, the child was reared at home. But from the age of seven boys were taken from their families and placed in 'herds' with boy leaders, while older men watched them play and provoked them to fight and quarrel so that 'they learned about character and struggles'. Although they 'learned letters', this was taught only so far as literacy was necessary to the rest of their training in responsiveness to command, endurance in hardship and victory in battle. Then their hair was cropped, they went about barefoot and played naked. At twelve they lived without tunics and were given only one cloak for the year. They slept in barracks on rush pallets which they made with their own hands. The older men believed they were fathers, tutors and commanders of all the boys and they encouraged them to take leaders from among the most valiant of the older boys. At twenty, a young Spartiate took command in battle while the younger boys served him at dinner and elsewhere. Dinners were provided for in messes and each member contributed monthly contributions of produce to be shared collectively. Only at thirty did they return home to their families, but they continued to dine in the military mess, as no Spartiate was allowed to dine at home.

While Spartan women did not go into barracks they received an education, based on physical exercise, that was similar to the men. They were not expected to weave or spin, were not allowed jewellery, had to keep their hair cut short, and they mixed freely and exercised with the men. Their role in Spartan society was to produce soldier-sons. In fact, married women could, with their husband's permission, bear children by men other than their husbands in order to ensure a supply of young Spartans for military service.[54] When we read Plato's *Republic* we will need to recall this.

The Spartan constitution showed anti-democrats how a strong *polis* could be maintained without *stasis* (civil strife) or tyranny. Almost all the debates which attracted the attention of non-Spartan sources dealt with foreign policy and here, although decisions were taken by shouting approval in the Assembly, the proposals and speeches were almost invariably made by kings, elders and *Ephors*. Many matters that, in Athens, were decided by the Assembly, in Sparta were left to *Ephors* and the *Gerousia*. Plato observed that the power of the *Ephors* was tyrannical[55] but, as we shall see, other aspects of their constitution would be paralleled in the provisions Plato made for the education of his guardian class in the *Republic*.

Where Perikles had praised the individuality and diversity of Athenian life with its many foci of loyalty to family, friends and private enterprise in economic affairs, Sparta seemed to stand for opposing values that allowed an individual to succeed only through service to the whole community, that is, through military service, patriotism, courage and devotion to the *polis* over individual pleasure and profit. The Spartan 'state' interfered far more than did the Athenian 'state' in what Athenian citizens considered to be matters pertaining more properly to the autonomy of the family. But Spartan values

---

53   Plutarch, *Lykourgos* 16, i–ii; the exposure of unwanted infants was a common practice throughout Greece but outside Sparta it was normally done only on the parents' initiative.
54   P. Cartledge, 'Spartan Wives: liberation or licence?', *Classical Quarterly* 31 (1981), pp. 84–105; MacDowell, *Spartan Law*, p. 85.
55   *Laws* 712d.

were the ones that left the rest of Greece in their debt when, at Thermopylae, and despite being massively outnumbered, the Spartans led the Greek resistance to the invading Persians at the beginning of the fifth century BC. And Sparta was able to defeat Athens at the end of the fifth century BC. Into the fourth century BC Sparta would continue to try to replace democracies with compliant oligarchies.[56]

Athenians Reject Oligarchy

The argument between democrats and oligarchs worked itself through the events of the late fifth century BC. Those who during the twenty-seven years of the Peloponnesian war with Sparta (431–404) insisted that the operations of a full democracy caused the lack of Athenian success, not least in prosecuting war, were able briefly to engineer an oligarchic revolution in 411. But with the violent excesses committed by these oligarchs and, in particular, the violence committed by the so-called Thirty Tyrants who were imposed on Athens by the Spartan victors in 404/3 in order to abolish its democratic constitution, Athenians thereafter successfully resisted and rejected oligarchy as a practical alternative to democracy. The democratic resistance to the oligarchy, led from outside Athens by a band of exiles, many of whom were artisans and shopkeepers,[57] had entered the *polis* under arms and defeated the combined forces of the Spartans and the Thirty in the port of Piraeus. Among those who died were Plato's relatives and associates.[58] The democracy was restored in 403/2 in somewhat less radical form than previously. A call for national reconciliation and an amnesty for those who had sided with the Thirty (except for their closest associates) was accompanied by an intensification of anti-aristocratic feeling.[59] But if good birth was now not seen as necessary to political ambition, a measure of wealth, inherited or acquired, appears to have been a prerequisite for most of those who aspired to *leadership* in order to sustain more than average political ambitions.

Ordinary Athenians appear to have believed that all Athenian citizens, and probably all Greeks, naturally had a measure of justice and good sense.[60] The further skills necessary for participating in the *polis* could be taught and developed through just legal and political arrangements. But only in a very minimal sense did democrats insist on an equality of 'nature' among male citizens, and this belief in a minimal natural equality encouraged them to trust in selection by lot, indicating that they considered all citizens to be capable of *learning* to rule and be ruled in turn. In itself, this may appear to us to be an extraordinary attitude which displays a remarkable trust in the capacities of one's neighbours, whether or not any of them ever realizes his acknowledged potentials. Over and above this minimal equality of nature, however, the *competition* for civic honours was a major characteristic of *politeia* (citizenship), a competition that was undoubtedly framed by differentials in wealth.[61] But more fundamental than wealth were the rules

---

56 Xenophon's *Hellenika* gives information on the continuous inter-*polis* warfare throughout mainland and eastern Greece into the fourth century BC.
57 Xenophon, II. 4.25, II. 4.40–2.
58 See *Republic* I.
59 Sinclair, *Democracy and Participation*, pp. 42–3.
60 Plato, *Protagoras* 319a–324d.
61 J. K. Davies, *Democracy and Classical Greece*, 2nd edn (London, 1993), p. 126.

and conventions, that is, the laws, which safeguarded the political activity of free agents within a community that practised a distinct form of political rule: rule by all. Therefore, fundamental to this democracy was the notion of freedom, in Greek *eleutheria,* a word whose resonances are only in part grasped by the modern English word 'liberty'.

Freedom

In general, Greek freedom (*eleutheria*) meant (1) not to be enslaved, not to serve another man.[62] It describes the autonomy of the self-sufficient peasant-farmer citizen. But it has been noted that the emergence of this concept of an autonomous individual, free from servitude, allows for and perhaps depends on its clearly defined opposite: the legal slave who, as an individual, was deprived of all rights to autonomy.[63]

The ancient world in general was comprised of slave-owning cultures and here the Greeks were no exception, embarrassing as this fact may have been to some modern scholars who could hardly believe that so extraordinary a culture, concerned as it was with justice, equality and freedom, could adhere to so evident an abuse.[64] But classical Greece would have been very different in many ways if it had not had slavery. Unfree peoples were part of its history (e.g. the *helots* in Sparta) and hence seen as *somehow* natural, even though at crucial moments slaves were offered freedom (although not citizenship)[65] if they participated in battle. From the time of the defeat of the Persians (480/79) the Greeks became increasingly disdainful of non-Greeks in general, whom they called barbarians from their evaluation of the sounds foreigners made ('bar-bar') when they spoke their own language, to say nothing of their inferiorly developed political systems. Slaves were overwhelmingly, though not exclusively 'barbarian' non-Greeks, for the most part war captives, and often associated with Thrace and Thracians to the north.[66] As we have seen, it is not simply that slaves were expedient for the classical Greek economy; they seem to have been necessary as an intellectual category by which a Greek could determine his own identity as 'free' and as autonomous within the limits, of course, of natural dependencies which, none the less, must never completely take him over. A Greek man defeated in battle was ideally never to allow himself to be captured and enslaved by the victors; he would prefer to die even at his own hands because life was not worth living at all costs, or at least, this is the way the ideal was represented by Aristotle in Book I of the *Politics.*[67] In contrast, those who allowed themselves to be enslaved after battle, like women and children, displayed a slavish mentality. But even here the issue was not so simple and Aristotle tells us that in his own day there was much

---

62   See M. I. Finley, *The Ancient Economy* (London, 1973), p. 28; also see R. G. Mulgan, 'Liberty in Ancient Greece', in Z. Pelczynski and J. Gray, eds, *Conceptions of Liberty in Political Philosophy* (Oxford, 1984), pp. 7–26, contrasted with M. H. Hansen, 'Was Athens a Democracy?', especially pp. 8–17.

63   See the discussions in J.-P. Vernant, *Myth and Society in Ancient Greece,* trans. J. Lloyd (London, 1980), pp. 81–2; Cartledge, *The Greeks,* ch. 6; Bryant, *Moral Codes,* pp. 136–7.

64   On the anachronistic intrusion of modern moralistic bias into this debate see M. I. Finley, *Ancient Slavery and Modern Ideology* (New York, 1980).

65   But see Rhodes, *The Greek City-States,* p. 107: near the end of the Peloponnesian war, at the battle of Arginusae (406 BC), Athenians offered freedom *and* citizenship to slaves willing to row in an emergency fleet.

66   Today this is modern Bulgaria; see Cartledge, *The Greeks,* p. 138.

67   See chapter 4.

discussion about whether enslavement could ever be justified on any grounds other than force and expediency.

In Athens, it may not have been possible to distinguish a slave from a citizen by his dress or bearing, and citizens and slaves worked alongside one another in a range of activities.[68] But a slave-owning citizen was able to treat slaves as items of property and were a slave to be mistreated, he had no recourse to legal action himself. The slave was entirely dependent on his master's good will and if the slave committed a wrong, he was punished bodily, whereas a citizen who broke the law had his goods confiscated, paid fines and appeared in court.[69] Demosthenes in the fourth century BC saw this as the real difference between a slave and a free man.[70]

Greek freedom also meant (2) that the community was not to be dominated by another, a freedom of the *polis*, whatever its constitution (be it democracy or oligarchy), to be autonomous in its self-rule and therefore to make its own laws and administer justice as it saw fit. The preservation of one's own state's autonomy was not seen as inconsistent, however, with depriving another state of its.

Added to this, however, was (3) a distinctive *democratic* understanding of freedom which, as a constitutional concept, was associated not only with freedom from factionalism but also with freedom of political participation in the public sphere where the laws, rather than an individual or factional group, were sovereign. This freedom was realized, in part, as a consequence of public pay for jurors, instituted by Perikles to counteract poorer citizens' dependency on the magnanimity of virtuous, landowning aristocratic patrons.[71] The *polis* also came to provide other forms of public pay, for holding public office, attending the Assembly, and rowing in the fleet. Indeed, for poorer citizens there were state stipends and maintenance grants for the disabled. Eventually, there was even a fund to enable poor citizens to attend major festivals. Linked to the democratic understanding of freedom was an expectation of personal freedom in the private spheres of life. This kind of democratic, constitutional freedom was not valued by oligarchies or monarchies, nor by political philosophers whose sympathies often attached them to these regimes. Disparagingly, they called this democratic freedom an anarchic, lawless, liberty 'to do what one likes', subsidized through public funds.

The notion of an Athenian citizen's freedom was both a privilege and a claim, reinforced by the myth that Athenians were autochthonous, that is, born of the soil and so unlike the descendants of ancestors who came from other lands. The Athenian citizen was also free from a regular direct tax and had a right to own land. But his right to attend the Assembly was not conditioned by his ownership of land. In the sphere of law, he enjoyed 'unrestricted capacity': at eighteen he was enrolled in the *deme* register, at twenty he could attend all meetings of the Assembly and participate in discussions and voting, from twenty to twenty-nine he gained military experience and at thirty he was entitled to offer himself for selection to the Council of 500 (*Boulē*) or to other offices of state and

---

68   Xenophon, *Athenian Constitution*, i.10 deplored the fact that Athenians could not be distinguished from slaves and metics by dress.

69   T. Wiedemann, *Greek and Roman Slavery* (Baltimore, 1981).

70   22.55, 24.167.

71   Aristotle, AP, 4.

serve on juries. Athenian freedom was therefore, both a negative *and* a positive concept, a *freedom from* certain impositions or limitations and a *freedom to* engage in certain activities.[72]

Behind all three notions of freedom was the idea of self-determination both at the individual and collective levels. But what was *not* emphasized in any of these ideas of freedom is the modern liberal democratic notion that the individual lives of citizens, determined by uniquely personal preferences, however acquired, were to be protected or enhanced by setting *limits* to collective, community control. The citizen's individual 'rights' were not spoken of as protected 'private possessions' nor was the preservation of these individual 'rights' understood as the reason for the subsequent foundation of political communities.[73] For Greeks, the political man lived not only for himself but, in the first instance, for his family and friends. The *polis* was not usually seen to be merely a utilitarian construction for the individual, autonomous self. Humans were thought to be, from the beginning, social.[74] Politics, thereafter, emerged from 'the social' as a consequence of both necessary and voluntary allegiances to others. Some Greeks appear to have floated the hypothesis that the state and its laws (as opposed to earlier forms of natural human associations, or natural societies) came into being as a contract between individuals for the mutual self-preservation of the contractees,[75] so that the political realm of the city-state was nothing more than a product of convention. Indeed, Plato has one of his main characters in the *Republic*, Glaucon, argue that this conventionalism is the common opinion on the nature and origin of justice in the *polis*.[76] But traditionally, Athenians seemed to prefer the notion that the *polis* with its laws and institutions, no less than society as its necessary precursor with its natural division of tasks, was natural to humankind. Politics was the natural outcome of human nature and its activity. Was Plato implying that this traditional view was no longer widely held or was Glaucon meant to reflect a minority view which not only misunderstood public sentiment but was, according to Plato himself, untrue?[77]

In another dialogue, set in the proud times before the outbreak of the Peloponnesian war, Plato has the Sophist Protagoras provide what looks like the traditional view when he has him tell the 'creation' story of how mortal creatures were created by the gods from a mixture of earth and fire. The gods Prometheus and Epimetheus were then charged with ensuring that no species should be destroyed. Epimetheus, however, foolishly distributed all the survival powers to the brute beasts, leaving none for the human race who remained naked, unshod and unarmed. Therefore, Prometheus stole from the gods Hephaestus and Athena the two gifts of skill in the arts and fire, and gave them to

---

72   This contrasts with Isaiah Berlin's discussion of ancient Greek liberty in his 'Two Concepts of Liberty' in I. Berlin, *Four Essays on Liberty* (Oxford, 1969), pp. 118–72.

73   But see later Hellenistic views on the state of nature as the war of all against all, in A. A.Long and D. N. Sedley, *The Hellenistic Philosophers* (Cambridge, 1987), vol. 1, translation 22 R, pp. 133–4 – but this is Plutarch.

74   But see G. B. Kerferd's interpretation of the Protagorean myth – in the beginning men were isolates – in 'Protagoras' Doctrine of Justice and Virtue in the *Protagoras* of Plato', *Journal of Hellenic Studies* 73 (1953), pp. 42–5, countered by P. Nicholson in P. Nicholson and G. B. Kerferd, 'Protagoras on Pre-political Man: an exchange', *Polis* 4 (1982), pp. 18–28 and M. Nussbaum, *The Fragility of Goodness, Luck and Ethics in Greek Tragedy and Philosophy* (Cambridge, 1986), pp. 101–2.

75   See Plato, *Republic* II, 359 below.

76   Ibid., II, 358.

77   See chapter 3.

humankind so that the species could survive.[78] With these skills men then discovered speech and constructed houses, made clothes and got food from the earth. Thus provided for, *they lived at first in scattered groups* (societies). But to save themselves from the ravages of stronger, wild beasts, they *then* came together to found fortified cities. Not being as yet endowed with political wisdom they fought with one another until Zeus got Hermes *to impart to all men alike* a share in the qualities of *respect for others* and a *sense of justice*. In this way order was brought into cities and a bond of friendship and union was created. Thereafter, humankind as a species with a final, determined nature which now includes a moral sense, *naturally* lives in law-governed *poleis*.[79] A 'person' who does not share in these moral, social excellences is not human and 'should not be among human beings at all'.

In this setting then, freedom did not mean independence in the sense of not having to depend on others. It was not simply that the Greeks observed that some of the best pleasures may come from dependencies. It was also that they thought dependencies were natural to men and not forced upon them by a state which had to be kept within a limited sphere of its own activities. Athenian social relations were founded on a system of reciprocal obligations between relations, neighbours and friends (*philoi*). The maximization of overall social objectives was not considered to be the job of the state, seen as an instrumental construction, but rather, it was the job of free, naturally dependent men who *were* the state.

Private and Public Life

This is the reason that their collective regulations protected individual citizens from violations of their person, property and home, from torture, from execution without trial, that is, from harm that could be inflicted by individual officials who might misuse their office and the collective power of the institutions of the *polis* and, thereby, *violate the laws*. It has already been mentioned that at the expiration of their term of office, magistrates were called to account and any citizen could bring a private suit against an official of the *polis* which would be heard by public arbitrators in the first instance, and in the case of an appeal, by a popular court. Athenians were known to be litigious. They emphasized that citizens were equally protected by the law (*isonomia*) and this seems to have meant something quite specific: in cases where *the law was violated*, they blamed magistrates and political *individuals*. They did not blame the *dēmos* or the *polis*. Individuals rather than collective institutions bore responsibility for violating law. Athenians do not appear to have pitted the individual agent against 'the state'. Instead, the laws *bound those in office* and protected citizens against their abuse by *polis* officials.

Athenians lived private lives and exercised private freedoms in the social and economic spheres without necessarily emphasizing those individual aspects of private life that *distinguished* one person from another. In the private sphere of life, one educated one's children (most Athenians learned to read and write in primary schools, although attendance was not compulsory), regulated family life and its economic survival in trade

---

78 Proto-humans, as Nussbaum, *The Fragility of Goodness,* calls them (p. 90); also see pp. 100–2. Nussbaum argues (p. 103) that Protagoras' speech provides a non-Humean picture of social virtue.

79 *Protagoras*, 320d–323a.

or agriculture, lived and worked side by side with women and children, slaves and foreigners and work colleagues — some free citizens, others free and Greek but not Athenian and therefore, non-citizens. The public, political sphere of the *polis* regulated those social activities that were judged to be connected with the city-state: its laws (on marriage, legitimacy, property), its policies of war and peace, its religious rituals and beliefs. Politics was not primarily about the reallocation of private economic resources, despite the considerable state transfers of money to poor citizens to enable them to engage in jury service and Assembly attendance. Politics was about the activities in which citizens participated when they were engaged in ruling and being ruled. Beyond this, the negotiation of economic well-being was a private, familial concern. The *polis* then, was an exclusive society of citizens whose own political activities were marked off from their activities in other spheres of life in the community and family. Once again, the *polis* of Athens *was* the Athenian citizens and not its territory or inhabitants in general. Here, the well-ordered city-state was believed to be realized through the publicly scrutinized behaviour of ambitious men whose ideal was meant to be the overriding of factional interests of rich and poor in the society. They were meant to serve the good life of the whole community in its interests as these were determined by collective public debate and decision.[80]

The *polis* was conceived as standing outside all class or factional interests despite their evident presence in society. Indeed, it was a criminal offence to be paid for political activity and there were no parties in the modern sense to which a citizen could be affiliated. The democracy's political goals were meant to transcend faction (*stasis*) and objectives were meant to express collectively held moral norms as well as to be pragmatic.

One of the most distinctive of the collectively held moral norms in Athens was the expectation of civic courage, for a free man to die on behalf of his *polis* whereupon his children would be publicly supported by the city until they came of age. This is emphasized in Thucydides' representation of 'the quintessential Athenian civic discourse', the funeral oration of Perikles, delivered in 430 BC at a state function to honour Athens' war dead, one year into the Peloponnesian war. Here Perikles expressed the ideals for which they had died. He also pointed to those collectively held moral ideals for which Athenians were meant to live:[81]

> We find it possible for the same people to attend to private affairs and public affairs as well, and notwithstanding our varied occupations to be adequately informed about public affairs. For we are unique in regarding the man who does not participate in these affairs at all not as a man who minds his own business but as useless.

Therefore, the Assembly, that mass meeting on the hillside called the Pnyx, southwest of the Agora, where, in the fifth century BC, a maximum of 6,000 citizens could be seated at any one time, was the heart of the system. At each meeting the composition was

---

80   See M. Berent, '*Stasis*, or the Greek Invention of Politics', *History of Political Thought* 19 (1998), pp. 331–62, who argues that the Greek *polis* was what anthropologists call a stateless community, characterized by the absence of public coercive apparatuses. Hence, the Greek concept of politics was very different from the modern concept. Similarly, Max Weber, *Economy and Society*, p. 1,364.

81   Thucydides, 2.40.2.

different so that policy-makers, concerned to win votes to secure a favoured decision on the day, needed to perfect their oratorical skills to sway the thousands in this outdoor audience. None could be certain that decrees (*psephismata*) made in a previous Assembly and relating to temporary or specific circumstances would not be reversed by the next.

Some people have found it difficult to imagine ordinary men having been actively engaged in politics and debate to the degree implied by Athenian ideals. There has similarly been much debate over who actually attended the Assembly, perhaps to sit there contributing only to the often raucous crowd response to the powerful rhetoric deployed in the string of speeches heard. In larger democracies like Athens, Aristotle noted that the multitude 'without resources' had sufficient, even too much leisure and were in receipt of state pay which enabled them to participate in the Assembly, perhaps even more regularly than did the rich who either had to pay attention to their private affairs[82] or, like Plato, chose to devote their time to philosophy.[83] But for the fourth century at least, there is evidence to show that those who were liable to the property tax that paid for wars *did* attend the Assembly in large numbers. And the payment which induced the poorer citizens to attend the forty or more meetings of the Assembly each year seems to indicate that in this democracy, leisure and its provisions *either* through private wealth *or* public subsidy *were* seen as crucial in involving a cross-section of Athenians in the communal affairs of the *polis*. Indeed, one of the marks of a developed democracy, according to Aristotle's *Politics* (1293a 2–7, 1294a 40–1, 1298b, 18), was precisely the provision of public pay to its citizens to sit in the Assembly. As he saw it, since democracies tended to have large populations of the poor, then if the state had no (imperial) revenues to hand out, it would not be feasible to hold many Assembly meetings. Hence, he says that the truly democratic statesman without access to continuous state funds for payments must consider how the poor may be saved from excessive poverty. Otherwise corruption will not be avoided. He suggests (*Pol.* 1320a 17–b4) that a central fund be set up by the richer (virtuous) citizens from which funds may be given to those in need so that they can buy a small plot or set up in trade. If Aristotle supposes a scenario where state funds are simply not available, or if we read him as criticizing democratic Athens and implying that a society's real virtue can *only* be exercised by *private, voluntary charity* to the poor, others would argue even more vigorously that the state, no matter how wealthy, ought not to provide public pay. Indeed, oligarchs repeatedly tried to abolish pay for public officials and to limit political activity to smaller numbers (e.g. in 411 BC). But if it is argued that this must have been an extremely costly system to operate, we need reminding that whenever Athens was on the verge of bankruptcy, this was not because of the democratic public expenditure but because of the high costs of its wars.

Leadership

Whatever the extent of ordinary political engagement, however, it was accepted that the *polis* needed to be led and Greek writers distinguished between good and bad

---

82   *Pol.* 1292b23–1293a11.

83   Sinclair, *Democracy*, p. 123; Aristotle possibly exaggerated (AP 24.1–2) when he said that more than 20,000 citizens received hand-outs and public pay from Athens' imperial tribute and internal revenues. It is doubted whether pay for jury service sufficiently compensated poor citizens for the time spent away from work.

character types who displayed certain essential qualities of leadership. Foremost was the distinction between a citizen who gives leadership with nothing else in mind but the good of the *polis* and whose skill in oratory leads to that end, and the man who puts himself forward out of self-interest and therefore panders to the worst instincts of the mob. The latter were attacked in the mid fifth century by 'the best people', who attached to the neutral term used for a leader of the *dēmos*, *dēmagōgus*, a pejorative connotation. Demagogues were, from then onwards, those who were said to have divided the community into factions. Instead of answering the crucial question: in whose interest does a leader lead? with reference to the good life of the whole, the demagogue was now said to answer it usually in terms of the poor faction in order to secure his own power base. At the same time the word *dēmos,* usually referring to all the citizens, came also to refer, pejoratively, to the common or lower people, the mob. And their right of free speech (*parrhesia*) whether or not they spoke in the Assembly, came to mean for the crypto-oligarch Isocrates in the fourth century BC, nothing more than slanderous behaviour.[84]

Aristotle noted that the character type of Athenian leaders underwent a great change after Perikles died (429 BC) and the Peloponnesian war ended with the Spartan victory (404/3). Until Perikles, Aristotle said that political leaders had largely been drawn from aristocratic families and it was many of these men, as we have seen, who were the architects of the reforms which completed the democracy itself. But after Perikles, leaders came from a different ancestry with different outlooks. Likewise, Thucydides (2.65), perhaps exaggerating, described an immense gulf between Perikles – as an astute, aristocratic leader, indeed, as a *stratēgos*, or general, ruling over a nominal democracy but where power was in his hands as its first citizen – and Perikles' successors, who instead of leading the people were led by them. A new breed of politicians whose wealth came from business and manufacture rather than agriculture was said to appeal directly to the poorer elements in the *dēmos*, thereby demonstrating the importance of *isēgoria* in achieving full control by the Assembly over state affairs[85] to the dismay of Socrates and Plato. Did these new leaders not only display non-traditional character traits but also hold to different values?

Heroic Politics versus an Amateur Citizenry: Character Formation

It appears that moral conduct, especially of those in authority, and morally correct legislation continued to be thought to be the determinants of a successful *polis*. As we have seen, Perikles argued that the democratic constitution was organized for the many but he also noted how political leadership fell to those worthy of it in that they were individuals with *aretē*, that is, the best, noblest and ablest. What kind of language is this? Scholars who have studied the heroic literature of ancient Greece have observed the evolution of an ideal character type from the eighth to fifth centuries BC, and they tell the following story as Greek society underwent alterations from being at first ruled by kings to later democratic rule.

In the eighth century BC when Homer is thought to have composed his epic poems

84   Millett, 'Patronage', p. 28.
85   Sinclair, *Democracy*, p. 41.

the *Iliad* and the *Odyssey*, the aristocratic military ideal man of excellence (*aretē*) was considered to have inherited certain qualities that were not wholly within his control.[86] He was portrayed as competitive among equals in a disorderly, unstable world. He was aggressive and courageous as a warrior and leader of fighting men, a hero whose honour depended in large part upon the good opinion of others so that he acted to avoid being shamed and dishonoured. His notion of justice was indifferent to any intent behind an action; it was the act that mattered and the more spectacular the better. This hero is presented as chafing at the restrictiveness of mortality itself, which he attempts to override by performing a monumental, immortal deed to win him undying renown.[87] His heroic ambition did not, however, bring him happiness. Rather, it brought him and his kin fame. Heroic pride and self-esteem often made this type of character prepared to run risks only on his own behalf and he was therefore an unreliable protector of those who were socially his inferiors.[88] His behaviour rarely fostered co-operative relations. He was irresponsible from a political perspective. So too the gods, while not acting at random, are portrayed as prone to fickleness, also pursuing their own honour and success but, unlike the hero, without suffering sorrow. Yet Zeus, in particular, is presented as concerned for justice in human society where the hero, in contrast, expresses little. Zeus is said to have put one superior, one king, in command of the people so that with his army, the king is Zeus's punishment of unjust men (Homer). Kings are seen as divine instruments. But kingly political authority is also shown to defer to one of his companions' heroic ambition for honour (as in the case of Achilles).

The literature of the subsequent Archaic age (seventh to sixth centuries BC), however, reveals a deepened awareness of human insecurity and helplessness combined with the notion that the gods are hostile and actively resent a man's success and happiness. It is a view found in the works of Hesiod and it represents the attitudes of peasant culture rather than those of an aristocratic elite. An *ordinary* man is said to be responsible neither for his ruin nor his success. *Hubris* (an almost untranslatable Greek concept, meaning something like the proud and deliberate attack on the honour of another to inflict shame and public humiliation, and hence, destroying the social fabric) becomes the worst sin. To be happy is considered dangerous in an age dominated by economic crises and warfare.[89] Zeus now becomes an active agent, avenging the poor against their oppressors, punishing the guilty and their heirs in this life or in the next. Justice is said to be Zeus's daughter and she tells him of the unjust minds of men until the people pay for the folly of their kings who do wrong with mischievous intent by giving 'crooked judgements'. Gradually, a man's behaviour comes to be seen as subject to his own personal responsibility. While on the one hand, his individual fortune attaches to him from birth and in part determines his individual destiny, on the other, he must purge and purify his blood guilt through ritual purification. This is because it is now said that he who brings evil on another does evil to himself. And so it comes to be thought that the insecurity of

---

86 In general, see T. Irwin, *A History of Western Philosophy, 1: Classical Thought* (Oxford, 1989), chs 1–2; E. R. Dodds, *The Greeks and the Irrational* (Berkeley, 1951); Campbell, 'Paradigms Lost', pp. 189–214 and Campbell, 'The Epic Hero as Politico', *History of Political Thought* 11 (1990), pp. 189–212; Nussbaum, *The Fragility of Goodness*; Bryant, *Moral Codes*, esp. chs 1–3.

87 Campbell, 'The Epic Hero as Politico', p. 189; J.-P. Vernant, *Myth and Thought Among the Greeks*, p. 331.

88 Irwin, *Classical Thought*, pp. 10–11.

89 Dodds, *The Greeks and the Irrational*, pp. 30–1.

a man's life can only be reversed to some extent by lawful institutions. But it is also recognized that a respect for law and justice will not be upheld in a world where there still exist admirers of the Homeric heroic ideals. Therefore, the heroic, aristocratic *aretē* must be institutionally and legally restrained and then refocused. This is what the reforms of Solon and Kleisthenes are thought to have achieved.

> *Solon*: I gave the *dēmos* power enough, neither subtracting nor adding too much honour. And those who had influence and were respected for their wealth I declared were not to be disadvantaged. I stood with my strong shield defending both sides and I did not allow to either an unjust victory. . . . [To the Athenians]: *Eunomia* shows everything well ordered and sound and often holds the unjust in bonds. She . . . checks extravagance, dims arrogance, . . . straightens crooked judgements and tames proud deeds. She ends civil strife and ends the anger of bitter dissension.[90]

If earlier the king was said to be the divine Zeus's punishment of unjust men, with Solon we see justice 'naturalized'. Solon's poetry and his laws, although surviving today only in fragments, seem to indicate that he believed that political destiny is, at least in part, to be regarded as a legitimate sphere of *human* agency. Furthermore, he reminds his audience that he declined the opportunity to become a tyrant (frag. 32–7) and for this reason he will be remembered for having believed that the good for the Athenian polity was the responsibility of the disinterested ruling statesman, the man of excellence.[91]

This schematic summary of the evolution of the heroic character is meant to illustrate that the *aretē* pertaining to the governing elite and the nature of political life itself were revised to restrict the previously unchecked power that had been in the hands of warring, dynastic, aristocratic groups. The hero was from now on to adapt himself to the civic setting. With the recognition that injustice and bad laws led to civil strife, the old heroic virtues which insisted on the advancement of the hero's interests and that of his supporters through aggressive and competitive behaviour at the expense of the community had to be constrained and neutralized. This gradually appears to have been achieved with Kleisthenes and subsequent reformers who co-opted the people and created democratic local government. Thereafter, the civic version of the epic hero became a dominant force in the consolidated *polis*; now he could see it as his task to construct a central polity as a monument to his own excellence.

Furthermore, the heroic view in which justice meant helping one's friends and harming one's enemies was known to lead to unending cycles of retribution down the generations. An appeal to the common interest had to override the allegiance to faction if a stable, collective life was to be established. By 458 BC this is the view that is expressed in the dramas of the playwright Aeschylus.[92] But here, the overriding of faction and the establishment of the collective good required the decisive intervention of the *goddess* Athena.

---

90   Solon in M. L. West, ed., *Iambi et elegi graeci*, 2 vols (Oxford, 1971–2), 5; also quoted in Aristotle, AP 12, 1–2.

91   G. Vlastos, 'Solonian Justice', *Classical Philology* 41 (1946), pp. 65–83.

92   Aeschylus, *The Oresteian Tragedy*, trans. P. Vellacott (Harmondsworth, 1956): *The Eumenides*: Athena's appeal, ll. 895–915. See H. Lloyd-Jones, *The Justice of Zeus*, 2nd edn (Berkeley, 1983), chs 4–6; O. Taplin, *Greek Tragedy in Action* (Berkeley, 1978).

Athene: Summon the city, herald, and proclaim the cause; / . . . And while the council-chamber fills, let citizens / And jurors all in silence recognize this court / Which I ordain today in perpetuity, / That now and always justice may be well discerned.(568–74)

Guard well and reverence that form of government / Which will eschew alike licence and slavery; / And from your polity do not wholly banish fear. / For what man living, freed from fear, will still be just? / Hold fast such upright fear of that law's sanctity, / And you will have a bulwark of your city's strength, / A rampart round your soil, such as no other race / Possesses between Scythia and the Peloponnese. / I here establish you a court inviolable, / Holy, and quick to anger, keeping faithful watch / That men may sleep in peace. (696–706)

Athene: Why should immortal rage / Infect the fields of mortal men with pestilence? / You call on Justice: I rely on Zeus. What need to reason further? . . . let persuasion check / The fruit of foolish threats before it falls to spread / Plague and disaster. (823–30)

But if / Holy Persuasion bids your heart respect my words / And welcome soothing eloquence, then stay with us.

(Here, Athena addresses the Furies, goddesses of old traditions, who wish to punish Orestes for having killed his mother and who must make amends for this blood guilt. Athena pleads for his acquittal and the end of blood revenge. All the jurors cast their votes. The votes are equal, both for and against Orestes and Athena casts the final vote. Orestes is acquitted of blood guilt and the Furies are persuaded to remain in Athens where the principle of retribution will be modified by an appeal to the common interest).

Chorus: Let civil war, insatiate of ill / Never in Athens rage; / Let burning wrath, that murder must assuage, / Never take arms to spill, / In this my heritage, / The blood of man till dust has drunk its fill. / Let all together find / Joy in each other; / And each both love and hate with the same mind / As his blood-brother; / For this heals many hurts of humankind. (977–87)

Athene: Let your State / Hold justice as her chiefest prize; And land and city shall be great / And glorious in every part. (993–6)

In general, Greek tragedy's critical consideration of public values, most notably through its dramatic attempt to moralize the heroic ethic,[93] was supplemented in the later fifth to fourth centuries BC by political philosophy doing much the same, but with a significant difference: where Aeschylus had insisted both on human responsibility *and* divine causation, now greater confidence was to be placed in men's reasoned debate and rational persuasion than in divine intervention and *holy* persuasion, if the common good was to be served in Athens.

Indeed, two of the pre-Socratic metaphysical innovators, Heraclitus and Parmenides, had helped to redraw the rigid boundaries between the human and divine. Before Socrates, these innovators were concerned with the question of how humans may attain knowledge and truth, and Parmenides in particular attacked an unthinking reliance on sense perception as a guide to reality. Knowing, on the one hand, and having an

93 See P. Euben, ed., *Greek Tragedy and Political Theory* (Berkeley, 1986); Nussbaum, *The Fragility of Goodness*, part I.

opinion, on the other, were said to come from *different* sources which enabled thinkers in the fifth century to *contrast* our ordinary sense perception of particular things in the external world with reasoned reflection of a more general kind. By emphasizing reasoned reflection they proposed that an intelligent human is already god-like. Knowledge that is revealed by reason is a kind of 'divine knowledge' and there is nothing better of the kind.[94]

And so it came to be said:

> [The early Athenians] conducted the city's affairs in the spirit of free men, by law honouring the good and punishing the wicked, for they thought it the action of wild animals to prevail over one another by violence. Human beings should make law the touchstone of what is right, and reasoned speech the means of persuasion, then subject themselves in action to these two powers – law their king and reason their teacher.[95]

During the fifth century when Socrates lived out his life in the democracy that had developed under the leadership of Perikles and his successors, aristocratic notions of an *exclusive* excellence continued to exist side by side with developing notions of citizen excellences. The excellences of citizens were seen to be a matter not of birth but of education and experience, enshrined in laws as *universal* expectations of the average man with subsidized leisure, who engaged not as a civic hero but as an amateur in politics. But the civically modified Homeric values still held sway for those with status and wealth. For them, the reconciliation of personal aims with the aims of the social order was circumscribed by an ideal of political leadership which was characterized by what was taken to be a good man's virtuous self-actualization, his *aretē,* within the political arena. We can observe this in the fifth century when the rich were required to undertake certain 'public works' (liturgies), for instance, paying for and arranging a group of performers in a festival or paying for a ship in the navy. Liturgies were seen as opportunities for men of wealth and good birth to compete in public spiritedness and there is evidence that some men performed liturgies in more extravagant ways than were expected.[96] Furthermore, it was said that one could recognize this character type, the man of *aretē,* from afar by his indifference to ordinary self-interest in his pursuit of some grand public cause. And in his indifference to his own economic well-being and that of his household, he displayed a magnanimity to the less fortunate in wealth as in knowledge.

Cimon, the Athenian aristocrat who dominated the political scene at the end of the second quarter of the fifth century BC, was described by Theopompus, the fourth-century historian (frag. 89), in the following way, a *topos* of magnanimity and aristocratic virtue:

> Cimon the Athenian stationed no guard over the produce in his fields or gardens so that any citizen who wished might go in and harvest and help himself if he needed anything on the estate. Furthermore, he threw his house open to all so that he regularly supplied an inexpensive meal to many men and the poor Athenians approached him and dined. And he

---

94   E. Hussey, 'The Beginnings of Epistemology: from Homer to Philolaus', in S. Everson, ed., *Companions to Ancient Thought, 1: Epistemology* (Cambridge, 1990), pp. 11–38.
95   *Lysias,* 2.18–1. See Nussbaum, *Fragility of Goodness,* pp. 94–5 on *Technē* as the deliberate application of human intelligence to some part of the world, yielding some control over *Tuche* (chance, contingency, fortune).
96   *Lysias,* 21, on a charge of taking bribes; 5 , speaking of one of his clients.

tended to those who day by day asked something of him. And they say that he always took around with him two or three youths who had some small change and ordered them to make a contribution whenever someone approached and asked him. And they say that he helped out with burial expenses. Many times also he did this: whenever he saw one of the citizens ill-clothed he would order one of the youths who accompanied him to change clothes with him. From all these things he won his reputation and was first of the citizens.[97]

In 461, however, Cimon was ostracized by democrats who wished to limit the power of aristocratic patronage.

Thereafter, it came to be discussed whether or not a man was born with this kind of character which then could be perfected by an appropriate range of relatively exclusive experiences. This character type was then contrasted with another, that of a rich and leisured young man who used his wealth to try to buy *aretē* from those who professed to teach *anyone* success in political life. These professors were said to make money out of their clients' discussions of their shifting opinions concerning what was right and wrong.

The Sophists

Imagine Athens at this time as the major intellectual and artistic centre for Greece. The economic transformation of the city-state during the fifth century in fact amounted to a revolution, as the economy of the *polis* became an economy of empire after the destruction of the Persians and the development of trade agreements and a protection alliance, the so-called Delian League of *poleis,* with Athens in charge. As private affluence increased and public building programmes made Athens a city of great elegance (the Parthenon was particularly notable), individual teachers, known in general as Sophists (from *Sophistes,* meaning 'expert'), arrived from all over the Greek world to offer their career-orientated services to the rich (if not always well-born), especially during the 'age of Perikles'. Indeed, Perikles was one of their main patrons and if the later Plutarch is to be believed, the Sophists Anaxagoras and Protagoras were his closest associates.[98] The Sophists were not merely precursors to the classical political theory to be developed by Plato and Aristotle. They were, instead, the culmination of a long tradition of political theorizing which had advanced to provide, not least, the foundations for the development of democracies and an understanding of procedural justice in communities.[99] Plato's dialogues, too, are filled with men who were in real life either patrons or clients of Sophists, or Sophists themselves; they are Plato's main philosophical antagonists. It is largely their views which must be overcome.

In the actual life of the city Sophists do seem to have set the agenda of Athenian debate in almost all areas of intellectual enquiry. From a political perspective it was precisely the variety of Sophist positions that required assessment and, in Plato's view, counteraction. In this, Plato appears to have shared some of the views of many of his contemporaries but for reasons that were not necessarily theirs. Indeed, Sophist

---

97   Cited from Millett, 'Patronage', pp. 23–4, who uses this as an example of private patronage.
98   G. B. Kerferd, *The Sophistic Movement* (Cambridge, 1981), p. 18.
99   For texts in translation see M. Gagarin and P. Woodruff, eds, *Early Greek Political Thought from Homer to the Sophists* (Cambridge, 1995).

teachings were not often well-received in the cities they visited; at best they were mocked in comedies, and at worst, as during the second half of the fifth century in Athens itself, they were prosecuted – some believe – in astonishing numbers, sent into exile and, possibly, their books burnt. The full democracy of Athens, this rich and affluent city whose citizens were equally entitled to exercise the freedom of public speech and to engage in debate and the taking of collective decisions, found certain views intolerable, despite Perikles' claim that in private they were tolerant. The charge brought against various Sophists was usually that of impiety (*asebeia*): not believing in the city's divinities and/or teaching astronomy as a kind of scientific rationalism to 'explain' traditional superstitions. The charge of impiety would also be brought against Socrates.

But some scholars think the real objection to Sophists was that they were willing to teach *anyone at all* about 'matters of state' in order that he might then become a success-ful politician.[100] To some Sophists, this might have meant that the character type re-quired to lead the *dēmos* could be *acquired* by their private instruction, not least in the techniques of persuasive public speaking. But what, if anything, was implied or actually taught concerning such a man's moral principles and values *prior* to his entry into public debate over policy issues of the day? And if it was held that *aretē* or the kind of excellence that merits public office can be taught, then was there any natural gift required by the pupil in order that he might benefit from the teaching? Or was money sufficient for anyone possessing it to come along to learn how to 'merit' high office and attain it? Were there personal qualities that a man, seeking to lead the *polis*, might be expected to possess or acquire? The appearance of certain Sophists in Athens raised questions not only about what a politician needed to *know* but also about what kind of man he needed to *be*.

From Plato's presentation of some of the Sophist positions in his dialogues, it appears they offered various answers to these questions, not all of which, by any means, implied a preference for democratic principles and equality of opportunity. If we look at some of the issues they treated we can see that whatever their final conclusions, Sophists were examining the beliefs and values of a previous generation and subjecting tradition to scrutiny, if not to outright attack. Plato presents some of their views as capable of be-coming those of the majority if they had not already done so. And we are reliant on Plato's generally hostile analysis of a variety of Sophist positions because Sophists' works have survived only in fragments.[101]

It appears that the Sophist agenda overlapped with that of the pre-Socratic natural-ists,[102] especially where some of them discussed not only the important problems con-cerning human knowledge and its relation to human perception, but also the nature of truth and reality and their relation to appearances. Some of them were concerned with whether moral values are relative to experience and social circumstance or are fixed despite these contingencies. Some of them wondered whether a *knowledge* of the gods was possible for humans or whether the human conception of the gods was necessarily based on and limited by the *human conception* of heroic humans. Some proposed the

100 Kerferd, *The Sophistic Movement*, p. 26.
101 Texts in H. Diels and W. Kranz, *Die Fragmente der Vorsokratiker*, 6th edn (Berlin, 1952); M. Untersteiner, *Sofisti, Testimonianze e frammenti* (Florence, 1949–67); R. K. Sprague, *The Older Sophists: a complete translation* (Columbia, SC, 1972). Also see W. K. C. Guthrie, *The Sophists* (Cambridge, 1971).
102 See introduction.

origin of politics as deriving from the social, but pre-political, expectation that all men are or ought to be considered equal in their relevant sensitivities to mutual social respect and to a concern for justice which can then be refined by education and good laws. Some queried society's attitude to punishment. If some people act against basic principles of mutual social respect and display little concern for justice, should they be subject to vindictive punishment and seen as social enemies who must be harmed, or should their punishment consist in rehabilitation and re-education so as to try to ensure that at some time in the future they can re-enter society as responsible citizens? Some asked whether the *polis* needs professional moral educators or whether it is the culture and institutions and laws of the *polis*, through its schools, family, military service, political participation, which educate young citizens so that professional teachers teach not moral education but a range of other skills. What then makes a good teacher and what makes a good pupil? And if a man seeks a political career, does he need some further education beyond the moral, which one might presume he has acquired from family and the social institutions, and beyond what he has learnt in studying language and literature, mathematics and athletics in school?[103] What should those aspiring to be statesmen be taught? And what kind of characters should they display?

Two of the most well-known Sophists were Protagoras (*c*.485–415 BC), the close associate of Perikles, and Gorgias (from Sicily), who came to Athens in 427 BC and was much admired for his rhetoric. It appears that there was a difference between the more generalist teachers called Sophists who spoke on all subjects, and rhetoricians.[104] Both men gave epideictic speeches, praising and blaming, and taught Athenian pupils privately for large sums of money. Along with Socrates, these were the major figures in that phase of Greek philosophy which most interests historians of political thought.

If the whole previous philosophical tradition, both cosmological and metaphysical, had assumed that rational argument and enquiry can arrive at the *truth* of how things are, Gorgias in particular appears to have argued that nothing can be proved one way or the other. Argument does not produce truth but, rather, persuasion and a man skilled in oratory is able to make an equally satisfying case for *every* position. Intellectual activity is therefore not concerned with the truth but with the persuasive, and similarly, the pre-Socratic naturalists' arguments about the *kosmos* must be thought of as neither right nor wrong but as more or less plausible, depending on the persuasive skill of the arguer.

A similar testing of some of the pre-Socratic arguments about the relation between reality and appearance, for instance, that how things *are* is different from how they *appear*, was taken up by Protagoras. For him, it was not possible to distinguish clearly between how things are and how they seem, so that all one can say is that what seems to be so to you, is so. Protagoras' most famous dictum was 'of all things, man is the measure – of what is, that it is and of what is not, that it is not' (frag. 1). Appearances are all that there are for us.[105] But unlike Gorgias, Protagoras did not present a sceptical position

---

103   This list of topics is adapted from Kerferd, *The Sophistic Movement*, introduction.

104   See Plato's *Gorgias* 465b–c, where Gorgias calls himself a rhetorician and defines rhetoric as 'the ability to use words to persuade jurors in a jury court and councillors … and those in the Assembly and in any other meeting of a civic nature': *Gorgias* 452e 4; in the fourth century the word *rhetor* was synonymous with 'politician'.

105   Plato's dialogue *Theaetetus* is the main source for our knowledge of these views; see M. Burnyeat, 'Protagoras and Self-refutation in Plato's *Theaetetus*', in S. Everson, ed., *Companions to Ancient Thought, 1: Epistemology* (Cambridge, 1990), pp. 39–59.

which eliminates the truth; instead, he argued that the truth is what each of us takes it to be. If we are a member of a minority group in society which thinks it right to break the laws of the wider society, then our belief is true just as is the belief of the majority. There is no way in which we can be told *with certainty* which of the different true beliefs we should accept. For Protagoras, there is no way of determining whether one moral outlook is truly preferable to another, for each is true. But he believes that a statesman who is a skilled orator can substitute opinions that are better (not truer) than others and, for example, can persuade minorities to act in ways acceptable to the majority. Hence, he argues that those practices which seem right and praiseworthy to any particular state, that is, to any community which decides and judges its own laws and customs, *are so* for that state so long as it holds by them. Only where the practices or conventions are, *in any particular case*, unsound for them, does the wise man try to substitute others that are better and which appear to be sounder.[106] It is evident that the wise man must be able to convince others by his rhetorical skill in argument. Each person is, of course, situated in a culture with conventions, and so, human convention, which is dependent on culture, is the measure of how things are. And 'how things are' is itself a measure of convention. Hence, for Protagoras, as Plato presents him in his dialogue of that name, *aretē,* a man's virtue, excellence or efficiency, can be taught and it is taught by experience; it is 'picked up' as a pattern of behaviour, the way a child 'picks up' language. And all men, more or less, have a capacity to 'pick up' *aretē* as it is transmitted by social conventions. Protagoras was an optimist and viewed human nature as capable of civilized progression: virtue could be taught, not by an intellectual discipline but by 'social control'.

However, what Protagoras takes *aretē* to be is not what Socrates understands it to be. According to Socrates, a man's excellence or virtue is an *intellectual discipline*, a consistent attitude of mind that emerges from an *unchanging intellectual insight into the true state of reality*. For Socrates, *aretē* is not simply habit or the ordinary man's intuitions and attachments but a branch of scientific *knowledge*, proceeding from within to guide external behaviour and perhaps, in some fundamental sense, it cannot be taught at all. We must note that he held this rational view while also taking both dreams and oracles very seriously.

As we shall see, there is an important contrast between the Socratic position and that of either of the two Sophists, Protagoras and Gorgias. For both Sophists, how things 'really' are is not discoverable by enquiry and argument. For them, philosophical activity simply does not get at *the* truth; for Gorgias it gets at no truth at all but at more or less good arguments and for Protagoras it gets at as many truths as there are men, culturally situated, who experience the world of appearances.

There were practical political consequences of these positions. If, according to some Sophists, all that men can attain is 'more or less good arguments' rather than the truth, then an examination of democratic principles might well raise questions about their justification. Better arguments might be put forward in favour of power to the 'better born'. In Athens, the Sophist Antiphon, in favour of the oligarchic revolution of 411 BC, criticized democratic conventional justice along just these lines and argued that democratic laws violated nature (*physis*). Arguments in favour of democratic justice, with their appeal to the interest of others, the weaker, the collectivity, were no more than bad

---

106   Alternative readings in D. Bostock, *Plato's Theaetetus* (Oxford, 1988); T. Irwin, *Plato's Moral Theory* (Oxford, 1977) and F. M. Cornford, *Plato's Theory of Knowledge* (London, 1935).

attempts at deceiving and preventing the 'naturally' stronger, more able men from pursuing their 'heroic', selfish, anti-social aims and their own more exclusive power. These arguments would surface in Plato's characterizations of Thrasymachus in the *Republic* and Callicles in the *Gorgias*. One of the major questions to be resolved was: were a society's laws (*nomoi*) necessarily in conflict with nature (*physis*)?[107]

During Socrates' adult life and in the early years of his student, Plato, the attack on Athenian conventional morality (*nomoi*) reached a revolutionary pitch, in part dictated by Athens' defeat by Sparta. Socrates, insisting that he was no Sophist, took up a number of the issues raised by a range of Sophists and their clients. With the reinstatement of democratic rule (403/2 BC) he was brought to trial, condemned and put to death in 399 BC. What did he teach and why did Athenian democracy kill him?

---

107 See Dodds on the difficulties of interpreting the many meanings of this antithesis: *The Greeks and the Irrational*, pp. 182–3; and A. W. H. Adkins, *Moral Values and Political Behaviour in Ancient Greece* (New York, 1972) on Antiphon.

2

Socrates

Conversation [with Socrates] did not turn on the nature of things as a whole, as was the case with most of the others. . . . With him, conversation was always about human affairs.

Xenophon, *Memorabilia*, I, i, 11

Socrates, a native Athenian, was charged and then tried by a jury of his fellow citizens when he was seventy years old. In the recently restored democracy of 399 BC three private individuals, Meletus, Anytus and Lycon, presented their case against him before a jury consisting of 501 citizens. The indictment and affidavit of Meletus read: 'Socrates is guilty of not duly acknowledging the gods in which the city believes and of introducing other, new divinities. He is also guilty of corrupting the young. The penalty proposed is death.'

Socrates was said to have spent a lifetime injuring Athens not only by his unorthodox views on a range of subjects, but in his insistence on propagating them. Because the proceedings in ancient Greek trials were oral and not recorded, all that remains to us are the indictment and verdict. Who the historical Socrates was, and what he taught in his lifetime, are almost irretrievably lost to the past. He wrote nothing. What we know of him comes from the traditions that grew up both around him (in the works of Plato, Xenophon, Aristotle and anti-Socratics like Polykrates) and over subsequent centuries, and not least from his students' and supporters' written defences (*apologia* means defence). The most famous of these is Plato's *Apology*.[1]

---

1   There are numerous translations of Plato's *Apology*. That used here is from *The Last Days of Socrates*, trans. H. Tredennick (Harmondsworth, 1981), pp. 45–76 and numerous reprints; for a brief introduction to Socrates see J. Coleman, *Against the State: studies in sedition and rebellion* (Harmondsworth, 1995), ch. 2; on the changing traditions of Platonic scholarship see E. N. Tigerstedt, *Interpreting Plato* (Stockholm, 1977); T. Penner, 'Socrates and the Early Dialogues', in R. Kraut, ed., *The Cambridge Companion to Plato* (Cambridge, 1992), pp. 121–69, a volume which also has an extensive bibliography; see the various studies in H. H. Benson, ed., *Essays on the Philosophy of Socrates* (Oxford, 1992) with extensive bibliography; G. Vlastos, ed., *Plato: a collection of critical essays*, 2 vols (New York, 1971); T. Brickhouse and N. Smith, *Socrates on Trial* (Oxford, 1989); C. D. C. Reeve, *Socrates in the Apology: an essay on Plato's Apology of Socrates* (Indianapolis, 1996); G. Vlastos, *Socrates: ironist and moral philosopher* (Cambridge, 1991); still the fullest introduction in English to Greek philosophy is W. K. C. Guthrie, *A History of Greek Philosophy*, vol.

This work gives a partial account of Socrates' activities and beliefs up to 399, set out as the three speeches Socrates was supposed to have delivered at his one-day trial: his defence, his counter-proposal for the penalty, and a final address to the jury. After the first speech the jury voted 281 to 220 to find him guilty as charged; the vote was a close one. After the second speech they voted again, 361 in favour of capital punishment, 140 against. One month later, in prison, Socrates drank the hemlock administered by the authorities and died.

Plato's *Apology* has been read in two interrelated ways: as representing Plato's (largely accurate) view of the gist of Socrates' philosophical message and 'teaching' method, and as representing what Socrates *should* have said (but possibly did not say) in his defence. Unlike Plato's other works which feature Socrates as the main character in conversation with friends, the *Apology* is not written in dialogue form. Plato inserts himself into the *Apology* (34a, 38b) as present at the trial and it is generally thought that he provides at least a faithful record *in substance* of what had gone on.[2] If, however, Plato's artistic portrait of Socrates is unfaithful to the historical Socrates, we are in no position to correct it. Even if we could correct it, it is with the Socrates of Plato's dialogues that we must deal because it is this Socrates who has been so influential in the history of political thought. In a sense, then, the history of political thought begins with an artistic myth designed by Plato. As we shall see in the next chapter, Plato's Socratic philosophy of the early dialogues shades into a Platonism that is more his own. There are, however, scholars who remain sceptical about the possibility of reconstructing a distinctively Socratic doctrine. My aim, here, is to attempt to make the distinction.[3]

It was once thought that the religious charges of impiety laid against Socrates should not be taken seriously and that the real charge against him was corruption of Athenian youth. This meant that his condemnation should be seen largely as an act of political vengeance. Not only were Charmides and Kritias relatives of Plato and associates of Socrates (Kritias was one of the Thirty Tyrants and Charmides one of the Ten sent by the Thirty to rule the port of Piraeus – both fell with the restoration of democracy), but Socrates was known to be critical of the values of Athenian democrats and often in the company of wealthy young Athenians who were pro-Spartan. Some of the earliest references we have to Socrates come from Aristophanes' comedies, and in *The Birds* (414 BC) we are told that 'everyone used to be Spartan-mad, long-haired, fasting, filthy, Socratising and carrying little batons'.

---

3   *The Fifth-century Enlightenment* (Cambridge, 1969), vol. 4: *Plato: the man and his dialogues, earlier period* (Cambridge, 1975) and vol. 5: *The Later Plato and the Academy* (Cambridge, 1978). For a range of different approaches to Socrates in context see various articles in the journal *History of Political Thought*, notably: F. G. Whelan, 'Socrates and the "Meddlesomeness" of the Athenians', *History of Political Thought* 4 (1983), pp. 1–30; M. Mion, 'Athenian Democracy: politicization and constitutional restraints', *History of Political Thought* 7 (1986), pp. 219–38; J. R. Wallach, 'Socratic Citizenship', *History of Political Thought* 9 (1988), pp. 393–414. The journal *Polis* (1977–) (originally the newsletter of the Society for Greek Political Thought) provides good bibliographies and brief articles on themes relevant to Greek political thought.

2   Guthrie, *A History of Greek Philosophy*, vols 3 and 4, pp. 68–80, but see C. Kahn, 'Did Plato Write Socratic Dialogues?' in Benson, *Essays on the Philosophy of Socrates*, pp. 35–52; there are, of course, Xenophon's *Apology* and the *Memorabilia*, which present very different pictures of Socrates.

3   I am grateful to Dr Richard Stalley of the Department of Philosophy, University of Glasgow, for reading and commenting on this and the following chapter on Plato, especially because he is more sceptical than I am about the possibility of reconstructing distinctively Socratic doctrine.

But in Aristophanes' comedy *The Clouds* (423 BC), Socrates is represented as a Sophist, concerned not only with teaching dubious rhetorical tricks of argument for money in order to help rich men with weak legal cases win lawsuits (making the weaker argument appear the stronger). Aristophanes depicts Socrates and his influence through the distorting mirror of the pronouncements of the peasant Strepsiades. Perhaps more importantly, he is also portrayed as not believing in the gods. Instead, he studies the natural phenomena of the heavens and earth in order to show that rain comes not from Zeus but from clouds filled with water. In the *Apology* Socrates tells the jury that he has no interest in such matters at all and knows nothing about the kind of 'natural science' attributed to him by Aristophanes. But he is being tarred with the same brush that previously had been applied to the kind of pre-Socratic rationalism that was thought to destroy collective, traditional beliefs in the powers of gods to influence men's lives. At his trial Socrates denied these 'stock charges against philosophers' but said he would, in his own case, have difficulty ridding the jurors' minds of the false impressions that were the work of many years.

> I have incurred a great deal of bitter hostility and this is what will bring about my destruction, if anything does; not Meletus nor Anytus, but the slander and jealousy of a very large section of the people. They have been fatal to a great many other innocent men and I suppose will continue to be so. (*Apology* 28b)

Indeed, in the times of crisis witnessed by Socrates and Plato, the fifth-century 'rationalist enlightenment' discussed in the previous chapter took on the appearance of rationalism for the few and religion or magic for the many: charges of irreligion were often selected as the surest ways of suppressing unwelcome views. Works may have been burnt, and Sophists were sent into exile and, some think, even killed. Professional diviners proposed decrees against the advance of rationalism and at moments of crisis especially, they were taken seriously.[4] Hence, Aristophanes presented Socrates as the archetypical intellectual of the time, the Sophist, who disturbed and was ridiculed by average Athenian men. And the charge seemed to stick in the minds of ordinary Athenians. There appears to be a very specific reference to Socrates' special powers in Meletus' charge of impiety.

After the restoration of democracy, atheism was highlighted as a chargeable offence. Anytus, the only accuser of Socrates whom we know to have been a prominent political figure, was involved not only in the declaration of the general amnesty for pro-Spartan sympathizers, but also in the complete revision and codification of Athens' laws. If Socrates was to be charged, it would have to be with respect to an alleged violation of the newly codified laws, one of which was a law of impiety. Athenian law did not prescribe the recognition of a clearly specified set of gods but it did forbid atheism, and included here was the teaching of a belief in 'new deities' or 'personal deities' which, in the end, was taken to be a belief in no gods at all. Indeed, this is Meletus' charge as he is made to

---

4 The famous victims of successful prosecutions from *c.* 432 BC included Anaxagoras, Diagoras, probably Protagoras and possibly the playwright Euripides; see E. R. Dodds, *The Greeks and the Irrational* (Berkeley, 1951), p. 180 on the breach between intellectuals and people, and ibid., p. 189 on prosecutions. During the fifth and fourth centuries BC foreign religious cults were brought to Athens (Plato's *Republic* I speaks of the cult of Bendis) and people continued to show they were afraid of magical aggression; also see K. Dover, 'Freedom of the Intellectual in Greek Society' (1975) reprinted in K. Dover, *The Greeks and Their Legacy: collected papers* (Oxford, 1988).

clarify it by Socrates. Therefore, the longstanding prejudice against Socrates as a Sophist, natural philosopher, and now, atheist is relevant. The formal charges against him, that 'he does not recognize the gods the state recognizes' are to be taken seriously so that the religious charge of impiety and its propagation among the youth of Athens constituted the nature of his corrupting influence as they saw it.[5] As we shall see, however, what Socrates really stood for, as Plato presents him at his trial, was something quite new even in the religious sphere. But he would be accused in old terms and categories.

We must note that these categories did not present him as a crypto-oligarch or as someone with an explicitly anti-democratic political theory. Strictly speaking, he is portrayed as having *no political theory at all*.[6] There are, however, huge political consequences of his ethical theory and we shall see that he has political sentiments and loyalties which he insists are pro-Athenian if not necessarily in favour of a democratic constitution. But he proposes no alternative constitution. Constitutions, as such, do not interest him. Constitutions are merely the consequence of prior questions that need to be asked: what are the qualities of good statesmanship? and what kind of life ought a good man to lead? Instead of propounding a theory of politics, Socrates studies the art of statesmanship and his vision is an ethical one: to open up the philosophic life, which he sees as the true art of statesmanship, to as many men who desire it, indeed to all men, although he is not optimistic that all will follow. Why? Because in Athens, especially, men are distracted by wealth, personal status and success. Plato will have him say in the *Gorgias* (521D–522A f):

> I believe that I am one of the few Athenians – perhaps indeed there is no other who studies the genuine art of statesmanship, and that I am the only man now living who puts it into practice . . . and if it is alleged against me either that I am the ruin of the younger people by reducing them to a state of helpless doubt or that I insult their elders by bitter criticism in public or in private, no defence will avail me, whether true or not, the truth being simply that in all that I say I am guided by *what is right* and that my actions are in the interests of those who are sitting in judgement on me.

Since the democratic determination of 'what is right' was collective and consensual, how did Socrates discover *what is right*? And how was he alone set on this path of discovery when his fellow-citizens seemed preoccupied with other concerns?

How Socrates Discovered What is Right: The Elenchos – Seeking Definitions

According to Plato, Socrates did not write anything because he believed that the value of philosophizing lay in the interaction between a 'teacher' and 'pupil', with the 'teacher' guiding the pupil by asking questions, not giving answers. The pupil would then become aware of his own beliefs and their relation to one another. Since books are not alive they can serve only as reminders of what the real philosophical experience is like and real philosophizing is, for Socrates, each person's commitment to a search along a certain path for self-understanding in the company of a teacher who asks the right

---

5 See the discussion in Brickhouse and Smith, *Socrates on Trial*.
6 See Coleman, *Against the State*, ch. 2 and R. Kraut, *Socrates and the State* (Princeton, NJ, 1984).

questions to enable this understanding to emerge.[7] This method of asking questions, at first in order to expose an interlocutor's confusions, is called the *elenchos*. It is a method of philosophical investigation the aim of which is to show someone not only that some of his beliefs can be disproved but also that they are inconsistent with others he also holds. Socrates' elenctic method tests a moral rule that is widely accepted in Athenian society against his interlocutors' beliefs about examples of the rule and also against general assumptions about virtues. For instance, he would ask a man who thought he had 'exact' knowledge for a definition of 'piety'. The definition would have to indicate the quality or qualities that *all* pious acts have in common. Socrates would refuse to accept a definition that simply gave one example of a pious act (*Euthyphro*). He then suggested a class of things of which piety is a part, that class being 'justice' or 'right behaviour'.

Now, to many modern minds, Socrates' investigation cannot even begin without the taking for granted of a number of undemonstrated or indemonstrable assumptions which, some today would argue, are themselves culturally rooted. Socrates' method of investigating presupposes that his interlocutors have ordinary, unreflective beliefs. It also sometimes assumes that there are other theories of morality than Socrates' theory and that these are worth investigating in order to show them to be insufficient. The Socratic *elenchos* is supposed to adjust his interlocutors' conceptions of the virtues to fit in with an overall view of what is generally taken, by all involved in the discussion, to be worthwhile in a man's life. Therefore, the *elenchos* is not simply a destructive method of investigating people's inconsistent opinions. The real aim of the *elenchos* is to discover stable definitions and thereby defend *true moral doctrine*. He does not himself offer his own moral definitions. But he starts from the assumption that there *is* a moral truth to be revealed and furthermore, that it is already *in* his interlocutors as true beliefs of which they are initially unaware. Moral enquiry is, therefore, for everyone. Furthermore, it is a rational discipline. All that is needed is a teacher who asks the right questions so that the truth can emerge. By the elenctic investigation, Socrates sought to affirm that the truth that was uncovered was not only true for him but true for *every human being* – citizen or stranger – who bothered to think about it clearly.[8]

Socrates uses an inherited vocabulary for discussing moral questions, a vocabulary with which we have already become somewhat familiar in the previous chapter. It assumes that all his interlocutors are *in* the ethical world, that no one opts out of ethical discourse. No one is a pure sceptic. It assumes that his interlocutors are concerned with questions of *aretē*, that is, human virtue or excellence. And it seems (at least in the way Plato represents Socrates' discussions in the early dialogues) that his interlocutors not only understood the questions he asked but, most importantly, that they also took for granted the *existence* of virtues, things like piety, courage and justice. The question was not whether these things existed – everyone seemed to agree that they did – but what was their nature, how should we *define* what they essentially are? The next question, after agreeing on their definition or nature, would be, how does any man (Athenian or Spartan, citizen or stranger) acquire them? The Sophists' agenda was significant here and

---

7   For someone who believes this, philosophical books are to philosophy as tennis manuals are to tennis, as Martha Nussbaum aptly puts it in *The Fragility of Goodness, Luck and Ethics in Greek Tragedy and Philosophy* (Cambridge, 1986), p. 125.

8   On the huge demands such a method makes on Socrates' interlocutors see G. Klosko, 'Rational Persuasion in Plato's Political Theory', *History of Political Thought* 7 (1986), pp. 15–31.

Plato does not present them as undermining the importance of traditional morality. In later dialogues he will show some Sophists to acknowledge the popular acceptance of the virtues but that this acknowledgement that *other* people play by the rules should be seen as instrumental to the acquisition of power by the few who have no need of exercising common virtues themselves. In other words, most people recognize that they exist in an ethical world but some wish to prosper by trying to deceive others about their commitment to common values. The Socrates of the early dialogues usually does not take on the ethical sceptic. Plato, however, will later feature ethical sceptics and show Socrates attempting, through rational argument, to demonstrate their position to be irrational and mistaken and, therefore, not sceptical at all.

Therefore, when Socrates asked his interlocutors, some of whom were Sophists, to define what they believed piety or justice to be, we ought not to be surprised that they thought they *could* give appropriate definitions of what they took for granted existed. Most of them, however, tended to give *examples* of what they took to be socially accepted ways of behaving virtuously. But by seeking *definitions*, Socrates wanted to affirm two things: first, that teaching men the skills of powerful, rhetorical persuasion or other political techniques, as the Sophists claimed they were able to do, did not solve fundamental questions about moral beliefs. Rather, the power of reason was what gave the ethical its force. If you engaged in rational argument with anyone, Socrates thought you could intellectually justify the ethical life. Through appropriate questioning, rational agents will discover for themselves that they are committed to the ethical life for their own good. And second, that instead of each person having his own private and different view on the *nature* or definition of these existents – justice, courage or piety – they were, in reality, all referring *essentially* to the same, stable thing: the virtues were unified. As we shall see, Socrates searched for universal definitions of the moral virtues that he and his community believed existed and he then affirmed that all the virtues were one. A person who has one virtue will, he said, necessarily have them all. Did the *elenchos* as a method of investigation have consequences for the practice of Athenian democracy?

Socrates did not reject the democratic entitlement of every citizen to join in discussion. Nor did he suggest that they should only be allowed to vote on final outcomes. It was rather that he believed that the truth was not to be determined by vote at all. In his democratically organized society, important decisions were made by majority vote, and political leaders, depending on majority support, courted popular appeal to secure their power bases. They used a kind of oratory in the courts and in the Assembly which Socrates refers to in the *Apology* as artificial, flowery language to sway the emotions. Socrates sharply distinguishes himself from these skilful speakers. This is because he believed that one could rationally explain away the power of the emotions in determining human behaviour. While most ordinary Greeks seemed to think that rational knowledge was not a dominant force in ruling a man and reasoning was, rather, a 'slave' to man's passions, Socrates thought that the emotions which most men thought motivated them to act could be explained and corrected in intellectual terms. Therefore, he says: 'Disregard the manner of my speech . . . and concentrate on whether my claims are fair or not'.

Socrates insisted that *before* one voted one had to spend a long time doing something else: one had to develop a serious, intellectual grasp of the ethical issues at stake and clarify one's own considered views on the matters of right and wrong, on the nature of justice, piety and courage. If you could not first *define* justice you would be in no position to determine, in specific circumstances, if a man had acted justly or not. Because Socrates believed that you had to have an ethics *before* you became politically active, he spent his life showing prominent public figures that their views on the nature of justice, piety and courage were unconsidered and unreflective. And he embarrassed them in public confrontations. He said that he was not paid for initiating these confrontations nor did he *teach* in the sense of instilling into his interlocutors a substantive doctrine to replace their own shaky opinions. This does not mean that he had no convictions of his own but they were, in crucial ways, different from those of Sophists like Protagoras and Gorgias. Everyone, even these Sophists, seemed to have accepted that the virtues existed but what they were and how they were acquired were disputed. Hence, Socrates went about trying to confirm *his* convictions by engaging anyone who would search with him for clarifications of that other person's strongly held views. He did this because he first of all insisted that, if a man had not reflected on his own values and on the more fundamental questions concerning what a good life is for a man, then he was poorly qualified to discuss the political ways and means to achieve any of his more political objectives. Socrates wanted to show that there are moral norms for all good men, whether or not they happened to be rich, well-born and powerful, and that moral norms are not guaranteed to advance the status, power or wealth of one man over another. But then, status, power and wealth were not of *primary* importance. He tells the court that in his own case, his necessary and beneficent mission to question the citizens of Athens has reduced him to extreme poverty and has led him to neglect his family affairs. This appears to be a variation on the well-worn theme of the man of true *aretē*, indifferent to ordinary self-interest in pursuit of some grand public cause. As Vlastos has noted, Socrates sticks to what in his Greek world (and that of Odysseus) would have been the rare deed of high moral resolve, but makes it into a rule of everyday conduct for everyone.[9]

At his trial he said the only thing worth considering in the performance of any action is whether a man is acting rightly or wrongly, whether he is acting like a good man or a bad one. That there is a right and wrong way of behaving, that there is a truth in such matters is not doubted and he furthermore believed that his fellow citizens accepted that there was a truth in these matters, a distinction to be drawn between a good and bad man, between pious and impious acts, between acting with justice and acting unjustly. Hence, he spent his life 'button-holing' fellow citizens in the *agora* and questioning them on a one-to-one basis about their views on certain moral concepts, on moral beliefs they said they held strongly. He then would show them, much to their annoyance, that they were not able to defend their views as they previously thought they could. And they certainly could not simply assume that their culture (any culture) had taught them, through instilling unreflective habits of behaviour, how to be virtuous and live well.

It was not that he offered them a new and original doctrine in the form of specific answers to the questions he asked. Indeed, he insisted that he was unaware of having knowledge in any absolute sense because he believed that real wisdom of an absolute kind is the property of god, not man. (*Apology*, 21b and d). Rather, he acknowledges that he was *thought* to have a kind of human wisdom, a practical knowledge (which people then believed he simply was not imparting when he questioned others but offered no answers) and that he was successful in disproving another person's claim to

9   Vlastos, *Socrates*, p. 212.

wisdom in a given subject by refuting him from the person's *own* beliefs. But Socrates insists that he has come to realize that his kind of wisdom, a human kind, is the recognition that human wisdom is limited. He insists he teaches nothing. But through his questioning of politically ambitious men he shows them to reveal the truth to themselves and others. This truth is 'that they are being convicted of pretending to knowledge when they are entirely ignorant'. He says that it is his plain speaking on this matter that has caused his long-term unpopularity. And a one-day trial would be too short a time to rid men's minds of their misconceptions about his kind of wisdom and method of interrogating others.

Socratic Ignorance and Moral Convictions

We cannot leave Socratic ignorance here, because it is a paradoxical kind of ignorance that disclaims special knowledge and yet gets people to contribute what he takes to be *true* answers to problems under discussion. His trial speeches show that Plato's Socrates did have moral convictions and we shall discuss the range of these convictions below. Vlastos[10] has taken his profession of ignorance to be a kind of irony which allows him to disclaim one sort of knowledge (absolute, divine) and distinguish it from another sort, the kind that begins with a recognition of human limitations. He held to his conviction that moral truth is what he did reach by means of the *elenchos*. Indeed, his method of questioning is meant to be a way of persuading others of the truth of his convictions. *One* of these convictions is that human knowledge comes from asking the right questions, because Socrates believed that people have within them *true* (as opposed to merely habitual) opinions of which they are unaware until they are asked the right questions. While he never seems to treat the question 'what is knowledge?', he does accept that knowledge is possible. He believes there is a truth of reality, and right questions can reveal to each individual the same, right answers from within their belief systems. Therefore, for Socrates, human knowledge is a rational discipline. In the communal life of the *polis* this is of great importance. Athenians were prepared to recognize doctors, architects, commanders of the army and navy as having special qualifications which they acquired through specific training in order to practise their skills effectively. But what kind of training did they require of politically ambitious men? Courses in successful public speaking, at most. Socrates believed that perhaps more than any other 'profession' a political leader required a kind of moral training and this could come about only after many years spent considering and clarifying what justice and human excellences (*aretē*) consist in. This intellectual consideration was not equivalent to having lots of individual experiences in the world of men and things. Moral training was an engagement in a rational discipline, an intellectual enquiry into one's own opinions concerning the distinction between what is good and what is bad. Only thereafter could a man sit in judgement of others in juries or make collective civic decisions in the Assembly. But it is not simply that one needed this intellectual enquiry for political leadership or in order to carry out civic functions. One needed this enquiry if one were to be happy as a man. Hence, he makes the astounding statement in the *Apology* that a life that is not spent in this kind of ethical self-examination is simply not worth living.

10 Ibid., p. 13.

Sophists of all kinds were engaged in similar questionings of ethical standards and how we come to have them. As we saw, some argued that although virtues existed, people simply held the views on right and wrong that they did because of social conventions and these were learnt as habits through the experience of being acculturated: at home and in school, where you read the poets (Homer) who recounted the exploits of the gods and man's relation to the divine; or in public, where you participated in civic administration and adhered to the laws and customs (*nomoi*) of your society; or, if you could afford it, you hired a teacher of rhetoric who taught persuasive techniques to enable you to sway a crowd to your own view. Socrates thought that none of these 'educational experiences' taught you to 'know yourself' and thereafter, to come to see that social justice, truly understood, was not mere arbitrary convention but natural and a universal value that was essentially the same everywhere. Stable definitions of the human excellences or virtues (*aretē*), for Socrates, could be naturally elicited by the elenctic investigation and this was so important an engagement that the philosophical life must take precedence over a life of political activity. This was especially the case in a society that accepted there was specialized knowledge to be acquired by doctors and military leaders but thought of politics as a sphere for non-specialist amateurs. Therefore he said: 'The true champion of justice, if he intends to survive even for a short time, must necessarily confine himself to private life and leave politics alone' (*Apology* 32a). The intellectualism of his approach to ethical standards is what is so astonishing. For Socrates, the virtues are cognitive achievements.

But this does *not* mean that one does not do one's public duties: Socrates did take up his office when he was selected for the Council (*Boulē*), and he did perform his military service. He shows himself to have been a model citizen. But if asked to commit a moral wrong, as he believed he was asked by the Assembly when he was a member of the Council, to try *en bloc* the commanders who had failed to rescue men lost in an otherwise successful naval engagement at Arginousae, he would not act unconstitutionally and unjustly. And later, when summoned by the Thirty Tyrants to fetch the wealthy metic, Leon of Salamis, so that he could be executed, Socrates again refused and went home. All that mattered to him was that he should *do nothing wrong and uphold the cause of right*, no matter what the consequences. He says that he would never submit *wrongly* to any authority through fear of death or through fear of being banished or deprived of civic rights. To be frightened of death was to pretend to know about what could not be known to a man. These are moral rather than political acts. And he clearly sees himself following in a long-established ethical tradition: the heroic consideration not to act so as to incur dishonour (he refers to Trojan heroes – *Apology*, c. 27b–28c) is seen by Socrates as akin to his own concern to act rightly and as a good man. For Socrates, to be both a good man and a statesman, a leader of the *polis,* requires a certain character type and a special training. These only come about through engaging in philosophy, living the examined life, revealing to yourself that you are a certain sort of man who lives the only life that is worth living.

Socrates Alone on His Path of Discovery

Socrates' first speech at his trial (*Apology*, 24b–28a), his attempt to answer Meletus' charge of impiety, indeed atheism, is an example of his use of the *elenchos*. He questions

Meletus, who answers under compulsion of the court, and Socrates believes that he has sufficiently cleared himself so that the jurors may judge with respect to the truth about the way in which the law of impiety applies in his case, that is, not at all. Was Socrates deluding himself over his potential victory? His real fear, he says, is of the older purveyors of false rumours, his invisible, unaccountable opponents, who have accused him over the years before the entire citizenry, from the time they were impressionable children. But both the older and the more recent accusers seem to be of one piece regarding 'impiety' and Socrates' elenctic method will prove to be of no avail, possibly for the following reason.

Socrates realized that his behaviour was considered abnormal. He shows in the *Apology* that even to those who best knew and loved him, he was not only unique but also strange. He made a self-confessed 'extravagant claim' about himself and called as his witness the god at Delphi. Socrates' friend Chaerephon, a good democrat, had gone to the shrine at Delphi to ask the god whether there was anyone wiser than Socrates. The priestess replied there was no one. When Socrates heard this, *he asked himself what the god could possibly mean* in asserting that he was the wisest man in the world, given that Socrates considered he had no claim to wisdom. *In attempting to answer the question for himself*, he tried to test the claim by interrogating men with reputations for wisdom and found them wanting. Although Socrates may have perfected his elenctic method by examining self-proclaimed wise men, Socrates' uniqueness apparently did not begin with the oracle of Delphi, but much earlier. He says that he pursued his investigation 'at the god's command'. He tries to 'help the cause of god' by proving that men, citizens or strangers, who consider themselves wise, are not so. Philosophizing is for him an active search in obedience to the 'divine command'. But the oracle questioned at Delphi had *commanded* nothing. Nor had the priestess at Delphi acted the part of teacher or questioner. If truth emerges in a search for self-understanding in the company of a teacher who asks the seeker the right questions, then who asked Socrates his questions? Who was *his* teacher? The priestess at Delphi did not ask a question but answered one. Socrates had long previously been asking his own questions of himself: what manner of life ought a good man to live?

He reveals that he had a prior experience in early childhood: he was subject to a divine or supernatural experience, a *daimonion*, a divine sign, a sort of voice that came to him alone to dissuade him from doing wrong. It did not tell him what to do but provided him with an intuition of what not to do. He says it somehow stopped him from doing wrong. And he then interpreted this as urging him on to pursue philosophy as self-examination. He notes that it is this personal deity that Meletus 'saw fit to travesty in his indictment'. It is not that Socrates has demonstrated that he does not believe in the supernatural or in the state's divinities.[11] He demonstrated to Meletus and the court that he believed in both – *in his way*. This way personally transformed Athenian custom and religion. He did not address the question of whether or not he had radically different views of the gods from those commonly accepted. Instead, he explicitly affirmed an allegiance to something beyond tradition, a personal, interior contact with his own divine sign and he says that this *daimonion*, this sign, as interpreted by him, debars him

---

11   Guthrie, *A History of Greek Philosophy*, vol. 4, n. 1, p. 83: 'The argument that one cannot believe in things *daimonia* without believing in *daimones* and that *daimones* are the children of gods, is so wholly Greek as to be scarcely reproducible in English.'

from entering public life. But Perikles, we recall, had said Athenians who were not concerned with the political were considered useless.

The centre of Socrates' defence is, then, the story of the oracle which leads to Socrates' revelation that he has his own private, divine sign *which his own fallible human resources must interpret.*[12] His divine sign combined with the oracle's pronouncement meant to him that he was divinely appointed, as a man and with a man's ability to reason about things human, to Athens 'as though it were a large, lazy, thoroughbred horse in need of stimulation from a stinging fly'. Was it possible for ancient Athenian society to tolerate not only this private, idiosyncratic contact with the divine, but also Socrates' intellectual interpretation of its meaning and his propagation of the views that were consequent on his private religious experience? This is what leads him to say that although he is a grateful and devoted servant of Athens, 'I owe a greater obedience to god than to you', and this duty is to lead the philosophic life, examining himself and others. He asserts that philosophical enquiry (and not political activity) happens to be the greatest good for men.

> I shall never stop practising philosophy and exhorting you and elucidating the truth for everyone that I meet. I shall go on saying [whether acquitted, or not], in my usual way: my very good friend, you are an Athenian and belong to a city which is the greatest and most famous in the world for its wisdom and strength. Are you not ashamed that you give your attention to acquiring as much money as possible, and similarly with reputation and honour, and give no attention or thought to truth and understanding and the perfection of your soul? . . . This, I do assure you, is what my god commands and it is my belief that no greater good has ever befallen you in this city than my service to the god; for I spend all my time going about trying to persuade you, young and old, to make your first and chief concern not for your bodies nor for your possessions, but for the highest welfare of your souls, proclaiming as I go, 'wealth does not bring goodness, but goodness brings wealth and every other blessing, both to the individual and to the state'. (*Apology* 29d)

Brickhouse and Smith have argued that his unorthodox belief alone constituted culpable guilt under the Athenian law of impiety. Others see the real difficulty as lying not in his idiosyncratic beliefs but in his active dissemination of his views with the purpose of making others like himself. Hence, to some, his aggressive public mission turned his moral enquiry into political activity and this was what Athens decided was intolerably dangerous. Dodds argued that part of the explanation for his trial and death was superstitious terror based on the perception that Socrates jeopardized the solidarity of the city-state. The other part of the explanation was that the new rationalism carried dangers for social order in that many people used it as an excuse to discard collective religious restraints that had previously held human egotism on the leash.[13] Still others[14] have argued that Athenian democrats found it intolerable to be questioned and asked to defend their beliefs and this was sufficient motivation to have Socrates removed if he would not agree to be silenced. At his trial he insisted that it was impossible for someone

12 Brickhouse and Smith argue in *Socrates on Trial* that the sign can override any decision reached on rational grounds. I agree with Vlastos, *Socrates*, p. 285 who argues there is no possibility for Socrates to allow his sign to trump a decision reached on rational grounds. Socrates believed that the sign and his reason were in accord.
13 Dodds, *The Greeks and the Irrational*, p. 191.
14 Kraut, *Socrates and the State* and in Coleman, *Against the State*, ch. 2 .

committed to moral truth to leave Athens or any other society alone. Although Athens prided itself on its greater tolerance than that of other city-states, some have thought that Socrates took Athenian *isegoria,* equality of public speech, and *parrhesia,* too far.

Socrates' fate raises unresolved questions about the threat his kind of rationalism (and moral absolutism) posed to his (or any other) state. Part of the irresolution for us, today, is surely the consequence of modern, secular societies finding the charge of impiety incomprehensible or 'irrational'.[15] Socrates' fate also raises the issue of the degree to which a philosopher with an explicitly ethical rather than political theory is responsible for the thoughts and actions of his disciples and students. In Socrates' case, he would rapidly be taken up by a wide range of ancient schools of philosophy who claimed him as their founder despite being at variance with one another (Cynics, Hedonists, Stoics, Sceptics). Plato, Aristotle and their philosophical and religious followers took Socrates, however they understood him or misinterpreted him, to be the true turning point in ancient Greek philosophy, religion and ethics. Furthermore, Socrates' uncompromising idealism appealed down the ages to men who none the less held to convictions that do not appear to have been his. As Dodds pointed out, the new rationalism and its frequent favouring of what some considered natural in man over the constraints of mere convention, a rationalism of which Socrates was taken by some contemporaries to have been a part, 'did not *enable* men to behave like beasts – men have always been able to do that'. Rather, it gave them tools to justify their brutality to themselves and others.[16]

In time, Plato's Socrates would be presented by early, philosophically minded Christians as a precursor to Christ and his *Apology* would be read as an ancient Greek version of the Sermon on the Mount. Furthermore, Plato's Socrates, as his character was to be developed in later dialogues, would be shown to espouse a political as well as an ethical doctrine so that Socrates would later be 'remembered' as having been explicitly critical of democracy as a constitution. As we shall see, Plato's *Republic* provides Socrates with a detailed training programme that would equip only an elite of political leaders, philosophers, to make the correct moral choices for the ideal *polis.*

But the Socrates of the *Apology* is presented as having no coherent programme to raise the level of democratic political discussion. Nor does he propose that Athens be ruled by the few. Rather, his moral theory is focused on true understanding prior to political power, a true understanding of moral well-being and human happiness. He is prepared to disregard the unreflective views of the many who have not engaged in philosophy and developed their moral expertise. Although he never seems to have offered a definition of what the good life for man is, he believed that the question 'how should a good man live?' was an *intellectual* problem. It was *the* question that must engage the human mind. And he seemed to be arguing as a consequence that no state, whatever its constitution, over and above moral individuals, can be a final authority to decide on moral

---

15 Much has been made of this in the case of the author Salman Rushdie and his book *The Satanic Verses*; and yet blasphemy is a crime in Britain – a state with a national Church.

16 Dodds, *The Greeks and the Irrational*, p. 191: '[Athenians'] fears [of the directions rationalism could take] were not groundless; but as people do when they are frightened, they struck with the wrong weapon and they struck the wrong man.' But see the portrayal of Socrates as a protagonist of 'landed reaction' in A. Winspear, *The Genesis of Plato's Thought* (New York, 1940) and the more nuanced discussion in Ellen and Neal Wood, *Class Ideology and Ancient Political Theory* (Oxford, 1978), ch. 3; there is a necessarily inconclusive discussion of rival readings in J. M. Bryant, *Moral Codes and Social Structures in Ancient Greece: a sociology of Greek ethics from Homer to the Epicureans and Stoics* (Albany, NY, 1996), pp. 193–200.

principles. He wanted to show that reflective men apply standards in judging whether a particular convention is just or not and this standard opened a society's conventions to rational criticism.[17] To recognize virtuous or vicious actions an individual first must know the *definition* of good and bad as a whole. Therefore, no public authority should be *wrongly* and unreflectively obeyed, as he said at his trial. Although Socrates presumed that the political community was a necessity and that one owed the *polis* respect and gratitude for its benefits, similar to those a child receives from its parents, a good man is obliged to try to explain or persuade the *polis* when he judges it appropriate to disobey those of its commands that he believes would force him to do wrong. This is not a result of subjective feelings. He does this on the basis of having come to know, through philosophical self-examination, what the definitions of right and wrong are. Socrates, as such a man, could not obey a court decision that required that he stop philosophizing because this would be a command to live the unexamined life which, he said, was not worth living. It would amount to doing wrong and self-harm. Examining one's intentions is undertaken so that one never knowingly harms or does wrong (at least) and one knowingly does right. As a citizen, however, he would accept the court's decision that he die while arguing that *they* were committing an injustice, doing wrong and harming, so that others, in the future, would take him for a martyr. Nor would he escape from prison when his friends said they would provide the means (*Crito*). In accepting death but refusing to stop philosophizing he would neither wrong the state nor his god because he believed that, for a good man, it is better to suffer wrong than to commit it. He was practising what he preached. Furthermore, he believed that a good man could not be harmed by a worse. Philosophizing made one realize this. If you did not engage in philosophical self-examination you were unwittingly living a trivial life, filled with self-harm, that was not worth living.

Socrates interpreted the Delphic inscription 'know thyself' as a divine injunction – first on himself and, through his questioning, on each individual to establish the limits of human thinking. One discovers one's own limits by discovering what one believes and then testing it to see how one belief connects with others. Humans cannot know either what the gods know or what the gods desire. They can only examine their own souls and ask: what can humans know about the life they most desire to live? Here we come up against yet another major, unargued, Socratic presumption: the Athenian Socrates assumes that every person's desires are focused on his own happiness and the best means of achieving it. This leads some to interpret Socrates' position as an egoist assumption about reasons and motives. 'Be concerned for your psyche' means 'be aware how your own real welfare is the ultimate aim of all your actions'.[18] Presumably, no Spartan could ever see it this way because, for them, self-interest was not only subordinate to the collective interest but was defined by the collectivity over and above the individual. And perhaps Socrates knew this, for he was unwilling to leave Athens, insisting that in other city-states he would probably receive even worse treatment as an irritating alien. But his rationalism seems to require that even Spartans could, perhaps with greater difficulty than Athenians, overcome their cultural prejudices and come to engage in rational self-

---

17   Plato's *Republic* would, later, close off this questioning of his ideal society's conventions; see chapter 3, this volume.

18   T. Irwin, *A History of Western Philosophy, 1: Classical Thought* (Oxford, 1989), p. 80.

examination. His more parochial loyalty to the Athens which had educated him and given him citizen identity was combined with a religious dedication to philosophical enquiry which aspired to be less culturally bound. His overriding conviction was that self-examination was an intellectual enquiry into the most desirable life for the good man and that the enquiry was a universal concern for individuals' true happiness. This is what tending your soul first, meant. Once you understood what was *truly* in your own interest as a man, what you truly desired as a human, you would never willingly choose what was not for your own good. You would never willingly do wrong.

Therefore, out of this purportedly universally shared concern for one's own true happiness emerges a range of other Socratic moral convictions, notably, that whoever harms or wrongs another, always damages his own happiness more than his victims.[19] According to Socrates, we must *assume* that all men (tyrants, victims, good and bad men) desire the same thing: their own happiness. What distinguishes them is their relative ignorance of what actually is worthy of desire so that it will lead to a man's happiness. Some, perhaps most men, commit deeds of moral misconduct but Socrates wants to show that this is none other than a failure of rational insight into what really is desirable and which will bring them happiness. No one voluntarily chooses his worst option. No one chooses to harm himself. 'Is there anyone who prefers to be harmed rather than benefited by his associates?' he asks Meletus.

> 'Of course not.' 'You have discovered that bad people always have a bad effect and good people a good effect upon their nearest neighbours; am I so hopelessly ignorant as not even to realize that by spoiling the character of one of my companions I shall run the risk of getting some harm from him? . . . The correct procedure in cases of such involuntary misdemeanours is not to summon the culprit before this court, but to take him aside privately for instruction and reproof, because obviously if my eyes are opened, I shall stop doing what I do not intend to do'.

When someone does choose wrongly, his judgement is faulty and he requires enlightenment.

Socrates' astonishing position, applied to himself and then generalized, is that *no one willingly does wrong*, that cases of wrong-doing are due to ignorance of the consequences for oneself, and that *knowing* what is right is so intimately tied to right or virtuous *behaviour* that a failure to act virtuously or rightly is an indication of one's moral ignorance. Virtue is knowledge and viciousness is ignorance. And he says his accusers have never shown any interest either in the young or in examining right and wrong, knowledge and ignorance.

Socrates was convinced that ignorance could be demonstrated and men willing to make the effort to demonstrate this with him would, then, be guided to the right path. From this Socratic conviction (a moral rather than an epistemic certainty, which Plato will later reverse) he encouraged some of Athens' most talented young men to steer clear of politics because they would *unwittingly* harm others and themselves if they had not first spent years in self-examination to discover their own moral convictions which, he undoubtedly believed, would conform to his own unified view.

19   *Gorgias*, 473ff.

Socrates' Ethical 'Egoism'

A first reading of Plato's *Apology* often leads to a discussion of whether a society – and especially ancient Athenian democracy – was justified or not in eliminating Socrates from its midst. Some students have found him to be an attractive idealist, while others have taken him for a self-righteous bore. Few today see him as socially dangerous and find it hard to see why such drastic steps were taken to silence him. Ignore him or offer him a soap box in some large park where people can listen to him if they wish. But the tradition of philosophizing from Socrates' own day to ours has focused less on what Athens took him for and more on analysing the man's beliefs, an adherence to which would effectively change the political world. For his aim was nothing less than a moral reformation of his fellows by means of individuals attaining a moral autonomy which, he believed, could come about only through intellectual enlightenment. Political force would not be required. Rationality itself would reveal to a man the kind of person he would find it most fruitful to be. Our political arrangements would, thereafter, look very different indeed. In what way?

Let us try to collect together some of the Socratic axioms or convictions in order to constitute his normative ethical theory in order to see what it implies.

A human being has a self that may be identified more fundamentally with the person's psyche or soul than with the person's body. Truly to know one's self or one's soul requires an investigation of a specific kind. We shall have to discover a method to investigate our souls or selves. One begins the self-investigation aware that one already possesses opinions concerning moral values. But the aim of the investigation is somehow to clarify how the various opinions one happens to have fit together and reinforce one another (or not, as the case may be) so that we may arrive at the truth. The self or psyche clearly responds to the acculturation of the society in which it finds itself, but it is not simply the creature of one particular culture or another. We must assume that there is a kind of human knowledge, a knowledge of the self, which is a mode of psychic functioning that transcends the specific responses a self might have to individual and local experiences in Athens or Sparta. We therefore start by assuming there must be a kind of human knowledge that is stable, independent of chance or contingent circumstances. Hence, there must be only one right definition of what all humans seem to agree really exists, e.g. a human virtue, in terms of its unchanging essence or nature. The *elenchos* can help us to get the right definition.

Given that our self or soul is what identifies us to ourselves as humans, we then ask if the self somehow is innately directed towards living in one way as opposed to another. What does the soul, our selves, most want for itself? It seems from a familiarity with what people tend to say when they discuss themselves with others, that all selves desire their own good, that is, all selves desire their own happiness. If this is the case, then what one really desires, one's good, cannot, by definition, be bad for oneself. Humans never desire actually bad things, since no one acts against what he would wish to do if he *knew* what really was his good. If no one willingly wishes to harm himself then *knowing* what is our good will defend us against self-harm. This means that no one *voluntarily* ever does wrong. To do wrong is to commit an act in ignorance (of the harm it will do to the self). Hence, no one is voluntarily or intentionally unjust, for to commit unjust acts is always more harmful to the agent, one's self, than to the victim. This then, is the reason that it is wrong to harm another, be he considered enemy or friend. Never retaliate. It is better to suffer wrong oneself than to commit it. No real harm can come to a good man and a good man is one who knows what is his self's own good, his happiness.

Socrates believed that through appropriate questionings of one's moral beliefs, an examination of one's soul, a person would come to adhere to the above ethical convictions. His enlightenment would equate virtue with knowledge. But this enlightenment had to be achieved by oneself and for oneself by means of moral enquiry with others. Socrates fundamentally insists on the individual attaining his own moral enlightenment but where the truths affirmed and then realized in a person's lived life are the same and true for everyone. There must be a sense in which virtue relates, not to the rules of one particular society and its view of success, but to a universally human way of living and to a person's success as a moral being. Each individual needs to rediscover for himself an existing truth that is true for all. (Plato will later elaborate on this rediscovery being a kind of recollection rather than a new teaching in the *Meno*). Socrates' focus is, then, on our psyche or soul as our very self. Socrates is, therefore, seen as the beginning of a tradition that sees philosophy as making a special, indeed unique claim to self-reflectiveness.[20] What should we, as humans, reflect on? Ourselves.

Socrates says that human selves want above all an ultimate end (*telos*) – their own happiness. There is then, what is called a teleological implication in Socrates' moral convictions. This teleological moral conviction assumes that there is a final, supreme, object of man's desire that is desired for its own sake and to which all other desires are ordered. The supreme and final object of desire is our happiness. It is attained by knowing what acts can deliver happiness, such acts are good by definition, this is what is meant by human excellences or virtues, and hence, moral wisdom, that is, knowing our good, is sovereign. Knowing our good is what leading the examined life is about. On this view we have, as humans, innate needs, and philosophical reasoning enables us to conceive of these needs as they truly are. Once we accept this, then we realize that we never *desire* the bad things we do when we mistake the bad for the good. An unjust man is operating under the mistaken belief that the bad things he does are what is good for him and in his interest. According to Socrates, he 'simply' has a mistaken object of his true desire as everyone truly desires his own good.

From here, Socrates can then go on to show that such a man needs correction, rehabilitating punishment rather than retaliation – by means of which he would be harmed rather than enlightened. Unjust men *do* desire to do evil, they perform vicious rather than virtuous acts, but they are under the mistaken belief that this is what is their good. Therefore, the punishment a man who has acted badly receives is for *his* sake, that is, for the sake of the man who has misperceived his own good and acted wrongly. Such a man is not an enemy, but one of us. We must, *in our own interests,* respectively, *do justice to all* and not follow the old 'heroic' way of doing justice to our friends but harming our enemies. Our formal systems of justice must not be vindictive. 'Enemies' are nothing more than men ignorant of their own true good or they are men pursuing their human good wrongly.

We have seen that the traditional discourse of the ancient Greeks accepted that there

20　But see B. Williams, *Ethics and the Limits of Philosophy* (London, 1985), ch. 1 on how this is no longer true only of philosophy in our self-conscious world.

was a general desire to be considered virtuous, to be a man of *aretē*. Moral conduct, they thought, offered the best prospects for happiness. But most seemed to think that the reason a man wanted to be moral had something to do with the *outside* social world, that is, because others would praise you as responsible, law-abiding, conforming to standards and this would give you pleasure in the form of wealth, status and recognition. Socrates, unusually, said the reason a man desires to be moral is an *internal* one, his own knowledge of his own character's consistent behaviour as a good man. Health, wealth and status *are* goods but only if we use them rightly, as a good man would. 'Wealth does not bring goodness but goodness brings wealth and every other blessing both to the individual and to the state.'

We have also seen that the Athenian social system was built less on explicit power relations than on the mutual exchange of benefices which one acquired in order to give some away so that one established status among kin, friends and fellow citizens.[21] It was thought that exchanges through virtuous behaviour bound society through reciprocity. Socrates' investigation into the question 'what manner of life ought a good man to live?' was predicated on the mutual exchange of moral benefits among men. This means there is no modern 'bare' self here of the sort we begin to see with Hobbes. To maximize moral benefits one needed to investigate patterns of desire and motivation in men as a species that lived in ethical collectivities, *poleis*, and Socrates believed that through the power of right judgement each individual could determine what it was in a man's life that was unqualifiedly in his interest, his good, so that a man's soul could not be misguided. Therefore, he begins his ethical considerations with the individual in self-examination (his first subject was himself), but he then relates this initial egoism to the demands, claims and desires of others. This is what is meant when Socrates is called an *ethical* egoist.

Beginning with the self, he then generalizes to all others so that the practice of the various virtues, some of which appear to us as distinctly ancient Greek – like manly courage, temperance and piety along with justice and wisdom – are acts that proceed from *inwards* to the outside and beyond the individual. He seems to speak as though his ethical constituency were a universal constituency of the human species. Once one discovers through self-examination how one has most *reason* to live, one cannot, he thinks, fail to live in this way in relation to others. The question 'how should I live my life?' becomes, upon reflection, a general question: how shall we, as humans in communities, live our lives? But Socrates believes that the question can only be asked by the individual himself and answered by *a someone* who has, upon reflection, come to see that to be just, as the quintessential virtue, is rational for him as a man with the sort of character type, the sort of self, that belongs to a man of true *aretē*.[22]

We have noted that there are numerous presuppositions from which Socrates begins his quest for self-knowledge and many of these were apparently shared by the ancient Greeks with whom he spoke. Is his rationalism founded on a peculiarly ancient Greek way of investigating and speaking about human excellences, character, and a kind of wisdom called 'moral'? To what extent is his view unique to him or shared by others? It is one thing to say that philosophical enquiry is the greatest good for men, and another

---

21   See P. Veyne, *Bread and Circuses: historical sociology and political pluralism*, trans. B. Pearce (London, 1990), ch. 2.
22   See Williams, *Ethics and the Limits of Philosophy*.

to assert the conclusions of this particular enquiry: that no one ever willingly does wrong; that one ought never harm another because it is self-harm; that the soul is the self; that a certain kind of human interpretation and enquiry is justified in seeking to establish the meaning of an oracle's cryptic response to a question.

We have seen that Socrates' moral confidence derived from a unique source (his *daimonion*, his sign) and this was distinct from the elenctic process. But his subsequent discovery of the *elenchos* shows him that it is rational to live a certain kind of life, the self-examined one and hence, it is rational to be a certain kind of person. No other life is worth living and no other kind of person is worth being. At his trial he says that he realizes how few people actually seem to hold to this view. But he optimistically believes that through the *elenchos* they *could* be made to see reason if enough time were given. A one-day trial was insufficient.

It is not that Socrates thought he alone expressed good opinions; he says in *Crito* 47a that he and his friends have always accepted in their past discussions that they should esteem the opinions of some men and not others. 'We ought to esteem the good opinions and not the bad . . . and the good ones are those of the wise and the bad ones those of the foolish.' There are experts with good opinions, for instance, in medicine or in architecture and their views do and ought to count. But this expert wise man in matters of statesmanship is not to be found, on Socrates' view, and in the *Gorgias* (521d–522a) Socrates is made to argue that *perhaps* he *is* alone of all Athenians who both studies the art of statesmanship *and* practises it.

What is most striking in his linking of moral reformation with intellectual enlightenment is Socrates' further assumption that once we know what is our own good we shall find ourselves bound to desire it and pursue it. Reason cannot be overpowered by anything. He has no room for the person who might *know* what is good and yet continue to do wrong. The Greeks called this incontinence (*akrasia*) and for Socrates it was a psychological impossibility, once a man recognized that acting virtuously was a cognitive, intellectual achievement. Aristotle will have more to say about this issue.[23] For Socrates, one *will* have happiness, what is most desired by each, *if* one is virtuous. Since Socrates believes that a man's proper concern is with the welfare of his own soul, that part of him that is most important, his psyche, must never be injured by acting unjustly. Morally bad acts harm the real self. To act unjustly is to harm others, doing wrong to others, by which you risk harming yourself. In doing wrong you have mistaken the bad for your good, since no one intentionally desires to harm himself. And so he says he will never stop saying:

> Make your chief concern not your bodies nor possessions but the highest welfare of your souls and let no day pass without discussing goodness and examining yourself. This is really the best thing a man can do. The real difficulty is not to escape death but to escape from doing wrong. (*Apology* 38a–39b)

This is what Socrates meant when he equated virtue with knowledge.

---

23 See chapter 4, this volume.

3

Plato

An ethical theory is a more systematic version of the interpretative schemes that ordinary people use to make sense of their own motivations to act within their social surroundings. As Socrates would have it, an ethical theory, investigated and confirmed through reason, is not an optional discipline for human beings. You simply must 'know yourself'. Without understanding your own motivations, your life would be anarchic and, unwittingly, you would come to grief, buffeted about by all manner of chance occurrences and wild responses to them. You would have one preference, one desire, after another.

An ethical theory would then give rise to a political theory because the self does not live alone. The political theory would be an articulate, systematic and explicit version of the often unarticulated, implicit or habitual interpretations through which ordinary people understand their experiences of the actions of others. The political theory, founded on the ethical theory, would more clearly enable people to respond to experiences through their own critically assessed and self-conscious actions.

Plato, Socrates' most famous student, saw this perhaps more explicitly than did his master: political theory was, for Plato, *the* major consequence of that central human activity – the contemplation of the *foundations* of the ethical life – to be carried out by the philosopher.[1] The philosopher was not simply some commentator on ordinary discourse and behaviour; he was no mere observer of pre-philosophical, common-sense beliefs, because, like Socrates, he would deny that ordinary men *were* pre-philosophical innocents. Innocence is ignorance and leads in each individual, ordinary life to a lack of virtue, to one's own unintended downfall, to personal unhappiness and it also brings down the society in which one is necessarily enmeshed. Therefore, it must be shown more directly than Socrates was able to achieve, that ordinary human agents are able to act in relation to others only *because* they first have a set of theoretical or philosophical commitments to living successful moral lives *together*, no matter how vague or unconscious these commitments may appear to them.[2]

Remember that philosophy is rooted, for Socrates, in a conception of the soul as one's true self for which one wants the best. Politics, the systematic pursuit of the collective and mutual well-being of individual souls or selves, is thereafter erected on what is most

---

1 See the doctrine of Forms, below, pp. 75–9, pp. 102ff.
2 For further general reflections along these lines see A. MacIntyre, 'The Indispensability of Political Theory', in D. Miller and L. Siedentop, eds, *The Nature of Political Theory* (Oxford, 1983).

dear to each person, his soul or self, and its well-being. Socrates believed that one's human happiness was only discoverable through self-examination by means of a rational deliberation with others on the best way for a self to live a human life, taking as given that he and his interlocutors accepted the *existence* of such things as the virtues of justice, courage, piety. His interlocutors also accepted that their contemporaries tended to speak about the individual as *tis*, somebody or other, a person who might be referred to as a standard of average agreement or dissent about any subject.[3] And this unidentified *tis*, this standard individual, was a member of society, an Athenian who was not subsumed under the city's name but whose name, Athenian, named the city. This *tis*, both when young and when mature, was agreed to be held in the grip of a morally bound collective more powerful than his unique, subjective oneness.[4] Therefore, there is no modern individualism here. In this milieu, humans as humans could not choose to be alone and remain human, but Socratic rational choice could help them to choose what kind of togetherness would best suit a collectivity of ethical selves. This was Plato's project in the *Republic (Politeia)*. But Plato saw that he had to make a few crucial changes to aspects of the original Socratic method of argument, the *elenchos*, and to Socrates' universal optimism that rational persuasion alone could reorientate men's characters and effect a moral revolution in everyone.[5]

Plato was born in 427/8 BC and died in 347 BC. His family was an old and distinguished one, and he was linked through birth and social connections to the most prominent men in Athenian public life, including Perikles, at the time of the Peloponnesian war and its aftermath. The two major influences on him were Socrates, his teacher, whom Athens put to death, and his disillusion with contemporary Athenian (democratic and radical oligarchic) politics. In the past, there has been much discussion over whether Plato should be read as Socrates' philosophical heir or as a political ideologue. Did his disillusion with Athenian politics come from his disinterested Socratic philosophical preoccupations and his own conclusions about how to know the truth and who can know it? Or was his philosophy a result of his politics, a justification and an excuse for what was of major importance to him – anti-democratic politics and its replacement with government by an intellectual elite?[6] There is an old argument that Plato really wished to be a practical statesman but was forced back into 'mere' theorizing and philosophy,[7] and hence, he should be seen as a statesman *manqué*. If he did not wish to be an active politician, then why, it has been asked, did he intervene, later in his life, in Syracusan politics (with disastrous results) when he abstained from political activity in democratic Athens?

Plato provides something of a defence of his life choices in his Seventh Letter.[8] He

---

3   *tis*, like *anthropos* (human being), are masculine adjective and noun, respectively, in Greek.

4   H. D. Rankin, *Plato and the Individual* (London, 1964).

5   See G. Klosko, *The Development of Plato's Political Theory* (New York, 1986), especially ch. 4, and on the failure of the *elenchos* in other Platonic works in G. Klosko, 'Rational Persuasion in Plato's Political Theory', *History of Political Thought* 7 (1986), pp. 15–31, 22–8; G. Vlastos, *Socrates: ironist and moral philosopher* (Cambridge, 1991) argues that the *elenchos* was abandoned rather than modified by Plato.

6   See E. and N. Wood, *Class Ideology and Ancient Political Theory* (Oxford, 1978) versus F. M. Cornford, *Plato's Commonwealth* (Cambridge, 1935) (reprinted as *The Unwritten Philosophy*, 1950).

7   U. von Wilamowitz-Moellendorff, *Platon*, 2 vols (Berlin, 1920).

8   E. N. Tigerstedt, *Interpreting Plato* (Stockholm, 1977) accepts it as genuine; also see G. Morrow, *Plato's Epistles: a translation with critical essays and notes* (Indianapolis, 1962) and P. Brunt, *Studies in Greek History and Thought* (Oxford, 1993), pp. 320–5, 341–2.

says that when he was young, like many others, he had ambitions to enter public life when he came of age. At that time Athens had lost the Peloponnesian war and the democracy had fallen. Athens was ruled by the Thirty Tyrants, some of whom were his relatives and they invited him to join them. He was tempted because he thought they were going to lead the city out of the unjust life she had been living (324d). But he soon observed a far worse state of affairs, and the Thirty tried to make Socrates their accomplice in crimes. 'I drew back from these evil men' (325a). After the restoration of democracy, Plato said he thought again about public life but then the democracy tried and executed Socrates. He came to the conclusion that public life was corrupt, although he did not cease to reflect how an improvement could be brought about. Yet he refrained from action, awaiting the proper time (326a).

> At last I came to the conclusion that all existing states are badly governed and the condition of their laws practically incurable, without some miraculous remedy and the assistance of fortune; and I was forced to say, in praise of true philosophy, that from her heights alone it was possible to discern what justice is, either in the state or in the individual, and that the ills of the human race would never end until either those who are sincerely and truly lovers of wisdom come into political power, or the rulers of our cities, by the grace of god, learn true philosophy (326a–b).

Plato then includes a lengthy philosophical excursus (342a–344a) showing his overwhelming interest in philosophy and systematic thinking as the necessary precursor to 'political' theorizing about society as a systematic whole. Only once one could show that philosophy was the foundation of a human way of being in the world could one then show that there was no distinction to be made between the statesman and the philosopher. He believed that both were engaged, in the same way, in ethical and political *theorizing* as the foundation of correct behaviour, although in the corrupt world of men, where the philosopher must live, political *activity* will always be a necessary sacrifice for the lover of wisdom. Philosophy as a full-time occupation *is* true politics for Plato, it is a skill (*technē*) of which most men are ignorant, it is the governance of selves, and the only sort of 'politics' worthy of the name. In contrast, foolishness is spending time on material, practical problems when one is confused about the state of one's own soul, one's character, and the true principles of right and wrong by which one acts. Philosophy must pose the most persuasive and radical challenge to the way corrupt power politics motivates men in their search for the good life for themselves.

After Socrates' death, Plato travelled and deepened his studies in Egypt, Italy and Sicily. We shall see that some of the philosophies he encountered on his voyages, notably that of the Pythagoreans, affected the ways he would come to modify his Socratic inheritance. Then he returned to found his Academy as a school for philosopher–statesmen.

One of the major questions we must keep in mind as readers of any philosophical theory that is generated from within a society that is not like ours, is to what extent may one say that this kind of ethical and political theorizing, as the foundation of what is taken to be correct behaviour, can be universalized to suit human beings living in other cultures, with other conceptions of the human self? If, in saying not simply that *there is a truth* about the human self but that *this one theory* offers the best account of that truth, are we not already speaking from within a culturally induced vision? Can a specific conception of the self ever be divorced from the implicit and explicit values of the culture within which it emerges? Is there an *essential*, fixed definition of the human self which only *appears* to vary as it expresses itself in different cultural milieux? When we read what Plato's Socrates has to say, are we reading what *only* an ancient Greek, with his set of cultural norms, could have said? Can one ever 'think' without a context and if not, are there certain contexts that, despite being historically and culturally discrete, none the less share specific features that give rise to shared or similar ways of thinking, for instance, about the human self, but which certain other cultures might not share? Is the Socratic–Platonic view of the essential human self plausible for us only because we have inherited a constructed history of our philosophy, a tradition of discourse, with the Greeks, and in particular Socrates and Plato, at the beginning? And yet we must be aware that this Platonic human self is no modern, subjective, unique individual but, by definition, a morally bound, objective reasoner, a communally dependent evaluator of the human good for a collectivity of ethical selves.

Contemporary historians of past political theories are troubled by these kinds of questions, and not all would agree with Guthrie when he noted that 'Plato can only be understood in his own setting'.[9] To understand Plato it is, of course, important to know that in the *Republic* he was still haunted by the 'primitive' logic of Parmenides, who was the first to distinguish the two modes of cognition, *doxa* (opinion/belief) and *epistēmē* (knowledge or intellect).[10] But to chart the origin of some of his ideas is not the same as affirming that what he says is 'true' about the human condition. We shall attempt to rephrase some of Plato's 'local utterances' in more normative terms in order to see if some of his insights can transcend their historical emergence, as Plato himself wished them to do. But we will still be left with a range of presuppositions, the truth of which he never even attempted to demonstrate, and some of these may still look odd to us today. None the less, people can and do consider themselves Platonists today and this should encourage us to consider what it is about certain theories that allows them to be absorbed by people whose experiences and values owe nothing *explicitly* to ancient Greece. We should also be encouraged to reflect on whether or not philosophical theories that are generated from within our own societies likewise begin in a range of presuppositions, the truth of which remains similarly undemonstrated.[11]

Plato's Early and Later Socrates

It is often said that in the dialogues of Plato there are two Socrateses, both of which were 'invented' by Plato, the earlier being taken for the more historically accurate rendering of the man's thoughts. We have come to know one Socrates from the early Platonic work called the *Apology*. But through an examination of stylistic criteria of Plato's later works scholars have tried to order and date the dialogues on the basis of their changing philosophical content. Most notably, Socrates' elenctic investigation ceases as a method in what are called the transitional dialogues. According to Vlastos,[12] we can arrange Plato's works in the following way:

9   W. K. C. Guthrie, *A History of Greek Philosophy*, vol. 4 (Cambridge, 1975), p. 492.
10 Guthrie, *A History of Greek Philosophy*, vol. 4, p. 496.
11 See the Introduction to this volume.
12 Vlastos, *Socrates*, p. 46, with whom everyone does not agree in detail, e.g. T. Irwin, *A History of Western Philosophy, 1: Classical Thought* (Oxford, 1989) and his *Plato's Moral Theory: the early and middle dialogues* (Oxford, 1977) and C. Kahn in H. H. Benson, ed., *Essays on the Philosophy of Socrates* (Oxford, 1992), pp.35–52.

Early (alphabetical listing)
Apology, Charmides, Crito, Euthyphro, Gorgias, Hippias Minor, Ion, Laches, Protagoras, Republic (Book I).

Transitional (alphabetical listing)
Euthydemus, Hippias Major, Lysis, Menexenus, Meno.

Middle (probable chronological listing)
Cratylus, Phaedo, Symposium, Republic (Books II–X), *Phaedrus, Parmenides, Theaetetus.*

Later (probable chronological listing)
Timaeus, Critias, Sophist, Politicus (Statesman), *Philebus, Laws.*

Despite the arguments over which works are to be ordered as truly early and which should be seen as transitional and early-middle, it is evident, in general, that a change did take place. In the early works we have a Socrates who is exclusively a moral philosopher with something of a populist conception of philosophy, a personal religion that is realized in ethical action (rather than in contemplation), no interest in the natural sciences or mathematics, and who investigates elenctically his interlocutors' propositions in the moral domain. He seeks knowledge elenctically, insisting that he has none. Although he thinks the soul is the most important aspect of man, he has no elaborated model of what it looks like nor how it functions, other than to insist that it can be persuaded by a rational investigation of held beliefs not to harm itself and therefore, to live well. He also has no explicit political theory. In seeking demonstrative knowledge he is confident only that there are a right and wrong, a good and bad, a virtuous and vicious, and that definitions can be sought by every person from within himself to enable particular instances of all virtuous acts to be shown to be unified.

But when we observe the Socrates of the middle dialogues, we see a man who is a moral philosopher *and* a metaphysician, by which is meant that he has a theory of cosmic order, of the first principles of nature and of thought. He also has an elaborated epistemology (a theory of how humans come to know and learn) and therefore a philosophy of education, a philosophy of science, a philosophy of language, a philosophy of religion and a philosophy of art. This means that when we confront Plato's *Republic*, we are dealing with a Socrates who has a metaphysical theory about the existence of Forms or Ideas or principles as *separate* from the material world.[13] We are shown two 'worlds' which, none the less, are *related*, a 'world of appearances' and a 'world of reality'. The world of appearances comprises the sensually perceived and the world of reality comprises the intelligible and conceptual. We meet a Socrates who has a belief in the immortality of the soul (*psuchē*) which, as separable from the body, comes to know about principles, Forms, Ideas, by recollecting pieces of knowledge originally acquired prenatally, that is, prior to the soul's birth into a body. Furthermore, the Socrates of the *Republic* has an elaborate exposition of the soul as divided into three 'parts', each 'part' of which has a specific function. We see a Socrates who values the discipline of mathematics as crucial in the process of leading the soul from the world of particular and transient things to an understanding of the unchanging principles by which such particulars are what they are. The Socrates of the *Republic* has exchanged his populist conception of

13   See below, pp. 102ff.

philosophy for everyone to a more elitist conception of philosophy for the few but with consequences for everyone. We see a new interpretation of what rational argument can achieve: now it cannot reorientate men's characters simply by providing the *reason* for living a good human life, because most people's characters are dominated by desires, and hence, it is their emotions, rather than their reason alone, that must be addressed. No longer is there the Socratic insistence that once any man comes to see, by rational persuasion, what is truly in his best interest, he will be bound to do it: moral weakness is no longer a psychological impossibility but a real and enduring problem. This is because it is now seen that there are other motivating factors in a person's psychology which can and do conflict with reason; it is too simple to say that knowledge (and ignorance) govern human behaviour. We need a theory of desire. Reason will therefore be shown to have a new function, to take the emotions seriously and to keep desire in its proper place, in order to ensure, both in the individual and in the *polis,* psychological and therefore, political order. Reason and those capable of it now must have the kind of political power that truly governs a collectivity of selves in the interest of each and all. And from this re-evaluation of reason's function we have an elaborated political theory which analyses a ranked hierarchy of different kinds of constitution, each of which reflects the kinds of souls of their respective citizen constituents. Democracy, for example, is shown to be the worst of constitutional forms except for tyranny. In sum, Plato has reworked Socratic ethical egoism and constructed a new moral psychology from which an ideal politics could emerge. With the *Republic* we confront Plato's Platonism, and it is this wide-ranging philosophical doctrine that would be taken up, reinterpreted and used by subsequent theorists of the political in the Roman and Christian worlds. It was once famously said,[14] and with some justification, that the history of philosophy consists of footnotes to Plato.

In order to interpret the *Republic*, we need to examine briefly some of the philosophical developments already found in the *Meno* but taken further in the *Phaedo*, because we shall see some of their doctrines re-emerge in the *Republic*. We shall focus on the *Phaedo* in particular because it contains discussions which are crucial to an understanding of the *Republic*'s political philosophy and because it is also central to Aristotle's later representation and criticism of Plato's views on psychology. The twin pillars of Platonism, its theory of Forms and its belief in the immortality of the soul, emerge in these two dialogues as doctrines that are united as the core of Plato's system. They develop from Socratic philosophy having demonstrated to Plato how to live as a man and to die as a philosopher.

The *Phaedo*

The *Phaedo* purports to tell the story of Socrates' last day in prison before his death, as recounted by an eye-witness, Phaedo of Elis. Plato says he was not present on this last day. The dialogue focuses on Socrates' attempt to encourage a belief in the immortality and reincarnation of the soul (*psuchē*). It speaks from within what we would call a religious or spiritual world of its time in its concern to understand life and death, the human soul (*psuchē*) as separable from the body and its centrality to human choices made when

---

14   By A. N. Whitehead.

embodied. Plato is original here, adapting and altering a number of Orphic and Pythagorean intuitions about whether or not the soul both exists before birth and persists
after bodily death. Plato describes the soul in an innovative way, as no longer passive and
subject to the play of emotions. Instead, the soul has choices and objects of its own. Nor
is the soul simply a breath of life, a mere phantom or ghost of a dead person which, for
ancient Greek contemporaries, could appear to the living only in their dreams. The
nature of the Platonic soul is best grasped by considering the activity Plato attributes to
it. Its pattern of conduct expresses the ideal, immaterial human essence in a life lived
naturally and correctly.[15]

In the *Phaedo*, what may appear to us to be a far-fetched subject for discussion – the
soul's immortality and reincarnation – is considered in order to try to understand why
humans can conceive of general, absolute ideas like Equality or Goodness and then
recognize instances of equality or goodness in particular entities or acts they see in the
material world. These absolute ideas must exist somewhere and somehow *come before*
any instances which are then called equal or good when they are perceived by the
senses. Only if we propose that the soul is immortal, that is, survives the body, and
therefore has acquired knowledge *prior* to its experiences in the world after birth can
we make sense, says Socrates, of the general acknowledgement that Beauty, Goodness,
the virtues, exist. What are these existents as standards or absolute categories of evaluation and how do we come to know them? Could we give an account of why two
things are considered equal if we did not first have a conceptual category of Equality
itself?

The Socrates of the *Phaedo* is still the rationalist of the earlier dialogues, without a
theory of motivation that takes the emotions seriously into account. The tripartite soul
of the *Republic* has not yet been devised. Instead, we are offered a dualist theory of soul
or mind versus the body. Here we see Socrates describe how the emotions must be
ignored in the search for knowledge of standards and absolute categories of evaluation,
that is, of the real and the true. This dialogue would have an enormous influence on
medieval Christian accounts of the divided human self, a fallen self that must be trained
to ignore bodily temptations in order to exercise that remnant, divine and rational spark
of intellect if it is to achieve salvation. The *Phaedo* along with the *Meno* would be the
only Platonic dialogues available in Latin translation until the fifteenth century.

The dialogue reflects the influence of Pythagoreanism which Plato is thought to have
learnt on his voyages to Sicily, and one of Socrates' interlocutors, Simmias, refers to
himself and Cebes, another participant, as 'we Pythagoreans'. Here Socrates makes plain
that, despite the views of ordinary people, those who apply themselves in the right way
to philosophy are voluntarily preparing themselves for dying and death (64a; 68a–b). He
also makes it clear that the philosopher is an ascetic, paying as little attention as possible

---

15   The text may easily be found in *The Last Days of Socrates*, ed. and trans. H. Tredennick (Harmondsworth, 1981
and reprints), pp. 97–183. See S. Lovibond, 'Plato's Theory of Mind', in S. Everson, ed., *Companions to Ancient
Thought, 2: Psychology* (Cambridge, 1991), pp. 35–55; J. Burnet, 'The Socratic Doctrine of the Soul', *Proceedings of
the British Academy* 7 (1915–16), pp. 235–59 and Burnet's commentary on the Greek text, *Plato's Phaedo* (Oxford,
1967); D. Bostock, *Plato's Phaedo* (Oxford, 1986); J.-P.Vernant, 'Aspects mythiques de la mémoire et du temps,' in
Mythe et pensée chez les grecs, études de psychologie historique, vol. 1 (Paris, 1981), pp.80–107 and Vernant, *Mortality and
Immortality* (London, 1991); W. K. C. Guthrie, *A History of Greek Philosophy*, vol. 3 (Cambridge, 1969), pp.467–70
and vol. 4, p. 555.

to bodily pleasures (or pains), so that the soul is to be conceived as the opposite of the body. Indeed, the body is a hindrance to the acquisition of knowledge because there is no certainty in seeing and hearing, while the soul, when concentrating on its own objects of thought, free from sensual distractions, searches for (and finds) Reality (65b–c). Wisdom, knowledge of Reality, is only found in its purity in the next world (68b). It is wisdom, the knowledge of Reality, that makes possible the virtues of courage and self-control, that is, true goodness, in the first place, and the presence or absence of pleasures and fears and other *feelings* make no difference at all.

Socrates states that a system of morality which is based on relative emotional values (physical pleasure or pain) is a mere illusion, a thoroughly vulgar conception which has nothing sound in it and nothing true. The true moral ideal, whether it be self-control or integrity or courage, is really a kind of *purgation from all these emotions* and wisdom itself is a sort of purification (69c–d).

If you have ever considered how you have come to know the discrete *natures* of things in the world, that is, if you have asked what it means for someone to be a human being as opposed to an animal, or for something to be a cup as distinct from a bed, and you thought that your knowledge came about simply through experiencing lots of individual, material things – different men, different cups – and then you somehow grouped them together through what looked to you like apparent similarities and you called them by one name (men, cups), you would be wrong! Socrates thinks you would be relying too heavily on an assumption that you, personally, had sensed the world of things *as they really are* in themselves. But we have all had the experience of making mistakes about what we thought we saw at a distance and then corrected our judgement when we came up close to the object we had (mis)perceived. Not only can our vision of particular things be faulty. According to Socrates, the apprehension of the *real natures* of what things are is not had through the senses at all, but, so far as possible, with the unaided intellect. The soul (psyche) is concerned with 'the real nature of any given thing – what it actually is, and not what it appears to be at a certain moment . . . and the aim is to *understand* that object *in itself*' (65c–d). The object of the intellect is the truth, that is, the true nature of something. The true nature of Socrates as a man is not whether he has a snub nose or is bald. To understand Socrates as a man is to understand the nature of his humanness. And you have to have an idea of humanness before you can judge whether or not Socrates is a human being. According to Socrates, pure knowledge of this kind is not possible in the company of the body (66e). Your ideas are not the consequence of sensual experience. For Socrates, it is the other way round. Rather, how you come to *know* about the material world which you see or hear, the reason you are able to recognize that there are discrete men, cups and beds is because you have a prior idea of humankind, 'cupness' and 'bedness'. The senses do not rule our understanding of what there is to be known; they simply confirm understanding by presenting instances of what is there to be known and is already conceived of, by the soul, as a *nature*, as a *kind* of thing. To hold to the view that our knowledge is sensually guided has, for Socrates, disastrous consequences in the world itself. Socrates insists that wars and revolutions and battles are due simply and solely to the body and its desires; all wars are undertaken for the acquisition of wealth and the reason we have to acquire wealth is because we have not permitted our souls to rule and instead our souls have become slaves in service to the body (66e). Hence, there are social and political consequences of defining man as soul-led rather than body-led.

Once the asceticism of the philosophical soul is accepted, the problem emerges of the soul's immortality and its separation from the body after death (69e).[16] Socrates describes a cyclical law of nature in which life comes from death and death from life (72b). We are told that the body is a temporary home, a tomb, of the soul which existed before it and will survive after it. Not only is the soul somehow eternal but the status of its reality is superior to that of the body and all the sense-perceived physical objects with which the body has come into contact throughout its mortal life. The soul is released upon the body's death and if it is pure, that is, uncontaminated by the body because it has never willingly associated with it in life, then the soul, having pursued philosophy and practised how to face the body's death, arrives in a place where it will be happy and released from human evils, change and uncertainties. The pure soul sees reality directly. It has been prepared by philosophy which has tried, by gentle persuasion, to set the soul free from the realm of change and material particulars. Philosophy has persuaded the philosophical soul that sense observation by the eyes and ears is entirely deceptive. The soul must concentrate itself by itself, trusting only its own independent judgement and when it investigates by itself it passes into the realm of the pure, everlasting, immortal and changeless. The soul refrains from attributing truth to anything which it views indirectly, that is, sensually, as being subject to change and variation. Its object is the invisible and the invariable, the unchanging truth in the realm of the absolute, the constant and invariable. It has contact with the unchanging beings in this realm, what Socrates calls the Forms, by being itself of a similar nature (78e–84a).

This is a theory that is couched in the terms of religious metaphor which, to us, may sound strange. It is derived from other theories, most notably a theory of what learning is, which has previously been set forth in the *Meno* and is repeated and elaborated upon in the *Phaedo*. In the *Phaedo* Socrates says that what we call learning is really recollection (72b–c). We can show that when people are asked questions they can give correct answers which they could do only if they already had a proper grasp of the subject. A questioner tries to get a person to remind himself of something he first knew at some time or other. Take for instance 'Equality'. Socrates says: 'We admit, I suppose, that there is such a thing as Equality – not the equality of stick to stick and stone to stone, but something beyond all that and distinct from it – absolute Equality [the idea of Equality]' (74a–d). Although we see equal sticks or stones or other equal objects we must already have a notion of absolute Equality which individual equal sticks or stones fall short of. And this means we must have had some previous knowledge of Equality before the time we first saw equal things which strive after Equality but fall short of it (74e).

> So before we began to see and hear and use our other senses [as babies] we must somewhere have acquired the knowledge that there is such a thing as absolute Equality; otherwise we could never have realized, by using as a standard for comparison, that all equal objects of sense are desirous of being like it, but are only imperfect copies (75a–e).

This knowledge of absolute standards, in this case, the idea of absolute Equality, must have been acquired before our birth (76a).

---

16   The possibility of a blessed immortality was familiar, not only from the more esoteric Orphic doctrines, but from the eleusinian mysteries which were an Athenian national cult. See Guthrie, *A History of Greek Philosophy*, vol. 4, p. 554.

And if it is true that we acquired our knowledge before our birth and lost it at the moment of birth, but afterwards, by the exercise of our sense upon sensible objects, we recover the knowledge which we had once before, I suppose that what we call learning will be the recovery of our own knowledge, and surely we should be right in calling this recollection (76a).

Hence, what we call learning is really a process of recollecting knowledge we somehow (today we would say, unconsciously) already possess.

Socrates says that he and his interlocutors are faced with a choice: either we are born with knowledge of absolute standards, ideas of Equality, Beauty, Goodness, *and retain a knowledge of these* all our lives, or a knowledge of these absolute standards is somehow *forgotten* and people learn them, become aware of them, by a process of recollecting. Socrates says that we can decide if we consider that in order to demonstrate knowledge a person must be able to explain what he knows. He must be able to give an account. We note that the only way he believes someone can demonstrate knowledge to others is through the use of logical argument, giving an account, in words. He is speaking with people who seem to agree with this, that the deployment of language is *the* means by which knowledge is revealed. But it is a very specific kind of language, and its function must be to reflect a pre-linguistic logic, a logic of thinking, a logic of the soul which itself reflects the logic of the way things are. It cannot be a language that appeals only to plausibility. This is what Sophists do without regard for the truth of what they are saying. But we must assume there is a way of speaking that does more than express what only *appears* to be the case at a particular moment. Socrates is always aware how mis-statements are not merely jarring in their immediate context; he also believes that mis-statements have a bad effect upon the soul (115d–116a). So there must be a proper way of speaking which demonstrates a knowledge of the truth.

Now Simmias is of the *opinion* that everyone cannot demonstrate that he has such knowledge; he does not *believe* (presumably from empirical observation) that everyone *can* give an account, and therefore a knowledge of absolute standards must not be re-tained throughout life. Within each person lies innate absolute standards but in order to gain access to them, to know they are there and to give an account of what one knows, something else must happen. In consequence, Simmias must agree with Socrates that people have to go through a process of recollecting what they once learned before birth, and that knowledge acquired pre-natally is not retained *as* knowledge but must be sought after by being asked the right questions to aid recollection (76b). The knowledge ac-quired pre-natally is non-perspectival and non-temporal; it is not a personal memory of doing or experiencing but, rather, it is a memory of truth, not acquired at any time but always possessed.[17] Hence,

If all these absolute realities such as Beauty and Goodness, which we are always talking about, really exist; if we refer all our sensations to these and compare our sensations with these as we re-discover our own former knowledge of them; is it not a necessary inference that our souls must exist too even before our birth, whereas if these abstractions, these absolute realities do not exist, our discussion would seem to be a waste of time? Is this the position, that it is logically just as certain that our souls exist before our birth as it is that these realities exist, and that if the one is impossible, so is the other? (76d–e)

17 See *Meno* 86a–b.

We are told that the same logical necessity applies to both and that our soul's existence before our birth stands or falls with the existence of Socrates' absolute realities. And these absolute realities, Equality, Beauty, Goodness, remain constant. The concrete instances of beautiful things like horses, men, clothes or equal things like sticks, vary. You can see or touch concrete instances but you can apprehend the constant, invisible entities, the ideas of Beauty or Equality, only by thinking. The soul, operating on its own, is thinking without the aid of the sensually perceived world, and is in 'contact' with its own objects of thought, the absolute realities, the ideas of Beauty or Equality. The thinking mind is said to be of a similar nature to what it thinks about, these absolute standards, principles, ideas, Forms, and these are objects of thought that exist *beyond* the soul.

That the soul is united to the body in life confirms that nature expects it to rule the body, and that the body serves the soul (80a). What then is the relation between soul's thoughts and the body's senses? Do the two worlds of Appearance and Reality not inter-connect? Socrates provides an 'autobiographical' interlude in order to show how he came to view the relationship between the soul's thinking, the senses observing the physical objects of the material world, and his theorizing or giving accounts. He begins by saying that humans hold to certain premises: they must suppose that there is an argument which is true and valid and capable of being discovered. Even if they have heard arguments that are sometimes true and sometimes false, they must not think that all arguments are of this kind and they must not attach responsibility to these changing arguments themselves but to the arguer and his technical ability or lack of ability (90d). Hence, we must consider that there is a *technē*, a skill, that an arguer is capable of demonstrating which enables him to give an account that is true and valid. We must not let it enter our minds that there may be no validity in argument (90e). Humans may be intellectual invalids but each must do his best to become healthy. Humans must assume that there is a truth and that one can, with effort, give an account of it. The first person who must be convinced with his account is himself and he does this by constructing a theory out of his own beliefs and opinions which then produces in him his strongest conviction (91a). Constructing theories is living the examined life. Socrates relates how he did this for himself.

His defence in the *Apology*, that he was never interested in the physical world and had no sympathy with the investigations of pre-Socratic naturalists like Anaxagoras, is here, surprisingly, reversed. Now we are told that in his youth he *did* have an *extraordinary passion* for natural science and wanted to discover the causes of things coming to be and ceasing (97c). But eventually he found himself to be unfitted for this form of enquiry (97c–d). Then he heard someone reading from a book by Anaxagoras that Mind produces order and is the cause of everything. 'In Anaxagoras I thought I found an authority on causation'(98a). But he was disappointed because Anaxagoras seemed to think that what caused *order in the world* was air, water, the ether and that what caused humans to act in the ways they did was their bodies, their bones and sinews. 'If it were said that without such bones and sinews I should not be able to *do* what I think is right, it would be true,' Socrates says, ' but to say that it is *because of* them that I do what I am doing, *and not through choice of what is best – although my actions are controlled by mind – would be a very lax and inaccurate form of expression*' (99c). Understanding motivates, not muscles. Your body is the instrumental means by which you perform acts which have previously been thought of. Socrates assumes all human acts are intentional acts. Hence, when the soul/mind functions, the proper objects of its thinking activity are ideas and not material things in the world. And because Socrates did not want to 'blind his soul' by observing physical objects which are not the proper objects of mind, he had recourse to *theories* to discover the *truth* about things (99d). The theory will have to concern soul/mind and its invisible objects of thought, given that it is agreed that absolute realities like Beauty and Equality are taken to exist but cannot be sensed and can only be thought. A theory of causation, that is, of human moral motivation to act in one way or another, will be worked out by minds starting from the premise that absolute standards such as Beauty and Goodness exist. Then, in giving an account, the theory will relate the ideas we have to the material things we perceive.

In general, he says his method is as follows: he starts by laying down the theory which he judges to be soundest and then, whatever seems to agree with it he assumes to be true and whatever does not agree with the theory, he assumes to be false (99d). Hence, he assumes the existence of absolute Beauty and Goodness (which everyone else seems to acknowledge) and then, if you grant him the assumption that they exist, and therefore that it is by these existents, Beauty, Goodness, etc., that beautiful and good things are beautiful or good, then he can prove the soul to be immortal (99d–101a). Here is how thought relates to concrete things. He assumes that whatever else is beautiful apart from absolute Beauty is beautiful *because* it 'partakes' of that absolute Beauty (100c). How do individual concrete things in the world 'partake' of their standard, their idea? What makes the object beautiful is 'the presence in it or the association with it (in whatever way the relation comes about) of absolute Beauty' (100d). Socrates says he does not insist on any one account of the precise details of this participation. But he does insist that his *theory* requires that the only way a given object can come into being is through participation in the Reality that is peculiar to its appropriate universal. You cannot distinguish a human from a horse unless you first have a general idea (an appropriate universal) of humanness and horseness. And he insists that you have to discuss the universal, the general, abstract idea, such as Beauty or Humanness, before you can discuss its consequences, before you can speak of individual, material things in the world being beautiful or human. First, then, we must agree both that the Forms, these absolute realities or Ideas, exist (and everyone does), and that they are the *reason why* other things are called after the Forms. The reason we *call* something beautiful is because it 'participates' in the Form of Beauty (102a). Furthermore, the *name* of a Form, like Beauty, is eternally applicable not only to the Form itself, but also to something else which is not the Form but invariably possesses its distinguishing characteristic (103d). This distinguishing characteristic is the essence or nature which enables the thing to be understood as what it is, be it a man or horse, beautiful or not. Thereafter, the *logos*, or account, expresses through words the world of appearances in terms of their essential intelligibility.

A Normative Account

Let us try to express this theory, couched as it is in the somewhat strange (to us) local utterances of fourth-century BC Greeks, in a more normative way: humans suppose that they have true beliefs about the material world that is independent of their minds and they therefore suppose that they have some knowledge of the world in which they find themselves. After all, they make judgements of all sorts about the world they see and experience. We cannot have specific thoughts or beliefs without having more general ideas or concepts. And without some *relation* between the world 'out there' and our minds, between receiving sense data from the outside world and our concept-exercising activity of understanding, there would be no reason to suppose that our intellectual constructions, no matter how internally coherent, had any bearing on independent reality at all, let alone conveyed any knowledge of it. We would simply be living in our heads. What, then, is the relation between what we sense and what we know? For Plato, sensible experiences must be not only a confirmation of our prior conceptualizations of what is there to be experienced, but the things to be experienced by the senses must also be what they are because they somehow are already intelligible: they have to possess characteristic natures or essences (distinguishing characteristics) which a reflecting mind recognizes by conceptually 'separating' them from their concrete manifestations in order to think about them. In themselves, concrete sensible things are *understood* to be what they are because essentially they share, or 'participate' in, their intelligible idea. The intelligibility of the world is what gives us rational grounds for forming judgements about the world. Things are bound together by intelligibility.

But the reason why things are intelligible is because they, like us, are part of what we must assume to be a general, metaphysical orderliness. For Socrates, humans are situated between two extremes, the apparent, material world on the one hand, and on the other, a world of formal, absolute, unchanging Realities (107c ff.). Within this larger, metaphysical framework, mind thinks of the Beautiful, the Equal, the Human because there are separable existents, formal standards like absolute Beauty and Equality. This supersensible Reality is beyond souls, it is a formal, universal, cosmic order, but it is, through thinking, within soul's reach as intelligible. This is Socrates' theory and he believes it renders an account of why men are able to judge things beautiful or equal, and more importantly, why they may make choices to act consistently on an understanding of motivating moral standards, that is, of what is best. Out of this comes his intellectualist, theoretical discourse on human motivation. It distinguishes between the cause of a thing, a man's actions, and *the condition without which* it could not be a cause (99c). The condition is the formal, intelligible nature of the Real. It is presumed that in order for human knowledge to be possible, men always do assume that there is a natural, essential order in all that is, and that humans are within that formal order. A thinking soul/mind has the capacity , through its activities, to grasp unchanging truths and have universal ideas of existents like Equality and Goodness.

In 'proving' the immortality of the soul Socrates insists that as a consequence of this immortality the soul demands our care, not only for that part of time which we call life but for all time. The soul can have no escape or security from evil except by becoming as good and wise as it possibly can, for it takes nothing with it to the next world except its education and training (that is, its degree of recollection of what it knew before birth and its ability to give accounts of its knowledge), and we are told that these are of supreme importance in helping or harming the newly dead at the very beginning of their journey there.

If the soul and the Forms complement one another, the argument for the previous existence of the soul seems to be based on the (prior) reality of the Forms or ideal standards. Reality is presumed to be independent of humans achieving a conscious access to it. And yet we can know the Forms, but only through recollection of what the pre-existent soul 'perceived'. Therefore, the *Meno* and its sequel the *Phaedo* provide us with a theory of the soul's education, of learning, which is a process of recollecting already existing and (unconsciously) known truths which are then 'tied down' by reasoned explanation. Learning is not the putting into one's mind of a systematic arrangement of information imparted by another, a teacher, but rather it is a technique of drawing out knowledge, through appropriate questioning, and this enables someone to recollect and then give a systematic account of what he now knows but had temporarily forgotten. That the human soul has access to a realm of unchanging and eternal realities and that philosophy is the means to reacquiring, or raising to conscious awareness as a systematic understanding, the innate standards by which it lives its life, is the central doctrine of the *Phaedo*.

The philosopher must be concerned with the release of the soul from its association with the body and in so doing he has access to an individualist ethics, the now conscious awareness of an innate moral sense that is to be guided by unchanging ideals of Goodness, Beauty, etc. in order to ensure a person's spiritual welfare. The soul, every soul, rises above the subjective and personal level by being orientated by objective, universally valid realities. Socrates emphasizes that when he speaks of soul he means absolute soul, since one soul is not more or less of a soul than another (94d). He is speaking of soul in general, that which all men have. In the *Phaedo*, he emphasizes that the nature of soul is such that it *opposes* the body in countless ways. The soul directs all the elements of which the body is said to consist and it does this by opposing them in almost everything through life. It tyrannizes (*despozousa*) over the body, sometimes inflicting harsh and painful punishments (through gymnastics and medicine) and sometimes it threatens or admonishes. But we recall that the body, for Socrates, is the instrumental means by which men act to express their psychological intentions. Men are *motivated* from within. If on the one hand, the body can be 'controlled' tyrannically, on the other, the emotions which motivate bodily acts must be spoken to and persuaded. Socrates says that although the soul is a unity and is non-composite, in that it is not actually made up of different elements or parts, none the less, the soul speaks to the desires and passions and fears *as if it were* distinct from them and they from it (94d). In the *Republic*, Plato will found his ideal city on this conception of the soul and its universally valid realities to which philosopher–rulers look in order to maintain the city in right order. In getting ready for its political task, however, Plato for the first time will provide the soul with a specified structure. And its desires and passions will have to be addressed by the kinds of persuasive arguments to which they can best respond. We shall see that these modes of persuasion include myth, analogy and metaphor.

The *Republic*

Plato named this work *Politeia* (constitution), by which was meant not simply the allotted roles of functionaries within the institutional structure of his ideal and just *polis* but, more significantly and globally, that which constitutes the political association founded on the self-understanding of its constituent members. It is less a work about institutions than about knowledge and education. That *we* call it the *Republic* tells us how much our Greece has been seen through later Roman eyes. A republic, in Latin *res publica*, emphasizes as Plato did not, a strict distinction between public things (*res publica*) and private things. What the Platonic political association looks like, writ large, as it were, in its institutions, necessarily reflects for Plato the prior degree of self-consciousness that the collectivity of selves manifests. But to distinguish sharply between public and private things, as we shall see the Romans to have done, is to posit the public sphere of the state as *against* the personal in the sense that the 'state' comes about as an agreement to protect a private sphere of possessions by establishing laws of legal entitlement to what is one's own. Taking this Roman understanding and reading it back into Plato has led to interpretations of his *Republic* as sacrificing individual, 'private' human freedoms to the 'higher good' of the state. By (incorrectly) reading back into Plato this private/public split, twentieth-century liberals like Karl Popper[18] were able to justify their fundamental horror at what they took to be Plato's purportedly totalitarian instincts that denied individual freedom to all but a select and elite philosophical few who ruled the closed, ideal society absolutely and, effectively, by force backed by a uniform Reason. This misconceives the Platonic enterprise.[19] But it will become clear to us that indeed there is no plurality of values in Plato's *Republic*. He does not believe that political conflict is something to be resolved through compromise. Other, compromising alternatives are mere (and dangerous) sophistry to him. For Plato, there must be only one right way to govern and it is not open to dispute.

As we read the *Republic*, it will become clear that one of the fundamental questions to be answered and which Plato does not ignore, is why all members of his ideal *polis* would *accept* his view of indisputable politics and therefore accept the rule of his philosophers. A good part of his argument deals not only with the means by which all members were to be *persuaded* (rather than physically coerced) to take this view of their own individual and collective best interest, but why such persuasion would be successful. At the very heart of Plato's *Republic* is an account of the distinction that is to be made between those corrupt political societies that do rule the minds of citizens by (threats of) physical coercion and fear, and the one that persuades each and every individual self that it is in his own best interest to desire and help to implement a collective governance of selves ruled over by those who have philosophical insight into human psychology and its true good. *We* must distinguish between, on the one hand, what Plato sought to convince men of – by education – and, on the other, whether or not his sketch of human psychology and the conditions under which it best flourishes is sufficient to achieve his ends.

The *Republic* is an attempt to define justice. As the story unfolds, we are shown Socrates looking first for justice in the *polis* because he believes that it is easier to discern just relations between different, functioning parts of an organized collectivity than it is to 'see' what justice in the individual human soul looks like. But his 'constitution' is based on a model of moral psychology, a model of the soul's structure, and hence, as we have already come to expect, he is trying to explain something internal to men, what motivates them to act in ways that can be observed, externally, as just behaviour. The virtues that are found present in the *politeia* are the manifestations of virtues of the individuals who comprise the city-state. Justice will be shown to be a *technē*, a skill, like medicine, mathematics, music and ship-building. But more than these, it is the sovereign *technē*, the true possession of which consists in the knowledge of good and bad, and the expert

18   *The Open Society and its Enemies*, vol. 1: *The Spell of Plato* (London, 1945); Popper's original intention was to call this work *False Prophets: Plato–Hegel–Marx*. See K. Popper, *Unended Quest: an intellectual autobiography* (London, 1976), p. 113.
19   For a refutation of Popper and a wider discussion see C. C. W. Taylor, 'Plato's Totalitarianism', *Polis* 5 (1986), pp. 4–29.

knower is a physician of the soul whose authority, for individual men and 'states', is unchallengeable.

We must be alert to the use of the word 'state' as referring to a historically variable concept. The modern, post-nineteenth-century 'state' is not in Plato. The state, as we use the term today, is a construction that is historically specific; it is associated with correlative concepts of 'sovereignty', 'positive law' , 'rights and obligations', the private versus the public, and in being associated with the public realm it has come to be seen as a point outside men by which to judge the particular sets of rights and duties which define their various roles within it. Modern political theorists do not always make clear the way our modern concept of the state rests implicitly on an individualist model of the human constituents of society, a model that emerged in historically specific circumstances. But Plato is not speaking of this kind of state because he does not see the ideal *politeia* as a realized bureaucracy with a 'public rationality' by which men *thereafter* functionally define their identities.[20] Rather, his ideal *politeia* emerges as a conscious, rational affirmation of what individual humans naturally bring to the collectivity, an affirmation of *what they already are* when living collectively. They already have the capacities to function in a collectivity of the sort he describes, they are not arbitrarily or conventionally allotted these roles, and this means his 'state' comes about because of what he takes to be the natures of its constituent members and is not something distinct or over and above them. The Platonic 'state' does not serve as an *external* point of reference for personal identity.

But if, as a consequence, we then say that his *Republic* should be understood as a society without a state we are doing no more than looking for ourselves in his ancient Greek construction and not finding ourselves there. Instead, we must see what kind of state he intends as a constitution that encompasses everything of which the political association is comprised. And if this is not what we mean by 'the state' we must ask ourselves why. After all, the ethical and political world has not been, and even today is not, uniformly liberal. Liberals presuppose that there are many different ends or personal visions of the good. They have a different conception of the self. But there is no room in Plato's *Republic* for the liberal notion that ethical and political disagreement is interminable. For Plato, there is only one vision of human happiness, collectively and individually, and this vision depends on true political knowledge which is a knowledge of what he takes to be the human self and its good. The focus on this notion of the self and its good is not a focus merely on how to stay alive, but on a *way of being* that is more than this, on how *to be a human self*. It focuses, first, on the *character* that it is appropriate for a man to have and then it tackles what manner of life such a man lives in a collectivity. It is the qualities of *psychological character* that help to determine, in the right contexts, what a man will do and how he will do it.[21] Plato posed his question about what kind of self a human self needed to be from within an ancient Greek civic context, but he meant the question and its answer to be timeless. We must always keep in mind, when we read his texts, whether his question can receive equally timeless answers in cultures that operate

---

20   See M. Berent, '*Stasis* or the Greek Invention of Politics', *History of Political Thought* 19 (1998), pp. 331–62.

21   Some argue, sociologically, that this focus on ruling elites betrays his aristocratic world view. In chapter 4 below we will see Aristotle taking this concern for character even further, arguing that in making the virtues forms of knowledge, Socratic intellectualism did away with both passion and moral character, while Plato correctly divided the soul into the rational and irrational 'parts' (*Nicomachean Ethics* and *Magna Moralia*). For Aristotle, the moral virtues are not knowledge but habits, dispositions of character.

with different conceptions of the human self that confirm its identity within the social and political structures in which that self lives its life.

The *Republic*, Book 1

The introductory first book of the *Republic* has sometimes been considered to have been composed earlier than the following nine books, and therefore it is thought to reflect an early Socrates engaged in his usual elenctic preoccupations with definitions, here of justice. The work is set, like many of the other Platonic dialogues, in the late fifth century BC when the traditional values of Athenian society were under siege. Whenever Plato composed the opening of his political *magnum opus*, it is clear that it focuses on common notions of justice which various interlocutors have difficulty sustaining with coherence. And it is this lack of reflective coherence that leads Socrates to construct his ideal 'state' of the subsequent books, in which justice, both writ large in the institutional functioning of its parts, and writ small in the psychological characters of its constituents, will be explained as the unified virtue which ensures the well-being both of individuals and the whole. How, we ask, do the various commonly held beliefs on justice relate to Platonic justice?

Book 1 achieves three main tasks: first, it outlines the problem that Plato is attempting to solve; second, it presents the common-view positions he is intending to counter; and third, it legitimates the method of the remaining nine books. It is the final debate between Thrasymachus and Socrates which most decisively establishes Plato's revised method and objectives.

First, we must recognize the speakers, and Plato meant to sound a note of sadness and impending doom of which the characters cannot be aware. They are men of substance and include prosperous metics, the brothers Polemarchus and Lysias (the famous orator), and their father Cephalus with a successful shield-making business. All of these men, during the rule of the Thirty, were either to lose their lives, their property or be sent into exile. Present also is Thrasymachus of Chalcedon, a Sophist, and the brothers (Plato's own) Adeimantus and Glaucon, among others.

We are first offered the views on justice of the old and wealthy Cephalus at a time of life when age has blunted his enjoyment of physical pleasures, and he tells Socrates that he now has a desire for intelligent conversation, enjoying it correspondingly more. This is a non-Athenian who has chosen to live his life making money in a city where he has no autonomous civic identity. But this does not mean he has no moral views and he certainly has a view on doing the right thing. He says that at this stage in his life he has time for reflection. Not only is he free of passions and his desires have lost their youthful intensity, but he insists, in his opening presentation of his philosophy of life, that it is not simply old age that solves the problem of becoming enslaved to one's passions, but character. You will be prepared for old age and much else if you have a 'sensible and good-tempered' character (329). He is not over-fond of money as Socrates says are those men who have made their money themselves and whose standards are, in consequence, only cash value. Instead, Cephalus believes wealth is valuable but only as instrumental to men already possessed of 'good and sensible' character. The fifth-century question, what kind of character ought a successful man to have and how may human excellence (*aretē*) be acquired, is answered by this first presentation of the common view of justice. Cephalus seems to be in possession of a kind of self over which he has no control: he believes that one either has this kind of character or one does not, and if one does have it, one has, throughout life, acted rightly. Wealth contributes only instrumentally to this kind of character's avoidance of unintentional cheating or lying and aids in the fulfilment of its various, traditionally established duties. Socrates leaps at this: 'are we really to say that doing right consists simply and solely in truthfulness and returning anything we have borrowed?' (331). Surely there are times when it is wrong to return something borrowed, say, a weapon from a friend who has subsequently gone mad. To return a weapon to this kind of man would be running the risk of harming him because he may harm himself and others. Therefore, telling the truth and returning what we have borrowed is not the *definition* of doing right.

It is not simply that Cephalus is morally complacent, following social rules without previously investigating what right and wrong are. His entire life has been led by unreflective rule-following; he is, after all, a foreigner who simply learns the rules of the society in which he hopes to make his money, but he also believes he is aided by the luck of possessing what he takes to be his own 'sensible' character and its sensible but unreflective deployment of equally fortunate wealth. Socrates is requiring a definition of right or just behaviour and alludes to his conviction that harm to others may never be included in doing what is right, no matter how unintentional the harm may be. We recall that for Socrates, unintentional harm is ignorance of how, in harming another, one harms oneself. Cephalus leaves, finding a traditional religious sacrifice to occupy him instead of self-investigation of character.

The next common view of justice follows on from that of Cephalus. It is presented by his son, Polemarchus, who, in a somewhat more sophisticated manner than his father, also draws on the maxims of traditional authority, now the poet Simonides, to establish a more general rule for doing right. Simonides says that it is right to give every man his due. Polemarchus understands this as doing good to friends to whom benefits are owed and harming enemies to whom harm is owed. This rule is most appropriate in times of war. But, Socrates asks, if one is not at war, does the rule of this kind of justice still hold? In general, in peace time, what do we get out of justice? (333). Polemarchus is unhappily made to follow through his views and he argues that, in the end, justice does seem to be rather useless in the real transactions of the world and one would rather be engaged with various experts like bricklayers or musicians or soldiers if one wanted to build a house, enjoy a concert or mount a military campaign. These skills aim at some end or good. But it looks as though the just man has no specific expertise of his own as do doctors, shipbuilders, bricklayers, musicians and soldiers. Although Polemarchus is made to concede 'I don't really know what I did mean', he still thinks that justice has some use and its end or aim is to be equated with helping one's friends and harming one's enemies. We note that Polemarchus adheres to a form of behaviour which entails obligations to some. He has nothing to say about why he is motivated to feel obligated to friends but he knows the social rule. As Socrates goes on to show, the determination of a man's true friends cannot be on the basis of who, for whatever apparent reason, *seems* to be good and honest; rather, a true friend must really *be* so whether one rightly recognizes him as such or not. For we all make mistakes and can think a man honest when he is not so and vice versa (334). And if one can make a mistake in recognition one can, in the end, harm a friend, thinking him to be an enemy, and this surely is not right. The correct definition of a friend must be one who both seems and *is* honest. And if justice is the standard of human excellence (which Polemarchus agrees that it is), even if we do not as yet know precisely *what* it is, then the just man will never use his skills to harm another and thereby make him a worse man, even if the man is a bad man and is thought to be an enemy. So the general rule of justice cannot be to help friends and harm enemies; it must be *never to harm anyone at all* (335). Again, Socrates has turned the argument back to character and its own insights into its own moral motivations. The common-sense views of justice, while recognizing that justice is some kind of human standard of excellence, do not investigate the nature of the kind of character one needs to have in order to know that just behaviour means never harming others and therefore, oneself.

The last and much more powerful articulation of another common view of justice erupts from the impatient Sophist Thrasymachus, who wants none of this elenctic question and answer. Thrasymachus' position will turn out to be Socrates' most formidable challenge.[22] He wants Socrates' own definition of what he thinks justice is. He thinks that Socrates does have a definition of his own but is shamming ignorance. And 'don't tell me that it's duty, or expedience or advantage or profit or interest' (336). Thrasymachus offers his own definition and he selects from the previously prohibited list: *justice or right is what is in the interest/to the advantage of the stronger party*. But what, asks Socrates, does he mean by interest/advantage?

Thrasymachus gives a sociological explanation based on the observation that power, in different kinds of 'states', is in the hands of their respective ruling classes, a tyrant in a tyranny, aristocrats in aristocracies and the people in a democracy. In each of these constitutions, whoever is the ruling class makes laws in its own interest, a democracy democratic laws, a tyranny tyrannical laws. This looks like the conventionalist argument that the laws of any state are simply the consequence of arbitrary definition established on the basis of what looks to those doing the defining as useful and efficient for the maintenance of peace and their power. The definition of 'right' for their subjects is what is in the interests of those who are not subjects but the ruling class. The latter is the stronger and what they define as right for the weaker, subject, others is in the interests of the rulers. Is this definition of 'right' true? asks Socrates. He does not ask whether the definition is plausible in given, apparent and contingent circumstances.

Socrates agrees that what is right is an interest/advantage but the nature of the stronger party is not yet clear. Nor is it clear that those who rule always know what is in their interest, for they can be mistaken. But Thrasymachus has no intention of agreeing that rulers as such make mistakes. He, like Socrates, defines a practitioner of some skill, be he mathematician or doctor, as someone with a certain expertise and if he does make a mistake he is not practising his defined skill but failing to practise it. 'To be really precise,' says Thrasymachus, 'one must say that the ruler, in so far as he is a ruler, [by definition,] makes no mistake and so infallibly enacts what is best for himself, which his subjects must perform' (341). From a Socratic point of view what is inadequate in this generally acceptable statement is that 'interest' is being assigned to only one player, the ruler, and he wants to show Thrasymachus that in every group there are not only leader

---

22   See various interpretations: G. B. Kerferd, 'The Doctrine of Thrasymachus in Plato's *Republic*', *Durham University Journal* 40 (1947), pp.19–27; G. Hourani, 'Thrasymachus' Definition of Justice in Plato's *Republic*', *Phronēsis* 7 (1962), pp. 110–20; P. Nicholson, 'Unravelling Thrasymachus' Arguments in the *Republic*', *Phronesis* 19 (1974), pp. 210–32; J. Annas, *An Introduction to Plato's Republic* (Oxford, 1981), pp. 34–57; T. Siemsen, 'Thrasymachus' Challenge', *History of Political Thought* 8 (1987), pp.1–19; Irwin, *Plato's Moral Theory*, chs III, 2.2–3; VII, 1–3.

but also led, and each group has its own particular interest (341). Thrasymachus has been insufficiently inclusive in his presentation of interest. Socrates wants Thrasymachus to see that no field of expertise focuses on the controlling party; rather, an expertise is focused on, is effectively defined by, its subject matter (what Thrasymachus, too narrowly, calls 'the weaker'). Instead of society being composed of human interests, individually manifested as selves seeking their own good, Thrasymachus appears to have a dual model of human psychology, the psychology of the led and the psychology of the leader, and his view is that their interests do not coincide. For Socrates, no ruler as such exercises his authority with his own (apparently unique and different) interest in view but rather his authority is exercised with regard to the interest of the subject of his skill, which for Socrates can only be human interest (342).

Thrasymachus then presents a second, more inclusive, rephrasing of his definition of justice, treating it, as it were, as seen from below. Now he says *justice or right is what is good for someone else, namely the interest of the stronger party or ruler and this is exacted at the expense of the subject who obeys him* (343). What he seems to mean by 'expense' is not only that the material well-being of the 'principled' man will be forfeited but that, by obeying, the 'principled' man has inflicted self-injury. Injustice, the opposite of justice, is what the stronger do when they dictate to the simple and 'just' subjects. The reason the subjects serve the interests of the stronger is simply that he *is* stronger. The *source* of his strength is not discussed (it is taken for granted), but its *exercise* is equated not with knowledge but with the power of physical coercion. This is the 'morality' of the bully in the schoolyard as seen from the perspective of his victims. And once again it seems that Thrasymachus sees a fundamental duality of character types in any given society, the natural leaders and the naturally led. Thrasymachan justice, therefore, is to the advantage of the stronger (other) and injustice is advantageous to oneself, *if* one has the nerve to pursue one's interests in this way, knowing that weaker others will not have a similar nerve.

It has sometimes been thought that, here, Thrasymachus has shifted position from his first stance as an *amoralist*, for whom justice is simply what different conventional social systems happen to define as the rules of acceptable behaviour and then implement. Justice merely *reflects* existing power distributions.[23] This amoralism, a form of extreme relativism, would assume that humans do not posit the existence of things like justice, or courage, or goodness and then disagree over what these are and how they may be acquired. Instead, a comparative observation of societies shows the amoralist that there always turns out to be, through nothing more than cultural imposition, a set of arbitrary rules that have been established for public utility and efficiency. Thrasymachus is sometimes thought to replace this amoralism with an *immoralist* position in which justice really is an ideal standard, some kind of existent, but in the world of 'corrupt' men, as a 'realist' would see it, it is an ideal standard of behaviour which happens not to be to the advantage of its practitioner. This would mean that Thrasymachus accepts that just standards exist, there is such a thing as Justice in everyone's intellectual toolkit (like Socrates' idea of Equality and Beauty in the *Phaedo*), but in the world of 'corrupt' men – and one only needs a few such – it has been found, at least by these wily creatures, that pursuing these just principles never pays.

---

23 See Annas, *An Introduction to Plato's Republic.*

Once again, we see him operating with two character types, but here their difference is not a soul difference but a difference that comes through a subsequent recognition, by a small group of men, of a disjunction between the soul's theory about the existence of ideal standards and the possibility of putting these standards into practice in the real world. Such men realize that while the mind may be 'ruled by ideas', the world is ruled by force. For such men, life is about harming but not getting harmed. This sounds like a perverse way of putting what Socrates himself had said in the *Phaedo*, that body is to be coerced but soul is to be persuaded. But where Socrates insisted that physical coercion and psychic persuasion aimed at the same outcome, the self's good, because soul motivates behaviour, Thrasymachus seems to believe in a disjunction between mind and action, theory and practice, so that character is a reflection of doing, not being, of acts not thought. For him, the world motivates man's behaviour, not mind and its moral principles. For him, once one experiences the world, one realizes that justice *is* a thing but of such a kind as always to be against one's own self-interest. It is what is to the advantage of another. The first formulation of justice as the advantage of the stronger (ruler) was a particular instance of this second, more inclusive definition. The final formulation applies to all people, from any perspective: justice between any two persons makes the person who *performs* justly vulnerable to exploitation and is, therefore, to the other's advantage. This is yet another variation on the theme espoused by Polemarchus but with a difference. In Polemarchus' world there are friends and enemies. In Thrasymachus' world there are only enemies and no friends. Therefore, it is in your interest to harm others. My gain is your loss.

Therefore, Thrasymachus has supplemented his original account by viewing the situation from the vantage point of the subject, having previously defined justice from the position of the stronger ruler as seen by subject 'victims'. In fact, we now have sketched for us what it looks like from *two* vantage points *within* the subject citizen body: one simple and just character type, that of the 'principled' weaker man, who pays his taxes, while the unjust character type will pay less on the same income. He proposes what, in the social world, are taken to be equal business partners and equal taxpayers but, as *characters* determined by their respective practices they are not equals: one lives his principles and the other does not. The argument has developed to show that even *within* the citizen body, that is, in all social relations, there are two types of character, each of which is recognized through his actions, and it is the unjust man who always comes off better. The just man's honesty will prevent him from appropriating public funds, his friends and relations will detest him because his principles will not allow him to push their interests to the exclusion of others, and if he takes on public office the just man will suffer from neglecting his private affairs. The conclusion is that there is much more private profit in wrong than in right and, what's more, *everybody* knows this. *The just is really the good of another, the advantage of the stronger who rules but the self-inflicted injury of the subject who obeys. Justice always serves another's interest and not one's own.*[24]

If we then transfer the unjust character type from the citizen body to that of the position of ruler, we shall find him to be the very definition of ruler as tyrant. 'Tyranny is not a matter of minor theft and violence but of wholesale plunder, sacred or profane, *private or public*' (344). If you are caught committing crimes in detail you are punished

---

24   See below, chapter 4, on the ways in which Aristotle deals with these arguments in the *Nicomachean Ethics*.

and disgraced and we give names such as sacrilege, kidnapping, burglary, fraud and theft to such petty forms of wrongdoing. However, when a man succeeds in robbing the whole citizenry, reducing them to slavery, no one speaks of these ugly names and instead *all* call him happy and fortunate.[25] It is not fear that prevents men from calling his large-scale tyranny criminal behaviour. Rather, he has achieved his own good, which is what everyone else seeks to achieve for himself. He is happy and *lucky*. Does his good luck consist merely in his having acquired the material benefits of power? Or is it once again (as with Cephalus and Polemarchus) that his luck consists in his possession of a kind of character type which he simply finds himself to have and over which he has no control? It's a gift. In short, according to Thrasymachus, what we are taught to call unjust behaviour is really a form of behaviour *that weak men are afraid of suffering from* but they are not lucky enough to find themselves possessed of the kind of character that enables them to implement large-scale injustice themselves. This reduces to a position that all men, when embedded in a social system with others, want their autonomy, not least from principles or standards of behaviour which they know to exist, but find irksome, particularly in the matching of these principles with lived practice. If they do convert theory into practice instead of preserving the disjunction, they can be assured of their own downfall. The strong man, however, knows that it is precisely in the disjunction between theory and practice that his freedom, autonomy and power lie. It will always be thus, justice for everyone else and injustice for him.

Socrates recognizes this character type but he is not persuaded that his fraud and violence pay better than justice (345). He tries to get Thrasymachus to categorize justice as either a vice or a virtue, as a good or bad human quality, but Thrasymachus is reluctant to see it as a *soul characteristic* at all (348). Rather, he calls justice 'supreme simplicity' and injustice is 'common sense good policy'. Furthermore, injustice is not, for him, a *moral* obligation,[26] but rather a logical *practice* of the instrumentally intelligent, socially embedded, self-interested actor. Thrasymachus argues that the unjust man is happier than the just man, not that the unjust man's acts are just. He maintains the moral absolutes of society in its definition of virtues (human excellences) but does not think they lead the just man to greater happiness than the unjust man. Socrates sees this as a 'tough proposition' that is not easily countered:

> For if you were maintaining that injustice pays but were prepared to admit that it is a bad and vicious quality, we could base our argument on generally accepted grounds. As it is, having boldly ranked injustice with intelligence and other good qualities, you will obviously attribute to it all the strength of character that we normally attribute to justice. (349)

Again, it is not that Thrasymachus does not understand what getting 'fair shares' means; he acknowledges the principle, but the unjust man *acts* in the way he does because he wants more than his fair share.

The end of Book 1 consists in four problematic Socratic arguments against Thrasymachus and all involve the question of whether justice is more advantageous to the individual than injustice.

---

25   Augustine uses a similar argument in his *City of God*; see below, chapter 6.
26   *Contra* Kerferd, 'The Doctrine of Thrasymachus'.

1   Socrates argues that rulers do not believe that ruling is sufficiently advantageous to do without payment, and therefore if ruling were done solely with the rulers' interest in mind, they would not require payment.

2   Socrates argues that the unjust man behaves as ignorant bad men do while the just man behaves like those who are wise.

3   Socrates argues that the unjust are incapable of organized action to their own advantage, always behaving as untrustworthy, mutual enemies.

4   Socrates claims that to be a good man one must be just, arguing that each thing has a function: 'that for which it is the indispensable or best instrument' (353); each thing also has a corresponding virtue without which it could not fulfil its function; the soul's function is life, and a good soul performs its function by wisely ruling and advising. Justice is, therefore, the virtue or excellence of a good soul, without which a man lives badly and so suffers rather than profits.

Throughout these final arguments with Socrates, Thrasymachus gets progressively more passive. He will not accept the Socratic belief that to know is also to *behave* in accordance with what one knows. For Socrates, a theory must be in harmony with practice: this is required by his metaphysics, and the metaphysics must be confirmed by a conception of the self such that it is the self's nature to be just. Here justice is not constraining but liberating. But for Thrasymachus, there is a fundamental disjunction between theory and practice; while it may be men's nature to be just, it is not to their advantage. Justice may be an intellectual constraint but it is not constraining on action.

In the end, not only have we been shown two modes of argument: Thrasymachus' more expansive, sophistic speeches, and Socrates' *elenchos*. We are also shown Socrates having achieved a not very convincing victory with his elenctic question and answer. It is apparent that neither Thrasymachus nor Glaucon and Adeimantus, with whom Socrates will continue speaking in Book 2, are persuaded that justice is in one's own interest. As Thrasymachus had said when he burst into the debate, 'it is much easier to ask questions than to answer them'. Socrates must revise his strategy and the *elenchos* must be rejected in the rest of the *Republic* in favour of what becomes a virtual monologue. 'Why do people appear to feel the need to be just?' will have to be more persuasively answered. The way one may best persuade, especially someone like Thrasymachus, requires a more thorough investigation of how different genres of persuasion suit the complex human psyche. Where Thrasymachus asked why he should constrain his self-interest to act according to the soul's abstract notion of justice, Socrates will have to show him not only that this is the wrong question to ask, because it is based on the belief that theory does not coincide with action, but also that he misunderstands what his self-interest is or can be. This is because he mistakes the nature of successful human character, which is not to be read off from behaviour but from motivating intention.

Plato needs to show that it is rational for people to be just no matter who they are or what their circumstances may be. Justice is in everyone's interest. It is in everyone's interest self-consciously to be a certain kind of person. Furthermore, what Plato has to show is that common views of justice which everyone seems to describe behaviourally, as 'act virtues', are actually, really, rationally and necessarily agent virtues, inward qualities of character, even though most people are not self-consciously aware of this. Plato must show that actions are always determined as vicious or virtuous in so far as they help to maintain the harmonious psychic disposition of a man's character. He does not want a mismatch between common and Platonic justice[27] and in the ideal state that he must now construct, the rational, philosophic man will act in such a way as not to embezzle money, commit sacrilege or theft, betray friends or country, break his promises, commit adultery, dishonour parents or be irreligious any more than will the commonly just man (442e–443a). It must be shown that there are reasons for abstaining from what are held to be common injustices. The just man would also heed society's prohibitions, but for rational reasons and not out of mere habitual rule-following. He will be both commonly just and, in his own best interest, more than commonly just to others. Plato will show that social rules can conform to man's nature and are not artificial, coercive impositions on that nature. But we cannot know which acts are virtuous or vicious, and which, therefore, conform to the laws that reflect man's true, ordered nature until we know which types of behaviour conform to a human self's inner harmony, its justice.

Socrates ends by saying that he considers his conclusion – that the just man is happy – to be somewhat premature. He has not yet examined the nature of justice itself and this is what he must do. Book 2 reaches a new stage where Glaucon and Adeimantus ask that he show that justice makes a just man happier than injustice makes the unjust man; that right is in all circumstances better than wrong (357). Glaucon wants to know what justice and injustice are in themselves, and what are their effects on the minds of their respective possessors, apart from the social consequences or rewards for appearing to act justly (358). 'I've never heard justice recommended on its own merits apart from its consequences', that is, good reputation and the rewards this reputation brings.

Book 2: Social Contracts

Glaucon presents the view 'which hundreds of others have dinned in my ears' that humans have a natural instinct to harm others and to avoid being harmed. So they calculate, *after* experiencing both harming and being harmed, that it is best to establish a compact, a *social contract,* to avoid both. The origin and nature of justice, then, is a conventional agreement, a compromise which naturally self-interested men establish, against their true natures or wills, between what is most desirable (to harm, do wrong) and most undesirable (to suffer harm, wrong, without redress). Justice is thought to be a *relative value,* established by those without the power to harm with impunity. The contract and its laws constrain men's natural motivations; it is only through punitive laws that men are forced to respect the claims of others. On this view, which is that of the moral sceptic, the social rules are utilitarian constructs and *always* suppress man's nature.

And if we posit two character types, a just man and an unjust man, we can, furthermore, show that if a man discovered that he could act unjustly, *but unobserved* (as in the example of Gyges' ring), even the just man would *never* stick to what is right. He would steal from shops without fearing detection, he would take other men's property, he would murder. Whatever a man's character, be it just or unjust, were he in a situation where his behaviour went unobserved, as though he had supernatural powers to render himself invisible, he would *not* act justly, *except* under compulsion. The skill of the truly

---

27 *Contra* Annas, *An Introduction to Plato's Republic*; and J. Annas, 'Plato and Common Morality', *The Classical Quarterly* 28 (1978), pp. 437–51; see N. J. H. Dent, 'Common, Civic and Platonic Justice in the *Republic*', *Polis* 5 (1983), pp. 1–33.

unjust man is to avoid detection in his wrongdoing. He must be perfect in his wicked-ness. If he makes a mistake, he must be able to cover it over and convince others that he has acted rightly. And furthermore, he must make the just man seem a simpleton, strip him of everything except his justice, punish him so that he would not, in the end, want to *be*, but only *appear to be* just. The point is that apparent reputation is all, and the best way of *being* is to be unjust but to contrive a reputation for justice. Appearance counts for more than reality.[28]

But if this is the way the social and political worlds appear to operate, then what do their requirements do to a person's psychology, his self, if he is to accommodate that self to the way of the world? Socrates wants to show that the self in this kind of world suffers from continuous internal conflicts, is continuously at war with its own nature and 'in-side' lives the most painful of existences. Instead of looking to its own greater good, its own real interest, it is tragically servile to its environment, lacks autonomy and unknow-ingly harms itself by pursuing momentary subjective preferences. These are based on what other people take you for, rather than what you truly are in yourself. Your 'suc-cess' depends on ceaselessly and restlessly maintaining a mask, a facade.[29] And where did Glaucon's model of the self as a natural harmer come from? Why is it assumed that there is a human instinct to harm others as well as not to be harmed? On what is it based if nothing other than a reading back from the corrupt world of behaviour in which men do, in fact, harm others? But is that human nature? Or is it what their characters become by having been moulded and disorientated by a corrupt outside? *All societies acculturate.* Plato believes that most acculturate us against our true natures; corrupt societies educate us against our true selves. This means that an ideal society would educate us *for* ourselves. The remainder of the *Republic* is an attempt to address the claims of the moral sceptic and it does this, in part, by proposing a revolutionary educational system to produce a soci-ety that truly is a collection of true selves.

The First Principles of Social Organization

We begin by looking for justice as a characteristic of a community where, as it were, it is writ large (369). We can see the just agent properly only in the ideal conditions of a just community. And the origins of community are in our nature. This means that in the debate over whether the political community is a consequence of *nomos* (convention) or *physis* (nature) Plato comes down on the side of *physis* in order to argue that the apparent opposition between a society's laws, customs and rules, on the one hand, and man's nature, on the other, can be reconciled. There are two aspects of that nature which, for Plato, are assumptions from which one must start: (1) *the individual is not self-sufficient*, having many needs he cannot supply for himself. He does not wish to be harmed. He needs helpers and partners. He does not naturally need opponents who are in competi-tion with him. Out of natural needs develops the natural association of the needy. Plato sees it as uncontroversial that humans are essentially social and find their most basic fulfilment in a survival association of co-operators. Collectively, men need food, shelter,

---

28   See the reprise of *aspects* of this argument in Machiavelli, in chapter 6, volume 2 of *A History of Political Thought.*
29   See Book 8, 562ff. where Plato discusses tyranny and the despotic character.

clothing and to satisfy these needs a farmer, builder and weaver will be required to constitute a natural community. Why does the individual not do all these tasks for himself, build his own house, grow his own food, make his own clothes? Why should he trouble to share with others and help to provide for common needs? Plato believes the answer is not simply a utilitarian one in that a farmer, for instance, can produce more if he sticks to farming, benefiting from an economy of scale and from the perfection of his own skill. There are other, more natural reasons for a division of labour in the most primitive of survival communities. This becomes clear when it is asked how it is decided who is to be a farmer, who a builder and a weaver: on the basis, again natural, that (2) *no two persons are born exactly alike. Each has a different aptitude which fits him for a different job* (370).

It is this second principle that will lead to an inegalitarian 'state' because, on Plato's view, people are born with their own, respective, natural talents which, in community, are deployed for the good of the natural association and for the individual who constitutes a contributing part. This appears, at first, to be a kind of natural determinism. That people may have natural talents exclusive to them and *prior* to an acculturation which may develop or even teach people talents, is itself a contentious statement for us. How could we possibly know whether observed talents are innate or acquired? Plato will argue that those who demonstrate a capacity to love what is really – as opposed to only apparently – loveable and therefore benefit best from the education system he will put in place in his ideal society, are those who reveal the best natural characters. For Plato, reason is a form of love, *philo sophia*, so that the real conflict is not between reason, as such, and desire, as such, but between the different kinds of psychological desires which motivate men's natural characters to live in one way or another. For him, education puts nothing in; it helps to mould character, eliciting an inner truth of the kind that Socrates had tried to help reveal through the *elenchos*. This inner truth, however, will be for Plato differentially manifested in terms of his categories of natural aptitude. That people should then only practise their one natural talent and therefore have one job and no other, is a leap Plato makes and only later justifies by his understanding of the true self. The self is capable of being only itself and, therefore, it is never to represent another self. Should a man do the latter he would be representing a character that is not his own (see 395). Human nature is, for Plato, such that it is impossible for an individual to play many roles, in real life or in representations on the stage (396). Each person must *be* only who he is and know only himself; indeed, this is the purpose for which he seeks knowledge, but in so knowing, the good man alone knows himself as an ideal type of character, his true self is that of *a good man*, and therefore, he alone can represent himself in narrative (396). To be master of oneself is, for Plato, to be subject to your true self so that you are both master and subject, 'for there is only one person in question throughout' (431).[30]

Does this not mean that in a world of differing natural talents only some men, and indeed a fairly exclusive number of them, have as their true selves the ideal character type of the good man and only they can know themselves as truly human? The consequence would be, *and is*, that in knowing the ideal standard of humanness, themselves first, only these men of talent should rule over other, less (and 'otherly') talented humans in community. For Plato, some talents are, clearly, sovereign over others. Plato's pessimism

---

30   We will see in chapter 5 how the Stoics and in particular Cicero keep this argument alive.

takes over from Socratic optimism and it is here that many have seen him attempting to justify what he takes to be a natural aristocracy of educated talent along *de facto* class lines.[31] The problem with this view is that Plato not only blames bad societies for orientating selves away from their natural talents but that he also wishes to reject what looked like an initial determinism in order to show that people are responsible for having *chosen* the natural characters they in fact have. In the end, the natural aristocracy of educated talent is an aristocracy that has, through its own choices (in some distant past), put itself in its position. Man's varying fortunes are not the province of the gods but of men responsible for the kinds of selves they are (380ff. and the Myth of Er in Book 10). There is no doubt that Plato is both arrogant and disdainful of those who, from within themselves, cannot be persuaded by *reason* to reorientate their characters. For the good of the whole, as well as for their own good, they will have to be reorientated from outside, within the context of the given limitations of their natural characters. Socrates' earlier, rational, personal ethics has been transformed into politics because Plato thinks there is evidence that certain kinds of psychologies do not respond to *reasoned* persuasion. These sorts of character will have to be addressed through their desires and Plato will have to find a means of persuading desires. Such characters will then be given a place in society which suits what they have chosen to be. To say, as Guthrie has said, that 'Plato certainly believed in the hereditary transmission of character and intelligence'[32] does not tell what appears to have been, for Plato, the whole story, the reason why people are to be regarded as responsible for having chosen the natural characters they in fact have.[33]

If we begin with the proposition that we are born with characters that display natural talents or aptitudes which distinguish us one from another, then this does not mean what Cephalus, Polemarchus and Thrasymachus took it to mean – that we have no control over our characters and we face the world, lucky or not. It is here that Plato supplements what at first looks like the argument for nature over nurture. He will insist that although there are natural character types with natural aptitudes, any community, through educational acculturation, has the power, not essentially to change but to reorientate that particular nature, either for the good of the person concerned or against his interest. Plato is looking for a political community that places people in the jobs that suit their natures. And he thinks that 'in the beginning' natural associations were of this type. In the most basic community of agriculturalists, wage labourers, craftsmen, traders and merchants there would have been a natural kind of justice between the parts which consisted in their mutual relations with one another, each doing what he was naturally most fitted to do. Plato sketches an ironic natural utopia, a golden age in which families feasted in summer on wine, cheese, olive oil and wholemeal, home-baked bread, and sat on couches of myrtle and bryony. Their simple needs were satisfied, constrained only by a fear of poverty and natural disasters. The first community was a society without politics and in its healthy, unchanging lifestyle it reproduced a natural harmony between functioning parts. There is no mention of any injustice here. Plato calls it the true norm. Glaucon, however, calls it a community of pigs. 'Give them chairs and tables and normal civilized food – the ordinary comforts' (373).

31   See E. Wood and N. Wood, *Class Ideology and Ancient Political Theory* (Oxford, 1978).
32   Guthrie, *A History of Greek Philosophy*, vol. 4, p. 466.
33   For another view, see G. Klosko, 'Racism in Plato's *Republic*', *History of Political Thought* 12 (1991), pp. 1–13.

Civilized Society and its Justice 'Writ Large'

The *necessary* society shifts to an overheated *civilized* society of luxuries. Socrates must try to discover how justice and injustice are bred in this kind of community. No longer confining themselves to necessities, the population embarks on the pursuit of unlimited material possessions, fights wars to obtain more land, and hence needs in addition to its 'producer' class (which effectively constituted the whole of the original, natural but primitive society) a Guardian class of soldiers with the natural aptitude to develop the skills of collective defence, being gentle to fellow citizens but dangerous to enemies. A final differentiation of the Guardian class into Auxiliaries with military, executive and policing functions, and philosopher Rulers who exercise the supreme authority in the 'state', establishes the completed *politeia*. It is based on a natural division of labour that corresponds to the collective needs of this whole, sophisticated society. Being in charge of instituting an education system that orientates citizens, training their respective characters in order to produce harmony in the functioning whole, the Rulers are distinguished by their philosophic capacity to benefit from the same, but increasingly abstract, education system which, at last, trains them in the kind of logical thinking that enables them to grasp the Form of the Good and hence, understand what justice is.

Educating Guardians and Producers: Myths and 'Lies'

Books 2 and 3 of the *Republic* are devoted to educating opinion. They focus largely on the Guardians as a military class and the aim is to train their bodies as well as their characters. But their character is the most important, and here Plato argues for the moulding of impressionable children's minds in ways that have struck liberals as nothing more than sinister mind-bending through censorship. But as Plato insists, all societies tell their children stories. Psychic moulding is the kind of 'persuasion' (usually, through fear) that all cultures are engaged in.[34] But where bad social ideologies refocus a person's moral sense and produce adults with divided selves, knowing what is right but doing what is wrong because they think it pays in the 'real' world, *his* society's stories will not misrepresent the gods and heroes. 'If we are to persuade the Guardians that no citizen has ever quarrelled with another because it is wrong, then our old men and women must tell children stories with this end in view.' The works of Homer, Hesiod and all the other poets who have told past generations of children about the gods and heroes must be expurgated whenever they speak of violence and harm. The founders of an ideal state must know what *kind* of stories teach the truth; they do not need to write them themselves. And what the stories must represent is that nothing good is harmful or can do harm; what is good is of service and is the cause of well-being. Indeed, the gods will only be represented as performing good and just actions and where they punish it must be shown that the sufferers benefited by being punished. The gods cannot cause harm or evil to any man.

---

34   See Klosko, ibid., and with reference to other Platonic works, Klosko, 'Rational Persuasion', pp.15–31; for another interpretation, D. Rice, 'Plato on Force: the conflict between his psychology and political temperance in the *Republic*', *History of Political Thought* 10 (1989), pp. 565–76, on Plato's sociology and his definition of forceful substantive reason suppressing and restraining desire.

Because Plato believes that children cannot distinguish allegory from literal fact, allegory must be capable of being read literally. Furthermore, it must be clear that the good is not the cause of everything. It is not the cause of evil – men are responsible for that. The gods who are equated with the good are responsible only for a small part of human life and if it is observed that we happen to have a far smaller share of good than of evil in us, we must account for the evil as not from god but in some other way: it is from the bad cultural orientation of desire. Man's varying fortunes cannot be in god's hands; we are responsible for our fates and hence the founders of an ideal state cannot allow the poets to make the mistake about the gods, saying that they are the ones who vary our fortunes. The gods can only be the source of good and this goodness is unchanging and perfect (380–1). And the gods and men have something in common. They both detest falsehood. Plato says that in things which touch most nearly the most important part of him, no man really wants to be deceived but is, rather, terrified of it. No one wants to be deceived in his own mind about things and not to know the truth.[35] But when he is deceived, we can call this ignorance of the truth 'true false-hood' and when a man utters a truely false statement he is merely using language, giving an account, to represent his ignorant state of mind (382). That state of mind is culturally induced.

But, it is asked, are not certain spoken falsehoods sometimes useful? There are, in-deed, certain kinds of noble lies (*pseudos*) that rulers of the city alone can use to deceive citizen or enemy for the good of the 'state' (389). But they are not the kind of falsehood that Plato calls 'true falsehood' which represents an ignorant state of mind. They are, rather, myths and stories that are essentially true but not as understood literally. A certain kind of spoken falsehood is not, for Plato, necessarily a rational untruth. Rather, it is a linguistic obscurity, a lie that is non-harmful. Whereas harmful lies are those which breed vicious habits in the young, a harmless lie encourages virtuous habits because it does not deceive about an essential truth. A harmful lie operates by force, and force is defined by Plato as the changing of our beliefs under the influence of pain and suffering. Evil propaganda entices people into changing their opinion by the promises of physical pleasure or they are terrified into it by physical threats (413).

The Myth of the Metals

But there is a kind of propaganda, a convenient story, a noble lie,[36] that persuades rather than forces people, including the Guardians, to adopt a conviction that is essentially equivalent to the one they would hold had they been educated by the society through its expurgated stories. Plato suggests the following convenient story of which the Rulers and soldiers are to be persuaded first, and then, the remainder of society.[37] Everyone is to be told that their education was a dream and in reality they were fashioned and reared in

---

35   Compare Socrates in the *Phaedo* on men always beginning with a premise that there is a truth.

36   For an alternative interpretation, see E. Andrew, 'Equality of Opportunity as the Noble Lie', *History of Political Thought* 10 (1989), pp. 577–95.

37   As with the Cave (below), as Guthrie noted: Plato did not usually invent the pictorial elements in his myths and allegories, but drew freely on the mystery religions and the Orphic writings, Pythagoreans, etc.; see Guthrie, *A History of Greek Philosophy*, vol. 4, pp. 517–18.

the depths of the earth.[38] All fellow citizens are brothers and born of the same earth. But they are distinguished by possessing one of three elements in their souls: gold, silver and bronze/iron, and correspondingly, rulers are those with gold, auxiliaries, those with silver, and the producers, those with bronze/iron (415). It is the role of the Guardian Rulers to watch the mixture of metals in the character of all the society's children and it is their responsibility to ensure downward mobility for those children with a metal that is 'lower' than that of their parents and upward mobility for those children with a metal that is 'higher' than that of their parents. The myth of the metals is a myth about society naturally constituting three classes which are the consequence of natural talent. We are told that this noble lie will probably not be believed by the first generation to whom it is told but if maintained, later generations of public opinion may come to accept it.

Plato distinguishes between reasoned explanation on the one hand, and fiction or myth on the other, in terms of genre and, more importantly, in terms of how each is understood. A rational narrative is, for him, an object of cognition, while a mythic narrative is an object of belief. Both can mean the same thing essentially. Myth is grasped as an object by certain parts of the soul that are not persuaded by reasoned discourse. It is only when he later provides us with the three-fold structure of the soul that we can determine which soul part is best addressed by myth. But it must be emphasized that mythical thinking has always been a feature of political life. Myths have occurred in all societies that have been sophisticated enough to boast a political culture which reaches back into the past and establishes links with the present. The rational discourse of politics is another genre of representation of the same thing that mythic discourse is about. Both are concerned with reality and its modes of representation. Where a mythic conscious-ness does not distinguish the symbol from what is symbolized, and so does not distin-guish between the image and the thing imaged, reason makes the distinction. But no society has members who think entirely in terms either of myth or 'science', so that the noble lie is not meant to be absorbed by those elements in society who are relegated to 'pre-scientific' selves. No one is excluded from Plato's convenient story. It is propa-ganda, an ideology, which not only suits a community's convictions but also is meant to be true of human communities in general. Plato says that humans do not know the truth about the past (383) and this is the reason we can invent a plausible fiction about it, but it must express essential truths about ourselves which we *can* know: we are born natural co-operators (rather than natural enemies), and no two individuals are born exactly alike; each has a different aptitude which fits him for a different job.

Plato provides an elaborate physical training for his Guardian soldier athletes which is aimed at character training. The character that is formed is of a recognizably Greek, aristocratic type, with perhaps more elements of the Spartan than the Athenian demo-crat in it. He is to become a man who is least dependent on others, who does not complain, can bear loss of property, loss of family members and general catastrophe better and more calmly than others. He does not laugh violently, will be truthful and self-contained, and has mastered his desires for sensual pleasures (389). It is here that Plato expresses his undoubted disdain for the kind of character democratic Athens had cultivated. The indiscipline in the community with its opening of the law courts to all offends him.

---

38 Athenians already believed themselves alone to be autochthonous; see chapter 1.

And when not only lower classes and workers but also those with pretensions to education need skilled doctors and lawyers, that is conclusive proof that the education in this state is thoroughly bad. For is it not a scandalous sign of a bad education if one's sense of right and wrong is so deficient that one has to seek justice at the hands of others as one's master and judge? And it is worse when a man not only spends most of his life in court as a plaintiff or defendant but is even ignorant enough to be proud of it; when he is convinced that he is an expert lawbreaker, up to every kind of twist, and that he knows all the tricks to wriggle out of a conviction. And all this for mean and unworthy ends without any idea how far better it is to arrange one's life so that one has no need of a judge dozing on the bench! (405)

Something like the Spartan model reappears in the depiction of the lifestyle of the Guardian class (Rulers and Auxiliaries) as a whole.[39] They have no private property beyond the bare essentials, receive no pay, their food is provided by the producing class of citizens in payment for their duties, and they live together in barracks, eating in messes as suits their military training and discipline. They have no private families and children are raised in state nurseries, not knowing their own parents, instead treating all as family members. He will later describe a eugenics programme where mating ceremonies ensure the production of the best Guardians, and children that are ill-formed, as in Sparta, are removed and exposed to die. Nor can Guardians touch gold or silver. Plato believes that, given their training, their character formation, they would be happy with this style of life but, for the purpose of the 'state', whose end is to promote the happiness and well-being not of a single class but of the whole community, it is necessary that the Guardians live in this way. It is in this community, with its sound educational system, that we are, at last, most likely to find justice. In having trained citizens of good and sound character there will be virtually no need of legislation and regulation. Good men need no orders, for education instils the spirit of good laws so that nature and nurture may combine (430). Such a state, founded on natural principles, will be wise as a whole in virtue of the knowledge inherent in its smallest constituent ruling class which exercises authority over the rest. It will be brave in virtue of the Auxiliary soldier class which works in harmony with the Rulers, executing tasks on the basis of their fixed convictions concerning the values of the whole. And it will be disciplined throughout. There is, says Plato, a better and worse element in the character of each individual, but when the naturally better element controls the worst, the man is rightly said to be a master of himself. When, as a result of bad upbringing or bad company, one's better element is overpowered by worse impulses, then one is criticized for lacking self-control. Hence, in the 'state', the better part is to rule the worse.

Here is the pessimism or, indeed, the intellectual snobbery that is driven by Plato's rational asceticism: even in this ideal state whose education system was meant to orientate citizens' characters correctly, there still seems to be a 'less reputable majority' with the greatest variety of desires and pleasures and pains. Their desires will be controlled by the desires and wisdom of the superior minority, a minority which Plato describes as having the advantages of natural gifts and good education (431).

Justice in this state, then, consists in one man doing his own, one job, the one he is naturally most suited to doing. When each of the three classes does its own job and minds its own business we have justice (433–4).

---

39   There are many parallels with Spartan practice but Plato expressly distinguishes the Spartan constitution from that of his ideal and he later ranks the Spartan *politeia* as the first of the inferior types: Book 8, 545a.

Individual Justice

Can the same definition of justice apply to the individual? Has the individual psyche the same three constituents in his character? Although Plato says we will never find an exact answer by the method of his present argument, he believes it sufficient to argue that the qualities that characterize the state must also exist in the individuals that compose it. And he argues that there are, in effect, three elements of psyche – appetite, spirit and reason – in *each* soul.

Justice in the individual, then, consists in the following: in the case of each one of us, whosoever is such that each of the three psychic elements in him does its own, he is a just man. Reason rules us with foresight, spirit supports and obeys reason and concord is effected by intellectual and physical training. These two, reason and spirit, are put in charge of appetite. Justice is therefore an internal harmony of psychic constituents of character of such a kind that intellect (and the objects of its desire) rules over the appetitive passions (and their objects of desire) (443ff.).

Political rule, for Plato, is not about *changing the nature* of the human being in whom there is the potential for both good and bad. Nor is it about *changing the natures of the characters* of the citizens. It is about moulding and refocusing the characters people already have and which, thereafter, can be modified by any society and its values. The sovereign *technē* of justly ruling a just and harmonious society begins, therefore, in the middle of things, as it were, by accepting that there already are three basic character types for each of which there is, respectively, a natural job because of the choices made to be the kinds of people that people show themselves to be. Plato only tries to explain how people make these character choices in the first place when he relates the Myth of Er which closes the *Republic*. Only at the end does this final myth speak about soul choices after bodily death in preparation for a new round of embodied life. The *Politeia*, however, must accept these choices as they have been made, and then, concentrate on character orientation. Therefore, for Plato, the sovereign *technē* is the intellectual skill of mastering the socio-political environment by first mastering, through an education programme, the respective psychological motivations of the three constituent classes.

For Plato, political *technē*, the skill of the true statesman–philosopher, is predicated on the statesman's own self-mastery through reason and the training of his passions. Because reason looks to the individual's greater good, calculating (*logizetai*) what is better or worse for the whole human soul, as such, there is a necessary invasion of the cognitive into all appetitive choices. This is not, however, obvious to everyone. Plato has come to accept the role of the irrational in most peoples' choice-making, and hence he accepts moral weakness in most people. He sees it not as an intellectual error, as did Socrates, but as a given problem of temperament or character which, thereafter, has been badly orientated by harmful environments. The latter have habituated desires against each character-self's true, long-term interests.

Appetitively dominated characters deploy their capacities to reason instrumentally for short-term, physiological gratification.[40] They will harm themselves and others in the long term if they are not refocused. Although they can be refocused in terms of how

---

40   See G. Klosko, *The Development of Plato's Political Theory*, part II, chs 5 and 7.

they pursue the jobs to which they are naturally suited, they cannot rule others because Plato now accepts they cannot rationally rule themselves. His education programme alone, Plato believes, can alter people's *beliefs* and refocus and discipline the characters they already have, so that each will make just choices within the spheres of life which suit their natures. But such people will only make these choices as a consequence of *doxa*, true belief, of which they have been persuaded by education, rather than through knowledge of the principles behind coherent moral choices. Civic virtue for most men, then, consists not in the philosopher's immediate knowledge, but rather in correct belief towards which the philosopher–ruler orientates them by means of a correct education. Even his strict education programme cannot change the dominant element in one's character – it can only reorientate it. For this reason the producer class, which, according to Plato, is such because it is comprised of people with largely appetitive characters, will find itself somewhat disciplined and its desires modified (in their own interests and that of the whole) by the Guardian rulers, but their styles of life will look rather like what most people's lives already looked like: private property, families, making things and growing things for themselves and the rest of society and being generally admired and materially rewarded – but not to excess – for practising their skills with excellence. However, they will now have no political power to rule over others, nor will they desire it, because they will not fear the injustice of those whose natural skill is to rule. They will believe they are ruled by those more consistently just than they are themselves and will reap the rewards of a just society in their own lives. The implication, not only for the producer class but even for the philosopher–rulers, is that men only seek involvement in the kind of politics in which democratic Athens excelled because they fear being ruled over and therefore harmed by those worse than themselves.

Plato's diagnosis of the source of communal unhappiness links social divisiveness with instability which, he believes, arises when those who are unfitted to rule are in power. In these cases, personal insecurity and the instability of general circumstances which are not bound by unchanging moral standards and, instead, are open to chance, lead to the disruption of the bonds of mutual benefit. Through education of the sort he describes the three character types will each be just in his own way – each doing his own – and each will desire that the Guardians rule, the Auxiliaries defend and the Producer–artisans provide for the economic well-being of the whole. If material and economic ambition were allowed to predominate in an unregulated, undisciplined manner, then, he believes, social life will hardly be social at all and instead the dominating acquisitiveness would become a predatory exploitation of competitive individuals where, just as Thrasymachus had said, my gain is your loss. Plato replaces this with a picture of Producers seeking economic rewards while their other ambitions to social power are moderated; with Auxiliaries seeking military honour and reputation through manly prowess while their competitive aggression is moderated by their heroism being placed in the executive service of the philosophic legislators/educators. According to Plato, a society ruled by the ethos either of economic man or heroic man does no good either for these character types themselves or for those who share (and suffer) a life in society with them. This is the philosophical justification for his rejection of both the democratic and radical oligarchic politics of Athens in his lifetime.

Women as Guardians

We have been spending our time discussing the three parts of the soul and the corre-sponding three classes of society to which the tripartite souls – that are respectively dominated by one element or another – give rise. The focus has been on men's charac-ters and natural aptitudes. But in Book 5 Plato introduces what Athenians certainly would have found preposterous – the education of women among the Guardians. As a consequence, he has been taken by some recent scholars to have been the first feminist.[41] But if we were to read no other Platonic dialogue (e.g. *Timaeus*) where Plato made absolutely plain his disdain for women as females, we would still be able to read through the *Republic* and find passages where women are characterized as over-emotional, irra-tional, hysterical and, if given power, dangerous. Indeed, in Book 8 (563b) he says that the freedom and equality for women (as females) are a mark of the excessive licence of the democratic state. What, then, could Plato possibly be up to in proposing not only that women Guardians exercise naked with the men (452), as in Sparta, but that they are to be similarly educated for a leading role in the ideal *polis*?

The discussion opens with Socrates' suggestion that for Guardians all things are to be in common as between friends, and this applies to women and children (449). Ought females to perform the same duties as males, or are they to stay at home on the grounds of bearing and rearing children, and therefore not take on the functions of war, nor be educated to executive and ruling tasks? Socrates agrees that there are great *natural differ-ences* between men and women (453) and it has previously been agreed that different *natures* need different kinds of occupation. But what Socrates means by natures being different (as opposed to natural differences) has nothing to do with biological character-istics (the female bears and the male begets (454)) any more than it has to do with superficial differences in appearance between members of the same sex, e.g. bald men and long-haired men (454). For Socrates, a person's nature, the inward character that is determined by psyche, determines social function, and there is no social function that is peculiar to a woman (or a man) as such (455). Plato's psyche may be thought to be based on a male model of the tripartite soul, but he presents it as genderless. Natural abilities (the respective dominance of reason or spirit) of the sort required for leading, functional roles in the state are, for Plato, similarly distributed in each sex, 'although in all, women will be the weaker partners', and at this point in the text this usually means in physical strength or stamina regarding military activities. A woman's psyche may be philosophic or high-spirited and should she demonstrate these qualities she will be fitted to be a Guardian. Certain men and women have the same natural capacity for Guardianship which, here, includes warfare, policing and other executive tasks, except that woman is the weaker of the two. Hence, those with similar characters will be similarly educated to be the best people for the best state. In fact, the best women seem mainly to be required to breed with the best men in order to provide the best children for the state (461), and this too is reminiscent of Spartan practices.[42] All live and feed together in common, have no private property and use the words 'mine' and 'not mine' in the same sense of the

---

41   See, for instance, N. H. Bluestone, *Women and the Ideal Society: Plato's Republic and modern myths of gender* (Oxford, 1987), who also cites other literature.
42   See chapter 1.

same things so that an individual's gain or loss is regarded as the gain or loss of the community (462).

Although Plato speaks of Philosopher–Kings and never of Philosopher–Queens, if a small number of women were capable of such intellectual development, it would not be as 'women' but as rationally dominated psyches. So too for the 'men'. Such people with the necessary qualifications will be philosopher–rulers (540b). Philosophical statesmanship has nothing to do with gender, for Plato, because for him, it seems that sexual difference is only a characteristic of body rather than psyche.[43] Hence, it is only in the ideal state that women, not as females but as rational souls, will ever be given the opportunity to realize what Plato takes to be their rational, human selves.

Plato's discussion in Book 5 refers to the Guardians as protectors and defenders of the common people. The discussion is a parody of Spartan institutions[44] without any reference, as yet, to the equivalent of the ideal state's Spartan *Gerousia*. No one is described, yet, as devoting their full energies to philosophy as a way of living their lives. Indeed, as Socrates makes plain (473–end) the society he has been describing will never become a reality until philosophers become kings or kings and rulers become philosophers and political power and philosophy come into the same hands. Hence, he needs to tell us now what defines the philosopher and how there is a Real world of Forms, as 'essential' realities', which exists independently of the philosopher's own mind (473). These Forms serve as the objects of his knowledge, the pattern from which he will take into himself the unchanging and absolute standards of reference by which particular things in the visible world are judged to be the kinds of things they are. Only after we are told of the philosopher's passionate love of unchanging, formal truth can we recognize that whenever knowledge of the truth is, thereafter, realized in practice, as in the construction of an ideal 'state', practice will always fall short of the precision of theory, but it is not disjoined from it as Thrasymachus believed it was. We are told that it is the nature of practice to be further removed (not disjoined) from truth or reality (*aletheia*) than theory is (473a). Since the visible world already 'participates' in the Forms, the philosopher's rational soul is the more motivated to try to reproduce the character of the Forms more fully in the ethical world of human beings.

Specially Gifted People and their Education

Plato has Socrates describe a rare character type whose mind can 'see' the essential nature of Beauty and who does not confuse a particular beautiful thing with the universal character of Beauty. We are familiar with this kind of account from the *Phaedo*. Such a man knows the fully existent (477); the object of knowledge is 'what exists' and the function of that reasoning part or faculty of the soul is to know the reality of existents. To have an opinion or belief about something is different from knowing it. Believing is intermediate between ignorance and knowledge, between non–existence and existence. Those who are able to see visible beauty or justice, etc. in their many manifestations in the physical world of multiplicity and change, but are incapable, *even with another's help*, of reaching absolute Beauty, may be said to believe but cannot be

43   See M. Nichols, *Socrates and the Political Community: an ancient debate* (Albany, NY, 1987), p. 122.
44   See chapter 1.

said to know what they believe (479e). But those whose hearts are fixed on Reality itself deserve the title of Philosophers (480). They can grasp eternal and immutable truth and they have, as a consequence, clear standards in their minds to refer to. Such philosophical Guardians have characters that demonstrate more than a familiarity with worldly experience; they have, in addition, characters that are motivated by a love of the whole of Reality, they love the truth and have shown this desire for the whole truth from their earliest years. Philosophers are 'coherentists' and they speak of knowledge as holistic.[45]

> So when the current of a man's desires flows towards knowledge and the like, his pleasure will be entirely in things of the mind, and physical pleasures will pass him by, that is, if he is a genuine philosopher and not a sham. (485e)

Plato describes a process of affective unintelligibility. Such a person, at last, finds unintelligible his earlier 'archaic' desires, so that he can no longer see what it is about the earlier objects of desire that makes anyone, not just himself, but anyone with a similar psychology, that is, anyone who has experienced previous desires but then gone on to other, more intellectual experiences, desire what was previously desired.[46]

Such a man will be self-controlled, not grasping about money, will show no pettiness or meanness but rather, generosity, will not think of death as anything to be feared and therefore will be courageous, will have a good memory (486ff.), will demonstrate a sense of proportion and be ready to learn. Education and maturity *then* round off this character, and it is only to such people, once they are philosophically educated, that the state can be entrusted (487).

Without the right education and environment such gifted characters will become particularly bad (491e). At present, however, and with an implied reference to Athens, Socrates says that it is the public themselves who train young and old, when they crowd into the Assembly or lawcourts or theatre. For this reason it is sheer folly to attempt, through private education of character as offered by Sophists, to produce a different type of character from the one praised or blamed by the crowd.[47] It has never been and will never be possible to educate someone to standards different from those of public opinion (493), so the aim must be to reorientate public opinion first, in order to provide the optimum environment in which the philosophic nature can best flourish. The common people of the present society will never believe the distinction between abstract beauty and particular beauty and so philosophy is impossible among them and they consequently disapprove of philosophers (494). But we are told that the common run of men can be reorientated. They can change their opinions and beliefs if, instead of bullying them, they are treated gently and their prejudices against philosophic learning are removed. They can be shown that philosophers are not what they have become accustomed to seeing in their own society but are, rather, defined by rationally dominated characters and habits and are men of moral rectitude, justice, reason and order, so that no

---

45   G. Fine, 'Knowledge and Belief in *Republic* v–vii', in S. Everson, ed., *Companions to Ancient Thought, 1: Epistemology* (Cambridge, 1990), pp. 85–115.

46   See R. Wollheim, *The Thread of Life* (Cambridge, 1984) for a discussion of the role of affective unintelligibility in Freudian psychology.

47   See C. J. Rowe, 'Plato on the Sophists as Teachers of Virtue', *History of Political Thought* 4 (1983), pp. 409–27 on Plato's treatment of Protagoras the Sophist specifically and Sophists' claims generally.

one can ever be harmed by them. The majority of men, says Socrates, are naturally amiable and good tempered and can be so persuaded (500). But the persuasion will have to begin very early.

Even in corrupt societies, the man with a philosophic nature will be recognized by all as especially gifted, physically and mentally, and he must try to remain true to his nature despite his friends and fellow citizens wishing to make use of his gifts for their own ends. But the very constituents of the philosophic nature, with its natural bent for reason, will be precisely what causes his companions to wish to secure his support for their ways of living and they will actively prevent him from being a philosopher. His gifts, in a bad environment, will destroy his very nature. 'It is men so gifted who inflict the deepest injuries on communities and individuals and, indeed, *if inclined that way, do them the greatest good*' (495).

Those with the natural philosophical gifts must be fostered by a suitable society that 'inclines' them to use their gifts for the greatest good. When this is not the case, then chance intervenes: there *will* emerge men with philosophical natures, even if all is left to chance.

> [But] there will emerge only a very small remnant that survives of all those worthy to have any dealings with philosophy – perhaps some honest man saved by exile from the influences that would corrupt his natural loyalty for her, or some great mind born in a petty state and so despising politics; or long ill-health that makes it impossible to engage in politics; and there may be a gifted few who turn to philosophy from other occupations which they rightly despise. . . . This small company, then, when they have tasted the happiness of philosophy and seen the frenzy of the masses, understand that political life has virtually nothing sound about it and that they will find no ally to save them in the fight for justice; and if they are not prepared to join in the general wickedness and yet are unable to fight it single-handed, they are likely to perish like a man thrown among wild beasts, without profit to themselves or others, before they can do any good to their friends or society.

To this extent, Socrates agrees with Thrasymachus, the immoralist, that in a corrupt society the good man is likely to suffer and even perish. But Socrates' aim is to show that justice still makes the just person, even in these conditions, happier than the unjust person; his aim is not to show that the just person is always happy. And so, when just men 'reckon all this up, they live quietly and keep to themselves, like a man who stands under the shelter of a wall during a driving storm of dust and hail' (496d–e). As such, he is self-sufficient. By adapting his desires to those that can be fulfilled in the environment in which he finds himself, the wise and just man secures his happiness, whatever the external conditions may be, more than does the unjust man who engages in the insecure conditions of a corrupt world. But there are, clearly, theoretically conceived optimum conditions in which this kind of wise and just character would flourish the better.

The Possibility of the Philosopher–ruler and the Ideal Constitution: Theory and Practice[48]

If there is, at present, no existing form of society which is good enough for the philosophic nature, then an ideal society must be found or constructed along the theoretical lines already laid down. Only then will it become evident as it has not been in the past, that the philosopher–ruler *is* a possibility and not some unrealizable fantasy. According to Plato, people seem ready to accept the existence of the philosophic nature but in corrupt societies they see him either as useless or they attempt to harness his talents to their own non-philosophic and corrupt ends. How can the common people be reorientated so that the philosopher finds his rightful place? Once one has the theory which gives an account of the kind of society in which the philosophic nature best flourishes for his own and others' good, then how does one start the process of constructing, in actuality, the perfect 'state'? Once again, this may come about if chance intervenes: either when chance compels that minority of uncorrupted philosophic natures to enter politics and they are able to compel society to listen to them, or when providence inspires some present rulers with a genuine love of philosophy. We are told that there is no reason to suppose that either of these chance occurrences is impossible.

But is this good enough? Is society and the philosophic nature to wait on chance? And which of these chance occurrences does Plato think to be the more likely? Ideally, chance must be superseded by the initiative of the founders of the ideal *politeia* who require a clean canvas (501a); the best and quickest way to establish the ideal society and constitution (541a) is to build a society from the beginnings, starting with children aged ten and under, and relegating their already-habituated elders to the suburbs (540d–e, 541a). It is the children, already showing the expected three-fold differentiation in natures, who are to be persuaded through being educated. The education will differentially appeal to the kinds of psychic dominance their respective characters or natures demonstrate, and for the majority, myths and stories will provide them with the true belief that accords with the kinds of cognitive operation of which their souls have demonstrated a capability. The education will prepare them to do the job that each is naturally suited to doing. For the exclusive minority with philosophic natures, Socrates specifies that philosophic training should be limited for children and, as they grow older, their chief attention should be devoted to the training of their bodies. As they mature, their mental training intensifies and, when their physical strength begins to fail and they are no longer fit for political and military service, they will, at last, devote all their main energies to philosophy.

The great majority of the Guardians, let alone the Producers, will never recognize Forms in the full Platonic sense. That is to be the goal of the highly select minority. Arithmetic and geometry and the other studies leading to dialectic, having been introduced in childhood as forms of play, followed by physical training, lead to a further selection for the best *aptitude* for dialectic when they are in their twenties and again, in

---

48   There is a large literature which asserts Plato was not serious about the realization of the political ideal and philosopher–kings. For a discussion and rejection of these views see G. Klosko, 'The "Straussian" Interpretation of Plato's *Republic*', *History of Political Thought* 7, (1986), pp. 275–93; also G. Klosko, 'Provisionality in Plato's Ideal State', *History of Political Thought* 5 (1984), pp.171–93.

their thirties. An aptitude for dialectic is described at this stage as an ability to take the comprehensive view, seeing how all their disconnected subjects of study, thus far, fit together (537c). At thirty, those selected are gradually introduced to philosophical discussions, but they are then sent into the world of political and military office for practical experience, which lasts for fifteen years. Only after they have reached fifty years of age will they be 'made to lift their mind's eye to look at the source of all light and see the Good itself' (540a) through dialectic.[49] Thereafter, they will be able to rule as philosophers, taking their turn in the weary business of politics, doing their duty as Rulers (540a–b).

No one is born a ruler. Statesmanship is a skill that must be learned, by which Plato means a certain kind of natural temperament can be trained to function at its rational best. The children who eventually become the rare philosopher–rulers are relentlessly tested in their resistance to pleasure and pain or other misfortunes. They are tested with regard to readiness to learn and remember, to determine their enterprise and breadth of vision as well as their steadiness, trustworthiness, reliability and their ability to be unmoved by fear in war. Their characters or natures are rare occurrences (503). Then they will work as hard at intellectual training as at physical training. Eventually, through an increasingly abstract education in various kinds of mathematical studies (arithmetic, plane geometry, solid geometry, astronomy and harmonics (524e–531c)), they will come to understand that the highest form of knowledge is knowledge of the essential nature of goodness, the Form of the Good, from which things that are just and beautiful, etc. derive their usefulness and value. The usefulness and value is to the human self.

The aim is to show that whatever a man desires so ardently that he will put it before everything else, is for him, the good. If you believe, as Plato's Socrates believes, that there is an Absolute Good, knowledge of which is a man's chief end or interest, then no other knowledge can be so important as the knowledge of what this is. Each human must concern himself with the final end of human interest first, his own good. Plato here tackles what the earlier Socrates left unanswered: an intellectual grasp of what must be present to every action and every possession commonly called good to ensure that it will be unfailingly useful and advantageous to the human self or psyche. This is the Good as superior to Being and as the sustaining cause of all the other Forms as virtues. Goodness justifies its own existence but it is the reason that we can recognize the good of other things as the final explanation of their existence, what they are *good for*, as useful and advantageous.

We are told that Goodness is higher than justice and other qualities or virtues (505). Goodness is what is to be understood as that existent which serves as the source of all other things called virtues and qualities. But what the Good is *in itself* is not something of which Socrates can here give an account (506d–e). He tells his companions that the truth of the matter is known only to god (517 c–d). At best, the Good can be spoken of analogously with light by which objects are visible to the eye. Just as the sun is the 'cause' of sight in the visible world, the Good is the 'cause' of intelligence and intelligibility in the Intelligible world (508b). The mind's eye, when it rests on objects illumi-

---

49   Compare below, chapter 4, where Aristotle prescribes religious–philosophical endeavours for those men who have passed through the military and political stages of their lives, indeed where theoretical activity is a necessarily post-political activity. Plato, in contrast, brings these men back into the *polis* to rule.

nated by truth and reality, understands them and the mind functions intelligently. What gives the objects of the mind's knowledge their truth and the mind the power of knowing is the Form of the Good, which is the cause of knowledge and truth. Knowledge and truth are *like* the Good but the Good is itself 'higher'. It is beyond reality but the cause of reality's existence and intelligibility (509).

What we need, and as yet do not have, is a description of the kind of discursive, synoptic knowledge that permits us to see how the Form of the Good explains the nature of the other Forms and gives an account of the nature of the sensible world which is as it is because it 'participates' in the metaphysical order of existence. Thereafter, reflection on the physical world that is perceived by the senses allows one to see what is good and rational in the physical world.[50] But at this point we are given Socrates' *opinion*, his theory or hypothesis: the final thing to be perceived by intellect is the absolute Form of Good (517d). Later it will be shown that the route to a grasp of the Form of the Good is through dialectic, the final stage of education. Dialectic alone enables the philosophic mind to give a logically coherent account to explain how the Good is the explanation of the structure of everything intelligible and sensible. *Epistēmē* (knowledge) recognizes the interrelations of the Forms themselves and their ultimate dependence on the Good as a self-authenticating principle and cause of all. The goal of the dialectic method enables the philosophic mind to see that the Good explains the intelligible world as an ordered whole. Socrates himself did not reach this goal because the refutational method of investigation – the *elenchos* – did not achieve what the Platonic dialectic could: a synoptic understanding of reality, attainable through a discursive knowledge about it. To understand this, we must begin with Socrates' opinion, that the *final* thing to be perceived by intellect is the absolute Form of the Good, an opinion that depends on there being two interrelated orders of things, the visible and the intelligible.

The Divided Line and the Cave

The continuity and relation between the visible and intelligible may be explained by using the static image of a line divided into two unequal parts. The Divided Line is an epistemology which shows the relation between the states of mind called opinion/belief and knowledge on the one hand, and on the other, between the physical and intelligible 'worlds'. The objects of *doxa* (true belief/opinion) are to those of *epistēmē* (knowledge) as a likeness of something to that which it resembles (509d, 510a). Resemblance is the clue. Plato is not arguing that the world we sense and about which we have beliefs and opinions has no reality at all, but rather that it is not total reality. The visible world is a world of change and is characterized by becoming, whereas the intelligible world is stable and changeless, characterized by being. The visible world resembles, is like, is in the process of becoming, what the intelligible world is. His image of the Divided Line is underwritten by his doctrine of Forms which 'saves the phenomena' of the sensible world and does not relegate the sensible world to a non-entity. All things depend on the Forms for such being as they have. The Divided Line depicts states of mind with their

---

50   See G. Vlastos, *Plato's Universe* (Oxford, 1995), ch. 3.

respective 'objects', seen in different ways and with regard to different degrees of understanding.[51]

How the human mind is enlightened is thereafter depicted by a dynamic simile, that of the Cave, which is meant to be connected with the Line analogy. The Cave simile shows how the unstable objects of *doxa* contain the semblance of stable realities. The difference between belief and knowledge is one of degree rather than kind, and educational reorientation – the journey out of the cave – makes this plain.

Men are shackled prisoners in the cave since they were children. They look straight ahead at the cave wall and behind them a fire burns. Between their backs and the fire various figures are moved about, but all that the prisoners see are shadows cast on the cave wall before them. They assume the shadows they see are the real things. If one prisoner (who is not described as any more rational, or naturally talented, than the others) is released from his bonds and compelled to turn round and forced to look at the fire, and then dragged out of the cave and into the sunlight, the experience would be painful, but after he had become accustomed to the light he would see things in the world outside the cave. We note that physical force is applied to the body but his mind is not forced to 'see'. Socrates later says that a free man ought not to learn anything under duress. Compulsory physical education does no harm to the body, but compulsory learning never sticks in the mind (536e–537a). The prisoner in the cave, however, is not a free man. Once he is released from his bonds and compelled to turn round, he becomes free. Once outside the cave he would first find it easier to look at the shadows, then at their reflections in water, and, finally, at the objects themselves. The last thing would be to look overtly at the sun and he would conclude that the sun was, *in a sense*, responsible for everything that he and his fellow prisoners used to see. He would now feel sorry for those in the cave and what they mistakenly took to be reality.

The ascent from the cave to the upper world and the sight of its objects is meant to be analogous to the Divided Line's depiction of the mind's progress from the visible to the intelligible realms. Once the absolute Form of the Good is 'perceived' by the mind, humans can only *infer* (we must reason: *syllogistea*) that it, like the sun, is responsible for everything right and good, indeed, of all other Forms, and that it is the controlling source of reality and intelligence. Anyone who is to act rationally either in public or private must perceive it. And this means that a *knowledge* of the Forms and therefore a knowledge of the principles which motivate men to moral action, is not acquired by means of the senses. The Forms exist separately from the sensibles, are unaffected by the visible world of change, and their source is the Form of the Good. They would exist even if sensibles did not, and even if we did not exist to 'perceive' them.

Once this is accepted, the view that education is a process of implanting into the mind knowledge that was not there before must be rejected. In *each* man's mind there is an innate capacity to turn away from the physical world of change and look at unchanging

---

51   As Guthrie noted in *A History of Greek Philosophy*, vol. 4, p. 496, Plato tried to disentangle himself from the consequences of Parmenidean logic where what is, is, and cannot not be; what is not, is not and cannot be. This leads to the Parmenidean view that nothing can change or come into being, for what is, does not become since it is already, and nothing could come to be out of what is not. See contrasting views on Plato's position in G. Vlastos, 'Degrees of Reality in Plato', in R. Bambrough, ed., *New Essays on Plato and Aristotle* (London, 1965), pp. 1–20. As Guthrie says, some of us may not believe (as Vlastos did not) in a gradational ontology but Plato did, and so did Descartes. For Plato, the world we can sense in ordinary experience has a quasi-existence only because things in that world share in the natures of the Forms.

reality which is what, Socrates says, he calls the Good. In the later *Phaedrus* (249b) Plato again says that only those souls which have seen the Forms can be born as men. *Every* man has had the vision of them and to recollect them is, in theory, possible for all. But clearly, to be consistent, Plato must still insist on differential ability. The great majority, in the *Republic*, are beset by the demands and temptations of life in the body, 'seeing many beautiful things or just actions but they do not see Beauty or Justice itself' (479a). That innate capacity in all men must somehow be overcome in most of us, so that natural talent is itself an indicator of whether or not a given person's character can actually benefit from the kind of higher, abstract education that orientates and focuses the reasoning element of soul on its proper objects. Most men, as the *Phaedo* had made clear (82e), are imprisoned by their bodies and the lower psychological desires motivate them to collude in their own ignorant imprisonment (*Republic* 519a–b). Some men, however, have the rare capacity for an intellectual grasp of the Good in order to be able to be turned round by education, which is described as no more than a turning of the mind towards, a training in a distinctive sort of reasoning about, the mind's proper objects. Somehow, such rare characters must not be easily (if at all), side-tracked by the other psychological elements in their souls which, if allowed to assume a controlling position, would amount to such characters being motivated by the irrational in the human psyche, so that they would remain imprisoned in the cave. Indeed, all the other qualities of mind, we are now told, are not innate so much as acquired by training and practice. But the power of knowing is innate, it belongs to some diviner faculty in man and it never loses its power. Its effects, however, are either good or bad according to the direction in which the mind is turned. And we are told that this is what distinguishes bad but clever men from good men. All men have the power to generalize from particulars, but unless they are informed by a knowledge of the Forms, their notions of justice will remain shadows or images of true justice. They will not be able to imitate in their own thoughts and actions the Form of justice because to imitate well one needs to have a comprehensive understanding of what one is imitating. Hence, the job of the lawgivers in the ideal 'state' will be to compel the best minds to attain the highest form of knowledge, the grasp of the Form of the Good, and then return to the cave.[52] The education system is compulsory but once they are in the system, what people learn is by means of genres of persuasion that differentially suit them.

> The object of our legislation is not the welfare of any particular class but of the whole community. It uses persuasion [of minds] or force [of bodies] to unite all citizens and make them share together the benefits which each individually can confer on the community, and its purpose in fostering this attitude is not to enable everyone to please himself but to make each man a link in the unity of the whole. (520)

To know what is good for anything, one must first know its nature; the good for humans requires a knowledge of ourselves as human natures, that is, a knowledge of the psyche. Only once a person knows what *is*, his self, can he feel obliged by an *ought*, and hence the philosopher, in particular, is obliged by what he knows to take his turn in political rule and show men how they ought to live.

The philosopher's justice, contrary to Thrasymachus' suggestion, is both good for

---

52   See Fine, 'Knowledge and Belief in Republic v–vii'.

others and good for himself. And having benefited from an education that turned the philosophic nature towards the human mind's true objects, the philosopher will realize that he owes it to society that has so trained his natural talents that he now can combine philosophy and politics in its service. Such a man will not refuse this just demand on his educated talents (520). It is, however, a demand and therefore a constraint. But it is one that is as much in the interests of the philosopher as in those whom he rules. The trained philosophic nature would prefer the pleasure of living a life of contemplation. But his self-interest lies elsewhere – in ruling. Philosophers alone, in love with philosophy rather than power, will be the only ones who least wish to possess the political power and its rewards that are pressed upon them (521). Their moral obligation to rule does not involve a sacrifice of self-interest when self-interest is properly construed.

Dialectic

Dialectic is the final stage in mathematical studies. It is for mature minds, otherwise training in this kind of logical argument will degenerate into the indiscipline of contradicting people just for fun (539a). It is a training in a distinctive sort of reasoning about the Form of the Good. It discovers the common features and the mutual relations between the various branches of mathematics in order to reveal the underlying harmony and order of the cosmos, and hence, for Plato, the order of values. It is a sort of reasoning that goes beyond the *elenchos*, beyond the hypothesis of opinion and refutation, and reaches the certainty of the self-authenticating first principle, the Good (535b–e), as the source of the existence of all Forms and their mutual interrelationships. Dialectic is the ability to give an account of the essential nature or Form of each particular thing and hence to demonstrate understanding. Furthermore, Socrates says that if a man cannot define the Form of the Good, distinguishing it from everything else, defending it not merely as a matter of opinion but in strict logic, then he does not know what the Absolute Good is or any other good (534d). Dialectic is the only rational activity whose method is to challenge its own assumptions so that it may rest firmly on first principles (533b–c) and, thereby, enable a person to 'take the comprehensive view' (537b–c). But we are never told what the Form of the Good is *in itself*. It is simply from where one begins. It is beyond words, but its effects are everywhere for the self and society.

Five Types of Constitution

The ideal constitution, ruled by philosopher–kings, is a constitution that is ruled by the best and hence is an aristocracy, which means 'rule of the best'. If only one philosopher can be found to be king, then it will be a monarchy. Other constitutions degenerate from this ideal into timocracy, oligarchy, democracy and finally, tyranny.

Plato here refers to the Spartan type of constitution as a timocracy (545a) and its failings are exemplified in the timocratic man, who is self-focused but through bad company yields to the spirited part of his soul and becomes arrogant and ambitious. A timocracy will degenerate into an oligarchy, the next-worse type, which is characterized by the dominance of property qualifications and wealth which determine social prestige. This, in turn, degenerates into democracy, which is characterized by free speech, liberty, each person doing as he likes according to his individual preferences. It is a 'supermarket of constitutions'[53] where no one is compelled either to govern or to obey those who do, where there are no fixed principles of behaviour and the 'rulers' rule because they call themselves 'the people's friends', offering equality to equals and unequals alike. The democratic personality is, for Plato, undisciplined, a chaos of wilful desires, 'governed' by caprice and making no distinction between more and less worthy pleasures. Indeed, the democrat is suspicious of all forms of control, be it from the law or from traditional moral principles. What Plato has described as the correct, harmonious order of the human psyche, its justice, is disrupted precisely by what we today would see as democratic virtues: tolerance of individual difference and the individual's insistence on determining his own preferences, based on his own subjective pleasure 'principle'. His 'state' takes no view on the moral good of the whole but, rather, allows this to emerge, piecemeal, and with no stability, as the consequence of individual choices. Plato acknowledges that the versatility of the democratic man and his society is what many men and women envy; it has so many possibilities (561e). Each part of the democrat's psyche, now the appetitive, seeking material, physiological pleasure; now the spirited, seeking recognition and honours; and even now the rational, suddenly recognizing long-term human interests, has its fling without any systematic precedence being established in motivation to behave in one way or another. The democratic man is many men in succession, a versatile personality. Why should he get rid of desires he cultivated when young but which, a more reasoned temperament might explain, were not good for him as he aged? (559c). He wants to make his own mistakes and successively 'be' different *personae*. This is his liberty, after all. And if he were not able to indulge his appetites when young – say, he had been brought up in a 'narrow economical way' – but he then gets into wild company and tastes a variety of pleasures, his father, not knowing how to bring him up properly, is replaced by his new associates. The young man's vacant mind is filled by an invasion of pretentious fallacies and back he goes to live with the Lotus-eaters (560d–e). Nothing is shameful, self-control is taken to be cowardice, and economy and moderation are abused as provincial parsimony (560e). Plato describes such a character as having an identity crisis.

This democratic character will need a great deal of *luck* not to be carried to extremes so that, as he ages, he will be able to establish a kind of equality of pleasures, where each pleasure of the moment, each preference, is exercised until satisfied and he then moves on to the next. If he is *lucky*, he will say that all pleasures are equal and should have equal rights. 'One day it is wine, women and song, and the next, bread and water' – a boulimia of the soul. But if he is *unlucky*, his psychological and physical dissolution will probably destroy him. In either case, his character will not be within his control. Indeed, his self's character will be divided against itself (560a). He will be a democratic 'state' writ small, a constitution that enshrines a conflict of factions. Plato admits that this looks like an agreeable, anarchic form of society with plenty of variety. Its modern version is Nozick's supermarket of protection societies[54] which one can join or leave as it suits the moment and one's preferences, with a minimum overriding 'state' that operates by procedure rather than fixed moral principles, a pluralism run mad. In this society, the just man is still happier than the unjust man but he keeps his head down and goes

---

53   To use the apt phrase of Guthrie, *A History of Greek Philosophy*, vol. 4, p. 531.
54   R. Nozick, *Anarchy, State and Utopia* (New York, 1974).

private. Indeed, it is virtually a 'stateless' society of private, shifting factions. And the real problem of this kind of society and self, for Plato, is precisely its instability. It can only degenerate into demagoguery and tyranny, the worst situation in which democratic men will find 'they have jumped out of the frying pan of subjection to free men into the fire of subjection to slaves, having exchanged their excessive and unlimited freedom for the harshest and bitterest servitude, where the slave to his own secret, bestial desires – the tyrant – is master'. Plato's real fear appears to have been that Athenian, democratic indiscipline would lead it straight into the arms of a 'saviour', the despotic personality. The despotic character inevitably becomes mad, is alone, fearful, friendless and cruel, 'ruling' by force without restraint or law. He is the perfect specimen of injustice (576b). He has the least capacity for self-knowledge and, therefore, the least capacity to pursue self-interest, his good. His appetitive character, dominated by the motive of gain (and his gain is everyone else's loss), never achieves the end for which all men strive, their human good. That Plato thought this to be the future trajectory of democratic Athens seems clear. Would Thrasymachus have disagreed?

It is noteworthy that Plato's account of the democratic character and the *politeia* the democrat constitutes with like-minded others, is not hateful but fearful. Socrates is made to reject a democratic constitution because, for Plato, it exemplified a woeful ignorance of its own instability in which individuals would not be as he wished them to be, disciplined and autonomous selves in a collectivity of selves, knowing their best interest *and achieving it*. For him, the democratic character has no stable self to be known, and what is worse, this would lead to him being harmed, inwardly, not only by his own lurchings from one preference to another, but by eventually being totally taken over by the demagogue whom the democrat at first believed to be his saviour.

Plato, unlike some early Christian writers, never believed that the human soul could be perfected in defiance of environment. Therefore, if men were to choose their destiny, and Plato insisted that this was their choice alone, then they would only be 'saved' by a politics based on impartial *epistēmē*, a knowledge of the good for men as they truly are, and where the power in society must be exercised for their good. If conflict, change, revolution and factions, the dizzy cycle of constitutional forms, were, for him, the stuff of Athenian history, a story of instability, unhappiness, worry about survival, then, as Plato saw it, the only way to ameliorate this irrational chaos and disorder was to realize that the world of political factionalism violated the dictates of cosmic order; it violated the Forms. We would not be alone, however, in wondering whether the aristocratic and disillusioned Plato read Athens' history and current situation aright.[55] None the less, for him, politics, as Athenians knew it, had to change from being a struggle between special advantages, factions, 'classes', to a symmetrical and static harmony of functioning parts, established and maintained not by amateurs, but by rare character types, strictly educated to exercise their rational intellects and grasp the Form of the Good. This would enable them to explain, logically, how human selves could live in harmony. It required that the community rid itself of politics, seen as a precarious equilibrium of opposing forces and momentary conciliations. For Plato, political order was produced by the true statesman–philosopher's skill (*technē*) of matching *praxis* to an informing theoretical vision. This came not from the contingent experience of men, corrupted by

55 See chapter 1, this volume.

social games, set in motion by bad and ignorant habit, but by an intelligible, eternal pattern, outside men, shaping the community to a pre-existent Good. From this came points of political and historical fixity: the size and population of the ideal *polis* would be stable and small; the structure of its vocations, fixed; education, moral and religious doctrines, controlled. If you regulated these, Plato believed, you could regularize human behaviour by regulating what you *could* regulate: psychological motivation. But then, of course, you would have to agree not only that the potentially conflicting psychological desires could be brought under the sway of rational desire, but that what was essentially human about the self was its reason.

The crucial difference between a democratic leader and the Platonic leader centres on the respective constituencies to which each is responsive. Plato's philosopher–ruler is not a politician as we understand the term, but a philosopher with political power, whose loyalty is not to a faction or interest group but to an orderly, synoptic, overriding truth – the Good for all. In the world of men, this Good is consistently valuable and useful and, therefore, in their interests. Some critics have argued, however, that the lack of participation in political decision-making in Plato's ideal state, but where citizens none the less benefit from the order that is imposed rationally, would create a severe kind of anomie. It would eliminate that sense of belonging to community which is, after all, what modern, liberal-democratic politics is supposed to be about. The argument is that a political community is not held together by truth (whatever that is) but by consensus, arrived at through participatory action and compromise. Surely, this has not always been the case, and subsequent chapters in this book will reveal how participatory action and compromise, even when considered, would be offered only to an exclusive elite.

Plato's answer to this kind of criticism took the form of a scepticism about the capacity for meaningful participation in collective governance by the many, and it seems to have resulted, in part, from his own observation and evaluation of what he took to be the failure of this kind of *politeia* in fifth- and fourth-century BC Athens. Tyranny was always on the agenda. But perhaps more fundamentally, the Socratic influence on him, which made the question of knowing the self – its good, and how it could ensure against harm – the centre of focus, led him further to analyse the psychology of men in order to determine the springs of motivational desire. This, in conjunction with the development of a doctrine of Forms that enabled the knower to give a coherent account, a holistic explanation, of men in nature, led to the destruction of human politics and its replacement by educational reorientation by reason.

Despite the inconsistencies and question-begging nature of many of his arguments, and which have been pointed out down the centuries,[56] his aim was to argue that the just person alone was psychologically stable, morally healthy and capable of a social integration that would serve his own interests and those of his fellow citizens in ways that no other character type was able to do. His arguments tried to explain to different types of

---

56   Annas, *An Introduction to Plato's Republic* is particularly good on this; also see J. M. Bryant, 'Enlightenment Psychology and Political Reaction in Plato's Social Philosophy: an ideological contradiction?', *History of Political Thought* 11 (1990), pp. 377–95: 'Pato's aristocratic animus against the masses overrides the logical social implications of his panhuman doctrine of the immortal, quasi-divine psyche' – a consequence, for Bryant, of philosophical discourse being embedded in wider contemporary, cultural norms and values which are not ours; Bryant observes a similar, aristocratic bias in his interpretation of Aristotle; see J. M. Bryant, *Moral Codes and Social Structure in Ancient Greece: a sociology of Greek ethics from Homer to the Epicureans and Stoics* (Albany, NY, 1996), pp. 356–4.

psychologies why certain 'facts' about the human situation have a rational claim on us, even if we have not previously been aware of this or cannot, without help, live according to such rational claims. As the Good explains what is intelligible about the ordered and harmonious 'world', so too, justice is the consequence of knowing a principle over and above it, the Good. It is from the Form of the Good that justice derives its usefulness and value for man. Justice, as a harmonious relationship in the psyche and in community, also explains how, each and severally, our interests are best served either by being a certain kind of self – the good man, or by being ruled by such a self in a certain kind of society – the ideal. This is the theoretical pattern that states and individuals must always keep in mind. For Plato, the 'civilized but "overheated" society' could only be saved and made secure by rational selves imperfectly imitating, through logical imposition, the formal order initiated by the first principle, the Good. His metaphysical epistemology prevented him from seeing any other options.

But this does not deny that the *Republic* is a political work, even if it is not exclusively political. It was certainly regarded in antiquity as political. The political principle, embedded in the *Republic*, and with which we may no longer have any sympathy, is that of consensus *without* compromise on the issue of who should govern and who should be governed. For most citizens this was to depend not on reason but on what Skemp has called 'an enlightened and disciplined desire for the common good of which all citizens are capable'.[57]

---

57 J. B. Skemp, 'How Political is the *Republic?*', *History of Political Thought* 1 (1980), pp. 1–7.

4

Aristotle

It has often been said that intellectually the world is divided into Platonists and Aristotelians. With hindsight, we can say that there has been an enduring argument between Platonists and Aristotelians down the centuries. The bottom line is a distinction that may be drawn between their respective approaches to understanding reality. Each thinker proposed different *sources* of knowledge and, consequently, each provided a different theory of *how* we come to know, and then define, what is essentially human about humans. This leads to two different accounts of human needs and capacities, and their respective visions of the 'state' differ accordingly.

Historically, the development of Aristotle's thinking could not have even begun and it certainly would not have progressed without Plato, his teacher. Many, if not most, of Plato's problems and the standards for evaluating successful answers to them comprised much of Aristotle's agenda. What we see when we read Plato's Socrates, Plato's Platonism and then Aristotle's responses, not only to both thinkers but also to the previous pre-Socratic and Sophistic developments, is the progression of the ancient Greek philosophical tradition through a reformulation of problems and ways of tackling them.

In discussing Aristotle's ethical and political theory my aim is to attempt a retrospective reconstruction, not only of the progressive development of his thought but also of its subsequent understanding and use. Political theories that have been judged important in the Western tradition of political theorizing, like Aristotle's, 'survived' in subsequent generations through later reinterpretations and commentaries. Especially in Aristotle's case we are often dependent on those commentaries to help us elucidate what he was taken to be saying in periods that were closer to his own times and culture than we are. There has long been a scholarly debate over the intellectual evolution of Aristotle's thinking.[1] In this chapter, I plan to emphasize many of his differences from, rather than his similarities to Plato. One of the reasons for this is that large parts of the two principal Aristotelian texts we deal with in courses in the history of political thought, namely, the *Nicomachean Ethics* and the

---

1   The genetic approach of W. Jaeger, *Aristoteles: Grundlegung einer Geschichte seiner Entwicklung* (Berlin, 1923) translated as *Aristotle: fundamentals of the history of his development*, 2nd edn, trans. R. Robinson (Oxford, 1948) versus I. Düring, *Aristotle in the Ancient Biographical Tradition* (Göteborg, 1957) and I. Düring, *Aristoteles* (Heidelberg, 1966).
2   Easily available translations are: Aristotle, *Ethics (Nicomachean Ethics)*, trans. J. A. K. Thompson, revd H. Tredennick with introduction and bibliography by J. Barnes (Harmondsworth, 1976) and reprints; Aristotle, *The Politics*, revd edn, trans. T. A. Sinclair, revised and represented by T. J. Saunders (Harmondsworth, 1981) and reprints; also see Aristotle, *Politics, Books I and II*, trans. with commentary T. J. Saunders (Oxford, 1995). Ancient commentators also grouped the *Ethics* together with the *Politics* and in that order as *practical* philosophical discourse.

Politics, come from the later stages of his life when Plato was long dead.[2] We shall see that many of Aristotle's views were the consequence of a critical reflection on Plato's teachings and that he often defended Plato's views against others. But we shall also see that Aristotle's approach led to another way of seeing and understanding the same world that Plato inhabited. He would come to reject some of Plato's explanations of that agreed world, by finding other causes that were more numerous, obvious and demonstrable than a single, separate, transcendent and unifying Form of the Good to elucidate the way things are.

This 'difference' between the two philosophers is often thought to be epitomized for any visitor to the Vatican in Rome who is able to admire Raphael's famous Renaissance painting *The School of Athens*. Here, Plato and Aristotle are depicted in discussion. Plato points to the heavens while Aristotle, holding a copy of his *Ethics* in his left hand, extends his right hand in front of him and appears, by this gesture, both to be restraining Plato's transcendental enthusiasm and to be encompassing the material world before him. It is most unlikely, however, that their difference was being underlined by a Renaissance painter, because we shall see that the more usual Renaissance position was that, in essentials, these philosophers did not differ.[3]

Now, some have argued (both in antiquity and today) that the differences to be found between Plato and Aristotle are the consequence of Aristotle, the student, fundamentally misunderstanding Plato, his teacher, and that his approach is a consequence of this misunderstanding. Some have attributed his other way of seeing and understanding to a temperamental difference combined with a different set of personal experiences.[4] Whatever view we come to hold we must approach Aristotle's *Nicomachean Ethics* and *Politics* as works which do not, in the first instance, attempt to answer *our* ethical and political problems but, rather, 'bear witness to an effort to solve problems raised by human life on Greek soil in the fourth century BC'.[5]

Aristotle's Experiences

In 384 BC Aristotle was born in Stageira, the son of a doctor who was the personal physician to King Amyntas of Macedonia in northern Greece. King Amyntas was the father of Philip of Macedon and the grandfather of Alexander the Great. Hence, Aristotle was to know life under two monarchies, that of Philip and Alexander. The ancient biographical tradition which provides the sources for what we know of Aristotle's life (Diogenes Laertius, Dionysius of Halicarnassus, various Neoplatonic, Byzantine, Syriac and later Arabic traditions)[6] tells us that Aristotle was left orphaned and that his education was completed under the supervision of a guardian, Proxenus. In 367 BC, at the age of seventeen, Aristotle went to the democratic *polis* Athens to complete his education and he joined Plato's Academy, where he remained for the next twenty years until Plato's death in 347 BC. Aristotle was not, therefore, an Athenian citizen in origin and he remained a metic. For a man who would become famous for having insisted that the activities of a citizen, taking turns in ruling and being ruled, was the optimum life for the

---

3   See volume 2, chapter 6 of *A History of Political Thought*.
4   W. K. C. Guthrie, *A History of Greek Philosophy*, vol. 6, *Aristotle: an encounter* (Cambridge, 1981).
5   R. Bodéüs, *The Political Dimensions of Aristotle's Ethics*, trans. J. E. Garrett (Albany, NY, 1993), p. 47.
6   See Düring, *Aristotle in the Ancient Biolgraphical Tradition*.

fulfilled man who, by nature, was a *polis*-living animal, his metic status in the Athens where he taught and lived was, at least, a notable irony.

When, by 347 BC, Demosthenes had already secured acknowledgement as a democratic political leader in Athens, and he challenged the increasing Macedonian peril, Athens became an uncomfortable place for a friend of Macedon and Aristotle left, with Xenocrates of the Academy, for Asia Minor. There he met his future wife Pythias, the niece and adoptive daughter of Hermias, a philosophically supportive 'tyrant-king', and with like-minded friends and collaborators he carried out scientific research, examining and writing about the flora, fauna and biology of that part of the world. In 343 BC he was called to the Macedonian court to serve as tutor to Philip's son, Alexander, who was then thirteen. He continued for three years until Alexander was made regent while his father campaigned against Byzantium.[7] With Philip's assassination in 336 BC, Alexander succeeded to the throne and thereafter left on his world-famous military campaigns in Asia, appointing Antipater as regent in Greece. Antipater, a friend of Aristotle, was to be named in Aristotle's will as his executor. From 347–335, then, Aristotle had been away from Athens, but he returned to teach independently in a precinct of Athens where not only Sophists and rhetors also gathered pupils around them, but where Socrates had spent much of his time. Each teacher had his own gymnasium, sometimes several adjacent buildings, and a favourite covered walk. Aristotle's school was known as the Lyceum, where it was said he collected an extraordinary library which later became the model for the famous library in Alexandria. His second and final Athenian period lasted twelve years.[8]

Aulus Gellius (a second century AD Roman) described how Aristotle taught. In the evenings he opened his lectures to any young men who were interested and he spoke, apparently more informally, on rhetoric, the cultivation of quick wit and civic education. But in the mornings his lectures were restricted to those whom he judged to have sufficient education, were keen to learn and to work hard, and they listened to his more exacting investigations of nature and dialectical discussion. It was at this time that he clarified his views on ethics and politics. He gathered round him a group of assistants to collect materials on all manner of subjects like botany, animal biology, medicine, the history of the exact sciences, arithmetic, geometry, astronomy and descriptions of 158 known political systems. In addition to his work on the natural sciences (zoology, biology, botany, physics), his erudition covered the fields of logic, language, human psychology, ethics, politics and law, constitutional history, epistemology and metaphysics. As Jonathan Barnes has put it: 'Choose a field of research and Aristotle laboured in it; pick an area of human endeavour and Aristotle discoursed upon it'.[9] Not only was the man a polymath but he was also a systematizer, categorizing bodies of knowledge in terms of the distinct intellectual dispositions or ways of thinking that were appropriate to their study. Many of his classifications of the disciplines remained in force in European university curricula until the modern era.

---

7   For a summary of scholarly findings on Aristotle's Macedonian political activities see J. M. Bryant, *Moral Codes and Social Structure in Ancient Greece: a sociology of Greek ethics from Homer to the Epicureans and Stoics* (Albany, NY, 1996), ch. 5: vi and J. Miller, 'Aristotle's Paradox of Monarchy and the Biographical Tradition', *History of Political Thought* 19 (1998), pp. 501–16.

8   F. Grayeff, *Aristotle and his School* (London, 1974). For interesting but contested views see H.-H. Chroust, *Aristotle: new light on his life and on some of his lost works*, 2 vols (London, 1973).

9   J. Barnes, *Aristotle* (Oxford, 1982), p.3.

The problem for us, however, is that his works can be grouped into two main divisions: those personal lecture notes which served as the basis for his morning oral presentations to critical collaborators in his School and not meant for publication, and those literary compositions for the wider public. Most of Aristotle's writings that have come down to us are the school papers, material for his various oral teachings, rather than the published works.[10] His various works on ethics and politics, in particular, appear to have been meant for the talented and prepared among his advanced students at his morning lectures. And the compilations of laws and political constitutions to which he refers in these works are now lost except for the *Constitution of Athens* which was (re)discovered in the nineteenth century.[11] What has survived, then, and what we read when we read the *Ethics* and *Politics* is 'the difficult stuff'. The style of composition of these lecture notes has little of the literary polish of Plato's works. Furthermore, we know from ancient references that many of his now lost published works, dating from his earlier years, included dialogues with titles similar to the titles of Plato's works and this means we cannot, with precision, trace his journey from Platonist to Aristotelian. Some of these lost works have, to some extent, been reconstructed from surviving fragments. But for the most part, we are left with about one fifth of his writings and most of these are advanced works from Aristotle's final Athenian period, the last twelve years of his life. They were written at a time when Aristotle's friends were the ruling powers in Greece and when Greek cities were chafing at the imposition of Macedonian garrisons.

In 323 BC, Alexander the Great died (at the age of 32) and Athens decided on war with Antipater. Aristotle was charged with impiety (*asebeia*) and he abandoned Athens for Chalcis, where his mother's family had some property. He went there with a freed woman, Herpyllis, with whom he had lived after the death of his wife,[12] and he died the following year in 322 BC. He was 62 or 63.

There is an astonishing story of the loss and subsequent recovery of Aristotle's lecture manuscripts and other notes, told by the Roman-period Greeks Strabo (63 BC–AD 19) and Plutarch.[13] Guthrie noted that the survival of all the Aristotelian works we possess once hung on the slenderest of threads[14] and the survival of the works is intrinsically bound up with the Roman conquest of Greece. Aristotle had left his library to the philosopher Theophrastus, who then left it to another who took it to Skepsis and whose descendants, not being philosophers, kept the texts in their cellar. It appears that barely more than one generation after his death, the original manuscripts of Aristotle's lectures and his scientific notes were to lie unknown, locked up and in disorder, damaged by damp and moths, in an underground cellar. Many years later, members of this family sold the texts to a bibliophile who tried to restore the damaged parts. Numerous errors are thought to have been introduced. The Roman conqueror of Athens, Sulla, annexed the bibliophile's library and brought it to Rome in the first century BC. There, Andronicus of Rhodes (between 40 and 20 BC) was supplied by the scholar (*grammatikos*) Tyrannio

10   W. Jaeger, *Studien zur Entstehungsgeschichte der Metaphysik des Aristoteles* (Berlin, 1912), pp. 131–63; also Jaeger, *Aristotle*. On the lost works see I. Düring and G. E. L. Owen, eds, *Aristotle and Plato in Mid-Fourth Century* (Göteborg, 1960).

11   P. J. Rhodes, *A Commentary on the Aristotelian Athenaion Politeia* (Oxford, 1981; with addenda 1993); Aristotle, *The Athenian Constitution*, trans. P. J. Rhodes (Harmondsworth, 1984).

12   Guthrie, *A History of Greek Philosophy*, vol.6, p. 45.

13   *Sulla*, 26.

14   Guthrie, *A History of Greek Philosophy*, vol. 6, p. 55, n. 1.

with copies into which had been introduced further errors, and Andronicus edited and published these. He also compiled a catalogue.[15] Hence, we owe to Andronicus of Rhodes the form of the Aristotelian corpus as we know it. This includes its division into whole treatises, made up of parts that Andronicus or his predecessors judged belonged together but which, originally, may have been separate lectures.[16] Recently it has been suggested[17] that considerably more than this was known of Aristotle's works through the writings of his followers. But most scholars have maintained that Aristotle's more advanced works remained unknown for some two hundred years until the time of the Roman, Cicero. As we shall see, Cicero himself seems to have been ignorant of Andronicus' edition and when he cites from or imitates Aristotle, he does so either from Aristotle's more public works on rhetoric or from the set speeches of the now lost, more 'Platonic' earlier dialogues, ignoring Aristotle's 'School works' which only later became so important to students of ethical and political theory. Andronicus' edition is one of the reasons why, when we read both the *Nicomachean Ethics* and the *Politics*, the books and chapters sometimes appear in the wrong order and repetitions or cross-references to other works or other passages are confusing. Modern editions and translations of these works do not, uniformly, order the books and chapters in an agreed way.[18]

The foundation of all modern, scholarly work on Aristotle's *Nicomachean Ethics* is the text prepared by Bekker in 1831, who established his text on the basis of six manuscripts, the earliest and most reliable of which comes from the tenth century AD.[19] The oldest surviving manuscript of the *Politics* is a literal, somewhat barbarous translation into Latin from the thirteenth century AD, while the five best surviving Greek copies come from the fifteenth century AD. This tells us something important about the date from which Aristotle's ethical and political writings began to have what would eventually become an overwhelming influence on Western thinking. During late antiquity and the first Christian centuries, Aristotle's more difficult works were only studied by a handful of professional scholars. Even by the fourth and fifth centuries AD, when his logical works were increasingly used and translated into Latin, both his scientific and his ethico-political works remained largely unexplored in the Latin-reading West of the Roman Empire. Plato and various Platonisms played a much larger role in the early development of Christian philosophy and it would be institutional Christianity which would replace the institutions of the declining Roman Empire from the early fifth century on in Western Europe. But thereafter, the Arab world preserved Arabic and Hebrew translations of many of Aristotle's works and Christian contacts with Muslim Spain would provide one of the means by which some of his writings would eventually reach the Latin West during the eleventh and twelfth centuries.[20] When Aristotle's ethical and political works

---

15   It is thought that Andronicus was influenced by earlier lists of Aristotle's writings, preserved by Diogenes Laertius (V, 22–7) and the anonymous author of *Vita Menagiana*.

16   Düring, *Aristotle*, pp. 41–51, 67. See P. Moraux, *Les Listes anciennes des ouvrages d'Aristote* (Louvain, 1951); H. B. Gottschalk, 'Continuity and Change in Aristotelianism', in R. Sorabji, ed., *Aristotle and After* (London, 1997), pp. 109–15, esp. pp.110–11.

17   J. Barnes in J. Barnes and M. Griffin, eds, *Philosophia Togata* II (Oxford, 1997).

18   See, for instance, W. L. Newman, *The Politics of Aristotle* (New York, 1973 [1887–1902]) in comparison with Aristotle, *The Politics*, trans. T. A. Sinclair, revd T. J. Saunders (Harmondsworth, 1981).

19   Laurentianus lxxxi, ii.

20   There was, however, no Arabic version of Aristotle's *Politics*.

became available he would be referred to as The Philosopher by Muslims and, thereafter, Christians. Some in the Latin West would take him to be the major, indeed dangerous, challenge to Christian Platonism.[21]

'Goodbye to the Forms'

Where Plato had given the abstract Form of the Good a leading role in his explanation of reality, and so was led to regard the intellect rather than sense perception as the key to a knowledge of the real, Aristotle, in contrast, placed sensible particulars at the centre of his enquiry. Aristotle firmly believed in the reality of the physical world and in its study as an indispensable instrument of knowledge. He believed that we need appearances (*phainomena*) for us to know anything. Although we will have to be more precise about what he means by appearances and phenomena, for Aristotle, the *source* of our knowledge is perception, which is the consequence of particular sensations. Sensation is an indispensable precondition of knowledge, although sensation on its own does not yield knowledge. Experience, for Aristotle, is a kind of knowledge of individual somethings; but the *principles* or foundations of this knowledge are reached or revealed by induction from sensation. Induction is the process of reasoning from particular cases to general conclusions. Knowledge relies on induction and observation, on things given or appearances, and not on the direct perception of some substance behind the given. Induction and observation give rise to commonly accepted views (*endoxon*) which can be subject to error, but it is only from these 'opinions' that the truth can be teased out. Knowledge, therefore, comes from the soul's (psyche's) capacity to generalize, based on its perception of particulars, and these generalizations are then subject to a kind of logical or rational testing.[22] Knowledge, then, depends on the correct interpretation of that direct acquaintance with individuals that is provided by the bodily senses. For Aristotle, actual things do exist and are, in some way, the cause of our being able to make true or false statements that refer to them.[23] Humans are 'immattered *psyches*', or 'ensouled bodies' – souls 'in' bodies, and when a person perceives and then thinks it is the whole 'composite' person that is involved. The problem that Aristotle thought needed solving was why, if everything real is grasped by the senses, can there be knowledge only from reason? What is the relation between the soul's perception and thinking, our speaking about our perceptions and thoughts, and our senses' sensing?

Between Plato and Aristotle's subsequent development of Platonic insights, a radical discontinuity has, therefore, been observed. Where Plato's is seen as the deductive, disembodied, formal and intellectualist account, Aristotle's is seen as the inductive, embodied, 'empirical' account. But we must be aware that his 'empiricism' is always situated within a discussion of how observations appear to humans, as they express this in language.[24] Both thinkers provide holistic theories but achieve universal explanations in different ways. Some scholars have argued, from late antiquity to the present, that their

---

21   See volume 2, chapter 1 of *A History of Political Thought*.
22   See below, pp. 128–35, on logic and dialectic.
23   *Categories* 12, 14b9ff.
24   On his kind of 'empiricism' see below, pp. 126–7.

respective doctrines may, in the end, be synthesized so that there is more agreement than disagreement between teacher and student. And there is no doubt that some of Plato's later works (after the middle-period *Phaedo* and *Republic*), most notably the *Laws*, provide parallels with some of Aristotle's preferences in his *Politics*.[25] But we are more concerned with what his ethical and political theory offers in contrast to the Plato we know from the middle dialogues.[26]

What Aristotle Means by 'Science'

For Aristotle, like Plato, 'science' is a *cognitive quality of persons* engaged in thinking. Science is knowing. But Aristotle goes further than Plato by dividing science or knowing into different modes or intellectual dispositions. This is because, although like Plato, Aristotle was interested in the permanence and invariability of truth, he also attended to change and its causes. He distinguished between the situation where things come into existence or cease to exist, and when they simply change. Change and plurality are in everything we experience. And he believed that the causes and principles of different things are *different*. We know this because we have experiences and reflect on these experiences. This means, for Aristotle, that there are different kinds of human knowledge, that is, different modes of thought or different intellectual dispositions. These different 'sciences' are distinguished by the activities performed by each mode of thought. He categorizes them as the *productive*, the *practical* and the *theoretical* kinds. For this reason, the discussion in this chapter will follow these distinct modes of thinking: the productive, the practical and the theoretical.

Each kind of knowledge, or mode of thought, or science, leads to the development of *independent*, systematic disciplines or 'sciences' which study different kinds of things in ways that are peculiar to their respective subject matters as these are determined by the mode of thinking about them.[27] A science refers to the *human* disposition or intellectual orientation towards something, be it the production of something, the determination of some (practical) action, or the contemplation of something.[28]

But this is not to say that human knowledge is a mere disconnected plurality of systematic disciplines. If one speaks very generally, universally and by analogy, one can say that human knowledge *is* unified rather than divided into productive, practical and

---

25   See R. F. Stalley, *An Introduction to Plato's Laws* (Oxford, 1983) and R. Bodéüs, *The Political Dimensions*, p. 48.

26   The literature on Aristotle is enormous. I have included suggestions for further reading below (p. 185–6, 226) which display the very varied traditions of interpretation of many themes, to which my own account is indebted, but also from which it often differs.

27   A science (*epistēmē*), in Aristotle's sense here, is a single or unified, consistent way of thinking about the elements of one single domain; each science has its own first principles or premises. One science is different from another if their principles do not belong to the same genus or if the principles of the one are not derived from the principles of the other. *Posterior Analytics* I, 28, 87a38–87b3.

28   For a more analytical, philosophical reading see C. C. W. Taylor, 'Aristotle's Epistemology', in S. Everson, ed., *Companions to Ancient Thought, 1: Epistemology* (Cambridge, 1990), pp. 116–42: Aristotle assumes knowledge is possible and 'he seeks to understand how it is realized in different fields of mental activity and how the states in which it is realized relate to other cognitive states of the agent' (ibid., p. 116). My reading of what demonstrative knowledge is and requires and the relation between what is true for the most part and what is probable, below, differs from Taylor's account.

theoretical kinds. But the way people think about the discipline or field of ethics, and the language they use to reveal their thoughts, differs from the way they think and speak about, say, the physiology of invertebrates. A concrete 'science' like physiology deals with human experiences in general of particular natures of individuals and what appears to be the case about them for the most part. From here we arrive at generally accepted opinions (*doxa*) about, say, the physiology of invertebrates. In ethical enquiry we also start from what is familiar to *us* and come up with generally accepted opinions. But here, the appearances or phenomena that are relevant are not simply observations of the natural world but, also, the common beliefs, charged with evaluations, that are widely shared by the many and the wise. What counts as an *ethical* phenomenon, familiar to us, and who is meant to be included in 'us'?

Aristotle's Audience

Aristotle investigates and addresses people who are experienced and talk about their experiences in ways that pertain to a community *like* his own, in Athens. He refers to them as 'listeners' (*Nicomachean Ethics* [NE] I, 1, 1095a2). From what he says at NE I, 1, 1095a2–4 they are not young men but men already experienced in the actions of life, although not yet experts (*technitēs*). He says that he gathers his phenomena from communities that are relevantly like 'ours', i.e. his own. The members of that group share with each other not only their membership in the human species, but also, more particularly, they share certain general features of a way of living communally in a Greek-speaking *polis*. And they share in a further interest in more formal discussion and debate of the kind that united them in their attendance at his lectures in the Lyceum. Aristotle not only begins the *Nicomachean Ethics* with a methodological statement on how each discourse or lecture must be appropriate to its subject matter – he says that ethics is not precise – but he also gives his listeners an indication as to how to receive what he says (1094b11ff.). Hence, his 'us' is not simply 'any man in the street' but those mature and experienced men who came to hear him as students in the Lyceum, having been accepted to attend his morning talks. He assumes a general agreement about what is familiar to 'us' (ancient Greeks), and, more specifically, those attending his lectures, men coming from *poleis*, perhaps with different institutions, but with similar values and ways of speaking and debating about people's characters and actions.[29]

According to Aristotle, when 'we' treat ethical issues, what is familiar to us is not simply our observations of people's behaviour and our inferences about their characters and the intentions that motivated them to act as they did, but it also includes what is usually *said*, especially by the experienced and wise, about human conduct in our community of shared experiences and evaluations. Aristotle contrasts this with physiological 'science' where we start 'simply' from visible occurrences as they appear to us, and the physiological account normally limits itself to the language of organs, sinews and bones, speaking of a biological necessity as the *cause* of fixed behaviour, without referring to an animal's intentions or external goals. Physiology usually concerns itself with the charac-

---

29   See M. Nussbaum, *The Fragility of Goodness, luck and ethics in Greek tragedy and philosophy* (Cambridge, 1986), p. 245, and further, Bodéüs, *The Political Dimensions*, who argues that the audience is the lawgiver(s)/educator(s) (pp. 45, 84ff. and 94–5) and thinks this extends beyond the students in the Lyceum.

ter of a particular species that is determined by its external appearances.[30] Aristotle's own practice of physiological science modified the more traditional materialist physiology of the sinew-and-bones variety of some of his forerunners, but he would still maintain that physiological science reveals reality in an *incomplete* way because concrete sciences, in general, are concerned with what can also be otherwise, rather than with what is necessarily true. Therefore, what we today call the empirical sciences, are for him, *inexact* sciences. Ethics, too, is an *inexact* science. We must keep in mind his distinction between what is necessarily true and what is true for the most part but can be otherwise, that is, what is contingent, in order to understand what he takes to be the domain of ethics and politics as *practical* science. A practical science is a mode of thought embedded in the moral action of someone with a disposition to act in some particular way in the contingent circumstances he is in.

Although he compares and contrasts the methods of physiological 'science' with those of ethical and political 'science', Aristotle's real target is Platonic political *technē* as *epistēmē*, which was defended in the *Republic*. Recall that for Plato, there is *no knowledge* (*epistēmē*) of the world of change, no knowledge of things that can be otherwise. Knowledge is only of unchanging universals, the Forms. But for Aristotle, the moral and social virtues simply cannot be studied with the kind of precision which alone deserves the name of that kind of true 'scientific' knowledge, *epistēmē*, which is a deductive system that is concerned with universals. Deduction is the process of drawing a particular conclusion from a universal or general premise – the reverse of induction. Like Plato, Aristotle does call *epistēmē* a state of mind or a mode of knowledge whose aim is to *demonstrate* necessary, unchanging truths, first principles and universals. But he says that the thinking that is engaged in when we study ethics and politics is not of this kind. Rather, it is of a practical kind, prudence (*phronēsis*)[31] and it deals with individual cases. It aims at *deeds* rather than the necessary and demonstrable truth. The ethical life is about *doing well* and is concerned, not with necessary and invariable things as is *epistēmē*, but with matters of conduct that admit of change and variation, that is, actions in relation to particular things that are good and bad for human beings (NE VI, v, 1140a24–1140b8). Instead of dealing with what is always and necessarily the case, it deals with what is probable, or true for the most part, in changing, contingent circumstances in which *human beings* live and develop the characters they each and severally display. For Aristotle, unlike Plato, there *are* inexact 'sciences' and one such, political science generally, is a philosophy of human affairs.

In effect, Aristotle insisted that the social sciences were *not* to be studied using the methods of deductive science as their models. The methods of the concrete sciences like physiology – observation and induction – were closer. But although ethics shares with physiological science an interest in building up a systematic account of particular phenomena, what count as *ethical* phenomena for 'us' are the already – socially – interpreted and evaluated 'facts'. He clearly believed that the concrete sciences also were 'invaded' by a human perspective (*doxa*) that was peculiar to the human species in general when it observed the natural world. Hence, an account of invertebrates in Lesbos would be much the same as an account of invertebrates in Athens. And this is the reason it could be taught didactically. But ethics is further circumscribed by a human perspective that is

30   See J. M. Le Blond, *Logique et méthode chez Aristote* (Paris, 1939), p. 245.
31   See below, pp. 140–2, 157–71.

always and necessarily *situated* in one distinct, cultural milieu or other. And one as opposed to another civic culture can and does, for him, help to determine whether or not
the human being as citizen is provided with an optimum setting to pursue his nature as
a human being. Humans do not simply live in nature; they live in *poleis* with different
criteria for determining who is and who is not a citizen. Ethics, therefore, tries to account for human motivations to action in a particular cultural milieu, and there are
many cultural milieux, even in the 'civilized' sphere of Greek *poleis* under review. But
Aristotle also sought to go beyond a discussion of motivation to action in distinct milieux: he wanted to distinguish the 'historical' question of who is and who is not a
citizen in different Greek *poleis*, from who ought to be, in the sense of who truly *is* a
citizen, according to an unchanging standard definition by which one might judge. He
believed one could determine who truly is a citizen only by *first* considering human
nature, its needs and capacities, as revealed through its practices in communities like his
own. Ethics investigates how practical reasoning and habitual states of mind lead to
certain observed and consistent ways of behaving, not only in distinct conditions or
cultural milieux but, also more universally, as identifiable human ways of behaving humanly. The *conditions in which* people come to have more fixed states of mind which
influence their social behaviour, contribute to (but do not wholly determine) those
chosen ways of living a life that enable a person to flourish (or not) as a fulfilled human
being. And he believed that the *conditions in which* a man lives are more easily changed
than are his more lasting states of mind or character (*Categories* 8, 8b26ff.).

Ethics studies human *character* (*ēthos, ethesin* = character traits) in and through its practices in a community where people share a common way of talking about and judging
practices. A person's character displays itself to others in a social environment which has
its standards but where moral decision-making and action are complicated if not down-
right messy. There are so many contingent circumstances, so many variables, over which
a good man either has no control or among which he needs to choose. Ethics, as an
inexact 'science', aims to discover the extent to which humans are not simply passive
entities, merely responding to natural forces or biological instincts, and it tries to discover the boundaries of the sphere of responsible agency where humans are able to act
on and in their world. Hence, on the one hand it provides a more complex account of
human behaviour than the 'science' of physiology can provide, and on the other, it is a
less universal, precise and stable account than that offered by a truly deductive 'science',
epistēmē, of the sort Plato provided.

Furthermore, he argued that a morally virtuous man's commitments could not be
attached to objects like Plato's eternal, separated, unchanging Forms, which remained
inviolable no matter how humans behaved or spoke about their behaviour. Aristotle
believed that there *was* a stability of the ethical life but it was of a kind that was revealed
in the stability of *human thought and language about* a presumed, stable world of appearances, rather than on something independent and 'higher'. He said that in ethical enquiry our aim should be to try to show, where we can, the truth of people's common
beliefs about their experiences. We start from the things people say about what appears
to be the case (*phainomena*). We start from what is more familiar to 'us'. These phenomena or appearances are already selected perceptions concerning what a given people take
to be relevant to a situation or experience. They are not neutral 'pure' facts. This, we
note, reverses Plato's argument that reality and true standards are not to be found in the
world of human belief and perception. And this is why Aristotle says (*Posterior Analytics*

83a32–4): 'we must say goodbye to the Platonic Forms; they are meaningless noises and if they exist, they are quite irrelevant'! Or, as Nussbaum puts it: the Platonist is 'just crooning away in a corner'.[32]

In the *Nicomachean Ethics* (1096b35–9) Aristotle says: 'even if the goodness predicated of various things in common really is a unity or something existing separately and absolutely [as Plato claimed] it clearly will not be practicable or attainable by man and we are seeking [in ethics] a good within human reach.' If, then, Plato's Form of the Good had to be rejected as *the* explanation, rejected as the self-subsistent paradigm prior to, separate from, and more real than the 'empirical' world of appearances which, for Plato, is only a reflection or imitation of Forms, then its consequences, not only in ethics and politics, also had to be rejected. Instead, as we will see when he discusses the existence and development of living beings, Aristotle speaks not of a separable Form but of an *immanent principle*, an essence. The essence characterizes each distinct species and which, as a specific form (*eidos*), defines what it is to be this thing. Hence, each species has its *own* good and its *own* perfect state of realization. And there is not a single kind of knowledge, not even that most finished form of knowledge called wisdom (*sophia*) that deals with the good of *all* living things (NE VI, vii, 1141a30–4). More generally (*contra* Plato), there is no one science which investigates everything.[33]

We will see that this leads him to find Plato's theoretical model of the *politeia* to be too unified; the optimum 'state' cannot be studied as a unified, single organism. Power should not, therefore, be concentrated in an elite, *philosophical* class because *ideally, all* citizens should share in ruling and being ruled precisely because part of the specific good of a state's citizens, as Aristotle saw it, is their engagement in political activity. Aristotle restores politics to the *polis*. For Aristotle, *all* men, *by nature*, seek knowledge and all have a potentiality of knowledge. The function (*ergon*) of man is to engage in moral and rational activity, seeking, not attaining, possession of their Good. And the aim of the 'science' of politics as a branch of philosophy is action, not knowledge of the truth in itself (NE 1095a6–7). Politics is not metaphysics.

Aristotle says that men like Perikles are judged to be the prudent political experts *par excellence* (NE VI, v, 1140b8). We shall have to examine this kind of man's character and discover how he comes by it. But we shall have to do more than this because Aristotle also notes (as did Plato in the *Meno*) that successful politicians have shown themselves to be incapable of teaching what they are presumed to know because they never get beyond the level of experience and action in order to study politics and then write or speak about it (NE X, 9, 1180b30–1181a9). A part of the reason is that active politicians do not have sufficient leisure to study politics and then write about it. Even Perikles had no pretensions to be a specialist and therefore was unable to teach his sons. Practical politicians do not know the general precepts, they do not possess the general knowledge in such a way as to transmit it to others. The successful among them seem to work on instinct. Aristotle insists that the rules of statesmanship, the science of legislation, can be transmitted only by one who studies and knows them, not by practical politicians who rely on empirical skill alone and who act on the basis of social custom which takes the place of a practical science. For Aristotle there *is* a practical science of politics and men of

---

32 Nussbaum, *The Fragility of Goodness*, p. 256.
33 *Sophistical Refutations* 9, 170a20–3; *Metaphysics* 1004a2–9.

the correct moral disposition and with experience can benefit from his teaching. The true statesman, the true lawgiver, will be shown to be *not* a philosopher but a practical, rational man who is not necessarily good at technical, theoretical argument and explanation (*epistēmē*, a mode of knowing which aims to *demonstrate* necessary and unchanging truths and which is achieved through deductive, demonstrative reasoning).[34] What he is good at is thinking not only about his own good but, *in general*, about what is good for humankind as a species. This is a mode of practical knowing whose last stage is *theoria,* reached by induction from perception of sense particulars to the universal and which is capable of being perfected by men of practical experience.[35] In terms of their natural abilities, *all* men are capable of thinking in this general way and do so, *if* they have already developed virtuous habits from childhood and are old enough to have had experiences which they have judged critically. These sorts of men can benefit from Aristotle's discourse on political science of which ethics is a part. To some extent this sounds like a return to the more inclusive Socratic optimism, but with a difference.

Aristotle and the Natural World

Aristotle's interest in the study of nature as a whole led him to examine the works of the first philosophers, the so-called pre-Socratic naturalists, whose methods he criticized and distinguished from those of Socrates and Plato. He is often interpreted as having contrasted the naturalist with the dialectical approaches to an understanding of nature in order to reconcile and refine them. But if he criticized the naturalists he also understood dialectic to be something different (and humbler) than Plato's dialectic.

Aristotle argued that the only way we can decide on a hypothesis or theory about anything in nature is to *start* from observation and experience. No argument in abstraction from observation can come up with a comprehensive view of the 'facts' as they appear to us. In his *De generatione et corruptione* 316a6 he says: 'those who have spent more time among physical phenomena are better able to posit the kind of principles which can hold together over a wide area, whereas those who through much abstract discussion have lost sight of the facts are more likely to dogmatize on the basis of a few observations'. And so he says we must study the phenomena, the appearances, before we theorize and then test our theory by confirming it, or not, against further observations.

The 'empirical' and classificatory 'sciences' of natural history and biology chiefly interested him but, as we have noted, this is an 'empiricism' of a special kind. Not only does it reverse Socrates' method as we saw it in the *Phaedo*, by *starting* with our observations of nature in order to get at the *logos*, explanation, or theory. It also insists that science or human knowledge can deal only with *classes* of things and not with individuals in themselves. We *sense* individual things but we *know* only universals or kinds. What does he mean?

A report of someone's observations gives us an account of how it appears to those who are experienced in observing and talking about their experiences of appearances. People talk about *kinds* or categories of things. And they know about kinds of things by

---

34   See below, p. 138, on demonstrative syllogism.
35   See below, p. 137, on induction.

trusting the evidence of their senses rather than theories, and they accept theories only if their conclusions agree with appearances (*De generatione animalium* 760b28). For instance, the observations of the heavens that are provided by those experienced in such observation give us the principles of astronomy. We then believe these observers' perceptions and arguments about them, the facts discovered by their research, which agree with the phenomena (appearances). Now, this does not give us a 'god's eye view' of the Truth. But it does give us some insight into how nature is for itself. It does this by giving us an inclusive hypothesis about *phainomena*, that is, about *our* beliefs and interpretations as these are often revealed in our linguistic usage about the kinds of things there are for us.[36] There is something very commonsensical about this. And it is of some importance to note that natural *and* political scientists' theories must be examined and tested against experiences, not by another specialist, but by everyman.

Aristotle speaks about scientific method from the point of view of an anthropocentrist because it is only from *our* point of view that we know anything at all. What other point of view can we possibly have access to? When we are engaged in a disinterested observation of nature, the appearances to *us* as a species – with our senses and minds to interpret our sensations, and language to communicate our thoughts about our experiences – are always filtered through *our* way of knowing what is there beyond us. There *are* actual things to be known and we happen to be capable of perceiving what actually exists. But perceiving is something *we* do in *our*, cognitive, way. Perception is a psychic state.[37] And what we perceive and then think about – perception and thinking being activities in which the human species engages – can be known more generally only by means of our capacity to communicate our perceptions and thoughts about them in language to others. The distinct disciplines or fields of enquiry are the consequences of different ways of thinking and then speaking about these domains. For this reason, even before we start to systematize the different 'scientific' disciplines and their respective subject matter, we need to study mind's own workings *as these are expressed in consistent argument*. This is logic. It deals with how we draw inferences and come up with conclusions deduced from premises.

---

36   See the different interpretations in G. E. L. Owen, 'Tithenai ta Phainomena', in J. Barnes, M. Schofield and R. Sorabji, eds, *Articles on Aristotle, 1: Science* (London, 1975), pp. 113–26 versus Nussbaum, *The Fragility of Goodness*, ch. 8.

37   I disagree with those (e.g. R. Sorabji, 'Intentionality and Physiological Processes: Aristotle's theory of sense-perception', in M. Nussbaum and A. O. Rorty, eds, *Essays on Aristotle's De Anima* (Oxford, 1992), pp. 195–226 and R. Sorabji, 'Body and Soul in Aristotle', *Philosophy* 49 (1974), pp. 63–89) who argue that in perception, the taking on of form without matter is a physiological process. It *can* be thus *described*. But in the De Anima, perception is a cognitive process of awareness *described as physiological* where the action of object and its perception are both *in the perceiver*. It is not that there is no physiological change that is needed for the eye, for instance, to become aware of its appropriate objects; it is that Aristotle is discussing here not physiological alteration in sense organs but, rather, what it is for the soul/psyche to be sensibly aware in its way of the outside world. The De Anima is not a treatise *De corpora*. See further, T. Irwin, *Aristotle's First Principles* (Oxford, 1988), p. 310, who rightly says De Anima is largely a dialectical account of the soul. Also see Nussbaum, *The Fragility of Goodness*, ch.10, pp. 290ff. Nor is ethics a psycho-biological science. In the De Anima perception is an activity that is a shared function of 'souls in bodies'. Soul is immattered form (*logos enhulos*); it is not merely housed in body. Likewise, emotions are forms of cognitive awareness, a type of perception. The soul is a functional structure in and of matter, it is the what-it-is-to-be for a body of a certain kind (*De Anima* II, 1, 412b4–25). See A. O. Rorty, '*De Anima*: its agenda and its recent interpreters', in Nussbaum and Rorty, *Essays on Aristotle's De Anima*, pp. 7–14; Irwin, *Aristotle's First Principles*, pp. 131, 304–5 on why, for Aristotle, psychological states correspond to but do not collapse into physiological states as they do for materialists.

Logic: The Productive Mode of Thinking

Productive knowledge: skills with general applications[38]

Logic, like rhetoric, is for Aristotle a rational quality of mind that, when developed as a technical skill or art, reasons *truly* about things that admit of variation (NE VI, 1140a21). It is a productive mode of thinking in that its aim is to bring something into existence, here, a set of rules, the purpose of which is to enable one to reason truly about variable things. Language speakers all have developed, to some degree, this rational quality of mind. Through speaking they display logical ways of thinking. But logic can be studied with greater precision by those who analyse what makes for consistent argument, and in Aristotle's intellectual world, Sophists and others were extremely interested in the properties of consistent argumentation, especially in order to prove an opponent wrong, often without regard for the truth of their own assertions. Aristotle, however, is more interested in proving opponents wrong when they are so, and he takes into account the character and intentions of the speaker.[39] But there are situations when the truth has yet to be determined and no one knows what the answer to certain problems should aim at. Aristotle says (*Topics* VII, 3, 159a25ff.) that no one before him has handed down what general method should be used to examine actual or possible theses, nor has it been made clear what an arguer should grant if he is to defend his position well or badly. 'Since we have nothing handed down to us from our predecessors we must try to say something ourselves.'

In doing precisely this, Aristotle is not only the founder of logic as an art or *technē*, prior to any discussion of the other kinds of knowing (practical and theoretical). He also insisted that without a reflection on the rules which govern the expression of our thought, we would not be able to say anything conclusive about our knowledge of reality. In other words, nothing would hang together for us if we did not examine the priority of logic. Logic enables us to analyse thought processes as expressed in language in order to expose inaccuracies and help us to reason correctly about anything at all. Because, following sensation, we perceive things one by one, but knowledge is of the universal (*Posterior Analytics* 87b38), according to Aristotle we do not *know* the individual things we sense. Experience is insufficient for knowledge. Only species, classes or higher universals can be the objects of discursive thought processes in so far as they can be put into words, and discursive thought is the subject of logic.[40] Without logic, the analysis of discursive thought, we would drown in the sheer bombardment of meaningless sensations. Our psyches have to 'process' sensations for them to be thought of and known and from which we draw conclusions. Logic, then, is preliminary and ancillary to all other kinds of scientific and philosophical investigation. It does not discover 'facts' about the world but provides a system to articulate what we think we know.

Logical rules can help us to guard against faulty arguments. But they cannot guarantee

---

38   Some argue – for instance, D. Keyt and F. D. Miller, eds, *A Companion to Aristotle's Politics* (Oxford, 1991), p. 7 – that since logic is applied to any subject matter it is not itself a science but an instrument of science, and therefore should not be included in the productive sciences which only include the mimetic and the useful arts. I do not think this is Aristotle's position.

39   See below, pp. 151ff., 170, on character formation prior to knowledge.

40   See Guthrie, *A History of Greek Philosophy*, vol. 6, p. 146.

that we start from the correct premises! Where *do* correct premises come from? From the observations and experience of earlier and current wise men. You must *start* from the most accepted premises available in the historically given discourse of experienced men. This is because Aristotle insists that 'all teaching and all intellectual learning come from pre-existing knowledge (*Posterior Analytics* I, 1, 71a1ff.), that is, 'facts' already recognized and purveyed by other men held universally to be wise. Aristotle distinguishes (true) opinion (*doxa*) from the vague opinions of the vulgar, and says that the authoritative opinion of those universally acknowledged to be wise is acceptable precisely because it is thought to encapsulate the common experience of humankind (NE X, 2, 1172b36ff.). There is nothing absolute in this; it is simply where one must begin.

Although Plato's metaphysics is an example of reflective thinking that is capable of logical analysis, Plato himself did not reflect on the logical structure of his thought. But without it, Aristotle believed you would not be able to distinguish the different kinds of thinking of which humans were capable and, as a consequence, you would not be able to see that there *were* different kinds of thinking, and consequently different ways of arguing, and hence different scientific disciplines which reflected the divisions of knowledge. If a human acquaintance with the world comes first through sensation of particulars, then it was only through the psyche's own workings, as expressed in language and investigated through logical analysis, that humans can be shown to be able to 'abstract' the common features which exist in things. These enable us to speak about our kinds of experiences, arguing 'if this is the case then the conclusion follows'.

Logic is the general term used for that set of general rules that emerges from an analysis of different kinds of argument. It presumes psychology but it is not about psychology. Aristotle's logical writings were grouped together in the sixth century AD under the name *Organon* (tool of analysis) and they provided the 'tools' or techniques by which one can see whether someone has reasoned and argued correctly or has made mistakes in his exposition on any topic of discussion whatsoever. It does not deal with a specific and substantive domain but is universally applicable to all forms of discursive reasoning as expressed in words. The *Organon* comprises the following works which would eventually come to serve as the preliminary subjects of study in medieval universities prior to taking courses in 'higher' philosophy: *Categories, De Interpretatione, Topics, Sophistici Elenchi (Sophistical Refutations), Prior* and *Posterior Analytics*. Aristotle's logical system was to serve the Western world until the nineteenth century.

It begins by asserting that our thought is expressed in words and we cannot make our thought objects of study without language. We cannot use a linguistic term correctly unless we can relate it to the reality which we wish to express by it.[41] Aristotle's *philosophical realism* is confirmed when he says that it is the truth about reality, about actual things, that leads to the truth of our indicative statements about reality. Hence, Aristotle takes it for granted that the logic of thinking and speaking rests on an unconscious metaphysics. This means that our conventional codes of signification, language, are assumed to fit the nature of things, names signifying or referring to actual things that exist in their own right (and not simply in our minds or as the products of logic). The world is filled with actual somethings and they have to be experienced by us more than one

---

41   See D. Charles, 'Aristotle on Names and their Signification', in S. Everson, ed., *Companions to Ancient Thought, 3: Language* (Cambridge, 1994), pp. 37–73, *contra* M. Nussbaum, 'Saving Aristotle's Appearances', in M. Schofield and M. Nussbaum, eds, *Language and Logos* (Cambridge, 1982), pp. 267–93.

time for us to 'process' them and thereby come to know their natures. When we use names or terms like 'man' or 'animal' we are already classifying the reality to which the terms refer, but the terms themselves *stand for* our classificatory *concepts about* the things we name or refer to. Language reflects *the way we think* of individual things and we think through naming things in common. This means that unique occurrences are unknown to us, and we can know and name only 'occurrences' or particulars which form a class, that is, which we are *intuitively aware* of having sensed more than once and then have cognitively grasped as a common 'form'. Behind logic is the psychology of perception of sensible individuals combined with an intellectual disposition (*Nous*) which acts as a kind of intuition, giving us a sense of recognition that there *is* a common form which unites present particulars, enabling us to pick out the universal in the particular.

Let us take a moment to see how Aristotle discusses *the way we speak* about 'man', the human being, because this will prepare us for his ethical and political discussion of human needs and capacities.

Aristotle believed that we can examine why things are named or referred to as they are and, thereby, investigate the ways we think when we reason either formally and 'scientifically' about necessary, stable truths, or when we reason in more ordinary discussion where we deal with 'plausible' or true-for-the-most-part statements. It is the latter, plausible or true-for-the-most-part statements that are appropriate to ethical and political discussion. Aristotle asks: what are we referring to that is common to Socrates and Plato when we refer to each as a 'man'? We can say things of or about a subject but these 'things' are not *in* the subject; for example, 'man' is said of a subject, the individual man, but it is not *in* any subject as a part that can exist separately from individual men. Note that we begin by assuming that the knowable is prior to knowledge. For, he says, as a rule, it is of actual things already existing that we acquire knowledge. Hence, the perceptible is prior to perception. And the existence of things does not depend on *our* affirming or denying their existence. Our statements about the world are precisely that, affirmations or denials about prior existing, actual things (*Categories* 12, 14b9ff.). What, then, is involved when we affirm, or state something as a property or attribute of a subject?

Aristotle says:

> It is clear that if something is said of a subject both its name and its definition are necessarily predicated (affirmed as a property or attribute) of the subject. For example, 'man' is said of a subject, the individual man, and the name is, of course, predicated (since you will be predicating 'man' of the individual man) and also the definition of man will be predicated of the individual man (since the individual man is also 'a man'). Thus both the name and the definition will be predicated of the subject. (*Categories* 2a19ff.).

When we state something about a subject, then, we do two things: we name it and we define it.

The subjects of all predication are sensible individuals. Whenever you observe a particular man, say Socrates, and you use the word 'man', you are making his substantial being known to you as a something, a category of thing, and you call it 'man' (if you are an English speaker), which refers to the common 'thing' he shares with others of his kind, that is, all other members of his species, 'man'. We cannot know an individual as a unique and unrepeatable instance. The individual is always *a something*. What always needs explaining are the individuals we perceive, but we cannot have knowledge of them as individuals. We can know them only as representative members of their classes or species. Language reveals to us that there has been a psychic process by which reality has become knowable to us, whereby we have examined a set of particulars, Socrates and Plato, for instance, and extracted their common 'form', here, 'man', what is called the *infimae species*, the 'lowest' or earliest universal or class by which sensible individuals can be known.[42] And for a particular something to be a something, it must have the universal nature of all somethings named by the noun, here, man. Hence, what you predicate of a subject (the sensible individual) is the species or genus to which the subject belongs. This is because there is something in virtue of which a named individual, e.g. Socrates, is a man, in the sense of human being. In order to provide the definition of Socrates as a man we need to state the genus to which 'man' belongs, which is 'animal', and distinguish how Socrates as a man differs from the larger category of animal to which, say, dogs also belong. The definition of man comprises the genus (animal) and the differentiae (what distinguish homo sapiens as a species from other animals). The most specific differentia is that which indicates the essence of 'man'. Now the definition states the essence of its subject, the what-it-is-to-be-that-thing and not something else. The definition of man, for instance, must point to what is exclusively human about the animal, man, as a distinct species. The essence or nature of man is a functional expression, in words, signifying what being a man is, and it does this by referring to the goal and intended function of this named something, man. The definition of man expresses the realized or actualized form which, somehow, nature intended a something, man, to embody and it represents the best of its kind. How do we come up with definitions in the first place?

Definitions are not in the natural world and cannot be empirically observed as already constituted elements of nature. According to Aristotle, they *arise* in us as a consequence of a *human way* of coming to think about, know and express, in language, what humans have perceived. The 'appearances' or phenomena that are relevant to every community of language users are then expressed in the commonly accepted beliefs, the assumptions widely shared by the many and the wise. The definition of man arises from observed and discussed tendencies and practices which enable observers to grasp the nature of man by observing human behaviour and representing, in the definition, the best, the most fully actualized example of its kind. Aristotle thinks that *we* can only understand a something if we regard it *as though* produced under the guidance of some purposive end. Once we have the definition, the functional expression that reveals the purpose of the named something, it remains fixed as a kind of ideal. The *logos* or set of words which indicates the essence of a subject, here, man, does not change over time or culture because the elements of the definition are prior, more universal and intelligible absolutely than any particular subject whose essence is thereby expressed.[43] Essences or natures are then

---

42   NE VI, ii, 1143b1–5 explains that *Nous* (intuitive perception) which all humans have, apprehends the *infima species* in practical inferences. Hence, we must have perception of particulars and this immediate perception is *Nous*. *Theoria* is the activity of *Nous*.

43   At the other end, *Nous* also *apprehends* definitions which cannot themselves be *proved* by demonstration. In demonstration, *Nous* apprehends the immutable and primary definitions which are themselves not reached by (logical) reasoning and then demonstration begins, taking definitions as givens (NE VI, ii, 1143b1–5). Again, *Theoria* is the activity of *Nous*. Contemplation (mental observation) is *Theoria* which is more perfect than demonstrative, deductive *epistēmē* as a mode of thought, and *Theoria*, mental observation, is engaged in by all humans and not only by those trained in the skill of deductive reasoning; see below, pp. 180ff.

made individual in a someone. But *we* become aware of essences or natures (as expressed by our definitions) by observing, here, particular or individual men and cognitively grasping that category to which humans and only humans belong.

Aristotle's Teleology

To grasp a category implies an ability to reject certain specimens as members of one category and place them in another. A tree is not a man, either in nature or in our thought about nature. Because there are many named somethings, there are many definitions or functional expressions of goal-orientated somethings. And the multiplicity of somethings or categories can be, and is, arranged by us constructively as a hierarchy which cognitively represents the hierarchy of goal-directed actual things in nature. Aristotle made this plain in all of his enquiries.[44] It is what is known as his teleological approach to nature. He was stimulated by what he took to be goal-directed activities – of trees, of men. This is because he started with the hypothesis that nature has a purpose (*telos*), whether conscious or unconscious, and is constructive, and its purpose is observable and it helps to explain reality as intelligibly structured. Aristotle did not argue (as did Plato) *from* design, but rather, from the point of view that regards purposive things as having the same result *as if* so designed. He conceived of nature as in process towards a series of end-states or goals and in so far as man is in nature, he moves from potentially to actually realizing himself as a something: man, not simply being, but being a man. Definitions express the actualized purpose of things, representing the most fulfilled manifestation, the best of a kind of something. The hypothesis, confirmed by observations, that man as a species is goal-directed in a way that uniquely suits his nature and no other, lies at the heart of Aristotle's discussion of what a good human life entails in the *Nicomachean Ethics* and *Politics*.

Definition and the Dialectician

Now, one of the productive modes of thinking in which humans may be trained to engage is the critical and constructive study of common beliefs, including proposed definitions, and its aim is to prove, as plausible and true-for-the-most-part, as many accepted beliefs as possible. This is the kind of logical technique known as dialectic. Aristotelian dialectic, as explained in his *Topics,* provides a detailed illustration of various methods according to which we start from what is intelligible to someone and then we move to ways in which we can avoid difficulties where there is an apparent conflict of views, say, over two proposed definitions of man, without losing insights which both parties in a dispute may accept. We move from the intelligible to someone to the generally or absolutely intelligible: the definition accepted as most suitable by the many and the wise. Aristotelian dialectic treats definitions, but that is not all it treats.

In order for reality to become knowable, humans examine a set of particulars in order to extract their common form. Socrates, we recall, suggested something similar in his

---

44   On design and final causes see T. Irwin, 'Aristotle's Philosophy of Mind', in S. Everson, ed., *Companions to Ancient Thought, 2: Psychology* (Cambridge, 1991), pp. 56–83.

search for definitions. By asking people 'what is justice, piety, etc.' and in getting people to give instances of that class of thing, the idea or form common to all such instances was revealed as the definition. Similarly, Aristotle says that when one has described by genus and differentia the *infima species* to which an individual belongs, one can go no further towards defining the individual. One cannot have a definition of an individual, sensible substance. We know a specimen when we understand its character as a member of a defined *infima species* and this is the unit that is expressed in words (which are predicates of a subject) and which the logician, using dialectic, studies. Socrates' search for definition is similar to Aristotle's dialectic. But while it is possible to go a long way in justification of Socrates' method, Aristotle thought he could not go all the way.

Socrates was correct in practising induction and reasoning. But Aristotle believed he was incorrect in thinking that the definition would arise, through proper questioning, as a universal that could be recalled from innate, pre-natal knowing, independent of our sensation, perception, memory and experience. For Socrates, definitions and universals simply *are the real* whether or not humans can be made aware of them through recollection. Aristotle, however, says that definitions grow out of a general body of authoritative ideas that are already in currency. And the reason they are in currency, the reason they have been accepted, is because people have tested them by first experiencing particulars and have intellectually extracted their common natures or forms and then named these in language. Definition is not, as Socrates believed, the basis of Socrates' reasoning. The basis of his reasoning is sensation of particulars and induction – the subsequent cognitive responses to these (getting from particulars to universals: *Topics* 105a13–14). For Aristotle, definitions are dependent on human thought and its mirror, in human language. And they are best provided by the experienced and wise down the ages, for these are the most accepted premises so far available because they are confirmed by experience. If there are several different definitions provided, then each can be tested against experience in order to find the best, for there is a best definition. Ultimately, the world determines what thoughts we have about it and in optimum conditions the thoughts are the same for all.[45]

In the *Posterior Analytics* (99b15–100b17), Aristotle says:

All animals have an innate faculty of discernment, that is, perception. In some animals perceptions persist. There is no knowledge, outside the moment of perception, for animals in which perceptions do not persist . . . but in some animals when they have perceived there is a power of retention. And from many such acts of retention there arises in some animals the framing of a conception. Thus from perception arises memory and from repeated memory of the same thing, experience. And from experience, that is, when the whole universal – (the one distinct from the many and identical in all its instances) – has come to rest in the soul, there comes the beginning of art and science, of art if the concern is with becoming, of science, if with what is. Thus the states of knowledge are neither innate in a determinate form [*contra* Socrates] nor developed from more cognitive states of mind [*contra* Plato], but from perception. . . . The soul is so constituted as to be capable of this. To be more precise, when an *infima species* has made a stand, the earliest universal is present in the soul; for while what we perceive is an individual, the faculty of perception is of the universal – of man, not of, for instance, the man Callias. Again a stand is made among these rudimentary universals till we reach the unanalysable concepts, the true universals;

45   *De Interpretatione* 16a6–8.

we pass from 'such and such a kind of animal' to 'animal' and from 'animal' to something higher [that is, the *summa genera* which are the ultimate categories of substance, quality, relation, etc. and these are the fixed and necessary principles of all that exists *qua* existence]. Clearly then, it is by induction that we come to know the first principles; for that is how perception, also, implants the universal in us.

Aristotle, therefore, believes that other creatures live largely by sense impression, perception and impulses of the moment. Some are capable of retaining their perceptions in their memories. But while humans also retain their perceptions in memory, humans, uniquely, seek to comprehend and grasp the world under some general principles that reveal a fixed order in multiplicity. They simply show themselves to behave in this way. They do this because they have a capacity to retain in their minds representations of particular experiences and they generalize these as concepts. 'The soul is so constituted as to be capable of this.'[46] Here, he is not speaking only of the most experienced and wise but of all humans as such. How does he know this about humans? By testing the opinions handed down of the experienced and wise against observation and experience. It appears true, at least for the most part, that the *infima species* 'makes its stand' in the mind and from this rudimentary universal the mind generalizes further to theoretical concepts. This process is called induction. Every human engages in it. But he notes that the natural tendency to theorize can lead humans to oversimplify and this is only prevented by our having recourse to experience to test the theory. We must always beware of becoming estranged from the beliefs about our experiences that ground our daily lives, where we are constantly reminded that we are not pure intellects but creatures of flesh and blood, body and mind, desirous and cognitive within a physiological state as well as members of cultural communities.[47] We are human animals. Hence, it is

> by the practical experience of life and conduct that the truth is really tested since it is there that the final decision lies. We must examine the conclusions advanced by bringing them to the test of the 'facts of life' and if they are in harmony with the 'facts' we may accept them; if found to disagree we must judge them mere theory. (NE X, 8, 1179a17–20)

Elsewhere, Aristotle explains that a definition is a set of words (*logos*) which *indicates* the essence of a subject. And a thing has an essence *only if* the expression which describes its nature is a definition (*Metaphysics* 1030a6–7). Essences do not float around out there or above us. They are the immanent principles in actual things, which arise in us when we, through perception, memory, experience and conceptualization of these internal psychic states, come up with the nature or essence of the something first perceived, and we provide a set of words, a definition, to indicate, through linguistic mirroring, our concept of this essence. Unlike Socrates and Plato, Aristotle argues that one must begin with an unargued premise that the nature of definition is a mirror, in language, of the nature of an essence. The definition is that set of words which shows the essence of a thing. It should be able to answer the question 'what is it?' and the predicates which

---

46 See J. Barnes, *Aristotle's Posterior Analytics* (Oxford, 1975). Also see *Posterior Analytics* I, 18, 81b2–6. For further discussion see Taylor, 'Aristotle's Epistemology', pp. 126ff.
47 Nussbaum, *The Fragility of Goodness*, p. 260.

make up the *logos*, or set of words, are of two types: genus and differentia. When we are presented with any item, whatever its category, to give the name either of the subject or of its genus is to indicate its nature (*Topics* 103b35–7). Definitions, as opposed to other ways of describing the nature of a thing, proceed in terms of the universal under which the subject falls. At the most fundamental level, the function of definitions is to provide all of us with unitary subjects of discourse. Definitions *represent* things in words. And because it is in terms of the *infimae species* that the world is presented to our understanding, dialectic approaches things through the forms of words, including definitions, in which they are portrayed.

Now, a dialectician is engaged in testing a particular, proposed definition, e.g. is a two-footed animal the definition of a man, yes or no? and in testing a proposed definition, he then provides reasons for choosing one definition as opposed to another. Dialectic is a method of testing plausible views that people already hold in any sphere of endeavour and it debates these without adhering to one doctrine of reality or another. The dialectician starts by assuming a given premise, not taking it to be definitely true or false. Where Plato had held dialectic to be identical with true philosophy, *epistēmē*, Aristotle says it is not involved with ontology, with being, but rather, more humbly, with ways of speaking about general attributes, without regard to that of which they are essentially attributes. Dialectic deals with definitions in general. And definitions, by which we grasp universals (e.g. humanity), arise in us as a consequence of perception and retention. Definitions and principles of all kinds cannot be proved or found by demonstrative logic. They are simply where logic starts from. And logic is not philosophy. Philosophy bases itself on demonstration from premises *already known to be true*. Dialectic, however, is a procedure which enables us to reason about any received opinion, simply assuming a given premise as plausible and taking no stand as to whether it is true or false.

Therefore, Aristotelian dialectic is a method of analysing the consistency of plausible arguments in general and is not limited in scope to any particular department of reality, having no special subject matter of its own. It *precedes* more specialized sciences, those called practical and theoretical, providing a means of investigating their foundations. Dialectic can never demonstrate the true or real nature of anything; it can start only from the premises that are in conformity with currently held and expressed opinions on some subject and it discovers a procedure whereby one can reason about any problem, from received opinions, and in turn stand up to the arguments of others without self-contradiction. It teaches a person to be able to argue consistently on both sides of any question, starting with currently held, reputable opinions and testing them for non-contradictions. Contradictions cannot be hunted out by oneself. This means that the convictions one holds as the result of an enquiry are not things a human being acquires alone and by himself. As we shall later see, someone who is alone and by himself is not, strictly speaking, human at all for Aristotle. One would define him as a beast or a god. What humans know is always based on pre-existing knowledge, which provides the premises, expressed in language, from which one starts, in order to discuss and test them against observation and experience.[48]

48   In general see Weil, 'The Place of Logic in Aristotle's Thought', in Barnes, Schofield and Sorabji, *Articles on Aristotle*, 1, pp. 88–112, and J. D. G Evans, *Aristotle's Concept of Dialectic* (Cambridge, 1977).

The Relation between Dialectic and Ethical Enquiry

The reason we have described the function of dialectic and how it tests proposed definitions as well as other, commonly accepted views, is that Aristotle says it is this kind of analytic method which can be used in testing arguments that occur in the domains of ethics, the natural sciences, and politics (*Rhetoric* 1358a12), which are inexact 'sciences'. Even though dialectic begins with commonly accepted, reputable views, and attempts to preserve them where possible, it is a technical discipline and not an amateur practice. The average citizen did not engage in this technical methodology. But students in Aristotle's Lyceum did. However, dialectic was seen as a technical refinement of what went on in the disputes of the average citizen in the lawcourts and Assembly where the aim was to beat one's opponent in debate. And it appears that dialecticians, including Sophists, put on debating shows before a public that was acquainted with the conventions of the argumentative game and enjoyed watching the experts attempt to defeat one another.[49]

When ethical and political arguments were examined dialectically the discussants were aware that dialectic, as a technique, never could tell them (or us) the true, unchanging and necessary nature of anything. The domains of ethics and politics are littered with particulars, changing circumstances and choices and the causes of all these variable things are themselves variable and therefore not necessary. A consideration of these domains begins with 'a laying on the table' of the premises that conform to the currently held and often varied opinions, whether lay or expert. In ethical debate one is seeking only to preserve these as plausible or probable, in so far as this is possible. Dialectic simply enables a discussant to reason more clearly and without contradiction in arguments with others in his community. It is a skill which is taught and learnt, and its only outward difference from rhetoric is that rhetorical speaking is public speaking to a crowd, whereas dialectical skill in speaking is between two, often competitive, 'opponents'.[50]

Dialectic, as a tool of analysis, does not contribute positively to the store of stable, philosophical knowledge. The only stability in the *ethical* domain is with regard to the way humans think and then speak about their experiences and appearances as these are presented in their commonly accepted views. Dialectic, which is a skill appropriate to the domains of ethics and politics, simply enables you to clarify the difficulties on both sides of a debate within any community in which people already share common ways of talking about and judging human character and behaviour. If we understand this it will help us to recognize what Aristotle is doing when he discusses slavery in the way he does and which strikes *us* as appalling and indefensible. It will also help to explain why Aristotle has no hope or enthusiasm for any particular society in which there is maintained a pluralism of differing values and a pluralism of ways of judging behaviour and character. One may start with a pluralism but it must be resolved in each and every community.

---

49 Weil, 'The Place of Logic', pp. 102–3.
50 Indeed, Andronicus of Rhodes grouped the two *Ethics* (*Eudemian* and *Nicomachean*) and *Politics* alongside the *Poetics* and *Rhetoric* to convey that they shared the same kind of philosophical preoccupation within the larger, rationally or systematically organized corpus of writings: Düring, *Aristotle*, pp. 224–5. Andronicus appears to have recommended beginning the study of Aristotle's works with logic, which he says is not a part of philosophy but its instrument.

Our contemporary liberal pluralism which works on the assumption that people can live peaceably and to mutual benefit in the same society with incommensurable value systems and where the 'state' makes no claim to favour one over another, would be either incomprehensible or anathema to a successful community as Aristotle and the commonly accepted views he presents understood this.

If we now have some understanding of Aristotle's dialectic as no more (but also no less) than a tool to help analyse commonly accepted views that emerge from premises within a given community, we may ask: is there a difference between a Sophist's methods and his lack of concern for the truth, and dialectic? They may seem identical: the honest argument of the well-intentioned dialectician and the knavery of the Sophist are expressed by the same means and in the same verbal forms.[51] They both deploy dialectical skills in argument. But Aristotle notes that the difference between them is regarding the *premises* from which each begins. Aristotle says the correct method of proceeding is to ask: is the thesis generally accepted by the many and wise? And we must also take into account the *intentions* behind engaging in dialectical analysis of views: we must ask whether it is our intention to further the search for truth by means of our common task – our research and our examination of a proposition – or whether it is our intention merely to exhibit our competitive skill in argument, whose aim is only victory, possibly by verbal tricks? Although the method is competitive, the aim of the true dialectician is to offer what 'we' believe to be true (*Topics* VII, 3, 159a25ff.).

We have seen that Aristotle believes that people start from particular experiences and through inductive reasoning they arrive at a universal and a theory. Induction and observation give rise to commonly accepted views which can be subject to error but only from these opinions can the truth be teased out. But people also draw conclusions by deduction from generally accepted, believable premises. When they do this, ordinarily, they simply assume one or another position to be plausible and try to refute someone who holds the contrary. He says that even the unskilled, ordinary language speakers in the *polis* use dialectic in some way (*Topics* 172a30ff.), since everyone, at some time, tries to engage in refuting the views of others. They do this by using syllogisms in their everyday conversations without realizing it. Syllogistic is the theory of discourse in which, given certain suppositions, something other than those suppositions follows necessarily because of them. When people draw conclusions deductively, Aristotle says they can be shown to be reasoning syllogistically in a very elementary way. He describes the case where there are three terms which are so related that the first two premises taken together imply the third as a conclusion: if A is predicated of all B and B of all C, then A is necessarily predicated of all C (*Prior Analytics* 25b32–26b3). It is an 'if . . . then' form of reasoning. 'If all animals are mortal, and all men are animals, then all men are mortal.' Every syllogism must be valid for every case and its validity must be self-evident, that is, following from the premises and leading to the necessary conclusion. But note that the premises, which is where one begins, are the *commonly accepted views of the community*, shared by ordinary men and the wise, the 'us' to whom he refers in Greek *poleis* and in the Lyceum.[52] He says, 'if we are merely seeking to gain credence, and are therefore,

---

51 Weil, 'The Place of Logic', p. 101.
52 A dialectical premise assumes either of the pair of positive or negative propositions, predicating a single predicate of a single subject, indifferently. *Posterior Analytics* I, 2, 71b9–72b4.

reasoning dialectically, we have only to consider whether the inference is drawn from the most plausible premises' (*Posterior Analytics* I, 19, 81b10ff.). When people are engaged in debate, they have already found plausible certain available theses which they have, presumably, tested by matching them with their experiences. Now they hold certain points of view, and debate these, including what people in the past have said and which have served as actual or possible theses or premises, and these are reflected in their general discourse. The *Topics* explains how they can defend these theses – which can be about all sorts of subjects – and argue successfully.

Therefore, Aristotle believed that we come to know or learn about things by induction and by syllogistic deduction. Experience (*empeiria*) is insufficient on its own. He opens the *Posterior Analytics* (71a1–10) with the statement that

> all teaching and learning that involves the use of reasoning proceeds from pre-existing knowledge. This becomes evident from a survey of all the branches of learning. . . . The two forms of *dialectical reasoning*, syllogistic reasoning and inductive reasoning, also proceed in this way for each makes use of old knowledge, 'facts' already recognized, to impart new; the syllogism assuming an audience that accepts its premises, induction exhibiting the universal as implicit in the self-evident nature of the particular. And the conviction produced by rhetorical arguments is, in principle, the same, since they use either example (a kind of induction) or the enthymeme (a form of syllogism).

The two forms of dialectical reasoning, syllogistic and induction, are what are presented to us in Aristotle's *Nicomachean Ethics* and *Politics*, beginning with the commonly accepted, reputable views in ancient Greek *poleis*, and proceeding on to Aristotle's testing them to preserve them, where possible.

But if we are aiming not at the credible, but at truth, we must start from those 'facts' which cannot be otherwise. And there is another kind of syllogism, called the *demonstrative*, which is employed. When people go on to give *reasons* for something being a *necessarily* true and universal conclusion that cannot be otherwise, they reason in a distinctive way. They are engaged in what Aristotle calls demonstration, where one logically demonstrates or proves the necessity of something being the case and that cannot be otherwise. Demonstration is from universals; induction is from particulars. But he insists that it is impossible to grasp universals except through induction and it is impossible to be led on inductively to the universals if one has no perception. For it is perception that grasps individual 'facts' and we cannot obtain scientific knowledge of them from universals without previous induction, nor learn them by induction without perception (*Posterior Analytics* I, 18, 81a38–b9). Demonstrative knowledge *starts* from a premise that is held by *everyone* (everywhere) to be true, primary and itself unprovable, which causes the conclusion that something is necessarily the case and cannot be otherwise. For Aristotle, observation plays a fundamental role in our grasping the undemonstrated universal premises of demonstrative explanation. Demonstrative knowledge is what we can explain; undemonstrative knowledge is the principle from which explanations are derived. The demonstrative syllogism, like dialectic, is a skill that can be taught and one can learn. The demonstrative syllogism is a kind of scientific reasoning (*epistēmē*) that Aristotle *contrasts* with the dialectical syllogism, discussed above, and we need to remember that it is the dialectical, and not the scientific, demonstrative syllogism that is applicable to questions in ordinary ethico-political discussion.

Demonstrable knowledge is *epistēmē*. Here, the proper object of unqualified scientific knowledge (*epistēmē*) is something which cannot be otherwise than it is. And Aristotle says that 'we think we know something without qualification when we think we know its cause to be its cause and that what we know could not be otherwise' (*Posterior Analytics* 71b9ff.). There is a kind of knowledge by way of proof or demonstration and this is by way of *scientific* syllogism which proceeds from premises that are themselves true, primary and indemonstrable, immediate, better known than, prior to and the causes of, the conclusion. The premises here are prior and better known by nature without qualification, rather than prior and better known simply relative to us. The premises of demonstrative syllogisms are, therefore, true and invariable and not simply possible or accepted because generally assumed because plausible. Especially in mathematics, geometry and astronomy, we need to validate our claims by providing systematic logical demonstrations of what is necessarily the case, and which indicate that the first principles from which we start our deductions are *a priori* truths that are universally grasped through a kind of intuition (*Nous*) by *all* humans. These *a priori* truths cannot be questioned or explained. They simply have fundamental status for us and we confirm this insight into their status through experience.[53] Experience provides principles, of which we are intuitively aware, with their content. There simply *are* features of the world that strike a human being as such no matter into which culture and community he may be born.

Now, there *is* a role for such demonstrative reasoning in the ethical and political domains too, as Aristotle makes clear in the *Nicomachean Ethics* (NE 1143b11–14), where he says: 'we must pay attention to the unproved assertions and opinions of experienced and older men, or of those men of practical wisdom, *as well as to those assertions and opinions which they support by demonstration/proof*, for through the eye of experience they see correctly.' But, in general, demonstrative reasoning does not play a very explicit role in discussions of ethical and political issues for the following reasons. We do not seem to need logical demonstration when we start from assumed and plausible premises about the ways we behave in particular circumstances or when we discuss people's characters. We are already acculturated and habituated in our community and have our experiences there. When we are born into a community we are born into a tradition of discourse and practices. No one starts from the beginning and alone. In common discussion, people display their convictions and largely rely on induction and on the plausible opinions of the experienced and older, from which they then construct their own syllogisms or inferences. They operate in this way not only because they find demonstrative reasoning too technical but because no one, in normal discussion, goes back to the necessary first principles as causes which underpin *why* one, as a human being, is able to affirm what one affirms. They simply accept these necessary first principles as a background to their discussions. People then proceed by relying on assumed but not *necessarily* true, accepted opinions, because in the domains of ethics and politics the *causes* of things – such as their behaviour, their characters, their situations – are *variable* rather than fixed and necessary.

This is not merely a sociological observation on Aristotle's part. It is a statement which distinguishes kinds of knowing and the conditions which enable one kind as opposed to another kind of knowing to guide our approach to the relevant phenomena

---

53   *Eudaimonia*, the species-specific unconditional end of man, living and faring well, is an *a priori* truth, a first principle of ethics, according to C. D. C. Reeve, *Practices of Reason: Aristotle's Nicomachean Ethics* (Oxford, 1992).

as we take them to be. Aristotle is distinguishing between *knowledge* of what is necessarily the case, on the one hand, and *true opinion* of what can be otherwise, on the other. And he does think that, with the aid of dialectical analysis of various accepted and plausible premises, we can arrive at true opinion. True opinion is thereafter the starting point for the deliberations about action of the practically knowledgeable and experienced prudent man who is the subject of the discussion in the *Nicomachean Ethics*.

As we shall see, Aristotle will distinguish between moral virtues or character traits on the one hand, and intellectual virtues or dispositions on the other. Moral virtue is not the same as intellectual virtue. For the most part, intellectual virtue owes its birth and growth to teaching (NE II, 1, 110315–17), e.g. one can learn how to analyse propositions dialectically, engaging in syllogistic and inductive reasoning. But moral virtue, initially dependent on certain natural factors like being born with a human rather than an animal nature, and therefore with a *capacity* for temperance, courage, etc., none the less proceeds from habitual practices. True moral virtue must be acquired; no one has it from birth. And it is from the *practice* of moral virtue that we learn to choose the right object, that we acquire a knowledge of the *principles* of good and bad which determine the rightness of the ends towards which we then make deliberate choices in order to act towards that end.[54] Reason is taught by argument (*logoi*) but character is taught by habits (habituation of the appetites: *ethismos*). We shall see that the prudent person must already possess a general conception of living well, an idea of the end which his actions should pursue. He owes this conception to the true opinion and the principles that have emerged in the acquisition of virtuous habits. True opinion, as such, is not a conclusion of scientific, demonstrable knowledge (*epistēmē*). True opinion is not a conclusion of an intellectual or theoretical study undertaken independently. Rather, it is an orientation that is grasped intuitively by an already morally virtuous agent in whom, through correct practices, the correct principles of conduct have come to be known to him.[55] Because people form their opinions about *eudaimonia*, living and faring well, from the kinds of life they lead, and not all lives lead to true opinions, Aristotle will place great emphasis on the correct kind of education in habit-formation which alone can lead to true opinions about living a successful human life. Aristotle will have a great deal to say about how people come to possess morally virtuous and vicious characters and the society – its tradition and norms – in which they are 'embedded' from childhood will be seen to play a dominant role. In the process, he will modify Socrates' claim that *knowledge* (*epistēmē*, in which Socrates included prudence (*phronēsis*)) *is the condition of virtue*, that is, that all the virtues are forms of knowledge. Instead, Aristotle will argue that *moral virtue is the condition of knowledge* of the human good, that moral virtues co-operate with (practical) knowledge or prudence and imply prudence (NE VI, 13, 1144b29ff.; VII, 9, 1151a17–20).[56] 'Neither in moral nor in mathematical science is the knowledge of first principles reached by logical means; it is virtue, whether natural or acquired by habituation that enables us to think rightly about the first [right] principles.'

---

54   See Taylor, 'Aristotle's Epistemology' and the literature cited therein on what he thinks are problems in Aristotle's account(s) of how the possessor of practical wisdom acquires a reliable grasp of principles (p. 131). Reeve, *Practices of Reason*, provides one approach to the answer, distinguishing ontological from epistemic first principles.
55   See below, p. 151, on correct principles being grasped not only by habituation but also by induction and perception.
56   See further, Bodéüs, *The Political Dimensions*, p. 51.

We have observed that Aristotle distinguishes between knowledge of what is necessarily the case and true opinion of what can be otherwise. In the domain of ethics and politics, what is fixed and necessary is the ideal or essential *definition* of man. Definitions are non-contingent propositions and demonstrative reasoning *starts* with definitions; it does not prove them. Definition portrays, in words, our *knowledge* of man in his essential nature. We can also have an opinion of man, but this is not of his essential nature. Our opinion can be, say, of someone's character. Although the object of knowledge and opinion is the same, *man*, the mode of knowing in which man is regarded when opinions are expressed is different from the mode of knowing when we provide a definition of man. Opinion is that state of mind that is concerned with what is true or false but *contingent*. A man's character is contingent rather than necessary. But man's nature is not contingent. Opinion, according to Aristotle, is the judging of a non-necessary proposition. It agrees with the observed phenomena and the observed phenomena in ethical and political life are contingent and so too are opinions. 'A man thinks he has opinions, not when he thinks the "fact" is necessary, for then he thinks he knows, but rather, when he thinks that it might be otherwise' (*Posterior Analytics* I, 33, 88b30–89b9). Were a man's character determined and necessary, as is the nature of man as expressed in the definition of man, then we could have fixed and necessary knowledge of it. But a man's character is the consequence of habituation and choices, and it is formed from his deliberation on what may or may not be morally done by him. Hence, there is a fixed and necessary definition of man, but ethical discussion is concerned with judging a particular person, observing him engaging in discrete practices, making choices among possible actions, responding to occasions, and we then draw (probable) inferences as to his character. In such contingent situations which depend on the particular man and his particular conditions, we can come up with only probable conclusions and these result from our having begun with probable premises (*Posterior Analytics* II, 12). Probable premises are where we begin when we try to give a true account of how to live well.

Let us sum up. In ordinary discussions that are concerned with how to live a successful life we start from within a tradition of practices and habituated responses. Our discussions *start* from generally accepted, plausible points of view as our premises, and in our community these are held to provide the *relevant* sum of knowledge acquired by men that enables us, thereafter, to draw our conclusions and confirm our convictions where we can. The dialectician enters to examine this common discourse, aiming to discover whether the expressions we use are correct. Our experiences, thereafter, supply the means by which we can judge between one proffered view or another. The dialectician does no more than examine how the given points of view (topics) in our community provide us with the matter from which we construct our ordinary inferences or syllogisms. His aim is to bring to light the weakness of any assertion that is not, for ordinary people as well as the wise, an immediately evident principle or a datum of experience. Aristotle is the dialectician at work in his *Nicomachean Ethics*.

But he is also more than this: we must realize that in writing a work *on* ethics, the author, Aristotle, is engaging in a moral discourse that is appropriate to a social science by using a tool that is at his disposal: the logical tool of critical analysis of common views, dialectic. As a moral philosopher theorizing about human things, he needs to state what the aim or goal or criterion is to which the prudent political agent looks in thinking out what he should do as a good man regarding the situation he finds himself in, and then Aristotle must *explain* why this is, for the most part, the case. Aristotle admits that studying and knowing general principles concerning the human good which is political science is not the loftiest kind of knowledge, and he says that it is extraordinary that anyone should so regard it, because man is not the highest being in the world (NE VI, vii, 1141a21–2). However, further distinctions must be drawn between (1) the loftiest kind of knowledge, (2) ethical/political science and (3) the living of a virtuous life. *Living* an ethical life, which is his subject matter, is *not* the same as writing as a moral philosopher and analysing the views of the many and the wise concerning the activities and character of the ethical man. Where the prudent man who is morally virtuous and has practical knowledge *can* see what is best, he is not able to explain the general principle, applicable to humankind, and therefore, teach it to others. The moral philosopher can. Aristotle is doing something other than Perikles, the archetypically prudent, political man, who is generally considered 'the expert in domestic economy or political science' (NE VI, v, 1140b8).

Virtue, Aristotle reminds us, is not merely a state or disposition in conformity with right principle, but is a disposition that *implies* right principle which, in moral conduct, is prudence. The moral virtues are not principles themselves; indeed many prudent political men practise moral virtue, seeming to act from experience and from the kind of knowledge based on careful observation of individual cases rather than by the exercise of reason (NE X, ix, 1181aff.). While prudence is classified as an intellectual virtue (NE I, 1103a4–8) it is not merely a rational state, because there are two parts of the soul that are susceptible to reason,[57] and prudence is the virtue of that part of the soul that forms opinions about doing well (NE VI, v, 1140b). Prudence is linked with moral goodness because the first principles of prudence are given *by* moral virtue, but a lack of reflection on these principles seems to be typical of most active political men. They are focused on an experienced familiarity with a succession of particular (and local) political problems. They tend to make correct judgements, forming opinions about what is to be done in this or that variable circumstance, and from there extend to general situations of like kind in which men may find themselves. The best of them is the *phronimos*, the practical, prudent man who knows the local conditions. Aristotle concludes that politics *as a science* is different from the other sciences like medicine in that the men with the practical political skills, the practitioners, do not study politics or give an account of its principles, but simply act on experience. They appear not to advance general principles or to acquaint themselves with the proper method of a science that deals with the universal (NE X, ix, 1180b15–23). The *phronimos* is not, then, a social scientist with general theories. But while those who aspire to a *scientific* knowledge of politics need practical experience as well, they also need a systematic analysis of what is involved in moulding characters of citizens and it appears that even Perikles could not offer this. Assuming that it is possible to make men good by the discipline of laws, Aristotle believes that men of practical experience should endeavour to acquire the science of legislation and be able to explain why this is, for the most part, a requirement of all men living in communities. It is for this reason that Aristotle has prepared his *Nicomachean Ethics*. Aristotle seems to believe that politicians, alone among the skilled practitioners in any society, need the insights and explanations of those trained in ethical and political 'science', whose moral critique and constructive suggestions about possible alternatives to local *nomoi* and behaviour will help statesmen to secure the best and most stable environments possible in which their

---

57   See below, p. 157.

citizens may develop morally virtuous characters and thereby live as fully human lives as conditions allow.[58]

In the *Nicomachean Ethics* Aristotle shows his students how the dialectical form of reasoning (and its type of syllogism – *not* the scientific form of reasoning and its syllogism) which begins with accepted, plausible premises about contingent matters and from which people draw inferences, is to be added to the results of inductive reasoning. For most men, Aristotle says, induction is found to be more persuasive than deduction. 'Induction (*epagoge*) is more persuasive, clear, and more easily grasped by sense perception and is shared by the majority of people (including practising politicians), but reasoning (*sullogismos*) is more cogent and more efficacious against argumentative opponents' (*Topics* I, 12, 105a16 ff.). In daily life, when men's characters and actions are discussed, we start from what is most familiar to us: we engage in inductive reasoning, that is, collecting the particular, relevant phenomena which give rise to the general, common beliefs about the human good and morality. Only thereafter, if we are so trained, can we engage in dialectic, the critical and constructive study of what we think follows from these common beliefs about values and behaviour.

But it must be realized that none of the common beliefs on ethical and political matters, shared by the many and the wise, no matter how central to their discourse on ethics and politics, is as deeply grounded in reality for us as are those logical laws which reveal the *a priori* first principles that strike all *polis*-living human beings as fundamental about the world, beyond their specific communities and the experiences of their group. Although these fixed, *a priori* first principles serve as the background to all human discourse, ethical discourse does not normally deal with fixed and fundamental principles. It deals with the practical and the particular. The domain of an ethically lived life is a domain of contingencies. This is because there are no facts without qualification, that is, there are no 'facts' that cannot be otherwise in the ethical domain. Ethics is a non-exact science. But ethics, in dealing with the variable, attempts to elucidate what, for a human being, are the best and most choice-worthy and, therefore, most praiseworthy ways to be a flourishing human being in community where there are so many contingencies – ranging from good or bad health, inherited wealth or poverty, sensible or unnecessarily restrictive laws, an education system that either instils good moral habits or thwarts natural impulses to act in ways that conduce to personal and collective well-being. Hence, it is Aristotle's task in his *Nicomachean Ethics* to preserve, where he can, the common beliefs on such topics of discussion after difficulties have been resolved.

When Aristotle comes to discuss what it means to live a human life, and he seeks to offer a definition of the good for man, he provides 'us' with 'our' starting point, the best, most inclusive definition of 'man' that the common opinion of the many and the wise has accepted. This definition emerges from his dialectical examination of the various reputable opinions that were already provided as plausible and seemingly true-for-the-most-part among the Greek-speaking inhabitants of *poleis* and tested against experience. He does not follow up his definition of 'man' with demonstrable proofs of the first principles from which such a 'man' tends to draw his daily inferences. This is because people do not draw daily inferences on how to negotiate the particularities of a well-

---

58 See S. G. Salkever, 'Aristotle's Social Science', in C. Lord and D. K. O'Connor, eds, *Essays on the Foundations of Aristotelian Political Science* (Berkeley, 1991), pp. 11–48.

lived life from first principles which they none the less know. The principles have simply come to be known through human living (through habituation, induction and perception). Instead, he will disclose the nature of practical wisdom (as opposed to scientific demonstrative wisdom), thereby discussing the kind of thinking that is required for a prudent man to calculate successfully about what is to be done with a view to some serious end. Nobody, he says, deliberates about things that are invariable or about things that he cannot do for himself. Whereas scientific knowledge implies the ability to demonstrate, *there can be no demonstration of things whose causes are variable because such things may be otherwise*. Hence, it is impossible to deliberate about things that are necessarily so. And because this is the case, in the fields of ethics and politics, where things like one's character, circumstances and choices *can* be otherwise, neither ethics nor politics as such deals with necessary and invariable truths. What is involved in practical reasoning, as opposed to *epistēmē* or scientific, demonstrable reasoning, is the calculation of what, in the domain of particulars, is good for oneself and for humans in general. Practical reasoning does not consider the Good without qualification. Practical reasoning, prudence (*phronēsis*), comes about through learning from the experience of managing households or 'states' (NE VI, 1140a24–b12). It is a kind of inductive thinking that is carried on in the midst of practices while an agent holds to the plausible premises of the community by which he seeks to evaluate such practices. Practical reasoning does not come about through having learnt the logical skill of demonstrating things whose causes are invariable, nor does it question those necessary and unchanging principles or premises from which humans reason about what cannot be otherwise. Hence, the concern with necessary and unchanging principles, what for Plato were the Forms that determine and structure all that is, is *not* the concern of the domain of ethics and politics for Aristotle. The myriad of decisions a human can make in the course of living a human life in a distinctively structured, cultural milieu can always be otherwise precisely because the causes of his choosing to behave in one way or another are variable. Life is complicated and, within the limits of what are capable of being reasoned about and acted upon, the constituents of a good life are not only choosable, if one has been well-habituated to correct, moral practices, but specific to the man and his circumstances. We shall be able to watch Aristotle take on board what ordinary people think about the constituents of 'the good life' and modify these views with the opinions of the experienced and wise, saving what he can of the views of ordinary observers and experiencers who share ways of speaking about how they evaluate human character in their community.[59]

This means that Aristotle is not interested in coming up with an original and new thesis 'out of the blue'; indeed, he thinks this to be impossible. Rather, he is concerned to describe a way in which to structure an enquiry, any enquiry, by collecting relevant 'facts' and resolving former difficulties. Once again, the relevant facts or phenomena in the domain of ethics and politics are probable, not necessary, and the premises from which people draw conclusions are themselves probable and they give rise to probable, not necessary, conclusions, that is, opinions, which are the judgements of non-necessary propositions (*Posterior Analytics* I, 33, 88b30–89b9). And we never start from pure beginnings. We always begin our enquiry within a tradition. In general, he says (*Metaphysics* B 995a24ff.),

---

59   See Irwin, *Aristotle's First Principles*, ch. 16, pp. 347ff. for a different argument that also focuses on the powers of dialectical argument underpinning *Ethics*.

we must, with a view to the knowledge we are seeking, enquire first what are the first questions to be asked. This includes both the various thoughts of others about them and anything they have overlooked. To those who wish to answer questions it is helpful to put the questions well: for the answer which is to come is the resolving of former difficulties and it is impossible to untie unless one understands the knot.

As we read the *Ethics* and *Politics* we may note that he offers us an ethical discourse that is the product of its time and place. But methodologically he seeks more than this. Formally, he offers a cumulative approach to human traditions of discursive knowledge which is meant to provide us, here, in the domain of ethics and politics, with true opinions about deliberations made in living a human life.

His approach to enquiry in all domains is based on a belief that, in a very general way, all knowledge has been perfected many times over and lost again in recurrent natural disasters. It is a version of 'there is nothing new under the sun'. But recall that there are different kinds of knowing. Applied to the political domain, there is a kind of knowing that arises out of certain necessary and stable truths about being alive as a human being and staying alive. There is also a kind of knowing that arises out of life's contingencies which help to constitute the kind of character a person displays beyond merely being alive and surviving. The kinds of characters that people display in their mutual interactions, not only are confirmed by the political institutions they erect but also indicate how they use these institutions and for what purposes. Ideally, the full actualization of a *human* life is matched by a political system that maximally enables the living of a fully human life. Despite those occurrences over which men have no control, we must regard humans and their political arrangements *as though* proceeding purposively towards their appropriate ends. Aristotle believes that the history of political institutions reflects this. He says:

> All other political devices also have been discovered repeatedly or rather, an infinite number of times over in the lapse of ages; for the discoveries of a necessary kind are probably taught by need itself and when the necessaries have been provided, it is reasonable that things contributing to refinement and luxury should find their development; so that we must assume that this is the way with political institutions also. The antiquity of all of them is indicated by the history of Egypt. (*Politics* VII, 9, 1329b 25ff.)

Human knowledge and the various 'sciences', therefore, progress out of traditions of discursive reasoning. Aristotle lists discursive thought and its species: intuitive reason, science, art, practical wisdom and metaphysical thinking. (*Posterior Analytics* I, 33, 88b30–89b9 and NE VI). He notes that all reasoning is *productive, practical* or *theoretical* (*Metaphysics* E, 1025b25): mathematics, natural philosophy (physics) and metaphysics (theology, first philosophy) comprise the three theoretical philosophies. But we are interested in that species of discursive thought: practical wisdom. In the ethical and political domain, this tradition is constituted by our probable, plausible premises, where we begin, tested against our experiences. As we shall see, there *are* necessary and invariable elements of living a human life: these include not only the 'facts' of surviving and procreating, the 'fact' of living in communities, but also engaging in the universally shared, species-specific activities of perceiving and experiencing the world, being intuitively aware of the presence of particular things, as well as grasping their essences and portraying these in definitions. But there are, in addition, variable elements in living a distinctively human life: these include making choices among alternatives in order to live virtuously as moral and rational agents, acquiring certain habitual dispositions of character and choosing the correct means to our end. It is the variability and contingency in human living that enable us to see political science and its part, ethics, as a distinct branch of knowledge, because it is in this sphere alone that humans are agents, responsible for the kinds of people they are. There is nothing we can do about the fact that we are human. But we are responsible for how we live. Ethics has its own principles or starting points: the reputable opinions of the experienced and wise concerning praiseworthy character and successful human living, tested by perception, induction and habituation. It does not deal directly with necessary, unchanging, eternal and universal truths. It is a practical science, not a theoretical science, and the character of the *polis*-living practical man, not the philosopher, is its subject.

Ethics as Practical 'Science'

We are now prepared to examine more closely some of the key issues raised and eluci-dated in Aristotle's *Nicomachean Ethics*. We must always keep in mind that the kind of reasoning that is appropriate to the ethical domain is practical not theoretical, even though all humans are natural theorizers. Practical knowledge issues in deeds in imme-diate situations. If we aim at practical knowledge, we must begin by setting out our premises, the generally accepted views about human life. Aristotle tells us that in Greek *poleis*, the generally accepted view of the many and the wise about the ultimate aim of human life, the end (*telos*) to which all our actions are directed, is happiness, that is, a peculiarly human kind of well-being (*eudaimonia*). But Aristotle also tells us that opin-ions differ in what human happiness consists. This means that we shall have to examine all the relevant views on what makes for a successful human life, which everyone agrees is that at which all of us aim. We must do this not only in order to come to some conclusions concerning what kind of character one needs to acquire in order to be a good man and according to which standards a good man then lives a good life, but also to save the generally accepted views where we can.

Studies with practical ends, like ethics, start by assuming that man has an end, a goal, and it is accepted that this is happiness (*eudaimonia*). We must now consider the means thereto with respect to a particular man in a range of circumstances. Similarly, medicine as a study with a practical end, assumes the end or goal to be health and considers only the means thereto with respect to a particular man. Practical studies require that you already know not only the general rule but also the individual case which falls under it. The *Nicomachean Ethics* deals with the good life as it may be realized by a plurality of good men who share ways of evaluating and discussing the good life in a good city or 'state', and the *Politics* deals with those constitutive principles of the good 'state' itself. The *Ethics* deals with two related topics: people's dispositions of character (and where these come from) and their practical thinking concerning their chosen means to the end of particular right actions. Hence it deals with the moral virtues and the intellectual virtues. The *Politics* deals with the *conditions* in which men, with certain dispositions of character, choose means to their end in order to flourish. One cannot determine what makes for a good 'state' unless one first has some idea of what humans as such need (not as individuals considered in isolation from the *polis*) and of what they are capable. 'States' are the conditions in which a man has the opportunity (or not) fully to actualize his human nature, so we need to know first what a successful human life lived in common with others would look like, as well as the kind of character disposition a man needs to acquire in order to live successfully and exercise his practical reasoning with others, if we then hope to be able to judge which situations (including legal systems and institutions) provide such a being with optimum conditions.

For this reason we may say that the *Politics*, as a work, follows the *Ethics*. But the political is always assumed to be prior logically, as a necessary and natural milieu in which human beings develop the characters they need to enable them to live humanly. Human excellence or virtue, according to Aristotle, can be realized only under the aegis of correct compulsive norms, the just laws of a political community. For this reason ethical discourse concerns itself with the moral virtues which presuppose some rule-based common life or other. Hence, the *polis* is necessarily (logically) prior to each of its members because it is that by which humans secure their living well. Aristotle argues that it is in the interest of each concrete, particular citizen to participate, co-operate and support the *polis*, even in situations which would be at the expense of his own immediate advantage. There is no liberal individualism here. As for Plato, so for Aristotle, there can be no moral formation of an individual's character that can be considered in isolation from the society in which he lives. No person's good can possibly be promoted without consideration for the society to which he belongs. Aristotle's ethics is a philosophy of the common human life. But unlike Plato, who said the happiness even of the Guardians was subordinated to the happiness of the entire *polis*, as an idea, Aristotle will not sacrifice the particular and actual members of the city to a unified abstraction of 'the state'. It is simply that the part, the citizen, does not exist without the whole, the *polis*. As we shall see, it is for this reason that the common good of a really existing *polis* must be secured, even if this means that the particular good of a citizen is sacrificed. Politics is about the good for man before it is about the good for this or that man. Aristotle did not think that any ancient Greek would take exception to this in the way that a contemporary liberal might because he did not think one could speak of the needs, desires and character of an isolated individual, prior to the 'state', and consider this individual to be human. Aristotle will argue that a man is not fully human if he is incapable of displaying and acting upon an impulse to form partnerships and associations. Someone who is 'clanless, lawless, heartless' and 'stateless' and is so by nature rather than through ill fortune, is a non-cooperator, war-mad, and hence, is either low in the scale of humanity or above it like a god. In either case this individual is not truly human, 'resembling an isolated piece at draughts' (*Politics*, I, 1253a1–6).

When we discussed Plato's *Republic* we said that political rule is not, for him, about changing the *nature* of the human being in whom there is the potential for both good and bad. *Nor is it about changing the natures of the characters of citizens.* Rather, it is about moulding and refocusing the characters people already have (displayed differentially even as children) and which, thereafter, can be refocused by any society and its values. Hence, the sovereign *technē* of justly ruling a just and harmonious society, begins for Plato, *in the middle of things* by accepting an already existing trinity of basic character types for each of which there is a natural job, so that political *technē* is about refocusing the characters people already display in order to ensure they pursue truly human interests.

Like Plato, Aristotle does not believe that people's characters, once habituated to ways of behaving, can be altered as readily as can the conditions in which these characters pursue their lives. Aristotle's solution is not so radical as to rusticate already formed adults to the suburbs, leaving the children with soul differentials to be refocused by philosopher–educators. Rather, his response to the question of human character is to start even earlier in the psychological formation of the human in order to emphasize, far more than does Plato in the *Republic*, the cultural responsibility for character through habit formation. Politics for Aristotle *is* about character *formation* because we are not born with characters, we acquire them. Politics is not about refocusing the characters people already have; it is about ensuring, through appropriate cultural rules, that humans have the opportunities to engage in the kinds of habitual practices from which they can acquire practical knowledge and so take responsibility for their actions and their characters. Cultural rules or laws are facilitators, enabling humans to actualize (or not) their species' potentiality and so develop a plurality of particular, truly human characters that enable each of them to flourish as human beings in the situations in which they find themselves.

Aristotle, then, agrees with Plato that politics is not about changing the *nature* of the human being; indeed, no human art or skill can do that. But for Aristotle, to study what politics is about you *start* from a cumulative, historically and culturally agreed definition of man as well as from a cumulative, historically and culturally agreed definition of what human flourishing consists in for that species, man, which has a potential to act well or badly within any social structure that necessarily prescribes rules of behaviour. It *concludes* that the true statesman is a legislator who aims to habituate men's characters to behave in ways that enable them to live successful human lives. In between the starting definitions and the conclusion is the domain of variability in lived life where good men deliberate about their choices to act so as to achieve particular good outcomes and an overall successful life. Here is the realm of responsibility, not only for one's particular acts but also for the kind of settled character one has – whose acts display to others a character that is open to praise and blame. So, in a sense, Aristotle too starts *in the middle of things*, with humans as *polis*-living animals with no more than a potential for moral virtue, where one society or another provides a better or worse environment in which people engage in practices that lead them towards what is considered the appropriate, because specific, human good. What Aristotle will not, however, agree with is the Platonic 'fudging' over the issue (in the Myth of Er) as to how people end up having chosen to be the kinds of characters they display which Platonic politics then simply refocuses. Platonic politics (if it can be called that) merely accepts them as character types and reorientates these to the best interest of humans. Although Aristotle is also concerned with the degree to which a particular person is to be considered responsible not only for his particular actions but also for his more settled character or disposition to act regularly in one way or another, he will be much more emphatic than Plato in assigning a prior responsibility for character to 'law'-structured cultures and their relative psychological insights into what is required for the actualization of human potential. Some cultures enable men to acquire a taste for what is fine and truly pleasurable, so that men do not simply live under the sway of their emotions (NE X, ix, 1179b11–18). Some cultures provide the right educational training by establishing the right laws which can nurture and discipline the young. Thereafter, it will be up to individuals to practise the lessons learnt and confirm them by habit when they have matured (NE 1179b30–1180a4). Only during the process of becoming habituated to the performance of *good* practices does one have the opportunity to reflect on becoming truly virtuous by *knowing* why one acts well, why one chooses what one chooses in specific circumstances, and not simply out of habit, which is (relatively) non-cognitive. For every agent, the knowledge or awareness of principles of behaviour emerges out of habitual practices and experiences. Legislators know this 'fact' about human psychology. That is why politics is a distinctive kind of science for Aristotle, being concerned with the human good, and it is not to be subsumed into a metaphysical concern for the unqualified, non-specific Good.

Nicomachean Ethics

The *Nicomachean Ethics* opens with a generally agreed premise which has emerged (historically) from people's discursive reflections on their observations and common beliefs. The Good is agreed to be 'that at which all things aim' because people consider that every art or investigation, indeed, every action and practical pursuit, aims at some good. People assess a premise by taking it back to perception and induction. However, the ends at which different things aim are clearly different. How do we know this? From our experiences in our milieu. We know that there are many actions, arts and sciences and hence, many ends; for instance, the end of medical science is health, the end of military science, victory, the end of shipbuilding, ships and the end of economic science, wealth. We must be living in a society where these discrete practices, these arts and sciences, are engaged in for us to know this, and 'we' do. If it is the case that as humans, among the various ends at which our various actions aim, there is one end which we desire for its own sake, and for the sake of which we desire all the other ends, such as health, wealth, social recognition and status, friends, etc., *then* this Good sought by us for its own sake is (by definition) the supreme and ultimate Good (*to ariston*). This is an all-embracing end which itself is partially constituted of prior ends and it is an activity that is undertaken for its own sake rather than as a means to some further end. Clearly, an understanding (*gnosis*) of *this* Good, our good as humans, is of great importance to us for the conduct of our lives as humans. What, then, is the Good and by which of the theoretical or practical sciences or modes of thinking is it studied?

We are told that the science that is most authoritative and directive in matters that concern the human good is the science of politics. This is because politics makes use of other (subordinate) sciences such as the arts of war, property management, public speaking and, by legislation, lays down what we should do and from what we should refrain. Politics is, for 'us', a master-craft because the end of politics must include the ends of these other sciences. The end of politics is the good for man. And because its subject is man, not particular individuals, the attaining and preservation of the good of the community, the good for man (not the good for this man Callias) is a greater and more perfect thing to achieve. Of course it is desirable to secure what is good in the case of the individual, but it is preferable to secure what is good for a people or 'state'. This then, is the aim of the investigation undertaken in the *Nicomachean Ethics*: to come to some view as to what constitutes the successful living of a human life.

From what has already been said above, it is clear that Aristotle believes you would not know what is good for a particular member of the species until you first clarified what was the specific good of the species of which he is a member.[60] This, then, is not to

60   Recall above on 'man' as predicate in the *Categories*.

be read, as many have read it, as a statement that the individual is subordinated to and by the state. It is a statement which seeks to clarify that a particular individual would not know his particular good without having first considered himself to be 'a man' and concerned for the good for man.

Now political science as a mode of thinking investigates particular instances of morally fine and just conduct. But there is such a variety of behaviour, and differences of opinion concerning instances of moral conduct, that people widely believe moral conduct to be due to convention rather than nature. Are they wrong? By what method of enquiry can we determine the extent to which the common view is correct? In discussing something uncertain, this variety of behaviour and difference of opinion concerning instances of human conduct and their sources, we must give an account that achieves such clarity as its subject matter allows and be satisfied with a broad outline of the truth. There is a similar uncertainty concerning the conception of the Good because, at the level of particulars, acknowledged particular good things can, none the less, be experienced as having harmful consequences: we know that people have been ruined by (an acknowledged good) wealth, and courage (another acknowledged good) can still cost men their lives. 'We' can only argue (dialectically) about what is for the most part true and our conclusions themselves must similarly be qualified as for the most part true. We are looking for true opinion. A trained mind, then, never expects more precision in the treatment of any subject than the nature of that subject permits, and the nature of the domain of instances of morally fine and just conduct is the domain of the contingent, just as the domain of character is widely considered to be contingent and conventionally formed. Demanding logical demonstration from a teacher of rhetoric is clearly about as reasonable as accepting mere plausibility from a mathematician. Therefore, from an investigation of human conduct and morally fine acts, it is appropriate to argue about what is true for the most part, not about what is absolutely and unconditionally true.

How are we to make headway in our investigation of instances of moral conduct and people's characters, be they conventionally or naturally constituted? Aristotle asserts that a person judges rightly only what he is acquainted with and understands and to judge correctly he needs to be a good critic. In specialized fields (such as shipbuilding or medicine) the good critic is himself a specialist practitioner; but in a general domain like politics, the good critic is a man with a general education, by which is meant having had experiences in living and having reflected on these with a view to action. To be possessed of a general education not only takes time but maturity of character. That is why a young man, not yet generally educated through having had experiences of the practical business of living, is not a fit person to attend lectures on political science. This is because politics draws its premises and examples from the experience of the practical business of life and conduct and only if one knows the appropriate premises and can give examples can one then draw appropriate conclusions. Furthermore, young men's lives and their pursuit of various aims are guided by their feelings. Were such people to study politics (in a lecture room) they would gain nothing from it; it would be of no use to them because the end of political science is not knowledge but action, not knowing but doing. Only men of mature and settled character disposition who are experienced in the practical business of living, men who have already learnt to guide their desires and actions by reasoned principle, can benefit from a study of moral science.

It is clear that Aristotle would not approve of his *Ethics* and *Politics* being studied in modern university courses in the history of political thought unless the room were filled with mature students who had returned to the lecture hall after a life of being in the world!

The end of political science, then, is the highest of all practical goods attainable by our actions. The majority of mature and experienced men, be they ordinary or more culti- vated, agree this good to be what is called 'happiness' or living and doing well (*eudaimonia*). We take this as our definition and starting point. Living well is something perfect and self- sufficient, being the end to which our actions are directed. But opinions differ concerning what living and doing well consist in. Our problem is that the account given by the wise is not that of the generality of humankind. Popular opinion takes the happy and successful life to be equated with pleasure, wealth and honour. Others (Plato) have held the view that over and above these particular goods there is another which is good in itself and the cause of whatever goodness there is in these other particular goods. Since we cannot review all the different views, let us consider at least the most widely prevalent opinions or those which have something that can be said in their favour. How shall we begin?

First, Aristotle advises us to be aware that there is a difference between arguing *from* first principles (deduction) and arguing *to* them (induction). In any enquiry we must start from what is known. But things are known in two senses: what is known to us and what is knowable in itself and absolutely. We, as humans investigating what is the human good, must start from what is known to us. Aristotle insists that if anyone is to make a serious study of fine and just things, and generally of the topics of political science, he must *already* know certain things and therefore have been trained in his habits. From this training certain things will have come to be known to him. The starting point or first principle of this study is the 'fact' that a thing is so, and if this is sufficiently clear there will be no need to ascertain the reason why it is so. To do the latter would be the domain of another kind of science–demonstrative proof (*epistēmē*), but in matters of ethics there is no demonstration because ethics presupposes that *a priori* first principles have arisen in us from practices, and thereafter ethics is concerned with the contingent rather than the necessary. First principles arise in us from perception and experience, from induction and from habituation; they cannot be demonstrated; it is simply ac- cepted *a priori* that this is where we begin and were we engaged in demonstrative reason- ing we would begin with these principles and give reasons why they are so. Here, we need not give the reasons. Aristotle believes that a man of good moral training already knows the first principles, the 'facts' that things are so, or he can easily acquire them. Aristotle will later indicate that first principles are cognitively grasped by us in different ways: some are grasped by induction, others by perception , and some by a kind of habituation (NE I, vii, 1098b1ff.). Through learning his community's language and through the moral education received both as a child in a family and, as he matures, in public encounters such as military training, participating in civic responsibilities and in discussion with those beyond his kin, a man will have acquired a range of morally guided experiences and evaluations which not only condition his behaviour but also establish the *a priori* principles that things are as they are for him. Political science is concerned largely with what follows from the first principles a man has grasped in the process of habituation.

The other ways of grasping first principles are treated in other kinds of discourses, some of whose results may be drawn on by ethical enquiry. We know (for instance from the *Posterior Analytics*) that from his innate faculty of discernment, that is, perception, which a man shares with some other animals, where retained perceptions collectively constitute his experience, he has come to know the (lowest) universal, the *infima species*, and thereafter, he arrives, by induction, at those fundamental and necessary *a priori* truths which strike him as such and which cannot be otherwise. From induction based on perception he also comes to know those principles that emerge as (true) opinion from experience in the domain of the contingent. Combining the results of induction with his socially tuned convictions about his daily experiences, themselves the result of his syllogistic (deductive) reasoning from pre-existing social knowledge or premises, he naturally tends to theorize and think critically. He tests and confirms or modifies his theories, by bringing them back to 'the facts of life'. But a well-habituated man does not need to have demonstrated for him or to learn how to demonstrate, logically, the reason why 'facts' are 'facts'.

Now, there are thought to be, broadly speaking, three types of life: the life of pleasure or enjoyment, which is the preference of the mass of men and even of some in positions of power; there is the political life where men of affairs often identify the successful life with honour, as this is, broadly speaking, their goal. Aristotle will spend most of his time treating these common views and the views of the political man. But because honour depends more on those who confer it than on those who receive it, and the Good, Aristotle says, we feel instinctively *must be an attribute of their possessor* and not easily taken from him, then honour is also insufficient as the end of a truly human life. In fact, intelligent political men seem to seek honour to convince themselves of something else – their own merit or virtue – so this virtue must be superior to honour as their end. And yet people think that the mere *possession* of virtue is compatible with being inactive or asleep.[61] Some think the possession of virtue incurs suffering and misfortune.[62] Even virtue proves, on examination, to be too incomplete an end, because no one would call a man living a life of misery, happy. In fact, the common view is that *eudaimonia*, living and faring well, is complete, and given that this is where we begin, then virtue is not sufficient for happiness (*contra* Socrates) because some further good can be added that is not guaranteed by a man's virtue – he certainly lacks some goods if he is persecuted. To say that a man is *eudaimon* under torture or in great misfortune, provided he is good, is false (NE VII, 13, 19–22). That *eudaimonia* is complete also means we cannot equate pleasure with living a successful human life because further pleasures can be added. Pleasure is not complete while *eudaimonia* is.[63]

The third type of life is the life of the *theoretikos*, the life of contemplation, which will be examined (much) later in the *Nicomachean Ethics* (book 10).

Before speaking further about the merits of the different types of life, Aristotle must examine critically the views of Plato and the Academy. He rejects Plato's doctrine of the Forms and therefore the notion that there is a common idea, the Good, that applies in the same way (univocally) to all uses of the word 'good'. He also rejects the position that there is a single universal goodness exhibited by all good things, since he argues that each thing specifically has its own good. For Aristotle, good things are prior to their goodness, for the existence of goodness is simply a matter of there being something good, whereas for Plato, goodness is prior to good things.[64]

But to say no more than that living and faring well is the supreme good (for man), the

---

61   Compare this with the view that it is a lucky gift of character; see *Republic* I: Cephalus.
62   Similarly, see *Republic* I: the argument of Thrasymachus.
63   See Irwin, *A History of Western Philosophy*, p. 135.
64   See J. O. Urmson, *Aristotle's Ethics* (Oxford, 1988), appendix to ch. 1 on NE I, 6.

end to which our actions are directed, seems to be a platitude. Aristotle suggests that we may perhaps give a more distinctive account if we consider that the human being has a function or specific activity (*ergon*) that is proper to itself, and the good of man resides in the function or specific activity of man. Only then can we decide whether the good for man is constituted by a life of pleasure, honour, virtue or perhaps something else. We want, then, a *definition* of man that grasps the species through its genus and its differentia. Aristotle tells us that all living creatures have a life force or psyche/soul which is a set of powers or capacities, and this soul is not separate from the body. The functions of the soul include nutrition, reproduction, perception, etc. The soul, then, simply is the functional state of a living creature. Now man is the kind of living thing we call an animal but of a certain kind. We must exclude from our definition of man the mere act of living life that consists of nutrition and growth because this is also shared by plants; and we must also exclude the sentient life because this too is shared by horses and cattle and animals of all kinds. Humans are animals but it is what distinguishes them from other animals that grasps their specific difference. What remains after we eliminate what humans share with other animals is what may be called 'the practical life determined by activity of the rational part of man'. This is not a definition that is meant to apply to, or be derived from, a specific cultural milieu. It presupposes that man lives in a cultural milieu but not necessarily in this one. Man is in the genus *animal* but he is differentiated from all other animals by his rationality, which is deployed in the practical business of living a human life.

But he is still an animal and not pure intellect or immortal intellectual soul. We must bring in what Aristotle says in the *De Anima* for further clarification (*De Anima* 412a3–28; 412b10–413a3; 403a24–67): soul, for Aristotle, is the form of the body, inseparable from the body it is 'in' and it is not an immaterial element that is *added* to the body's material constituents. In other words, what we might call 'the self' is distributed throughout the body. There is no sharp separation between mind and body (as Descartes was later to propose) since mind cannot exist or function at all without body. Soul and body are one, just as wax and its shape are one, although one can *think* about the psyche separately from the body. Now, *if* the function or activity specific to man is an activity of the soul in accordance with or implying a rational principle, and *if* we assume that the function or activity specific to man is this kind of life or series of soul activities, and *if* the function or activity of a good man is to perform these soul activities well and rightly, *then, we define* the good for man as an activity of soul in accordance with virtue/excellence (*aretē*) or, if there are more than one kind of virtue/excellence, in accord with the best and most perfect kind. And this soul activity in accord with the best virtue/excellence must be exemplified over a complete lifetime.

Human beings, then, are defined as the only ethical agents in their genus. Ethics, being about the virtues of character that are acquired by habituation, is not reduced to a science of behaviour modification through training based entirely on pleasure and pain, as is the case with other animals. This is because we shall see that human virtue and vice are *voluntary* activities, and people's characters, as exhibited by their actions, are the objects of praise and blame. In order to act voluntarily the agent has to exercise an intellectual virtue or excellence of soul, that is, to think rationally in a certain way, to deliberate between possible alternatives with a view to an end, and Aristotle does not think animals (or children) think so universally in this way.[65] Aristotle believes that

---

65   See Irwin, *Aristotle's First Principles*, p. 340.

humans only come to actualize this way of thinking rationally and deliberatively after having become habituated to moral practices by which they will have acquired a view as to their end.

We now have an account defining the good for man in outline. Is Aristotle's definition adequate? We have already noted that people come to first principles and definitions by induction, perception or habituation and political science deals largely with the first principles acquired through habituation. Political science cannot affect the specifically human way in which human minds happen to function when they come to know things through perception and induction. Instead, Aristotle says that 'we' who are studying political science must examine these *a priori*, already grasped first principles or definitions, not only as reached as logical conclusions deduced from (generally and historically accepted) premises, but also in the light of current opinion as this is expressed in what people say (NE I, viii, 1098b9–11). The dialectician enters here. If a *proposition* be true, all the 'facts' harmonize with it, but if it is false, it is soon found to be discordant with them.

The goods have been classified (by Plato) as external, of the soul, and of the body. But it is our actions and the soul's active exercise of its functions that Aristotle posits as that which determine the definition of the good for man, *eudaimonia*. Hence for the purposes of investigating human successful living, he focuses on the good of the soul. Aristotle tells us that this is also a view of longstanding and is accepted by the philosophers; hence, he takes their view to support the correctness of 'our' definition. 'Our' definition is also supported by the (common) belief that the successful man lives and fares well because what we have described – the good for man as an activity of soul in accordance with the most perfect virtue over a lifetime – virtually identifies *eudaimonia* with a kind of good life or doing well. 'Our' definition is inclusive: all the various characteristics that are looked for in a successful life, lived well, are included in it, for some think *eudaimonia* is virtue, others prudence, others wisdom, some add pleasure and others include favourable external conditions. Aristotle says that some of these views have been held by many people and from ancient times, others by a few distinguished men. He says that neither group is likely to be entirely mistaken. The probability is that their beliefs are at least partly or indeed mainly correct. Hence, there is no inconsistency in understanding human flourishing, *eudaimonia*, as an inclusive *and* as a dominant end of life.[66] Indeed, humans want honour, pleasure, wealth and every possible kind of excellence, and humans want these for their own sake (NE 1097b2), but they are all parts of *eudaimonia* (NE 1129b28) *and* humans want them in order to live the successful human life.[67] In other words, there is a class of acts that are ends in themselves and also constituents in some wider end. *Eudaimonia* is a compound of ends, rationally ordered, to achieve the complete good for man, which is a successful life as a man.

Now Aristotle asks whether the supreme good consists in the *possession* or in the *exercise* of virtue, that is, in a disposition or state of mind, or in the manifestation of the disposition in an activity? It surely is the latter because it is, after all, possible for someone to possess a disposition without its producing any good results. Virtue actively exercised

---

66 For a range of interpretations of Aristotelian *eudaimonia* see the various essays in A. O. Rorty, *Essays on Aristotle's Ethics* (Berkeley, 1980).
67 Urmson, *Aristotle's Ethics*, p. 13.

means that a man necessarily, that is, by definition, acts and acts well. The type of life that is worthwhile must depend on the actions it contains rather than simply on one's (unexercised) abilities and presumed character. Of course, there are many things that happen to a man that are out of his control, but he can to a great extent choose his own actions and it is from these that his character is evaluated and his life judged *eudaimon* or not. We need to carve out a space where we believe that a person can make a difference to the kind of life he actively leads.

Although Aristotle's focus is on the good of the soul, he believes that it is clear to everyone that the living of a successful human life, that is, our soul's exercise of its functions, needs the addition of external goods because one cannot do morally fine deeds without any resources. Many morally fine acts can only be done with the help of friends, or wealth or political influence. It is also advantageous to have good ancestry, good children and personal beauty, for the lack of these mars one's felicity. It is held to be unlikely that a man will live a successful human life if he is very ugly or of low birth, solitary or childless. This is why he tells us that some identify *eudaimonia* with good fortune; others with virtue. But Aristotle argues that personal beauty, good ancestry and the like should be considered to be necessary *preconditions* which serve only as *instruments* to flourishing. That the most important and finest things about a successful human life should be left entirely to chance he thinks would be a gross distortion of the tendency in nature to order things in the best possible way. This is why he believes that the definition he has proposed can shed some light on this: that the living of a successful human life is to be described as a kind of virtuous activity of the soul. Since it was agreed that the end of political science is the supreme good (for man) *and the principal concern of this science is to endue citizens with certain qualities of character, namely, to make them virtuous and able to do fine deeds*, then *eudaimonia* is a form of *our* activity over a whole life. Perhaps it will be easier for one to acquire a virtuous character and perform fine deeds if one happens to have been born handsome, is not of low birth nor childless. But these chance factors are not the sole determinants of whether or not one lives a successful human life. One's success is more centrally determined by one's own agency. Hence, a dead man is not appropriately called *eudaimon*; nor, of course, is a man who suffers reverses and vicissitudes in the course of life and experiences disasters in his declining years. Since our commonly agreed conception of *eudaimonia* is of something permanent and complete, and not readily subject to change, then true prosperity and adversity do not depend, essentially, on fortune, although a good life does require fortune in addition.

The heart of this issue is that to live and fare well is down to the active exercise of our faculties in conformity with virtue. Short of calamities over which we have no control, there is a certain way of living a human life that is within our power to achieve and it depends largely on our actions. The successful man possesses the element of stability in his disposition to act virtuously since he will be always or at least most often engaged in doing and thinking about the things that are in conformity with virtue. This kind of man will then bear changes of fortune most nobly or finely; anyway, for the most part, success or failure in life do no depend on the sorts of things like fortune, wealth, personal beauty for Aristotle; these are mere complements of a human life. The truly good and wise man bears his fortunes with dignity and always takes the most honourable course that circumstances permit. This kind of man never becomes miserable although, if he suffers disasters like those of Priam, he cannot be called entirely *eudaimon*.

Aristotle's final definition then, is that the man who lives and fares well is one who is active in accordance with complete virtue and who is adequately furnished with external goods through a complete life. Such men are supremely successful, but as humans (and not as gods) (NE I, ix).

One further clarification is required for an ethical enquiry which starts from what is familiar to 'us', that is, from what is said about human conduct by the majority and the wise, because it is within a realm of collective evaluation that we become habituated and adopt our premises. Aristotle asks whether *eudaimonia* is something that is praised or something that is valued. He answers by observing that everything we praise seems to be praised because it has a certain quality and stands in relation to something else. We praise the good man and virtue, we praise just and brave men, *because* of their actions and the results they produce. Praise, then, belongs to what is relative, that is, we praise a fine act by praising the character of the man who performs it. But we already know that *eudaimonia* is not relative; it is complete and perfect. In effect, we view it retrospectively as a completed achievement. No one praises a life lived well as he praises justice. Rather he calls *eudaimonia* 'blessed' as being something better, more divine, than, say, justice. Praise is concerned with goodness as an appreciation of a *quality in an agent* and praise enables men to do fine deeds. Praise acts as a form of persuasion; it motivates in the present with a view to the future. We praise or blame the quality of men's characters, their virtuous or vicious dispositions, by praising or blaming their actions. We praise or blame what we think is within a man's power to determine. But the *eudaimon* life is 'a way of living' which *already* constitutes success. It is prized rather than praised. Where the morally virtuous life is to be praised, the *eudaimon* life is an achievement to be congratulated.[68] An ethical enquiry then, must focus on human virtues and their lack which are the subject of praise and blame or some other evaluation which motivates us by 'persuading' us to behave in ways that we are responsible for determining. Our aim in life is to live and fare well. Ethical enquiry is concerned with the means to that end.

Moral and Intellectual Virtues as Moral and Intellectual Excellences

What sort of character is needed to make sound choices and how does one develop it; that is, where does one's character come from?

Aristotle suggests that we examine the nature of human excellence or virtue to help us in our investigation. He tells us that the true statesman is thought of as a man who has taken special pains to study human virtue because he wants to make his fellow citizens good and law-abiding and therefore worthy of praise. He provides comparative examples of historical legislators in Crete and Sparta. He reminds us that we are considering human goodness, for it was the good for man that we set out to discover. Human goodness concerns the soul or psyche rather than the body (the latter is, in effect, what the doctor studies) and the statesman ought to have *some* acquaintance with human psychology; he ought to study the soul, not as would a psychologist but with a view to politics as the supreme practical science. With a view to politics, he will observe that there are two kinds of virtue or excellence which humans as such display: virtues or excellences of intellect and virtues or excellences of character. Most of the remaining discussion in books 2–5 will deal with virtues of character but, as we shall see, although

68   Ibid., p. 12.

the two kinds of virtue, moral and intellectual, can be thought about and discussed separately, there is a rational component, a virtue of intellect, that must be brought into play as a necessary component of displays of virtuous character. The legislator deals with the two kinds of virtue separately because over one kind (character) he has more influence than over the other (intellect).

The statesman is reminded that there are aspects of psychology that are treated adequately in other discourses but that political science should make use of the results; these are, for instance, that the soul consists of two 'parts', one part irrational and the other part capable of reason. The irrational 'part' is the cause of nutrition and growth and is common to every living being that receives nourishment. The excellence or virtue of this 'vegetative' or 'nutritive' soul is not confined to man. There also appears to be another element of the (human) soul which, while irrational, is in a sense receptive to reason. For instance, if we look at the types of man (whose character) we call self-restrained or continent and unrestrained or incontinent, we say that they have a principle, a rational element in their souls, which urges them in the right direction and encourages them to take the best course of action. We praise this. But we can also observe another element besides this rational principle which struggles and strains against the rational. The impulse of the incontinent man takes him in the direction contrary to reason. This irrational element, however, seems to be receptive of reason and in the continent man, as in the temperate and in the brave man, it is obedient to reason. Now we can say that this irrational 'part' of the soul itself consists of two 'parts': the nutritive, a kind of impulse which has no association with reason, on the one hand, and on the other, the desiring and generally appetitive 'part' which does somehow participate in reason in the sense that it takes account of or is submissive to reason. This is why the appetitive or desiring 'part' of the irrational 'part' of the soul is in some way capable of being persuaded by reason, for instance, when one is admonished or encouraged. Aristotle notes that it may be more correct to speak of the appetitive part of the soul as rational, so that the soul may best be considered as divided into two (rather than three) 'parts'. Indeed, later (NE VI) he will divide the rational 'part' of the soul similarly into two: one kind of reason which calculates or deliberates about variable things and the other, or scientific reason, which contemplates invariable first principles (NE 1139a1–15). But it is useful to know this here because the calculative or deliberative reason will be brought in to determine the means by which the desiring 'part' of the soul is, in each particular and practical situation, accommodated to or persuaded by reason to fix its desire and so take pleasure in acting in ways that contribute to one's long-term best interest, one's good.

According with the first differentiation of the soul into rational and irrational 'parts', virtue, a soul quality, is likewise divided into classes. Some virtues are therefore called intellectual (of the rational 'part') and others moral (of the irrational 'part' that is none the less receptive to reason). *It is the appetitive, irrational 'part' of the soul, capable of being persuaded by reason, that accords with the moral excellence of character.*

We can now turn to the intellectual virtues. These are distinguished as wisdom (*sophia*) and understanding (*sunēsis*) and prudence (*phronēsis*), all of which are ways of thinking. But Aristotle notes that when 'we' speak of a man's character, whether he displays, for instance, liberality or temperance, we are not referring to his intellectual but rather to his *moral* virtues. We are referring to what he consistently *desires* and finds pleasure in. We do not describe him in terms of his ways of thinking – as wise or understanding – but rather in terms of his behaviour – as gentle or temperate. Moral and intellectual virtues are distinct and yet related. Aristotle notes that we do praise a wise man on the grounds of what we take to be his settled mode of thought or state of mind, that is, his *disposition to choose* to act in a morally virtuous way, since those settled states of mind that are praiseworthy we also call virtues. These two kinds of virtue or excellence, the intellectual and the moral, need to be discussed in terms of the ways in which each may be acquired. To choose well is caused by *desiring* the right end, which is doing well, and *then* deliberating about the various means that are in our power to secure the rightly desired end. To be able to choose well in the sphere of action involves both a certain mode of thought (deliberation, that which is directed to one end as opposed to another among possible alternatives) and a certain habituated and stable disposition of character which desires and finds pleasure in doing well (NE VI, ii, 1139a32–37). The problem is to decide which develops first, the mode of thought (intellectual virtue) or the settled character disposition (moral virtue).

Nicomachean Ethics Book 2

Aristotle tells us that the intellectual virtues or different modes of thinking such as wisdom, understanding and prudence, are generally thought to owe their inception and growth chiefly to instruction, and therefore this kind of virtue needs both time and experience. One is not born with wisdom, understanding or prudence; given that we are born with the relevant capacities to learn, we are then taught to *exercise* these different capacities, to think in different ways by instruction and experience. Didactic instruction and experience teaches humans to think necessarily as humans in the different ways that humans do think: for instance, prudentially, abstractly, theoretically. Such ways of thinking are fixed for the species and are not capable of alteration by habituation. Aristotle seems to believe that even if you treated a healthy human being like an animal, he would not think like one, although his potential for thinking either abstractly or practically in a human way would remain largely unexercised and unactualized.

On the other hand, moral goodness is the result of habit (*ethos*). The excellences of character, according with the irrational or appetitive 'part' of the soul, are acquired by the training of *behaviour to desire* the right end. We are not born with the moral virtues, since nothing that is what it is by nature can be made to behave differently by habituation. But we *can* be made to conduct ourselves differently as a consequence of habit formation. If you treated a human like an animal, he would not think like an animal although, through his capacities to learn by imitation, he might behave like one. The moral virtues are engendered in us neither by nor yet contrary to nature. We are constituted by nature to receive them as is no other animal, but their full development in us is due to habit. We are, therefore, potentially morally virtuous as humans but actually so only through habituation.

In effect, Aristotle is dealing with the common view that morals are merely conventional and he is suggesting that this view is too simplistic. He is arguing that there are *correct*, psychologically insightful conventional moral rules that enable humans to actualize their natures as moral agents. Convention must work with nature, not against it. This means two things: no human is simply a social product. And no one simply comes to know what is right from accepting unexamined social opinions. People come to know the principles of right and wrong both from syllogistic deduction from social premises and from perception and induction based on experiences. But, as we shall see, if a child becomes habituated to bad practices in a society with bad (psychologically wrong and unnatural) social rules and opinions, his character will be sufficiently distorted by his habituated practices so that his ability to reason to correct first principles, distinguishing between good and bad, is likely to be corrupted.

Most men are born with the relevant capacities to actualize their human excellences, both intellectual and moral. This means that neither Aristotle nor the discourse of the common and wise which he analyses conceives of man as initially a bad or anti-social creature; there is no original sin of later Christian doctrine, where habituation 'converts' us from 'naturally' bad (after the Fall) to 'conventionally' good. Rather, Aristotle and his community appear to believe, in general, that humans are born on the one hand, without any character at all and, on the other, with a capacity, as yet unrealized, to think in different ways. Nature endows humans with potentialities which are later actualized through different processes.

Now, virtuous and vicious *characters* are held to be the result of repeated practices. A good character is acquired by practice. Men become good builders as a result of building well and bad ones as a result of building badly. Otherwise, Aristotle says, there would be no need of anyone 'teaching' them this craft and such 'teaching' comes in the form of showing young builders how to imitate what master-craftsmen builders do so that 'practice makes perfect', as it were; if this were not the case then they would all be born good or bad builders. This, he thinks, holds for the moral virtues as well. Anything we have to learn to *do* we learn by the actual *doing* of it among our fellow men. We become just by performing just acts, temperate by performing temperate ones, brave by performing brave acts. He notes that this view, that we learn to do from actually doing, is supported by what happens in *poleis*. No one simply learns to do from doing in a vacuum or on his own. Nor does he learn to do simply from thinking or reading a handbook. One learns to do in a milieu of practitioners. It is the intention of legislators, by definition, to make their citizens good by habituation. Those who do not carry it out fail in their objective and this is what distinguishes the laws of a good constitution from a bad one. It is the way we behave in our dealing with others that makes us just or unjust, and the way we behave in the face of danger, accustoming ourselves to being timid or confident, that makes us brave or cowardly in character. Similarly with situations involving desires and angry feelings. It is their conduct in such situations which make people temperate, patient, licentious, choleric. Like activities produce like dispositions. It is the qualities of our actions which determine our resulting character dispositions. And it is for this reason that it is a matter of no little importance what sorts of habits we form from the earliest age; it makes a vast difference, or rather, all the difference in the world (NE 1103b23–5). Hence, legislators concern themselves with child education because it is at this time that character formation takes place through habituation to practices.

For the most part, then, the environment in which one becomes habituated, in which one learns to do from actually doing, has more observable effects on one's character than does heredity for Aristotle. It is the environment of practices which is of primary importance. In his *Rhetoric* Aristotle would place great emphasis on people learning how to behave first and best from imitation.[69] Here one observes norms of behaviour

---

69   See volume 2, chapter 1, pp. 65–9 of *A History of Political Thought* for a fuller analysis of Aristotle's *Rhetoric* and the ways in which it was understood in the middle ages.

exemplified by good practitioners, men who are well-habituated and who teach by doing, their behaviour being seen, in retrospect, to have provided correct guidance, rather than coercion, for other doers, so that they are exemplars in enjoying doing things in the right way. But as we shall see, human agents, responsible for their actions, live within environments that may *enable* them to behave well or badly. As mature agents they still make choices to behave in one way or another, to engage or not in one practice or another. Some environments, with bad practitioners as exemplars, simply make it harder to live humanly.

Since Aristotle's ethical enquiry has a practical aim, for he reminds us that we are not investigating the nature of virtue for the sake of *knowing* what it is but in order that we may become good and so *behave* well, we must ask how are we to act rightly, since it is our actions which determine the quality of our dispositions (NE II, ii). We begin with the premise, the commonly accepted 'formula': 'to act in conformity with right principle' and ask how this may be achieved (ibid.). Aristotle does not think he or anyone else can provide a theory of conduct with hard and fast rules for acting. A discourse on moral action cannot be a handbook on ethical etiquette. This is because questions of conduct and expedience have as little fixity about them as questions of what is healthful, because both vary with the particular person and the circumstances. If this is true of the general rule, it is even more true that the application of the general rule to particular instances of conduct admits of no precision. Here an (already habituated) agent (in an environment of practitioners) must at every step think out for himself what the circumstances demand. And since the circumstances are virtually innumerable he thinks that all that can be provided is a general outline.

How do we judge whether someone else acts in conformity with right principle or whether we have ourselves guided our own actions in this direction (NE II, iii)? We must realize that another person's inner character or disposition is not visible to us. For this reason ethical enquiry is always based on inferences: we infer a person's disposition from his actions and the visible pleasure or pain with which they are performed we take as signs of such a person's disposition. We have to use the evidence of visible 'facts' to throw light on those that are invisible. First we observe the 'fact' that it is in the very nature of moral qualities, themselves the product of habituation, to be destroyed by deficiency and excess. For instance, strength is destroyed both by excessive and by deficient exercise. Likewise, the man who fears everything becomes a coward; the man who is afraid of nothing at all but marches to every danger, is foolhardy. One's character, as judged both by others and oneself, is open to a certain alteration if one engages in practices that unsettle a previously more or less settled disposition acquired from an earlier set of habituating practices. This means that settled character dispositions have to be actively and voluntarily maintained.

Another 'fact' that we must keep in mind if we are to come to some general guidelines about how a person comes to act in conformity with right principle, is our consciousness of pleasure. A consciousness of pleasure has grown up with all of us from our infancy. Our life is so deeply imbued with this feeling that it is hard to remove all trace of it and for this reason alone Aristotle does not think that humans can temper behaviour entirely by a reasoning that is divorced from the emotions. To follow a rule has to include a person's *desire* to follow it. Pleasure and pain are the standards by which, more or less, we regulate our actions. It is, then, the concern of both morality and political science to be aware of the role played by pleasures and pains in a man's behaviour. Given that Aristotle is trying to say something general about what it means to act in conformity with right principle, then he thinks we can say that it is the man who *treats* pleasures and pains rightly who will be judged good and the one who *treats* them wrongly who will be judged bad. Political science is not really concerned with pleasure and pain as 'facts', but rather its concern is with a person's *attitudes* to the emotions, dealing with what a man shows himself to like or dislike doing. Recall that moral virtue and political science are concerned with the appetitive 'part' of the soul that can be 'persuaded' to act in conformity to reasoned principle. What is distinctive about man is that he can guide his desires so that he can come to feel pleasure and pain in the right things, that is, those things that conduce to his living and faring well. Moral virtue or excellence of character, then, depends not merely on acts but on what one likes doing. Character is concerned with our emotional inclination to act well and pleasure, what we like, motivates us. This is revealed to others through the consistency of our behaviour. Therefore, if the moral virtues are concerned with actions and emotions and every emotion and action involves likes or dislikes, then the excellence of character will be concerned with one's likes and dislikes. No one develops a consistency of 'preferences' and 'aversions' in isolation from a community. Moral virtues, acquired by habituation from infancy, to feel joy and grief at the right things, disposes us to act in the best way regarding pleasures and pains, likes and dislikes. When we are mature, we then display a settled disposition to want to act and to choose to act in a way that is appropriate to each particular situation. It is for this reason that Aristotle thinks we assume that moral virtue is the quality of acting in the best way in relation to pleasures and pains and that vice is the opposite.

Therefore, we can now state what moral virtue or excellence is generically. The moral virtues are dispositions acquired by habituation to certain practices as opposed to others. By this is meant that they are the formed states of character in virtue of which we are well- or ill-disposed to the emotions, such as desire, anger, fear, envy, friendship, etc. Such emotions are generally states of consciousness accompanied by pleasure or pain. Note that Aristotle says that we are not called good or bad on the ground of our emotions. Nor are we praised or blamed for the fact that we have feelings. Ethical judgements evaluate what we show ourselves to take pleasure or pain *in* and our biology does not determine this; habituation and our choice to respond to circumstances in one way or another, do. Again, we possess certain capacities by nature, that is to feel pleasure and pain; indeed, so do other animals, but we are not born good or bad by nature. We become good or bad by habit and choice. We are, therefore, praised or blamed for our expressions of choice and for being disposed to certain emotions in one way or another. The virtues, then, are certain modes of choice or involve choice (NE II, v, 1106a7–11). A disposition or virtue or excellence causes its possessor to perform its function well. Excellence or virtue in a man, therefore, will be the disposition which renders him a good man and will also cause him to perform his function well. Since moral virtue concerns the emotions and actions in which one can have excess or deficiency, we are looking for the 'mean' somewhere between such extremes which is of positive value in and for itself. One can, after all, feel pleasure and pain in general, either too much or too little. In other words, it is possible to feel fear, confidence, desire, anger, pity, too much or too little. Both are wrong. More precisely, we are looking for a way of describing what it is to act in certain ways and to have accompanying appropriate feelings at the right times, on the right grounds, towards the right people, for the right motives, and in the right way. This takes some consideration and will, given the circumstances. If excess and deficiency in the field of actions and emotions are failings, then it is the 'mean' which is praised and recognized as success.

The Mean

Now, moral virtue is a settled disposition, an already formed state of character, that observes the 'mean' between excess and deficiency *relative to us*. How may any particular individual determine what is the 'mean' in any situation? Aristotle gives no further guidance than to say that this 'mean' is determined by a rational principle, that is, by what an already prudent man would use to determine it. Such a man does this by deliberately exercising the irrational appetitive 'part' of his soul that takes account of rational persuasion by responding appropriately to admonition or encouragement, blame or praise, taking pleasure in praise and feeling pain at being blamed. He makes choices not only in the circumstances but also with a familiarity with the kind of person he has become, taking into consideration whether he is more or less prone to certain excesses than to others. One of the characteristics of choosing the 'mean' in any particular circumstance is a recognition that it is *not* always equidistant from either extreme. In fact, as a guiding rule, and for the most part, we should assume that one of the extremes is always more erroneous than the others (NE 1109a30–4). Virtue is a settled disposition that enables a person purposefully to determine the choice of his own actions and emotions which are right in each and every situation (in the present and future) for him. Hence, the disposition is essentially the observance of the 'mean', but as an excellence or virtue it is itself an extreme (good rather than bad). A virtuous disposition enables a man to display appropriate anger, fear, confidence, etc. And for this reason Aristotle's teaching on 'the mean' is *not* a doctrine of moderation. Moral virtue, the settled disposition, does not ensure he displays *moderate* anger, fear, confidence. While the virtuous disposition observes the 'mean' not every action or feeling admits of a mean. There are certain actions and emotions that are always wrong in all circumstances and Aristotle says we know these by such names for emotions as malice, shamelessness, envy and for such actions as adultery, theft, murder. And there are occasions when one cannot be too indignant. Again, the emotions, like anger, are not themselves excellences/virtues or defects/vices of character. Virtues or vices are settled states or dispositions to choose to act with regard to exhibiting the relevant emotions to the appropriate degree in the circumstances.

Such a disposition to choose those acts appropriate in the circumstances relative to 'you' is directed by practical reasoning, an intellectual virtue which is a consequence of perception. You have to be present at the particular situation to judge appropriately. To determine in a given situation what the excess or deficiency in one's response would be requires the exercise of a mode of practical reasoning, an *intellectual virtue*, which men learn to exercise and actualize simply by having perceptions which constitute their experiences of particulars and then, from induction, they arrive at (true) opinions as these pertain to variable things (not fixed necessities). Recall that rational principles are grasped in various ways, by perception, induction or habituation. We need experience of the business of living life and we reason to first principles, coming to know them from what is known to us, not known absolutely.

When we respond to admonition and encouragement and accept praise or blame as motivations to behave in one way or another, we begin by accepting the premises of the community, accepted by the common view and the wise, as the rational principles of behaviour, the (true) opinions from which we start, and then we match these with those rational principles – also (true) opinions – which have emerged from our prior engagement in repeated, now habitual practices. This means that the man with a virtuous disposition or character, which is the consequence of correct habituation, is thereafter responsive to the rational principle he has intellectually discovered precisely by engaging in particular, repeated practices. As a result he observes the emergence of a general rule that is, for the most part, applicable to all such like practices. Not only does he now have a kind of knowledge of the principle but he can and does apply it to further particular like circumstances. This is the practice of a practically knowledgeable man of prudence who lives in a society whose master practitioners have helped him become habituated to acting well.

The general hypothesis that virtue is a 'mean' must be shown to be applicable to particular facts, and in so far as actions are concerned with particular facts, then theories or general definitions, here of virtue as a settled disposition that observes the 'mean' relative to us, must be brought back into harmony with 'the facts' if they are to hold up as true. Aristotle thereafter shows how, in practice, one can draw a diagram to illustrate how people tend to evaluate conduct, that is, the expression of actions and emotions as reflected in social intercourse, by the words used to refer to excessive, to deficient and to virtuous behaviour – the 'mean', situated somewhere between but not always equidistant from relevant extremes.[70]

Aristotle closes his discussion of moral virtue as a disposition which aims at hitting the mean point (not the average point) in emotions and actions by remarking how difficult this is to achieve for each and every case. It is not only that circumstances are so varied, but that coming to know how to behave correctly, given what one has come to know about oneself and one's own foibles, makes the management of one's emotions and actions a complicated affair (even with correct habituation). It is a difficult business to be good, to function well and truly as a man, to live up to the definition of man. Aristotle explicitly tells us that to be angry with or give money to the right person, for the right amount and at the right time and for the right purpose and in the right way, is not within everyone's power and is not easy. To do these things properly is, in fact, rare, praiseworthy and noble. In order to do them consistently you must consciously *know* how to do these things properly; you do not do them out of sheer habit. And one of the things you must know in order to do these things properly is the errors or failings, that is, the excesses or deficiencies to which *you* are yourself most prone, because different men are inclined by nature to different faults. Aristotle thinks that we can discover our own faults by observing the pleasure or pain we experience and then drag ourselves in the opposite direction aiming for the middle course which would exemplify what a good man, by definition, would do in the circumstances. This will only become obvious to any particular individual as a consequence of the business of living; not by contemplating action but by choosing and acting. Aristotle is not, then, describing the class-determined Greek gentleman as has often been thought, so much as the non-neurotic man in something of an ideal Greek *polis* who knows not only his own temperamental failings but also, through his own experience of agency, the principle by which to judge morally fine behaviour. We should be aware that Aristotle is in favour of the character that displays even temper, bravery, modesty, temperance, fair-mindedness, justice, liberality,

---

70   For further discussion of particular moral virtues see NE III, vi–V.

truthfulness, friendliness, dignity, pride and magnificence. Not all of these moral virtues are what we, in Western European culture, influenced by Judaeo-Christian norms, have learnt to accept as admirable character traits, not least because of Christianity's 'fallen' model of man where pride, in particular, is considered a vice.[71]

Aristotle later discusses in book VII the four possible dispositions that one might encounter in Greek *poleis* even with admirable and correct habituating norms. This gives us not only an intrinsically interesting vantage-point from which to view what was admired, but it also provides us with a set of character vignettes that would be reinterpreted and transformed by later commentators in Roman, medieval and Renaissance times. He describes:

1   The man who displays the kind of excellence of character we have been discussing.
2   The man who displays strength of will, desiring to act improperly, but who makes himself act properly.
3   The man who displays weakness of will (*akrasia*), desiring to act improperly – in accord with his appetite for the immediately pleasant – who tries to make himself act properly because he knows what is good as a general principle, but who still fails to act in accord with what he knows because he cannot see how the immediate situation falls under the universal or general principle of what is right. (This is how Aristotle reinterprets and reconciles on the one hand, Socrates' insistence that when a man acts against his own interest, he does so in ignorance, and on the other, the common view that holds one *can* know what is best but still not do it).
4   The man who displays badness of character, who wants to act improperly, thinks it a good idea to do so, and does so without internal friction. The bad man deliberately chooses to follow his appetite. Like the profligate, he chooses to pursue excessive pleasures for their own sake and not for some ulterior consequences. He is certain to feel no regret for his excesses afterward and, this being so, he is considered incurable, since there is no cure for one who does not regret his error (NE VII, vii, 1150a16ff.). He does not feel regret because his vicious habits have destroyed the first principle or starting point in matters of conduct. Aristotle reminds us that neither in ethics nor in mathematics are the first principles imparted by a process of reasoning, but rather by virtue, whether natural or acquired by training in right opinion as to the first principles. The bad profligate man has lost all principle. His vices have perverted his mind, causing him to hold false views about the first principles of conduct, that is, about right and wrong.

Urmson has provided an apt modern illustration of these four character types:

There is the even-tempered man who has no difficulty in waiting coolly in a traffic jam; there is the hot-tempered man who can make himself act properly and he successfully restrains himself. There is the hot-tempered man who tries to remain calm but cannot; and finally there is the kind of character who curses and hoots at all and sundry with complete self-approval.[72]

---

71   Machiavelli, as we see in volume 2, chapter 6 of *A History of Political Thought*, had something to say about what Christianity in his own times had done to what he took to be the original Christian virtues which, he thought, were more in line with those described by the pagan Greeks and Romans.
72   Urmson, *Aristotle's Ethics*, pp. 31–2.

Only the first displays excellence of character, the mean, which is the dispositional state of the man who wants to act appropriately *and does so, effortlessly, without internal friction.* Excellence of character is, then, an intermediate disposition towards action and not a disposition to intermediate action. Men can only achieve this excellence of character through habituation to *good* practices and thereafter voluntarily choosing to act, knowingly, in conformity with principles that have emerged from good practices.

Aristotle warns us especially to guard against pleasure because we are not impartial judges when it comes to making our choices which necessarily involve pleasures. In so far as we can be impartial judges, we should try to be. It is easier to be impartial with regard to the behaviour of others. And we use as our standards of impartial, unimpassioned reason, the tested conclusions of the experienced and wise as framed in the law which has, from our earliest initiation into the family and community, habituated us to practices from which we have established our moral virtue, our settled disposition to do well.

Of course, the question that will have to be addressed is whether all laws, or social rules, succeed in habituating us to acting well *as humans* so that we can then function best as what we are, by nature, and so realize the good for man as a rational activity of our soul in accord with the best human excellence or virtue. The answer is, of course, no. Only the best laws, not only intended but actually achieved by the best legislators, result in the possibility of the good citizen coinciding with the good man. Others can secure good, that is, law-abiding citizens but not good men. This will be treated in the *Politics*, where Aristotle will maintain that most decent-enough societies (and they are such if they have endured) instruct in moral beliefs and habits, only some do so better than others. The consequence is that some people are enabled to live more humanly than others.

Voluntary Acts and Responsibility

How do legislators in societies like 'our own' actually determine to whom should go praise and, therefore, honours and to whom should go blame and, therefore, punishment? Aristotle tells us that legislators, concerned with moral virtues, that is the emotions and actions of citizens, praise or blame those emotions and actions that are considered *voluntary*, and those that are involuntary receive pardon and sometimes pity. Legislators need to know how to distinguish the voluntary from the involuntary in order to reward or punish. Book III gives us an extraordinary insight into the practices and evaluations of conduct in fourth-century BC Greek *poleis*.

Book III[73] provides an analysis of degrees of human responsibility, not only for the consequences of certain acts performed but for one's own disposition or character that led to the choices so to act. As agents, people are treated as the originating causes of their voluntary actions, be they fine or discreditable acts. In this kind of society there is no room for excuses that someone simply acted from his irrational feelings, temper or desire, that is, there are no special circumstances for what we might call *crimes de passion*; nor is there any distinction between premeditated acts of violence and sudden violent

---

73   Also part of book V, viii ff. and book VII.

acts due to emotion. Both are blameworthy.[74] Aristotle insists that the irrational feelings are considered by legislators and people in general to be no less a part of human nature than are our considered judgements. As humans we are responsible for both and therefore rewarded or punished accordingly.[75] If a man is thought to be in some sense responsible for his ignorance as an offender, he will be punished. Aristotle says that penalties are doubled for committing an offence in a state of drunkenness because the source of action is the agent and he was capable of not getting drunk. In choosing to get drunk, he caused his own ignorance of his subsequent acts and their consequences. When it is in our power not to be ignorant we are culpable.

This includes being punished for displaying ignorance of any point of law that ought to be known and is not difficult to ascertain. He does not mean that it is up to the citizen to go to the equivalent of the public library to find out what has been promulgated in positive law. He means that from the business of living a life and from having become habituated to practices from the doing of them, a man in his right mind will come to know the universal principles of right action, not simply from social norms but from perception, experience, induction and conclusions reached thereby. He will have taken the trouble to ascertain the 'facts'. Principles will necessarily emerge in him from the repeated doing of the act in specific circumstances and he will follow on by rationally deliberating on the practical alternatives in a present situation. Then, in choosing to act in one way or another, he will have chosen to express himself as a certain kind of character. In every sphere of conduct, Aristotle repeats, people develop qualities of character corresponding to the activities they pursue. Only an utterly senseless person can fail to know that our characters are the result of our conduct. It is unreasonable to suppose that a man who purposely acts unjustly or licentiously does not wish to be unjust or licentious. But we must note that this is distinct from someone considered totally bad and incurably vicious – the brutish character. Aristotle considers he is rare among human beings, although he says that sometimes we use the term 'bestial' as a term of opprobrium for a surpassing degree of human vice (NE VII, i, 1145a30). Bestiality, however, is considered less evil than vice because in a bestial man as in an animal, the highest part, intellect, is not corrupted as it is in a man who is wicked in a human way; instead, it is entirely lacking. Aristotle insists that a bad man can do ten thousand times more harm than an animal or a brutish man! (NE VII, vi, 1150a2–8).

He makes it clear that there is no room for the Socratic excuse of ignorance of the human good in the assessment of blame, because it is commonly held that a man *can know* what is right and still *not* do it; in so far as Aristotle accepts it to be true that no one willingly wishes to harm himself, one cannot say that a man does so out of ignorance of what is right. An unrestrained or incontinent man does not wish to be harmed, but Aristotle thinks that in his acting in a way he thinks he ought *not* to act, he voluntarily harms himself. One can explain how this may come about, what intellectual state such a

---

74   It appears that the following situations would be the subject of blame and therefore punishment: a woman who killed her violently abusive husband would be considered as having deliberately done wrong both in the case where she waited to kill him later and thought about how to do it, and where she killed him in the heat of the moment. 75   In *Politics* IV, 1300b13–1301a15 Aristotle discusses the types of court, of which there are four, that deal with homicide concerning deliberate killing, unintentional killing (manslaughter), offences with justifications, and homicides by those exiled with a view to their return. Also see Plato's *Laws* 865–7 on homicide as voluntary acts and those done without deliberation.

man is in, that is, that he voluntarily acts improperly because he does not see how his immediate desire to act improperly falls under the principle which he does know of what is right (and wrong). But this does not excuse him from blame.[76] If anyone acts in a way that will make him unjust, he will be voluntarily unjust. There can be no excuse of the sort that says 'he is probably the sort of person who does not take care'. People get into this condition, Aristotle says, through their own fault by having chosen to live careless lives, making themselves unjust, licentious and dissipated characters. *If* man is the originator of his actions, *then* the actions whose sources are in him are themselves in his power, that is voluntary, and therefore, it is these that are open to praise and blame, and to reward and punishment.

To us, this may seem harsh. But it does mean there is no philosopher who, through appropriate questioning, can elicit an unconsciously known truth in men. For Aristotle, it is not there before one has had perceptions and experiences and one has reasoned inductively to universal conclusions. It means that the truth will emerge for oneself only if one lives a life of practices and reflects on them oneself in the course of making further deliberate choices in particular circumstances. Does this include becoming habituated to practices in morally impoverished environments? Are *we* to blame even if our upbringing is defective?

Cultural rules, for Aristotle, are facilitating occasions, providing the normative parameters in which agents and practitioners have become habituated to acts and attendant emotions. But there is a point where cultural rules, as the contingent, varied and conventional contexts in which a person becomes experienced and learns to think about what he is doing, must be recognized as no more than better or worse opportunities. If and when the person is considered mature enough to be an agent within a given milieu, he must be considered capable of choosing to engage in practices. He cannot, and society will not allow him simply to blame bad upbringing for his having done wrong. Even within the most compulsive of situations or regimes, where events are not within a man's control – say, stormy weather carries his ship somewhere and he is forced to jettison his cargo, or a tyrant has him in his power and commands him to do a base act by threatening the lives of his parents or children – Aristotle tells us that it is *debatable* and *is* debated whether his compliance is voluntary or involuntary. After all, one still prioritizes and makes choices even in dreadful situations. And the terms 'voluntary' and 'involuntary' are used with reference to particular times and circumstances in which an action was performed.

This means that even if you have been brought up in a miserable, morally impoverished environment, Aristotle thinks it is still *possible*, despite one's bad training, to recognize the 'facts' and retrain yourself to better ways. *But with great difficulty*. It does make a difference, that is, it *is* easier for us to become good if our early opportunities are of the better sort and we receive the right sort of training (NE 1179b23). But as agents, responsible for our acts in the last resort, culture is not everything. A legislator, however, who studies politics as a science, must think it is at least the necessary (if not sufficient)

---

76 Aristotle distinguishes (V, ix,1136b5–9 etc.) between voluntarily harming oneself and suffering injustice voluntarily. One who gives away what is his own cannot be said to suffer injustice: giving depends on oneself, suffering injustice does not; it depends on another person acting unjustly against the other person's wish. Not even the incontinent man is voluntarily treated unjustly. Aristotle later confirms that it is not possible to treat oneself unjustly although one can voluntarily harm oneself.

condition to provide those laws which enshrine cultural practices which *will* enable men not only to become responsible agents but actually achieve their good. Aristotle says *we* must by some means secure that the character shall have at the outset a natural affinity for virtue, loving what is noble and hating what is base. No one, of course, has these affinities from birth because one has no character at birth. And it is difficult – but not impossible – to obtain a right education in virtue from youth up without being brought up under the right laws.[77] For this reason Aristotle believes that the nurture and exercise of the young should be regulated by law, since temperance and hardiness will not be painful when they have become habitual. But he does not think it is sufficient for people to receive the right nurture and discipline in youth. They must also practise the lessons they have learnt and confirm them by habit when they are grown up (and considered responsible agents) (NE X, ix, 1179b30–1180a6). Therefore, Aristotle concludes that in order to be good, a man must have been properly educated and trained, and must subsequently, on his own initiative, continue to follow virtuous habits of life and to do nothing base whether voluntarily or involuntarily. Mature initiatives are themselves to be guided by good laws backed by sufficient coercive sanction. He says that a man's continuing to follow virtuous habits in maturity will be secured if men's lives are regulated by a certain intelligence (their own) and by a right system (their society's), invested with adequate sanctions (of the law that has compulsory force) (1180a14–19). We shall see that Aristotle reinforces this view in *Politics* I, 1253a30–4 where he says that man is the best of the animals when perfected by, and the worst when divorced from, law and justice. That is why societies praise and blame, reward and punish and legislators need to know when to do so, how and why.

Aristotle tells us that sometimes an action is performed which is wrong, but none the less it will be condoned because the man acted out of fear of penalties that are too much for human nature and which no one could endure. Similarly, a man may act in a particular way due to an ignorance of certain details of a situation which he could not reasonably be presumed to know, and therefore the consequences of his act could not be foreseen. He is not ignorant of the universal principle of right and wrong but of the details of the circumstances or objects of his acts. His particular action is wrong and blameworthy but this does not necessarily mean that his character is wicked or will be judged so (see NE V, viii, 20ff.). His act will be judged involuntary if, the bad consequences becoming known to him, he feels distress for having done it. He will be pitied or pardoned as an involuntary agent. But there seem to be some acts which a man cannot be compelled to do, that he must sooner die than do, though he suffer the most dreadful death. In the *Politics* Aristotle will describe the values of the *polis* where men refuse to be taken captive in a war fought to defend their own community. For such citizens, a human life is not worth living at all costs and certainly not in the conditions of slavery. The larger principle here is that merely surviving, without freedom, is not what makes humans and their lives, human and choice-worthy.

Choice

When we make ethical assessments having to do with judging men's characters and the overall goodness of their lives, Aristotle believes that we only do so appropriately of

---

77   Compare the chance emergence of a philosopher in Plato's *Republic*, above.

adults who already have formed characters and have chosen a way of living. As adults, we are capable of making choices in the sense of having deliberated about how our own acts fit into our view of our ultimate ends or values. What, then, is the nature of deliberate or rational choice (*prohairesis*) (NE III, ii)? Aristotle provides an analysis of how ancient Greeks used the word.

He tells us that (rational) choice is felt to be closely related to moral virtue and a man's choices are considered a better test of his character than are his particular actions. Choice is the determinant of the limits of human responsibility, an attitude to which reveals the reasons for praise and blame, reward and punishment in *poleis* like 'our' own. Choice is a species of the genus voluntary act, that is, what is chosen is voluntary but not everything that is voluntary is chosen. According to Aristotle, children and animals share in voluntary actions but not in choice. Their sudden actions can be called voluntary but they cannot be said to be done by choice. Choice is not a possibility for irrational creatures, either animals who remain irrational and children who as yet have not learned how to think rationally. Furthermore, choice is not concerned with pleasure or pain (as is appetitive desire). We are being made aware of what appears to be the 'common view' that an educational process begins in the family with children, who are not manipulated only behaviourally by physical punishment and reward. Children are viewed as already capable of responding selectively to their world in species-specific ways: by cognition and desire. They are like animals but are more than animals. They act voluntarily and are responsive to the kind of rule-bound, external and therefore rational parental 'persuasion' which is listened to by their irrational psyches, such admonition attempting to 'persuade' them to modify their views on what is good. But they are not seen as yet capable of choosing whether or not to follow the advice because they have not collected enough experiences to have arrived for themselves at a general knowledge of the principles of right and wrong. They are still at a stage of development where their appetites can be amenable to reason but that reason is not yet their own.[78] They have not yet established a conscious continuity in their behaviour to make them responsible single selves.

Choice concerns the practical means to an end which is already conceived as good or bad (not true or false). It is our choice of good or bad that determines our characters, not our opinion about good or bad. Aristotle distinguishes opinions as true or false, whereas choices are good or bad. Choice concerns possibilities, not impossible wishes; whereas we can have opinions about what is impossible as well as possible for us, choice only concerns what one can bring about oneself by one's own acts. The same people are not equally good at choosing best actions and forming best opinions. The latter may be intellectually clever but they display a moral defect and fail to make the right choices, while the former are morally virtuous and Aristotle has already made it clear that one needs to be morally virtuous, to have a settled character disposition, in order consistently to choose those actions that one can perform as the best means to an already known end. Humans wish for ends but they deliberately choose means to their end. Humans do not choose to be *eudaimon*, they wish to be. They choose acts that lie in their power, that is, they choose *means* to living and faring well as their human end.

Choice, then, is a voluntary action preceded by deliberation since it *involves* reasoning and some process of thought. One's moral virtue as a settled disposition ensures the

---

78   Note the parallel with Plato, who treats every adult in this way except the philosopher.

rightness of one's choice of the end aimed at, whereas deliberative excellence concerns calculating what is expedient as a means to that end, enabling an already morally virtuous man to arrive at the right conclusion on the right grounds and at the right time. For Aristotle, character formation is prior to knowledge. Hence, the true and supreme good for man appears only to the good man of moral virtue. His virtuous disposition is regulated by a specific mode of thinking, prudence (*phronēsis*). *Phronēsis* is that mode of thinking where a man of experience deliberates about the good and advantageous in each situation, not only for himself but for men in general. His deliberation concentrates on those calculations concerning a variety of variable, non-necessary, particular acts he and other humans can do themselves in relation to things that are good for humans.

This means that people do not, because they cannot, deliberate about everything. They do not deliberate about things eternal, such as the order of the universe, nor about things that change but follow a regular process whether from necessity or by nature or some other cause. None of these results can be effected by our agency. We only deliberate about practical measures that lie in our power, not about Nature, Necessity or Chance. Each particular set of men, be they Spartans or Scythians, deliberates respectively about the things attainable by their own actions. Spartans do not deliberate about the best form of government for Scythia but about the best form of government for Sparta. We deliberate about things in which our own agency has effects but which are not always produced in the same way. Therefore, we deliberate about those matters where what happens does so for the most part (not necessarily) and where the result is uncertain and the right course not clearly defined. We deliberate about what we ourselves can do among various ways of doing it. We deliberate about possible alternatives. We deliberate prior to forming opinions as affirmations concerning probable conclusions. Again, we deliberate not about ends, but about means. A doctor, for instance, by definition, does not deliberate whether to cure a patient but about the means so to do. A statesman, by definition, does not deliberate whether to produce good government, that is, law and order, but about the means to this end. Aristotle describes them as first setting some end before them; as an end it is an object of rational wish, and they proceed to consider how and by what means it can be achieved. If they then encounter an impossibility in the various proposed means – say, if money is needed and cannot be provided – they give up trying to secure the means but not the goal. If, however, the means to their end appears possible by their agency they set about doing it.

This description of the way statesmen proceed will have important consequences for our understanding of the *Politics* and indeed of what Aristotle takes political agency to mean. We shall see that politics is about setting rational goals that are judged to be truly beneficial to the community as a whole and then discussing the ways and means of their achievement. On this view, a politician does not start with a budget and then decide what he will spend it on. Only in states that are dominated by factional interest and therefore have deviant, that is corrupt constitutions, does Aristotle acknowledge that this can and does happen, but it is notable that the common good is not served. If a decent general education is a collective good, a rational wish, and Aristotle has made clear that it is fundamental to all legislators' intentions, then a political office holder's job is to find the ways and means of realizing this collective good. The statesman, by definition, is not an accountant. The modern world has moved rather far away from this understanding of politics by collapsing it into the economic realm and divorcing political means from a specified common good. As we shall see in the *Politics* Aristotle will acknowledge the economic view but classify it as a pre-political perspective. Here he says that when we speak about possibilities achieved through our own agency we include things we do through the agency of our friends – other citizens – because this counts in a sense as done by ourselves since the origin of their action is in us. What a *polis* collectively achieves is the consequence of the responsible agency of each of its citizens.

In deliberating, a man stops enquiring how he shall act as soon as he has traced the origin of action to himself and to the dominant part of himself, reason, for it is this part that chooses, in the sense that a course of action is chosen as a consequence of deliberating on alternative means or courses of action to a defined end. Since the object of choice is something within our power which, after deliberation, we then desire, Aristotle concludes that *choice will be a deliberate desire to act in one way or another that is in our power* (NE 1113a9ff.). First we deliberate, then select, and finally fix our desire according to the result of our rational deliberation. Choice, then, includes both the desire for an end and practical reasoning about how to achieve it. Children do not deliberate and make choices because their practical reason is not yet actualized through sufficient experiences and practices. Not only do they not yet have the realized intellectual capacity to plan their lives; they are unable to deliberate and plan wisely because they are not, as yet, morally virtuous, that is, they have not yet developed stable dispositions through sufficient habituated practices. They are not yet prudent. Aristotle makes clear that prudence (*phronēsis*) is not limited to an excellence in deliberation about specific means to some desired end. Rather, prudence requires a more complex capacity to sum up a situation and judge it critically and know what is right in *this* situation and *do* it. This comes only from experience and maturity of character (NE 1143b11–14).

Let us recapitulate: the end is an object of wish, and what is rationally wished for in a true and unqualified sense is the good for man, *eudaimonia*. But the means to it are objects of deliberation and choice, so that the actions dealing with the means are done by choice and will be voluntary. The good man, by definition, wishes for what is truly wished for, judging everything correctly; the bad man for anything as it may happen (NE 1113a23–31). The good man already has a conception of the good for man as a form of activity over a whole lifetime. That activity consists in the exercise of his faculties in conformity with moral virtue. This requires a stable disposition to act virtuously and the stable disposition proceeds out of habituated practices and is confirmed by deliberate choices to act well in every situation. The activities in which the moral virtues are exercised, then, deal with means to our end. Therefore, virtue as well as vice, that is our character dispositions or states of mind regarding actions and appropriate emotions, lie in our power. *Where* we are free to act we are also free to refrain from acting. If it is in our power, and therefore, we are responsible, to do a thing when to do it is right, we are also responsible for not doing it when not doing it is wrong. It is in our power to do and to refrain from doing right and wrong and if, as we saw, doing right or wrong is the essence as expressed by the definition of being a good or bad man, then it is in our power to be decent or worthless, virtuous or vicious in so far as this is determined by our deliberate choices of means to our (unchosen) human good or end. *If* it is manifest that a man is the author of his own actions and we are unable to trace our conduct back to any other sources than those within ourselves, *then* the actions whose sources are in us, that is, our deliberate choices to act in ways that serve as means to our human end, are themselves in our power and are voluntary.

Aristotle says that this conclusion is supported by men's behaviour in private life and by the practice of legislators themselves. They impose punishments and penalties on malefactors (except where an offence is committed under the kind of compulsion or ignorance for which the agent cannot be considered responsible). And they bestow honours on those who do fine actions, encouraging the latter and restraining the former (NE 1113b22). No one tries to encourage us to do things not in our power; no one can persuade us not to feel heat, pain, hunger, because we still feel them all the same. Punishment and honours proceeding from blame and praise, 'persuade' only those aspects of ourselves which can be changed by habituation and it is these aspects – our moral virtue as a quality in an agent, our character disposition, and our acts reflecting that disposition – which develop through habitual practices. These are guided by good coercive laws and our stable dispositions are then capable of reinforcement by encouraging or restraining persuasion.

How easy is it to stop being the kind of person you have voluntarily become? Aristotle says it is extremely difficult. You cannot merely wish not to be, say, unjust, any more than a sick man can get well by wishing, even if his illness is voluntary in the sense of being the result of his having chosen to live intemperately. While *in the beginning* he may have avoided getting ill, once he has let himself go he can do so no longer. But Aristotle insists that he was responsible for having chosen a way of living that led to his illness. The unjust and profligate might at the outset have avoided becoming so, and therefore they are what they are now, voluntarily – recall that no one is born with character but develops one through practice, habituation and choice. Aristotle insists that when they have become unjust and profligate as settled character dispositions it is no longer open to them not to be so. An agent is responsible as the origin of actions is in himself. When, however, is one considered an agent?

We are discussing why and when societies blame or praise people and Aristotle emphasizes that, as with physical defects, so too with moral defects of character, blame is apportioned to those defects for which humans may be held responsible as the origin of their own actions. You are pitied if you have been born blind but if you have become blind through alcoholism you are blamed. The hypothesis is that each man is *in a sense* responsible for his moral disposition and therefore he will *in a sense* be responsible for his conception of the good (NE 1114b2–5). In what sense? Some might say a man needs to be born with moral vision, a good natural disposition as a gift, bestowed on him at birth. But then, Aristotle asks, how can virtue be considered voluntary any more than vice? Both the good man and the bad will have their view of their end determined by nature. But Aristotle rejects this determinism: he says that both the bad and the good man equally possess spontaneity in their actions even if not in their choice of end. Neither can choose not to be members of the human species with the end or good that is specific to man, but each can choose the quality of the actions they perform as means to that end.

Praise and blame, reward and punishment, focus on the particular, voluntary and responsible agent (where he is so regarded) within a culture of practices. A culture's laws are not critically evaluative of the culture itself but of those practitioners who live within its bounds. The virtues as dispositions render us apt to do the same actions (in the present and future) as those by which they are acquired (through practices and habituation); they depend on ourselves, are voluntary and we do them (now) in a way that accords with the right principle. But Aristotle reminds us that we can control our *actions*, because we are their source, from beginning to end. Our *dispositions*, however, are not voluntary and totally dependent on us *in the same way* as are our actions. We have not chosen to have been born into a particular society of practices but have found ourselves there. We control only the *beginning of our settled states or character dispositions,* but each separate addition to such settled states, each addition being the consequence of our deliberate choices, is imperceptible (as is the case with the growth of a disease). At what point in our lives can humans be said to reach that stage where they take control of the beginning of their settled character dispositions? Aristotle believes this comes about after childhood, that is, when they have gone beyond childhood's unreflective, voluntary but not chosen practices and have had sufficient experiences of the business of living life as mature men. Responsibility begins when they are free agents in the relevant sphere of action, building on the practices to which, as children, they have become habituated and now, with experience and induction to universal principles of moral conduct, they have become cognitively aware of why they choose to act as they do. It is these mature and cognitive deliberations to choose to exercise our human capacities in one way or another that determine that we are voluntary agents of a certain kind and open to praise or blame. Children, for Aristotle, are not praised or blamed by society. They are not given honours, nor are they subject to legal penalties. They are not rational agents. Children who commit murder would not be brought to trial in the society Aristotle describes.

It seems clear that on Aristotle's view, if a person has grown to maturity in a society which has not provided the opportunities to engage in practices that lead to practical knowledge, he will not have developed a character for which he can be assessed as worthy of praise or blame and therefore as a truly responsible agent. Such societies treat their citizens as children or youths, as mere subjects or slaves, coercing them irrationally rather than persuading and encouraging them according to a rational principle to behave in one way or another. Such coercion is applied not for the development of citizens as moral agents, but simply in order to maintain, unsuccessfully as it turns out (*Politics* V), a kind of imposed stability. We shall encounter such types of society as extremes in the *Politics.* But in the *Ethics,* Aristotle is speaking to 'us' who come from *poleis* like his own and which, more or less, share ways of talking and behaving and, perhaps most notably, consider citizens to be free, responsible agents. Not all societies are like 'ours'.

Justice as a Moral Virtue or Character Disposition: Justice in its Universal Sense

Aristotle's discussion of justice both as a character disposition and as a particular action illuminates his way of treating many of the same issues encountered in book I of Plato's *Republic.* When people speak of justice in a generic or universal sense, Aristotle says they mean that moral disposition or state of character that not only *disposes* someone to perform just acts but ensures that he *acts* justly, and that he also *wishes* for what is just. In its widest meaning, justice is righteousness in general and covers all right conduct in relation to others. The previous discussion of moral virtue in general, what it is and how it is acquired, was, in effect, an examination of this general righteousness of behaviour from the point of view of the agent, and now (in book V) his moral virtue may be considered in terms of its consequences for other people. When it is so considered, people call this moral virtue 'justice'.

But Aristotle is aware that the words 'justice' and 'injustice' are also used in a wide variety of senses. For instance, he tells us that 'we' call the law-breaker unjust, the law-abiding man just. Therefore, all lawful things are just in one sense of the word, for what is lawful is decided by legislators (in whatever kind of constitution) and their decisions are called rules of justice (for that particular polity). The law prescribes for all departments of life and all the various pronouncements of the law, by definition, aim at the common interest, either of all the citizens, or of the best of them, or of the ruling class, or in some other similar way depending on the polity and its criterion of who constitutes the political community. So that in one of its senses the term 'just' is applied to anything that aims at producing and preserving the *eudaimonia*, or the component parts of *eudaimonia*, of the political community.

The law taken to mean 'general rules of justice' always prescribes certain conduct; that is, it takes a view on men's actions and attendant emotions which exemplify the various particular virtues and vices, commanding the former and forbidding the latter. Legislators, by definition as men in possession of the knowledge of the principles of right and wrong, are themselves best able to establish laws that rightly command the former and forbid the latter, *if* they enact the law rightly. But if they establish the law at random or if they enact an inappropriate rule, the law will command and prohibit not so well (NE 1129b13–25). Aristotle thinks that the aim of legislators is to work with men's nature and not against it. The laws or regulations are meant to be productive of virtue in general among citizens. Some are more successful than others in *achieving* this aim. In seriously morally impoverished societies, the prescribed norms of behaviour, despite their intentions, will actually serve to encourage men to develop those habitual practices that are so irrational and destructive that their capacity to come to a knowledge of the right principles of conduct will be corrupted. But by definition the laws do not intend this; they mean to produce virtue in citizens. In this sense, 'justice' as behaviour towards others in conformity with the general rules of *correct* behaviour as enshrined in law is considered a complete virtue, not unqualified (as a Platonic form) but always as actively exercised in relation to someone else. Justice in this sense, Aristotle says, is perfect virtue because it is the practice of perfect virtue.

This justice is thought to be the only moral virtue that is regarded as someone else's good, securing the advantage for another person.[79] Aristotle believes it is best exemplified in the practices of someone in public office because his actions are always performed and judged in relation to someone else in the community. Justice in this universal sense is not a part of virtue but the whole of it. Its opposite, injustice, is the whole of vice. Both reflect the qualities of character of the performing agents. Justice in its universal sense is coextensive with virtue in general, being the practice of virtue in general towards someone else (NE 1130b18).

Particular Justice

Since everyone more or less understands universal justice as a complete virtue, Aristotle wishes to discuss those situations where justice may be considered a part of virtue, that is particular justice (and injustice) (NE V, ii, 1130a14ff.). To discuss particular justice is not to discuss character but, rather, to discuss individual actions where people get their fair share. He says that there are more kinds of justice than one and the term has another

79   See *Republic* I: Thrasymachus.

meaning besides virtue as a whole (NE 1130b6–9). If, broadly speaking, most of the acts laid down by law are enjoined from the point of view of virtue as a whole, directing citizens to live in accord with every virtue and refrain from every vice, then the law acts as a general normative framework. But in the complexities of life, particular decisions must be taken which are more specific regarding circumstances and persons and those citizens who hold public offices must make these kinds of decisions in the field of particular justice. They will be faced with particular justice, divided into two kinds: distributive, and corrective or rectificatory.

Distributive justice is exercised in the distribution of honours, wealth and other divisible assets of a community which may be allotted among its members in equal or unequal shares. Corrective justice, on the other hand, rectifies the conditions in private transactions. Because some private transactions are voluntary and others involuntary, corrective justice itself has two parts. Examples of voluntary transactions are selling, buying, lending at interest, pledging, lending without interest, depositing, letting for hire. All of these are voluntarily entered into by both sides. Examples of involuntary transactions are those that are *secret*, for instance, theft, adultery, poisoning, procuring, enticement of slaves, killing by stealth and false testifying; or *violent*, for instance, assault, forcible confinement, murder, robbery, maiming, defamation and public insult. Aristotle observes that in distributive as with other kinds of particular justice one who is charged with taking a decision in the matter is looking for a kind of mean in his decisions. But the mean is achieved differently when one is engaged with matters of just distribution from the way the mean is achieved in matters of just rectification. Both kinds of particular justice depend on establishing proportions.

Distributive Justice as a Kind of Particular Justice

Where a just distribution of, say, honours is to be made, Aristotle describes a situation in which there are two persons and two shares in the assets which will exhibit the just distribution. A ratio between the shares will be established which is equal to the ratio between the persons. The distribution of the shares is based on an evaluation of the proportional desert of each person. In distributive justice one looks to the equality or lack of equality between the persons under consideration. If the persons are not equal they will not receive equal shares but proportional ones. But equal regarding what? Here is what distinguishes one kind of constitution from another. While all agree that justice in the distribution of social assets like honour and wealth must be based on desert, they do not all mean the same sort of desert. Democrats, for instance, make free birth the criterion on which desert is determined – everyone of free birth is equal and gets equal shares of social assets, for instance, honour and wealth; those of oligarchic sympathies make their criterion wealth (or sometimes birth), so according to them the wealthiest person receives proportionately more of the social assets than the proportionately less wealthy; aristocrats take virtue to be the criterion, so that honours go only to the men of proven excellence of character and action. This means that particular justice of the distributive kind is always determined as a *geometric proportion*, the proportion being the equality of ratios of shares to ratios of persons. We are talking about how different communities acknowledge social worth and reward accordingly through distributing social assets. Desert is determined by the political system in force and its values. In every case of distributive justice, what is just for each person is proportional and lies in the mean between extremes where each recipient receives proportionate shares which are neither too large nor too small for him. But this depends on what the community in question takes as its criterion of equality between persons.

As we have come to expect, Aristotle will examine further (in the *Politics*) the respective criteria of various constitutions and come to the most probable conclusion as to which gets it right. If you have read the *Nicomachean Ethics* you already know his answer: the correct criterion by which one judges social worthiness is the display of moral virtue. A society that rewards men in proportion to their virtuous contribution to the community is one in which a larger number of men is encouraged to pursue their natures and live well as humans. But this means that prior to the rewards it dispenses to men of virtuous character and actions, it must have enacted laws that have enabled men to become habitually virtuous and to engage in practices that lead to practical knowledge and responsible agency.

Corrective Justice

Rectificatory or corrective justice is a different sort of particular justice from the distributive kind. Rectificatory justice is concerned with private transactions of the voluntary and involuntary sorts and is determined as an *arithmetical proportion*. The characters of the individuals concerned and their respective merits are *not* considered. This is because in such situations it makes no difference whether a good man has defrauded a bad man or a bad man has defrauded a good man. The law (concerned with rectification) looks only at the nature of the damage. The parties are treated as equals and the law only asks whether one has done and the other suffered an injustice. The judge tries to equalize the situation between the parties by imposing penalty or loss on the damagee and recompense for the victim or sufferer of damage. Rectificatory justice tries to rebalance loss and gain or restore fair shares where some unfairness has occurred. We note that the victim is awarded damages but the perpetrator is *not* criminalized. Furthermore, no question is asked about whether the original positions of either party are justified. These are taken for granted by the judge engaged in this kind of rectification; the parties are already living in a society and have what they have, entering transactions on this basis. Justice in rectification will be an equalization, an attempt to return to some original position by legal means, and therefore the judge in such cases of damage will seek the mean between loss and gain. Aristotle says that this is why when disputes occur men have recourse to a judge – that is, recourse to justice – and an ideal judge is justice personified. He serves as a middle term, a mediator who is meant to decide the mean between gain and loss and thereby restore equality. He is impartial regarding the personalities or social standing of the parties. Hence, the equal here is a mean by way of *arithmetical proportion* between the greater and the less, as when a whole line is divided into two unequal parts and one takes from the greater segment that portion by which it exceeds the lesser segment.

Aristotle asks us not to equate either distributive or rectificatory justice with what some (Pythagoreans) call reciprocity, by which they mean that justice is simply suffering reciprocally with another, that is, retaliation or an eye for an eye. This is pre-political behaviour for Aristotle. In Aristotle's *polis* if an officer of the 'state' strikes a man it is wrong (an injustice) for the man to strike him back. And if a man strikes a *polis* official it is not enough for the officer to strike him back for justice to be achieved. The man must be punished (by the *polis*) as well (NE 1132b28–31). This is not a statement about how some men, as men, are more valued than others, but a statement about how those who serve a community in an official capacity assume a kind of public status over and above their being simply men. The political realm is privileged and Aristotle will have much more to say about this in the *Politics*. Aristotle says that reciprocity in the interchange of services in a *polis* is based on proportion, not equality, and this kind of reciprocity is the bond that maintains the community. The very existence of the *polis* depends on proportionate reciprocity and within this political community, where men are not merely men in households, bound by kinship ties and concerned with mutual survival, but are instead part of a collectivity that is different in kind from the household, they are citizens with proportionate public responsibilities. Hence, they demand a system of proportionate reciprocal exchanges of benefices, requiting evil with evil, good with good. Otherwise, they feel they are nothing more than slaves.

To live in a *polis* of which one is a member is to live according to laws that encourage or restrain certain kinds of morally evaluated public behaviour in the service of a communal human good. Aristotle remarks in *Politics* I that the political association and the role of a statesman in it is not the same as that of a household manager or a master of slaves. There is a *qualitative* difference between even a large household and a small state and the difference between them is not determined by numbers of inhabitants. The difference is determined by the good at which each type of human association aims. The good at which a political association aims is specific to it as a *polis* and the *polis* is not simply a household writ large. Public responsibilities, public rule, is concerned with securing the *good life* of its members through laws that habituate citizens to virtuous practices *over and above* securing life itself, which is the primary aim of households (*Politics* I, ii, 1252b27ff.). In the sphere of public rule the proportionate reciprocal exchanges of benefices take place between citizens and, he says, this is the reason we set up a shrine of the Graces in a public place: it reminds men to return a kindness which is a special characteristic of grace, since it is a duty not only to repay a service done but another time to take the initiative in doing a service oneself.[80] In the political sphere where mature men are engaged in the business of living life, they exercise their moral virtue in relation to others, most notably when they take on public office and serve the community. They serve by engaging in the system of justice which is constituted as a proportionate, reciprocal exchange of benefices. They make public judgements of the distributive and rectificatory kinds in order to achieve proportionate requital or a rebalancing and restoration of equality.

This proportionate requital or rebalancing and restoration of equality operates not only in the domain of political exchange of services but also in the economic exchange of different commodities. According to Aristotle, proportion runs all the way down in human relations. His terse discussion of money and the reciprocal exchange of goods has generated an enormous literature. He argues that in order to meet the requirement that different commodities be compared in some stable way, money was introduced as a measure of superior or inferior value. Money has been introduced as the conventional standard that enables exchange and association, determining, for instance, how many

---

80   See Cicero, *On Duties*, below, chapter 5.

shoes are equivalent to a house or a given quantity of food. The reciprocal proportion between these exchangeable goods or products is based on demand, and demand has come to be conventionally represented by money. When people exchange their products they reduce them to the form of a proportion. Money serves as a measure which makes things commensurable and so reduces them to equality. Indeed, if there were no exchange Aristotle says that there would be no association, and hence there must be an accepted and agreed standard (here money) which makes all things commensurable. For our purposes, his emphasis on the need for agreed standards to establish commensurability is what is important.[81]

Political Justice

Justice in principle and regarded universally, then, is that quality in virtue of which a man is said to be disposed to do by deliberate choice that which is just and, when distributing things between himself and another or between two others, not to give too much to himself and too little to his neighbour of what is desirable, and too little to himself and too much to his neighbour of what is harmful, but to each what is proportionately equal. Similarly, when he is distributing between two other persons. He uses a geometric proportion to establish the mean, that is, the just deserts owed to each of two men in terms of allotting public assets, and he uses an arithmetic proportion to rectify cases of damage and loss between two parties in a private transaction. These are practices which comprise what Aristotle means by political justice (NE 1134a25ff.).

When 'we' speak of political justice 'we' mean justice as between free and actually or proportionately equal persons living a common life for the purpose of satisfying their needs. Between people not free and (proportionately) equal, Aristotle says that *political* justice cannot exist. 'We' *do* speak of a kind of justice between master and slave, between father and child, between husband and wife, but this is not identical with absolute or political justice – it is a kind of justice that is *analogous* to political justice. This means that *political justice* does not cover household relations; it means that a father cannot be considered in an unqualified or absolute sense unjust to his child or wife. Political justice is defined by law and it only applies to members of law-governed communities who share, as citizens, in ruling and being ruled. Women, children and slaves are not, in *poleis* like 'ours', sharers in public ruling and being ruled. They are not citizens. But this does not mean that there are no considerations of justice in the domestic association. Aristotle is not speaking of a private sphere where public moral rules have no influence and where each *paterfamilias* simply exercises his untrammelled will. Domestic justice is understood to be analogous to political justice precisely because Aristotle believes that men's concept of justice, their morally virtuous behaviour towards others, derives from men's *polis*-living experiences and practices. These will necessarily affect their conception of justice in familial relations. Those societies which do not enable men to develop their practical reasoning and their exercise of morally responsible behaviour will create analogous scenarios in their households. As he says in *Politics* I, barbarians tend to treat their wives as slaves, a reflection of the way their society treats them. He says that by defini-

81   See, further, A. N. Shulsky, 'The "Infrastructure" of Aristotle's *Politics*: Aristotle on economics and politics', in Lord and O'Connor, *Essays*, pp. 74–111.

tion *political justice* can exist only between those whose mutual relations are regulated by law and the law exists among those between whom there is a possibility of injustice; this is the case only when citizens are regarded by the law as responsible agents.

He tells us that responsible agents are engaged in *administering* the law when they take on certain public offices. The administration of the laws means the discrimination of what is just and what is unjust in situations where a just distribution of social assets is required or where a rebalancing and restoration of equality is required through rectification. Persons between whom injustice can exist can act unjustly towards each other, assigning themselves too large a share of things good and too small a share of things evil. This is why Aristotle says 'we' do not permit a man to rule but the law. It is too easy for a man to rule in his own interest and become a tyrant. Hence, the function of a statesman or ruler is to be the guardian of justice, the guardian of the laws, and therefore of (proportionate) equality. Knowing the principles of right (and wrong) and the rules or laws which encourage moral virtue and restrain moral vice, such a man makes nothing out of his office. He does not allot to himself a larger share of things good unless it be proportionate to his merits, a judgement which is not a matter of subjective and private evaluation. He therefore labours for others and this is why Aristotle says 'we' say justice is the good of others. His recompense is precisely what is decided in distributive justice: honour and dignity. It is those whom such rewards do not satisfy who make themselves tyrants (NE 1134b35). For those whose relations are regulated by law, that is, persons who share equally (but not simultaneously) in ruling and being ruled – and these are the citizens of a *polis* – however each type of constitution respectively deploys its criterion concerning who is to be a citizen and therefore their proportionality, political justice applies.

Aristotle notes (NE V, vii) that in our world, as opposed to that of the gods where justice presumably never changes, everything is subject to change. However, he does think we can speak of such a thing as natural justice or natural law that applies to a world of changing contingents. In our world, to which political justice applies, there are some things that admit of being otherwise; they change, and they do so by nature; then, there are other things that are changeable but by legal convention. There are also those rules of justice or laws that are established by a kind of universally accepted convention based on expediency and we can see their utility as conventionally established standard measures, similar to the establishment of money. Now while it is true that the rules of justice, the laws, ordained not by nature but by man are not the same in all places since forms of government are not the same everywhere, *yet in all places there is only one form of government that is natural and this is the best form.* This form of government operates according to what we can call natural political justice because we have seen that there is a universal principle of what is right and it is not culturally relative. The morally virtuous man is not merely a social construction, although he is enabled to become morally virtuous by correct cultural rules which habituate him to good practices. Those rules of justice, established by men of moral virtue who know what constitutes human behaviour in conformity to right principle, constitute the system of political justice, the laws. These best conform to human nature in *poleis*. Aristotle's approach is to insist that legislators work with human nature, not against it, and by definition they intend to endue citizens with the moral virtues that enable men to become responsible, choice-making agents and achieve their human end. Of course, it is true that in so far as there are different constitutional forms of government and hence different systems of political justice, the different systems of justice will praise or blame actions in conformity with their own laws. But as was noted previously, there is a difference between being a good citizen and being a good man. Only in the best constitution, that which has the most psychological insight into what constitutes and fosters human excellence, will the laws be such that the good citizen will also be a good man, and it is these laws we can call natural political justice, operating in a world of changing contingents.

Contemplation or Theoretical Science

Recall that Aristotle differentiated the sciences in terms of the activities performed by each mode of thought, calling them respectively the productive, the practical and the theoretical sciences. Each science is a cognitive quality of persons engaged in different modes of thinking. We have discussed the productive mode (e.g. logic) and the practical mode (e.g. political science or prudence (*phronēsis*)). Does the theoretical mode of thinking, theoretical science, play a role in human flourishing? What is the place in an ethical life of what is normally translated in English as 'contemplation' (*theoria*), an intellectual activity of pure thinking in and for itself which does not motivate to action? Aristotle had already noted that, broadly speaking, there are thought to be three types of life, the life of pleasure or enjoyment preferred by the mass of men, the political life of men of affairs, and lastly, the life of the *theoretikos*, the life of contemplation. In book 10 of the *Nicomachean Ethics* he at last treats the nature of a life of theoretical activity and his discussion has caused a great deal of confusion, not least because he asserts that the life of moral virtue is a secondary way of flourishing, whereas the contemplative life is perfect *eudaimonia* for man. If the purpose of his whole enquiry in the *Ethics* was to determine how a choice-worthy life could be lived by men, then it has appeared to many that Aristotle changed his mind to argue that moral agency and political engagement were lesser components of a successful, *eudaimon* life than had previously been thought.

In order to clarify what Aristotle means by *theoria* we need to look briefly at some very condensed analyses in book 6 of the *Ethics*, where he shifts his attention from the moral virtues to the intellectual virtues. The psyche, we recall, is thought to be divided in two, an irrational and a rational 'part'. The moral virtues were developed as a consequence of the irrational 'part' taking notice of, or being directed by, a kind of practical reasoning of the 'rational' part. The aim of the moral virtues is the good (good conduct), whereas the aim of the intellectual virtues is the truth.

In book 6 Aristotle assumes that the rational part of the psyche itself consists of two parts or faculties, one with which we 'contemplate' or (more literally) mentally observe those things whose first principles are invariable, and another with which we contemplate or mentally observe things that are variable. The assumption is dialectical; Aristotle is not giving us a psycho-biology. But cultural habituation of one sort or another plays no fundamental role here. Humans simply think in these ways and they learn how to do so by having experiences and cognitively responding to them. (The *De Anima* treats this more fully.) He says that the two parts of the rational psyche are *naturally* adapted to the cognition of their respective and different objects. The part with which we contemplate things whose first principles are invariable and necessary we call the scientific (*epistemic*) part and that with which we contemplate things that are variable we call the calculative part (*logistikon*). Calculation, the activity of the calculative part, is the same as deliberation and Aristotle reminds us that we never deliberate about invariable things or about things not in our power to do. We can best determine what is the best state, that is, the virtue or excellence of each of these two rational parts, by grasping the function or activity which each faculty performs. The calculative faculty aims at truth as rightly desired by the exercise of choice and, we recall, that choice involves not only a kind of purposive practical reasoning – deliberation about means to an end – but also a moral disposition that is already acquired, through habituation, and is stable, *desiring* to act well as an end and choosing to do so. Man, considered as an originator of action, is a union of desire and practical thinking to an end which is action. A consideration of man in this light makes him the subject of ethico-political science.

But we can also consider man in terms of the varied ways in which his species happens to think about different domains and therefore the ways in which he arrives at true principles, not by habituation, but by perception and induction coupled with syllogistic deduction. Whereas in the moral domain of conduct, acts and emotions are involved so that we pursue things we *desire*, in the domain of reasoning, we seek the truth through affirmation and denial. This is the kind of consideration Aristotle engages in here when he examines the different modes of thinking or states of mind by which the soul is able to arrive at truth by affirmation and denial, that is, by reasoning. He lists five modes of thought: productive art; demonstrative, epistemic science; prudence; wisdom; and intuition. Our capacity to exercise these intellectual virtues as different states of mind is not the consequence of any legislator or any constitution. Wherever a human is, so long as he is in some community, he can think productively, demonstratively, prudentially, intuitively. But as we shall see, certain polities give him the opportunity to engage and perfect certain of these intellectual capacities better than do others. Certain polities enable a man to integrate his moral and intellectual virtues so that he lives the kind of life that is suited to the kind of being he is.

Now a mode of thought is not itself a faculty or 'part' of the rational soul. Rather, it is an activity *by which* the faculty or part of the soul functions as it does. Let us examine the activities of *epistēmē* and intuition because Aristotle says it is these intellectual virtues which the wise man (not the prudential, political man) exemplifies, and the wise man is the *theoretikos*. It is notable that his wisdom (*sophia*), which Aristotle calls the most finished form of knowledge, studies none of the things that go to make a man *eudaimon*; only the prudent man does that by being concerned with particular acts that are just, admirable and good for man.

A scientific, epistemic mode of thinking has as its object what is necessary, eternal, unchanging, such as definitions and first principles. It is held that scientific knowledge is communicated by teaching and its necessary and immutable object is capable of being learnt. But all teaching that involves the use of reasoning starts from pre-existing knowledge (he cites *Posterior Analytics* (71a1)) because we come to know things either by induction or deduction, induction introducing us to first principles and universals, while deduction starts from universals and first principles. There are first principles from which deduction starts but which cannot themselves be proved by deduction; they have been reached by induction founded on perception that grasps individual 'facts' (*infimae species*). Epistemic scientific knowledge, then, is a mode of thinking whereby we demonstrate, using the demonstrative syllogism (as explained in *Posterior Analytics*), those things that necessarily follow from indemonstrable first principles, that is, from premises or 'facts' known by everyone, everywhere, to be true because they cannot be otherwise.

Demonstration then gives reasons for something being a necessarily true and universal conclusion.

Since this kind of scientific, epistemic mode of thinking depends on and derives from first principles and these first principles cannot themselves be reached by this mode of thinking (nor by the productive or practical modes of thinking, the latter, prudence, being concerned with variables), then what mode of thinking is it by which we reach invariable first principles which cannot be otherwise?

Aristotle speaks of *Nous* or rational intuition. *Nous* or intuition is that faculty or rational part of the soul whose activity is to apprehend correctly (by the process of induction based on perception) indemonstrable and fundamental first principles that strike all humans as such. It is infallible. In effect, Aristotle merely asserts that *Nous* is that part of the rational soul which is engaged both at the beginning and at the end of cognition. (To enquire into *how Nous* is thought to act one reads the *De Anima,* not a treatise on ethics.) Intuition (*Nous*) starts as perception, it grasps and identifies the ultimate particulars, the 'facts' or *infimae species*, the immanent essence of a something, and it ends with the primary definitions or first principles that are not reached by reasoning but by induction from perception. The activity of *Nous* in grasping first principles from induction is *theoria*. It is very important to understand that *Nous* and its activity, *theoria*, is species-specific. *All* humans can theorize based on induction from perception.

Prudent men who are older and experienced and make assertions on that basis as well as those who demonstrate or give reasons for the 'fact' being as it is, rely on the insight of intuition which enables them to see correctly. This is the reason we should pay attention to *both* (NE VI, ix). Aristotle notes, however, that prudence is the opposite of intuition. Where intuition apprehends first principles and definitions which cannot be proved by reasoning, prudence deals with particular things which are only apprehended by perception. Prudence, dealing with the variable, is a knowledge of human interests and concerns itself with the means to some good human end attainable by one's own action. Taking part in politics is exemplified by the actions of persons dealing with particular facts, a knowledge of which has been derived from their experience of managing households and official administration of the *polis* so that one pursues not only one's own welfare but that of the whole community. Prudence is a deliberative and judicial science applied to the whole community of which one is a part. A prudent man needs a knowledge of particular facts even more than he needs the kind of knowledge of general principles that enables him to explain and teach such principles. Perikles was thought to be the prudent man *par excellence* despite his being unsuccessful in teaching his sons to be similarly prudent. But we are reminded that the 'eye of the soul' cannot acquire the quality of prudence, a man cannot develop this mode of thinking, without already possessing moral virtue. We cannot be prudent without being good, no matter how potentially intelligent we may be.

Now wisdom (*sophia*) is generally thought to be the most finished form of knowledge, far more so than is prudence (*phronesis*). The wise man not only knows all that follows from first principles but he must also truly understand these principles. Aristotle sees wisdom as characterized by two modes of thinking, intuition and epistemic knowledge, and these are perfected by their objects being the most precious truths which are over and above what is true and good for man. Man is not the highest being in the world; there are beings more divine in nature than man – the gods and, most evidently visible, the celestial bodies such as the stars. The wise man thinks about these.

All the states of mind or modes of thought, not only the epistemic mode of thinking and the intuitive mode of thinking, are natural gifts or capacities in humans. They can be perfected by being actualized through the opportunities afforded for their exercise. But if wisdom is not concerned with the process by which man can act to be *eudaimon* and live successfully, then why is it desirable? Wisdom does not produce results in the political world; indeed, Thales and Anaxagoras are called wise rather than prudent and men have observed that such wise men can be ignorant of their own advantage. Since the objects of their enquiries are not human goods, their knowledge has been called useless (NE VI, vii). But Aristotle says that the state of mind or mode of thinking called wisdom, not only as a natural gift or capacity in man but as the most finished mode of thought because its objects are higher than man, makes a person *eudaimon* simply by his possession and exercise of it. This is true of all the other modes of thinking as well, although prudential thought has consequences in our world whereas *sophia* does not. But the activity of the highest part of intellect has a pleasure peculiar to its own activity (NE X, vii) and human beings simply are theorizers and explainers.

Humans move from a confused mass of appearances to an ordering of perceptions, they move from a grasp of the way things appear, attained in practices, to an ability to give reasons. There are no principles which humans know that hold independently of all their experiences and their cognitive conceptualizations of these. Indeed, in the *Metaphysics* (982b12 ff.) Aristotle says that philosophy began with human wonder, it began in humans initially failing to grasp something and their intellectual desire, their seeking or reaching out for understanding. He then goes on to modify Plato's image of the cave by saying that our encounter with the world is like what happens when we attend a puppet show performed by mechanical marionettes who appear to move without any visible human control. We *all* wonder and look for an explanation for this apparently wondrous movement. We *all* theorize and seek to explain what must be happening. No one is 'forced' or luckily led out of the cave; we all naturally take this journey outside and theorize. But we all return to the cave of appearances, testing our theories against the facts of life, the appearances, in order to ground our theories as true and comprehensive.[82]

Wisdom and its exercise may not be what directly interests the legislator in his attempts to endue men with those habits that will enable them to be morally virtuous in their conduct and live successful human lives, but this means no more than that politics is not concerned with legislating for the intellectual virtues. It legislates for character and affects what can be affected: habitual dispositions. The highest kind of human thinking, the epistemic and intuitive modes of thinking trained on the highest, most divine objects, goes on despite constitutional forms and their attendant systems of justice. Men theorize about the most divine things whether or not they live in good *poleis*. Even in dreadful 'states' the stars and the divine remain unaffected by the absence of prudence – developed oneself or in others. Humans can contemplate them no matter what else is happening. But as A. O. Rorty has observed, the benefits assured to the contemplator by contemplation in the worst of times give only a confused understanding of its excellence in the best of times.[83] What the prudential man, either as legislator or as guardian of the

82   See Nussbaum, *The Fragility of Goodness*, p. 260.
83   A. O. Rorty, 'The Place of Contemplation in Aristotle's Nicomachean Ethics', in Rorty, *Essays on Aristotle's Ethics*, pp. 377–94.

laws, can assure is the political conditions that allow man as a natural theorizer and seeker after explanations to discover and exercise his intellectual potentialities.

But there is one thing about the practical, prudential life which prevents its also being contemplative,[84] although it would be enhanced by being contemplated, and this is the lack of leisure (*scholē*) enjoyed by most political men in most *poleis*. There is no doubt that in its truest sense *eudaimonia*, as perfect human flourishing, consists in the proper exercise of all the potentialities of the soul, actualized for their own sakes, because this actualization simply *is* living the life of a human. *Eudaimonia*, having been defined as the activity in accord with the highest virtue in us, the exercise of the best part of us, would be the exercise of *Nous* which possesses intuitive insight, not only into 'our world' but into things above us, the noble and divine (NE X, vii). But Aristotle notes that it is difficult to contemplate the moral life in activity as well as those things higher than men when one is engaged in the nitty-gritty of judicial and deliberative decision-making. *In principle,* the most general ends of human life, in so far as these are defined by the species, can be contemplated, and these ends are the actualization and exercise of those essential activities which define humans. But the wise man no less than the just man of practical, prudential reasoning needs the necessaries of life because neither, as a man (by which is meant a composite of soul and body) is what he is because of his natural capacity to theorize alone. The difference between the wise man and the just man is that the latter can be just only if he has someone else to whom he is just, whereas the wise man can practise his epistemic and intuitive thinking by himself. *Were* both types of men adequately supplied with the necessaries of life, then it would be the wise man who could be called more self-sufficient. Aristotle says that *if* it is evident that self-sufficiency and leisuredness and such freedom from fatigue as is humanly possible along with all the other attributes assigned to the supremely *eudaimon* man *are* those that accord with this theorizing activity, *then* this activity will be perfect *eudaimonia* for man if it is allowed a full span of life. *But such a life will be too high for human attainment.* A man who lives it will do so not as a human being but in virtue of something divine in him. If the intellect is divine compared with man as a composite being, then the life of the intellect must be divine compared with the life of a human being. All we need do is accept that we do have this divine capacity to theorize, although we cannot sustain it continuously as might the gods. Aristotle enjoins us to try, in so far as we can, to live in conformity with what is highest in us.

What raises man above the other animals is this highest capacity, to think in and for itself, the enjoyment not the acquisition of knowledge, and this activity of theorizing is held to be the true self in action of each man. Only in this sense is the life lived in conformity with moral virtue *eudaimon* in a secondary degree (NE X, viii). Among the human activities, that which is most akin to the activity of god – pure thinking for itself – is the most perfect and hence the more people contemplate the happier they are. But in a work on ethics there is no room for a detailed treatment of the separate mode of flourishing of the intellect (read the *De Anima* for this). Legislators are prudent men. Society is ruled by the standards set by the man of practical reason, the *phronimos*, not by the wise. Hence, we need reminding that human nature is not self-sufficient. In so far as a human is and must be a member of society his specific function is to choose to act in accord with moral virtue and this means he needs all those external goods, including other men to whom he can be just, to enable him to live as a human being.

84   *Contra* Rorty.

The moral philosopher studies what the wise man does not study. He studies the activity of the *phronimos* in the light of general human ends (NE 1094a1–1094b11); he studies the formation of human character which can assure right desire rather than the purely theoretical capacities of man. The *only* theoretical activity in which the *phronimos* or prudential, political man engages with regard to the practical order is his thinking that his own interests as ends are specifications of the interests of all other men in the community.

Is there a time in a human life which is likely to provide more leisure for theorizing than others, so that the more limited theoretical activity of the *phronimos*, focused as it is on human interests in general, can be extended to theorizing or contemplating the moral life in activity as well as the celestial bodies and the divine? In book VII, ii of the *Politics* Aristotle says that both in earlier and modern times men most ambitious for virtue seem generally to have preferred either the life of the statesman or that of the philosopher. He thinks it makes a great difference which of the two is correct because we must direct ourselves to the better of the two aims, as individuals and collectively as members of a rule-governed polity (*Politics* 1324a23ff.). If *eudaimonia* is to be equated with doing well, then the active life will be the best both for any state as a whole community and for the individual. The active life, however, need not, as some suppose, be always concerned with our relations with other people, nor is intelligence 'active' only when it is directed towards results that flow from action. On the contrary, thinking and contemplation that are their own end and are done for their own sake are more active because the aim of thinking is to do well in the sense of thinking well (*Politics* 1325b14ff.). And in the *best* constitution, that which follows nature and makes a 'state' the setting for the most flourishing of lives, not only will citizens be those who have sufficient leisure to develop their human excellences but the tasks or offices of 'state' will be allotted to the same men but at different stages of their lives (*Politics* 1328b33ff.). The young who have strength will be engaged in the military, the older who have practical knowledge will be engaged in deliberative and judicial offices. And lastly, since it is only right and proper that the gods be worshipped by the citizens, it is proper that those who have spent their lives in long service, first in military service, then in deliberative service, should serve the gods and enjoy their retirement. They are appointed to the priestly office. Apart from their engagement in ritual worship their time is theirs to theorize and become wise.

Aristotle is an ageist. He has most confidence in older men because their lives of experience in the business of collective living have provided them with opportunities to actualize their potentials, both moral and intellectual. But there seems no doubt that man, the natural theorizer and seeker after explanations, if living in a morally impoverished polity, stands a poor chance of ever developing those habits that enable him to become morally virtuous and live successfully as a human among others. And because he has not been given sufficient opportunity to develop his practical reasoning, not having been treated as a responsible agent, his theorizing will most likely be limited to the other-worldly.

Further reading which indicates the very wide range of alternative interpretations of issues in NE

Acrill, J. L. *Aristotle's Ethics* (London, 1973).

Anscombe, G. E. M. 'Thought and Action in Aristotle', in Anscombe, From *Parmenides to Wittgenstein: collected philosophical papers* (Oxford, 1981), pp. 66–77.

Barnes, J., M. Schofield and R. Sorabji, eds, *Articles on Aristotle*, vol. 2 : *Ethics and Politics* (London, 1977).

Bostock, D. 'Pleasure and Activity in Aristotle's *Ethics*', *Phronesis* 23 (1988), pp. 251–72.

Charles, D. *Aristotle's Philosophy of Action* (Ithaca, NY, 1984).

Clark, S. R. L. *Aristotle's Man: speculations upon Aristotelian anthropology* (Oxford, 1975).

Cooper, J. M. *Reason and Human Good in Aristotle* (Cambridge, MA, 1975).

Engberg-Pedersen, T. *Aristotle's Theory of Moral Insight* (Oxford, 1983).

Gauthier, R. A. *La Morale d'Aristote*, 3rd edn (Paris, 1973).

Hardie, W. F. R. *Aristotle's Ethical Theory* (Oxford, 1963).

Heinaman, R. 'Eudaimonia and Self-sufficiency in the *Nicomachean Ethics*', *Phronesis* 33 (1988), pp. 31–53.

Hutchinson, D. S. *The Virtues of Aristotle* (London, 1986).

Irwin, T. H. *Aristotle's First Principles* (Oxford, 1988).

Kraut, R. *Aristotle on the Human Good* (Princeton, NJ, 1989).

Lear, J. *Aristotle: the desire to understand* (Cambridge, 1988), ch. 5.

Nussbaum, M. C. *The Fragility of Goodness, Luck and Ethics in Greek Tragedy and Philosophy* (Cambridge, 1986), part III: Aristotle: the fragility of the good human life, pp. 235–378.

Reeve, C. D. C. *Practices of Reason: Aristotle's Nicomachean Ethics* (Oxford, 1992).

Rorty, A. O., ed., *Essays on Aristotle's Ethics* (Berkeley, 1980).

Rowe, C. J. *An Introduction to Greek Ethics* (London, 1976), chapter 7: Aristotle's *Ethics*.

Rowe, C. J. 'The Good for Man in Aristotle's *Ethics* and *Politics*', in A. Alberti, ed., *Studi sull'Etica di Aristotele* (Naples, 1990), pp.193–225.

Urmson, J. O. *Aristotle's Ethics* (Oxford, 1988).

The *Politics*

From the *Nicomachean Ethics* we have learnt that the living of a successful human life, where the soul exercises its functions, both moral and intellectual, needs the addition of a range of external goods because one cannot do morally fine deeds without any resources. Furthermore, humans are composite in that they are souls 'in' bodies and they need the material and social world to live a life suited to the kinds of beings they are. Such resources include the help of friends, sufficient wealth, one's family. But these additions serve only as the means to human flourishing. They are preconditions for, but do not constitute the actual living of, a successful life.

Aristotle was at pains to discuss the ways in which human flourishing is manifested in the active, self-conscious exercise of a person's faculties in conformity with moral virtue. His final definition of the successful man was one who is active in accordance with complete virtue and who is adequately furnished with external goods through a complete life (NE I, ix). He is, *to the extent that this is possible for a man*, a self-mover among others of his kind. Hence, the morally virtuous life ought to be, and *is,* praised because such a life exhibits a person's behaviour which demonstrates to others his character's disposition to make sound choices in a responsible manner.

We recall that legislators are more interested in encouraging the development of moral, rather than intellectual, virtue because their laws influence the habitual development of a person's character. They can do rather less to encourage the development of intellectual virtues, ways of thinking the way humans do think, because the intellectual virtues cannot be altered by habituation. But the moral, as opposed to the intellectual, virtues can be altered by habituation and they describe a man's *behaviour*, what he consistently *desires and finds pleasure in*. And because choosing well is caused by *desiring* the right end, which is doing morally fine acts, then that 'part' of the soul which affects the moral virtues is the appetitive, irrational 'part' capable of being persuaded by reason, and this 'irrational' part accords with the moral excellence of character no matter how intellectually clever one may be.[85]

Recall that the intellectual virtues or different modes of thinking such as wisdom, understanding and prudence develop, not through habituation, but rather through experience and instruction. Although humans are born with relevant capacities to learn to think in recognizably human ways, it is only through instruction and experience that we can actualize the potential to think in different ways. But psychologically insightful laws or conventional moral rules do something other than instruct humans in how to exercise their reasoning: they can enable humans to actualize their natures as *moral* agents and thereby *desire* to do the right thing. The laws train one's habits of behaviour by training one's desires. Rational principles, enshrined in laws, both persuade men of reason and also (coercively) habituate the desires of the young prior to a child's development of the mature and experienced capacity to deliberate on what is to be done. If the aim of legislators, by definition, is to work with human nature and devise rules to channel human propensities so that each person may develop, through habituation to given practices, a character of the sort that will enable him to live humanly, then laws are meant to be productive of moral virtue and are not simply coercive rules to maintain order. For this reason Aristotle's philosophy of human conduct is completed in the *Politics*. This is where he examines the legislation of different constitutions in order to arrive at some view as to what preserves and what destroys *poleis*. We shall see how he determines which regulations, laws and customs are best absolutely for the kinds of beings humans at their best and by definition show themselves to be, and which are best relative to a given constitution in local circumstances.

According to Aristotle and the generally accepted views in his society, humans are constituted by nature to *become habituated* to act well. No one is born morally virtuous. The moral virtues are not engendered in us by nature – we are not born with characters – and yet the moral virtues, once engendered in us, are not contrary to nature. Humans are unique among animals to be so indeterminate. They cannot rely on biological instinct to do the right thing for themselves. Without the habituation to moral virtue, a 'human' would, Aristotle thinks, be worse than all other animals, having no instincts to limit, for instance, sexual drives or gluttonous over-eating (*Politics* I, 1253a33–6). But humans by nature are possessed of an impulse to form that kind of partnership in which they can become habituated to act well. This instinctive social impulse to partnership is independent of rational calculation to personal advantage, although it is advantageous to the species. This instinctive social impulse to friendship, co-operation and solidarity with others is the *natural precondition* for social justice and law: for Aristotle (like Plato) the social impulse is not a byproduct of law and positive justice. And if a human is, by definition, constituted by nature to become habituated to moral virtue and act well,

---

85   Note Aristotle's development of Plato's reflections on how the soul's 'irrational' part may be persuaded to desire what is good (for man). Where Plato used myth, Aristotle uses law. In contrast, Socratic intellectualism which, according to Aristotle, did away with passion and moral character, thereby denied the irrational 'part' of the soul so that moral virtue for Socrates was knowledge, whereas for Plato and Aristotle moral virtue is rationally orientated desires.

then a 'man' who is *by nature* (and not merely through ill-luck) without a *polis* precisely because he is incapable of entering into an acculturating partnership of this kind, must be either too bad or too good, a lower animal than 'man' or a god (*Politics* I, 1253a1–5). He is, *by nature*, a non-cooperator and a lover of war. Are there such 'men'? Homer seems to have thought so, and with revulsion called them 'clanless, lawless, heartless'. Such a brutish 'man' for Aristotle is rare, certainly in *poleis* like 'ours', resembling as he does 'an isolated piece in a game of draughts' (*Politics* I, 1253a6–7).[86, 87]

Aristotle does not think that man is, by nature, naturally evil, anti-social or uncooperative. What is distinctive about the species 'man' is that he has more indeterminate freedom to become the different kinds of characters that co-operate in the ways that they do. If one compared the study of other creatures with man, Aristotle thinks it would be easier to observe a relative stability of performance in, say, dogs than in man. That is why human ethical and political discourse is imprecise. Humans are capable of making an exceedingly wide range of choices of ways of acting, amid all sorts of contingencies, towards their human end – a successful human life. While man may be the most versatile of animals, finding pleasure in a wider variety of practices than any other animal, yet man is not so unique individually as to be incapable of communicating through language to his own kind about what constitutes a human life lived well, about good practical activity, about functioning well as a man. This is why there can be found certain stabilities, indeed, necessities in the domain of ethical and political enquiry. One such stability is that humans, like all other species, have an end peculiar to their species and can have no other. Another stability is that humans discover what constitutes the living of a specifically human life only by already being within a social partnership of a qualitatively distinctive kind, the *polis*, and it is here that humans discover what constitutes a human life – through experience and social discourse. Moral knowledge is the condition of knowledge of the human good, and hence one must have developed moral virtues in order to know what one's human end is. While the original impulse to social solidarity is instinctive, the motive for further political evolution derives from social experiences and discourse concerning what is useful to personal and collective advantage.

Social discourse, which is unique to humans, is an ethical and political discourse. It is not simply grunting about the pleasurable and the painful. When we speak of others as

86   See the interesting discussions of Salkever, 'Aristotle's Social Science', pp. 11–48 and C. Lord, 'Aristotle's Anthropology', pp. 49–73 in Lord and O'Connor, *Essays on the Foundations of Aristotelian Political Science*; also S. G. Salkever, *Finding the Mean: theory and practice in Aristotle's political philosophy* (Princeton, NJ, 1990).

87   Hobbes, in the seventeenth century, argued that *everyone* is a naturally self-interested, non-cooperator (who none the less reasons that he would prefer to be a co-operator if he could be assured that others could be relied on to co-operate); only by convention, the social contract, could each be made actively to become co-operative, it being rationally in his interest to perform co-operatively when an overarching sovereign power has been set up to keep him and his fellows in awe: *Leviathan* I, c.13: 'From this equality of ability ariseth equality of hope in the attaining of our ends. And therefore if any two men desire the same thing which nevertheless they cannot both enjoy, they become enemies; and in the way to their end, which is principally their own conservation and sometimes their delectation only, endeavour to destroy or subdue one another. … From this diffidence [fear] of one another there is no way for any man to secure himself, so reasonable, as anticipation; that is, by force or wiles. … Again men have no pleasure, but on the contrary a great deal of grief in keeping company where there is no power able to over-awe them all. … So that in the nature of man we find three principal causes of quarrel. First, competition, secondly, diffidence, thirdly, glory.'

ambitious, envious, proud, courageous, just, we are speaking of passions that are essentially socially – and rationally – evaluated and are praised or blamed because they are *acquired* dispositions or attitudes to the emotions rather than simple biological feelings as 'facts'. Social conversation, then, is a *consequence of* ordered societies (*Politics* I, 1253a19ff.). We can be individuals as moral agents only because we are social.[88] Such kinds of ordered society are therefore prior to the individual man, for without the possibility of communication concerning right and wrong the individual is no man. Aristotle notes that anything that no longer performs its function cannot be said to be the same thing and they bear their names – here, 'man' – in an equivocal sense (*Politics* I, 1253a20–5).[89] Should he cease to desire to share his perception of what is useful, right and just through ceasing to desire to communicate about such things with his own kind, Aristotle tells us that he is no human but must be either a lower animal than man or a god.

Since the whole must necessarily be prior to the part, then the *polis* is to be considered prior in nature to all other partnerships and to each of us individually (*Politics* I, 1253a19). Speech would be superfluous without an ordered community and it would be swiftly abandoned were there not the already actualized possibility of communication concerning shared perceptions of the human good. The individual is not, therefore, subordinated to the 'state', in the sense that his interests are of less importance than those of the 'state'. Rather, as we have already seen, Aristotle believes that an individual would not know his own particular good without having first considered himself to be 'a man' and concerned for the good for man. And he could only undertake this consideration if he were already embedded in a moral community of a qualitative kind. Humans are and also wish to be *polis*-living animals. Although humans may first hear this discourse within the family, its origins are in a way of thinking and acting that can only manifest itself in a sphere of practices beyond the household, a domain in which law and justice among equals is already actualized through practices. The impulse to form this kind of partnership is present naturally in all men but the actualized political community is the result, so to speak, of the benevolence of that man who first united people in this kind of partnership. Aristotle postulates a lawgiver who enabled men to be conditioned by laws by means of which they could become what their potential impelled them to be. Aristotle seems to be saying that the *polis* comes into being through a discontinuous act, and it is one which has not and does not occur everywhere (*Politics* I, 1253a30–4).[90] For instance, he notes that foreign nations have never, strictly speaking, realized it and so remain like Greek primitive monarchies, ruling over willing subjects along the model of household governance. This kind of kingly rule is not political rule for him. The ruled in such primitive monarchies are within a natural hierarchy of (one) ruler and (many) ruled, but they have not developed that qualitatively distinct kind of social partnership called a *polis* where there is a true balance of power in the polity under law. They have not developed a taste for Greek liberty, to rule and be ruled in turn.

The ethical and political discourse of Aristotle and those who come from *poleis* 'like ours' is not concerned with what man 'is' but with what man does. Man, like other animals, is in the end, what he *does*. Man alone is known by what he does as a consequence of his own decisions. What he does which defines him distinctively as man and

---

88   S. R. L. Clark, *Aristotle's Man: speculations upon Aristotelian anthropology* (Oxford, 1975), p. 98.
89   See below, pp. 198ff, on natural slavery.
90   Lord, 'Aristotle's Anthropology', p. 60; compare Cicero below, chapter 5.

apart from other animals, is to act not only in terms of the naturally pleasurable and painful but in the rationally guided moral domain of what is right and wrong. The right and wrong colour his disposition to things that he finds pleasurable and painful. He alone can become habituated to find pleasure in what is also right. When a man functions at his best he pursues a goal that he has come to desire as his good. And to recognize the character of another human is to infer what a particular man is from what he is presumed to have chosen to do. For this reason, cultural environment, expressed through *nomoi* or prescriptive cultural habits, must (and always does) play a huge role in providing the opportunities to become the kinds of characters humans display in their actions. In fact, social rules that are not psychologically insightful, despite, by definition, intending to instil moral virtues, can sufficiently distort a person's character by encouraging the wrong habituated practices to the extent that his human ability to reason intellectually to first principles, distinguishing between good and bad, may be distorted. One's performances in the moral domain can, in the last resort, affect not one's thought processes (the way humans happen to think) but what one thinks about, one's very end, with a view to action.

In book 7 of the *Politics* Aristotle says that for each individual to be virtuous entails the collective virtue of all. How, he asks (once again), does a man become virtuous? He states that the three things by which men are made good and virtuous are nature, habit and reason. First, one must be born with the nature of a human being and not of some other animal (one cannot do anything about this) and 'what each thing is when fully developed we call its nature' (*Politics* I, 1252b32ff.); more specifically, one must be born of a certain quality of body and psychology.[91]

> But there are some qualities that it is of no use to be born with for our habits make us alter them: some qualities are made by nature liable to modification by habits in either direction, for the worse or for the better. While other animals live chiefly by nature, although some in small degrees are also guided by habits, man also lives by reason for he alone of the animals possesses reason. In him, nature, habit and reason must be harmonious, one with another, because men often act contrary to their acquired habits and contrary to their nature because of their reason, if they are convinced that some other course of action is preferable.

This is why the legislator's task of educating habits is so important, because men learn some things by practice, others by precept (*Politics* VII, 1332a38–1332b11). Neither children nor animals display deliberative desire and choice. But when experienced and mature, men have their reason to reflect on the habits they have formed as children within their culture and, *with effort*, they can alter their deliberative desire and choice, changing their habitual behaviour. Recall that this is *not* easy to do and most men do not do it. Hence, the most influential of effects on our characters come from the habits we have formed in the process of developing cultivated characters from childhood (no one is, for whatever reason, 'bronze', 'silver' or 'gold' from the beginning).

The *Politics* is Aristotle's attempt to discuss systematically *those conditions in which* man becomes well- or less well-habituated to morally fine practices which are the precondition of coming to a knowledge of the human good. He and those to whom and with

---

91   See below, pp. 198ff, on natural slavery.

whom he speaks believe that all *human* communities acculturate their members with *nomoi* that intend to instil the moral virtues and thereby train the habits of behaviour so that one desires the right things. But some cultures do this less well than others. Aristotle is interested not only in those cultures that 'get it right' but also in what is required for a less good set of enabling conditions to alter in the direction of the more good. Those constitutions or 'enabling conditions' that are considered by him are all, in effect, Greek, more or less contemporary, and are or were established among people who are like 'us'.

Amelioration of the sort he offers in the *Politics* is not on the cards either for those 'human', Greek communities that are prehistoric (about which he can do nothing and which, in any event, evolved into that final, qualitatively distinct partnership, the Greek *polis*) or for those non-Greek societies he refers to either as foreign nations or as barbarians. There appears to be a distinction between the latter. For Aristotle and his students, neither prehistoric Greek nor contemporary foreign nations, both of which were/are ruled by kings in a manner similar to the way in which senior (male) members of the household rule their wives and children, defines the essential nature, or the final actualization of human community. 'If what each thing is when fully developed we call its nature' then such communities were not or are not fully developed. But there seems to be a distinction drawn on the one hand between some foreign nations 'today' who are ruled by kings on the model of the household and where the senior member rules and has 'the power of law' over wives and children and, on the other, certain barbarian partnerships where no distinction is made between females and slaves and furthermore, where there is no class of natural rulers. The entire barbarian community is considered a partnership of female and male slaves and Aristotle tells us that the poets see this as the reason for Greeks ruling barbarians, implying that barbarian and slave are the same in nature (*Politics* I, 1252b5–9). The prehistoric, scattered settlements described by Homer had kings who ruled their people just as the senior member rules his blood relations in the household. Foreign nations rule in this primitive way 'today'. There appears to be a ruling element here. There is none such in barbarian partnerships. They are not political, have no recognizable constitutions or laws, and in Aristotle's and his students' view, they seem to operate by a pre-political survival instinct that values only brute physical force to contend with contingency and adversity. These 'barbarian' networks cannot be improved from within themselves because, having no constitutions, and therefore no laws as such, they are not the product of deliberative choice. He seems to view them as instinctual survival networks based on nothing other than physical strength in response to procreative urges and violent circumstances, all of which are taken by their members to be entirely within the province of chance/natural disaster. They are communities that are constantly ready for or engaged in war. The good of their members can only be served by a natural ruler, who rules by reason, and in not being able to provide this from within their own ranks, Aristotle tells us no more than that it is said in his culture that they should be (and historically often have been) taken over (*Politics* I, 1252b5–9). This appears to be Aristotle's only application of the Platonic rule of reason imposed from 'without'.

If there is one thing Aristotle was not (and did not intend to be in his ethical and political discourses), it was an anthropologist with a sensitivity to forms of governance that were not like anything he and his fellow Greeks had experienced. But then, he had already made plain that definitions do not float around over and above us. They arise in us, according to Aristotle's epistemology, as a consequence of *our* experience and *our* dialectical examination of social premises which are themselves based on the accumulated wisdom of the many and the wise thus far, tested against the 'facts'. If our experiences are limited and our social premises are only as good as the experiences and inferences from them of the past, thus far, then this is simply as far as 'we' have been able to get. He is of the view, however, that the distance come by Greeks could be assumed to represent the full development of the nature of man and the nature of his political community and that barbarian cultures could, in the light of the Greek standard, be judged to have failed of their 'human' promise. In this domain, today we would argue that the ancient Greeks seem not to have got very far by Western, twentieth-century standards. But we need reminding that their cultural heirs during more than 2,000 subsequent years hardly progressed any further. The attitude to those *not* like 'us', called barbarians and without recognizable 'constitutions' and laws, would enable European nations to justify their benevolent (or otherwise) forceful domination of native peoples wherever they found them right into the twentieth century. Aristotle was the teacher they acknowledged with alacrity.

But when considering societies like 'ours' and their different constitutions or enabling conditions, Aristotle considers there to be only one form of government that is natural to man, whose nature he has defined, and this is the best form. We have seen that it operates according to what he judges to be the best criterion of social worthiness, which is the domain of distributive justice, by valuing above all the display of moral virtue in service to the community. The 'best' political community which rewards men in proportion to their virtuous contribution to the community is also one in which the greatest possible number of men is encouraged to develop their natures as moral agents and live well as humans. It is, as we shall see, his standard by which he will evaluate the range of possible and experienced *political* communities in the ancient world.[92]

Partnerships and the Sovereign Partnership

Book 1 of the *Politics* opens with a discussion of the Greek *polis* or 'state' as a distinctive kind of partnership. It has in common with all kinds of partnership the intention of aiming at some good purpose and it, like all partnerships, is formed by men with a view to what they think to be good. But he assumes as he did when attempting to define 'man' in the *Nicomachean Ethics* that the 'state' has a specific end (*telos*), revealed through its function and hence, from observation, its distinctive goal-directed associative activity emerges in us when we understand the nature of the *polis*. *Humans must already be in such a partnership for this to arise in them.* Pre-historically, as well as observations of some contemporary social formations, indicate to him that some men have not lived and do not 'now' live in this qualitatively distinct kind of partnership. He identifies the *polis* or 'state' as that kind of partnership which is the most sovereign of all as it aims at the most sovereign of all goods: the common good.

If we begin by analysing the *polis* by looking first at its parts – since we observe the

---

92   For a collection of previously published articles on different subjects raised in the *Politics*, see Keyt and Miller, *A Companion to Aristotle's Politics*, with an extensive bibliography on Aristotle's *Politics*; a good introduction is R. G. Mulgan, *Aristotle's Political Theory: an introduction for students of political theory* (Oxford, 1977); also see J. Barnes, M. Schofield and R. Sorabji, eds, *Articles on Aristotle, 2: Ethics and Politics* (London, 1977).

polis to be a composite whole of different parts (families, extended kinship groups, villages) – then he hopes that systematic knowledge can be acquired about these functioning parts and how they differ one from another in purpose. His method has much in common with his treatment of biological subjects, where a specific animal is examined in terms of the functions of its constituent parts as they contribute to the functioning of the whole. He aims to show that they are mistaken who think of the natures of statesmen, of kings, of household managers and masters of slaves as the same, differing only in the quantity of people over whom they exercise control. There is for Aristotle a *qualitative* difference between even large households and small 'states'. The nature of the *polis* is not that of the household 'writ large', although certain (presumably some foreign) cultures appear to believe that it is. This is because living is qualitatively different from living well as a human being, for Aristotle and 'us', and it is in the *polis* (and not simply in the family household) that men are engaged in the practices which constitute living well (*Politics* III, 9 supra 1281a).

That distinctive kind of partnership, the *polis,* does not originate, according to Aristotle, as the result of war and conquest. He claims that those practical activities of leisure which express the human's function – performing morally fine acts – are more determinative of the quality of a human life than are the activities of war. The *polis*, as a coherent set of recognizably human practices, is the consequence of men being natural co-operators.[93] But men naturally display two qualitatively different capacities for co-operative solidarity, that based on the family and kinship, and another based on comradeship as a special kind of moral partnership among those who are free and equals. The political is a privileged environment where one engages in qualitatively different practices from some of those which are performed in the household, although the moral principles which guide certain family practices are determined by the moral principles that are discovered and established in the *polis*. Politics is not economics. Politics is about living well as a human being and not simply about surviving in a partnership with and among one's kin.

The nature of the *polis*, like the nature of man, is the culmination of a process. Like the definition of man which, when arrived at, provides the best and most complete encapsulation of the specific differences that functionally distinguish man from other animals and, as a definition, provides a unique descriptive content which highlights the best example of its kind, so the *polis* is, by definition, a natural end of earlier or prior partnerships. The *polis* is in the genus *partnership* but is defined by its specific differences. The *polis* is not the product of convention. It is the product of nature and of natural processes.

Some call this Aristotle's *organic theory* of the 'state'. But all too often this risks becoming oversimplified through too literal a reading. Rather, what the *polis* is, known through what it *does*, owes more to Aristotle's definitional method of procedure where, to define the nature of anything requires a teleological process of 'growth' by analogy, tracing the realization of potentials *in* final actualizations. If his theory of the 'state' is organic then everything defined by Aristotle would be 'organic'. In one sense, this is true in that his insistence that nature does nothing superfluously enables him to consider the world as a unitary and animated whole. His organicism is systematic. But to call his theory of the state organic and to provide too literal an understanding of his biological analogy would

93   Compare Plato.

reduce every project in which he engaged, and for which he provided definitions, to a biology and a deterministic biology at that. Neither the *Ethics* nor the *Politics* is a biological treatise. The *polis* is not an organic body but *like* one. Biology affects the *polis* but does not determine it. Nature is a whole and the various distinct natures which are components and constituents of the whole, like the *polis,* and men, are part of that organic unity. But man's nature is given as indeterminate potential. To become actually what his definition (or nature) prescribes, man must create circumstances in which his awareness may become instructed and where his moral virtue may develop as the product of cultivation. Aristotle is too certain of the naturalness of human reasoning and of man's capacity to orientate his passions by reason to diminish the freedom that derives therefrom and so submit to biological determinism. Both the nature of the *polis* and the nature of man are matters of experience. To realize either, as a living entity, has taken and continues to take time. Aristotle is saying *more* than that certain processes, like the full development of man according to his nature, happen naturally and by biological determination. He is attempting to explain how something without a determinate nature, man, comes to have a determinate nature by functioning in a way specific to his capacities: man is that sort of being which has, given the *political* opportunity, the capacity to acquire habits of behaviour that reveal his nature to be a 'compulsive' deliberative chooser. The kind of interaction that is essentially political is, therefore, structured by *nomoi* (laws, custom) rather than by unstructured individual choice, and decisions are made according to some procedure for ruling and being ruled in turn rather than by force, chance or theoretical wisdom.[94]

Hence, the *polis* is to be viewed as the final stage of natural growth of prior, necessary partnerships. Aristotle takes the *polis* to be the defining end-product from which prior partnerships can be viewed and their functional purposes (*tele*) discerned and distinguished.

The *polis* is a qualitatively distinctive kind of partnership but is preceded by other, more necessary partnerships like households which, in also being *like* organic bodies, have a ruling and a subordinate element, what he calls a combination of natural ruler and ruled for the purpose of preservation. His systematic organicism is structured by hierarchies of ruling and ruled elements. Therefore, any association, even for preservation, that is a partnership without a natural ruling element is missing a capacity for self-direction. It is ripe for take-over. The household partnership is thought of as a composite unity of long-term intelligence and physical capacity with the aim of engaging in practices guided by rational purpose in the interest of the unit's self-sufficiency. The *polis* is the final stage of natural growth, originating in the pairing of male and female who, by natural impulse, come together to reproduce their own kind. That this initial pairing to reproduce the species is a natural impulse makes its occurrence one of necessity rather than choice, just as the propagation of their kind is a natural necessity for other animals and plants as well.

But the impulse to reproduce, and hence to pair, is not sufficient to make a household. Some animals mate and then return to a solitary existence. Others, however, namely gregarious, communicative animals like bees, stay together to form partnerships

---

94   S. G. Salkever, 'Aristotle's Social Science', in Lord and O'Connor, *Essays on the Foundations of Aristotelian Political Science,* p. 13. The parallels with Hegel are instructive – Hegel knew what he was coming from!

with natural rulers ('king'! bees) and ruled (drones) for the sake of security. Humans like bees are gregarious animals and they too communicate for the sake of security. But alone among the gregarious animals man possesses speech (*logos*) over and above voice, and speech is designed to indicate the advantageous and the harmful and therefore, for man, also the right and wrong, the just and the unjust. Hence, the partnership that comes about subsequent to the reproductive urge is the household and it serves the everyday needs of the unit. The partnership made up of several households with the purpose of satisfying not merely daily needs is the village, which seems to be a colony from the extended household. In early times, Aristotle tells us that such colonies were made up of parts under royal rule since men, who were living in scattered settlements, lived in households where the elder member ruled. Analogously, village colonies, whose members were united by blood relationships, were ruled by a king, 'giving law to sons and spouses'. Some foreign races are still living under this kind of royal rule.

Human Household Partnerships

Human households are typified by their internal relationships and they provide us with a *definition,* the nature of the human household and its functional 'parts'. In human households there are three distinct types of relationship, that of the master and slave, that of the husband and wife, and that of the father and children. The differing functional parts are the consequence of the recognition of the distinct natures of the individuals of which it is comprised, and this enables Aristotle to distinguish between the respective *roles* of the man as master, husband and father, the woman as wife and mother, and the household slave as an instrument of action. Each in its own way serves the purposes of the household, the self-sufficiency of the unit and therefore its security into the future.

In 'barbarian' conjugal partnerships, however, which Aristotle does not dignify with the name household but considers rather as a result of the reproductive impulse and no more, one none the less finds an imperfectly differentiated set of relations where the male assigns to his female and to his slave precisely the same status. This is not a humanly defined household and it is not even analogous to the 'king' bee as natural ruling element and 'his' family of slave/drones. Instead, the male in the barbarian conjugal partnership is considered by Greeks to be as much a slave as his females and slaves. Hence, under this kind of rule by what amounts to instinctive physical force rather than reason, the male is himself slavish and imposes his will on the female slave in a slavish partnership. This is a 'human' partnership that has no natural ruler, by which Aristotle means it has no one who naturally is capable of using reason to look ahead for the benefit of the unit. He tells us that this is the reason the (Greek) poets give when they say that it is proper that Greeks should rule over non-Greeks. Aristotle will include an analysis of the poets' view indirectly by later asking if it is true that all non-Greeks should be ruled over by Greeks. Effectively, he answers no; it would only be just to rule over non-Greeks with the barbarian characteristics specific to natural slaves.[95]

In contrast, a humanly defined household not only has three distinctly differentiated relationships, but, most importantly, its members share a common view in matters of what is useful and harmful and in the expressed perception of what is just and unjust.

95   See below, pp. 198ff.

The human household is a sphere of deliberation. Humans alone have perception of good and evil, just and unjust, and it is the power of speech, not simply voice which expresses pleasure and pain, that enables humans to share a common view in *these* matters and this sharing makes a household. A shared common view in these matters of the just and unjust also makes a *polis* (*Politics* I, 1253a14–19). There is a deliberative continuity between the kind of partnership that defines a human household and that which defines a *polis*. But they are not the same kinds of partnership because they aim to satisfy qualitatively different human needs: living, on the one hand, and living well, on the other. They are part of the same flexible generic continuum of 'partnership' which ends in the fixity of the specific difference, *polis*. And when the *polis* is in existence, its concerns – living well – penetrate back into households. The *polis* is the best name or predicate which reveals the common properties, the single nature of those enabling conditions required for men to live sufficiently and well. We shall see that there is a range of actual *poleis* but the *polis,* by definition, is the critical standard by which they may be judged in relation to human needs to live sufficiently and well.[96]

The *polis,* then, is the final stage of the natural growth of partnership, retrospectively analysed and defined. Prior and qualitatively different kinds of partnership have their origin in human impulse, but they go on to evolve through experience and reflection on the personal and collective advantage of different kinds of solidarity in search of collective self-sufficiency. Aristotle insists that while the *polis* came about as a means of securing survival, it continues in being to secure the good life, which is a life of fine actions that typify civic virtue. Because humans show themselves to be and are, by definition, uniquely political over and above being familial, the chief and continuing purpose of politics is not to make living biologically together possible but to make living well as humans possible. Politics is not, therefore, a spontaneous, biologically determined drive as is the impulse to friendly partnership. Friendship is the motive of social life but a *polis* is the partnership of clans and villages in a full and independent life, a life characterized by deliberation and moral action, so that political comradeship exists for the sake of fine actions and not merely for living and surviving in common (*Politics* III, 1280b32–1281a9).

Aristotle, however, believes that those factors responsible for the *actual* development of political society have been neither universally nor uniformly actualized. What is required for political society's actual development is that faculty of the soul – practical reason (here, called spirit or *thymos*) – whose activity it is to govern desire by reason because 'it is from this faculty that power to command and the love of freedom are in all cases derived' (*Politics* VII, 1328a6–7). We recall (NE VI, 1139a27–36) that the efficient cause of action is choice and the cause of choice is a desire and reasoning to some end. Choice involves reasoning and a certain acquired disposition of character. This calculative or deliberative faculty functions at its best only when a man enables it to achieve its function by having acquired a disposition to do well, and we know that Aristotle has argued that this can be achieved only by a man having become habituated to acting well in a law-governed political community of a distinct kind. Prudence is that rational qual-

---

96   Presumably, primitive monarchies modelled on the household's hierarchical structure were 'human households' and therefore to be considered deliberative, moral units. They are still qualitatively distinct from the *polis* although certainly not similar to barbarian partnerships.

ity, that intellectual virtue, concerned with action in relation to things that are good and bad for human beings (NE VI, 1140b6–8).

That practical reason's activity is a requirement of political living and that it is not on display everywhere are matters of induction from observation and of deduction from social premises, taking into account the experience and reasoning of the wise concerning the range of social formations around the world. But to answer *why* this is the case, why nature has not achieved her intention universally or uniformly, requires a less secure kind of speculation. In *Politics* 7 (1327b18–39) Aristotle speaks of the effects of climate and other, contingent physical factors. He says that observation of Greek cities and observing how the inhabited world is divided among nations can give us a *fair* idea of the situation, accounting for differences among peoples and hence for their tendency, or not, towards a display of the kind of political organization (as opposed to some other form of social partnership) that would institutionally suit the rule of man generally as a distinct and fully actualized species. But climate and geography cannot provide the whole answer. If they did, then we could not observe, as we do, the differences among the Greek nations themselves when we compare one with another: some are by nature one-sided, in others intellect and courage are well combined (*Politics* 1327b34). This argument about the observed diversity among Greek races compared with one another acknowledges but modifies Plato's: only some seem to have the intellectual and spirited natures that enable them to respond to the lawgivers' guidance to virtuous behaviour. Climate and geography are presented as plausible arguments based on Greek observation and induction. Their form is rhetorical. They are the phenomena as they appear to ordinary Greek observers. Whether or not all such phenomena can be saved were they dialectically scrutinized, there is no real answer to the question why nature has not everywhere fulfilled her intention for the species 'man'. It is none the less the case that wherever there is a *polis,* it exists by nature, just as do the earlier partnerships.

Differently organized *poleis* have different views about what human lives require as means to achieving an agreed end, human well-being. Who and how many actually deliberate about the means to the collective end, distinguish one *polis* from another. But the *polis,* as such and in itself, not only is the end-product of those other, prior partnerships but the *polis* defines the very nature of human partnership in the activities which seek the *chief good* of all partnerships aiming at self-sufficiency. Differently organized *poleis* are judged against the standard definition of the *polis* as essentially political. Politics is a way of living by laws and customs, where taking turns in ruling and being ruled is not determined by human biology. Rather, it is a deliberate ordering of human perceptions of the good and bad, the just and unjust as means to an agreed human end, well-being and doing. This way of living indicates that the *polis* with this kind of political activity has been found, retrospectively, to be the best, reasonably possible way of organizing human needs and inclinations. The *polis* is not in opposition to our biological capacities. But its laws are deliberately imposed on men generation after generation.

When Aristotle says the *polis* is by nature, then, he is claiming not merely that it is the conclusion of a process of generation but that it displays essentially the human partnership. Aristotle sums up what is, in effect, a complex, condensed and much qualified argument by stating that the *polis* is a natural growth and man is such a being whose nature it is to live in a *polis. Man is by nature a political animal* (*Politics* I, 1252b27–1253a4).

Slaves, Natural and Conventional

We are transported to the 'otherness' of the ancient Greek milieu with its experiences and discursive social premises in a startling way when Aristotle examines the household in greater detail. In particular, his discussion of slavery, natural and conventional, is notorious. For he tells us that the complete (Greek) household consists of slaves and freemen. This is historical fact but, as we shall see, it was, even in Aristotle's day, a contentious issue. Apparently there were some who thought that the household partnership as practised was not what should be practised. Aristotle's conclusions may still be offensive to our ears, but it is not at all clear that he was making an argument that justified the *de facto* economy of Greek slave labour. Aristotle never simply reproduces the standard Greek views on ethical and political subjects. And he does not do so on slavery either. However, some, if not most modern scholars, have read him as doing no more than justifying Greek practices that are obnoxious to us and should have been obnoxious to him if not also to them.[97]

The ancient Greeks, and specifically the Athenians in their time, would have been very unusual had they not sanctioned slavery and we have seen how their language expressed what they took to be the necessary dualities of free and slave.[98] Aristotle, however, presents an analysis that finds its place in his philosophy of human action. He will 'save the phenomena' *where and if* he can. Hence, he begins as he must, given his audience, with a *de facto* description of the household as a whole made up of parts, and the primary parts are partnerships: namely, the master–slave partnership, the husband and wife partnership and the father and children partnership. Aristotle examines the character of these three relationships: mastership, matrimonial, paternal. How does the master–slave partnership bear on the provision of the essential services required by the household unit's needs of enduring self-sufficiency?

Aristotle tells us that some think household management or mastership is the same as statesmanship or kingship. Others say that mastership of one man over another is contrary to nature and that it is not nature but convention alone that makes one man free and another slave. This would make their partnership unjust because it is based on force rather than reason (*Politics* I, 1253b15–23). Aristotle intends dialectically and rhetorically to analyse these two contentious views: (1) that political rule has no specific differences from household rule, and (2) that there are no men who by nature are unfree. His aim, as usual, is to discover *if and under what conditions* the common opinion, reflected in *de facto* practices, may be preserved and also to establish what is true for the most part.

If we begin by recalling that the purpose of the household partnership as a whole is to attain the unit's living necessities then the art of acquiring property is part of household management. The manager of the household must have the proper sort of tools and one can say he is in a partnership with them. Any piece of property can be regarded as a tool enabling a man to live. Living is not production; living is action. Life, says Aristotle, is doing things, not making things. This is fundamental, not only to Aristotle's discussion of slavery but to his whole view about the exercise of moral virtue in political self-rule.

---

97   See, for instance, P. Cartledge, *The Greeks* (Oxford, 1993), chs 3 and 6; Mulgan, *Aristotle's Political Theory*; E. Wood and N. Wood, *Class Ideology and Ancient Political Theory* (Oxford, 1978).
98   See above, chapter 1.

Indeed property is that sort of tool with which its owner does something rather than makes something. There are, of course, other sorts of tools that are instruments of production. Now, tools for doing things rather than making things may be inanimate or they may be animate: Aristotle asks us to think of the ship's helmsman who uses the rudder as an inanimate tool and the same helmsman whose look-out man is his animate tool. The household slave is, like the helmsman's look-out, a sort of living piece of property, enabling the master to do, rather than make, something. What the helmsman does is steer the boat to its final destination, making use of his tools, rudder and look-out man, in the course of his journey to his end. What the master of a household does is to put his slaves to use so that he has sufficient time and leisure to engage in political activities and achieve his end, beyond household management for self-sufficiency. Tools of inanimate and animate kinds are assistants. If man were self-sufficient and not impelled to partnerships then he would need no assistants. Indeed, if shuttles could weave by themselves and the plectrum self-moved could strum the strings of a harp, then craftsmen would have no need of assistants and masters no need of slaves. The need of slaves is a need for assistance in the activities of living a human life within a household. The master of a household's needs have been established without Aristotle as yet saying anything whatever either of the slave's needs or, indeed, whether there are such men whose need is to enter into the partnership to act as assistants to *other* men's living (*Politics* I, 1253b23–1254a8).

Aristotle informs us that Greeks speak of 'an article of property' in the same way as they speak of 'a part' in that a thing that is a part of another absolutely belongs to that other. 'Slaves' as articles of property are 'parts' of the master. There is an imbalance observed: the master does not belong to the slave but the slave belongs to the master. None the less it is a partnership. He tells us later that Greeks in fact speak of several kinds of 'slave', and one kind is the manual labourer who usually is a free man. For anyone to be under the authority of someone or something that rules them absolutely, that masters them, is slavish and this includes anyone who is bound by necessity. In the case of the labourer, he is forced to live a life of labouring, of making, acquiring or producing material things in order to live. Since a human life is about doing not making, since a human life is the exercise of moral and intellectual virtues, anyone who is in the situation where he cannot exercise the peculiarly human excellences is slavish.[99] Where the free-man labourer is a slave to *circumstance*, however, the natural slave is such because he appears to lack within himself the capacity to be an autonomous chooser were circumstances different. These considerations show the nature (or definition), that is, the essential qualities of the slave and his functions (*Politics* I, 1254a14–15). Any human being that *by nature* belongs not to himself but to another is *by nature* a slave, and a human being belongs to another whenever, in spite of being a man, he is a piece of property, that is, a tool having a separate existence from his owner and meant for action. Is there anyone of this character who, none the less, is human? This is precisely the question Aristotle himself asks: 'But we must next consider whether or not anyone exists who is by nature of this character and whether it is advantageous and just for anyone to be a slave, or whether on the contrary all slavery is against nature' (*Politics* 1, 1254a15–20).

He says it is not difficult to discern the answer, either by theory or by experience.

99   See below, pp. 222ff, on banausic labourers, mechanics.

Recall from the *Topics* that 'induction is more persuasive, clear and more easily grasped by sense perception and is shared by the majority of people, but syllogistic reasoning is more cogent and efficacious against argumentative opponents'. In daily life when men's characters and actions are discussed, we start from what is most familiar to us: inductive reasoning, collecting the particular, relevant phenomena which give rise to the general, common beliefs about the human good and morality. Aristotle begins with these common beliefs which constitute 'our' theory or the premises which structure our daily discourse. He rehearses his view that all of nature is hierarchically arranged according to the principle of ruler and ruled. All partnerships operate following the principle of ruler and ruled; indeed, man, the composite of ensouled body is, as we have already seen, a being of such a kind as to seek his human well-being by exercising his reason and rationally orientating his desires so that he desires to do what is also right. Throughout nature there are many varieties of ruling and subject factors combined to make a single common whole – this is especially characteristic of living things. An animal consists of soul and body, of which the former is by nature the ruling factor over the latter. To discover what is natural we must study the best of a kind of thing. In studying man, we ought to consider one who is in the best possible condition regarding body and mind. If we instead considered those in permanent or temporarily bad or degenerate condition we would infer from their behaviour that the body often rules their mind. But in a man in good condition the mind conspicuously rules the body like a master's rule, the intelligence persuades the appetites like constitutional or royal rule. It is both natural and expedient for the body to be governed by the soul and for the emotional 'part' of the soul to be governed by the 'part' possessing reason. Aristotle has already discussed at length in the *Nicomachean Ethics* why he believes this is so.

In the case of humankind generally, whenever there is the same wide difference between humans as there is between soul and body or between the human being and a lower animal, then those whose condition is such that their function is the use of their bodies and nothing better can be expected of them, are by nature slaves (*Politics* I, 1254b15–21). The definition of a natural slave is one who is capable of belonging to another, of being another's property *and this capacity in himself is why he does so belong to another*. He is such a 'man' as to *participate in reason so far as to recognize it but not so as to possess it himself.* Aristotle says that the use made of this sort of man hardly differs from that of tame animals; both help with their bodies to supply our household's daily needs. But this is not to say that household slaves, being used like tame animals, *are* tame animals. The difference between men and their animals is clearly marked and observable in their respective physical differences. And one would think that if slaves were so by nature then it would be nature's intention to make the bodies of free men and slaves sufficiently different as well, with the latter's bodies strong for the necessary actions within the household economy while free men's bodies would always be erect and unserviceable for the necessary tasks which achieve household self-sufficiency. On this view, the bodies of the free are intended to be serviceable to the life of political agency, both in war and peace (*Politics* I, 1254b–33).

But in fact, Aristotle tells us, the very opposite often comes about; that is, that slaves have the bodies of free men and free men have the right soul but not the body. So the real criterion, as we have come to expect, must be the state of the soul rather than the body and we cannot see the mind except by inferring its character from moral behaviour and deliberative choice. Only from observing and judging practices can it become manifest whether there are cases of people of whom some are free men and others slaves by nature. The fundamental issue is the inferred psychological criterion for determining the natural distinction between ruler and ruled. For those who are slaves by nature the institution of slavery, Aristotle concludes, is clearly both expedient and just. But nature's failure to match bodies with minds so that we could, without controversy, distinguish the higher and the lower in *human* associations means that the political order of ruler and ruled is constantly open to dialectical examination and challenge.[100]

This is not an argument to every Athenian that his household slaves, or those slaves who were Athenian policemen, bankers and recorders of law, are such because they are deficient in that definitional human capacity to reason autonomously, and hence are incapable of making deliberative choices. Instead, it is an argument of the form: *if* slavery is natural *then* there must exist certain persons who are essentially slaves everywhere (how many we cannot say), even if they happen not to be slaves, and similarly, there are certain persons who are essentially slaves nowhere. Aristotle comes as close to naming those who appear, by their behaviour, to be naturally slavish when he says that one (we Greeks) cannot admit that a man that does not deserve slavery can really be a slave. Greeks, the archetypical *polis*-livers abiding by the law as the principle of justice, if taken as prisoners of war and sold, cannot be said (by Greeks) to be slaves because we cannot admit that they deserve enslavement, but barbarians *can be said* to be slaves because they deserve enslavement. When people say this, Aristotle says, they are merely seeking for the principles of natural slavery.

Aristotle's remarks about barbarians and natural slaves are not intended to demonstrate that barbarians *are* natural slaves; it is not historical redescription. Rather, he argues from common Greek opinion to a deeper analysis of what Greeks despise in non-Greeks who appear to display a certain kind of character. It is not their non-Greekness as such that is despised but their apparent failure to show themselves to be the valued man who makes up his mind and who can internalize law. Such deficient men, if they exist and are among 'us', have a claim on 'us'. Not least, they would serve to remind 'us' that a life of drudgery is not the best life for men and if there are some whom it suits, then the best life for them is to be in partnership with someone who finds the good life through self-determining and mutual practices.[101]

Principles arise in us as a result of experience and induction. Induction exhibits the universal implicit in the self-evident nature of the particular – here, the barbarian. It is the initial social premise, the as yet unexamined 'definition' or 'nature' of the natural slave, provided by already morally virtuous *polis*-living agents, and derived from these kinds of Greeks observing the character of the apparently naturally slavish, read against the definition of man. Nature intends men to fit their definition but sometimes, Aristotle says, she is unable to realize her intention. This is the reason the definition of 'slave' comes within the definition of 'human' but the 'slave' falls short of actualization as a man. *If* they exist, they do not, by nature, actualize the specific difference that separates men from their genus *animal*. But in so far as they are within the spectrum of the species 'man'[102] they are, even like the best examples of man, impelled to form partnerships such

---

100   W. J. Booth, 'Politics and the Household: a commentary on Aristotle's *Politics* book 1', *History of Political Thought* (1981), pp. 203–26.

101   Clark, *Aristotle's Man*, pp. 106–7.

102   'No Aristotelian classification can be other than flexible in the nomenclature employed' (Clark, *Aristotle's Man*, p. 32).

as friendships. Not all friendships or partnerships are between equals. Only the perfect friendship is one between true equals, where each sees the other as 'another self'. The political partnership or friendship is said to be one of equals, but even here all men who are free and equal are not equal in all respects. So too, pre-political partnerships in the household, formed for mutual but distinct benefits on the part of the partners are not relationships of complete equals. There is no problem of the possibility of a utilitarian rather than perfect friendship between a master and a natural slave as men,[103] any more than there would be a problem between the different but still unequal, although more equal, partnership or friendship between husband and wife who are equal in some respects but not in others.[104]

Aristotle characterizes the rule by the husband and father over women and children as free, but where the matrimonial relationship is permanent rule of the wife by her husband as though by a statesman, and over children, as kingly rule. In the household, which is a product of deliberative choice and not simply of the impulse to solidarity and reproduction, the male assumes the role of natural ruler and the female of the naturally ruled, each free and sharing in virtue but in those virtues specific to their respective natures *where such natures are considered in terms of their functional contribution to the household*. We always need reminding that *Politics* I is about interconnected *partnerships* of distinct kinds and Aristotle's discussion is always carried out in terms of the proper organization of human partnerships with qualitatively distinct characteristics. Indeed, the whole of the *Politics* treats the proper organization of partnerships as its background theme, since these peculiarly human associations are the conditions in which man's intellectual and moral virtues, as discussed in *Ethics*, can be, and always are, brought to actuality.

Now, in this household partnership the rule of husband over wife and children who are free is, despite Aristotle's terseness, a much more ambiguous argument than the rule of master over slave. Rule over the free hints at the potential problems of the political partnership, to be taken up later, where the differences between rulers and ruled are far from evident because in virtue of being free, men tend to see themselves as equal in *all* respects, and this is something we know that Aristotle rejects (NE V). Indeed, he insists that the *polis* as 'state' is not merely a plurality of men but of different *kinds* of men; you cannot make a 'state', he says, out of men who are all alike (*Politics* II,1261a22 ff.). This is one of his major criticisms of Plato. Hence, he argues for a reciprocal equivalence that keeps the 'state' in being. Is there a similar reciprocal equivalence between a husband and wife in the household?[105]

The fixed place Aristotle establishes for women in the household is recognized as contradicted by Plato's *Republic* and by Sparta, both of whose political constitutions will be critically discussed by Aristotle in book 2. In fact, Aristotle concludes book 1 of the *Politics* with a discussion of wives and children, saying that certain questions concerning the character of their relationship and education must be treated later when he treats of various forms of constitution. The education of women and children depends on the political organization of the 'state' of which they are, loosely speaking, 'parts' (*Politics* I,

103 *Pace* E. Barker, *The Political Thought of Plato and Aristotle* (London, 1918), pp. 359ff.; see NE 8 on the types of friendship.
104   See below, pp. 202–3, 206–12.
105   See below, pp. 206–12.

1260b8–20). 'For just as man and wife are each part of a household partnership, so we should regard a "state" also as divided into two parts approximately equal numerically, one of men, one of women' (*Politics* II, 1269b12ff.). From the point of view of the ultimate partnership, the *polis*, a constitution must provide for the good regulation of each part. The 'state' as a plurality depends on education to bring about its common unity (*Politics* II, 1263b5ff.) and that education must be provided, by legislators, not only to a Guardian class, as he understands Plato, nor only to men, as in Sparta, but to all who can benefit from it. The legislator's aim is somehow to moderate appetites by training desires, for there is no *natural* limit to desires (*Politics* II, 1266b30 and 1267b4ff.). The legislator's aim is to provide those laws that enable the aims of a 'state's' constitution to be achieved as well as the attainment of the happiness of the 'state'. Hence, women as well as men must be well-regulated, and he argues in *Politics* II that Sparta's constitution did not achieve this, because, with the men absent for long periods on military service, their women were left to exercise an unregulated kind of freedom that led them and the whole of the society into lives of luxuriousness and dissolution. This kind of military society's constitution usually honours wealth in times of peace. In the times of the Spartan empire, the women ruled and when this military society turned to peaceful pursuits, handing themselves over to a lawgiver who was prepared for obedience from men who had lived a military life, the women were not similarly regulated. What, asks Aristotle, is the difference between women ruling and rulers ruled by women? This question is not specifically targeted at the inadequacies of women as rulers, but rather at the very notion that a society ruled by women *or* men and not by law is inadequate. The result is the same: admiration of luxury and wealth on the one hand and bravery, largely on the part of men, in times of war, on the other. But Aristotle, like Plato, believes that bravery is of service for none of the regular duties of life, except perhaps in warfare, and even here Spartan women caused more confusion than the enemy (*Politics* II, 1269b19–29). Aristotle concludes that the Spartans were stable enough while at war but declined once they achieved supremacy; they did not understand how to be at leisure, as Plato too had noted in his *Laws*, and they never engaged in any kind of training higher than training for war. They only valued one part of virtue, military valour (*Politics* II, 1271a41–1271b7). But a state's constitution must properly regulate all of its 'parts' by means of laws educating desires and this ought to include being concerned for the role of women's contribution to that *perfect* partnership, the well-regulated *polis*.

Of course, the best *polis* will organize its constituent households according to the needs of the political man who is also a self-sufficient householder. The household, by definition as the self-sufficient unit, itself made up of distinct partnerships, themselves characterized by the qualities that define mastership, matrimonial and paternal relations, is what it is because of the respective natures of men, women, children and slaves *when considered in terms of their functional contribution to that deliberative partnership, the household, that seeks to endure.* But once there is a *polis* whose aim is not simply to achieve the sufficient life but to live well, then the household itself is (re)organized with a view to that higher end. If men are political animals because they already are in the political and engage in practices there, then women are wives and mothers because they already are in the household and engage in practices there. But in so far as households are parts of *poleis*, then the principles that emerge from moral practices within a law-governed political sphere of activity have their effects at home in the formation of and continued display of character.

Character, the evaluation of observed practices, is the external judgement of inferred internal dispositions that is appropriate to ethical and political discourse. Hence, if it is the case that from the practices of the female in the household, we infer that the deliberative faculty of the soul is present 'but ineffective'(!) or 'without authority',[106] then from what has so far been said, it must in the case of the (natural) slave not be present at all (*Politics* I, 1259b21–1260a20). All that can be inferred from a *polis*-living 'man's' behaviour is that he is somehow deprived, or not, of the capacity to make long-term plans for living well, and if so deprived he acts only to achieve present satisfactions. A 'human' who lives thus, as though in nature and not in *poleis*, is not by definition the best example of his kind. His performances show him not to be master of himself, a self-mover, and hence he exhibits characteristics that indicate to others that he would benefit from 'belonging' to a man who is master of himself. Aristotle suggests that such a slave will be trained in cookery and other forms of domestic service.

It appears that for Aristotle, *if* there are individuals who exist to exemplify the category 'natural slave' *then* barbarians come about as close to this, *for ordinary Greeks*, as it is possible to come. He says that a man *is called* master not in virtue of what he knows but simply in virtue of what he is. And by now we know that when we engage in ethical and political discourse, an imprecise mode of argument but one which enables us to grasp the modes of social evaluation in order to make explicit the ends and means of agency in *poleis*, what a man is, is inferred from what he does. Similarly, says Aristotle, with slave and free.

But when the slave–master relationship arises out of force or conventional law, Aristotle says that it is unjust, unnatural and neither slave nor master can be said to share a common interest.

The wider question that emerges from this is whether there are people, judged on the basis of their moral behaviour within the society in which they live, about whom it is inferred that they are not deliberative choosers. Whether or not there is an institution of slavery, are there people who behave in such a way as to be judged by others in the community as actively preferring to be taken over by others? They would appear to be people unconcerned for social honour, indifferent to praise and blame, uninvolved in social discourse about the means to the human good, indeed, apparently indifferent to there being an inward guiding principle that channels what men do in order for them to consider how to be happy as men. For instance, are there people who, no matter what the moral values of their community may be, strike other members of the community as never getting beyond the notion that labouring *is* living? If, no matter how rewarding in some senses, labouring is not what truly human living is about according to Aristotle and those who come from *poleis* 'like ours', then are there people who are thought of as never realizing this? If they existed they would be people without characters formed from doing good or bad actions voluntarily, from which arise those virtues and vices which display our dispositions to desire to act in one way or another. Aristotle insists that such a person is not to be judged vicious and blameable but rather is one who is treated benevolently by being taken over. Aristotle describes him in *Nicomachean Ethics* VII as the brutish man whose intellect is not corrupt but lacking. This is not a character who has been corrupted by impoverished social practices because he is judged not acculturated at all. His life is that of a drudge, performing little tasks which help others attain material self-sufficiency and the leisure to engage in truly human practices in the *polis*.

106   See below, p. 209.

This description of the partnership between the natural master and the natural slave looks like a more benevolent version of modern policies for 'care in the community'! The real problem with Aristotle's argument, it seems to me, is not the argument itself but the imprecision of ethical and political discourse, a problem acknowledged numerous times by Aristotle himself, a problem that arises in all human communities precisely because men draw inferences about dispositions from behavioural acts. Today, it is not that such persons are not judged to exist, but rather that *we* consider the kind of character described by Aristotle and his community to be the product of socialization. Currently, sociologists call them 'the underclass' or the 'socially excluded'. Clearly, in Aristotle's world, the common opinion of such men's character, constructed from inferences drawn from their behaviour, led to the opinion that they were somehow naturally so constituted. From Greek experience, 'barbarians' were not *polis*-livers, the norm. Indeed, they were not even judged to be deliberative householders. However problematic their status, the ancient Greeks certainly judged them to be useful. And those who argued that slavery was not natural but conventional none the less never seemed to argue for the dissolution of the status quo of slavery in Greek households.

Aristotle is perhaps an exception even here, however. In *Politics* VII he discusses the best constitution, constructed exactly as one would wish within the bounds of possibility, that constitution which has considered what is the most desirable mode of life and has duly organized social and political life among similar and equal people in order to provide the conditions in which the good life can be achieved by those who have the opportunity to take at least minimal advantage of the leisure required for moral agency. He argues in favour of private ownership of the land by citizens, but a community use of the land (*Politics* VII, 1329b40–1330a25). Although 'states' need property, the property is not a part of the 'state'. Those who cultivate the land are not the citizens but slaves drawn from a variety of peoples and preferably from those without a spirited character so that they will do their work and abstain from insurrection. We recall that spirit (*thymos*) is precisely what Aristotle believes is necessary for desire to be governed by reason, spirit being that soul-capacity from which the love of freedom is derived (*Politics* VII, 1328a6–7). The Greeks, we also recall being told, speak of an article of property as absolutely belonging to the owner and hence these slaves who work the land are the private possessions of the private owners of the land. But then he says cryptically, 'how slaves should be employed and why it is advantageous that *all slaves should have their freedom set before them as a reward,* we will say later' (1330a26–34). But he never takes this up again. It appears that these slaves cannot be those considered *by nature* slavish because anyone for whom freedom is a good could not, by Greeks, be considered natural slaves! But freed slaves can never, for Aristotle, be true citizens (1278a2) because they have not developed the citizen's virtue of the capacity for governing. Neither, as we shall see, have free labourers.

The nature/nurture debate is still not over although *our* common opinion has arrived at the position that nature probably is subordinate to nurture. Neither position appears to be demonstrable (although some have tried) but we have observed that the consequences for holding one view rather than the other are immense. And most of us in liberal societies would prefer to be consequentialists in these matters. In part, this is because many are also social contractarians of one form or another, believing that in origin, unlike Plato's and Aristotle's beliefs, we are all naturally self-interested non-cooperators so that politics is an artificial rather than natural construction. This brings other problems concerning the nature of politics to our agenda which were not on

Aristotle's, one of which is that we are constantly trying to construct a 'state' which will *never* draw the conclusion that its constituent natural non-cooperators are slaves by nature, and treat us accordingly as 'taken over' non-deliberators either about the means to our human good or about that good itself.

Aristotle and Women

Aristotle's understanding of the requirements of citizenship is intermingled with his treatment of gender. His biology is interwoven with his ethico-political discourse, but to what degree? Undoubtedly he presents a notion of participation in political activities, beyond the concerns for household economics, as an exclusive domain of males. He is, after all, both speaking to ancient Greeks and methodologically beginning with the common opinions of his culture.

There is no scholarly consensus on how to interpret Aristotle's brief, sometimes ambiguous and often imprecise views about the proper social and political role of women.[107] An older tradition saw him as the loving family man alive to the mutual affection and friendship possible between husbands and wives, and this tradition had no difficulties concerning his restriction of women to the household and in a subordinate role to their husbands.[108] More recently, Aristotle has been targeted as the ideologue of sexism, marshalling his biological theories to demonstrate his belief in male superiority, both in reproduction and in political engagement.[109] There is more of a consensus about his negative views of females in his biological writings, but the degree to which these views have a direct or indirect bearing on what he says about women in the *Politics* (and *Ethics*) is not agreed. Nor is it agreed that by depriving women of opportunities for political engagement Aristotle is arguing that men, who do have such access, are engaging in the highest form of human activity. For some,[110] Aristotle is not a whole-hearted advocate of the superior value of political activity above personal and family life: on this view, he neither upgrades political engagement nor downgrades the family and household to the degree that some have maintained. Indeed, citizenship as political participation – sharing in deliberative and judicial office – is thought not to be necessary for the good life. According to this interpretation, Aristotle's famous statement that humans are *polis*-living animals does not require that they engage in holding office; all that is required is that they do not live alone, and that they live in a community that has moral law and order, that is, that the political community is fairly stable, offering security of life and property, and that they live within the context of social institutions which include the family.

Furthermore, it has been argued by some recent scholars[111] that Aristotle's position is

107   See the summary of the literature provided by R. G. Mulgan, 'Aristotle and the Political Role of Women', *History of Political Thought* 15 (1994), pp. 179–202.

108   Barker, *The Political Thought of Plato and Aristotle*; A. Bloom, *The Closing of the American Mind* (London, 1988 [1987]), pp. 112ff.

109   P. Cartledge, *The Greeks*, pp. 66–70 and A. Saxonhouse, *Women in the History of Political Thought: ancient Greece to Machiavelli* (New York, 1985), ch. 4, provide good overviews.

110   Mulgan, 'Aristotle and the Political Role of Women', pp.183–4; T. Duvall and P. Dotson, 'Political Participation and *Eudaimonia* in Aristotle's Politics', *History of Political Thought* 19 (1998), pp. 21–34.

111   S. G. Salkever, 'Women, Soldiers, Citizens: Plato and Aristotle on the politics of virility', in Lord and O'Connor, *Essays on the Foundations of Aristotelian Political Science*, pp. 165–90.

far less mysogynistic than either the common opinion of his day (recall that Aristotle never simply presents the common view but tries to save what he can where he can) or the later European tradition of political theory and practice, with the latter's completely dismissive attitudes regarding there being any relation whatever between women and the political.

We have already observed in chapter 1 that ancient Athens connected its political freedoms with the male courage of soldier citizens.[112] But Aristotle's *Ethics* and *Politics* are not uncritical hymns to Periklean or any other period in Athenian history. For instance, Aristotle believes, unlike Periklean Athenians, that the best exemplification of human activity is not to be observed in war but rather in leisure.[113] And the best teachers of virtue are not warriors but legislators with a correct insight into human psychology and a concern to establish those laws that will habituate agents in the household *and polis* to co-operative, reasoned and correctly desired peaceful, specifically human ends.

Neither Plato nor Aristotle was trying to answer what would become modern liberal questions: are women equal to men? Ought they to have the same rights? It has been claimed, plausibly I think with regard to Plato,[114] that even with Plato's disparaging remarks about women as females being emotional, indeed hysterical temptresses, none the less some of the desirable qualities of character required of that Guardian philosopher–citizen who justly merits social recognition and who can be trusted to rule justly for the common good, are precisely those qualities which ordinary ancient Greeks normally attributed to women: peacefulness, playfulness, a realization of human mutual dependence and a conscious will to engage in rationally guided co-operative moderation for the good of the partnership. These characteristics were opposed, by Plato, to the more traditional ones of war-making and courageous spiritedness in the service of competitive (aristocratic) honour-mongering in his own society.[115] Aristotle takes this aspect of Plato's implicit critique of common Greek male attitudes concerning the necessary qualities of citizenship somewhat further.

In so far as the distinguishing characteristics of humanness are reason and *logos*, the exercise of which define the specifically human virtue or excellence, Aristotle does not deny these to women. Women possess the deliberative capacity and they live according to a rational principle that takes into account the overall interest of a human (*Politics* I, 1260a13). Women, like men, are rational animals and like men they require education to virtuous behaviour; both men and women, when children, receive this habituation to moral practices at home. Humans of both sexes learn by imitation. But do little girls and little boys engage in the same practices which none the less habituate them to virtuous behaviour? Aristotle never tells us directly, but the answer must be 'no'. Little girls are habituated to virtuous practices by imitating habituated practitioners – their mothers. This does not mean that it will never be required of women that they develop the intellectual virtue of practical wisdom or prudence. Although there will be no call on them to have experiences of the sort that will engage the kind of choice-making that

---

112   See Perikles' funeral oration for Athenian soldiers in Thucydides' *History*, where it is said that the virtue of Athenian women was to remain silent and at home.

113   See above, p. 203, for his criticism of Sparta.

114   A. Saxonhouse, 'Philosopher and Female in the Political Thought of Plato', *Political Theory* 4 (1976), pp. 195–212; also Saxonhouse, *Women*, esp. ch. 4.

115   S. G. Salkever, 'Women, Soldiers, Citizens'.

will issue in decisions and actions that affect the 'common good' of those outside their home, women, when mature and as wives and mothers, are described as deliberators with a view to a human end. Their sphere of activity, however, is sufficiently filled with the *particular* moral and organizational demands of child education and household management that their prudence will be characterized by the agenda (what is to be done and how ought it to be done) of the field in which it is exercised. The question that remains is whether women remain in the household as deliberators with a view to a moral end because this sphere of their agency is determined for them by their biology and psychology.

Recall that in order to develop into a prudent agent in the *political* world one most already be habituated to the practices of moral virtue, those practices that are praiseworthy and are thought to reflect the stability of one's character dispositions. The mature deliberative choices made by the *phronimos*, the man of practical wisdom, amid the contingencies of lived life are guided by the already grasped principle of what is good for man that has arisen in him as a habituated practitioner. Habituation to moral virtue is constituted by the rational education of one's desires. The training of any individual's desires begins, for Aristotle, within the household. Mothers as well as fathers, both as deliberators, are essential to the moral education of their children. Therefore, it is essential to Aristotle, and a major part of his rejection of Plato's abolition of the biological family for Guardians, that the household be maintained as the necessary preparatory sphere of experience and desire-habituation prior to engagement in moral and political activity. But the child's household remains only a necessary preparatory educational experience for men – it is not the limit of the experience suited to their sex; for women the household serves as both preparation for the roles of wife and mother as well as the limit of the experience suited to their sex. Aristotle's functionalism emerges here: the human excellences are further differentiated into the more particular excellences of men and women. Even within the household, there are certain matters which befit a woman and the husband leaves these to her (NE VIII, 11, 1160b33–5).

Furthermore, he says that husbands rule their wives by a kind of rule, *political rule,* that is, the kind of rule that is proper among free and equal men of independent value in the *polis.* This political rule of husband over wife is contrasted with the kingly rule of father over child, and the despotic rule of master over slave. Women should be ruled as fellow citizens: they have independent interests and have independent value, existing for their own sake and not for the sake of another. But where fellow (male) citizens take turns in ruling and being ruled, women are never to rule. Within the household men have unquestioned authority. Women and men in households are equal in some respects but not in all. Aristotle also believed that men in political relationships in the *polis* were free and equal but this did not mean they were considered equal in *all* respects either. Men engaged in politics were to be considered proportionately equal, depending on their merit. This was made clear in Aristotle's discussion of the proper operation of distributive justice (NE V). However, even this recognition of proportionate equality does not provide scope for women to enter the political sphere, even as junior citizens, and apply their deliberative capacities there. He does not see women in the household as men's slaves or to be treated as children, and this enables him to contrast barbarian practices with those of the Greek household. But a woman is definitely to practise her moral life under the authority of her husband. Aristotle sees no incompatibility, as we may do, between a woman's capacity for virtuous action and her being under the overall authority of men. It appears that women have not developed a taste for liberty, to rule and be ruled in turn.

Today we ask why are Aristotle's women not full participants in political life and why are they permanently ruled by their men at home? Is it simply that Aristotle's biology now intrudes? It does appear that aspects of women's biology, as with men's biology, lead to distinctions concerning what Aristotle takes to be the separate spheres in which the species-specific reasoning capacity functions. The particular virtues or excellences of women *as* women in households are different from the excellences of men *as* men in households. Women, he insists, do deliberate (unlike slaves and children) but they do so 'without authority'. The problem arises as to what this lack of authority (*akuron*) means and the degree to which his biology is meant to penetrate his ethical and political discourse to provide an answer. Is the characteristically human capacity to deliberate separate from the social conditions which may or may not acknowledge the authority of this capacity? Is this lack of authority, as Fortenbaugh argues, an *interpersonal* relationship so that women's psychology lacks authority in their relation to men who rule over them?[116] Or is the lack of authority linked to the female deliberating capacity itself and therefore a distinguishing characteristic of the possessor's psychology alone? The former solution seems more likely than the latter. Aristotle says enough to generate our questions but not enough to enable us to be certain as to the answers he would have given in his ethico-political discourse. But in so far as he argues that there is no specific difference between men and women, we may think he believed that in being born human, women as well as men shared exactly the same intellectual virtues: the capacity to learn to develop ways of thinking the ways humans do think. Their difference would be rather in the moral virtues to which each sex had respectively become habituated. If the difference between men and women is with regard to the emotions specific to each sex, then reason would have to work on female emotions in order to habituate desires in ways different from the way reason worked on male emotions. The *Politics* tells us nothing that can enable us to decide. Whatever the answer, Aristotle grounds his ethico-political analysis as applied to women in concrete social behaviour rather than in abstract rational principles. Practices are for him the origins of the principles we come to live by. Hence, this problem of interpreting an ambiguous remark about the location of women's deliberative 'authority' has led, in the end, to some interpreters arguing, probably justly,[117] that Aristotle's biological works, which definitely present females as of inferior status to males, allowed him in his ethico-political writings to maintain some of the typical prejudices of Greek men as an unthinking sexism. None the less, Aristotle allows women more scope for moral agency in the household than typical Greeks allowed.

Aristotle's biology is a functionalist biology, guided by a teleology and penetrated by natural hierarchies. Because Aristotle argues that unlike wild beasts, humans form household partnerships, then male and female excellences are different with regard to that partnership. In his *Historia Animalium* (9.608b11ff.; also see *De Generatione Animalium*, I, 729a28ff.) Aristotle presents a list of natural (emotional) differences to the effect that women are more sensitive to heat and cold than men, are more affectionate towards their children than men, and are better fitted to life indoors. The woman is

---

116   W. Fortenbaugh, 'Aristotle on Slaves and Women', in Barnes, Schofield and Sorabji, *Articles on Aristotle, 2: Ethics and Politics*, pp. 135–9.
117   S. R. L. Clark, 'Aristotle's Woman', *History of Political Thought* 3 (1982), pp. 177–92.

more compassionate, more emotional, easily moved to tears, more jealous, more queru-
lous, more apt to strike and scold. She is more prone to periods of depression, less
hopeful, less concerned with shame or self-respect, more false of speech and deceptive
and has a better memory than men. She also sleeps less, is more difficult to rouse to
action and needs less food! In short, Aristotle fills out Plato's more general statement that
women are weaker than men. Clark argues[118] that Aristotle's recognition that women
have a capacity for deliberation but without authority, is easily understood even if not
argued for by Aristotle: women were observed to be less able to withstand their own
passions so as not properly to be considered responsible for their incontinence (*akrasia*) at
all. This, however, was the common view (from observation and induction) and it can
be found expressed in much contemporary literature. But Aristotle does not himself
argue that women cannot be considered 'incontinent' and therefore are not responsible
for their emotions. If he did so argue for an incorrigible lack of emotional control in
women he could never criticize those 'states' whose constitutions forgot to legislate for
women as well as men: he would have to admit that women could not be habituated to
moral virtue through the legislator's efforts. Aristotle also noted (*Metaphysics* IX, 1058a29)
that humans are one species and that between the male and female there is no specific
difference.

In his biological work *De Generatione Animalium* (IV, 766a18ff.), however, he says
that females are infertile males. If the paternal principle of motion fails to master the
maternal material, thereby moulding it to the father's form, the result is a female. Because the female is wetter and colder than the male her blood cannot produce a living
being; and her coldness and wetness apparently leads the female to be less confident, less
strong, open to temptation, and like children, she has a high voice. To what extent does
this bizarre (to us) biology lead him to be unaware of certain observed characteristics of
women as products of social conditioning? Recall that his complaint against Spartan
women was that their love of luxury was the consequence of a failure of constitutional
discipline which, in a military society, was imposed on the men alone. No human is ever
blamed for having emotions as such. Blame and praise accrue to one's character, to
what, through one's choices, one shows oneself as desiring or avoiding. None the less,
Clark argues that 'Aristotle clearly thinks that the gap of achievement and character
between male and female is not merely a cultural but a biological datum.'[119] This is
probably true.

But when Aristotle argues that the difference of sexual *role* is greatest in humankind,
not simply because humans are the most perfect of animals or because in humans it can
be observed that the two sexes are most clearly distinguished and most fully collabora-
tive (*Historia Animalium* IX, 608b5ff.), he is forecasting an observation that is typical of
ethico-political discourse: that human males and females come together in households
not simply out of the procreative urge or the urge to solidarity but because they alone,
both of them, have a capacity for long-term co-operative deliberation about the unit's
moral and economic self-sufficiency. They share the rule of the household by role division and each can live and act well as responsible agents. This means that women are
eudaimones too. Aristotle does not offer women the opportunity of becoming Guardians,
as did Plato, reducing them in effect to a male model of rational but genderless beings.

---

118   Ibid., p. 179.
119   Ibid., p. 182.

Aristotle's women's *eudaimonia* is clearly of another kind. And Aristotle is simply not concerned with it because women, for him, are less of a problem in a 'state' with good laws.

Clark suggests, in general, an interesting reason for this: he argues that politics and civic engagement are particular efforts 'by the male cohort isolated from the female lineage to provide its members with a sense of being and belonging. Patriarchalism involves a corresponding effort to break up female nexuses, to bring daughters to the husband's home, and create a new male lineage, the household.'[120] But why?

Instead of arguing that in relegating women to the male-ruled household sphere (for whatever reasons, biological or social) Aristotle was providing an answer to what Greeks may commonly have seen as their 'woman problem', we might argue plausibly that Aristotle's ethico-political project is concerned more with their 'men problem'. If there is an indirect line between Aristotle's biological works and his *Ethics* and *Politics* then it traces a route defined by a species-specific set of partnerships where, ultimately, the males have to find something to do with themselves beyond going to war. Recall that everyone learns from doing. On this view, men have to *learn* how to care for others; this is what the good man of prudence is and what he gets from the experience of household management and *polis*-living. Women, on this view, at least in households, learn more readily how to care for others: their natural emotions become tuned to caring for their children, they show themselves to be more compassionate and jealously focused on blood of their blood. But they too, like men, need the larger moral framework of a law-governed *polis* where law works with nature rather than against it. This kind of *polis* as a perfect partnership would enable them to actualize their potentials, and that of their progeny, in the home.

Whatever we think of this kind of argument, we must always recall that his very discussion of women along with slaves in *Politics* book 1 is set within the larger discussion of the nature of that deliberative partnership that is, for him, the definition of a proper household. Here he is not primarily focused on analysing women as females or slaves as humans. Hence, whatever he says about women, as with slaves, is to be understood in terms of the respective natures of men, women, children and slaves *when considered in terms of their functional contribution to that deliberative partnership that seeks to endure as an economic and moral entity*. In the end he is not offering in the *Politics* a biology or a psychology of slaves or women but an ethico-political discourse. From this perspective, in ethics as in politics, the nature of someone, what someone is, is inferred from what he or she does; from practices we infer dispositions. The Greek household exemplified the practices of a partnership of a qualitatively distinct and, Aristotle believed, highly evolved kind. As such it served as the most evolved form of partnership for human self-sufficiency in the economic and moral domains that was capable of continuing in existence for the good life, carried on within the law-structured *polis* and working with, rather than against, human nature for the common good. Since the life which is best for humans, both separately as individuals and collectively as 'states', is the life which has virtue sufficiently supported by material resources to facilitate participation in the actions that virtue calls for (*Politics* VII, 1323b40), no discussion of any *politeia* (be it the absolutely best constitution or the various possible and actual constitutions which organize the inhabitants of any given 'state' (*Politics* III, 1274b39)) can be divorced from society made

---

120   Ibid., p. 190.

up of family households, (foreign) residents of the *polis,* as well as citizens. The *polis* as the supreme partnership is, after all, a composite of less perfect partnerships.

The 'State' and its Citizens

Statesmen and legislators are concerned with the *polis* or 'state', particularly in terms of the ways in which *all* the inhabitants of a *polis* may be organized (*Politics* III, 1274b37–9). The social, economic and political organization of *all* the inhabitants of a given *polis* is generally referred to by ancient Greeks as a 'state's' constitution (*politeia*) and hence the word *politeia* conveys a much larger range of meanings than our modern notion of a written or unwritten constitution.

That there are or have been different constitutions among 'us' reflects a lack of agreement as to what essentially the 'state' is, or rather, what the 'state' is for, and it is Aristotle's aim in the *Politics* to come to a fairly comprehensive, plausible, indeed true understanding of the nature of the 'state'.[121] Since we have been told that the 'state' is classed as a composite thing, then Aristotle suggests that perhaps we can best approach the nature of this supreme partnership by focusing on what everyone can come to agree on: that the 'state' is an aggregate of its citizens, an aggregate of those with the fullest sovereign power over the *administration* of public affairs. As is to be expected methodologically, we can discover the definition of the 'state' by examining the whole by way of its citizen parts.

But what unites the aggregate citizens or 'parts' is the constitution itself. The 'state' is not a chance aggregate of people but one that is self-sufficient for the needs of human life (*Politics* VII, 1328b16). If we ask why people form this qualitatively distinct partnership called the 'state' the answer is that they seek not simply an association of people living in the same place, nor do they simply seek to prevent members from committing injustice against each other. The *polis* is not simply a mutual protection society. Neither do people associate simply to promote economic or commercial transactions. All these functions must be present as preconditions if there is to be a 'state', but even the presence of all of these factors does not make a 'state' in its truest sense. Rather, the 'state' is formed as a a partnership to enable its members in households and kinship groups to live well by living a full and independent life (*Politics* III, 1280b29ff.). It is for the sake of morally fine, mutual actions, which are the products of exercising what is best in humans, their moral and intellectual virtues with and for one another. For this reason, those who contribute most to this kind of partnership and with this higher, mutually reciprocal purpose in view are for this reason seen to be entitled to a larger share in the 'state' in the sense of having public office or honours accorded them, than those who, though they may be equal or even superior in free birth and family status, are inferior in the virtue that belongs to a citizen who understands and acts upon these aims of the

---

121 Curtis Johnson argues for a logically prior set of questions – why do varieties of the state exist? How many varieties are there? What is the natural order among the varieties? – and second-order questions which cannot be answered until the first ordered ones are. Second-order questions involve particular forms of constitution: what is the best state absolutely, what is the best constitution for most states, what is the best constitution under given conditions, and how are constitutions established, preserved and destroyed. Unfortunately, Aristotle pursues both types of question at the same time. For an attempt to disentangle the first- and second-order questions see Johnson, *Aristotle's Theory of the State* (London, 1990), p. xvi.

partnership (*Politics* III, 1280b29–35). Aristotle does not defend a traditional aristocracy of birth. He defends the virtuous character. To understand the end of political partnership is to understand why distributive justice is based on proportional merit.

But as we already know from *Nicomachean Ethics* (V), different constitutions hold different views as to the criteria of distributive justice. To administer public affairs in whatever constitution requires that you operate on prior principles that suit the kind of people being governed and these are revealed in your 'state's' laws. The laws have to be well-enacted so that a given people may abide by them; it is not enough to have laws which no one obeys (*Politics* IV, 1294a3ff.). Constitutions depend on the kind of people to be governed and not on some posited universal, theoretical principle (*Politics* VI, 1317a35ff.,*contra* Plato). A people is one because it shares in a given conception of law and virtue; hence, it is important for them to know one another's characters in order that they can trust those in office to administer the laws and make judgements which conform to their values (*Politics* VII, 1326b15ff.). Principles of justice exist in all 'states' and are relative to the constitution. Aristotle does not, however, stop at this relativist observation. Some constitutions establish laws which are unjust, while others use the term 'justice' in too limited a sense, reflecting the experiences and practices of the people governed. Only one 'state', the best, and therefore providing the conditions for the best experiences and practices, holds the correct view on what a *polis* truly is for, and establishes a constitution with the kind of distributive justice outlined above.

If a 'state' is a collection of citizens then we need to examine what, by definition, a citizen is. We do this by beginning with common opinions, discussing who is judged to be entitled to the name of citizen in different 'states'. We already know that not all the persons who are indispensable for the existence of the *polis* are called citizens *in the strict sense* in *poleis* like 'ours', despite there being different constitutions or ways of organizing the *polis*; for instance, women, children and slaves are never, strictly speaking, citizens because each is said, by Greeks, to suffer from one (more or less permanent) disability or another, and only some constitutions admit foreign residents to citizenship ('we' often call children citizens but they are incomplete ones: 1278a4). By definition, and this applies more or less to all constitutional arrangements, Aristotle says that a citizen is defined by the recognized capacity *actually to participate in giving judgement and in holding office*. This is what sovereign power is taken to mean: the participation in the administration of public affairs. Especially if his tenure of office is of an unlimited length he notes that this description best fits a democracy.

In different constitutions sovereignty may be in the hands of one, a few or of many (1279a26). But in different constitutions there are differences of *opinion* concerning who is a citizen; for instance, someone judged to be one in a democracy (rule by all free and usually poor men who make up the majority) is not judged a citizen in an oligarchy (rule by the rich who are usually a minority). Different 'states' have different criteria for admitting men to citizenship, so defined: some determine citizenship by wealth and have property qualifications, others by birth, either in terms of class or in terms of whether both mother and/or father is a citizen, and some by merit. *Generally, a 'state' is a sufficiently numerous collection of such persons participating in deliberative and judicial office so as to secure a self-sufficient life (Politics* III, 1275b18–20.) In so far as the citizen aggregate aims in different ways at a collective good – the securing of the sufficient life of the whole – rather than at partial or individual goods, it deliberates, judges and administers for that purpose. In this active sense, the citizen-body *is* the constitution (1278b9). More particularly, the constitution is its ordering of public offices, and the ways in which its offices are distributed, along with the principled aims of the community, enable us to distinguish one constitution from another (*Politics* IV, 1289a15ff.).

There are, schematically, six constitutional types ranging from monarchy, aristocracy, polity, to democracy, oligarchy and tyranny. There are several varieties of each type. The participation of one, few or many in deliberative and judicial office determines both the number and the quality of those deemed sovereign citizens and held responsible for public administration of the *polis*. Who actually is a citizen varies according to the constitution in which he is one. But Aristotle is interested in discovering the standard – what are the correct criteria by which we can determine who truly ought to be considered capable of participating in public office and deliberating about public matters? – and thereby defining the citizen proper and demonstrating the degree to which one constitution or another measures up to this standard.

Aristotle sets out a rough classification of three 'correct' and three 'deviated' or mistaken constitutions. He attributes priority to 'correct' constitutions and posteriority to the 'deviated' ones, not in the sense that 'correct' constitutions chronologically or historically emerged prior to their deviations; rather, the deviations are bad and are to be conceived of as falling away from their true, correct definitions. A deviated constitution is conceptually dependent on its correct form and their deviancy is with respect to their not being true to the essential nature of what a constitution is: an organization of all inhabitants in such a way as to aim at the well-being of all.[122] Now, depending on the constitution, sovereignty can reside in one man, in a few or in many. Whenever the one, few or the many rule with a view to the common good or the general advantage, which is what the *polis* came into existence to provide (1282b14–17), we have 'correct' constitutions, and the usual names for these are monarchy, aristocracy and polity. How each achieves the well-being of all through the criteria established for admission to public office (citizen participation) is separate from the unity these 'correct' forms display in being properly orientated to that collective well-being.

On the other hand, those constitutions ruled over by one, few or many that look only to the private or sectional interests of the one, few or many respectively, and not to the good of the whole community, are deviant and are called tyranny (deviated from monarchy), oligarchy (deviated from aristocracy) and democracy (deviated from polity). Tyranny is a rule of one man for his own benefit, oligarchy is rule of the rich for the rich alone, and democracy is the rule of the mass of the poor only for themselves (1279b4ff.). There are varieties of each type.

A monarchy can be justified when there is rule of one man of superior moral virtue who rules in the interests of all. Theoretically, it is the best in that such a king would be a man of almost divine qualities. Aristotle believes it is virtually impossible to find him. In effect, there is only one 'citizen' here, the monarch, but his divine qualities make him something of a law unto himself even to the extent that he would not be part of the 'state'. 'There is no law that can regulate men of that calibre' (*Politics* III, 1284a3–12; 1288a15ff.).[123] But there are other kinds of monarchy which do not imply a man of superior, near divine moral virtue: there is kingship according to law which is acquired

---

122   W. Fortenbaugh, 'Aristotle on Prior and Posterior, Correct and Mistaken Constitutions', in Keyt and Miller, *A Companion to Aristotle's Politics*, pp. 226–37.
123   In effect, this would be the rule of the philosopher–king of Plato's *Republic*.

by birth or election; there is kingship as among non-Greeks which is legally established and ancestral, but where the king has powers akin to tyrants. He rules over willing subjects (but more slavish than the Greeks) according to law; there is kingship as among the early Greeks, which is also akin to an elected tyranny over willing subjects, where such a king rules by law; there is similarly a royal monarchy as existed in heroic times, both ancestral and subject to law and ruling over willing subjects (*Politics* III, 1284b 35– 1285b 33). Since in these other cases where the kings are not men of superior moral virtue Aristotle believes it is better to be ruled by law than by one man, 'because the judgement of one man is bound to be corrupted if he is in a bad temper or has strong feelings about something', then the king must be a lawgiver and establish the law as sovereign in all cases. It is better to be ruled by law than by any one citizen and those who govern must be appointed as guardians of the laws and be subordinate to them. Law is wisdom without desire, for passions corrupt the rule even of the best of men (*Politics* III, 1287a19ff.). Aristotle believes that in general, and among 'us', rulers are not so superior to their subjects and when there are men who are equal and similar it is neither just nor useful for one single man to be sovereign over the rest, whether he rules with or without laws (*Politics* III, 1288a1ff.).

Aristocracy is justified either because there is rule by the few who are unconditionally the best, morally virtuous men, or it can be justified because these absolutely best men rule by aiming at what is best for all the 'state' and its members (1279a32ff.; *Politics* IV, 1293a35ff.). Virtue is the sole defining principle of true aristocracy. Some Greeks use the name aristocracy more loosely, however, to describe a constitution in which election to public office depends on merit as well as wealth (1293b7). In this kind of 'aristocracy' the claim to equality is freedom, *wealth* and virtue, where wealth and noble birth are traditionally seen as leading to the virtues characteristic of an aristocracy. Aristotle refers to this as a 'so-called' aristocracy and sees it as a mixed constitutional form showing affinities with his third 'correct' constitutional form: polity. But the true aristocracy, an ideal, has regard to virtue alone.

Aristotle considers aristocracy – rule by the best *or* the constitution which is led by the few best men who aim at the best – to be the best constitution, by definition, because its principles are congruent with the very definition of the *polis,* what the 'state' is for. A people that is capable of being governed by an aristocracy is one of free men, ruled by those who are unconditionally more virtuous than anyone else so as to be capable of taking the role of leaders in government (*Politics* III, 1288a10). But this makes the leaders or rulers permanently separated from the ruled, although likewise subject to the law. The permanent rule by the unconditionally best men appears to be a definitional and historical ideal and, as we shall see, not one suited to that *polis* which has evolved as a perfect partnership of like-minded and equal free men (discussed in books 7 and 8). A true aristocracy, Aristotle says, is not an achievement open to most states. Furthermore, that there were true aristocracies in the historical past, may have been a matter of luck.

In all forms of constitution the laws are laid down to suit the constitution and its prin- ciples (*Politics* IV, 1289a13ff.) and hence must suit the people and their principles. Princi- ples emerge from experience and practices. Legislators need to know this. But citizen–rulers – here, an aristocracy – are, like all rulers, guardians of the laws. For an aristocracy to aim at what is best for all would require that there were the best, morally virtuous men in place to legislate in the sense of not beginning again with a model constitution but, rather, supplementing or correcting rules and traditional uses so as to improve a regime/constitution in line with greater stability and goodness, discerning which laws are best according to the best principles. The laws themselves would evolve to enshrine values that reflected men's true needs, the laws having laid down the correct criteria for selecting those who should rule and justly dividing the public offices among men of proven virtue with the highest offices going to the best, that is, these aristocratic, virtuous men. This *polis* possesses an already proven and ensconced set of guidelines for moral and political practices. Aristotle favours constitutions that are ruled by law rather than by the personalities of individual men, no matter how virtuous. He states that it is the laws, if rightly established, which ought to be sovereign while the citizen(s) when acting as ruler or rulers in office should have supreme powers over matters where the law cannot pronounce with precision, since it is difficult for general rules to cover all cases (1282b2–6). If such laws, rightly established, are already in place, then Aristotle seems to have satisfied his definition of an aristocracy where the constitution aims at what is best for all.

When this is the case, he welcomes the idea of the mass of ordinary citizens, provided they are not too slavish in character, collectively judging specific issues. This he makes clear when he treats the obviously democratic view put forward by some that the mass of people ought to be sovereign rather than the best few (1281a39ff.) and he says there is, perhaps, some truth in this. 'For even where there are many people, each has some share of virtue and practical wisdom, and when brought together . . . they become one in regard to character and intelligence.' While this may not be true of all peoples, he concludes that 'there is no reason why in a given case of a large number we should not accept the truth' of this view. He will not want to take the risk of opening the highest offices to the mass of men, who have no claim to virtue or even to the wealth that would provide them with the leisure to develop and exercise the virtues, but he sees there is also a risk to the stability of the 'state' in not giving them some share in sovereignty. Hence, he says it should remain open to them to participate in deliberating and judging, but not to a share in the highest offices (1281b15–31). Could such a constitution, if it had rightly established laws which aimed at the best for all, and led by men of outstanding virtue, 'aristocrats', be an aristocratic constitution?

Citizens are, after all, administrators; they are not legislators, and if well established laws that habituate to moral virtue are already in place, then the opportunities for the good life of each and all are so as well. The diversity of men in such a 'state' need only avail themselves of the opportunities, or not, and here it is a matter of experienced individuals, amid contingencies, choosing to act on what they have become habituated to feel is the correct end of their actions. Human autonomy and individual responsibility take over within this 'correct' frame and this leads to a 'state' in which some are truer citizens than others, given that the 'state' is made up of unlike parts. 'The virtue of all the citizens cannot be one' (*Politics* III, 1277a5ff.). This aristocracy, a constitution led by the best men but providing opportunities to participate in lower offices for the more extended mass of men, has many affinities with Aristotle's next best 'correct' constitution, polity, and in particular with the kind of polity that he most admires: the polity with a middle constitution.

Polity: Mixed and/or Middle Constitutions

A polity, which is for him the best practicable constitution capable of being achieved in most circumstances and which will suit pretty well all states, is one where the many rule in the common interests of the whole. He notes, however, not only that Greeks tend to use the term polity (*politeia*) to mean *all* constitutional government, but that in common usage, polity is often used to refer either to a kind of aristocracy, which is more like an oligarchy that takes account of merit, or else what are today called polities were formally called democracies (IV, 1297b23ff.). People are seeking the *principle* of polity (just as they were seeking the *principle* of natural slavery), starting from observation, experience and induction. Hence, we can begin to grasp what polity is, as a 'correct' constitution, by describing it as a mixture of aspects of two 'deviant' constitutions, oligarchy and democracy. Deviant constitutions are conceptually dependent on their respective correct forms. Correct forms, by definition, all aim at government for the interests of the whole *polis*.

A polity, in general, is defined as that constitution where a large number of men share the most common virtue, military virtue, and hence the most sovereign body, its citizens, is constituted by those who bear arms (*Politics* III, 1279a39–1279b5). Here, these people rule in the common interest. But Aristotle's polity is more than simply a military pact of mutual protection. It must, for it to be a 'correct' constitution, genuinely be concerned with moral virtue. Is it sufficient, to satisfy the concern for moral virtue, that the most widely shared virtue among rich and poor (but not destitute) is courage, a military virtue that is directed by the collective aim of the 'state's' cultural and material survival? Is there a more specified definition of polity which goes beyond commonly shared military virtue? He says that the people suited to polity as a distinct constitution are a people who possess military virtues and are also capable of being governed by a government under a law that distributes offices among the sufficiently well-off but in accordance with merit (*Politics* III, 1288a13). It is not the absolutely most correct constitution (true aristocracy based on moral virtue alone) but is similar to the kind of constitution people call aristocracy where there is election to office based on merit and wealth (*Politics* IV, 1293a35ff.).

Aristotle says polity is rarely found in practice. Instead, what is found are varieties of oligarchies and varieties of democracies. But it can best emerge in most of these circumstances because it is a constitution that takes into account the characteristics of the kinds of people suited to it, and most free peoples or *poleis* are internally differentiated by those who possess wealth and those who lack it. This, in fact, is why the real differentiation between oligarchies and democracies is based on wealth or its lack. In most cases, the wealthy are few and the poor are many, but all share freedom (*Politics* III, 1279b26ff.). In small states in particular, it is easy for the whole body of citizens to be divided into two, where nearly everyone is either rich or poor. Hence, claims to equality in a polity are normally grounded in wealth and freedom. But in larger states there is a large 'middle element' which acts as a kind of buffer to prevent factions (*Politics* IV, 1296a10). Polity, then, in its *generic* sense, is that constitution in which free men, with wealth sufficient to enable them to possess military arms (hoplites), share in office. It is a mix of the rich and the 'poor' who are wealthy enough to bear arms, and offices are distributed on the basis of free birth, wealth and the virtue of military courage.

Aristotle will propose a *method* to constitute a polity by judiciously mixing certain elements to be found in the two most commonly found constitutions: oligarchy (rule by the rich few) and democracy (rule by the many poor). A polity can be achieved as a *well-mixed constitution* if it is based on certain best practices that are already prevalent in democracies and oligarchies respectively, but where these practices are not supported by the best reasons for engaging in them. This is why Aristotle considers these constitutions to be deviants of their original, correct forms: oligarchy is a deviant of aristocracy, and democracy is a deviant of polity. Methodologically, a polity might mix or combine certain practices, taking for instance from oligarchies their practice of filling public office by electing officials (although oligarchies do this on 'incorrect' criteria – wealth alone – believing that since the rich are unequal to the poor in respect of wealth, then they are unequal in every other respect as well), and taking from democracies their practice of enabling all free men, regardless of wealth or property, to attend the Assembly (although this too is based on the 'incorrect' criterion that all free men, as free, are equals in everything). This eclectic mixture of practices would ensure that those *elected* to public office are not subject to any or only a *minimum property qualification* for office. The 'oligarchic' election of officials and the 'democratic' freedom from property qualifications results in a polity which has the structural features of a constitutional, rather than best, aristocracy (1294bb12–13).

This polity, as a mixed constitution, makes claims to a proportionate equality which takes into account freedom, wealth and merit, but where merit is commonly understood as widely shared military courage and, presumably, election to high office will be open to those who share in this virtue, giving those elected an opportunity to rule as a general would rule his army. In this it is similar to, but also differs from, so-called aristocracies where merit is conceived of as characteristics not widely shared, based as they are on noble birth and reputation for virtue as a consequence of traditional status, wealth and education. The polity can still be described as either an oligarchy or as a democracy, although as a mixed constitution it combines both into a unity. Since its stability would be maintained by rich and poor (for different reasons) no section would wish to have a different constitution (*Politics* IV, 1294a30–1294b42).

Another way to constitute a polity would be to mix legislation of both oligarchy and democracy when, for instance, a jury system is to be established. Oligarchies fine the wealthy for not attending as jurors in law courts and do not pay the poor for their attendance; democracies do not fine the rich for non-attendance but they do pay the poor. A polity as a mixed constitution would both fine the rich and pay the poor (IV, 1294a35–1294b13).

Polity is the best generic type of constitution to provide the best life for the majority of states and the majority of men. The majority of men do not possess extraordinary virtue, nor can they avail themselves of the conditions necessary to acquire it. Aristotle is speaking about those men whose education depends neither on the luck of exceptional natural ability nor on the luck of having resources. Neither do such ordinary men live in an ideal constitution. What is the mode of life able to be shared by most men? He says that true aristocracies are not within the competence of most states, although certain so-called aristocracies approximate to polity (*Politics* IV, 1295a25–33). If the best life is a life of virtue, and as was stated in *Nicomachean Ethics*, virtue is a mean, then we need a mean that is open to all kinds of men to attain. At its most basic, this is military virtue.

But Aristotle says that a 'state' aims, *in so far as it can*, to be a partnership of men who are equal and similar. In *poleis* where there are a minority rich and a majority poor, the oligarchic and democratic understandings of equality and similarity differ and these two 'parts' of the 'state' can only be brought into a unity by mixing legislative practices from each, such as election to office but with minimal property qualifications.

Ideally, and Aristotle says that this has never occurred in the Greek world, or only seldom and sporadically (*Politics* IV, 1296a37ff.), a 'state' that has a minority of rich and a minority of poor, but with a predominant majority of the middle sort of people, would best satisfy the 'state's' aims to consist of those who are similar and equal. Aristotle calls this a middle constitution. Is this an ideal version of polity as a mixed constitution or is it a different constitution altogether?[124] Some interpret Aristotle as arguing that the middle constitution is the perfected form of the mixed constitution. Others argue that they are separate.[125] None the less, the middle constitution is closest to the best constitution which could be achieved *within the bounds of possibility*, as described in books 7 and 8.

Where the virtue shared by both rich and poor in polity is military, in the middle constitution the virtue of the middle citizens is their living a middle way of life. The middle people are *not* a bourgeoisie. Instead, they have characters that locate them between the extremes of the characters of the poor (who are often either subservient or excessively concerned with a kind of liberty that means living as they like without restraints) and the rich (who are often haughty at best and ungovernable at worst). Aristotle says middle citizens are most secure, they do not covet, as do the poor, the possessions of others, nor do they have wealth and possessions in amounts which others would covet. They therefore live without risk and neither scheme nor are schemed against. Having a middling amount of wealth, like other moderate conditions between extremes, makes its possessor more amenable to obey reason. Their financial and property situation acts as a kind of natural constraint on their desires. He says that the *best* partnership in a 'state' is the one which operates through its middle people and ideally it should be large, certainly stronger than either the rich or poor. The middle regime, then, does not have to mix elements of democracy and oligarchy *in the same way* as that polity does which has virtually no large middle group. But Aristotle says that it is more likely to find the middle people in a democracy where they take a larger share of public honours than they do in oligarchies (1296a15–16). Middle people show themselves the least inclined to run away from the duties of public office, and at the same time they are less inclined to covet office. A 'state' that comprises *a majority* of middle people is one which has a middle constitution, meaning that the community is administered by them as the sovereign citizen body in the interests of all, the rich, the poor and the middle sorts. Aristotle says that this is the *best* of polity (*Politics* IV, 1295b28–1296b12).

To govern a people well it is necessary to know what kinds of people there are in a *polis*. Both legislators and statesmen cannot directly affect the individual economic positions of members. Their policies can and should take into consideration public health and they should plan, for instance, ways of securing pure water and clean air (*Politics* VII, 1330b11ff.). The statesman's policies should also attempt to increase the 'state's' prosperity. Aristotle seems to be suggesting that certain varieties of democracies, with a numerous if not preponderate group of middle people, stand a good chance of developing opportunities for the middling people to grow in numbers. And should they finally constitute the majority, the polity will become that superior middle constitution.

Indeed, this middle constitution of middle people is remarkably similar to Aristotle's description of that best constitution (book 7), among equal and similar people who know one another and take turns in ruling and being ruled, constructed 'exactly as one would wish' within the bounds of possibility (*Politics* VII, 1325b33–1326a4). This is the best constitution beneath the ideal true aristocracy.

124   See J. Creed, 'Aristotle's Middle Constitution', *Polis* 8 (1989), pp. 2–27.
125   C. Johnson, *Aristotle's Theory of the State*, part III.

Depending on the constitution, then, a citizen's virtue, that display of character through practices for which he is praised, will be commensurate with the criteria which are established by that constitution in order to judge practices and character with a view to constitutional aims. The virtue or soundness of someone considered to be a 'good citizen', depending on the constitution under which he lives, coincides with his functional contribution to *maintaining the stability* of that particularly organized association and its values. For instance, a 'good citizen' in an oligarchy is one who actively seeks to maintain the stability of the rule of the rich and exclude from consideration the well-being of all others in the *polis*. Because there are several kinds of constitutions, there cannot be a single and perfect virtue of the sound citizen. His citizen-virtue is a function of the values that underpin the constitution he serves as a participant in deliberation and office holding. Aristotle believes that one can be called a 'good citizen', obeying the laws, in a state whose values and practices are distorted. In such a 'state' one could argue that 'one was only obeying orders' and this would indeed make you a 'good citizen' but not a good man (*Politics* III, 1276b33ff.). To be both a good citizen and a good man depends on two things: voluntary deliberative actions and the setting of the best 'correct' constitution. A particular citizen would have to be a free deliberator engaged in ruling rather than being ruled, actively exercising his moral and intellectual virtues in public office; he is the *phronimos*, governed by laws of such a kind that enabled him and his fellow citizens to have developed habits and dispositions to choose, and hence to become morally responsible agents in the first place. This would happen in the best constitution within the bounds of possibility (not the ideal true aristocracy) and all others are judged in relation to it as a standard.

If a citizen lives in such a state with a constitution *whose citizens are free men and of similar birth* then he participates in taking turns in ruling and being ruled (1277b7ff.). Aristotle does not always elaborate on what is meant by similar birth. From the context in *Politics* III, it appears to mean something like 'of the same culture' and where there are no fixed divisions of status. But primarily what is implied throughout is that a 'state' as such is constituted on the basis of some determined and accepted notion of equality and similarity between citizens where, despite their personal diversities, they agree in an almost unconscious way about the aims of their partnership: the welfare of all who are part of the culture. There is no pluralism of ultimate values here. Such a 'state' is not a matter of utility of the sort which serves as no more than the frame for prosecuting what are individual, private and different goods, individually arrived at. Aristotle tells us that this principle of taking turns is an old one, having emerged in the awareness of men of equality and similarity from practices which led them to expect, when in public office, to look after the welfare of others who had, when in office themselves previously, looked after them (1279a9).

In such a constitution where there is an alternation in ruling and being ruled, the virtue or excellence of the citizen–ruler is not the same as the virtue of the ruled citizen. This is because what a citizen does when ruled is different from what he does when ruling. As a citizen in this kind of constitution he has learned from experiencing both positions: he has lived by the laws and acknowledged the administrative applications of the laws in particular circumstances that have been decided on by those taking their turn to rule, and then he has taken up office and become a deliberator himself, applying the laws and making judgements regarding specific cases before him, all with a view to the common welfare. Parallel with Aristotle's discussion in *Nicomachean Ethics* concerning habit formation to moral practices and deliberative choice, Aristotle speaks of the citizen learning the habit of ruling *by being ruled*, and he provides an analogy with learning to command cavalry by serving under a cavalry commander. The citizen's virtue or excellence is not the habit as such but precisely his mature understanding of what his habits have led him to desire and now to choose these in the acts he voluntarily and deliberatively engages in. He comes to know, in this way, what is required in the governing of free men from both points of view, that of ruled and ruler. He comes to such an understanding from engaging in practices that serve the welfare of his fellows as well as himself. When he is in the position of being ruled he exercises *correct opinion* but when he takes his turn to rule, he engages in *practical reasoning or prudent choice-making* in the circumstances.

Hence, there are several kinds of citizen, depending on the constitution and also within the same constitution. Even in a constitution that governs men who are free and similar, citizenship behaviour depends on whether one is engaged in being ruled or ruling. A 'state' is made up of unlike parts and the virtues of all the citizens as citizens are similarly diverse, depending on their functional contribution to the whole. Aristotle repeats, in effect, the conclusions of his argument in *Nicomachean Ethics* V that the man who is the citizen *in the fullest sense*, as an active prudential deliberator for the public welfare, is the one who has a share in honours, that is, public office. Here their equality is one between equals in virtue rather than being determined by some other exclusive means, such as property or birth. A constitution that governs free and similar men by giving them the opportunity to engage in taking turns in ruling and being ruled, and hence to become practitioners of the moral virtues which enhance the public welfare, is the one, for Aristotle, that can best come to exemplify distributive justice based on proportionate merit. This proportionality comes to be realized even where citizens are free and similar, because their characters and circumstances are diverse, having been effected through a range of local contingencies, good and bad luck, sheer persistence on the part of some and not others, and the functional requirements of the different public offices. Where the majority of men are of the middling sort, with a middle amount of property and moderate characters to match, then the relatively rare public benefactors as prudential, politically active men of whom Aristotle spoke in *Nicomachean Ethics* have a better chance of emerging under the middle constitution which suits these kinds of people, than under any others. This is because it will enable more men to have public experiences and thereby it will have a larger base of proven deliberators on whom to bestow praise and public honour through the truly virtuous among them being elected to high office.[126]

What then is the essential nature of the 'state'? Recall that a definition is achieved by locating the species through its genus and differentia. The 'state' is a qualitatively unique partnership (genus) with a distinctive end (differentia): the supreme good for the community, and this is the self-sufficient and good life of its members, which is itself constituted by the actualization of their moral and intellectual virtues. Hence, its territory, its walls, its population are *not* fundamental to what a 'state' essentially is. Fundamental to the 'state' is its being a human partnership of the type where the plurality of kinds of men is brought into a unity by laws that habituate actions: the 'state' is an association of citizens in a constitution whose laws structure values and such values penetrate the

---

126 Cicero's later discussion of a mixed constitution, his republic, is *not* of this kind; see below, chapter 5.

citizens' administration of the public welfare. It is easiest to do this if the *polis* is comprised of men who are equal and similar. The main criterion of the continued identity of a 'state' is, then, its constitution (1276b10–12), defined both in terms of its orientation towards the common good, and in terms of its criteria for admission to the roles of judging and administrating. Through examining varieties of correct and deviated constitutions he secures an answer to the question: which best secures the well-being (*eudaimonia*) of all those whom we ought to call citizens?

The constitution that best provides the conditions in which a plurality of men can be moral deliberators, making choices, depending on character and circumstances, to engage in actions of moral fineness with others, is the one that achieves these conditions *as a matter of policy*. Such a constitution has laws that express a set of principled preferences whose overall aim is the greater and higher goods for man as a moral agent rather than simply aiming at the lower but necessary goods. This is because Aristotle believes that a society should be capable of engaging in war and business *but still more* be capable of living in peace and leisure (*Politics* VII, 1333a35ff.). The principled preferences of a constitution determine (through its laws) what matters to its citizens.

Aristotle insists that a proper understanding of what humans are and what a human life is, leads to the conclusions that external goods are tools and have a limit. One can have too many of them and this can even come to be a positive injury to their possessors. Living well is not concerned with material acquisition as an end. While men form and continue to maintain the political partnership for the sake of life itself (for there is a good even in mere living), living well, the good life, is what brings men together and sustains them in that distinctive partnership. The good life is, therefore, the chief end of men, communally and individually and they desire this kind of life together even when they have no need to seek each other's help (*Politics* III, 1278b18ff.). The good life is a life which seeks to acquire and exercise the goods of the soul, which are the peculiar virtues of humans. Unlike the goods of the body, the goods of the soul are *unlimited* so that a constitution that is interested in providing the conditions in which citizens can exercise their species-specific excellences is the one that enables them to acquire and keep the virtues and live humanly. The acquisition of material possessions, land and money, is properly to be seen as the *means* to ensure sufficient leisure to engage in activities that are peculiarly human, the practices that serve public welfare. Aristotle believes that the successful human life is to be found in larger measure with those who, having had the opportunity, have bothered to achieve an extremely high cultivation of character and intellect but who have been moderate as regards the external acquisition of goods. He says that to each man there comes just so much happiness as he has of virtue and of practical wisdom and performs actions dependent thereon (1323b21).

Labouring and Life as Work

What happens if, despite man being a naturally indeterminate species with a two-fold human potential (a) to acquire a moral character from habituated practices and (b) to learn to exercise his intellectual capacities, a man is born into the world without the means to ensure the sufficient leisure that is required to engage in morally fine acts and thereafter to think in a sustained, goal-directed way? Some men are unlucky enough to have been born into a life of labouring and they never escape. These are Aristotle's *banausoi* ('mechanics') – handicraftsmen, men engaged in labouring – and this category is extended to include those in commerce and even in agriculture (*Politics* VI, 1328b33–1329a1). Some 'states' enable them to become citizens. Extreme democracies have workmen participating in public office (*Politics* III, 1277b1ff.). Aristotle thinks this is a mistake. But he acknowledges that they have their place, even as citizens, in less than the best constitutions.

He tells us that 'we' speak of several kinds of slave and one kind is the manual labourer. Greeks call them slaves because they are under a kind of authority akin to that of the household master, but here the authority is more abstract; it is the authority of necessary work. They serve necessity. No good citizen or statesman ought to learn how to be subject to labouring *as a way of life*, although he may engage in work for the personal use he may need to make of it (*Politics* III, 1277b3–8). Aristotle is mindful of the virtues that are useful for leisure and 'civilized' pursuits as well as being useful in a period of work. He says there are many essential things that need to be provided before leisure becomes possible (*Politics* VII, 1334a17–18). A man must be able to go to war to defend his *polis* and he must be able to work, to do the necessary and useful things (*Politics* VII, 1333a30ff.) But the peculiarly human excellence is not work, for Aristotle. Human life is not about making, producing or acquiring material things but it is about moral action which makes use of made, produced and acquired things with a view to a human end.

However, some constitutions do count 'mechanics' as citizens, indeed, in some constitutions this will be necessary (*Politics* III, 1278a15–22). But the best 'state' will not do so since in this kind of 'state' the honours that accrue to holding office depend on merit and proven moral virtue. Although the labourer may be a free man he is not relieved of performing necessary tasks and this makes it impossible for him to occupy himself in deliberative moral choice-making, since he has no leisure to do so nor, in having lived a life of labouring, subject to necessity, has he developed the moral habits that would enable him to be a trustworthy evaluator of other men's character. In the best 'state', then, freedom and wealth are necessary but not sufficient conditions for true citizenship. It is not that all mechanics are poor; indeed, Aristotle notes that in oligarchies with high property qualifications required for participating in public offices, mechanics may get the opportunity since most skilled workers become rich (*Politics* III, v, 1277b33–12788a25). The problem is not wealth but leisure to have become a certain kind of character. The oligarchical constitution of Thebes appears to have recognized this and there was a law requiring an interval of ten years to have elapsed between a man's giving up trade and being able to participate in office (*Politics* III, 1278a25–6). Aristotle is dubious that this would be sufficient time to retrain one's character disposition, acquired over a lifetime.

Men who labour and, over the years, accumulate wealth tend to become habituated to seeing wealth as an end rather than a means to something else. The acquisition of goods and wealth is limited by its end, what it is for, and this is household management. But those who are engaged in acquiring goods as a way of life go on increasing their money without limit. Aristotle provides a plausible reason for this: it may be that such people are eager for life but not for the good life, and since desire for life is unlimited they desire an unlimited amount of what enables life to go on (*Politics* I, 1257b40ff.). Allowing these kinds of men into public office would ensure that issues requiring moral decisions, and which ought to be guided by concerns for the moral and intellectual collective welfare, would be reduced to economic ones, guided only by the lower necessities. Mechanics and businessmen tend to mistake means for ends, not having become habituated to limiting material desires, and therefore they spend their lives trying to satisfy these (*Politics* II, 1267b4–5). Since there is no natural limit to desires, most people spend their lives trying to satisfy these. <u>Good laws intend to ensure that those</u> <u>with the leisure and sufficient means to take the opportunity to become habituated to</u> <u>moral virtue,</u> do so by educating their desires so that *they do not wish* to get more than their share. The laws should likewise prevent those without the opportunity to become virtuous through practising virtue, *ever to be able to get* more than their share (*Politics* II, 1267b5–10).

Those constitutions that set up laws to redistribute wealth, and thereby effect an equality of possessions, like that of the Chalcedonian Phaleas (*Politics* II, 1266b24ff.), tend not to be successful, according to Aristotle. The legislator needs to equalize *appetites* rather than possessions and this can only be done by an adequate education enforced by laws. We are told that Phaleas established equality of possessions because he thought that no one would then resort to stealing out of cold or hunger, and this would be sufficient to prevent crimes. Aristotle sees it differently. To secure the necessities of life is not the only, or even major, reason that men become criminals, developing bad dispositions of character. They also wish to enjoy things and not go on desiring them and if their desire goes beyond mere necessities, they will remedy this through crime. *The primary fact is that naturally, and without law, human desires are unlimited. Furthermore, men wish to enjoy pleasures that bring no pain.* This is what legislators need to know, and not a redistributive administration of 'things' which will be unsuccessful anyway.

Aristotle says that there are 'cures' for all these types of men and their dilemmas, and the cures are *political* considerations, that is, matters of 'state' policy, all of which seek to regulate man's desires for his own good and the good of the *polis*. For the man who steals out of want of necessities, the 'state' should encourage employment and provide the conditions in which he may acquire moderate possessions. In a constitution whose majority of citizens comprise the poor, namely a democracy, the man who steals out of necessity is likely not to be rare. To preserve this kind of democratic constitution from corruption the true democratic citizen ensures that the population is not destitute. He administers policies that perpetuate the prosperity of the rich as well as the poor, and what accrues from the 'state' revenues is collected into a fund and distributed in block grants to those in need, preferably so that they can acquire a small piece of land, or start a business. Men of wealth and virtue are encouraged to make it their concern to provide the needy with a start in some occupation (*Politics* VI, 1320a35–1320b8).

For the man who wishes to enjoy things beyond necessities to the point of extravagance, and who desires not to go on desiring them, the 'state' should educate him to have some self-control. Greed and excessive competitiveness are not the consequence of private property but of vice (an attitude to desires) and vice can only be prevented by a moral education that makes it reasonable to show some restraint.

For the man who wants to enjoy pleasures without pain, and if he is the sort who wishes to find independent enjoyment by himself, then philosophy will provide the cure because it alone is an activity that stands in no need of other people. It appears that the best 'state' will include in its policy a place for the philosophical life (*Politics* II, 1267a9ff.). In the best state, there will be several functions required: defence, deliberation about expedient policies and deliberations about matters of justice. These roles are best assigned to the same people, with sufficient leisure to practise moral virtues, but at different stages of their lives. The young with strength and as yet without political experience go into the army; the older with practical wisdom administer policy and judgement. And those who have played both roles and who have arrived at a certain age should be 'state' priests, serving the gods and enjoying retirement (*Politics* VII, 1329a3–19; 1329a29ff.). In ideal conditions, none of these men should have had to labour to live.

Aristotle believes that to operate a good constitution requires freedom from necessary and laborious tasks (*Politics* II, ix, 1269a34) and he argues (in his discussion of the Carthaginian constitution, book II, 1273a31ff.) that it is essential that from the very start provision be made by the legislator for the best people to have leisure and that the laws be of such a kind that these people do not depart from the standards of what is right, both while in office and as private citizens. Wealth is required for the sake of leisure to develop and enable the exercise of virtuous activities of a citizen (*Politics* VII, ix, 1328b33–1329a1). Someone who must spend most of his time and effort working for a living, or who lives dependent on the favours of another, will never develop the right virtues of character required of a citizen. Indeed, Aristotle assumes that a life of menial work has a ruinous effect on a person's character so that moral education, of the sort required by the true citizen, cannot have a countervailing effect.

Aristotle is certain that *all* men aim at happiness and the good life, but some have an opportunity to get it, others have not (*Politics* VII, xiii, 1331b39). This opportunity or its lack may be due to their nature (clearly, brutish men haven't the opportunity; one must be born a man and not some other animal or some defective specimen of a man where the body rules the soul (1332a38ff.)); humans do not choose to be born humans.[127] This opportunity or its lack may be due to some stroke of fortune such as being born into poverty, for he reminds us that the good life needs certain material resources for one to be able to engage in morally fine acts, such as liberality, even magnanimity to others. When a man's character disposition is comparatively good, which means he has become habituated to desiring the right things in the right ways and at the right times, his need is for a lesser amount of these material resources, but a moderate amount must, none the less, be available. There are, however, some people who start with the opportunity but go wrong from the very beginning of the pursuit of human well-being, either by having misconstrued the means for the end (bad habituation) or by having misconceived the nature of living well itself and thereby having aimed at the wrong sort of life (either bad habituation or the character failure of possibly knowing what is right but failing to do it, not seeing how what is right applies in particular cases and choosing wrongly or not at all).

Aristotle reminds 'us' that all life can be divided into work and leisure, war and peace and some things done have moral worth while others are merely necessary and useful. But human living is more than being concerned with utility. Work falls into the domain of necessity and utility and when one asks what does a man work *for*, the answer should be, leisure. Leisure is the end of work, and it is a fundamental mistake to think that what is distinctive about a human way of living is work. Production and accumulation are not positive goods; actions directed to public office and the welfare of the polity are positive goods. Some things must be there, as preconditional, fortunate opportunities from the start. But others are provided by the lawgiver, namely a sound constitution which results

---

127 Although the laws can regulate the age of marriage partners and other aspects of bodily health to ensure, to the extent that one can, the physical health of children (VII, 1334b29–1337a32).

from knowledge and deliberate choice. For a state to be sound its citizens must be sound and both capable and desirous of sharing in the constitution.

We have come full circle: to become sound is by nature, habit and reason. We cannot do anything about our nature, but we can be habituated and we do reason. 'State' education, of the sort that liberals find unacceptably intrusive, and the leisure to be able to benefit from it, are the means by which indeterminate humans can become determinate and therefore what they actually and naturally are.

Further reading exemplifying a range of approaches to Aristotle's *Politics*

Ambler, W. 'Aristotle on Nature and Politics: the case of slavery', *Political Theory* 15 (1987), pp. 390–411.

Arnhart, L. 'Aristotle's Biopolitics: a defense of biological teleology against biological nihilism', *Politics and the Life Sciences* 6 (1988), pp. 173–229.

Arnhart, L. *Darwinian Natural Right: the biological ethics of human nature* (Albany, NY, 1998).

Barnes, J., M. Schofield and R. Sorabji, eds, *Aristotle on Aristotle, 2: Ethics and Politics* (London, 1977).

Fondation Hardt *Entretiens sur l'antiquité classique IX: La Politique d'Aristote* (Geneva, 1964).

Huxley, G. L. 'On Aristotle's Best State', *History of Political Thought* 6 (1985), pp. 139–49.

Irwin, T. H. 'Moral Science and Political Theory in Aristotle', in P. Cartledge and F. D. Harvey, eds, *Crux = History of Political Thought* 6 (1985), pp. 150–68.

Irwin, T. H. 'Permanent Happiness: Aristotle and Solon', *Oxford Studies in Ancient Philosophy* 3 (1985), pp. 89–124.

Irwin, T. H. *Aristotle's First Principles* (Oxford, 1988), chs 16–22.

Keyt, D. and F. D. Miller, eds, *A Companion to Aristotle's Politics* (Oxford, 1991).

Kraut, R. *Aristotle on the Human Good* (Princeton, NJ, 1989).

Lear, J. *Aristotle: the desire to understand* (Cambridge, 1988), esp. the master–slave dialectic, pp. 192–208.

Miller, F. D. *Nature, Justice and Rights in Aristotle's Politics* (Oxford, 1995).

Nussbaum, M. C. *The Fragility of Goodness, Luck and Ethics in Greek Tragedy and Philosophy* (Cambridge, 1986), chs 9–12.

Patzig, G., ed., *XI. Symposium Aristotelicum: Studien zur Politik des Aristoteles* (Göttingen, 1989), including: J. Barnes, 'Aristotle and Political Liberty' with commentary by R. Sorabji; J. M. Cooper, 'Political Animals and Civic Friendship' with commentary by J. Annas; C. Lord, 'Politics and Education in Aristotle's *Politics*' with commentary by D. A. Rees; M. C. Nussbaum, 'Nature, Function and Capability: Aristotle on political distribution' with commentary by D. Charles.

Salkever, S. G. *Finding the Mean: theory and practice in Aristotle's political philosophy* (Princeton, NJ, 1990).

Springborg, P. 'Aristotle and the Problem of Needs', *History of Political Thought* 5 (1984), pp. 393–424.

The Legacy of Plato and Aristotle: A Pause for Thought

Let us pause for a moment. As twentieth-century readers of Plato's *Republic* and Aristotle's *Nicomachean Ethics* and *Politics* (in translation) we are dropped into this tradition of discourse. We may think it a simple matter to determine for ourselves whether or not it may be accepted as *our* tradition, to which subsequent European discourses merely added, refining and nuancing fundamental ways of speaking about human nature and its tendencies as these have been observed and discussed in human communities differently structured from the Greek *poleis*. But it is not a simple matter at all, for some of the reasons to which I pointed in the introduction. The later and retrospective construction of a European tradition of discourse with Plato and Aristotle taken to be the beginnings (rather than, say, the Sophists for whom we only have fragments, or ancient Egyptian or Persian sources), irrevocably makes what Plato or Aristotle tell us and the ways they tell it an integral part of the way we have been taught about ethics and politics as distinct domains of lived life and discussion. This means that something extraordinary occurred between the time when Plato and Aristotle presented to their students their respective but related perspectives on fourth-century BC common views on the nature of living a successful human life and our own times, even if none of us ever bothered to read either of their writings or had even heard of these philosophers. The tradition of ethical and political discourses into which *we* are born when we learn our language and grow up in our society is an unwitting inheritance from a more recent, nineteenth-century past which did know the texts of Plato and Aristotle, on to which were grafted the insights of a tradition of earlier – but subsequent to the Greeks – interpreters and theorists who accepted or rejected what they had to offer. In engaging with what they thought these philosophers had to tell them, they passed on the agenda in no matter how substantively modified a form. In fact *A History of Political Thought*, focusing as it does on the history of Western political thought from the ancient Greeks to the Renaissance, will enable us to see how this agenda was selectively absorbed and reinterpreted. It deals with a period in which medieval Christians asked themselves whether what they inherited concerning the pagan Greek views on human flourishing could be accepted by those who believed in human perfection as a post-historical state, not achievable by a rationally guided human will nor by human action in history, but rather by the selective and unpredictable gift of divine grace. The question remained as to what constitutes the good life, but the answers that came were to be couched in terms of another community's common views 'of the many and wise'. And these altered the very question itself. Consequently, the answer would come to consist of a range of other, often contrary beliefs: in fallen humanity; in salvific 'happiness' achieved for humans by a god–man, crucified for 'all' who believe in him; in a 'city of God' after history; in human nature as not capable of living by reason. We shall observe how men like Augustine in the fifth century AD and Thomas Aquinas in the thirteenth century used the ancient Greek pagan legacy to structure their own understandings of the ethical and political, read against the Old and New Testaments. These would be filtered through their own experiences, and notably through their inheritances not only from the Bible but from ancient Rome. It is to Cicero's Rome that we now turn.

5

Cicero's Rome and Cicero's Republic

The gradual disintegration of the ancient Greek system of independent and free *poleis* – often at war with one another or in temporary alliances, but without outside interference – is often linked with, indeed blamed on, the massively successful conquests begun by the Macedonian king Philip (II) in the mid-fourth century BC and continued by his son, Alexander, Aristotle's 'tutee'. In 338 BC Philip decisively defeated the armies of Thebes and Athens at the battle of Khaeronea and imposed peace and his own policy on most of the *poleis*. But he did not interfere with the Athenian constitution nor destroy democracy. His son Alexander expanded his conquests through Asia Minor and Egypt and thereby changed the face of the Greek world, initiating what has been called the Hellenistic period, where the Greek language was spoken everywhere, including by non-Greeks. The effect on Greek culture of 'barbarian' peoples in this now expanded empire was considerable. On Alexander's death in 323 BC the Athenians led a Greek revolt against Macedon and were utterly defeated. Antipater, the Macedonian general, regent in Greece and executor of Aristotle's will, put an end to Athenian democracy and from 322 BC subjected Athens to constitutional changes which prevented the *polis* from deciding its own destiny.[1]

But from the late third century BC another power appeared in this world: Rome. Rome was to have *the* decisive impact on the minds of all who came into contact with it. By the mid second century Rome's part-time army of peasant-farmers, led by a ruling oligarchy, had conquered Italy and the Mediterranean, and Rome continued to expand its sweep. It was the effects of the Roman intrusion, dating from *c.* 229 BC and the First Illyrian War, that resulted in the subordination of all the Hellenistic centres of power to the Roman senate.[2] The historian Polybius (*c.* 200–118 BC), a Greek who had been brought to Rome as a hostage (167 BC) and who acquired Roman friends and patrons, began his narrative of the events which led the Romans in 220 BC from the war with Hannibal and Carthage (called the second Punic or Hannibalic war) to dominance over 'nearly the whole inhabited world in less than fifty-three years'.[3] Rome destroyed and yet was the heir of ancient Greece.

---

1 For a good general introduction see J. Boardman, J. Griffin and O. Murray, eds, *The Oxford History of Greece and the Hellenistic World* (Oxford, 1991).
2 Rome's equivalent of the Athenian *Boulē*.
3 Polybius, *The Histories*, trans. W. R. Paton, Loeb Classical Library, 6 vols, I, i, 5. See F. W. Walbank, *The Hellenistic World*, 3rd revd edn (London, 1992). On the effects of Hellenization on the 'barbarian' world, and their effects on Greeks when they wrote in Greek, see A. Momigliano, 'The Greeks and their Neighbours', in Momigliano, *Alien Wisdom: the limits of Hellenization* (Cambridge, 1975), pp. 1–21.

The highly militarized Roman state, whose values were those of a ruling 'aristocracy' linked to military achievement, set Rome apart not only from the Greeks but from all other peoples of the Hellenistic world. It has often been said by scholars comparing Greece and Rome that the Romans were the more pragmatic, concrete, if not brutal, in their thinking and action, demoting philosophical theorizing to second place in a life devoted to activities tied up with the acquisition of property and laws to protect it. But they were remarkably successful in developing their own language, Latin, as an instrument of thought which could translate Greek ideas and also provide alternate visions of politics to those of the Greeks. Cicero would provide an eclectic mixture of Hellenistic philosophy and Roman practice in his reformulation of the ideal of republican politics. According to Cicero, the *res publica* (their nearest equivalent to our concept of the state) meant the *res populi* – the people's business – where 'the people' (*populus*) is 'a union of a number of men, acknowledging each other's rights and pursuing in common their advantage, utility or interest'.[4] Although it is not clear that his contemporaries shared his interpretation of 'the people', the aggressive common pursuit of their advantage or interest was the guiding principle of Roman policy.

Indeed, the Roman character was determined by an adherence to a very specific form of praise, public renown (*gloria*), which was the reward of manly courage and skill (*virtus*) as manifested in service to the 'state', the *patria* . A Roman sought *dignitas* and *auctoritas*, standing and influence, both through holding high office and waging wars. Roman heroes were recognized by being awarded a triumphal procession for having won the spoils of war, slain enemies and enslaved peoples.[5] Such men were given governorships of Roman provinces, where they massively increased their personal wealth. The preoccupation with personal achievement and competition for the greatest glory stands out as the most conspicuous characteristic of the Roman ruling class traceable over more than 300 years, from the third century BC, through the middle and late Roman republic and into the early Empire.[6] The pursuit of glory was intimately tied to the pursuit of wealth.[7] This 'corporate' sense of a ruling group's interests bound to the interests of the 'state' is said to have lost coherence during the last century of the Roman republic, to be replaced by the naked competition of individuals' self-interest and their use of physical force to achieve it. The changing political alliances which characterized republican politics were not necessarily dangerous in themselves, but when they were linked to individuals with great military power the republic came to be threatened. This in turn led them into the arms of dictators and a loss of their liberty.

Through Roman influence in Greece and Asia Minor, through annexations and reductions of former free cities, confederations and kingdoms to Roman provinces, Ro-

---

4   Cicero, *De re publica* I, xxv, 19: 'res publica res populi, populus autem non omnis hominum coetus quoquo modo congregatus, sed coetus multitudines iuris consensu et utilitas communione sociatus.' The text used here is Cicero, *De re publica* and *De legibus*, trans. C. W. Keyes with facing Latin text, Loeb Classical Library (London, 1977). A very useful commentary in English with selected Latin texts is J. E. G. Zetzel, ed., *Cicero, De re publica, selections*, Cambrige Greek and Latin Classics, (Cambridge, 1995).

5   Cicero records in his letters that he hoped for a triumph after his late-in-life military campaigns when briefly governor of Cilicia: *Ad familiares* XV, 4, 5, 6, 10, 13; *Ad Atticus*, vi, 3.3, 6.4, 8.5, 9.2.

6   A good brief discussion of the various political and military 'theatres' of competition is given by T. Wiedemann, *Cicero and the End of the Roman Republic* (London, 1994).

7   T. P. Wiseman, 'Competition and Co-operation', in T. P. Wiseman, ed., *Roman Political Life 90 BC–AD 69* (Exeter, 1985), pp. 3–19; also K. Raaflaub, *Dignitatis contentio* (Munich, 1974).

man domination became unchallengeable by the middle of the second century BC. After 168 BC the cities of mainland Greece and the Aegean were deprived of their main leaders, who were carried off to Italy. Corinth was sacked in 146 BC and with the massacre of those inhabitants who were not sold as slaves 'free' Greece was at an end and became a Roman province.[8] Not only were Roman wars immensely profitable but Roman domination exploited the political divisions in the cities of mainland Greece, favouring on the whole those groups who supported oligarchic government. Rome received a regular stream of taxes or tribute imposed, we are told, by the private greed of Roman officials. Polybius describes them as members of a class for which huge expenditure and conspicuous consumption had become a way of life.[9] He singles out only one man, his own patron Scipio Aemilianus (Africanus the Younger), the adopted grandson of Scipio Africanus who had defeated Hannibal in 202 BC, as someone of complete, if not unique, integrity. Aemilianus took nothing from the rich Carthaginians whom he defeated in 146 BC and then governed, despite Scipio not being particularly rich by Roman standards.[10] The victorious general had the legal right to the spoils of his victories and although it was expected that he would deliver a substantial portion to the Roman public treasury and distribute rewards to his officers, what was left was legitimately his. Scipio could have become a very rich man without breaking any laws. We shall meet this exemplary Roman warrior and statesman again, in Cicero's *De re publica*.

But then Scipio Aemilianus was a man who displayed the other, more positive side of the Roman–Greek relationship. Although he was not as virtuous as either Polybius or Cicero made out,[11] like other soldiers returning from eastern military campaigns he became familiar with the Greek language, Greek customs and gods. Cicero says of him in *De re publica* (iii, 6) that 'he and his friends added to the native usage of our ancestors the teaching of Socrates coming from abroad'.

The decisive period of the Roman assimilation of Greek language and culture occurred between the two Punic wars, *c.* 260s–202 BC. It was thereafter common for educated Romans of the second century BC to become bilingual in Greek and Latin. Rome's very success in bringing Greek hostages, envoys, traders, professional men and even philosophers – often as slaves and tutors in the homes of the wealthy – to Rome, enabled it to absorb the Greek pattern of education and various professional skills, like those of Greek medicine and architecture. Greek works of art were plundered and brought to the homes of wealthy and powerful Romans. Roman literature itself, under the influence of Greece, began with Greeks who taught Latin and Greek, themselves writing Roman poetry, plays and history, in the interests of constructing a Roman past for their patrons to defend Roman policy in the present.[12] It has been argued that the historian Polybius could not have written his Roman history as he did if he had not found in Rome an aristocracy which he understood because he shared its attitude to life,

---

8   Walbank, *The Hellenistic World*, p. 242; on the beginnings of a policy of economic imperialism *c.* 148 BC when Scipio Aemilianus was elected consul, and the subsequent rebellion and submission of Greece, see M. Le Glay, J.–L. Voisin and Y. Le Bohec, *A History of Rome*, trans. A. Nevill (Oxford, 1996), pp.96–9.

9   *Histories*, xxxi, 25, 6–7.

10   Polybius, *Histories*, xviii, 35, 9; Cicero would say the same of his own policy when he governed Cilicia and Cyprus.

11   A. E. Astin, *Scipio Aemilianus* (Oxford, 1967); Polybius knew him, Cicero did not.

12   See E. D. Rawson, *Intellectual Life in the Late Roman Republic* (London, 1985).

an attitude that had been crafted by the large-scale infiltration of Hellenistic thoughts and customs into Rome the previous century.[13] Nor is it surprising that the distinction of founding Roman drama and of being the 'father' of Roman literature belongs to a Greek ex-slave, Livius Andronicus.

The culture of Greece provided models and encouragement for what would eventually become the growth of an indigenous Latin culture. As the poet Horace had said, 'Captive Greece, captivated her barbarous conqueror'.[14] But as we shall see, Rome's numerous differences with Greece produced a political system, a political history and a political theory which created institutions and values that were more easily passed on to a Romanized posterity than many institutions and values which the Greeks, and most notably the Athenians, had previously underwritten. Later Europeans thought they understood Roman values and institutions despite having adapted what they found in Roman histories and in the writings of Cicero to later and different circumstances.[15] It was through Rome that so much of the ancient Greek legacy came down to a Romanized Western Europe, and especially the values and workings of republicanism culled from the numerous writings of Cicero, not least the *De officiis*, and not simply from his *De re publica*, most of which they did not directly possess until the nineteenth century. This means that much of the meaning of the legacy of ancient Greece has been unconsciously read through Romanized eyes, be they medieval, Renaissance, early modern or ours.[16] As Walbank has noted, 'eventually, with the setting up of the [Roman] empire, the whole Mediterranean was to coalesce into a single cultural continuum in which many aspects of the Hellenistic world lived on, adapted to the provincial organization imposed from Rome'.[17]

When medieval, Renaissance and later Europeans came to speak of the blessings of a mixed constitution, they meant what they understood to be the Roman Cicero's republic, not Plato's *politeia* (which *we* translate as 'republic'), nor Aristotle's *polity*. Indeed, as we shall see, when they rediscovered Aristotle's ethical and political writings in the thirteenth century, they would often read his analysis of best and worst constitutions in the light of what they already knew about the history and the workings of Roman law and Rome's constitution, a knowledge they gained from Ciceronian texts on rhetoric and philosophy, with their numerous examples of Roman practice and historically great orator-politicians. Where Cicero's *De officiis* would reappear in numerous encyclopedias of excerpts or *florilegia,* so too his *De Inventione* would survive as a seminal text which taught medieval men how to acquire Latin grammar, logic and eloquence in the medieval schools. The by-product of being taught eloquence by these texts was a familiarity with Latin, Roman political ideas, exemplary persons and practices which would serve as the frame in which the newly rediscovered Aristotelian writings would themselves *initially* be understood.[18] It has only recently been acknowledged by specialists in Hellenistic philosophy that Cicero's *De officiis* tells us more about Cicero's politics than

13   A. Momigliano, 'Polybius and Posidonius', in Momigliano, *Alien Wisdom*, pp. 22–49.

14   Graecia capta ferum victorem cepit.

15   See *A History of Political Thought* volume 2, chapter 6.

16   For instance, when we speak of the influence of the classical tradition on the framers of the US Constitution we must mean, on the whole, Hellenistic and especially Stoic ethical thought as revealed in the writings of Cicero, Seneca and Plutarch. See M. Nussbaum, *The Therapy of Desire: theory and practice in Hellenistic ethics* (Princeton, NJ, 1994), p. 5.

17   Walbank, *The Hellenistic World*, p. 249.

18   See *A History of Political Thought* volume 2, chapter 1.

anything else he wrote. As Neal Wood rightly said: 'Cicero may be all but forgotten, but in the period of our past that gave rise to distinctly modern institutions and attitudes, he of all ancients was possibly the most esteemed and influential'.[19]

Indeed, the English word 'republic' derives from the Latin res publica, meaning literally 'the public thing', that is, 'the public concern' or the 'people's business'. Roman historians apply the word 'republic' to that period of Roman history from the late sixth century BC, when the early monarchy ended, and the late first century BC, when a new monarchy, the principate, was established.

If we ask the important question of Roman or any other society: who were the political theorists and what effect did they have on the practical policies of their society? we are seeking those responsible for the systematic presentation of values. Thereafter, we might ask how these values were learned and how the current ideology, the most prominent view of the way things were taken to be, operated in a sophisticated and highly structured society. In looking for the relation between theory and practice in Rome, we cannot ignore the position of Roman slaves and their relationship to free-born men who were full Roman citizens. We shall see that the famous phrase 'captive Greece captivated her vanquisher' is in part a key to much of Cicero's understanding of Roman republican politics. Cicero presents what he takes to be the ideals of Rome, a description of 'ancestral ways' (the mos maiorum), from which, as usual, the present generation has fallen away but which they should imitate. His presentation of the ideals, however, is couched in a moral language that owes much to his Greek education. And this gives rise to problems for us, since there is considerable debate among scholars as to whether Cicero's writings are accurate reflections of attitudes and practices 'on the ground'. He is often taken to be rather good on the day-to-day negotiations of late republican politics (in his letters and some speeches), but it is not so clear that his presentations of the moral and historical underpinnings of republican values and practices were widely shared.[20] But as we have already noted about the later European reception of the writings of Plato and Aristotle, Cicero would also be seen to have been exemplary for his culture and the question of whether he was telling it 'as it really had been' was largely ignored.[21] There is little doubt, however, that the influence of 'captive' educated Greeks on Roman citizens was extensive. The Hellenization of the Romans was carried out on on their own soil largely by freed men and slaves imported mainly from captive Greek lands, and education as Romans in the second and first century BC knew it was a Greek import. The privileged Roman citizen was, by the very nature of his society, debarred from scholarship as a career and consequently he gathered highly educated slaves into his household to teach himself and his sons, or he went abroad for a few years to study philosophy, grammar, rhetoric, in Greek with the Greeks. Cicero was no exception. He

19   N. Wood, Cicero's Social and Political Thought (Berkeley, 1988), pp. 1–2; also see A. A. Long, 'Cicero's Politics in De Officiis', in A. Laks and M. Schofield, eds, Justice and Generosity: studies in Hellenistic social and political philosophy (Cambridge, 1995), pp. 213–40, esp. p. 214. See the illuminating review of this volume by Paul Cartledge in Polis 14, 1–2 (1997), pp. 198–205. All of Cicero's extant philosophical works survive in Carolingian manuscripts. Wood provides a brief summary of Cicero's rise and fall in modern Europe beginning with the Renaissance.

20   E.g. on the origins of Rome and its historic destiny, Cicero and others gathered together the literary sources that passed on the traditions but he, like Livy, Virgil and Dionysius of Halicarnassus were all far removed from the events 'and, moreover, prepared to embellish what they received, in order to serve the cause of the Roman "nation"' (Le Glay et al., A History of Rome, p. 2).

21   See introduction to this volume.

typified the educated Roman who lived in two worlds, the Greek world of rational, intellectual speculation, and the Roman world of sentiment and ancestral tradition; the two were never completely harmonized.[22]

Marcus Tullius Cicero (106–43 BC) was born into a wealthy family in an Italian town, Arpinum, south-east of Rome. He was to become one of the leading figures in the last decades of the Roman republic, remarkably creative but violent times which came to a violent end in 27 BC, whereafter the *principate* was established by Julius Caesar's adopted son Octavian, who ruled as Augustus Caesar. Members of Cicero's family had held public office in Arpinum and his ancestors were intimates of members of the ruling elite in Rome, but they were not themselves of that elite.

Social and Political Organization in Rome

Roman society of the second century BC was organized by status and wealth into, broadly speaking, three ranks or 'orders': the *traditional senatorial nobility,* whose wealth was founded on land ownership; the *equestrians* (or knights) whose wealth might be other than land (they were privileged citizens whose status was signified by their entitlement to a horse supplied and maintained by the 'state'); and the lower class or *plebeians.* While the senatorial class held the monopoly of high office (Senate and magistracies) and retained its land-based fortune and wealth, there developed a tendency for certain families to retain high office whose ancestors had received it and this led to a group of *nobiles* to whom high office was increasingly confined. By the end of the second century BC this group of *nobiles* was limited to the descendants of former consuls and the same families (*gentes*) came to monopolize all the high offices.[23] They intermarried and shared the competitive ideals to enjoy abundant wealth and control the business of the 'state'. They monopolized, either by tenure of office or by patronage, the highest governing positions, military, political and religious. There was also a lower 'aristocracy' in the Senate who were not nobles but drawn from a wider circle of ambitious and sufficiently wealthy men.

Cicero's inherited rank was *equestrian*, which placed him in the wealthy, often commercially minded group who were not in the Senate. One especially profitable area of their business activity was the collection of taxes under state contract from the provinces.[24] Others were bankers and money-lenders as well as landowners, including the governing classes of the municipalities in Italy, outside of Rome. Cicero's father was an example of the latter group. The equestrians sought influence with the traditional nobility who were in theory prevented by custom from commercial activities and state contracts.[25] The senatorial elite were landowners and this was seen as an essential ingredient of their integrity of character. In Cicero's time it was not unusual for young men of equestrian status to aspire to the lower public offices, but they would not expect to reach the summit of a senatorial career in the first generation. Even small success in these

22   For an interesting general account of Roman values, see M. I. Finley, *Politics in the Ancient World* (Cambridge, 1983), chapters on Rome; and M. Crawford, *The Roman Republic* (London, 1978) for the historical background to Cicero's Roman republic.

23   Le Glay et al., *A History of Rome*, pp. 108–9.

24   *Publicani*: the publicans of the New Testament.

25   Although during the late republic many senators engaged in agriculture and trading for profit.

matters would require the patronage of a leading senatorial family and the 'new man' in politics would forever be made to feel an obligation to the ruling oligarchy.

Magistrates, Senate and People: The Polybian Ideal 'Mixed Constitution' of Rome

The functions of Roman republican government were nominally split between three elements: (1) the *magistrates*, the most powerful of whom were the annually elected two *consuls* who were the Executive of the 'state' with 'royal' power, commanding unconditional obedience with judicial and coercive powers; (2) the *Senate*, a self-regulating assembly of the aristocracy or ruling elite with non-elected, life membership and accountable to no one, giving preference in free debates to the senior members or ex-consuls – the *nobiles*; (3) the 'democratic' sovereign assemblies of the people (e.g. *comitia centuriata*, the largest assembly of the whole body of citizens) which were distinguished from the *plebeians* in their own assembly (*concilium plebis*), convened by a tribune. The decisions of the latter were acknowledged as those of the *populus*, when assembled in the *comitia tributa* (the tribal assembly which represented the *populus* divided into tribes). In Cicero's time there were four assemblies of the people (*comitia curiata, comitia centuriata, comitia tributa* and *concilium plebis*).

The Senate, from a legal point of view, was only an advisory body, convened by a consul and without legislative powers. It could only pass motions or resolutions (*senatus consulta*), unlike the popular assemblies which passed laws (*leges*). But by constitutional convention magistrates consulted the Senate on important issues and, before introducing a bill to one of the popular assemblies, the magistrate was meant to set it before the Senate. This made the Senate the only deliberative body; hence, it had a firm grip on legislation and it defined the sphere of activity of magistrates.

This is an oversimplified but schematic picture of the early republican constitution of the mid-fifth to the end of the fourth centuries BC to which Polybius refers[26] and it reflects the victories of the plebs in their successful attempts to gain access to those offices that had previously been uniquely in the hands of the patricians. This patrician–plebeian settlement is what Polybius thought gave Rome its equilibrium. The fifth- and fourth-century reforms and democratic victories made Rome an aristocratic republic. 'A Senate governed, and by its side magistrates ran the state, while the assemblies of the people had their say in the election of magistrates and voting on laws.'[27]

Ideally, and again according to the Greek historian with Roman patrons, Polybius,[28] this 'mixed constitution' guaranteed stability by 'sharing' power, ensuring that none of the three elements had sufficient power to dominate the other two and that each of the separate elements depended on the other two for the successful discharge of its respective functions. Rome's aim was a 'balance of powers', an unequal mixture of monarchical, aristocratic and democratic powers, designed to prevent any one element from seizing control of the 'state'. It was not a balance between organs with separate functions but between organs with overlapping functions.[29]

---

26   See Le Glay et al., *A History of Rome*, pp. 46–54, 60.
27   Ibid., pp. 61–2.
28   Book 6.
29   F. W. Walbank, *Polybius* (Berkeley, 1972).

Polybius was convinced that the Roman constitution was open to analysis in these Greek terms. Was it? He was, after all, writing to explain to the Greeks why the Romans were victorious as well as referring to Roman readers. He sought to persuade Romans to behave in such a way as would not alienate their subject peoples and consequently would not imperil the position of those Greek upper-class provincials who had identified their interests with Roman rule. He presupposed that Romans were eminently reasonable, and that the nobility was not divided by conflicts of interest and convictions and that it controlled the lower classes in Rome and the provincials without difficulty.[30]

Furthermore, Polybius related the development of the Roman political system, a result of gradual collective effort by the community as a whole, to a Greek theory of constitutional origins and cyclical development. He said that all states undergo a cyclical process, where a primitive (unconstitutional) monarchy gives rise to true monarchy which degenerates into tyranny; tyranny is replaced by aristocracy which then degenerates into oligarchy, and oligarchy degenerates into democracy; democracy in turn is replaced by mob rule, a period of anarchy, and the subsequent emergence of primitive monarchy again. Rome alone had succeeded in breaking this cycle of constitutions by achieving a stable blend of monarchy, aristocracy and democracy. This was the Roman mixed constitution, although in the fragmentary account we possess he never explained exactly how this was achieved. In writing favourably about Rome's political genius 'Polybius paved the way for the other Greek intellectuals who accepted Roman rule and collaborated with it'.[31]

More importantly for us, Polybius's representation of the Roman constitution in Greek terms and as a mixture was once thought to have much in common with Cicero's own presentation of republican history and ideals. Cicero also applies a cyclical theory of constitutions to Rome's constitutional history, but he modifies the Polybian cycle[32] sufficiently to destroy it. Cicero also shares the idea that Rome's actual constitution was inclusive, one that truly shared power and was therefore mixed, with elements of monarchy, aristocracy and democracy, despite its decided emphasis on its aristocratic element, the power of the senior magistracies and the Senate. Polybius, however, emphasized the wide-ranging and fundamental powers of the people[33] and we shall look in vain in Cicero's De re publica for a similar and extensive popular balance to his ideal republican mixture of monarchic and aristocratic elements.[34]

---

30   But see Livy's discussion of Roman conflicts: *The Early History of Rome* (books i–v), trans. A de Selincourt (Harmondsworth, 1971); *Rome and Italy* (books vi–x), trans. B. Radice (Harmondsworth, 1982).

31   Momigliano, *Alien Wisdom*, p. 30. 'Yet we are still left with the impression that these two Greeks [Polybius and Posidonius] never quite understood what was really happening in the social organism which had become the guarantee of their own survival' (p. 36). See D. E. Hahm, 'Polybius' Applied Political Theory', in A. Laks and M. Schofield, eds, *Justice and Generosity: studies in Hellenistic social and political philosophy* (Cambridge, 1995), pp. 7–47.

32   *De re publica* i, 65–8.

33   *Histories*, vi, 14; see A. Lintott, 'The Theory of the Mixed Constitution in Rome', in J. Barnes and M. Griffin, eds, *Philosophia Togata II* (Oxford, 1997), pp. 70–85.

34   See below, pp. 275ff. Polybius' influence on Cicero's *De re publica* is thought by some to be especially notable in book 2, somewhat less so in book 3 according to C. Nicolet (see note 35). See also J.-L. Ferrary, 'Cicéron entre Polybe et Platon', *Journal of Roman Studies* 74 (1984), pp. 87–98. As Wirszubski writes: 'The form of government between the Second Punic War and the Gracchi, which Polybius and Cicero described as a mixed constitution, was in fact an aristocratic republic in everything but name. This fact was apparent to contemporaries, and even frankly admitted by the very supporters of that regime.' C. Wirszubski, *Libertas as a Political Idea at Rome During the Late Republic and Early Principate* (Cambridge, 1950), pp. 31–2.

The question that has taxed scholars over the past one hundred years is, therefore, threefold: whether in reality Rome's republican constitution was a true mixture of elements of kingship, aristocracy and (especially) democracy; whether Polybius was accurate in his representation of the Roman republic as such a mixture; and, most important for historians of political ideas, whether we can rely on Cicero to provide, if not strict historical accuracy, then at least some plausible account of the values and practices of Rome's golden age which he sought in his own later times to revive.[35]

It has been argued by many generations of scholars of Roman history that in reality sovereignty only nominally belonged to the people in their assemblies. Economic, political, military and religious factors ensured that they deferred to the traditional elite who controlled the Senate and the magistracies. Political power was in the hands of an oligarchy.[36] During the fifty years that followed the victory of the second Punic war, the fifty years to which Cicero referred as the 'golden age' of the republic, the Senate gained control of foreign and financial affairs to such an extent that the magistrates, who alone could summon the Senate and control its agenda, became near absolute rulers. This was because in meetings of the plebeian assemblies the people were controlled by the presiding magistrates, the tribunes, whom they had the power to elect and who originally had the task of protecting the interests of the plebeians against the magistrates. Tribunes were often wealthy plebeians or 'plebeian nobles'. While recent, more nuanced, accounts have tried to present a much more powerful influence of 'the people' in their assemblies, the salient point is that the people had no freedom of discussion nor the power to initiate business from the floor. A Roman popular assembly was not, therefore, a deliberative body. It listened to speeches and made policy by approving or rejecting policy made

35   For the debate over whether Rome's *was* a mixed constitution as well as on Polybius' accuracy, see Momigliano, *Alien Wisdom* and C. Nicolet, 'Polybe et la "constitution" de Rome: aristocratie et democratie', in C. Nicolet, ed., *Demokratia et aristokratia* (Paris, 1983), pp.15–35. Momigliano: 'We may suspect that if Polybius had done his job properly modern scholars would have had less difficulty in finding a way into the Roman mind. We would consequently have to register some losses: we should be deprived of the 490 pages of Kurt von Fritz, *The Theory of the Mixed Constitution in Antiquity* (1954), which would be a pity because, against all probabilities, there is much incidental wisdom and knowledge in this preposterous attempt to compare the surely non-existent mixed constitution of Rome with the doubtfully existent mixed constitution of the United States' (*Alien Wisdom*, p. 44). Nicolet insists, on the contrary, that Polybius gives a refined and correct reading of Roman institutions, speaking of democratic elements but not of true democracy as he never says Romans had equality or freedom of speech, and the Roman people do not deliberate in any true sense of the word; they attended deliberations to hear them only: 'Liberté de parole donc, mais non exactement pour le peuple: pour ceux [tribuns] qui ont charge de parler en son nom' ('Polybe et la "constitution"', pp. 28–9). Nicolet notes how Polybius never speaks of the method of recruitment to magistracies or to the senators, nor of the groupings of Roman people in wealth classes (via centuries) which severely limited their capacity to participate equally. Nicolet says this is a deliberate 'silence', and instead, Polybius discusses differentials in the army to explain centurial classes (ibid., p. 30). For a subtle and wide-ranging continuation of Nicolet's position see Lintott, 'The theory of the mixed constitution at Rome', pp. 70–85. Lintott argues for Polybius' originality which goes well beyond Greek political thought (ibid., p. 79) precisely because he was in contact with Roman politics. Also see Hahm, 'Polybius', pp. 7–47.

36   Perhaps the strongest argument against Roman popular sovereignty came from the nineteenth-century German historian Mommsen, when speaking of the so-called 'golden age'. See T. Mommsen, *History of Rome*, vol. 2, trans. W. Dickson (London, 1868), p. 381: 'Never even in the most limited monarchy was a part so completely null assigned to the monarch as was allotted to the sovereign Roman people'. R. Syme, *The Roman Revolution* (Oxford, 1960), p. 15, called the Roman constitution 'a screen and a sham'; with regard to the provinces, E. Badian, *Roman Imperialism in the Late Republic*, 2nd edn (Oxford, 1968), p. 87 says: 'No administration in history has ever devoted itself so whole-heartedly to fleecing its subjects for the private benefit of its ruling class as Rome of the last age of the Republic'.

elsewhere. However, those in attendance at a plebeian assembly could vote, not as individuals, but through being divided into groups (*tribes*).

The official designation of the Roman 'state' was SPQR (*senatus populusque romanus*, Senate and People) and reflected the true status of the Senate. While the 'Senate and People' formally decided on matters of war, peace and treaties, the detailed aspects of the conduct of policies lay in the hands of annual magistrates elected by the people from Rome's ruling elite. Since magistrates served for only one year, elections were frequently held and the Roman people was divided into constituencies or centuries which voted as a single entity. Voting in Rome was always by groups rather than individually. The poorest citizens were grouped together in a single century and voted last, which effectively meant not at all, since voting stopped when a majority was achieved. A candidate who was unanimously favoured by the rich had no need to gain the support of the poor. When he did require their votes, they were more effectively courted by 'bread and circuses', especially as the massive expansion of Rome's population made the traditional social relationships of patronage impossible. However elected, once a magistrate, he was not obliged to act as a delegate of the electorate.[37] Those elected to the most important magistracies could try and sometimes succeed in delaying the implementation of legislation indefinitely.

In theory, then, the people alone made laws by voting yes or no to a magistrate's proposal. In practice, the decrees of the Senate had overriding executive force in many spheres. In theory, the people chose the magistrates. In practice, they tended to elect men from already distinguished families and were influenced by their obligations of clientship and by their patrons' wishes and wealth.[38] In theory, the ten tribunes could veto the act of a magistrate or propose legislation to the people. In practice, unless they were near revolutionaries, and there were a few, they consulted the Senate first. The *libertas* or freedom of the people meant, politically, no more than the freedom to vote in person in their own tribe. And in Cicero's day they were 'free' to jeer or applaud.

Roman Freedom (*libertas*) and Roman Civil Law

The freedom (*libertas*) of the Roman citizen consisted in the legal capacity to possess rights of his own, possible only if he was not subjected to someone else's mastery (*dominium*). A free man, in Roman law, was free only because he was a member of the civic body; hence, Roman liberty was an *acquired* civic right, resting on positive laws. It was not an innate right of man. Roman civil law did not apply to non–citizens, *peregrines* who were instead governed by the law of nations, *ius gentium*, which were rules considered to be part of the laws of all civilized people and hence also applied to Roman citizens as well. But civic freedom was an acquired civic right, dependent on citizenship, itself determined by the 'state's' law, and this civic freedom is one of the most enduring legacies of Rome to European government.

Romans identified their freedom with the republic's constitution and the extent of that freedom was therefore determined by the constitution. Since the Roman constitu-

---

37 Wirszubski, *Libertas*, p. 48: 'The government [i.e. annual magistrates] of Rome, although elected by all the full citizens, was essentially non-democratic because, once in power, it was largely independent of the popular will'.
38 See below, pp. 243ff.

tion was not a written document but a product of gradual development and evolution, constitutional changes affected the form and extent of citizen freedom over the years. In the fifth century BC the law of the Roman republic was a set of unwritten customs, applicable to Roman citizens, and called the *ius civile* (civil law). Tradition has it that plebeian agitation caused the customary law to be written down *c.* 450 BC as rules (*leges*), known as the Twelve Tables, and approved by the popular assembly. These were memorized by schoolboys and served as the foundations of subsequent civil law which was modified and adapted to the increasing complexity of society by the praetor's law. The praetor, an annually elected law officer, issued an edict which revised the laws of his predecessors. From the late republic the praetor set out the issue between parties in legal terms and instructed a judge (*iudex*) to condemn or absolve the defendant if certain allegations were proved. Neither the praetor, nor the judge, nor the advocates who represented the parties, were professional lawyers. But from the middle period of the republic a class of Roman citizen jurists, aristocrats who were amateur legal experts, advised the praetor as members of his council. These amateur legal experts expounded the law to those who sought their advice. Their common opinion was embodied in successive court decisions and hence Roman law was adapted on a case by case basis. Like the English common law, Roman law was elaborated through discussion of cases by amateur legal experts who then collected and published their opinions. The continuous legal development of Roman law reached its peak during the 'classical period', that is, the first two centuries AD. During the last century of the Roman republic, the first century BC, alterations in the traditional law which derived from custom and the Twelve Tables were the result of magisterial innovation and the views of those amateur legal experts whose views were considered authoritative.[39] Hence, freedom was the sum of civic rights *granted objectively* (not subjectively to an individual) by the laws of Rome, and these evolving laws were conceived as positive restraints in order to distinguish the unqualified power to do whatever one likes (licence) from the restraining moderation of liberty.

Roman freedom (*libertas*) could only be enjoyed under the law. All citizens were equally subject to the law and it was intended not only that the law would be equal for all citizens but that 'state' justice was accessible to all. Without the law there would be an unrestrained, unregulated free-for-all. But the law could also withdraw freedom: 'from a purely legal point of view there was nothing to prevent even the enslavement of a citizen'[40] although in ordinary circumstances *civitas* and *libertas*, citizenship and liberty, were practically inviolable so long as the citizen remained at Rome. The law guaranteed the *liberty of a citizen*, who was already conceived of as a member of an organized community, that of the Roman republic, and not simply the liberty of an individual against the authority of the community. Roman liberty was viewed in terms of social relations, as a duty no less than a right, a right to claim what is due to oneself and a duty to respect what is due to others.[41] But within the law a distinction was established between the rich (*assidui*) and the poor (*proletarii*) rather than between patricians and plebeians.[42] The issue

39   For a brief summary see Peter Stein, 'Roman Law', in D. Miller et al., eds, *The Blackwell Encyclopaedia of Political Thought* (Oxford, 1987), pp. 446–9.
40   Wirszubski, *Libertas,* p. 30.
41   Ibid., p. 8.
42   Le Glay et al., *A History of Rome*, pp. 51–2.

of what is differentially due to one citizen as opposed to another, and the criteria used to judge, are essential for an understanding of the republic's legal and social relations. It is also essential to an understanding of Cicero's political theory, as expressed in his *On Duties* (*De officiis*) and in the *De re publica*. In theory, to benefit from Roman freedom one obeyed the law (not other men) because Roman freedom existed only under the rule of law.

Freedom of the Roman people was not absolute. Individuals were free from arbitrary arrest; they could claim protection, even in the provinces, against arbitrary actions by magistrates which affected their person or possessions. They were guaranteed civic rights and personal freedom under the laws, and their rights to possessions legally obtained. But to maintain their rights citizens and subjects were constrained to seek the protection of powerful men.[43]

Romans insisted on citizens being equally subject to the law, meaning equality of all personal rights and equality of the fundamental political rights, but they simultaneously rejected complete egalitarianism. Romans were equal before the law but not to equal things. They insisted on a proportional fairness or *equity*. All citizens had a right to participate in public life, but not to participate equally, only according to rank. A Roman citizen's liberty was the *lower limit* of his political rights and the right to govern was not a civic right of all citizens.[44] The actual exercise of governing required in addition authority and standing, *auctoritas* and *dignitas* (which determined rank) and which were not equally possessed. Romans appear to have accepted this, in that they did not interpret their right to enact laws and elect magistrates as a right actually to govern themselves.[45] As we shall see, Cicero, following a Greek understanding of worthiness to rule, would seek to equate *dignitas* and *auctoritas* – normally accorded on the basis of ancestral birth, wealth and the traditional habit of public achievement that was associated with birth and wealth – with the proven merit or virtue of the rulers. For Cicero, as we shall see, this proven merit would not require ancestors but educated reason and a true understanding of Roman history. In practice, however, Romans equated these with customary ancestral standing and wealth, *dignitas* adhering to a man permanently, inherited from ancestors and passed on to descendants.[46]

Roman *libertas* was forever in tension with Roman *dignitas*. This tension was not concerned with the individual against the 'state'; rather, it was a tension between the Roman citizen and other citizens who were stronger and wealthier.

The difference between Roman *libertas* and democratic Athenian *eleutheria* (freedom)[47] is important, because whereas Athenians exercised equality of political 'rights' the Roman republic never intended to be a democracy. Nor did Roman citizens enjoy freedom of public speech (as did the Athenian democrats: *isegoria*). Romans could not address a public meeting without the consent of magistrates and tribunes. In the plebeian assemblies popular decisions were achieved by majorities of the voting groups and the voting

---

43 See below, pp. 243ff.

44 Compare and contrast Athenian democracy.

45 Wirszubski, *Libertas*, p. 35: 'Libertas is not so much the right to act on one's own initiative as the freedom to choose an "auctor" whose "auctoritas" is freely accepted.'

46 Wirszubski, *Libertas*, p. 14 astutely notes that 'whereas Cicero declared that the composition of the government determined the character of the constitution, Aristotle deduced the various types of constitutions from the various possible bases and extents of equality'; also see p. 36.

47 See chapter 1.

groups themselves were so arranged as to ensure the predominance of the wealthy. The decisions of the *concilium plebis* – *plebiscita*, from where we get our word 'plebiscite' – bound the plebs and if the consuls agreed were passed upwards to become law. Tribunes of the plebs could use their relation with the plebeian assembly to secure their own personal dominant power base in Rome, as was famously attempted by the younger Tiberius Gracchus (133 BC), who introduced a law in the assembly, going against custom in that he by-passed the Senate to take over public land held illegally and redistribute it in smallholdings to landless citizens. Tribunes could be cynical manipulators of the plebeian assemblies or more committed reformers who, none the less, had personal political ambitions of their own. The ambitious individual, whether a plebeian noble or a patrician, was driven by the desire to acquire and use power.[48]

Populares versus Optimates in Cicero's Rome

During the last century of the republic the Roman 'state' was ideologically divided between two major tactical approaches to government: that of the *optimates* and the *populares*, reflecting the two broad status divisions of rich and poor in society. The *populares* (panderers to the mob) were themselves from the ruling elite and were originally called this by their opponents to refer to their promoting popular causes by manipulating popular institutions against the Senate. The first great *popularis* was the tribune Tiberius Gracchus. *Optimates* (the best men) were, likewise, from the ruling elite, but their approach was more traditional and favoured the primacy of the Senate. Each claimed to be champions of Roman *libertas*.

In terms of competing visions of structural control and power in the 'state', the *optimates* believed in (and practised) oligarchical government by a 'state's' elite (the *senatorial aristocracy* with power, and the *equestrians* with influence on the *nobiles*) with only limited control by the people. The *populares,* on the other hand, believed that the people should play a more active role in shaping government policy as well as sharing more equitably in the tangible benefits (spoils) of empire. This is no modern left–right political distinction. Freed men and wealthy plebeians could adopt the 'optimate' position as could nobles and equestrians take on that of the *populares.*[49]

The terms *populares* and *optimates* came into being to refer to what had previously occurred during the second century BC when the old noble, ruling elite had already hardened into an exclusive, arrogant, even complacent oligarchy, determined to maintain its power and perpetuate its rule at all costs. The *optimates* and the *populares* were *not* like modern parties representing discrete and local constituencies with cohesive political programmes. The *populares* were certainly not men who favoured democracy. They were politicians who sought to break the inner ring of the ruling oligarchy which was supported by propertied interests, and they attempted this by supporting popular

---

48   D. Shotter, *The Fall of the Roman Republic* (London, 1994); W. K. Lacey and B. W. J. G. Wilson, *Res Publica: Roman politics and society according to Cicero* (Oxford, 1970), pp. 1–15.

49   Ironically, in real life the proud and ambitious aristocrat Scipio Aemilianus was, in practice, a *populais* who repeatedly violated customary procedure and created extreme factional hostility in which popular appeal was a key factor, despite Cicero presenting him in the *De re publica* as an advocate of strict constitutionality! Astin, *Scipio Aemilianus*, p. 226 and Zetzel, *Cicero,* p. 13.

measures like the redistribution of land for the landless, corn subsidies and debt relief. Roman politics did not produce stable political groupings and the Roman political leader (be he *popularis* or *'optimate'*) had no other constituency than himself and his own self-aggrandizement, *dignitas* and glory. In Cicero's time, the objective of a Roman senator was to maintain his own *dignitas*, not to uphold some political principle. The loyalty (*fides*) that existed in Roman society was not to a party, or even to the 'state', but to a variety of specific individuals or families.[50]

Indeed, the Roman 'state' did not usually intervene in a great many aspects of citizens' lives. In Cicero's time, citizens were not subject to direct taxation although provincials were, and 'social services' were minimal. The 'state' had no mechanism for providing financial credit. Loans, health care, support in old age, education for one's children, all required help from wealthy and powerful patrons. Nor were salaries paid for government duties so that these offices, in practice, could only be exercised by the wealthy.[51]

As there was no standing professional army, Roman citizens of different status formed the legions. Hence, typical of the republic was a *citizen army*, where soldiers were seen as having a physical stake in the republic for which they fought. But military service hit farmers more severely as campaigns became longer and were fought at greater distances from Italy. Originally, there was a property qualification for military service, so that the main burden fell on farmers who, with the increasing riches acquired by the Roman 'state' from their successful military campaigns, sought a greater proportion of war booty. When the property qualification was abolished, recruitment was open to all citizens of whatever status. But where, in the past, farmer soldiers could return to their land, the Roman 'state' now had recruits who had no land to which to return: the 'state' made no provision for the distribution of land to discharged recruits. Furthermore, from the mid second century BC Roman armies were made up of Italian allies as well as Roman citizens, and Italian soldiers felt increasing resentment at their being excluded from the benefits of the empire they were helping Rome to win. Italians were not integrated into Rome until during Cicero's lifetime, when the rebellion of the Italian allies – the Social War – forced Rome to grant citizenship to every community in Italy. Roman generals were now responsible for the resettlement of all their troops and each general returning to Italy after each campaign had to arrange for an *agrarian law* to be passed by 'Senate and People' in order that land be provided. By Cicero's time, the ruling elite no longer shared the sympathies of the troops or had their interests at heart.

For members of this governing class, the growth of empire provided opportunities for amassing large sums of money and property. The money was 'invested' in financing bribes to the people during the times of election to magistracies or in acquiring ever larger private agricultural estates. Agricultural instability caused many farmers to leave their lands and drift to Rome or other cities, in the process losing their tenure and making their lands available to those with the money to increase their holdings further.[52]

---

50   See below, pp. 243ff.

51   Cicero, *De inventione* II, xxxix, 115 (common rhetorical topics considering rewards for behaviour, actions and deeds): 'the national resources should be increased rather than diminished, and that he is a shameless man who demands wages for his service to the state, rather than gratitude'.

52   Cicero's letters show the Roman nobility as not only deeply concerned with real property, their main form of investment, but feverishly engaged in property deals, property frequently changing hands. See E. Rawson, 'The Ciceronian Aristocracy and its Properties', in M. I. Finley, ed., *Studies in Roman Property* (Cambridge, 1976), pp. 85–102.

During the late republic, the Senate and consuls initiated hardly any major pieces of social legislation to cope with these problems, many failing even to recognize their existence, and they put up tremendous opposition to land reform bills. Instead, ad hoc private patronage was seen as the cure for most social and personal grievances. By Cicero's time, however, the fracturing of the ruling class into fluctuating cliques comprised of fiercely competitive individuals was soon to lead to the traditional ruling families having all but disappeared.[53]

Patrons and Clients

Roman social relations were constituted by the patron–client relationship. Roman traditions, as expressed in the law of the Twelve Tables, were affected by Rome's remote past as a struggling community of rural farmer soldiers, and placed particular stress on the unity and continuity of the family and its method of extending the area of protection, based on kinship, through the *patronus* or patron as 'father'. The Roman father had, by judicial sentence, the power of life and death over his children (not merely at birth, as in Greece) and could sell, repurchase and resell his child up to three times, after which the child was 'emancipated'. But within the family the limits of paternal authority came to be fixed and a certain amount of female emancipation was provided for. In Cicero's time, some of the older traditions had been broken down or modified, especially in respect to women. If her father was alive, a woman not placed in her husband's power would be in that of her father. Likewise, if in her husband's power, upon his death she was 'emancipated'. Women who were not in the power of their father or husband still required a guardian to enable them to perform legal acts, but they had the ability to put pressure on their guardians to allow them considerable freedom of action in respect of their property.

Further modifications to more traditional social relations occurred in Cicero's time so that the original ruling families were expanded to include members of the equestrian order in the realm of power. But the form of patron–client relations remained intact. The *patronus* served as an advocate for less powerful clients who were in the legal position of infants by reason of age or status. He had a natural area of powerful clientage where the less powerful were more dependent on him than he was on them. Cicero describes the great noble of an earlier generation: 'both walking about in the Forum and sitting at home on his throne, he was approached, not just about questions of law, but about marrying a daughter, buying a farm, cultivating the land, in fact about any point of social obligation or business'.[54]

All non-criminal litigation trials took place before private individuals whose judgements were binding, without any right of appeal to the public courts. A patron spoke for his clients if they had to appear in court. Clientage, where the more fortunate members of society 'protected' those less well-off in return for the latter's political loyalty, characterized the 'corporate' relations of stability and harmony of the Roman republic. We are told that patronage as an *ideal* ensured that the ruling class and the ruled were held

53 P. A. Brunt, *Social Conflicts in the Roman Republic* (London, 1971); P. A. Brunt, ' "Amicitia" in the Late Roman Republic', *Proceedings of the Cambridge Philological Society* n.s. 11 (1965), pp. 1–20, reprinted in P. A. Brunt, ed., *The Fall of the Roman Republic and Other Essays* (Oxford, 1988).
54 *De oratore* 3. 133.

together by mutual bonds of affection.[55] But the bonds of affection were strongest between those of similar status. Around the noble patron would gather his *consilium*, a group of friends who advised him and helped him in his public life. It was these ties of *amicitia*, meaning a prudential use of friends in defending social claims over rights and property especially in the law courts, that was a key concept in daily life in Rome. *Amicitia* was more than merely a political alliance with those who could do one a favour; it was not devoid of personal or emotional content. Roman patronage was primarily a moral rather than a legal relationship, clearly seen as fluid and where each client had many links to different patrons to whom he was obliged, some inherited from ancestors, and where they could pick and choose to suit the moment.[56] One man's patron could be another man's client. It was a kind of 'friendship' that was practical, active and useful.[57] If Cicero reveals the true nature of this 'friendship' in the *De officiis* then it is clear that one's obligations were largely circumscribed by friends of like status.[58]

This system failed for *some* of the reasons Cicero himself gives in the *De re publica*: greed, ambitious corruption and the failure to support and maintain the institutional authority of the republic against the domination of military individuals as 'kings' or dictators. But during the last century BC the fault was as much individual as global: the majority of the poor no longer enjoyed active protection from their patrons for no other reason than that the poor were too numerous and the republic's debt crisis was, by then, immense.[59] A significant body of social legislation had to be brought in to deal with the severe problems of debt, land settlement and the dwindling food supply suffered by ordinary Romans. It is significant that popular legislators, from the time of the tribune Tiberius Gracchus onwards, who made themselves universal patrons through the distribution of public resources, were viewed negatively by Cicero because they replaced the social power of the ruling class as patrons with a dependence on popular demagogues as patrons for alleviation in times of poverty and crisis.[60] But this had already occurred well before the time when Octavian established the *principate*. As Augustus, he was able to break completely and finally the pluralist power base of dependents of the nobility in the city of Rome. He replaced it with imperial patronage, where the ultimate control of public resources was in his hands. The end of the Roman republic meant that the senatorial elite would become his collaborators, dependent on him.

If the *optimates* and *populares* signify approaches to securing shifting 'group interests', these interests were taken up and forwarded by important and powerful, competitive *individuals* who were deeply attached to their ancestral and political traditions (the *mos maiorum*). Such men could look back to consular ancestors in their families, real or fabricated, and on this basis defend their notion of membership in the Senate and tenure of magistracies as a birthright. They conceived of their position as a 'freedom' (*libertas*) which was not to be infringed by the over-ambitiousness (*dominatio*) of others. Hence, it was the noble individual's view that his was both a right and a duty to serve the *patria* in

---

55   A. Wallace-Hadrill, 'Patronage in Roman Society: from republic to empire', in A. Wallace-Hadrill, ed., *Patronage in Ancient Society* (London, 1990), pp. 63–88.

56   Wallace-Hadrill, 'Patronage', p. 67.

57   See Brunt, '*Amicitia*'.

58   See below, p. 264.

59   P. A. Brunt, 'Clientela', in Brunt, *The Fall of the Roman Republic*, pp. 382–442.

60   Wallace-Hadrill, 'Patronage', p. 70 argues that the universal patron was perceived to be the 'state' and its revenues.

leading military campaigns but especially in government, through which service he enhanced his own glory. The equestrian Cicero was unusual in that his political career was achieved, consciously, through the law courts, without commanding an army or governing a province, but he too held to this older 'corporate' ideal which bound the nobles to the interests of the republic. Cicero's view was that all who had the welfare of the 'state' at heart were, in fact, *optimates*.[61]

Cicero was not initially in the position of a member of the political class, the traditional Roman noble, aptly described by Paterson as 'a one-man band'. Expecting to be elected to high office, the Roman noble had to 'put together an elaborate but entirely temporary, coalition of interest-groups and individuals who would anticipate favours and rewards from the successful candidate'.[62] A retinue was required and largesse was expected by members of one's circle. They also had to contribute towards the expenses of their friends for them to reciprocate and the ambitious and unscrupulous borrowed large sums to enable them to distribute bribes to secure election. Bribery of electors and of jurors was illegal, although it was widely practised, as was extortion in the provinces. The Roman system of criminal jurisdiction had permanent courts to deal with these offences. Cicero would make himself famous by appearing in cases dealing with bribery, extortion, violence and rioting. He charted a career for himself that, in the end, gave him considerable executive authority and control of the major affairs of state as well as the opportunity to win glory for himself and for dispensing favours and rewards to others. But he did this in an unusual way.

Cicero the Lawyer: The 'New Man' on his Way to the Top

Cicero's father had moved the family to Rome when Cicero and his brother were still boys. From an early age he was determined to seek office in Rome. He was given the best education available, much of it from learned men from the captive Greek world.[63] Although he was a junior officer in the Roman army, he resumed his studies and took up civil law instead of pursuing a military career. He decided to seek political power by his exercise of his tremendous talents as an orator, developed in part through his family's connection with the consul Crassus – an expert in Greek rhetorical theory and a fine orator[64] – and when he was taken into the home of Scaevola, another noble ex-consul and a practising Roman orator and jurist.[65] Scaevola's marriage to the daughter of Laelius, a friend of Scipio the younger's, enabled Cicero to build up a picture of Scipio Aemilianus and the previous generation of warrior-intellectuals whom he represents in his *De re publica*. The place in which rhetorical skills could be exercised was in the Roman law courts and Cicero began his career as an advocate, winning influence and friends (*amicitia*) through his defence of and, exceptionally, in his prosecution (for extortion: C. Verres) of famous politically active men.[66]

---

61 See below, *On Duties*.
62 J. Paterson, 'Politics in the Late Republic', in Wiseman, *Roman Political Life*, pp. 21–43.
63 E. D. Rawson, *Cicero: a portrait* (London, 1975 and reprints).
64 *De oratore*.
65 Plutarch, *Life of Cicero* – *Cic.*, 3.1.
66 The consequence of prosecution and conviction was loss of status since the convicted man went into exile to avoid punishment and hence relinquished his public career.

The public courts were held in Rome in the open air at various positions in the Forum, so that this central space in the middle of the city of Rome could, at times, be full of courts simultaneously in session. One could, and did, become widely known to spectators and well recognized for rhetorical performances under these conditions. Cicero did not rise to high office by representing one political viewpoint or another. Instead, he described himself as daily increasing his popularity and resources by devoting himself to his legal cases, for he saw this as the road to favour in the eyes both of clients as well as the general public.[67] He made it clear that his rhetorical skills were at the disposal of all sorts and conditions of men who needed him in the courts.[68] Simultaneously, he progressed rapidly through various lower public offices and finally ran an election campaign which brought him extraordinary (and unusual) success: he achieved the highest office in the Roman 'state', that of one of the two *consuls*, in 63 BC.

He was in charge of the republic for a year and the office of consul made him and his descendants nobles. As a 'new man', meaning not from the rank of the traditional senatorial elite, Cicero promised to give 'what the *res publica* needs above all else, the long-awaited restoration of the traditional authority and prestige of the senatorial order'.[69] Cicero took it upon himself to seek a balance of the interests of the many and the few to ensure the dominance of the latter. In his *Pro Sestio*[70] he outlined an idealized version of the political programme of the *optimates*,[71] and his *De re publica* is a reasoned defence of this position.

He spent his life, thereafter, arguing that the republican constitution as a 'mixed' form is the best, because there is a balance of rights, duties and functions (offices) so that the magistrates have sufficient power, the Senate – the council of eminent citizens – sufficient authority, and the people sufficient liberty, the latter being entirely dependent on the Senate and magistrates for their liberty and welfare.[72] This institutional ideal, in effect an 'aristocratic' republic, what *he* meant by *optimates* as men of personal merit who were devoted to senatorial government regardless of ancestry, emerged out of a realization that this kind of constitution was the only practical compromise to allow for strong government, without absolutism, and which also would satisfy 'the people', without democracy. He believed it to be essential to maintain the princi-

---

67   *Ad Attic.* ii, 22.3; he also notes in *De officiis* ii, 69–71 how the obvious financial and political advantages that derive from 'friendship' with the wealthy and influential in preference to the poor but worthy man, is well recognized by others, so that few, in practice, hesitate to lend their support to the wealthy. But he argues that there is a strong case for taking the opposite line, for the patronage and 'friendship' of the poor but upright man appears disinterested and wins widespread and lasting support, whereas the wealthy dislike being held under obligation and hate 'like death' to be treated as clients whether in deed or name. It is of some interest, however, that this is his only reference to clientship in the *De officiis* and in general he expresses no interest whatever in relations with social inferiors in this work, implying that true friendship, where no one is called a 'client', can only occur between men of similar status who pursue mutual moral obligations to one another.

68   For an interesting discussion of how Cicero's use of oratory's techniques coincided with his political career see Wiedemann, *Cicero*; also see G. Achard, *Pratique, rhétorique et idéologie politique dans les discours 'optimates' de Cicéron* (Leiden, 1981).

69   *De lege agraria* i, 27.

70   *Pro Sestio*, 96–143.

71   See Wirszubski, *Libertas*, pp. 40–2 on this, *otium* (political inactivity and peaceful security for the people) and public peace with *dignitas* for the ruling, senatorial elite; also pp. 93–4, that ordinary people preferred peace and security to liberty if they had to make a choice and could not have both.

72   *De re publica* II, 57.

ple that the greatest number should not have the greatest power.[73] As a 'new man' Cicero advocated breaking down the exclusiveness of the ruling oligarchy, opening it up to 'new men' like himself, but without altering the pre-eminence of the governing class.

Cicero's Debts to Captive or Client Greeks

When Rome acquired her empire, just prior to and during Cicero's own lifetime, oratory came to be much in demand and it was taught in Greek first, to Romans.[74] In this way Greek ideas were Romanized and rendered into Latin. Even the formal study of grammar was introduced in Rome by an embassy of Greeks and such men were taken into households like Cicero's. Cicero's own greatness was to adapt the lessons to the Latin language and to Roman political circumstances, in a social milieu in which the best-qualified Latin orators were Roman citizens, not professional orators, but lawyers and landowners with senatorial rights. In addition, a knowledge of Greek literature enabled educated and wealthy men to compete for status with their rivals. Cicero's linguistic and rhetorical achievements were so great that he is justly regarded as one of the moulders of the Latin language and his skills in oratory ensured him fame and a reading public for the next 1,600 years, in fact, beyond. He wrote numerous works on philosophy, rhetoric, the position of the orator, politics, religion and the good life, and he edited and published his trial speeches which served as models of Roman forensic display. His numerous private letters to friends were also edited and published. His letters to his life-long friend Atticus, filled with acute observations of contemporary politics and the revelations of the personal griefs and joys of Cicero, served as a primary influence on some of the most famous confessional works in Western literature, the *Confessions* of St Augustine, the letters of Petrarch and the *Confessions* of Rousseau. Most notably he summarized for his own and subsequent generations the development of Greek philosophy to his own day. When, several centuries later, the Western Roman Empire was gradually to forget its Greek, Cicero's Latin writings served to sum up for future generations of educated Western Europeans all that the Greeks had stood for, especially in the realms of rhetorical theory and practice and theoretical philosophy. His contribution to Greek political ideas was to insist that philosophy was useless if it was not somehow activated by individuals who lived according to philosophical precepts in their private and public political lives. He insisted that the chasm that, in his own times, had been opened between oratory – which he took to be practical statesmanship – and philosophy – the contemplation of the universe and how a man ought to order his life – was a disaster. It had, he believed, been unified in Socrates and in certain Socratics,[75] but Socrates' death had tragically turned Plato away from practical affairs into the realm of pure theory. Hence, the ideal man, the perfect orator as politician, will combine philosophy with oratory, the contemplative with the active life.

In the cultured circles in which Cicero moved, freed men were literary collaborators

---

73   *De re publica* II, 39.
74   Cicero, *De oratore* I.14.
75   Ibid., II.270.

or authors, scholars and historians in their own right. Educated Romans like Scipio Aemilianus, Laelius and others whom Cicero portrays in his *De re publica*, were flattered by their learned slave tutors who allowed their patrons to take part credit for the authorship of their tutors' writings. The deliberate education of an intelligent slave, his intelligence winning him his education,[76] then freedom or manumission and finally the patronage of eminent Romans[77] can be seen in the case of Cicero's own secretary, Tiro, who was his research assistant and later edited an anthology of Cicero's letters and other works. Tiro was manumitted and Cicero provided him, in later life, with modified citizen rights. Freed men contributed to much of the systematic history which Cicero transmitted in his *De re publica* when he speaks of a Rome he never knew, prior to his own times, the Rome that led up to what Cicero believed was the 'golden age' of Scipio Africanus and Scipio Aemilianus Africanus the Younger. Indeed, what passed for the earlier political history of Rome was the creation of later historians who had no means of obtaining an authentic insight into the actual political conditions of the time.[78] This mattered little to Cicero, because history was not, for him, primarily a recording of what had merely happened but was, rather, a narrative of the past's meaning to be judged in the present. It was none other than an exemplary record of universally fine behaviour, imitable in the present. History was oratory and as such was the inspiring teacher of the virtuous life: *historia magistra vitae*.[79] Cicero the orator's attitude to history as exemplary would affect European historical writing, and its rhetorical and political purpose, for nearly two thousand years.[80]

Romans and Greek Philosophy

The position of the ex-slave, freed man in the profession of philosophy was similar to his position in oratory. Athens was still the centre for philosophical studies and Romans went there, as did Cicero, to pursue their educations.[81] What philosophy was being taught at the time? Hellenistic Greek philosophy had developed by taking up and pursuing certain themes found in the writings of Plato and Aristotle, notably, on the possibility of certain knowledge based on sense data, and on the role of virtue in ethical theory: specifically, a doctrine of right conduct. A variety of 'schools' arose to provide systems for the complete understanding of the world's basic structure and man's place in it. As was already noted with regard to training in oratory, rhetorical methods of arguing were taught by the heirs of Plato's Academy and Aristotle's Lyceum, known respectively as Academics and Peripatetics. Aristotle's ethical and political ideas largely survived as mediated through later Peripatetic authors, and in their attempts to accommodate key con-

---

76 Plutarch, *Cato Maj.* 20. 5ff.
77 Suetonius, *Vita Terentiae*.
78 T. P. Wiseman, 'Introduction', in T. P. Wiseman, ed., *Roman Political Life 90 BC–AD 69* (Exeter, 1985), p. 1.
79 In *De inventione* I, xix, 27 Cicero defined narrative as an exposition of events that have occurred or are supposed to have occurred ('Narratio est rerum gestarum aut ut gestarum expositio'). He distinguishes between *fabula*, *historia* and *argumentum* and the form of narrative concerned with persons where both events and the conversation and mental attitudes of persons are plausibly reconstructed.
80 J. Coleman, *Ancient and Medieval Memories: studies in the reconstruction of the past* (Cambridge, 1992); see above, Introduction.
81 Cicero, *Acad.* i, 13; Rawson, *Intellectual Life*.

cepts of their own 'school' they diluted Aristotle's strong conception of the *polis* and its emphasis on political activity as central to his moral ideal.[82]

Stoicism was a complex and diverse philosophical movement which exercised a deep influence over Greece and Rome for more than five hundred years. For Stoics, right conduct in life was derived from a knowledge of the physical world which was knowable. As physicalists with respect to the soul and the body, Stoics believed that 'to exist' is 'to be a body', but all matter is imbued with an intelligent force called 'reason' or 'god'. Man could correctly develop individual goodness and happiness (*eudaimonia*) by reasoning from the primary information he obtained from sense data, so that the wise man is perfectly in harmony with the moral perfection of the pre-ordained scheme of things. Stoics accepted the assumption of most ancient Greek moral philosophy that agents desire their own *eudaimonia* and this is the only intrinsic good. But they disagreed with their predecessors over the relation between virtue and *eudaimonia*. They insisted that moral virtue is both necessary and sufficient for happiness, and virtue is an intrinsic, complete and final good sufficient for *eudaimonia*. Certain other goods which run along a continuum of the 'preferred' to the 'dispreferred' (the 'preferred' being, for instance, health or wealth), they considered to be *indifferent* with respect to an agent's *eudaimonia*. A rational agent prefers good health and wealth (to ill-health or poverty) but they are not of intrinsic value in themselves although they can be of *instrumental* value in moral development. Indifferents, however, do not cause or produce wisdom.[83]

The difference between the Stoic view and that, say, of Aristotle, is that Aristotle did not think virtue to be the sole constituent of *eudaimonia* and he understood virtuous activity to involve the external world. Stoics, however, normally took virtuous activity to consist entirely in the exercise of *ethical dispositions* or *intentions*. An agent's actions, accomplished in the world, are of less concern than the dispositions formed by reason to perform acts in a certain way, whether or not they accomplish what they intend. Stoic philosophical teaching addresses the soul 'from within' so that the mind is vigilant and awake, and 'learns to repossess its own experiences from the fog of habit, convention and forgetfulness'.[84] For Stoics, the morally virtuous agent is guaranteed *eudaimonia*, regardless of health, wealth, status or anything else external to his own power.

Epicureans, on the other hand, argued that the only proper object for man's consideration was his own pleasure, to be obtained by a retired and simple life. The only reason that the virtues should be valued was in so far as they provided pleasure. Their view of society was that it arose out of a natural agreement between men for mutual protection and security but they had no interest in the respective merits of particular types of constitution. Indeed, the active political life was not usually worth the trouble and they tended to despise public office.

---

82   See A. A. Long and D. N. Sedley, *The Hellenistic Philosophers*, vol. 1, *translations of the principal sources with philosophical commentary* (Cambridge, 1987); introduction on 'the Schools' and 'the systems'. On the different 'schools' in Rome and Romans' 'low estimate of philosophy as a preparation for public life' see M. Griffin, 'Philosophy, Politics and Politicians at Rome', in M. Griffin and J. Barnes, eds, *Philosophia Togata I* (Oxford, 1989), pp. 1–37. For an excellent collection of essays on Hellenistic social and political philosophy see Laks and Schofield, *Justice and Generosity*.

83   B. Inwood, *Ethics and Human Action in Early Stoicism* (Oxford, 1985). See especially G. Lesses, 'Virtue and Fortune in Stoic Moral Philosophy', in *Oxford Studies in Ancient Philosophy* 7 (1989), pp. 95–128.

84   Nussbaum, *Therapy*, p. 340.

In contrast, a New Academy scepticism emerged to argue that nothing can be known with certainty to be true. This was taught by Carneades (*c.* 154 BC). The New Academy adhered to the view that absolute truth is unattainable but that probability was a sufficient guide for life: examine the arguments and go with the one that seems the most persuasive. Carneades, when part of a philosophical embassy to Rome, argued on the role of justice in international affairs. On the first day he argued that there is such a thing as natural justice which should be followed; on the second day he said that natural justice does not exist.[85] He told the Romans that their empire was based on self-interest, which for him was wisdom. Justice, he taught, was not natural but relative, and different for each state. Rome's justice was her might. Cicero studied with Philo of Larissa, the head of the New Academy and a refugee in Rome. From him he probably learned the radical scepticism of Carneades.

When Cicero wrote his more philosophical works he was influenced by certain teachings of the New Academy as well as by certain Stoic doctrines. Never wanting to side dogmatically with either, he would later expound Stoic arguments for, and Academic arguments against, the possibility of certain knowledge and the reliability of sense perceptions.[86] He would refute the Epicureans[87] and support, but modify, Stoic moral theory which argued that virtue was not only the ultimate good but the only thing properly to be called good.

For our purposes in coming to terms with Cicero's moral and political works (*On Duties* and the *De re publica*) certain Stoic doctrines will be fundamental; hence, we must keep in mind that Stoics insisted that all those things popularly called good, be they wealth or pleasure, are morally indifferent. Generally, we should seek them out but not as ultimate objectives. Virtue alone is the cause of human happiness, and all virtues are one and the same. A man's virtue or excellence does not depend on his success in obtaining anything in the external world. It depends on a correct mental attitude towards what is morally indifferent. Moral improvement rests on the primarily *intellectual* nature of our *passions*. Emotions are themselves natural, but the passions, which are the morally bad state of our emotions, are false judgements. Our passions can be modified, indeed 'extirpated' by reason.[88] Hence, a wise man accepts misfortune without resentment. When we use the word 'stoic' today this is normally what we mean, reducing it to the 'stiff upper lip'.

Cicero's Stoicism

Cicero had been personally influenced by the unorthodox Stoic philosopher Posidonius with whom he studied at Rhodes, and he had taken a Stoic, Diodotus, into his house. Panaetius, the teacher of Posidonius and another unorthodox Stoic who visited Rome as a guest of Scipio,[89] wrote a work (*On Duties*, sometimes translated as *On proper func-*

---

85   Griffin, 'Philosophy, Politics and Politicians', p. 3.
86   *Academica; Academica posteriora*, his part-surviving historical survey of Greek philosophy.
87   In *De finibus*, which also provides a great deal of information on orthodox and non-orthodox Stoic positions, and in *De re publica* 1.
88   See Nussbaum, *Therapy*, pp. 316–401 on selected Stoics.
89   Cicero, *De oratore* I.45ff., II.155; *Pro Murena* 31.56.

tion/on appropriate actions, c. 140 BC) that especially influenced him, because Panaetius was concerned to give practical advice to the good man who was not perfectly wise, but who could be trained in so far as he had any mark of virtue.[90]

Posidonius had argued that in the golden age, nature gave power to the wise rather than the strongest, and that the irrational part of the soul was to be subjugated by the rational for the good, indeed health, of the inferior. Rome, in consequence, had a civilizing mission with a right to subdue peoples who could not see where their own good lay. The best (not the strongest) must rule the worst. This was a Stoic interpretation of Plato, tailored to the conquering Romans, and Cicero absorbed it.

However, the more orthodox Stoic position, unlike that of the earlier Platonic and Aristotelian political philosophy which focused on the independent small *polis*, was instead a world philosophy which held that all men were brothers, alike in their capacities to reason. They linked this to a belief that all men were tied to an overarching cosmological ordering principle of the universe which all men could perceive, no matter what incidental culture in which they were raised. The Stoic idea of a universal respect for the dignity of humanity in each and every person, regardless of nation, race, class or gender was to become central to the later Western political tradition. Cicero absorbed this too. As we shall see, Cicero's teachings on the *natural law* stem from this Stoic cosmopolitanism but he mixes it with a vision of Rome's civilizing mission, bringing peace to the world through just wars. In different works he would reformulate Stoic teachings to suit the legal and social conventions of Rome.[91]

On Duties (De officiis)

Contemporary students of the history of political thought are usually advised to study Cicero's *De re publica* to obtain a grasp of Roman republican values and practices. But A. A. Long is surely correct in arguing that his *On Duties* is, above all, Cicero's political testament and that this is the work that provided later Europeans with Cicero's Republic.[92] Although not in all things indebted to the Stoics (he frequently thought of himself as a devoted follower of Plato), Cicero none the less argued in *On Duties* as did his Stoic forebears, that all good men feel a natural urge to increase the resources and prosperity of humankind in general.

In his early work *De Inventione* (I, 2), which argues for the supreme importance of eloquent and rational persuasion in all areas of life, Cicero imagines a time when men wandered at large in fields, like animals, doing nothing by the guidance of reason. They relied mainly on physical strength. There was as yet no ordered system of religious

---

90   Briefly, on Panaetius and Posidonius see F. H. Sandbach, *The Stoics*, 2nd edn (London, 1989), pp. 123–39; on Cicero's use of Panaetius in *On Duties* see Long and Sedley, *The Hellenistic Philosophers*, p. 368; A. Erskine, *The Hellenistic Stoa* (Ithaca, NY, 1990), esp. chs 7 and 8; I. G. Kidd, 'Posidonius as Philosopher–Historian', in Griffin and Barnes, *Philosophia Togata I*, pp. 38–50.

91   See the various contributions in J. G. F. Powell, ed., *Cicero the Philosopher* (Oxford, 1995).

92   A. A. Long, 'Cicero's Politics in *De officiis*', in Laks and Schofield, *Justice and Generosity*, pp. 213–40. This is an excellent essay on Cicero's reinterpretation of Roman attitudes to glory so that when justly pursued, glory benefits the community no less than the individual; it also treats Cicero's defence of private property. See also the discussion in Wood, *Cicero's Social and Political Thought*, pp. 70–119 and the interesting analysis of *De officiis* in D. Burchell, 'Civic Personae: MacIntyre, Cicero and moral personality', *History of Political Thought* 19 (1998), pp. 101–19.

worship nor of social duties. None had learned the *advantage* (*utilitas*) of an equitable code of law. Their ignorance led their *unreasoning passion* to be satisfied by a misuse of bodily strength.

> But at this juncture, a man – great and wise – became aware of the power latent in man and the wide field offered by his mind for great achievements, if one could develop this power and improve it by instruction. He assembled men in accord with a plan and despite their initial resistance to his novel introduction to them of every useful and honourable occupation (yet) through reason and eloquence they listened to him with attention and he transformed them from savages into a kind and gentle people.

They were persuaded by eloquent speech of the truth discovered by reason.[93]

In the *De officiis* he says that man's reason enables his natural impulses to be realized in sociability. He says that men are naturally social and seek fellowship not only through common discourse but by the mutual exchange of obligations or duties, such as keeping to one's promises and assigning to each what is his due. It is assumed that social men acknowledge that what is due to one man is not the same as what is due to another, although all men seek for themselves and for others what is due them. In his early *De Inventione* II, liii, 161 he had argued that by nature there is implanted a kind of innate instinct in man which includes religion, duty, gratitude, revenge, reverence and truth. Reverence, a natural instinct, he defines as that feeling by which men of distinguished position are held worthy of respect and honour; in a similar but variant version earlier in *De Inventione* II, xxii, 66, he had said that the innate instinct of reverence is the act by which we show respect to and cherish our superiors in age or wisdom or honour or any high position. The assumption, which Cicero will later clarify in the *De officiis*, is that natural gifts which enable us to be possessed of differentials of talent, when crafted in the context of one's status and circumstances, emerge as differentials in character, and along with the luck of having the ancestors one has or the wealth they have acquired, are all parts of social men's evaluations from the very beginning. Although men share a common nature through their share in reason and their superiority to brute animals, their different traits and talents, realized through a calculated comportment that is affected by status and circumstance, determine their differential *dignitas* and desert.

From a Stoic point of view, these 'inheritances' (status, wealth) are themselves, for the most part, matters either morally indifferent or simply instrumental but of no intrinsic worth. What is most important to a Stoic is the degree to which a man can best use whatever he has when guided by reason in order to be virtuous and self-sufficient, and hence do what is right or appropriate (*honestum*) as a result of a stable ethical disposition.

Cicero, however dependent he is on aspects of Stoicism, actually reverses the direction of their ethics by placing greater weight on these inheritances and circumstances as useful, and they are not for him, as they were for Stoics, morally neutral or simply preferred indifferents.[94] Indeed, wealth for Stoicism as an external commodity has no

---

93   This argument would be put to use in medieval and Renaissance political theories. See *A History of Political Thought* volume 2, chapters 4 and 6.

94   M. Colish, *The Stoic Tradition from Antiquity to the Early Middle Ages* (Leiden, 1985), vol.1, p. 148 argues that 'The elevation of legal and social conventions above nature, the limitation of the moral horizon to members of his own polity, class, and sex, and the exaltation of patriotism as the chief criterion of virtue bespeak Cicero's adherence to the Roman tradition'.

moral value at all, but it can have instrumental value for living in agreement with nature and therefore should be preferred to poverty. But for Cicero's Romanizing Stoicism, it is the useful as practically advantageous which appear as ends in themselves and what is useful (rather than what is right, *honestum*) helps man to withstand the vicissitudes of fortune. As we shall see, Cicero advises that a man take into account his individual situation, his character, talents, status, age, circumstances and personal commitments, inherited or contracted, in order that his display of virtue is itself useful . Cicero will argue that there is, in the end, no real conflict between what is intrinsically right *(honestum)* and what is useful *(utile)*.

Where Panaetius had observed that moral choices involve three considerations: is the act intrinsically right and appropriate *(honestum)*? is it conducive to utility *(utile)*? and can there be a reconciliation between what is right and what is useful?, Cicero notes that Panaetius never answered the last question and he proposes to do so in *On Duties*. He adopts Panaetius' arguments only in so far as he can use them to confirm and illustrate them from Roman experience. Panaetius had thought that the *honestum*, the intrinsically right and therefore honourable, was the only good, and only a small group of wise men could achieve this. Cicero, however, redefines the right and the useful for more ordinary men living in a political community, so that the right is equated with the common good and the useful is equated with individual interest, where neither conflicts with the other. Although he will hold to the Stoic notion that the right *is* to be preferred to the useful, the common good to the private advantage, the reason he gives is *because* men recognize the reasonableness of *social utility,* so that what is right serves as a means to the useful. Where Stoics would not allow any conditions to the good as the desirable or preferable, Cicero ends by making social utility the highest good. Therefore, he departs from Stoicism in redefining what is right as a species of what is useful. Virtue, for Cicero, is useful and expedient.

We shall see that he does not think it usually necessary for private rights to be sacrificed so long as they do not interfere with the rights of others or the public good and so he elevates the norm of expediency to analyse what is useful. Cicero reconciles what is right with what is useful by saying, as no Stoic could have done, that virtue *is* public service to the 'state' through offices and this does not conflict with individual interest, the useful. In contrast, all that a Stoic would say is that a wise man will prefer a career that involves him in public life. The preferred, for a Stoic, is morally indifferent and of no intrinsic value to Stoic *eudaimonia*. This is because the stable disposition that is moral virtue is something in addition and intrinsically good, and not equivalent to preferring appropriate actions. What a preferred indifferent can do is motivate natural impulses of desire and aversion in men so that they perform the appropriate moral action *(officium)*.[95]

In *On Duties* he adapts the views of Panaetius for whom justice is the virtue that arises naturally from innate social instincts. These instincts need reason's guidance, especially in determining differentials in what is due. Justice, arising from innate social instincts,

---

95   Colish, ibid., p. 149 is surely correct when she says 'Cicero's *utilia* are clearly not Stoic *adiaphora*; nor are they evaluated, as are middle Stoic preferables, in the light of their relative conformity to reason or their relative capacity to conduce to the *honestum*. What is perhaps most striking about Cicero's argument in the second book of the *De officiis* is his use of a strategy which he also discusses in his rhetorical works, that of making the good seem attractive by presenting it under the guise of the useful, in order to make it appealing to an audience that can be counted on to respond out of self-interest.'

forbids one man to injure another, take his property, or take what belongs to the community. It actively promotes the bonds of society through benevolence.

In his youthful *De Inventione* (II, lii, 157), in speaking of the rules for deliberative oratory, Cicero had presented the Stoic position that

> there is something which draws us to it by its intrinsic merit, not winning us by any prospect of gain but attracting us by its own worth; to this class belongs virtue, knowledge and truth. But there is also something else that is to be sought not because of its own merit and natural goodness but because of some profit or advantage to be derived from it. Money is in this class. . . . The things in the first class are called honourable [*honestum*] and those in the second, advantageous [*utile*].

He went on to say (II, liii, 160) that

> justice is a habit of mind which gives every man his desert while preserving the common advantage. Its first principles proceed from nature, then certain rules of conduct became customary by reason of their usefulness; later still, both the principles that proceeded from nature and those that had been approved by custom received the support of religion and the fear of the law.

There appears to be a distinction, between natural first principles and those customary practices found useful, which requires resolution.

Cicero argues in like manner in the first of the three books of *On Duties*: every creature in nature has a tendency to preserve itself, to avoid the harmful, and to seek everything necessary for life. Animals share the impulse to unite for reasons of procreation and care of the young. Nature has distinguished between men and beasts by endowing man alone with reason which enables him to foresee consequences and the future direction of his life; by the same force of reason he is united to other men for the fellowship of common speech and life. And above all, what distinguishes man is his investigation of and search for truth. Cicero follows the Stoic principle that links man's possession of reason with the divine and hence man alone has an insight into the regulated workings of the universe. Man, furthermore, is the only animal capable of perceiving order, decency and propriety in words and deeds: he can moderate his instincts. What is right, appropriate and honourable (*honestum*), therefore, emerges from this perception of order and that order should be preserved by being reflected in one's decisions and acts. Impulses must be made obedient to reason. He argues that the honourable is the outline of virtue and everything that is honourable can be said to have its source in one of the four characteristic virtues of which humans are capable: (1) their capacity for the perception of truth, (2) their capacity for preserving human society by giving each his due and observing contracts, (3) their capacity for displaying greatness and strength of mind, (4) their capacity for order and limit in everything said and done.

Cicero focuses on the virtue or human excellence that enables human society to be preserved, and here there is a kind of reasoning by which this may be achieved. Reasoning applied to the preservation of human society is one of the sources of our obligation to do the right, appropriate and honourable thing and it is the most wide-ranging because by this kind of reasoning the fellowship of men with one another and the community is held together. Later, he will elaborate on this kind of reasoning, which turns out to be a quasi-utilitarian process of calculation (*ratiocinatio*) that takes into account the

relative value of ties of fellowship (*societas*) which are dependent not only on circumstances but also on the complex social landscape where the citizen is required to match
different duties with different interpersonal and legal roles (*personae*). Cicero exhorts his
audience (i.e. his wayward son to whom he addressed this work) to become ethical
calculators or accountants of their duties (*officia*) (I, 59).

Justice is a part of this social virtue to preserve human society and its first concern is
that no man should harm another unless he has been provoked by suffering a wrong;
second, the concern of justice is that one should treat common goods as common and
private ones as one's own.[96]

The second concern of justice, the distinction between common and private goods,
has inspired an enormous literature. A. A. Long and others have recently argued that
Stoics had extended the idea of property and property ownership to that of a human
being's relation to himself with important implications for their conception of the autonomy of individual human beings and the appropriate ways in which they should treat
one another. They connected property ownership with being a 'person' or being properly human and with being a member of a human community. The important thing to
notice in this Stoic doctrine, however, is the *egalitarian* implications of every self-owner.
Cicero provides something different, indeed, hierarchical.[97]

In *On Duties* Cicero explains how common goods and private goods came about. His
argument here, along with his discussion of customary law in *De Inventione* II, liv, 162 as
(a) a principle derived in a slight degree from nature and fed and strengthened by usage,
or (b) laws proceeding from nature but strengthened by custom, or (c) *any principle which
lapse of time and public approval have made the habit or usage of the community,* would be read
again and again in Western Europe until the modern era. He says that no property is
private by nature. Rather, it becomes private by long occupation and hence by custom
(men having come into unoccupied territories); or by victory, as when acquired in war;
or by law, settlement, contractual agreement or lot. He makes no distinction between
these modes of private acquisition in terms of the justice or injustice of the initial acquisition.[98] Each of these modes of acquisition is simply a kind of arrangement men have

96 This reflects Roman law divisions between *res publicae* and *res privatae*, where public things are all citizens'
property and *res privatae* are privately owned; A. Watson, *The Roman Private Law around 200 BC* (Edinburgh, 1971).
Colish, *The Stoic Tradition*, vol. 1, p. 146 notes 'in effect, the criteria that govern the duties pertaining to justice are
non-philosophical ones; they are Roman legal and social conventions'; but clearly Cicero sees these social and legal
conventions as underpinned by a more fundamental philosophical Stoic principle of the natural impulse to self-
preservation, and a corollary principle of non-harm to others. Also see P. A. Brunt, 'Cicero's *Officium* in the Civil
War', *Journal of Roman Studies* 76 (1986). For a somewhat different interpretation see J. Annas, 'Cicero on Stoic
Moral Philosophy and Private Property', in Griffin and Barnes, *Philosophia Togata I*, pp.149–73. On pp. 168–9 she
treats justice in *De officiis* I as a single virtue with two parts: justice proper, which she takes to be concerned with
matters of legal obligation and rights, and justice as benevolence, which is concerned with moral duties which we
have towards others as fellow human beings. Cicero presumes that they do not conflict.
97 A. A. Long 'Stoic Philosophers on Persons, Property Ownership and Community', in R. Sorabji, ed., *Aristotle
and After* (London, 1997), pp. 13–31; also see A. A. Long, 'Representation and the Self in Stoicism', in S. Everson,
ed., *Companions to Ancient Thought, 2: Psychology* (Cambridge, 1991), pp. 111–20. A. A. Long, 'Cicero's Politics',
pp. 233–40 notes the tensions in Cicero's arguments to harmonize individual and community interests and sees
Cicero's politics as an 'intriguing precursor' of conservative liberalism. See also Annas, 'Cicero on Stoic Moral
Philosophy', pp. 151–74.
98 Annas, 'Cicero on Stoic Moral Philosophy', p. 170, although I do not take Cicero to be arguing for purely
legal entitlements here but something prior: customary acknowledgement.

either customarily agreed to as useful or, through defeat in war, been forced to accept. Private property is therefore not a principle derived from nature; it emerges, rather, out of the customary usefulness of collective habits. But Cicero seems to be implying that as custom it derives somehow from a prior natural principle of justice (self-preservation) and is fed and strengthened by the utility of usage and custom. He is presenting, in effect, a Stoicized reading of Roman legal views on the right to private property based on ancestral custom or conquest. Romans think them reasonable because they are useful.[99]

Later (*De officiis* I, 51), he will argue that the law of the community, that is civil law, establishes the criteria for distinguishing between what is communal property and what is private.[100] The *rights* to private possessions, then, are the creations of law just as are Roman *libertas* and *civitas*, liberty and citizenship. From the common there has been, historically, and before the institution of the 'state', a simple and *de facto useful* division into mine and thine which *follows from* a *natural appropriation* to serve the natural impulse of self-preservation. The law of nature safeguards the moral (rather than legal) claim to one's own. But, as we shall see, men went on to construct the 'state', the republic, out of and above natural society where mine and thine came to be distinguished from what was common, in order to *preserve and stabilize agreements* (as civic *rights*) to mine and thine by enforceable and equitable law. Consequently, Cicero says, since what becomes each man's own comes from what had in nature been common, each man should hold on to whatever has fallen to him. If anyone else should seek any of it for himself, he will be violating the law of human fellowship (I, 21).

It is important to realize what it is he believes is being violated here: the universal instinct to social fellowship, an instinct that is within all men. If one takes wrongly what is someone else's property, one is not violating the state's laws in the first instance; as we shall see, the state's laws are themselves built positively on the more fundamental principles of natural justice which men already know: never harm another but preserve yourself, and know the difference between, and respect, common and private property. Cicero proposes a harmony between public and private interests by basing it on an ideal according to which the individual and society are equally bound to the protection of each other's rights, where the the common good and private interest are reciprocal, even identical.

This argument extends the Stoic observation that nature provides, in animals and man, 'a programme of "impulsive activity" which is both immediately self-sustaining and also other-related'. The principle of 'appropriation', even at the level of animal behaviour, extends beyond the self to affectionate 'ownership' of offspring.[101] There is, then, common ground in nature between animal and human behaviour in preserving oneself and looking after one's young. Natural appropriation is then extended by custom based on the useful or advantageous to men who live in organized communities, which are themselves a discovery of reason.[102] But for Cicero it seems that custom establishes not only mine and thine but the further advantages of differential property

99   See A. A. Long's argument that Cicero, particularly in *De officiis*, is indebted to (unorthodox) Stoicism's (i.e. Panaetius and his students) position on private property as central to a conception of self and its autonomy. Long, 'Stoic Philosophers on Persons', esp. pp. 18–19. See Wood, *Cicero's Social and Political Thought*, esp. pp. 111–19.
100   Compare *De inventione* II, liv, 162 (c), above.
101   Long and Sedley, *The Hellenistic Philosophers,* vol. 1, p. 352.
102   Compare Cicero, *De finibus* 3, 62–8.

ownership from what was originally a natural, egalitarian appropriation for self-preservation as explained by Stoicism.[103] In his early *De Inventione* Cicero had already argued for a natural instinct of reverence for those of higher social standing and office. And he had included a third kind of customary law which no more than lapse of time and public approval had made habitual.[104] For Stoics, self-preservation will promote justice if it is recognized that concern for other people is a natural development of concern for oneself. But for Cicero even natural appropriation along with the mutual recognition of self-owners with property admit of degrees.

The tensions between prior self-interest and extended social obligation in the Stoic argument have been pointed out over the centuries, often to no avail. Indeed, the question of the origins of and justification for private property would figure as some of the most debated issues in political and legal theory in Western Europe until our own days. In the seventeenth century John Locke would elaborate further on Cicero's position in saying that by occupying a piece of common ground a man mixes his labour with it and it becomes his by right. Cicero, however, does not here make an argument for a labour theory of rights. Instead, private property is customary – from time immemorial – or by conquest. But he will later say (II, 12–14) that without the labour of men's hands the fruits and benefits of civilization would not have been possible. But his point is that men collaborate in their labours for private and social utility, not that they derive rights from solitary pursuits. Indeed, for Cicero the Roman, there are no private, individual *rights* as stable entitlements without the construction of the 'state' because rights are objective legal grants by the republic to its citizens.

Cicero, however, seeks more than simply to assert the civilized right to what is one's own. He seeks to enlist Stoics in his justification of Rome's laws, themselves based, he believes, on a natural instinct for society's preservation. Hence, he insists that all men know that they are not born for themselves alone. No man is an island. Their country and their friends make claims on them and on what is their own. He tells us that the Stoics believe that everything produced on the earth is created for the *use* of humankind for the sake of men so that they may be able to assist one another. To Cicero, this means that private owners must contribute to the common stock of things that benefit everyone together and, by giving and receiving expertise, effort and means, they bind the fellowship of society together. This is a doctrine of private ownership and communal use and benefit. Cicero is modifying the Roman law of private property with an argument that seeks to persuade (but cannot, likewise, be enforced): those with private means should learn how to act on their communal instincts and do the honourable thing. Contribute time, effort and personal wealth to the community. Most men in his own times, he says, are led to a forgetfulness of justice (for which they have a natural instinct) by falling into the bad habits of the times: violent ambition, seeking after empire, personal honours and glory. Cicero the Roman, of course, believes that the pursuit of honour, empire, power and glory are precisely what the most exalted genius and greatest-minded man does seek. But such a virtuous man seeks these not as ends in themselves, but in order to influence and establish bonds with others. One engages in these pursuits *for* fellowship, they have social utility. The pursuit of honour, empire, power and glory must be underwritten by the principles of justice: preserve yourself, do

103   Long and Sedley, *The Hellenistic Philosophers*, vol. 1, pp. 352–3.
104   A. A. Long, 'Stoic Philosophers on Persons', p. 24, admits that Cicero deviated from Stoic egalitarianism.

no harm to another unless your self-preservation is threatened, and serve the common advantage (I, 31). Roman law can clearly prevent citizens from harming one another or at least provide remedies should harm be done, but it cannot induce one to serve the common advantage. For this to occur, a good man must be individually, voluntarily inspired and persuaded by the orator. Cicero insists on the Stoic concern for the rhetorical and literary dimensions of arguments that move and change the individual's soul.[105] It is to this argument that Renaissance civic humanists would turn.[106]

Human Communities and the Origins of the 'State'

Cicero's *On Duties* was meant to be a work on practical ethics, emphasizing the acts of social and political morality because he believed that society is the natural and best condition for human life. But it is clear that Cicero's main interest in *On Duties* is in those individuals who take an active part in public life. He has almost nothing to say about obligations to recognized social inferiors – slaves or clients – although he says justice must be maintained even towards the lowliest. By this he means slaves should be treated as if they were employees: one should require work from them and *grant* them just treatment.[107] He speaks of those who will take up civil and military office and he attempts to 'codify' those cohesive social virtues of a republic which he wished to preserve. All good men are concerned to make life both safer and richer, through their thought and effort, and this concern impels men to the fulfilment of their natural desires. For Stoics, as for Cicero, there is one way of life and one order under a common law, not an organized world state, but rather an order which makes it plain that men everywhere should be ruled by reason which is universal. Universal reason, which men share with the divine, is evident in the common law of nations (*ius gentium*) in the sense that the laws of all civilized people are dictates of common sense or natural reason, shared by all men.

> For there is a fellowship that is extremely widespread, shared by all with all . . . a closer fellowship exists among those of the same nation and one more intimate still among those of the same city. For this reason our ancestors wanted the law of nations [*ius gentium*] and the civil law to be different: everything in the civil law need not be in the law of nations, but everything in the law of nations ought also to be a part of civil law. (III, 69)

This seems to mean, in the case of self-owners with property, that according to universal common sense all men as persons are property owners, living in accord with nature which instinctively impels each to his own self-preservation through the use of and appropriation of what is common. But civil law further distinguishes between greater and lesser 'persons', an equitable rather than egalitarian division of *rights* to property.

Cicero wants to persuade his readers (I, 49ff.) that there are natural principles of human fellowship and community which cannot be altered. These can be seen in the fellowship of the whole human race through the universal bond of reason and speech which reconciles men to one another through teaching, learning, communicating. The

---

105   See Nussbaum, *Therapy of Desire*, p. 330.
106   See *A History of Political Thought* volume 2, chapter 6.
107   They are not legally owed just treatment; see Griffin and Atkins, trans., *On Duties*, p. xxiii.

human fellowship in its most extensive manifestation is revealed in its reasoned discourse. In this most natural kind of universal society we must preserve the communal sharing of all the things that nature brings forth for the common use of humankind, (but) *in such a way that they may be possessed in the manner prescribed by statutes and civil laws*. Once again, Cicero is making a distinction not only between common use and the private possession of goods, but between all men as appropriators and men as legally entitled, unequal possessors under civil law. Instead of taking further the interesting possibility that teaching, learning and communicating are for universal use but, by law, the teaching materials, the acquisition of personal knowledge and the very communication itself – as a speech or text – are all private possessions, he further refines what he means by things common to all men (and hence, commonly to be used) in the following way.

He advises (following Ennius) that if any assistance can be provided, *without detriment to oneself*, it should be given, even to a stranger. What, then, is to be for common use? Fresh water, fire kindled from one's own fire, trustworthy counsel to someone seeking advice. These are useful to the receiver and *cause no trouble to the giver*. Our obligation to humankind is restricted by a principle that we do no harm to our own interests. The *honestum* is reconciled with the *utile*. Cicero believes this is balanced by the restriction on the pursuit of our own interests: that we do not damage the interests of others. Were he thinking of a world in which all men were considered equal as to what they were owed, then this could well be made to look like the principle of 'do unto others as you would be done by'. Cicero knew that both Plato and the Stoics taught that there is no such thing as private property or social inequalities of rank in the natural order. But he prefers the Roman model of 'natural' justice and does not think everyone is owed the same. One man's due is not the same as another's. He explains this (I, 107–20) by suggesting, following Panaetius, that we consider humankind in terms of their four *personae* or roles, and their relation to necessity, chance, circumstance and individual will. Machiavelli would later rework this in his teachings on princely *virtù* and for this reason it is useful to present Cicero's position at some length.[108]

The Four *Personae*

Cicero argues that nature has dressed us, as it were, for two roles, one being common to all men and arising from the fact that we all have a share in reason and in the superiority by which men surpass brute creatures. This, he says, is the source of all rectitude and propriety and the basis of the (subsequent) rational discovery of our proper functions or duty. For humans to assume this role it is required that they exercise their share in the universal stock of reason, in the way that the Stoic wise man (*sapiens*) was required to pass beyond the limits of individuality in order to recognize himself as part of a cosmos penetrated by reason.[109]

But the second *persona* or role for which nature has 'dressed' us is specifically assigned to individuals and their personal traits and talents. Cicero is following the Stoic position

108   See Machiavelli in *A History of Political Thought* volume 2, chapter 6.
109   See Long and Sedley, *The Hellenistic Philosophers*, vol. 1, p. 424; C. Gill, 'Personhood and Personality: the four-personae theory in Cicero, *De officiis* I', *Oxford Studies in Ancient Philosophy* 6 (1988), pp. 169–99; Wood, *Cicero's Social and Political Thought*, pp. 84–9; P. Hadot, 'Spiritual Exercises', in P. Hadot, *Philosophy as a Way of Life* (Oxford, 1995).

according to which nature endows animals including man with certain dispositions which enable them to do things for themselves. All purposeful action, from self-preservation to self-knowledge depends on each agent having a self-perception in relation to the world. But we are not born with this actualized self-perception; we must acquire it. Cicero goes further and makes this actualized self-perception dependent on a capacity for calculating what is suitable for each of us to appear to be in terms of our status and circumstances. He argues that we see that men differ in bodily strength and there are even greater mental divergencies.[110] Some men are witty, others exceptionally serious; some are jolly, others ambitious and earnest; some are cunning and crafty and find it easy to conceal or to keep silent, to dissemble, set traps and anticipate an enemy's plans; others are straightforward and open and think that nothing should be done through secrecy and trickery, cultivating the truth and a hostility to deceit. Others again would endure anything, devote themselves to anyone, provided they acquire what they desire. All of these are observed performances. Hence, there are clearly countless dissimilarities of 'nature' and conduct, and Cicero insists that each person should hold on to what is his, so long as it is not vicious, but peculiar to himself.

> For we must act in such a way that we attempt nothing contrary to universal nature in general; but while conserving that, let us follow our own 'nature' [the second of the two initial *personae*] so that *even if other pursuits may be weightier and better, we should measure our own by the rule of our own* 'nature'. (I, 110)

It is appropriate neither to fight against nature nor to pursue what you cannot attain. A person cannot preserve what is consistently honourable in his own whole life and in his individual actions if he copies someone else's 'nature' and thereby ignores his own. It is the huge differences between those individual 'natures' that account for men's lives being so different. 'Everyone ought to weigh the characteristics that are his own, *and to regulate them*, not wanting to see how someone else's might become him; for what is most seemly for a man is the thing that is most his own' (I, 113). How do ordinary men, prepared by nature to assume this second role, come to know what it is to be?

Some have interpreted this reference to each man's 'nature' as an invocation of some ineffable uniqueness which our modern theories of personality insist on.[111] Others, however, understand it as not unlike the notion of 'character' familiar from the Greek conception of *ēthos*,[112] derived initially from the stage and the set-piece speeches attributed to heroic characters based on the Homeric epic.[113] If Cicero is referring to something like Greek *ēthos*, as seems likely from his numerous references to the stage and to characters like Ulysses and Ajax, then this 'nature' or second *persona* is not possessed as an inward quality, an ineffable uniqueness, but rather it is a set of 'presentations of self' through stage-like 'roles'. Cicero's second *persona* is one's character.

Cicero, we recall, is addressing only those men who take part in public life. Each is obliged to acquire a knowledge of his own talents and then exert himself in those things

---

110   Long and Sedley, *The Hellenistic Philosophers*, vol. 1, p. 424.
111   See the discussion in Gill, 'Personhood', pp. 170–2.
112   See above, chapter 1.
113   C. Gill, 'The Character–Personality Distinction', in C. Pelling, ed., *Characterization and Individuality in Greek Literature* (Oxford, 1990) and C. Gill, *Personality in Greek Epic, Tragedy and Philosophy* (Oxford, 1996), esp. chs 1 and 2; D. Burchell, '*Civic Personae*', pp. 101–18.

to which he is most suited. 'Nor ought we so much to strive to acquire good qualities that have not been granted to us [!] as to avoid faults' (I, 114). The second *persona* for which nature has dressed us must be deliberately fashioned out of one's natural impulses and capacities, through a process of weighing one's own characteristics and *regulating* them so that a match is found between one's talents and the most fitting presentation of self, given one's status and in the circumstances.

To the above two roles (*personae*) Cicero adds a third that distinguishes the entirely accidental determinants of one's public identity: this is imposed by some chance or circumstance. He finishes with a fourth *persona*, 'which we assume for ourselves by our own decision'. 'Kingdoms, military powers, nobility, political honours, wealth and influence, as well as the opposite of these, are in the gift of chance and governed by circumstances. But in addition, in assuming a role that we want ourselves is something that proceeds from our own will.' The latter is demonstrated by some taking up (the roles of) philosophy, others civil law, others oratory and, he says, people differ as to which virtues they prefer to excel in (115). What does he take to be the relation between chance circumstances and the scope of individual choice? While chance or circumstance may grant that an individual be born into a family where fathers or ancestors won glory by outstanding performance – and their heirs generally tend to devote themselves (out of habit and imitation) to excelling in the same way themselves – Cicero observes that it sometimes turns out that some people decline to imitate their ancestors and pursue some course of their own. Cicero, the new man, makes a case for himself when he concludes that 'those who exert themselves the most in this way are, on the whole, men born of unknown ancestors who aim for great things themselves' (116). Such men adopt shifting *personae* which are tied to their social positions, relationships and circumstances as well as to the often incompatible responsibilities associated with their different occupations and statuses. They do this in order to fulfil their functions (*officia*).

He acknowledges that to decide what kind of life one wants and what one wishes to be is the most difficult of things. How do we discover what is appropriate to each of us? Cicero appears to adopt the Stoic understanding of our natural *orientation* to our own good or self-perception (*oikeosis*), which becomes more accurate only as we mature, that is, as we try to fashion our self-presentations (*personae*) given our status and circumstances. Such deliberations on the kind of life we want to lead unfortunately but usually occur as adulthood is approaching, that is, at a time when a person's counsel is weakest, and he decides on and then engages in a fixed manner and course of life before he is able to judge what is best. For Cicero, it is only when each of us learns what our natures call for, can we enable our motivations to evolve in the direction proper to us. Only the mature adult can grasp moral order *and* his role(s) in it.[114]

Cicero observes that most men, instead of deciding who and what they wish to be and what kind of life is appropriate, 'tend to imitate those whom each of us thinks he should and we are drawn to their pursuits and practices. We are also generally imbued with our parents' advice and led towards their customs and manners'. Others, he says, are swayed by the judgement of the masses and long especially for the things that seem most glittering to the majority. Cicero then turns to a rarer individual, cut loose from social habit, who does decide on the basis of what is intrinsically good. He is the one who follows 'the right path of life', whether by good fortune or by the goodness of his

114 Compare Cicero, *De finibus* 3.

own nature or through parental guidance (118). He is exemplary, produced by good fortune and outstanding personal capacity. For him alone, status and circumstance are 'indifferent' to his *eudaimonia*.[115]

Cicero insists that it is an extremely rare type of person who is endowed with outstanding intellectual ability or a splendidly learned education or both, and who has also had time to deliberate over which course of life he wants, above all, to follow. He is like Hercules, of whom the story is told that he went out to a lonely place, deliberated on the path of life to take, pondering between pleasure and virtue. But Hercules had 'sprung from the seed of Jupiter', and it is not the same for us (118). Cicero emphasizes that for ordinary men, in such deliberation all counsel ought to be referred to the individual's own 'nature' (second *persona*) and hence the individual must have a knowledge of his inclinations and talents, and then decide on the best roles to play, regulating those inclinations and talents accordingly. He must develop a calculated self-perception in the circumstances that goes beyond the instinctive behaviour that is peculiar to humans. This enables his motivations to evolve in the right directions so that he exerts himself in those things to which he is most suited. Cicero reminds the reader that just as actors do not choose the best plays but rather those that are most suited to themselves, so too a wise man observes this in his life (114).

> For just as in each specific thing that we do, we seek what is appropriate *according to what and how each of us has been born,* we must exercise much more care when establishing our whole way of life so that we can be constant to ourselves for the whole length of our life, not wavering in any of our desires. (119)[116]

What is 'seemly' for each person, then, depends on the roles appropriate to his age, status, circumstances and the approval of those with whom he lives (122–6). In fact, one's duties, what is appropriate for one to perform, depend on whether one is a magistrate, a private individual, a citizen or a foreigner. It is significant that Cicero advises that a private person ought to live on fair and equal terms with other citizens, and to want public affairs to be peaceful and honourable. He is to be neither submissive nor give himself airs (124). Whereas the magistrate assumes the *persona* of the city and imposes his views in accord with this role, the private person is a more passive agent, aware that the preservation of the laws, the administration of justice and the maintenance of the city's 'seemliness' are entrusted to others (124).

Cicero concludes explicitly that 'nature' carries the greatest weight in such calculated reasoning about which role(s) to assume, and after that fortune (120). A successful, ordinary man (unlike the Stoic wise man) is not an inwardly unified moral personality:

115   Compare Aristotle's *Nicomachean Ethics* I and his views on young men, for whom the science of ethics/politics is unsuitable because they have as yet had insufficient experience of life. It is notable that where Cicero leaves the quest for self and its roles to the individual alone, depending on his status and circumstance, Aristotle enlists the legislator as moral educator of a society's youth, going well beyond the happy or otherwise chance of parental supervision of character development. For an interesting but different perspective on Cicero's individualism see R. D. Cumming, *Human Nature and History: a study of the development of liberal political thought* (Chicago, 1969).

116   Some have seen this as directly parallel with Aristotle's seeking the mean relative to us in the *Nicomachean Ethics*; but the 'us' for Aristotle is the character that has developed through the deliberated practices of a stable disposition, preferably guided by best practitioners in the first instance, and is not a role that is appropriate as a consequence of 'what and how each of us has been born'.

he plays roles which enable him to appear virtuous in his behaviour, having regulated those natural impulses that are peculiar to him by performing his appropriate duties, given his position and circumstances.

The focus of much of his argument on the relative weight of the four roles or *personae* is, then, on the second personal character or assumed role, *for* which nature has 'dressed us', and this differentiates one man from another. Nature does not determine our roles; we craft them to suit our place in society and the circumstances. Cicero believes that a man ought to adopt a plan of life entirely in accordance with his 'nature' or character (second *persona*)- if it is not vicious - and he ought to maintain a constancy, unless he comes to realize that he has made a mistake in choosing his type of life. Then, Cicero advises that he ought to change his behaviour and plans. When circumstances are favourable to such a change, then he says it shall be effected more easily; otherwise the change is to be made gradually (120).

We can compare this view with Aristotle's, who believed it to be extremely difficult – although not impossible – to change one's habituated character, men not being born with a character but having to acquire it through deliberate choice which follows from a settled disposition, itself the result of repeated good practices. For Aristotle, it is easier to change the *circumstances* and this is the legislator's task. Aristotle's legislators aim to make their citizens good by habituation and this is the reason they concern themselves with child education when character formation takes place through habituation to good practices.[117] Not so for Cicero: Roman legislators neither change circumstances nor involve themselves in child education; instead, they adapt themselves to shifting circumstances. Cicero is clearly more optimistic, especially if the chance circumstances are propitious, about changing one's type of life. This is because calculated role-playing in changing circumstances, as well as according to status requirements, differentiates men and is recognized in social evaluations. Whereas for Aristotle the moral agent has a stable disposition, recognized in a range of practices throughout his life, for Cicero, ordinary moral agents are unstable 'personalities', successful only if they can adopt roles that regulate their talents according to their status and the circumstances. The man who has developed his second *persona* to suit his status and the times is the man who knows how to perform his duties.

Cicero appears to make a much stronger statement about the role of calculative reasoning to serve utility than the usual Stoic understanding of normative innate preconceptions which most Stoics thought had no definite content at birth but were assumed to develop naturally in the course of early human experience.[118] Cicero does not seem willing to adopt the view of some Stoics (and Aristotle) that it is overwhelmingly external circumstances which prevent the good from manifesting itself to most men who are imperfect. Instead, his argument is that precisely because there are status differentials and circumstances change, a good role-player is one whose ethical requirements change, depending on his social function, as he slips in and out of roles.[119]

---

117   See above, chapter 4.
118   Long and Sedley, *The Hellenistic Philosophers*, p. 375.
119   Wood, *Cicero's Social and Political Thought*, pp. 92–4 argues that Cicero believes 'we are born with equal rational potential and thus are equally capable of being moral but we do not equally realize our rational and moral natures. Some acquire bad habits and false beliefs preventing them from fully actualizing their rational and moral capabilities. ... Because human beings are appetitive as well as rational, all are subject to desire, to the pleasure that accounts for our evil tendencies ... [and] this depravity ... is controlled in some men and not in others, owing to differences in circumstances ... [but] Cicero is never clear as to whether the superior in virtue and wisdom are

From this it is clear that natural justice, which takes account of what each is owed, cannot conclude in egalitarianism: that one man's due is the same as another's. The universal obligation to humankind must, for Cicero, be balanced by an awareness of one's own character's specific deserts and due so that in pursuit of the common advantage a good man does not jeopardize his own interests, given his status and circumstances. Specifically, he acknowledges that the means of any one individual are limited, and the numbers of the indigent are boundless. Consequently, our distributive generosity is bounded not only by our interest in retaining possession of what is ours but in order that we may be generous to those close to us and enable them to use it. Our commitment to others, as a foundation of justice, seems as it was for the Stoics, to be grounded first in our instinctual love for our self and our own (e.g. offspring) and then is generalized to all fellow humans, but it is clearly weakened by the extension.

For Cicero, those close to us constitute a more bounded fellowship than the previous universal, unbounded kind. They are men of one's own race, tribe, language; even closer is that society of men inhabiting the same city as citizens, sharing in the forum, the laws and legal rights, law courts and political elections. Fellowship still closer is that between relations and family. Indeed, he tells us that from the propagation and increase of kinship relations, through marriage, and the sharing of ancestral memorials and religious rites, political communities have their origin.[120] And of all the fellowships, none is more important and none stronger than when good men of similar conduct are bound by familiarity. These good men of similar conduct are the primary beneficiaries of our private generosity and from whom we expect to be, similarly, in receipt of theirs. These are the natural social instincts of men playing themselves out in social communities of differentiated rank. Such social instincts must, however, be guided by reason. Cicero therefore goes further and says that upon rational reflection, of all fellowship none is more serious than that between the individual and the republic. No good man would hesitate to face death on her behalf if this would be of service to the republic. In sum, reason's guidance of natural social instincts to fellowship demonstrates that those to whom we, as individuals, are most obliged are our country and our parents. It remains unclear, however, whether primary self-interest can ever be overridden by an equal regard for others and Cicero appears to be arguing in the end for the ego seeking its own utility in a law-governed community.

Cicero is speaking here of intense affective and reasoned bonds between a citizen and the institutional structure of his 'state', an allegiance to decisions of the Senate over and above the virtuous individuals of similar conduct who fill the republic's offices. When the 'state's' good is at issue, he insists that services to individuals *are* to be

---

"naturally superior".' Wood rightly argues for the conflicts here in Cicero's social outlook. But he ignores the explicit distinction Cicero draws between everyone being capable of a kind of virtue relative to himself and his circumstances, and those rare men who are, by natural gift, capable of true reasoning and therefore capable through their own unique natures of overriding circumstance. This is not simply a matter of individual will and good education but, in addition, of some natural and unique gift that enables the rare person to benefit regularly from propitious circumstances because all circumstances are, for him, propitious. He is a Hercules and not one of us. Machiavelli will turn this argument to favour his prince with princely *virtù*: see *A History of Political Thought* volume 2, chapter 6.

120   1.53–4; compare this with Aristotle's different understanding of the relation between the household and the political.

considered but in such a way that the matter benefits, *or at least does not harm*, the republic (II, 72). This 'state', however, is not for Cicero some transcendent entity over and above its citizens and especially not over and above the citizens who truly comprise it. This is why he says that any man who administers public affairs must first of all see that everyone holds on to what is his and that private men are never deprived of their goods by public acts (II, 73). Self-regarding intention must always be prior to, and the origin of, other-regarding intentions. Anyone, like the tribune who in proposing an agrarian law claimed that there were not two thousand men in the citizenship who possessed anything, deserve, according to Cicero, to lose their civic rights, advocating as they were an equalization of property. Cicero rhetorically asks: what greater plague could there be than that? The reason this is a plague on the republic is that political communities and citizenship were, he says, constituted especially so that men could hold on to what was theirs. Redistribute private possessions and the 'state' and its reason for existing disappear. He says that it may be true that nature first guided men together in groups, but it was in the hope of safeguarding their possessions that they sought protection in cities.[121]

Regulated political societies are not simply the result of men recognizing the utility of a collective enterprise to secure natural necessities to survive. They emerge out of man's social instinct to fellowship, from their desire not to live alone even if they require no help in securing the necessities of life. Men recognize the social utility of law-regulated political societies because they are social beings seeking fellowship. They are rational consensus-seekers living among their fellows who are differentially 'owed' their respective due. They are self-aware agreement-makers, and they seek to formalize customary agreements with a regulatory law that preserves and stabilizes customary agreements about mine and thine. What is right and what is useful, the common good and private interest come together in the 'state' where they cannot conflict because men are part of a larger social and moral whole and they recognize that acts based solely on *radical* individualism are neither useful (serving self-interest) nor right (conducive to social utility and the common good). Hence, Cicero argues that a redistribution of private possessions by the 'state' is precisely the opposite of the reason for the 'state' having come into existence. Those who govern the 'state' should, of course, plan how to provide an abundance of necessities and Cicero says he need not discuss how these are to be acquired, 'for that is obvious enough': tax the empire.[122]

Cicero, the orator, stirs the emotions especially of equestrian and optimate possessors when he says those who wish to present themselves as *populares* and attempt agrarian legislation so that landholders are driven from their dwelling, or want to excuse debtors for the money they owe, are undermining the very foundations of the political community. Concord cannot exist when money is taken from some and bestowed on others; equity utterly vanishes if men cannot keep what is theirs. It is the proper function of citizenship and a city to secure for everyone a free and untroubled guardianship of his possessions (II, 78). How, asks Cicero, can it be fair that when a piece of land has been

---

121   This, I would think, is Cicero's accommodation of Panaetius' belief that states came together not out of nature but out of reason.

122   II, 85: 'by whatever means they can, [those who are administering and protecting the republic] whether in war or at home, [will] increase the republic in power, in land and in revenues. Such are the deeds of men who are great.'

owned for many years, or even generations, a man who has none should take possession of it while he that had it should lose it? What is the point of cancelling debts and wiping slates clean unless it is so that you can take my money in order to buy a farm which you will have, while I no longer have my money (II, 84)?

Although no man is perfectly wise, Cicero shares with the Stoics a recognition that if life is not to be a random and disordered thing, there must be fundamental rules or laws (over and above the positive laws of a particular society) and from these a man knows that certain actions must be recognized as those to be done. Among the things that ought to be done are acts of benevolence extended, in principle, to all humans. The Stoic identity between the honourable and the beneficial is equated with 'the rule' by which a good man lives. Human rationality enables man to see as natural the promotion of the interests of his fellow men. But men's interests are not the same. Among the things that are held universally honourable as one's obligations are efforts towards preserving fellowship among men, assigning to each what is his own, and faithfulness to agreements one has made (I, 15). Cicero adapts this Stoic notion of benevolence to the requirements of Rome's society of orders, so that benevolence has to fit the recipient's status and merits and the benefactor's means. In administering the republic a governor, similarly, must seek to preserve property differentials which underpin the society of orders.

Cicero further extended the Stoic understanding of history as demonstrating how all good men in all cultures are guided to honour and fame, *dignitas* and *gloria* through engaging in political and virtuous activities which build on the natural instinct in men towards friendship (*amicitia*) for all humankind. This is the Stoic gloss on the patron–client relations of Romans. On this view, all men accept the naturalness of the acquisition of private property, and come to institute the 'state' in order to entitle men to their possessions and preserve their right to what they have already acquired. Out of such universal principles was to emerge the justification of Roman law as universally applicable to Rome's body of citizens, made up of the free born and those of freed status from a wide variety of captive cultures. This is but one example of Cicero's attempt to interpret and apply Greek thought for the practical Romans.

Rome's Freed Men and Slaves

Passing from the teachers of oratory, grammar, history and philosophy to other professions in Roman society, the overwhelming effect of foreigners, most notably Greeks, is again evident. Roman medicine, for instance, relied on Greek science and nearly all medical practitioners were Greeks. As slaves or as freed-men doctors, employed in the personal service either of their owners or in public practice, doctors were to be found as part of the household staff of any Roman of standing. So too were architects, a very large proportion of whom were foreign recruits and slaves. The household management of a wealthy Roman was entrusted to a servant who was often a manumitted slave. This indicates that the sons of freed men were almost wholly integrated into Roman society, a fact that highlights what has often been regarded as the near genius capacity of Romans for integrating men of differing race and culture into *Romanitas*. Romans seemed to have been able to accept diversity, up to a point, and to harmonize it through the law. What served as a model for future European cultures, theoretically and sometimes practically, was Roman law's sensitivity to the position of the legally naturalized foreigner.[123]

But while freed men were not to be deprived of the basic rights of citizenship, these rights were, in subtle ways, limited.[124] Although the recruitment of freed men into the citizenry was advantageous to the 'state' in providing it with recurrent influxes of soldiers, it was also recognized as having a radical effect on the culture. But generally, freed men and foreigners Romanized themselves, emulating the upper classes who were often their patrons. And no educated Roman would have taken seriously as worthy of investigation, as Aristotle did, the Greek cultural belief that *natural* slaves existed, even if Aristotle was not arguing that natural slaves, in appreciable numbers, justified the *de facto* Greek slave-based economy.[125] Romans shared the Greek notion that slaves were chattels, but to educated Romans the concept of *natural* slavery was incoherent; hence, they manumitted their slaves in vast numbers. The Stoic doctrine appears to have been influential in that for Stoics the real slave is no legal or biological category but, rather, refers to a man who is a slave to his own passions. Some Stoics, however, allowed for different kinds of slavery including slavery in the conventional sense.[126] And in Rome slavery *was* a legal category.

When Romans used the word *persona*, meaning not what a human being is but rather a role or status a human being has or maintains or undertakes or bears, they were signifying a status or role some human being has as a legal right, for instance, freedom and citizenship. Notoriously slaves, according to Roman law, were distinguished from free citizens by their lack of *persona* in this sense: slaves were 'things' (*res*), items of property and not legal persons with rights to property ownership.[127] Furthermore, Stoics like Posidonius had argued that the best should rule the worst who were inferior, clearly not rationally in control of their passions, and educated Romans did not doubt their own civilizing mission to bring peace to the world, defending empire against rivals. Cicero himself strenuously tried to show that Rome's wars through which she acquired empire were undertaken as just wars to establish peace.[128] His extraordinary justification for the destruction of Carthage and Corinth by 'our forefathers' (in 146 BC by Scipio Aemilianus) – although he says that he wished they had not destroyed Corinth – is that they had some specific purpose in doing so, in particular in view of its *advantageous* (*utile*) situation, to prevent the location itself from being some day an incitement to war (!) (*On Duties*, I, 35).

Educated Romans do not appear to have argued that slavery devalues a man's character or worth. Slavery for them was utilitarian and inevitable, a consequence of imperial military conquest which, in itself, was a good. But these educated views must not obscure the fact that the hardship and brutality they actually visited on slaves was notorious and slave revolts were frequent. Slavery in Roman law was a legal institution where the slave was subjected to the mastery (*dominium*) of another person. Slaves were almost entirely without rights and could not be entitled to possess or do anything, nor to contract

123 See *A History of Political Thought* volume 2, chapter 1.
124 S. Treggiari, *Roman Freedmen during the Late Republic* (Oxford, 1969), pp. 237–45.
125 See above, chapter 4.
126 Long and Sedley, *The Hellenistic Philosophers*, p. 436.
127 Long, 'Stoic Philosophers on Persons', p. 13.
128 *On Duties* I, 35–6, 38; see below, chapter 6 on St Augustine's response to this argument in his *City of God*.

liabilities.[129] Roman law allowed the slave-owner to punish, sell or even kill his own slave with impunity. The slave was defined by law as one who did not have the legal capacity to possess rights of his own. To possess one's own rights meant one was not subjected to someone else's *dominium*. The slave did not, therefore, have *libertas*.

However concerned about the effects on Roman society of the indiscriminate admission of ex-slaves to citizenship, the Roman 'state' did little other than to encourage masters to pause before manumitting.[130] In a society which required a period of probation in Roman households and where most slaves who won freedom were of Hellenistic culture anyway, educated Romans seem to have suffered far less from worries about race difference than about internal divisions of status. Rome had been a society of distinct orders or rank and by the late republic what was viewed as the ancient and traditional harmony between the orders had become unstuck.

The Destruction of the Concord between the Orders

During Cicero's own lifetime there would be an explosive rise to power of the moneyed classes who were not part of the senatorial elite. Freed men with highly placed patrons or with their own wealth would acquire important roles in commerce and trade, more so than did free-born Romans. Freed men, dependent on the growth of the republic's empire, became more common and more important to Roman society in general, as artisans, business agents, in the civil service. But although Cicero was aware of a breaking down of social barriers through wealth alone and he insisted on a return to a 'golden age' of the republic, his real fear was of maverick nobles (like P. Clodius) against whose radical individualism he sought to elaborate a political theory which focused on constitutional cohesion. It was to be maintained by an upper guardian elite of wealthy property owners. This group alone, wealthy *and* virtuous, with rights and duties to govern, would have the appropriate sense to see that the survival of concord between the orders meant, not least, their own survival so that it was in their interest as well as their duty to take an active role in politics. They would maintain the law and thereby justice, harmony, security and a status quo that was, at the end of Cicero's own lifetime, no longer possible.

Cicero insisted that these men exemplified true humanity (*humanitas*), by claiming justice for all members of society, best achieved by consensus government for the good of the whole. He was trying to 'remember' the principles which he imagined had sustained Roman social life prior to the breakdown of the so-called 'golden age', exemplified in the Roman quality called *consilium*, that is, common sense or good sense, a capacity for compromise and self-restraint. But increasing luxury and the disruptions of impatient reformism and selfish reaction emerged from the increased affluence of only a certain, small proportion of the population. In Cicero's own times the gulf between the rich and poor had so widened that the plot of late republican political history focused on a recurrent dilemma: inefficient freedom with local riots and disruptions of stable, elitist senatorial politics by upstarts wanting agrarian reform, on the one hand; and efficient, peaceful

---

129 *Institutes* I, 3, 2; *Digest* I, 5, 4, 1.
130 Treggiari, *Roman Freedmen*, p. 238.

dictatorship on the other. This dilemma would be replayed in a new key in the period of the late medieval and early Renaissance city-states of Italy.[131]

Cicero's Career During the Last Days of the Republic

Freed-men individualists and equestrian entrepreneurs were only reflecting what had come to pass by the 80s BC in the scramble for careers of many ambitious men on their way to the office of consul.[132] The ongoing debate between *optimates* and *populares* over the nature of republican government (was it the preserve of the elite deliberating in the Senate, or the business of magistrates, and especially the tribunes dealing directly with the plebeian assembly?) was fuelled by bitter personal rivalries and civil war. Sulla, an *optimate*, had become dictator and consul after his *coup d'état* following the Social and Civil War. On his previous military campaigns in the east he had brought to Rome Aristotle's library; Cicero would make use of some of Aristotle's public works on rhetoric and cite from the set speeches of Aristotle's more 'Platonic' earlier period. He appears never to have known or used directly Andronicus of Rhodes' edition of Aristotle's *Politics*, although Barnes has recently argued that it is likely that he had some version of the *Ethics* and certainly was in touch with book collectors who had access to a library of Peripatetic works.[133] Sulla and his supporters perceived their common interests to be best realized through ensuring the primacy of the Senate and he added new members, many from the equestrians, to increase its numbers and ensure its political sympathies. The politics of the next generations would be in the hands of those who could mobilize the support of these new senators.[134]

He also made the Senate an indirectly elected body for the first time in its history. At the same time, he was ruthless with the tribunate, most notably legislating that those who held the tribunate would thereafter be ineligible for any further public office. In effect, no ambitious noble would ever seek to preside over the plebeian assembly again. Furthermore, he reformed the judicial system, removing the administration of justice from the popular assemblies and extending the system of permanent courts whose jury members were to be exclusively senatorial. The young Cicero undertook the first case to be tried in the newly reconstituted criminal courts to defend the wealthy landowner Sextus Roscius against one of Sulla's freed men whom Sulla appears not to have protected, and the jury acquitted Roscius.[135] Only years later did Cicero make it clear how Sulla had been destroying the republic. Sulla's constitutional reforms would be largely undone during the next ten years amid plots and counterplots at home and military campaigns abroad. But the Senate had been opened to a wider social permeability simply through the increase in numbers and Cicero would argue in his prosecution of the

---

131   See *A History of Political Thought* volume 2, chapter 6.
132   T. P. Wiseman, *New Men in the Roman Senate 139 BC–AD 14* (Oxford, 1971).
133   In Barnes and Griffin, *Philosophia Togata, II*, pp. 1–69; Laks and Schofield, *Justice and Generosity*, p. 2 believe that it is unlikely that Cicero actually read Aristotle's *Politics* itself but instead received some ideas mediated by Peripatetic authors (Theophrastus et al.). Rawson, *Intellectual Life*, p. 290 had noted that Cicero attributed a *Politics* to Theophrastus and an *Ethics* to Nicomachus; also W. W. Fortenbaugh and P. Steinmetz, eds, *Cicero's Knowledge of the Peripatos* (New Brunswick, NJ, 1989).
134   Crawford, *The Roman Republic*, pp. 139–54.
135   *Pro Roscio Amerino.*

extortionate governor of Sicily, Verres (70 BC), how it was more important for the
Roman republic that more 'new men' of honesty and merit get on in politics than those
who merely came from families with influence. Furthermore, Cicero's later criticism of
Sulla could not allow him to support the overthrow of Sulla's constitutional settlement.
He maintained his belief that the integrity of government and support for law and order
were the prerequisites of stable government.

The joint consulship of Pompey and Crassus (70 BC) followed by Pompey's being
given the command of the army against Mediterranean pirates, and successfully contain-
ing them, made him widely popular and the ambitious saw him as the route to their own
success. Pompey was further given commands in the east which he settled successfully.
Cicero made a speech (*Pro lege Manilia*) expressing the general belief that Pompey was
the only guarantor of Rome's prosperity and stability. Cicero became a member of the
network of his supporters: he was attempting to make way for the return of Pompey
from the east. Cicero saw this immensely powerful warrior–statesman as an ally of the
Senate and he appears to have imagined him as something of an ideal leading citizen, the
rector or *moderator* of the republic, even if he could not fully sympathize with Pompey's
personal ambitions. As we shall see, the *De re publica* culminates in the republic being led
by such a man of proven, practical virtue. If Pompey suited Cicero's political vision,
historically, this was a remarkably inaccurate view of Pompey's own cynicism, his ruth-
lessness and utter lack of idealism. Although it is often observed that Cicero's career as a
political thinker is largely detached from his career as a politician, there is a surprising
degree of philosophical principle, idealistic naivety and oratorical excess that links the
two together. Political theorizing, based as he insisted it must be on the experience of an
active political life, proved retrospectively in his own case to be an exercise in extraordinary idealism. For a man who had fought so hard to rise in Roman politics and to
survive there, Cicero read the signals wrongly numerous times, and ultimately paid a
terrible cost.

By the time Cicero was a candidate in the 64 BC election for the consulship of 63 BC,
the complex corruption of Roman politics was beyond repair, but Cicero seemed to
think otherwise. He campaigned on a platform of unity and harmony between senators
and equestrians with the slogan *concordia ordinum,* a concord of the orders.[136] Some have
argued that Cicero wanted the support of Pompey, but if this could not be achieved he
wanted the consulship more. His rival for the consulship, the aristocrat Catiline with
links to Pompey's patronage, had in a previous election been disqualified by a charge of
malpractice during his time as governor in Africa. In a letter of 65 BC to his friend
Atticus, Cicero says that he was hoping to defend Catiline in his trial and that the public
prosecutor was prepared to collude with the defence. Cicero seems to have had in mind
avoiding a rivalry with Catiline in the election to consul. But Catiline appears to have
declined Cicero's offer and was defended by someone else. In his own consular election
address (64 BC) some have argued that Cicero embellished the situation as it now suited

136   See various (sometimes discordant) accounts of his political life: in T. N. Mitchell, *Cicero, the Ascending Years*
(New Haven, CN, 1979) and T. N. Mitchell, *Cicero the Senior Statesman* (New Haven, CN, 1991); C. Habicht,
Cicero the Politician (Baltimore, MD, 1990); J. Boes, *La Philosophie et l'action dans la correspondance de Cicéron* (Nancy,
1990); E. Rawson, *Cicero*; D. Stockton, *Cicero, a Political Biography* (Oxford, 1971); Wiseman, *New Men*; M. Crawford,
The Roman Republic, pp. 154–84; and relating the life to his political theory, Wood, *Cicero's Social and Political
Thought*.

him: rather than admitting that he had hoped to defend him, Cicero accused Catiline of being part of a conspiracy to murder the previous year's incoming consuls. Cicero, as a 'new man', sought the support of the *optimates* who feared Pompey, in order to secure election to the consulship. He publicly demolished Catiline, was himself elected, but Catiline reappeared.

Cicero was now convinced that Catiline would seriously attempt to assassinate him although the Senate was unconvinced of the threat. During Cicero's year as consul Catiline stood for the consulship again, to be taken up the following year, with a platform to cancel debts, a programme with which Cicero could not agree as he believed it would destroy the financial order of the 'state'. Having formed a private bodyguard for himself, Cicero appeared at the election wearing protective armour as was permissible for citizens gathering for elections, following the tradition of this being a military assembly where soldier–citizens were, in the past, to have the preponderant influence. Catiline lost again and this time prepared for an uprising with his own troops. Cicero, as consul, revealed the plot to the Senate and brought troops into the city to secure law and order. He was able to have Catiline's co-conspirators arrested.

Constitutionally, the role of the Senate was to decide the charges against them. But Cicero took the view that the Senate should go further and condemn them without trial. It was a well-known principle that punishment without formal trial and conviction was a violation of Roman freedom (*nulla poena sine iudicio*). Cicero, however, saw a higher principle at stake than strict constitutionalism: the possible destruction of the 'state' itself and the very safety of 'the people'. Furthermore, he argued that Catiline and his co-conspirators had become public enemies and thereby forfeited the protection of the law afforded to citizens. Hence, the Senate must accept that there is a higher law to protect the 'state': 'reason of state' could override acting unconstitutionally.

Indeed, in the *De re publica* he attempted a more theoretical, Stoic-inspired explanation of the reasoning behind 'reason of state'. He argued that the various laws of different peoples, if they are just, derive their power and reason from a primal, universal and unchanging law, the natural law.[137] Natural law as the formative and controlling standard by which all states' positive law codes are evaluated, can never be altered. If an attempt is made to alter these universally known standards, then the justification of the 'state' itself dies and one is left with nothing more than a 'state' brought together and unified by force. Hence, all good men must be obliged to act to ensure that the controlling standard of statutory law, which is the natural law on which the state is itself justified, is never destroyed. The fundamental laws, those underwritten by the natural law and which are at the heart of any constitution that can be rationally justified, ought to be above ordinary legislative power. Appeal to a higher principle (indeed, the Stoic principle of self-preservation, here applied to the people and their safety) must be in reserve to protect the unalterable and immortal principles of a constitution, because without the moral basis behind a constitution no state could ever be justly established and maintained. Whenever there is a crisis, law as universal reason must override law as will. The survival of a people is the supreme law, since the death of 'a people' is incompatible with its nature.

In the Senate a debate over whether the conspirators should receive imprisonment or death ensued and Cicero and others argued for the death penalty. He won, and the

---

137 See below, pp. 275ff.

conspirators were killed, Cicero personally supervising their execution. Cicero did not invoke the authority of the Senate to authorize emergency and temporary suspension of the law – this was beyond senatorial capacity; rather, he argued for an appeal to a higher law, the salvation of 'the people' and the survival of the city.[138] Catiline was killed at the head of his army the following year. Cicero says he was immediately hailed as 'father of the country', he had saved the republic from destruction, but his actions were neither universally approved of, nor were they legitimated by the Senate. He was naively surprised and hurt at Pompey's subsequent coolness towards him. His execution of the conspirators without trial was to create tremendous problems for him.

The events of 63 BC seemed to demonstrate to Cicero how the stability of Rome depended on the rule of law, underpinned by a higher law than those promulgated. In eliminating the Catilinian threat to the republic he believed he had played the major role in restoring the republic to its proper functioning. Law was an expression of reason and the Senate expressed it and were joined by the equestrians in a concord of the orders (*concordia ordinum*). Cicero believed that, just as in former times, there had been a harmony of senators and equestrians and others whose concern was the corporate good of the republic. After his consulship he published his speeches to remain in the public eye and remind the Roman people of his efforts on their behalf.[139] But the priorities of senators were not those of Cicero: in reality he had great difficulty in convincing them of the danger of Catiline, a patrician after all, and their support for him would prove to be temporary.[140]

By 60 BC Pompey, in alliance with Julius Caesar and Crassus, formed the first (informal) triumvirate to govern Rome with the intention of dominating the machinery of the 'state' through consulships and combined patronage and wealth. Cicero, the constitutionalist, who feared this powerful coalition, seeing it as destroying the freedom of the Senate, was seen as dangerous and expendable in the factionalism of the next few years. The urban plebeians had been captivated by the aristocrat P. Clodius who assumed their leadership and became the spokesman for social reform. Cicero had slighted the honour of Clodius and thereby made a powerful future enemy. When elected tribune Clodius was able in 58 BC to have a law passed outlawing those who had executed citizens without trial, clearly aimed at Cicero, who was then deprived of his citizenship and exiled. His house was destroyed, and in its place they established a shrine to the goddess of *libertas*.[141] Cicero's friends arranged for his return the following year and secured the support of Pompey. The Senate decided in Cicero's favour and awarded him compensation, but very inadequately. For his part, Cicero seemed to hoped for the dissolution of the triumvirate, leaving Pompey alone as the sole directing force in the republic. In 56 BC he delivered an elaborate defence of his own career and of the traditional constitution based on a concord between the different orders (*Pro Sestio*) and insisted that civilization must be based on the replacement of violence with the law. But he had come to accept the use of political violence by those whom he

138   J.-L. Ferrary, 'The Statesman and the Law in the Political Philosophy of Cicero', in Laks and Schofield, *Justice and Generosity*, pp. 70–2.
139   See T. Wiedemann, *Cicero*, pp.42–6 on Cicero's consulship and how all the speeches we have (including the four *Catilinarians*) were Cicero's published, revised and edited versions of the originals.
140   *Ad Att.* vii, ii, i; viii, ii, 1.
141   See A. Lintott, *Violence in Republican Rome* (Oxford, 1968).

supported[142] and the philosophical underpinning of his political theory justified legitimate violence for the sake of self-defence and a people's survival.

He completed his *De oratore* (55 BC), whose theme is the extreme importance of public political discourse and the central role of the orator. It would remain one of the most important treatises on oratory, its techniques and its purpose, for the Western European tradition because it emphasized how the orator must also be a philosopher as well as someone skilled in arousing emotions. It made an overwhelming case in favour of linking, rather than separating, the rhetorician and the philosopher. Politics was about the skilled manipulation of emotions by the orator for a reasoned cause.

During the period 54–52 BC he wrote his *De re publica* and began work on his (unfinished) *De legibus* (*Laws*). He seems to have inferred from the politics of his time that the people were out of control and that republican institutions could not be brought back to correct functioning without some form of guidance by one man: a *rector* of the republic. Some believe he was thinking here specifically of Pompey, others that he was arguing more generally and theoretically for an ideal, virtuous man like the Scipio Aemilianus whom he portrays as the main protagonist of his *De re publica*. He may even have been thinking of himself, of his own devotion to duty and his service to the republic in 63 BC when he rid the 'state' of Catiline's co-conspirators and preserved the constitution. He was certainly thinking of an ideal philosopher–statesman along Platonic and Stoic lines, but tailored to the needs of contemporary Rome.[143] Although much of the text was lost in later antiquity (and only rediscovered in the nineteenth century) major fragments and summaries were provided for future Europeans by early Christian writers[144] who were living in an imperial Roman period which, they believed, had lost the republican values of an earlier, idealized Rome as presented by Cicero. Christian authors were also attracted to the final book of the *De re publica*, known as the 'dream of Scipio', which argues that military glory and political success are of little value in relation to the importance for eternity of a good man's keeping to his principles. The text of 'Scipio's dream' would alone survive intact into the Middle Ages along with an influential fifth-century commentary by Macrobius. But Latin-reading Europeans would also know Cicero's various rhetorical works (*De inventione*, *De oratore*, *Topica*, etc.) as well as his *On Duties* (c. 44 BC) and the surviving books of his *De legibus*.[145] They would glean from these varied writings the workings of an idealized Roman republic which, increasingly, they saw reasons for trying to revive.

The triumvirate proved short-lived. The tension between Caesar and Pompey escalated and Rome slid towards civil war. Cicero made public his *De re publica* at the time of his reluctant departure for Cilicia in 51 BC, where he had been made a governor. He returned

---

142   A. Lintott, 'Cicero and Milo', *Journal of Roman Studies* 55 (1974), pp. 8–14; Crawford, *The Roman Republic*, p. 170. See N. Wood, '*Populares* and *Circumcelliones*: the vocabulary of "fallen man" in Cicero and St Augustine', *History of Political Thought* 7 (1986), pp. 33–51, on Cicero's attack in his *Pro Sestio* on *populares* as irrational, immoral, reckless, violently disrupting social unity with the aim of overthrowing government.

143   A. E. Douglas, *Cicero* (Oxford, 1968), p. 32, argued that Cicero could not have had any contemporary in mind, himself or Pompey as *rector*. Crawford, *The Roman Republic*, p. 170, argued that he was unable to resist the fascination of the charismatic leader of his day. For the view that Cicero's intention was to write *De re publica*, not as a theoretical treatise on republican government, but rather as a remedy for the contemporary evils of Rome, see Wirszubski, *Libertas*, pp. 79–87.

144   Notably Lactantius, Augustine, Ambrose and Jerome.

145   The relationship between the *De re publica* and the *De legibus* is very different from that between Plato's *Republic* and *Laws*.

to what he called the war-thirsty madhouse of Rome the following year. Caesar crossed the Rubicon into Italy and the civil war began in 49 BC, Caesar arguing that he was fighting for his own *dignitas* against the *optimates* who were forcing him to fight. Agonizing over which side he should take, Cicero opted again for that of the *optimates* and Pompey. Pompey was decisively beaten in battle and later murdered. Caesar survived and some see evidence that briefly Cicero came to think of him as the *rector* who would stabilize the concord of the orders. Caesar's 'monarchy' did accomplish much-needed social reforms but this was at the price of a loss of liberty for all Romans. And his temporary dictatorship, meant to preserve the republic after its civil war, turned into an indefinite, some thought a perpetual one. Caesar was murdered by his 'friends' on the Ides (15th) of March 44 BC. Many of Cicero's more philosophical works, notably his *On Duties*, the *Tusculan Disputations*, the *De finibus bonorum atque malorum*, had been written during and just after Caesar's dictatorship when Cicero had retired from politics. This was also a time in which Cicero's daughter had died in childbirth, leaving him emotionally devastated.

But Caesar's death provided Cicero with his last political opportunity. He later recalled the arbitrary character of Caesar's and his circle's rule in his fourteen *Philippic* orations. These were to be his last fight for the republic and his own *dignitas*, where he saw himself as its champion against Caesar's replacement, the would-be tyrant Antony (whose step-father had been one of the Catilinian co-conspirators whom Cicero had had executed in 63 BC). He presents the *optimate* opposition to Antony as analogous to the opposition of Athenians led by Demosthenes against Philip of Macedon. Cicero attacked Antony for offering Caesar the crown and Antony, in turn, asserted that Cicero had attached himself to the conspiracy against Caesar which led to Caesar's assassination. Cicero responded: 'Apart from those who were happy that Caesar had absolute power, there was no one against the plot; everyone is equally to blame for all men of *dignitas* slew Caesar, to the best of their ability – no one lacked the desire to do it'.[146] Everyone of standing had realized that the republic's rule of law and order had given place to the rule of the stronger. In waging a verbal war against Antony, Cicero was once again representing the *optimates* who felt threatened by Antony's earlier agrarian law which made possible the appropriation of land for distribution to the poor. It was during the previous year that Cicero had written his *On Duties*, after Caesar's death,[147] where he argued that the first duty of the statesman is to safeguard the rights of private property, not least against invasion by the 'state'. Indeed, 'states' owe their origin to citizens' concern to protect their possessions, especially from the 'state'. In the *Philippics* Cicero defended the republic against Antony and his 'shameless profiteering' and he tried to get the Senate to name him a public enemy. He next declared his own support for Octavian, Caesar's great-nephew, adopted son and legal heir. The *optimates* were hoping that Octavian would restore the status quo. But in 43 BC a triumvirate (a triple dictatorship for the restoration of the *res publica*) of Antony, Octavian and Lepidus was established by law and their first action was to murder their respective opponents. The elderly Cicero was killed.

Octavian would come to dominate and, following his victory at the battle of Actium in 31 BC, he was left as the only remaining leader, a virtual dictator. In 28 BC he formally abolished the triumvirate and legitimized an extraordinary position for himself as Caesar Augustus, the *princeps*.

---

146   *Phillipic* II, 29.
147   *De officiis* II, 79.

★

We may well ask whether Cicero's life story, as revealed in his various writings, is a narrative about naivety, or about extraordinary political misjudgements on the part of an immensely talented and ambitious man whose legal and political manoeuvring could make him a match for the later Machiavelli. Or is it about the impossibility of reading Rome in Greek philosophical–political terms and trying to justify one culture's behaviour in the untranslatable terms of the values of another? The influence of Cicero's Greek education on him appears to have been so deep that what Momigliano said of Polybius appears even more true, if somewhat modified, of Cicero: that we are left with the impression that he never quite understood what was really happening in the social organism which had been the guarantee of his survival, success and finally, death. Most scholars accept that Cicero is very good on the day-to-day mechanics of Roman affairs, indeed he could hardly have been otherwise as he was so successful an advocate. But it is arguable whether powerful Romans in the 50s could ever adopt the values he asked of them and he certainly appears to have had little insight into the motivations of those below him. He presented his hopes for an ideal republic and an ideal citizen in his *De re publica* to which we now turn. But we must not be under any illusion that this accurately represents or was intended to represent the mere historical record of the Roman republic: Cicero is far more original than that. He *interprets* the historical experience of Rome in order to discover the essence of the ideal 'state' and its founding principles. We shall see that he consciously emulates Plato's attempt to offer an idea of the ideal 'state', but he thinks that Plato's ideal was too utopian and impractical to guide actual human conduct. And where Plato's successors, Aristotle and the Peripatetics analysed existing states, he believed they never came to any definite conclusions about which might serve as the best model. Instead, Cicero's plan is to use a real 'state', Rome, as the best practicable 'state' and modify it to produce an ideal which consisted in an inheritance of the thoughts and actions of the great men who helped to realize the ideal over generations. It is his originality, in this and other works, in combining an eclectic philosophy with contemporary Roman problems as he saw them, that influenced later Europeans when they came to reconstruct the Roman past in the cause of constructing their own futures.

In terms of his self-understanding, at the end of his life at least, he held to the Stoic belief that happiness depends on what is entirely a man's own doing, the operation of the mind: if he judges correctly and holds steadfastly to truth he will be a perfect being, whom misfortune may strike but will never harm.[148] This reiterates the sentiments of the final book of the *De re publica*, the 'dream of Scipio'.

Cicero's *De re publica*[149]

The setting of the *De re publica* is that of a generation before Cicero's own, where Scipio Aemilianus and his friends are imagined engaged in a conversation early in 129 BC. The background to their discussion is the crisis over the legal powers of the *popularis* tribune

148   Cicero, *De finibus* iii, 75–6.
149   The texts used here are Keyes and Zetzel (see note 4, above). Zetzel also has a good bibliography. For a useful discussion of Cicero's stated intentions in writing the work and an overview of the contents of each book, the aims of the uncompleted *Laws* and the importance of *On Duties*, see Wood, *Cicero's Social and Political Thought*, pp. 63–9; also pp. 120–75.

Tiberius Gracchus's land commission. Cicero substituted the period of the Gracchi in order to deal with troubles of his own times because he thought the Gracchi had begun the conflict that ended by dividing the republic. Scipio Aemilianus, consul in 147 BC, destroyer of Carthage, patron of Polybius and Panaetius, opponent of the Gracchi, and who was murdered in the year in which the dialogue is set, is his principal speaker. Cicero said that he placed the dialogue in the past in order to avoid offending contemporaries, but he also was using Plato's model in the *Republic* to guide him, as the dialogue form was something of a new departure for Latin literature.[150] And as Plato had set his own dialogue in the past with Socrates as protagonist, so too Cicero uses Aemilianus to establish his own intellectual ancestry. It has been said that the crucial difference between Plato and Cicero, however, is that Plato was interested in a universally applicable theory of individual justice, whereas for Cicero an individual's justice (what he is due) has no meaning apart from the 'state' in which he is a citizen.[151] That the Roman 'state' had emerged to display 'perfect' principles of justice, correctly establishing differentials as to what is due, according to law, meant for Cicero that its criteria were universally applicable to all societies seeking the best, the fairest and the most stable constitution.

Most important is that Cicero wished to present Roman ideals in what he imagined to be their last moment of nobility, when Roman senators were military heroes, Greek-educated intellectuals and virtuous public-spirited governors. Cicero was establishing his own intellectual pedigree and at the same time presenting Scipio (who in reality had opposed Gracchus and yet had built his own career on popular rather than senatorial support) as a leader of the senatorial opposition to Gracchan land redistribution. In truth, Scipio had only led the senatorial opposition during the last year of his life.[152] Some of the other interlocutors represented, like Laelius, Philus, Manilius, Rufus, Scaevola and Fannius, had all been consuls. But in general Cicero's historical accuracy is at best questionable, at worst fabrication. He aims for plausibility rather than historical accuracy, where his exposition is not meant to go beyond what he believes to be the accepted facts.[153]

Scipio's Definition of a *res publica*

Book 1 of *De re publica* is concerned with the urge to community that is innate in man, on the one hand, and the need for some form of government that can best assure the continuity of the 'state', on the other. Cicero's preface insists that humans are naturally in need of virtue that is active and have an innate desire to defend the common safety (i, 1–2). Philosophers are not the only ones who have discovered the principles of what is

---

150   See R. W. Sharples, 'Cicero's Republic and Greek Political Theory', *Polis* 5 (1986), pp. 30–50 on similarities between Plato's *Republic* and Cicero's *De re publica*, but where Cicero's is Plato's 'turned inside out' (p. 30); also see Zetzel, pp. 14–15 for the differences; J.–L. Ferrary, 'The Statesman and the Law', pp. 48–73.
151   Zetzel, p. 15.
152   Astin, *Scipio Aemilianus*, pp. 227–41.
153   See Zetzel, p. 12: 'C.'s dialogues have long been used as evidence for the reconstruction of second-century intellectual history, in particular for a "Scipionic circle" which was the centre of diffusion for enlightened Greek ideas, composed of men who were patrons of letters as well as models of *humanitas* and *urbanitas*. That idea has been generally discredited.' Cicero's portrait of Scipio as an advocate of strict constitutionality is most innaccurate.

just and honourable: these principles have also been discovered by those who have drawn up codes of law or by men who have been educated by social rules, the principles having been confirmed by custom or enforced by law (i, 3). That leading citizen who compels all men by the authority of magistrates and the penalties imposed by law to follow the rules whose principles philosophers have also discovered but could never enforce, is superior to philosophers who have come up with the principles alone. Philosophy is useful but knowing Roman history is more so (i, 31) because the history of the many great and active military statesmen of Rome's past has demonstrated that great Romans have always required a knowledge of those things that could make them useful to the Roman 'state'. According to Cicero, the Romans who could adapt Greek philosophy to their own government and law were far superior to the Greeks.

We are introduced to Scipio's views which are pushed further by, for the most part, the interventions of the Stoic Laelius. We are prepared for the more narrowly focused discussion of the best constitution based on a notion of justice that gives to each what is differentially his due, when Scipio argues about a universal kind of justice which transcends what the civil law obliges: it is only a very special kind of man who can claim all things as his own by virtue of the decision of the common law of nature which forbids that anything should belong to a man except to him that knows how to employ it and use it (i, 27). This common law of nature is known to the wise: it stipulates that a knowledge of how to employ and use possessions is the condition of recognition to entitlement.[154] It is significant that natural, human social instincts are insufficient to establish a 'state' whose principles, enshrined in its laws, make it a reflection of the higher, rational order displayed in this common law of nature. We need the wise who are not passive philosophers but active, prudential men who know how to employ and use principles rationally discovered. Cicero holds to the Greek belief in the primacy of mind over body, and hence reason must rule the 'state' and it does so through laws that are *understood* (if not discovered) by all rational creatures. The Roman constitution, as an artistic creation, is not imported from elsewhere but has grown up on native soil, following nature's road, and it has been discovered and realized by Rome's great and active men generation after generation. Indeed, we are given a selective history of the road taken by such men in the *De re publica*'s book 2. We shall see that learning and knowledge must be added to whatever universally shared natural faculties of the mind enable men everywhere to follow reason and act virtuously for the social fellowship.

First, however, we need a working definition of the 'state' and Scipio defines the republic, the *res publica*, in terms of its people, who have come together not as a random assemblage but rather as an association because of its agreement as to what is in the common interest. The correct definition of 'a people' is an association which acknowledges a common idea of what is right (*iuris consensus*) and hence each other's rights under shared laws, and pursues in common their advantage, utility or interest. The 'state' is identified with its people's *concern*, its people's *business*, through an agreement over *ius,* meaning both what is agreed to be right and hence, normatively, what is law, where there is a shared advantage, interest, utility (*utilitas*) being served. The emphasis is on an agreement, an acknowledgement, of what is in the collective interest. We shall have to discover how passive this agreement is, since to agree to something can either mean that

---

154   This is about as close as one gets to the seventeenth-century Locke's statement in the *Two Treatises of Government,* ii, 34 that the world was given by God to men in common for the use of the industrious and rational.

one has come up with the principles oneself or they have been placed before one and then accepted as useful. Those who accept the law as rational do not necessarily discover it. The meaning of *res* as 'things', 'property', 'interest', 'business', 'concern' and therefore the *res publica/res populi* is best approximated as 'including all interests of the community of the people'. This has been taken to be a contractual theory of the state, involving the acceptance of the rule of law and implying an equitable (not equal) distribution of rights and duties.[155] The agreement is said to originate not out of human weakness but out of innate sociability (i, 39).

Scipio distinguishes between *res publica/res populus* and the *populus*, however: the state as a constitution is not strictly identified with the organized people who make it up, because the Roman republic was not a popular sovereignty. The 'state' is concerned with the people's advantage or interest and this cannot best be achieved by popular rule. Hence, Cicero distinguishes between a 'state' and its 'government' which is its deliberative body serving as guardian and administrator (i, 22). The 'state' does not govern, but those responsible for its management and policy do.[156] The ruling functions of its deliberative body enable 'states' to be classified. Loosely speaking, all forms of government, good or bad (monarchy, aristocracy, democracy on the one hand, and tyranny, oligarchy and mob-rule on the other), may be considered *res publicae*, but are not truly so. A true *res publica* must exhibit justice and justice is proportional equity, giving to each what is his due. A true *res publica* identifies justice with interest, *ius* with *utilitas*.

Since every 'state' must have some direction in order to last, the direction must always be related to the particular reason, made plain in ancestral customs and traditions, for which the state came into being. States directed by one man, the few, or the many, if they were able to maintain the bond which originally bound men into a 'state', would not be perfect nor best, but might be considered tolerable. But since the most natural system in society is one which recognizes three distinct orders, then the rule of any one order is undesirable, and especially rule by the people as in democracy is the least desirable constitution. We are presented with the vices specific to each form of constitution determined by whether one, few or the many, respectively, direct it: monarchy fails to seek counsel or share power, an aristocracy denies popular liberty since the people are excluded from any deliberation and power, and there is no *dignitas* or standing, no distinctions in rank accorded to noble birth or merit in democracy, even if the people exercise their power with justice and moderation (i, 43). Taken individually, none of the simple constitutional forms is suitable as each has failings specific to it, and furthermore, they are all liable to degenerate into their corrupt equivalents.

Cicero modifies the Polybian cycle of constitutions, increasing the variations and permutations of constitutional forms and their degenerate counterparts (i, 65; ii, 45).[157] While Scipio, if he is to choose one of the simple forms of constitution, is most in favour of monarchy as a strong executive (i, 54), he is made to confront arguments against monarchy from the point of view of democracy and aristocracy. Each form of government is then characterized by its most distinctive attribute: in democracy it is *libertas*, which means political equality rather than equality before the law (equity). If democrats

---

155   Zetzel, p. 129.
156   Wood, *Cicero's Social and Political Thought*, p. 133.
157   See ibid., pp. 152–5; Hahm, 'Polybius', pp. 7–47; Lintott, 'The Theory of the Mixed Constitution', pp. 81–2.

are asked to define the 'state' they see it as an aggregate of individual citizens with juridical equality.

Scipio asks the following question: since the law is the bond of civic society, and right is equivalent to law, then by what right can a society of citizens be bound together when the *status* of citizens is not the same? On the one hand, the unequal status of citizens is a simple fact, because the historical cycle of constitutional change, as well as Rome's own history, demonstrate that status differentials have always been recognized. On the other hand, history demonstrates that different criteria have been used to try to get some agreement among all the people as to the proper weight of differences of status. History shows that men have not agreed about how a 'state' should factor into its constitution the differing views on status. Scipio concludes that we cannot agree to equalize men's wealth; nor can we agree on an equality of innate abilities. What we can agree on is that the legal rights of all those who are citizens are equal (i, 49). This is what Rome discovered, a useful kind of compromise concerning irreconcilable approaches to status. This is the agreement that defines the 'state' as an association in justice: equality before the law but not to equal things. Scipio insists that men of the highest and lowest honour must exist in every 'state' and hence treating them equally cannot be fair (i, 53). But treating everyone equally before the law is the minimum to which everyone, with his different view of status, can accept.

Scipio asserts that any true 'state' based on justice chooses its leaders on the basis of virtue, so that it is neither at the mercy of the limited judgement of one man nor subject to the folly of the masses. Cicero at last makes his claim for the superiority of virtue over noble birth and wealth (i, 51). Although virtue may be possessed by only a few it is not the case that it can be distinguished and perceived by only the few. This parallels his notion of universal agreement to the law which is not universally discovered. A virtuous man who rules the state imposes no laws upon the people that he does not obey himself (i, 52). And in a state ruled by its best men, he says that the citizens enjoy the greatest happiness, being freed from all worries when they have entrusted the preserving of the peace to others whose duty it is to guard it vigilantly and never allow the people to think that their interests are being neglected by their rulers.

It is when there is a failure of justice, a lack of a *iuris consensus,* that essential agreement by a people in what is right, and hence what is lawful, that the constitution degenerates. Only a fourth kind of constitution, which is a true mixture of the best elements of the three simple good kinds, can serve justice because only here is each order held in its place by the other two. There is a royal executive element in the 'state', power granted to the leading citizens, and certain matters left to the judgement and desires of the masses. There is a supreme, royal element with *potestas* (power) for the magistrates, *auctoritas* (authority) for the notables and *libertas* (liberty) for the people (i, 69; ii, 57). It is more stable than any of the three simple kinds, there being no reason for a change when every citizen is firmly established in his own order (i, 69–70). It is not simply a mixture but a 'well-regulated' mixture. Cicero devotes much of book 2 to a historical analysis of the development of Rome's mixed constitution which achieved its practical ideal realization as 'well-regulated' with a 'fair balance' in the 'golden age' just prior to the time in which the *De re publica* is set.[158]

---

158   See Wood, *Cicero's Social and Political Thought,* pp. 159–75.

Natural Law

Because Cicero believed that nature had implanted in the human race so great a need for active virtue and so great a desire to defend the common safety, the strength of this natural *amicitia* and its expression has enabled men to choose to fight for their country and for the common good, conquering thereby whatever selfish attractions there may be to private pleasure and ease. That the active public life is not only virtuous but natural, and that it is natural for men to want to express love and friendship in a protective way to all members of their community, is one of the central ideas of his *De re publica* and also of his vision of Roman political ideals in the past. This reading of Rome's history, philosophically supported by the Stoic doctrine of a unity and brotherhood of men, enabled him to develop a notion of a natural sense of moral duty, in the first instance innate, but requiring an educated reason to enable social men to learn from history: nature and history, that is, the efforts of educated and exemplary men in the past, have combined to demonstrate, especially in Rome's case, how men have been guided to honour and fame, through politically virtuous acts of regulated friendship. The doctrine of public service over private desires is one that men who are aware of an ancestral inheritance of public service, consciously and rationally engage. Only an educated reason and regulated habits can build on the universally shared natural instinct to sociability and the natural tendency to come to agreements through consensus. The reflective and educated man can recognize that there is no occupation in which human virtue approaches more closely the functions of the gods than that of either founding a new republic or preserving those already in existence.[159] This is not open to all men. Since Roman society developed naturally to establish three orders in society, each order is recognized as having its own competence and its own sphere of interest. Hence, the ideal 'state' in practice must have an even balance of rights, duties and functions where the magistrates have sufficient power, the councils of eminent citizens sufficient influence, and the people sufficient liberty. This concord of the orders, where each order has its own sphere of interest as well as function, is derived from historical observation as to what humans can and have agreed to: men cannot agree either to equalize wealth or innate talent, but they can agree that a people ought, in law, to have equal rights (but not to equal things). The single body of Roman law, ruling over and hence binding together a harmony of diverse interests based on rank or order, is itself a reflection of a higher, universal law, and order which is evident in nature itself. This is the natural law.

In book 3 Philus puts the case that different laws exist throughout the world and that laws are successfully imposed on men through their fear of punishment and not by their sense of justice. This argument, reminiscent of Thrasymachus in Plato's *Republic* and probably derived by Cicero from its more recent incarnation among Epicureans and the sceptical Carneades, concludes that there is no such thing as natural justice and that men are not just from nature. They obey whatever laws there are out of utility and fear. Out of mutual fear, man fearing man and order fearing order, and because no one is confident in his own strength, a sort of pact or contract is struck between the common people and the powerful. Philus argues that the mixed form of government, described by Scipio,

---

159   This is a sentiment that would reappear in Machiavelli's *Prince*, although Cicero's *De re publica* was not available to him. See *A History of Political Thought* volume 2, chapter 6.

actually derives from this (iii, 23).[160] Weakness is the mother of political justice. Plato's arguments for the good, just man are rehearsed and rejected, for no people would be so foolish as not to prefer to be unjust masters rather than just slaves (iii, 27).

Cicero, however, has the Stoic Laelius argue (iii, 33) that the different laws in the world represent the variety in the utility and application of what is, in fact, a single principle of justice and such a single principle is the inexorable, foundational, natural law. He defines true law as right reason in agreement with nature. True law, the rational regulating principle of all societies, is of universal application, is unchanging and everlasting. As a rational rule, obliging all humans, it enables men to come to know what their duties are and similarly enables men to avoid wrongdoing. It is innate in human nature, and humans need only look inside themselves to know it and interpret it. The natural law does not require experts to expound it or interpret it. This unchanging and eternal law ensures that there will not be different foundational laws at Rome or Athens, or different principles now and in the future. God is the author of this unchangeable law, valid for all nations and all times, and its enforcing judge. As written into man's nature it is unalterable and it cannot be abolished. The 'Senate and people' cannot release humans from these naturally and rationally known obligations. Whoever disobeys this innate natural law is fleeing from himself and denying his human nature. By this very fact he will suffer the worst penalties even if he escapes civic punishment.[161]

A constitution like that of the Roman republic is founded on higher, more universal and unchanging principles, those revealed to men in the natural law. Any 'state's' positive laws must be judged against these principles. Cicero expands on this theme in his *De legibus* (i, 19) where again he says that law is the highest reason, implanted in nature, which commands what ought to be done and forbids the opposite. But he emphasizes the Stoic requirement that reason, only when firmly fixed and fully developed in the human mind, is law. The origin of justice is to be found in the law as the highest reason, and law, as a natural force, is the mind and reason of the rational and prudent man (*mens ratioque prudentis*), the standard by which justice and injustice are measured. The people, however rational, do not seem to have access to this highest reason. Law for them is the written form which decrees whatever it wishes, either by command or prohibition. This, Cicero says, is the crowd's definition of law. To know what justice is one has to have access to the supreme law, the highest reason, and this again only emerges in minds that are fully developed. We have already been told that the principles of what is just and honourable have been discovered not only by philosophers but also by those who have drawn up codes of law or by leading citizens. The latter, because they could compel men to follow the rules by the authority of magistrates and the penalties imposed by law, are superior to philosophers (i, 1–3).

Should we think that Cicero is merely making a sociological observation, that the mass of men simply have not had the education and training to develop their reason to the extent that the universal principles are known to them *as* supreme law, we would be

---

160   Compare Glaucon's restatement of Thrasymachus' position in Plato's *Republic*, II.

161   Compare the early *De inventione* II, xxi, 65, where Cicero says the origins of law seems to be in nature. Certain principles, either obvious or obscure to us, have by reason of advantage passed into custom; afterward certain principles approved by custom or deemed to be really advantageous have been confirmed by statute. The law of nature is something implanted in us not by opinion but by a kind of innate instinct, and it includes religion, duty, gratitude, revenge, reverence and truth.

mistaken. He is not offering a doctrine of perfectibility through education so that all men may become wise. His position is, rather, that of a Platonically nuanced Stoic determinism. We already know that Scipio, at least, believes that innate talents are not subject to equalization. Furthermore, all humans share in reason but not to the same extent. If we allude to his *On Duties* in the expectation that his views would not change substantially on these matters during the ten years that separate these works, we could use his advice that each individual should acquire knowledge of his talents and fashion his character, that second *persona*, for himself: the unique (and shifting) roles appropriate to his status and circumstances. He should not strive to acquire good qualities that have not been granted to him. Instead, he should know his own 'nature' and qualities and thereby lead a life in the 'state' that enables him to remain true to his own character and interests.

But that innate moral capacity in all men (the first, non-individuating *persona*) ensures that the moral law predates the existence of 'states'. Cicero says:

> That animal we call man, endowed with foresight and quick intelligence, complex, keen, possessing memory, full of reason and prudence, has been given a certain distinguished status by the supreme god who created him; he alone has a share in reason and thought, while all the rest of living beings are deprived of it. But what is more divine, I will not say in man only, but in all heaven and earth, than reason? And reason, *when it is full grown and perfected*, is rightly called wisdom. (*De legibus*, i, 22–3)

Those who share law and justice are to be regarded as members of the same republic. But the question remains as to the nature of that sharing, since men are distinct in virtue; they are not all wise. Are we to understand that it is only those whose reason is perfected that truly share law and justice and are the only true citizens of a republic? In Stoic terms, only these wise agents are not vulnerable to chance or fortune, but in Cicero's application of Stoicism it was the leading citizens of Rome's past, with the customary authority to compel compliance with the principles, whose reason was full grown and perfected.[162]

In line with Stoic teaching Cicero tells us that nature, *when perfected and developed*, makes man like god. One can, of course, provide a single definition applicable to all men: for no single thing is so like another, so exactly its counterpart, as all of us are to one another. Man is identifiably one species. But then he says if bad customs and false beliefs did not twist the weaker minds (*non imbecillitatem animorum torqueret*), turning them in whatever direction they are inclined, no one would be so like his own self as all men would be like all others. But men are not all exactly the same. Some have weaker minds. To have a weaker mind does not mean that such a mind is evil or is, from nature, twisted concerning what is morally right and appropriate. Rather, the share in reason on the part of each and every mind can be corrupted if improperly cared for; psychic pathology is not from nature.

Cicero's individualism requires that each person become knowledgeable about his own capacities and the role (second *persona*) for which nature has 'dressed him', given his status and circumstances. In the process of fashioning the roles which suit him, he even acknowledges the comparative weakness of his own mind with its specific natural ten-

---

162   For a different approach see W. Nicgorski, 'Cicero's Focus: from the best regime to the model statesman', *Political Theory* 19 (1991), pp. 230–51.

dencies towards intemperance. The achievement of such a self-knowledge on the part of most men will only be possible if a suitable guide is found. Cicero appears to hold with Stoics that bad habits and pathological passions constitute the 'vice' of a mental sickness and the foundation of such sickness or weakness is ignorance or errors of value judgements. Stoics believed generally that becoming virtuous or vicious was in the power of those determined by nature to achieve mental health or mental sickness. Weaker minds, then, are not irrational but are naturally so constituted as to tend more easily to succumb to unrestrained 'pleasures' which can lead to vice. They require guidance. Indeed, Cicero tells us that only the beginnings of intelligence are imprinted in our minds alike[163] and that all humans, of whatever race, can achieve virtue if properly guided.[164] This virtue must be one that is proper to each and in accord with his own moral character (itself actualized through roles appropriate to status and circumstance). The virtue proper to each is not wisdom, since this is a quality of the very few.[165] Not all men are wise or can serve as guides. But it is only the wise who attain the virtue of governing.

For Stoics, rationality and the good coincide in god and can coincide in man *if* he perfects his reason. As Cicero would explain in the later *On Duties*, such men are extremely rare, naturally endowed as they are with outstanding intellect or a learned education or both. Nature's fate comes before fortune to Cicero and it appears to be most men's fate to have weaker minds. Hence, if this is the best possible of worlds, as Stoics and Cicero believed, then each individual is in it to perform a specific role and this must mean that one's moral virtue consists in living willingly and to the best of one's ability the life assigned to you by fate.[166] But that self-knowledge as to what life has been assigned to you and is appropriate will only be realized in most men if they are directed to it by rare men of insight and reason, and in *De re publica* they are not Hercules 'sprung from the seed of Jupiter' but Rome's leading citizens of the past. The Stoic teacher as psychic healer with his therapy of self-awareness becomes, for Cicero, the therapist who as leading citizen either directs the 'state' in times when customs are maintained, and thereby maintains the state, or in corrupt times when customs have been lost, brings it back to mental health in accord with reason. Cicero seems to have this in mind when he says that not all men can be directors of the republic, understanding the natural law foundations of the civil laws and the mixed constitution. Hence, if Rome's constitution is founded on ancient customs and on men of military and political virtue, then its failures in 129 bc, as Cicero says in *De re publica* v, are due to the loss of our customs, which in turn is due to the lack of appropriate men with the combined insight into highest reason and historical ancient custom (v, 2). Here, Cicero transcends Stoic teaching by arguing that a specific governing class must apply the law and ensure the survival of the ideal republic.

In this corrupt situation a *rector* is needed to bring the republican constitution back on course. The governing statesman required needs to become familiar with justice and law and their origins; he is not a lawyer but he must be fully conversant with justice in its highest aspects for without that no one can be just (v, 5). He must, therefore, educate his mind to the highest reason, knowing the natural law as the foundation of the 'state's' civil law. The pilot of this 'state' ensures that the *optimi*, the best men, seek praise and glory and

---

163   In *De fin.* 3.23 Cicero says that we are first introduced to wisdom by the *initia naturae*.
164   *De legibus* 1, 29–30.
165   See above, pp. 251ff, *On Duties*, the four *personae*.
166   See Long and Sedley, *The Hellenistic Philosophers*, p. 392.

avoid disgrace and dishonour. The pilot also strengthens the feeling of shame from justi-fied censure *by the force of public opinion*, shame deterring the citizens from crime no less effectively than fear (v, 6).[167] His skills regarding the people are, clearly, rhetorical, stirring the emotions to an end *he* (alone) sees as true reason, in harmony with universal order. The 'state' which has lost its ancient customs because it has lost its men of virtue is best directed by someone who can lead the people to emotional compliance with the law.

This best 'state' *weighs* its citizens rather than counts them (vi, 1). And those accorded most weight are those who have actively preserved, aided or enlarged the republic through ruling and preserving the 'state'. In the afterlife it is such men who, in actively being associated with justice, are gathered together again (vi, 14). In the 'dream of Scipio' such men, when removed from their mortal bodies, will know that they are gods, 'if a god is that which lives, feels, remembers and foresees and which rules, governs and moves the body over which it is set, just as the supreme god rules this universe' (vi, 26). Ultimately, those who engage in preserving the republic will be rewarded with an immortality that infinitely surpasses the recognition, or lack of it, achieved in the political world.

Cicero believed that laws are imposed on social humans and are held by them to be obliging, not out of fear of punishment but rather from a human sense of justice and collective utility. The human law of nations (*ius gentium*) had to be in consensus with the more foundational principles, the universal law of nature (*lex recta ratio naturae congruens est*). The standard of judgement is reason and out of an educated reason come just civil laws to rule society. The universal law of nature encompasses and directs the law of nations which, in turn, encompasses and directs the civil law. The civil law is more specific to a given people but it has within it the principles of the foundational law of nature. This natural law is written into men's innate capacities, but only rulers with educated reason have access to it *as* highest reason and true law. Everyone else simply accepts the rational utility of rules that promote human fellowship and agreement.

The effect of the natural law on the republican constitution is clear: there are rational discoverers of the higher law and rational agree-ers to the civil law. Society is naturally ranked not only in terms of wealth but especially in terms of virtue and intellect. The republic needs such men, all the better if they are 'new men' as true *optimates*, who have bothered to learn what Rome's ancestral history means along with the values that under-pin her ancient customs and ancient constitution. The present nobility has lost its way.

Cicero's Mixed Constitution Compared with Aristotle's Mixed Polity

It has often been said, especially by historians of later European periods, that Cicero's mixed constitution owes much to and is a continuation of Aristotle's mixed constitu-tion, polity.[168] There are, however, more contrasts than similarities.

---

167   It is important to note that when Polybius considered the power of the people (vi, 14) he said that they had authority over honour and punishment, trying men who have held the highest office for capital crimes of a political nature. Despite the Senate's power, it still had to rely on the people to ratify legislative proposals to restrict the Senate's power and privileges (xvi, 1–3), as well as investigations of political crimes. Cicero notably endows the *rector* with an ability to guide and direct the people's emotions in these matters and therefore exercise control over their 'authority'. He likewise directs the *optimi*.

168   See Lintott, 'The Theory of the Mixed Constitution', pp. 70–85, who sees Cicero's ideal as comparable to Aristotle's aristocratic 'mixture' in *Politics* IV 1293b.

Aristotle's mixing of constitutional features in the practicable polity is concerned with a blending of oligarchic and democratic practices and ideologies to promote among citizens an equally shared liberty to *engage to some degree in self-rule* on the one hand, and on the other, the recognition of the wealthy as having a limited amount of privilege. As Lintott has observed, Aristotle 'is thinking in terms of fusion, not of holding in balance conflicting forces'.[169] Aristotle's emphasis is not on checks and balances, a confrontation of constitutional elements that he probably would have regarded as civil conflict. Are we to understand Cicero as similarly describing a well-mixed constitution as non-conflictual in its achieving of consensus?

Wherever the idea of a mixed constitution derived from, as Cicero depicts it, it seems to have been an idea in circulation among Rome's Hellenizing aristocracy.[170] Whether or not we accept Polybius' accuracy and knowledge of Roman politics and ideas, and therefore accept or not his description of the actual workings of the early Roman constitution, it is clear that in the mixed constitution he described, and which appears to have coincided with the Romans' own construction of their political mythology, the salient aspect of this naturally evolved mixed republic is its having been a product of conflict.[171] Cicero absorbed but also transformed this conflictual, dynamic notion of the naturally evolving mixture. Aristotle's mixture, however, was a prescription to lawgivers that has rightly been called static and perhaps more importantly the product of practical reason in given and appropriate circumstances.

Cicero's modification of the conflictual evolution of the republic emerges in his historical reading of Rome's past.[172] Instead, Cicero presents the mixed constitution[173] as the invention of *kings*, and the subsequent tide of popular antagonism to the people's lack of liberty is said to have been *managed* by leaders through legal restrictions on consular power. Notably distinct from Polybius' approach is Cicero's favourable presentation of monarchy (Scipio's position) and his desire to present a vision of the mixed constitution in which popular agitation, or even opinion and habit, not only have no significant part to play in the present but had no role in the past.[174] Cicero consistently 'minimized the length and intensity of the conflict which had produced the constitution that he himself enjoyed'.[175]

But what the republic *is*, is a 'reconciliation' of irreconcilable conflicts of interest, of irreducible views on merit and status, a constitution held together by means of a law that is agreed to be just for all and thence produces the concord of orders. For someone inspired by Stoic moral teaching as was Cicero, conflict is always there, but is to be overcome, not as was the case for Aristotle, by a legislator who seeks to re-educate all men's emotions from the beginning through 'state' moral education, but by a law that accepts natural mental and emotional distinctions, as well as distinctions of status, and does nothing to change men's circumstances. Furthermore, Cicero's mixed constitution

169   Lintott, 'The Theory of the Mixed Constitution', p. 72.
170   At the time of Cato the Censor. Lintott, 'The Theory of the Mixed Constitution', p. 73.
171   Ibid., p. 79.
172   Although historically, through patrician–plebeian conflict, is precisely how it does seem to have evolved; Le Glay et al., *A History of Rome*, p. 47.
173   *De re publica, II.*
174   Lintott, 'The Theory of the Mixed Constitution', p. 81.
175   Ibid., p. 84.

is not an analysis of the relationship between assemblies, Senate and magistrates but rather describes a balance between the many and the few to ensure the latter's dominance.

Let us compare in greater detail Cicero's mixture with Aristotle's mixed constitution, the most practicable polity. First, Aristotle says the 'state' aims, in so far as it can, to be a partnership of men who are equal and similar. This is impossible for Cicero's 'state', founded precisely to formalize and entrench differences, most specifically regarding what is one's own and therefore one's due. An apparent similarity appears, however, in that Aristotle too held the notion of equality to be sustainable only when equals were equated with equals. While Aristotle believed it to be impossible in most *poleis* to attempt to seek perfect equality among men in all things, most *poleis* being characterized as either oligarchies or democracies, he none the less believed that the development of a 'state' made up of unlike parts, where a plurality of citizens had an amount of property sufficient to secure a good life for each, was the greatest barrier against the division of the state into two mutually hostile factions of very rich and very poor. Hence, Aristotle directs 'state' policy of the mixed polity to economic amelioration. Cicero, in contrast, thinks this is precisely what the 'state', mixed or otherwise, did not come into existence to do.

Aristotle's polity mixes elements of oligarchical practice and democratic practice and has a 'state' policy which encourages employment and provides the conditions in which a poor man may acquire moderate possessions. Indeed, the element of democracy in his mixed polity requires that the democratic citizen helps to make policy which ensures the population is not destitute. He administers the policies that perpetuate the prosperity of the rich as well as the poor and what accrues from the 'state' revenues is collected into a fund and distributed in block grants to those in need, so that they can acquire a small piece of land or start a business. Cicero, on the contrary, during all of his political life, argued against 'state' redistribution of 'state' revenues.

From the oligarchical side, Aristotle encourages men of wealth and virtue to make it their concern to provide the needy with a start in some occupation (*Politics* vi, 1320a35–1320b8). It is only here, in the guise of patron–client voluntary, personal relations that Cicero would agree. Furthermore, Aristotle says that in larger states there is often a large middle element. When there is a minority of rich and a minority of poor, with a predominant majority of the middle sort of people, the 'state' has, for Aristotle, the best chances of satisfying its aims to consist of those who are similar and equal. This is the middle constitution, his ideal version of polity as a mixed constitution. Cicero, on the contrary, sees no virtue in a large middle element because his understanding of a directing senatorial elite is founded on a view of Rome's history as having been made by a smaller elite of politically active and virtuous men. Indeed, his concord of the orders as described in *De re publica* makes no mention whatever of the equestrian 'middle' group.

Cicero's mixed constitution, then, is different in crucial ways from Aristotle's mixed polity. The 'state' does not, for him, aim to consist of those who are similar and equal. Nor is there a 'state' policy for wealth creation other than plundering the empire. The 'state' indeed, came about to secure an unequal distribution of property and power and his mixed constitution balances the discrete and immutable interests of each social order. Consensus is achieved between irreconcilable interests and each order or rank enjoys the benefit of what Cicero takes to be the particular good of each. The royal power sought by consuls is separate from the aristocratic authority sought by the Senate and different again from the liberty sought by the people. The group interest of the people is perceived to be largely a negative kind of liberty: not to be oppressed by the nobles. They do not share in the positive liberty to take their turn in governing or self-rule. Through their tribunes they have a constrained right to agree or not to laws which affect their interest. Cicero insists that all will agree that there is no reason for a change in the constitution when every citizen is firmly established in his own order. And when the greatest number of votes goes to the rich rather than to the common people, he says that we have established in practice the principle that the greatest number ought *not* to have the greatest power. No one is deprived of the vote but those with the most votes are in that social order to whom the highest welfare of the 'state' is most important. Given the reasons Cicero offers for the republic having been established in the first place, the preservation of one's own, this is not unreasonable: those who have the greatest interest in maintaining the status quo are those whose interests are best served by the 'state'. They are obliged to rule and maintain the law if they hope to realize their just entitlements. Cicero is in favour of retaining the tribunes of the people (in *De legibus*) so that their (narrowly conceived) interests are at least represented in the authoritative and powerful councils of state, but their powers are very circumscribed.

Cicero's is not a sociological theory which argues that one's social rank accustoms one to a fixed vision of what the 'state' is for, so that those not born into a ruling elite with the requisite ancestral inheritance, simply come to want from the 'state' what they have socially become accustomed to wanting: not self-rule but living as one likes without oppression from the stronger in society. He does not argue that this social experience can be altered by education to effect mobility between orders. Nor is it clear to him from his own times that those born into the rich and powerful have, as a consequence, the requisite virtue for governing. His theory is, in structure, more Platonic than this. It is a theory that society has natural leaders, not necessarily those from an inherited aristocracy but those who, like himself, have been granted the intelligence and have gone on voluntarily to exercise their ingenuity to discover what Rome's history really means. Such men, in any age, are rare, but they have always made the 'state' what it is and Rome's history (and good fortune) has been down to them. The Roman 'state' has been made by flexible men capable of a set of 'presentations of self' through stage-like roles that were appropriate to their social positions and circumstances, enabling them to fulfil their functions. They were excellent calculators of effect, assuming the very role of the city itself, preserving its laws and administering its justice.[176] When Cicero's writings would come to be seriously revived during the Italian Renaissance he would be appreciated for having shown Italians precisely this. By then, they would read him and other Romans selectively and partly through the lens of Aristotle's *Politics*. Just as later ages would assimilate Plato to Aristotle, so too Aristotle would come to be harmonized with Cicero. This is what readers do to texts when they live in circumstances and according to values that their 'ancient' author could not have known or shared.

Cicero in Retrospect

In the first century BC when power politics were unusually dominant and unscrupulous, Cicero is now thought to have been unusually principled, relatively speaking. But

---

176   See *On Duties* I, 124 above, p. 262.

during the nineteenth century, when Roman history was studied rigorously especially by German scholars, Cicero's reputation was eclipsed because, some have argued, those German historians writing under the influence of Hegel could not sympathize with the nature of the republican ideal, nor of a harmonious concord between the various social orders of society. This, however, was not the heart of Theodor Mommsen's brilliant, although 'loaded', criticism. It was rather that anyone who represented the Roman constitution as a mixed constitution and derived from it the success of Rome, was a fool.[177]

Furthermore, Mommsen, the greatest German historian of Rome, considered Cicero, like so many of his contemporaries, to be a dishonourable politician and an incompetent advocate in law cases where he defended often guilty members of the public. Cicero certainly did the latter and he was prepared to ignore established procedure in Roman law when it suited the case of a client.[178] He indeed admitted as much when in *On Duties* (II, 51) he says 'scruples should not prevent us from occasionally defending a guilty man provided he is not wicked and impious. The masses want it; custom permits it; humanity tolerates it. In lawsuits, a judge should always strive for the truth, but an advocate may sometimes defend what looks like the truth, even if it is less true.' This, says Cicero, was acceptable to the Stoic Panaetius.

Mommsen also considered Cicero to have been a philosophical journalist without anything original to contribute. He believed that if Cicero was to be studied at all, it was for his Latin style alone. One should learn to read and write Latin as an exercise using Cicero as a model for form but not for content.

The twentieth century, however, has been more generous. We recognize, even feel comfortable with the man, not least because of the way he develops Stoic individualism and his emphasis on the natural links between personality and property, self-interest and social utility. Much more has been uncovered concerning the conditions of first century BC Roman history and Cicero has come in for a more sympathetic re-evaluation as a man of his times, and unusually principled at that. His contributions as a philosophical thinker have attracted sustained scholarly interest only in the twentieth century and recently it has been asserted that his philosophy cannot be detached from the other aspects of his political career and personal life.[179] The reputation and influence he acquired during the Middle Ages and heightened during the Renaissance, and which survived into the eighteenth century in a European society which was constituted everywhere by differentials in social rank,[180] has therefore been revitalized and, in part, has countered the mid-nineteenth century demotion of his work to the status of dabbling.

There has been a reassessment of his philosophical and rhetorical works as well as his letters to various friends.[181] They reveal not only the trials and tribulations of a 'new

---

177   T. Mommsen, *Romische Geschichte*, 7th edn, vol. 2 (Leipzig, 1854–6), p. 452; Mommsen, *History of Rome*, trans. W. Dickson (London, 1868): 'To the later generations who survived the storms of revolution the period after the Hannibalic war appeared the golden age of Rome, and Cato [the Censor, one of Cicero's heroes; M. Cato, who championed the Roman people and got on in politics by his own merit and not by family influence; Cicero, *Acti secunda in Verrem*, v, 180] seemed the model of the Roman statesman. It was in reality the calm before the storm and the epoch of political mediocrities, an age like that of the government of Walpole in England'.

178   *Pro caecina*; see B. W. Frier, *The Rise of the Roman Jurists* (Princeton, NJ, 1985).

179   Colish, *The Stoic Tradition*, vol. 1, p. 61.

180   See the writings of Edmund Burke.

181   See Colish, *The Stoic Tradition*, vol. 1, pp. 65ff. for the waves of reassessment.

man' in the process of making it to the top, but also his own political vacillations, made necessary by the process of legal defence of clients, the desire to be successful and liked, and most importantly, they tell us of Cicero's desire to be a moderate, constitutional conservative. He attempted time and again to return to a consensus government when the various powerful and shifting interest groups of his day were themselves altering their own stands because of personal greed for wealth and power. Hence, the complaint by contemporaries and by posterity that Cicero did not practise what he preached, and that he was inconsistent in politics, can to some extent be mitigated by the vacillation of his opponents.

It has also been said that his eclectic vacillations regarding various philosophical schools were no more than a reflection of Hellenistic philosophy itself at the time, so that he ought not to be judged according to standards alien to this own conception of the philosophical enterprise.[182] It is in this light that one understands his undoubtedly backward-looking ideals in the *De re publica* which were unable to prevent the fall of the Roman republic. But as we have seen, the work is not merely nostalgic: in seeking an understanding of the dynamics of Roman political life, *De re publica* goes beyond a constitutional definition of the ideal republic by focusing on moral categories which describe the ethos of rulers and citizens who make up the political community. It was Cicero's emphasis on the proper ethical attitude of Rome's great public men, who were, for him, the animating minds that vivify and regulate the 'state', that served as the lesson which later Europeans absorbed from his linking of the Stoic-educated statesman personality with the republican constitutional form.

Furthermore, twentieth-century readers of his letters have been much struck by his revelations of moral dilemmas that seemed, astonishingly, to be repeated in more recent European history. From his letters to Atticus, and at the outbreak of the civil war when he was seriously in danger, not having sided previously with Julius Caesar, he listed several essay topics for his own consideration:

> Should a good man remain in his country even under a tyranny? Are all means justifiable to abolish a tyranny even if there is danger of ruining the state? Should one take precautions to prevent the man who has killed a tyrant from becoming one himself? Should one, if one's country is under a tyranny, try to help it by words and biding one's time or by war? Is one doing one's duty if one retires to some other place and remains there so long as one's country is under a tyranny, or should a good man brave all dangers for the sake of his country's liberation? Should one enrol oneself in the ranks of the loyalists even if one does not oneself approve of war as a means of abolishing tyranny? Should one, in public matters, share the dangers of one's benefactors and friends, even if one believes their policy to be mistaken? Should a man who has done great service to his country and has, for that very reason, incurred envy and injury, go out of his way to continue to run risks for it, or should he be permitted eventually to take thought for himself and his loved ones, abandoning endless struggles against those who have the power?[183]

It is in this light that he is seen as one of the most significant political voices in republican Rome. He has also been rightly recognized as a political and philosophical mentor for later Roman history and literature, his influence extending beneficially to

182   Ibid., p. 68.
183   See L. P. Wilkinson, *Letters of Cicero: a selection in translation* (London, 1966).

the troubled times of thirteenth-century medieval urban self-government and to the politically restive times of the Italian Renaissance during the fifteenth and sixteenth centuries. His influence as an active politician who also wrote down his political, legal and philosophical ideas enabled his views to serve as the basis of the Christian re-evaluation of Rome's significance and its ideals. His writings helped the Western political tradition to build up a complex legal and political vocabulary which would stand as the substratum of social organization until and beyond the early modern period in European history. As we shall see, for St Augustine, writing at the end of the Roman empire in the fifth century AD, as for the fifteenth- and sixteenth-century Renaissance, Cicero would be taken to have been the guide to the educated and active good life, the presenter of an ideal life to be lived in the ideal political community based on a consensus government led by the rich, the great and the good. That later Christian Europe would also recognize his naivety, not simply in terms of Roman politics but perhaps more so, in terms of his optimistic view of human nature, if well-educated to virtue, none the less made his views the ones to be reckoned with and, if possible, modified by later political theorists. His fate was to be christianized rather than rejected outright as a pagan.

His ideal statesman as *rector*, was a skilled orator who had more than mere forensic virtuosity. He was a man conscious of Rome's customary constitution and laws and he helped to build an ideal 'state' by being aware of Rome's exemplary past and the wise decisions made, not by one genius, but by many prudentially wise and politically active men, over centuries, concerning right governance. Adherence to 'the ancient constitution', brought into being and sustained by politically active men, ideologically begins with him. The larger message was that decent politicians, who aim at the good of the commonwealth which they have the privilege of governing, need to know some history. It is history of a peculiar sort, in that it charts the lives of relatively rare, even heroic, virtuous men and demonstrates, more often than not, the victory of their publicly expressed virtue over vice.[184]

In the *De re publica* Cicero came up with his own utopia to answer Plato's more imaginary ideal, and Cicero's was modelled on what he imagined, creatively, to be a 'real' period of Roman history, that of the 'golden age'. It had existed in the past and its values he wished to revive. He believed himself to be shoring up a tried and tested set of traditional values and institutions which had been built on the unwritten Roman constitution, underwritten by a universal, moral natural law. Aside from the Twelve Tables, which every Roman schoolboy memorized, we have seen that the Roman constitution was a hodge-podge of compromise and revision, a product of legal evolution and custom. This was taken to be its virtue, especially if one could read history in the exemplary and rhetorical way Cicero read it: as a progressive story of the great men in every generation knowing what was right *and doing it*. He has Cato argue in the *De re publica* (ii, 2):

> Our constitution is superior to those of other states because every one of them has been established by a single author of their laws and institutions. . . . Ours is based on the genius not of one man but of many. It was established not in one generation but in a period of centuries and ages. For there never lived a man possessed of so great genius that nothing

---

184   In rejecting this lesson, Machiavelli would provide his own peculiar reading of history. See *A History of Political Thought* volume 2, chapter 6.

could escape him; nor could the combined powers of all men living at one time possibly make all necessary provisions for the future, without the aid of actual experience and the test of time.

Cicero's legacy to Europe would be (1) his natural-law underpinnings of civil law and the 'state', (2) his justification of a harmonious 'mixed' constitution that comprises different and irreconcilable social interests based on rank, and hence maintains a society of orders, where all are subject to the law, and (3) his rationalization of the very existence of the 'state' as having been created by private owners to protect, through legal entitlement, what they have already acquired. Later European political theorists would adapt one or more of these positions to their own historical and political circumstances as their societies emerged from their Roman past. Rome set the parameters for the future and the constitutional debates would, henceforth, be in terms of imperial monarchy/tyranny on the one hand, or republicanism on the other. The contrast would be between the absolute and arbitrary exercise of government, and its limitation by law and the represented will of the people. As we shall see, by the later Middle Ages and the Renaissance, Cicero would be reread through Aristotelian eyes and a defence would be mounted in favour of the relationship between rhetoric as the art of persuading, and politics as the art of ruling a city. Ruling a city, it would be claimed, requires the ability to speak in a way that suits a community of free and equal citizens, by which would be meant republican *libertas*, freedom and equality under the law but not to equal status, wealth or power. The thirteenth to sixteenth centuries would also glorify the great political man or the *rector civitatis*, the moderator of the city's different passions and interests, who establishes and preserves the *civitas*, following Cicero's 'dream of Scipio'.

In a Rome-saturated world, Athenian democracy, as a theory or as a practice, did not stand a chance against either Roman imperialism or republicanism. It still probably does not for at least the reason that Wiedemann has given: that we are brought up to see the republic as more like the pluralist parliamentary system through which we ourselves are governed.[185] The number of contemporary states that call themselves republics, ranging geographically from North America across the European continent, are the historical, practical and theoretical heirs of ancient Rome.

---

185 Wiedemann, *Cicero*, p. vi.

6

St Augustine

The view of ancient ethics, shared by Socrates, Plato, Aristotle and the Stoics, was that the moral life *is* the good life. But the distinctive, qualitative characteristics of a given individual's moral and, therefore, good life were, for them, dependent on his own character. Dissimilar characters were themselves the products of different circumstances and the choices made within these circumstances of the means to an agreed end or value. The acknowledged dissimilarity of characters did not, however, lead ancient ethics to presume an incommensurability of values if one were to achieve moral individuality. They did not posit a radical, uniquely personal view of subjective ends as some sacred zone never to be invaded by the public, outside view.

The Stoics in particular began instead with an *a priori* claim that all animals possess pre-rational impulses of self-love, self-interest and self-awareness.[1] They then provided an account of how, for humans, reason enables a change in the understanding of the goals of action and leads to a grasp of what is truly good. Through rational self-reflection on our self-love, self-interest, self-awareness and our earlier acts which distinguish what belongs to the self and what is outside the self, a man acquires a belief about the good for man. He comes to see rationality as constitutive of his own self, so that the good is a guide to his actions, and rationality allows him to build on his subjective self-awareness so that he also develops an objective view on or about himself. This rational, objective view is open to external debate and public criteria because man is a speaker and communicator who is uniquely capable of agreeing with others, through language, about what is truly valuable and choice-worthy.

Indeed, Cicero had argued[2] that as one comes to understand one's own nature better, understanding the natural functions of one's human impulses and reason, one comes to understand that one's nature is conducive to treating the practice of virtue, the *honestum*, as an end in itself. However, this reason that supplements and guides pre-rational impulses does not exist in a vacuum. It is bound by the world as it is and by one's circumstances, and hence the freedom of deliberation and choice-making that reason gives man is circumscribed by the way things are.[3]

---

1 Cicero, *De finibus* 3.5.16: animals could not feel desires towards anything unless they possessed self-awareness and consequently felt love for themselves.
2 *De finibus* 3.7. 23–4.
3 See Cicero's theory of the four *personae* in *De officiis* (pp. 259ff, above). In general, see T. Engberg-Pedersen, 'Stoic Philosophy and the Concept of the Person', in C. Gill, ed., *The Person and the Human Mind: issues in ancient and modern philosophy* (Oxford, 1990), pp. 109–35.

If this is the case, then it was asked: in what way can one account for man's *freedom* of action and will? What is the relation between a natural determinism and free decisions? How can a reference to an individual's character or 'nature' (understood as both determining particular actions on the one hand, and being itself determined by external factors of heredity, status and environment on the other) point to a man as a morally responsible individual, free to choose and act as he freely wills? We have observed that Stoics regarded theology as the foundation of ethics and they defined the end for man as living virtuously and in conformity with nature, and in nature the divine reason was everywhere immanent. Indeed, Cicero thought Roman superiority was realized in their surpassing other peoples in piety and religious wisdom of the sort that comprehended that everything was ruled and determined by the will of gods. Some philosophers questioned whether the gods were anything but indifferent to human fortune, but Stoics insisted that the world was divinely governed for man's benefit. For them, the divine penetrates nature which man can see from the design and structure that is intelligible to reason, and this reason man shares with the divine.

There is much scholarly discussion of the Stoic doctrine of fate, that chain of events which include human volitions and which Stoics tried to accommodate to the freedom of the will or at least to the subjective 'illusion' of freedom. Cicero, while acknowledging the argument that gods foreknow men's fates, held that if the gods were truly benevolent (as he believed they were) then they would 'from all creatures hide the book of Fate' so as not to increase human misery by aggravating the pains of suffering with those of anticipation.[4] Hence, the answer to the question concerning the scope of human responsibility and free will for much of ancient ethics as a whole and, in particular, for Stoic ethics, came in their *refusal* to consider any impulses or desires as inaccessible to rational guidance and discourse.

The gradual triumph of Christianity from the first to the fourth centuries AD would change all this. By the late fourth century, for the Christian Augustine, ancient ethics would be seen as part of a perverse human fantasy of self-perfection, self-sufficient omnipotence and self-dependent autonomy. Ancient ethics exemplified man's original sin, that of pride which rejoices in private goods and a perverse self-love. Augustine would argue that for man's will to be free, it cannot be understood as autonomous. For Augustine, man's own nature and his will are mysterious to man himself and he must, therefore, recognize his dependence on an inscrutable but loving God. For Augustine, our powers of introspection lead us only to a knowledge *that* we exist, but we are not capable of a clear idea of *what* we are. If we are mysterious, even to ourselves, then we need to be freed from our 'free choice' to do as we like.

Augustine considered the ancient ethical themes concerning moral responsibility, rationality, impulse and will, and weighed them against the truths he believed to be in the Bible and the Christian tradition. Indeed, Augustine would argue that the consequences of the Fall of Adam, as related in the Old Testament book, Genesis, are that we have lost the sense and in practice, the reality, of our unity as individuals. A unified personal identity can now only be understood 'in logic'. In reality and in this life, without Christian revelation, we are nothing more than bundles of competing selves.[5] This appears to

4   See P. A. Brunt, 'Philosophy and Roman Religion', in M. Griffin and J. Barnes, eds, *Philosophia Togata I* (Oxford, 1989), pp. 174–98.

5   *De Libero Arbitrio voluntatis.* See, in general, the remarkable analysis in W. E. Connolly, *The Augustinian Imperative: a reflection on the politics of morality* (London, 1993).

be a strikingly negative and generalized reading of Cicero's description of the ordinary man who, unlike the Stoic sage or Hercules, is not and cannot be on his own an inwardly unified moral personality but, rather, plays roles which enable him to appear virtuous in his behaviour, having regulated those natural impulses that are peculiar to him by performing duties that are appropriate to his position and circumstances.[6]

Now some ancient writers like Plutarch and Seneca had already argued that instead of a continuous self there was only a series of momentary selves. In order to achieve tranquillity one avoids the disintegration into momentary selves by consciously weaving one's past life into a whole through the use of one's memory to create a biography of a continuous self.[7] But Augustine would find it impossible to sustain, through autobiographical memory, a personal continuity and a stable, objective self-knowledge. Although he believed that memory is where one meets oneself through recalling what one has experienced, Augustine thought he could not totally grasp all that he is.[8] Contrary to the view of ancient ethics that proposed man's ability to 'know himself', and his responsibility either for self-perfection in the creation of a unitary moral self, or for successfully crafting his character to suit his circumstances, Augustine insisted that we could only be inwardly certain of self-existence but not capable of grasping what we are. We remain, in this life, uncertain about the information acquired through accounts constructed by mental re-readings of our own narratives of previous events that are lodged in our memories. We can obtain no objective knowledge of ourselves. And what we know of others is even less secure. He therefore concluded that our impulses and desires are largely *inaccessible* to rational guidance and discourse. Humans may desire, but through their own efforts can never achieve, tranquillity and moral wholeness.

Hence, one of the central problems for Augustine was that of human autonomy. He took this to be a delusion of self-determination, so that politics was no more than a symptom of the multiplicity of fallen man's partial and often competing loves. He addressed the ancient question of the extent to which it is possible to treat man as having a measure of rational control over his political environment or even over his conscious, moral intentions. And he thought the extent of control was much more limited than some of the more optimistic, perfectibilist doctrines of the ancients.

But in the ancient tradition he also found a scepticism about the extent of human control over environments and selves. He was to rework aspects of Cicero's presentations of the positions of Stoicism and Scepticism to arrive at his own mature views. If one's nature, after the Fall, is mysterious, then man will always be frustrated in a search to understand whether or not his nature *is* conducive to the practice of virtue as the ancients said it was. Augustine concluded that the only 'nature' that is conducive to the practice of virtue is one which can view an account of moral development, where the moral good is seen as a priority, as intelligible and plausible. It would be intelligible and plausible if it answered this kind of person's own experiences and understanding of himself as a moral agent. But Augustine insisted that our experience of the world and others is precisely the opposite: we continuously encounter in ourselves and others inconsistent and irrational 'agents' rather than men for whom the moral good is given absolute priority. The kinds of beings we now are do not, he thought, see the moral

---

6   See above, pp. 259ff, on the four-*personae* theory of Cicero's *De officiis* (124).

7   Plutarch, *On Tranquillity* 473B–474B.

8   J. Coleman, *Ancient and Medieval Memories: studies in the reconstruction of the past* (Cambridge, 1992), chs 6 and 7.

good to be consistent with our natures. The person for whom moral good is a priority then, had to be one in whom God's grace had 'prepared', indeed, 'repaired' his nature so that he could now see moral development as intelligible and plausible. It is impossible for fallen man, autonomously and based on his experiences, to see moral development as anything other than meaningless.

We have seen that Cicero required that one be a certain kind of person, that is, have a certain kind of character that could see that other-related virtues are natural, but he clearly indicated that this is itself a divine-like quality and is differentially possessed by the wise man when compared with the ordinary, or the foolish. In the *De finibus* (3.18.59–3.22.76), Cicero provided the picture of a universe governed by divine will and where the wise man looks to the general interest rather than his own. He says that it is only men of exceptional gifts and of great ability who have a 'natural impulse' to protect humanity and, hence, are like god (3.20.66). But the wise man, even if he is taken as normative and somehow embodying the state of character to which all people, including the ordinary mass of the foolish, should aspire, *cannot* be aspired to nor his state of character achieved by the foolish, since his wisdom is a divine gift. Augustine seems to have taken this over and Christianized it. The kind of person who believes that other-related virtues are natural, plausible and intelligible, for Augustine, shows himself to be a man who has been aided and prepared for this ethical state of character by God.

During a lifetime of intense intellectual activity, Augustine undertook to present a range of interpretations of ancient philosophy, some more enthusiastically in favour of ancient wisdom than others. It was his versions of Christianized ancient philosophy that were to become the most powerful and comprehensive for the European West. Some have considered him to have been handicapped by his lack of knowledge of much of the best of ancient philosophy. His originality of mind was consequently less constrained than it might have been.[9] But Augustine was undoubtedly a genius, rhetorically and theologically. It is our concern here to discuss some of the consequences of his reflections in his later works, and notably his *City of God*, where his most consistent observations about politics may be found. It is important that we grasp something about the earlier stages in his journey before he came decisively to his final positions.

The lifetime of Augustine (AD 354–430) spanned one of the most turbulent and decisive periods in the history of the Roman 'state' and we shall see him to have been very much a Roman of his times.[10] He was one of a generation that absorbed in a highly eclectic fashion the themes that had been on the philosophical and theological agenda of pagan Graeco-Roman and Christian thinkers for more than four centuries and which stretched back to pre-Christian Stoicism and Hellenistic Judaism. Each of these 'philosophies' was influenced by a kind of Platonism that continued its development roughly contemporaneously with the rise and development of Christianity. The eclectic nature of both Christianity and Platonism in the early centuries of what we now call 'the

---

9   For one of the best philosophical studies of Augustine see J. M. Rist, *Augustine: ancient thought baptized* (Cambridge, 1994).

10   For a brief introduction see J. Coleman, 'St Augustine: Christian political thought at the end of the Roman empire', in B. Redhead, ed., *Plato to Nato: Studies in Political Thought* (Harmondsworth, 1995 [1988]), pp. 45–60; H. Chadwick, *Augustine* (Oxford, 1986); P. Brown, *Augustine of Hippo: a biography* (London, 1967). For a comprehensive historical study of the world into which Augustine was born, see R. L. Fox, *Pagans and Christians in the Mediterranean World: from the second century AD to the conversion of Constantine* (Harmondsworth, 1986).

Christian era'[11] reminds us that Christianity was not a fixed quantity from its inception to *c.* AD 600, that is, well after Augustine's death. The philosophical world of fourth-century North Africa and Italy from which Augustine came was primarily Stoic and Platonic, often in unusual alterations of these systematic teachings. Augustine appropriated an amalgam of ancient philosophies whose principle ingredient was Platonism, but Augustine's Platonism was only one kind of Platonically influenced Christian thought, arguably the most influential for the Latin-speaking and Latin-reading West. He learned much of what he knew of classical and Hellenistic Greek philosophy from Cicero's deliberate Latin popularizations, especially of Scepticism and Stoicism, while his own Platonism came largely from only a second-hand acquaintance with Plato's works, again, much of it through Cicero's writings (e.g. the *Tusculan Disputations*), from Varro, and possibly from the older Platonism of Apuleius.[12] With hindsight, we can understand the historical development of Christianity and especially its ethical and political doctrines during its first centuries as a process of continuous 'translation' of its sources.[13]

The Origins of Christianity and its Development into the Fourth Century AD

After the crucifixion by the Roman authorities in Judea of the Jew Jesus of Nazareth, Christianity as a religious sect had small beginnings. Initially it attracted the lower orders of Graeco-Roman society, men and women who left no mark on classical literature and culture of their time, other than cemeteries, burial inscriptions, some buildings and letters describing intermittent persecution by their neighbours. Born into an imperial Roman 'state' that initially had no policy of widely persecuting Christianity's adherents, early Christians likewise had no quarrel with the 'state' authorities of the Roman Empire. Those who believed that, like Jesus, they must imitate his passion and death and hence suffer death in order to be perfected and worthy of the name of Christian martyr, largely saw their acts in terms of salvation from *all* society rather than in narrowly political terms. The Christian was to undertake a life of positive witness because, with Jesus, it was believed, the final era of world history had dawned: the long-awaited messiah of Judaism had come, the day of the Lord was at hand and, as the New Testament book of Luke (chapter 12) records, 'Christians are to live like men awaiting their master', awaiting the imminent Second Coming of Christ.[14] The problem which early Christians posed to the Roman Empire was similar to that posed by Jews. Both proclaimed a universal theology for a divinely chosen people, emphasizing citizenship in an unworldly 'state' that transcended the temporally and geographically more limited boundaries of the Roman Empire.

11   AD = anno domini; the division of chronological time into BC and AD was crystallized only during the sixth century and became widespread only in the eighth century.
12   C. Stead, 'Augustine's Philosophy of Being', in G. Vesey, ed., *The Philosophy in Christianity* (Cambridge, 1989), pp. 71–84.
13   J. Coleman, 'The Christian Platonism of St Augustine', in A. Baldwin and S. Hutton, eds, *Platonism and the English Imagination* (Cambridge, 1994).
14   For a general discussion of the mentality of early Christian martyrs see J. Coleman, *Against the State: studies in sedition and rebellion* (Harmondsworth, 1995 [1990]), ch. 3. On the confrontation between ancient paganism and early Christianity see E. R. Dodds, *Pagan and Christian in an Age of Anxiety* (Cambridge, 1965); R. MacMullen, *Christianizing the Roman Empire* (New Haven, CN, 1984).

Two famous and complementary texts of the New Testament, written during the first century AD, provide a clue to the major problems with which Christianity, as a break-off sect of Judaism, would have to deal in its confrontation with Rome. The first is from Matthew 22:15–22, and the second from St Paul's Letter to the Romans:

> Then went the Pharisees and took counsel how they might entangle him in his talk. And they sent out unto him their disciples with the Herodians, saying, Master, we know that thou art true, and teachest the way of God in truth, neither carest thou for any man: for thou regardest not the person of men. Tell us therefore, what thinkest thou? Is it lawful to give tribute unto Caesar or not? But Jesus perceived their wickedness and said, Why tempt ye me, ye hypocrites? Show me the tribute money. And they brought unto him a penny. And he saith unto them, Whose is this image and superscription? They say unto him, Caesar's. Then saith he unto them, Render therefore unto Caesar the things which are Caesar's; and unto God the things that are God's. When they had heard these words, they marvelled and left him and went their way.

Caesar has a certain authority over men, but not total authority. In contrast to the unity of paganism in which religion and 'state' were one, the Christian had a dual allegiance, on the one hand to the 'state' and on the other to God, whose representation on earth and in historical time would come to be the institutional church. To Caesar, the 'state', the Christian renders up the money on which is engraved the image of secular authority. He pays his taxes, obeys governors and the law. But to God, he renders the image of God that the Bible says is in man, man having been created in God's own image.[15] He does this by suffering no less patiently for his faults as for his good deeds for which he may suffer wrongly in the world. Two kinds of obligation of unequal value are demanded of him by two independent institutions to which correspond the duality of the human being, his spiritual and his material nature. But the obedience to governors and masters is not an end in itself; it is a means by which the Christian accepts his suffering servitude to God, following in Christ's own steps. In the case of a conflict of duties, he is to follow the duty that he owes to God rather than to men.[16]

In chapter 13:1–7 of his Letter to the Romans St Paul elaborated on the lessons of obedience to superiors, saying:

> Let every soul be subject unto the higher powers. For there is no power but of God: the powers that be are ordained of God. Whosoever therefore resisteth the power, resisteth the ordinance of God: and they that resist shall receive to themselves damnation. For rulers are not a terror to good works, but to the evil. Wilt thou then not be afraid of the power? Do that which is good, and thou shalt have praise of the same: for he is the minister of God to

---

15 Genesis 1:26–7: 'And God said, Let us make man in our image; after our likeness. . . . So God created man in his own image, in the image of God created he him; male and female created he them.'

16 1 Peter 2:13–23: 'Submit yourselves to every ordinance of man for the Lord's sake: whether it be to the king, as supreme; or unto governors, as unto them that are sent by him for the punishment of evildoers and for the praise of them that do well. For so is the will of God that with well doing ye may put to silence the ignorance of foolish men: as free, and not using your liberty for a cloak of maliciousness, but as the servants of God. . . . Servants be subject to your masters with all fear; not only to the good and gentle but also to the froward. For this is thankworthy, if a man for conscience toward God endure grief, suffering wrongfully. . . . For even hereunto were ye called: because Christ also suffered for us, leaving us an example, that ye should follow his steps. [Christ] committed himself to him that judgeth righteously.'

thee for good. But if thou do that which is evil, be afraid: for he beareth not the sword in vain: for he is the minister of God, a revenger to execute wrath upon him that doeth evil. Wherefore ye must needs be subject, not only for wrath, but also for conscience sake. For this cause pay ye tribute also: for they are God's ministers, attending continually upon this very thing. Render therefore to all their dues: tribute to whom tribute is due; custom to whom custom; fear to whom fear; honour to whom honour.

These first-century messages to Christians advocated submission to human institutions in virtue of their moral, indeed, divine mission. The duty of obedience to secular powers set up by God as ministers of his ways in the world is proclaimed, rather than resistance to secular and pagan authority. Order in the world is instituted by God's will and authority, and especially if it appears just, it is the true instrument of the divine will. If it appears unjust, it is none the less a true instrument of the divine will, either as a chastisement to fallen men or as a means to suffering, like Christ, as God's servants. Furthermore, an acceptance of status hierarchies in the political world was to be reconciled with a more universal, spiritual claim that a distinction between Greek and Christian, Jew and Gentile, slave and master was no longer to be observed.[17] Each is individually obliged before Christ, who recognized no distinction of person. Baptism was the means to transcend all temporal frontiers of race, sex, nation and social rank. Transforming the Stoic tradition of the equality of human nature among all men, free or unfree, Christians insisted that it was Christ's recognition of each and all that ensured universal equality. In historical time, slaves indeed submit to their masters, but each is regarded, in terms of eternity, as equal before God. As St Paul said (1 Corinthians 20–2), 'Let every man abide in the same calling to which he was called. Wast thou called, being a bondman? Care not for it, but if thou mayest be made free, use it rather, for he that is called in the Lord, being a bondman, is the free man of the Lord'. Early Christian liberty was, no less than Socratic and Stoic liberty, an internal disposition.

One might think that the Roman authorities would have been satisfied with this outward allegiance to secular authority. But by the third century at least, many Romans came to see Christianity as a new social movement and a secret society. Roman authors (e.g. Celsus, Minucius Felix) noted the abhorrence that Christians felt for other religions, pagan and Jewish, throughout the empire, which went against imperial toleration of the polytheism that was paganism. They also observed the exclusive Christian love for one another and their sometimes heroic endurances in the face of violence and torture. The emperor Domitian charged them with atheism, by which was meant their apparent uninterest in the survival of the Roman 'state' and its law, and their lack of conviction, even disdain, for the belief that the Roman 'state' was immortal. Instead, they were perceived as having a noxious psychology of an exclusive, gathered church with its martyrs and saints, living in the hope of a millennial triumph over all earthly kingdoms. Christ had said, after all, that his kingdom was not of this world. But unlike the Jews, who had a story to tell as an existing nation with a tradition of obedience or disobedience to God during centuries of organized political life, Christians considered themselves to be a new nation, created through voluntary baptism rather than through a 'state's' laws. Their own sacred writings showed them to rejoice in their own suffering, afflictions and persecution (Acts) and to have adopted a

---

17   Paul's Letter to the Colossians 3:10–11.

policy of non-resistance, suffering the wrongs inflicted in the present world, rather than retaliating.[18]

If Socrates had not been able to convince Athenians of the virtue of the position that it was better to suffer than inflict suffering and wrong, and Cicero, likewise, through his philosophical writings had failed to impress fellow Romans that retaliations would only destroy the republic and would not serve men in terms of what is both useful to them and true in itself, then the uneducated women, slaves and the lower orders who were attracted to this Christian message had even less of a chance. Their adherence to a belief that history would soon end, probably in the conflagrations described metaphorically in the Bible's Book of Revelation by St John, likewise alienated them from contemporary Roman culture. And their belief in the resurrection after death was seen as an incomprehensible cult which treated torture with contempt. Gradually, but seemingly inevitably, Christians came to be perceived as threatening Roman social stability. When third-century Roman emperors attempted to unite the empire by a religious reform which instituted the cult of the unconquered Sun, *sol invictus*, as a national religion that would absorb all the different sects of paganism but without excluding other gods, Christians refused. They would not take part in public cults and worship the state as a religious entity as was now required of Romans who had come to see their historical embodiment as divine, their history as a religious and natural necessity, united to a divine Caesar.

The Roman world was polytheistic: one sees this even in the writings of Cicero who uses the Stoic language of a single, all-encompassing divine power from which natural law for men and nature flows. After Cicero's republic was destroyed, Rome, pagan but religious, became a divine-right, absolutist monarchy. The peace that had endured for several centuries in Rome's empire, from the principate that was inaugurated by Caesar Augustus just after Cicero's death until the third century AD, was known as the *pax Romana* and it was thought to be ensured by a combination of the institutions of the Roman 'state', enshrined in Roman law, and its civic religion. A Roman's religion and his contribution to the preservation of the 'state' were intertwined. Morality and religion were public expressions, as were political activities in the Senate and law courts. But Christianity was thought by pagans to teach a private religion on the one hand, and a public political stance on the other, and this was regarded as somehow treasonous because it implied that Christians, like the Jews, in their very hearts cared little for the survival of Roman institutions, customs and values. Their eyes were fixed on an apocalyptic vision after history, on another united society in heaven and after Rome.

Educated, upper-class Romans continued to study the Greek philosophers, and a revived Platonism, often with mystic elements, attracted them.[19] The few educated men who became Christian, like Clement of Alexandria (*fl.* 192–217), thought of Christianity as the revelation of the ultimate reality, the final philosophy for all men. Especially in the Greek-speaking East of the Roman Empire, in places like Antioch and Alexandria where the ancient philosophical Greek traditions were strongest since the language of philosophy was the same as that spoken daily, an Apologist tradition developed to show

---

18 M. Whittaker, *Jews and Christians: Graeco-Roman views*, Cambridge Commentaries on Writings of the Jewish and Christian World 200 BC to AD 200 (Cambridge, 1984).

19 For an overview see C. Stead, *Philosophy in Christian Antiquity* (Cambridge, 1994).

how Christianity was the further step along the road to truth that had been begun by Plato and his followers: Stoics, middle Platonists and Neoplatonists. In the second and third centuries these Apologists employed an allegorical method of interpreting the Bible in order to argue that Christianity was in fact a highly sophisticated philosophy that could and should appeal to any well-educated Hellenistic population. It is largely due to Alexandrian efforts that the Christian message was gradually adopted by the learned and powerful in the extended Roman Empire.

Early Christian Philosophical Theology

Indeed, the precursor and to a great extent source of Christian Platonic thinking was the Jew Philo of Alexandria (*d.* 50 AD), an older contemporary of St Paul.[20] As a prototype of the Jewish philosopher who absorbed the Greek philosophical tradition of his day in order to render Jewish religious teaching as a philosophy to Greek-speaking Jews in Alexandria, Philo spoke of the 'philosophy' of Moses as set forth in Genesis. He used the Greek translation of the Hebrew Bible (Septuagint) and perfected an allegorical interpretation of the biblical texts to demonstrate an inner, spiritual meaning about the human condition and man's quest for salvation. His language is shot through with elements of Stoicism and Platonism, providing us with a type of discourse that would become prominent among early Christian philosophical theologians, aspects of which would reappear four centuries later in Augustine's own meditations. Philo allows us to become familiar with one of the dominant ways in which the ancient philosophical tradition was to be absorbed by the early church.

Philo, St Paul and Platonism

Philo was convinced of the hierarchically arranged and numerical orderliness and uniformity of nature and the cosmos. He thought that the beginning of a knowledge of God's existence could be deduced from the design and rationality of nature to which all races assent. Hence, the world/cosmos is in harmony with the divine law (ten commandments) and the law with the cosmos, this law regulating man and nature. The human mind is somehow akin to God being made in the image of the divine Logos or reason, and therefore has some capacity for the reception and discovery of the transcendent truth about realities beyond time, space and the text of Genesis. The human mind that is possessed by love and longing for wisdom has within its reach some understanding of those ideas that transcend our capacity for speech and hearing; Philo, like Augustine, believed that there is no creaturely language that is adequate to express the being of the transcendent Creator who wills only the good.

Philo spoke of how God's voluntary benevolence creates the cosmos out of nonbeing by ordering formless and chaotic matter and by not denying a share in his own nature and goodness to his creation, which is capable of becoming all things but which,

20   R. Williamson, *Jews in the Hellenistic World: Philo*, Cambridge Commentaries on Writings of the Jewish and Christian World 200 BC to AD 200, vol. 1, pt 2 (Cambridge, 1989).

apart from the divine generosity, could obtain nothing by itself. He argued that God stamps a pattern of order and rationality – his Logos – on his creation, which is a dependent, material, mutable and non-eternal world. But this material, sensible world mirrors an intelligible realm of ideas which are God's incorporeal thoughts. Philo, like Plato (*Timaeus*) draws an analogy between God and an architect who sketches the details of a perfect city in his own mind, and this is possibly the earliest reference to identify the Platonic doctrine of Ideas *as* God's thoughts. Furthermore, he distinguishes between the two Platonic sensible and intelligible worlds, with God as the One transcendent Creator who, although loving, personal, and the cause only of good, is also too remote for any direct contact with his creation. The remote transcendent God of late Platonism requires a second, metaphysically inferior aspect of himself to contact the lower world; the gulf between the Creator and his creatures requires mediation. But God, being both above the world and also a vital force pervading it through his Logos – also called the idea of ideas or the first begotten Son of the uncreated Father – ensures that his Logos serves as a pattern and mediator of creation. The Logos is the archetype of human reason, serving as God's mediating revelation to the created order, standing midway between the transcendent One and his creation. The created cosmos is arranged as a hierarchical continuum of grades of being and is held together by the immanent power of the Logos, a second God, the 'man of God', the image of the divine word, the interior divine teacher of Moses. Philo's Logos not only anticipated the Christological terminology of St Paul in Colossians 1:15, where Paul refers to he 'who is the image of the invisible God, the first born of every creature', but also the terminology of later Platonisms (notably that of Plotinus). Philo's Logos would have a great future in Christian doctrine. That the divine word could be mediated through its image, a gift of inspiration to man, would also lead Augustine to emphasize the importance of language as a means to the ineffable truth beyond oral speech and written text.

The goal of the religious quest, for Philo, is the vision of God, an absorption in the thought of the divine and a union with it. This is a mystical experience of mind contemplating God's immutable being in wordless mental prayer. Anticipating St Paul, he speaks of the transcendent God as a dazzling light that blinds the soul. What the human mind is capable of is the knowledge *that* God is but not *what* he is. The beginning of the mind's knowledge is a philosophical contemplation of the world, ascending upwards from the sensible to the intelligible and eternal world by means of a rational control, a spiritual discipline, of the body. The Platonist opposition between mind and body reappears as an antithesis between spirit and matter, one law for the mind and another for the senses, a view reiterated by St Paul.[21] Philo describes a true inwardness of the contemplative soul, possible through a frugal life that inclines towards an ascetic and strict self-control, a way of virtue that is learnt first by dealing with others, sharing God's gifts with neighbours and fellow men. This is the beginning of a true assimilation to God which parallels the ideal in Plato's *Theaetetus* (176 A–B). Thereafter, a withdrawal to a higher contemplative life, a true inwardness takes over to which externals are irrelevant for the pure soul which dwells in the body as a tomb. Here, as with St Paul, circumcision must be that of the heart (Romans 2:29). And if God is to be known it is because he makes himself

---

21   Romans 7:23: 'But I see another law in my members, warring against the law of my mind, and bringing me into captivity to the law of sin which is in my members.'

known by grace when he grants revelation in accordance with the varying capacities of the recipient.

For Philo, the Socratic maxim learnt from the divine oracle, 'know thyself', is an awareness of creaturely dependence on God. We are nothing which we have not received. Philo argues that if, by his fall, Adam lost immortality, and sin is now congenital even in the best of men, then a philosophical journey must be undertaken where the soul is a pilgrim in this life, using but not possessing the world, living a life of spiritual self-discipline of the body . This philosophical journey is superceded by faith, the decision of the will to restrain the passions until there is an absence of passion, and he takes Moses as an example. The faith which supercedes philosophical self-education ends in a knowledge of God that ultimately is not achieved through a *paideia* of the soul, the quest of inferential philosophical reasoning, but rather, by an intuition that is offered by God's grace.[22]

Philo draws on the oracular and ecstatic language of Plato's *Ion, Phaedrus* (244e, 245e) and the *Symposium*, describing the soul's frenzied rapture as it is caught up in contemplation of the eternal ideas. His description of the mystical union with the ineffable One through a final negation of thought and a negation of consciousness will contribute to the Neoplatonism of later centuries. To the contemplative soul, free from the distractions of the senses, God appears as a triad which foreshadows the Christian doctrine of the trinity. In the end, the soul, having risen from the sensible to the invisible, immaterial world of God and, when filled with grace, will 'go outside itself', mind being displaced by the divine spirit.

Philo's elaborate correlations of biblical revealed religion and Platonist philosophy are not thought to have greatly influenced Judaism, but they were to have a profound influence on the form and content of Christian Greek and later Latin writings. It is not surprising that this Platonizing Jewish exegete would be seen by those charged with the development of Christian doctrine to have been something of a 'naturally Christian soul'. In the fourth century, the Greek-reading St Ambrose, whose influence on Augustine we shall see was decisive, quoted from and paraphrased Philo's writings to a considerable extent, and noted how Philo's language matched that of the Gospel of John, the Epistle of James, and especially St Paul, the other decisive influence on Augustine.

Philo frequently referred to atheists and sceptics in his time who were unmoved by philosophical–religious assertions of a divine creation and an ordered hierarchy of being from the sensible to the intelligible, overarched by a transcendent, creative One. But against this scepticism, most ancient Greek and Roman people lived, like Jews and early Christians, in a universe which included a large and varied unseen world integrated into the visible. The holy was not remote and the divine was always there. The varied and non-cohesive range of cults and observances of educated paganism taught, as did, for instance, the Stoics who became increasingly open to Platonist influences, how the divine principle and cause of the world, the Logos, penetrated all that exists. They also believed that the cosmos was somehow divine in character, that the Old Testament and ancient Greek 'prophets' along with Socrates had heard the divine voice, that a more personal relationship to God was possible for educated religious people, and that a certain *paideia*, an education of the soul that was relieved from the fetters of the body, was

22   *Legum Allegoriae* III, 135–6.

available in the doctrines of the various philosophical religions on offer. Cicero, we recall, had himself spoken of a city common to gods and men.[23]

But if Stoicism placed high on its agenda the relationship between determinism and providence, attempting to locate the place of man's free will within a larger cosmic determinism, both Philo and St Paul stopped short. For them, to have free will was not the same as to be free. Freedom in God was not achieved through a wilful toiling towards spiritual perfection but was dependent on the additional gifts of revelation and grace. A process of self-perfection according to a literal adherence either to the laws of religion or to the philosophical laws of spiritual ascent would not be successful. The Plato of the *Republic* who spoke of the strict education of a selected group of naturally capable minds, educated in mathematical and ultimately dialectical methods that would enable them to pierce the intelligible realm and see the essences or Forms, the immutable truth, had little to say either to Philo or St Paul. For them, true religion superceded all philosophy. For them, an intuitive knowledge of God came by grace, written in the heart, not in books or stone tablets. But where Philo appeared to speak of a select few who are sufficiently pure to receive God's grace, Paul opened out the field of the truly saved to all who converted to Christ, so that 'all may be inspired'. Early Christian churches, then, answered the Hellenistic Jew's question about how to reconcile Hebraic religion with Greek philosophy by following St Paul, a converted Hellenized Jew himself, who told them to outgrow Palestine and extend the Christian mission not only to Greek ears but also to the Romans (Gentiles).

For we know that the law is spiritual; but I am carnal, sold under sin. (Romans 7:14)

Now the Lord is that Spirit and where the spirit of the Lord is there is liberty. But we all, with open face, beholding as in a glass the glory of the Lord are changed into the same image from glory to glory even as by the Spirit of the Lord. (2 Corinthians 3:17–18)

But though our outwards man perish, yet the inward man is renewed day by day. (2 Corinthians 4:16)

While we look not at the things which are seen but at the things which are not seen, for the things which are seen are temporal but the things which are not seen are eternal. (2 Corinthians 4:18)

Platonism's two realms, the sensible and the intelligible, the changing and the eternal unchanging, underlie St Paul's vision in his writings (especially to the Romans and the Corinthians). Indeed, St Paul says of himself: 'I am debtor to the Greeks and to the barbarians; both to the wise and to the unwise' (Romans 1:14). He was also proud to be a Roman citizen. But where the Pythagorean influence on Platonism encouraged a rational correlation between number and order in the cosmos, St Paul accepts the divine order but does not think it open to rational scrutiny. Instead, men must *believe* in God's orderly disposing of all things in number, weight and measure but God's judgements are often inscrutable. It is for this reason that St Paul establishes his attitude to superior powers and sets in train the Christian perspective on political obligation, saying: 'Let every soul be subject unto the higher powers; for there is no power but of God; the

---

23 'The dream of Scipio', *De re publica* vi, and *De legibus* I, 23; see R. A. Markus, *The End of Ancient Christianity* (Cambridge, 1990).

powers that be are ordained of God' (Romans 13:1–7). Instead of a confidence in the noetic capacities of the rare philosophic mind, St Paul assured his readers that *true belief* was sufficient for the vision of God. True believers may be inspired with a knowledge that surpasses the rational knowledge of the philosopher. For St Paul, 'the just shall live by faith' and 'having then gifts differing according to the grace that is given us, whether prophecy, let us prophesy according to the proportion of faith' (Romans 12:6). As we shall see, St Paul's conclusions would be those adopted by Augustine after Augustine's own long and arduous philosophical journey that, in the end, he would come largely to repudiate.

The Pagan Philosopher and the Educated Christian

The traditional figure of the philosopher, however, continued to furnish late antiquity, both pagan and Christian, with the model life. It was the philosopher who could come as near as possible on earth to the good life and his dedicated pursuit of wisdom pointed the way to its full realization in the next. This ought not to surprise us since Christians and pagans underwent the same education. A cultivated education meant a knowledge of the Greeks – Plato and Parmenides – and the Romans – Virgil and Livy. Perhaps the chief difference was that for the Christian, his interest in philosophy was not a professional one since he already believed he had the ultimate religious philosophy in the gospel.[24] But when Christian literature addressed pagan literates, it used Socrates and Plato as philosophers and parallels were drawn between Socrates and Christ. With the second century, a great revival of Plato occurred everywhere in the Greek-speaking part of the Roman Empire and 'the divine Plato' was presented as the supreme religious and theological authority; but this was not the Plato of the *Republic* with his social theories, but rather the Plato of the *Timaeus* who spoke of Forms, the Ideas, which could be interpreted as the thoughts of God.

If the sacred texts of the Bible were read at first not in Hebrew but in Greek, Christianity's future would be expressed in the language of its sacred texts, interpreted by philosophical minds who could appeal to those who would reject the numerous alternative religious sects in the empire. Through the writings of second- and third-century Christian Apologists, particularly in Alexandria and Athens, namely Clement, Origen, the Cappadocians and Porphyry, the gospel message was first adapted to the ears and minds of Greek speakers. Adopting the Stoic desire to see all mankind as a brotherhood, in some sense capable of perfection and thus salvation, they argued first against the polytheist pagan Greek populace, then against those Gnostic Christians who affirmed that salvation and *gnosis* was available only to an elect, uninstitutionalized, perfect few, and finally, they set out a specific analysis of the Christian life of perfection, capable of fulfilment in this life as preparation for the next. Clement of Alexandria was foremost in broadcasting a message of philosophical hope to all men, Greek and Gnostic Christian alike, that an appropriate interpretation of the sacred texts of the Old and New Testaments could lead to the perfect life where men would be made one with God.

Greek-speaking Christians were told to study Greek literature and especially to quote from Plato's dialogues, rejecting much of the moral and religious content but praising its

---

24   See Markus, *The End of Ancient Christianity*.

form and emphasizing how a true Christian spiritual education is the fruit of a trained nature. True Christian *paideia*, an education of the soul, purified it, turned it away from self-delusion and ignorance, and could lead to a final restoration and assimilation to God, which was undoubtedly the life-long quest of he who wished to contemplate God in perfect union with him. Begin the education of the soul with the rhetoric and philosophy of the Greeks and pass on to the study of the Bible. Through a literal, then historical, and finally a spiritual reading of texts, a Christian is gradually transformed, his soul perfected, ascending through the grades of a mystical way until he reaches the highest point in his journey.

The best environment for this spiritual ascent was held to be that of the ascetic movement, based on a monastic ideal that became popular during the third century in Asia Minor and the Near East. This monastic, ascetic tradition would soon attract the Latin West. Its philosophical mixture of Platonism and ascetic Christianity, where the body with its desires becomes increasingly detached from the soul and its desires, was held to lead to that inner freedom of which Paul had spoken when, in Romans 12:2, he had advised: 'Do not be conformed to this world'. Through ascetic restraint and introspective contemplation the soul would be led to its true fulfilment, its enjoyment of God. For this kind of Christian Platonism there was to be no frontier between philosophy and theology because the subject of true philosophy was said to be nothing less than the study of God and the human soul.

This Greek-speaking Christian Platonism would come to Rome, having been preceded by non-Christian Platonisms, and especially that of the Egyptian Greek Plotinus (who died in 270 AD at Rome). For those Latin-readers whose Greek was perhaps inadequate, Platonist texts would be subject to excerpts and translations during the fourth century. Italy, in contrast to the Greek-speaking Eastern part of the empire, had been an intensely conservative, under-Christianized region where active pagan worship played a major part in public life until the end of the fourth century. There was not a different culture to distinguish Christians from their pagan contemporaries other than their religion. But extraordinary things were to occur in the Latin West of the fourth century which encouraged an increasing insecurity over the question of where religion ends and long-enduring secular customs and traditions begin.

Christianity in the Byzantine Greek East and in the Latin West

Early in the century the emperor Constantine had issued his so-called Toleration Edict of Milan (313), which established the Christian faith on an equal footing with other, pagan religions. Constantine, thereafter, personally converted to Christianity.[25] Post-Constantinian Christians, in what was still an overwhelmingly pagan society, thought that they could now take for granted not only that they would no longer be persecuted but that the church would receive due recognition. If Christianity had begun as a lower-class religion, by the mid-fourth century it had succeeded in converting members of the middle classes. It had become increasingly advantageous to be a Christian in order to win status in civil service positions: Peter Brown has written of Christianity having seeped upwards to create

---

25 The evidence of much that culminated in the Constantinian age comes from two Christian authors, Lactantius and Eusebius.

a court aristocracy of *parvenus*.[26] And these opportunities had themselves been created because Constantine had done something that was of more long-term importance than officially tolerating Christians. He had also moved the administrative centre of the empire out of Rome and eastward, to Constantinople (today, Istanbul), because Roman Italy maintained, in contrast to the Byzantine East, a relatively more sustained pagan adherence to non-Christian traditions. Constantinople was the New Rome and it had been designed to replace Old Rome, heralding the separation of East from West within the Roman world. There was to be no permanent imperial presence in the city of Rome (the Western imperial residence had been moved to Milan in 383) and a pagan administration in Rome was perpetuated. Constantine thereafter brought the church within the ambit of imperial 'state' authority, not least by summoning and closely supervising various ecclesiastical councils to resolve doctrinal questions (at Arles and Nicaea). In the relative backwater of Italy, the church was to emerge as the major institutional organization in a 'state' whose centre was elsewhere, until the imperial 'state' itself became Christian.

When this was decreed in 380 AD, Roman military control in the West was in the process of being lost. This is because, well before the fourth century, Germanic Gothic tribes had disrupted imperial control on the Rhine and the Danube, and after numerous advances, by the 370s, the Visigoths were permitted, by treaty, to occupy lands south of the Danube. They were settled in large numbers within the empire and although many had adopted Christianity, they had been drawn to the heretical form known as Arianism. Tribes occupied imperial territory in both the east and west as federates and their leaders were granted imperial titles, while their sons were given a thoroughly Roman education at an imperial court. By the later fourth century, many Christianized Goths had long been exposed to Roman traditions and had made successful careers, particularly in the Roman army or as mercenary forces. Military commanders of non-Roman origins became respectable, rose in Roman society and intermarried with Romans. But the Gothic tribes continued to seek fertile lands, notably in Italy, and the Roman Senate refused either to make compromises or to buy them off. The consequences were that Alaric, the Arian Christian Visigothic leader, was able to defeat the imperial army and he captured and sacked Rome in 410.[27]

Christianity had succeeded in becoming the official religion of the entire empire by imperial decree in 380 AD, but especially in the Latin West this occurred amid increasing pressure from Gothic tribes on the one hand, and a rear-guard traditionalist set of attitudes in an emperorless Roman Senate on the other. Rome had remained the largest and richest city of the West, and aristocratic families, having been excluded from the life of the court and imperial power, sought to maintain the old pagan traditions. A great senatorial debate ensued over whether the altar of the Roman goddess Victory, taken to be a symbol of Rome's honourable expansion and extension of Roman law to all her territories, should be removed from the Senate. Christians argued that a newly Christian state would not wish to worship pagan military victories and virtues and the altar was removed. Christian intolerance of pagans and Jews reached something of a resolution by 392, when all pagan cults were declared illegal. The church had increasingly found itself in a position to clarify what precisely was Caesar's and what was God's, inaugurating the beginning of a conscious delimiting of spheres of influence of secular political power and

---

26   P. Brown, *Religion and Society in the Age of St Augustine* (London, 1972).
27   For the historical background see J. Herrin, *The Formation of Christendom* (Oxford, 1987).

universal spiritual power. Thereafter, Christian theories of government and rulership were to be developed, especially in the imperial East, to accommodate a Christian imperial power. The debate over the rightful jurisdictions of church and state began in earnest, and, with the help of Augustine's views, the debate – if not his proposed resolutions – would last well into the modern era.

When Rome became Christian at the end of the fourth century, several Christian theologians and historians, among them St Ambrose, Orosius, Prudentius, Lactantius and Eusebius, the Bishop of Caesaria, became intoxicated with the vision of the Christian empire having been realized in their own times. Eusebius set about writing the history of the first three centuries of the church in the belief that Rome itself had been revitalized, redivinized and resacralized as a political order. A Christian Rome would indeed make Rome eternal and this was seen as the next step in the divine history of humankind. Augustine would gradually come to disagree with this view and he would make his views known in his *City of God*.

But a century after his death, Augustine's own considered and mature views about the less than perfect natures of the historical church and state would be modified, even rejected, in favour of a theory of the theocratic state. In structure, this theocratic theory would owe a great deal to Byzantine political thought and the optimistic views of Eusebius on Constantine's having established a Christian empire as a turning-point in human history. The classic exposition of the divinely derived power of the Christian Roman emperor would thereafter be expressed in the sixth-century emperor Justinian's collection of the *Corpus iuris civilis* (the codification of Roman civil law) with its emphasis on imperial power, entrusted to the Christian emperor and derived directly from God's command. Imperial law would come to be regarded as sacred and the emperor's will expressed itself as a 'living law'.[28] As we shall see, Augustine was not to go this far, in part because he was addressing another range of issues peculiar to Christian perspectives in the Latin West, most notably in North Africa.[29]

The 'Ascetic Takeover' in the Latin West: St Ambrose

We are able to grasp something of the temper of the mid to late fourth century in the Latin West by observing the increasing polarization of pagan and Christian public opinion around an old pagan aristocracy that was itself penetrated from below by new families who had risen to nobility through service and patronage. A striking number of women from these newly ennobled families were converted to Christianity. As patrons of individual writers and distributors of wealth, numerous rich and aristocratic widows acted as lay patrons to the church and as arbiters of intellectual life to a degree unknown in the Greek East. In this milieu St Ambrose was born, the son of a Christian praetorian prefect.[30]

28 See *A History of Political Thought* volume 2, chapter 1.
29 Brown, *Religion and Society*; Herrin, *The Formation of Christendom*; A. Momigliano, ed., *The Conflict between Paganism and Christianity in the Fourth Century* (Oxford, 1963); R. L. Fox, *Pagans and Christians*; MacMullen, *Christianizing the Roman Empire*; Markus, *The End of Ancient Christianity*, all for detailed background on this period. Also see the contributions of H. Chadwick, D. M. Nicol and R. A. Markus in J. H. Burns, ed., *The Cambridge History of Medieval Political Thought c. 350–c. 1450* (Cambridge, 1988) and the extensive bibliography therein.
30 P. Brown, *The Body and Society: men, women and sexual renunciation in early Christianity* (London, 1989), especially ch. 17 on Ambrose.

Ambrose had been a child in Rome during the 340s but his career led him to Milan where he became governor of Liguria. In 374 he was chosen bishop of the church in Milan. During his earlier career as a Roman senator he had become aware of philosophical study groups and he was unusual among his aristocratic contemporaries in having learnt Greek. He had read the works of Philo, Origen and Plotinus, perhaps in predigested Christian extracts. He was also familiar with the sermons of the Greek Christian Apologist tradition and his own sermons, when bishop, would be comprehensively indebted to their Christian Platonism. He wrote his sermons in a Latin that was didactic and displayed the declamatory eloquence that had been expected in the Senate. Like Cicero, who had addressed the world through his letters to his friend Atticus, Ambrose also wrote letters to his sister Marcellina, a consecrated virgin who lived at home with their mother, and through these letters he spoke to Roman Christians. Along with sermons, the epistolary tradition so dear to educated Romans would flower abundantly among fourth- and fifth-century Latin-speaking Christians, to produce those models of public self-revelation as St Jerome's letters to various aristocratic Roman women, and supremely, Augustine's most famous autobiographical letter to God, his *Confessions*.

From Philo, Origen and Plotinus, St Ambrose absorbed the fundamental antithesis between soul and body and he identified St Paul's war between flesh and spirit with the Platonist opposition between body and mind. He argued that man's mind is superior to his body which is a mere 'veil'. Not only is the body a veil but a 'perilous mudslick' symbolizing the tragic frailty of the body, enticing the will to slip. But because Christ sits in the inner person, having come to humanity in human flesh and thereby mediating the antithesis between heaven and earth, man can, even in this life, still the body's instincts. Through baptism, 'the putting on of Christ', the weakened human flesh could be mysteriously exchanged for reformed flesh that was made perfect by having been taken up in Christ by God himself. St Ambrose believed that Christ's body was 'unscarred' by sexuality, for through the virgin birth he was an example of life untainted by sexual origin and sexual desire. Ambrose considered that baptism and sexual continence promised man restoration at the Resurrection, when the flesh would have all its flaws removed from it. Human nature would then rest in the high happiness of life untouched by death.

Two notable and influential Ambrosian positions are clear and they characterize a Latin, Western development in Christian understanding. He emphasizes, far less than the Greek tradition, that long purification of the soul through spiritual *paideia* and he replaces it with a swift transformation in baptism. And he narrows the Platonist notion of general bodily continence to the sexual. Both positions struck his contemporaries in one of two ways. An increasing number of extremely ascetic Christians, some demanding clerical celibacy and others, mainly pious, virgin women who regarded chastity as sacred, saw the Christian life measurably perfected through a withdrawal from sexual activity. But others, primarily successful Roman public men, rejected the explicit Ambrosian model of a hierarchy of Christian perfection, led by virgins of both sexes first, then continent widows and widowers and lastly, the married. They asked: were not all baptized Christians equally holy? The debate over the relative perfection of the married versus the celibate, virginal state, erupted and would be repeated throughout the Middle Ages and beyond, drawing on the texts of St Ambrose and St Jerome on the one side, and Jovinian (the hero of later Protestant historiography) and Helvidius, their antagonists, on the other. Augustine's own discussions of these issues, which show his views to have evolved during his lifetime, were taken as support for one side or the other.[31]

The markedly ascetic image of the Ambrosian church, a symbol of the battle of mind with sensuality, would constitute one of the main ways in which the earlier Neoplatonist concern to control the appetites through rational discipline would be transformed into a distinctive, near dualistic reading of the Platonic tradition that would enter the Latin West. Educated Romans were already prepared for the doctrine of the ascetic morality of detachment as a means to inner freedom from a reading of Cicero and Stoicism. In fact, the idea of self-mastery that results from an inner combat in which the self emerges victoriously free from passions and mundane concerns was a well-established pursuit familiar to cultivated minds.

We can also see here the beginnings of the role of the clergy in creating a spiritual elite along with different statuses among Christians that would influence the structure of church institutions during the Middle Ages and beyond. With the image of the virgin woman, body sealed but mind and heart open – to scripture, to Christ, to the poor, to Christian cultural patronage – the image of the church as a whole as virginal bride of Christ would come to dominate Christian imaginations. And the ancient philosophical discussion of the relative merits of the politically active, the theoretically contemplative and the mixed lives, so prominent in Cicero's writings, would be read increasingly as a discussion of the relative perfection of the married and celibate states.

The end of ancient Christianity occurred precisely with this fourth-century 'ascetic takeover', the desecularization of the world and discourse about it. There was a contraction in the scope that the educated, clerical representatives of Christianity allowed to the secular during the fourth and fifth centuries in the Latin West. The spread of the ascetic mentality throughout Christian society had much to do with this redrawing of the boundaries between sacred and secular in the age of St Ambrose and St Augustine. By the end of the fourth century, when Christianity was declared the religion of the Roman Empire, what had once been seen as the Constantinian reformation became for Christians – and not least, Augustine – a revolution. With the intellectual and spiritual journey undertaken by Augustine throughout his life and retold, stage by stage, in his *Confessions*, and supplemented by his mature views in the *City of God* – his encyclopedic analysis of the relation between secular history and philosophies and religious faith, God's grace and providential, predestining will – we are able to see the reformation become a revolution. What was at first an easy shift from Neoplatonism to Christianity became for Augustine a cavernous divide, a painful break with old ways, and finally, a taking of sides. If, in the pagan non-Christian Roman world, religion had touched everything, the *distinction* between the sacred and the secular was to become an essentially Christian one. Augustine is both witness to and deviser of the fourth- and fifth-century formulation in the Latin West of what was now to constitute a properly Christianized society. Augustine's lifetime spanned the beginning of a trend in which much of secular government, provincial and local administration, and secular education were running down in the western Roman provinces. With the growing prominence of the military and clerical at the expense of the civil powers, secular education was being eclipsed by a scripturally orientated culture, and this led to what Markus has called a 'draining' of the secular from

---

31 See Markus, *The End of Ancient Christianity*, pp. 41–3 for a good discussion of Augustine's middle line in these matters, his 'defence of Christian mediocrity'.

Western Europe. The spread of an ascetic mentality throughout Christian society had much to do with this redrawing of the boundaries.[32]

The mixture of a Neoplatonically inspired philosophy with an increasingly ascetically coloured Christianity would characterize Augustine's final vision of man and his relation to God. In the end, he would no longer have confidence in man's rational and moral capabilities, no matter how well educated the soul. From this late perspective, Augustine insisted that God does not command what he knows men simply cannot perform. Perfection is a very distant goal and within history, *im*perfection is man's inescapable condition. He would come to view the only virtue appropriate to man to be humility and the rise of this alternative to human pride has been seen as what truly transformed ancient ethical and political virtue to Christian virtues.[33] The consequences for Western Christianity's attitudes to the purpose and function of the 'state' and the political, to the fulfilment of a man's individual self in collectivities, to the shaping of his character as morally responsible, and notably, to the good life that was judged choice-worthy, as ancient ethics had emphasized, would be immense.

Augustine

Augustine was born in 354 in what is today Algeria. He was a rural North African Roman born to a non-Christian father and a Christian mother of humble means. Both were ambitious for their son to make something of himself through success in his studies. The atmosphere of his home appears to have been Christian but Augustine was not baptized and despite his mother Monica's constant entreaties, he found it difficult to accept her faith. He had a local, traditional, Roman education in Latin grammar and rhetoric, and went to Carthage to become a student of Latin rhetoric and then professor. This eventually led him to Rome (383) and thereafter, he became a professor of Latin rhetoric in Milan (384). His doting mother Monica followed him to Milan and stayed with him until her own death, despite Augustine having tried successfully to slip away from Carthage to Rome without her knowledge. He had been made to learn Greek as a small boy but found learning a foreign language drudgery and he hated it, preferring Latin literature, although he insists he was forced to learn that too, disliking learning as well as hating to be forced to it. It is not clear whether or not he ever mastered sufficient Greek to read Plato in the original[34] and instead he appears to have benefited from the Latin translations of Neoplatonist texts, some of which were probably produced by his near contemporary Marius Victorinus, when Augustine came upon them in Italy (*Confessions* 7, ix).

Augustine experienced a series of intellectual and spiritual conversions throughout his turbulent life. These are eloquently recalled in his work known as the *Confessions*, which he wrote *c.* 399, thirteen years after his final conversion to Catholic Christianity. It is one of the most extraordinary and moving tales of inner turbulence and self-revulsion, a quest for tranquillity that evaded Augustine all his life except once, when, after his conversion to Catholicism, he and his mother sat together in Ostia just prior to her

---

32   Markus, *The End of Ancient Christianity*, p. 17.
33   See Machiavelli's views on this, in *A History of Political Thought* volume 2, chapter 6.
34   He says he read Aristotle's *Categories*, but without formal instruction and without any profit: *Confessions* 4, xvi.

death, and lost themselves in a contemplation of God that went beyond words and beyond self-awareness. Among the many and varied things he tells the reader about his persistently divided self as he grew from infancy to adolescence and then maturity, one overriding issue concerning self-understanding is prominent: Augustine asks, 'Who will open and discover to me this most intricate and crooked knot of my perverse nature? It is deformed, I cannot endure to behold or to reflect upon it' (*Confessions* 3, x). Writing with the hindsight of a convert to Catholic Christianity more than thirteen years after the event, and reading himself as he would be read by others, his life becomes the archetypical story of man's seeking answers about his own perverse nature, seeking the sources of evil and good, and concluding with man's final inability to discover the answers about this mysterious and perverse self without divine help. His faith in the Christian God alone will enable him to secure a whole and undivided self, and he 'demonstrates' this by outlining the false starts and stops of his successive conversions. His early optimism, consisting in the belief that the goal of human striving was attainable by human effort through rationality, gets replaced by a dramatic renunciation of his past confidence in man's rational and moral capacities.

While studying Latin eloquence and, as he tells it, seeking to shine more than others, Augustine at eighteen years old came across Cicero's (now lost) *Hortensius* which exhorted him to study philosophy in order to attain immortal wisdom. His first conversion – to philosophy – established his belief in having been set on the road to discover Wisdom itself, 'whatever it might be' (*Confessions* 3, iv).

While still a young man in North Africa he then became attracted to a dualist Christian sect known as the Manichaeans, whose complicated theology centred on a battle between two opposed cosmic principles of Good and Evil, manifested as light imprisoned in matter. He tells the reader that the sect was divided between a celibate, purified Elect, and a much larger group of unpurified believers or Auditors of whom Augustine became one. Augustine's own discussion of Manicheism is an interesting revelation of what attracted Roman North African minds of the mid-fourth century: he reveals its 'puritanism', which divides the flesh from the spirit, the material darkness from the immaterial light, its belief that Adam's fall consisted in his yielding to the seductions of sex, and that Eve is eternally damned for seducing Adam. Despite this, Manichaeans held that individuals did not sin but some other nature was sinning in them, that the forces of evil, being foreign powers working within man, were not man's responsibility. Augustine describes how he too found it acceptable at the time to think of evil as bodily substance, and therefore he feared to believe with his mother that the word had been made flesh. At this time, Augustine could not see Catholic Christianity as anything other than degrading in its belief in God having taken on human flesh, so that when he left Carthage for Rome he kept up his Manichaean links.[35]

But Augustine's confidence in their doctrines after nine years of adherence began to fade and in Rome he was thereafter drawn to the study of the scepticism of the New Academy as he found it largely in Cicero's writings. When he moved to Milan he was introduced to some Platonic books (we do not know which) and he fell in with Christian Platonists. He heard bishop Ambrose preaching a Platonizing Christianity, attacking the Manichaeans, and urging his congregation to think of God and the soul as distinct

---

35   See the interesting discussion on Augustine and Manichaeaism and Platonism in B. Stock, *Augustine the Reader: meditation, self-knowledge and the ethics of interpretation* (Cambridge, MA, 1996), pp. 43–74.

from material reality. In the books of the Platonists, Augustine says he found that God and his word were everywhere implied (*Confessions* 8, ii). On hearing Ambrose, Augustine did not at first think that his own ideas on man and the universe, absorbed from Cicero and the Platonists, required any serious change. In short, Neoplatonism was not far from Christianity, focusing as each did on the soul and the intelligible world. He found it easy to move from the philosophical distinction between the sensible and the intelligible to the biblical distinction between flesh and spirit. Plato, Cicero and St Paul seem to be speaking with one another. He converted to Catholicism in Milan in 386 (*Confessions* 8, vii–xii). He had no difficulty in reconciling Plato with the Bible, identifying the stages of God's providence in history with the stages of the Platonist soul's ascent. Jewish history, as rehearsed in the books of the Old Testament, could be read as an image of the Christian people and, in consequence, he was able to provide an outline of human history in terms of universal progress. At this time, and not unlike the views of those optimistic Christians who glorified Rome's conversion, he understood history to be God's gradual education of the human race.[36]

But during the 390s Augustine took it upon himself to study scripture intensely and to re-read St Paul, following a request from his friend Simplicianus for enlightenment on the mysteries of divine election to salvation. Between the period of his conversion and his reply to Simplicianus, Augustine had returned to North Africa and by popular acclaim had been ordained to the priesthood and asked to preach. He became the bishop of Hippo. He gradually found it difficult to see how a pagan *rhetor* or a neo-platonist philosopher could pass so easily into the ranks of the Christians. He made this plain *c.* 400 when completing the *Confessions*. From then onwards, his 'philosophical models' grew increasingly to be theological hypotheses learned from scripture (e.g. the Fall of Adam), along with the authoritative beliefs and practices of the then contemporary church, although Platonism was to permeate his thought until the end.

The Gradual Emergence of Augustine's Mature Thoughts on Politics and Authority

The aim in what follows is to observe some of the shifts from philosophy to theology and the increasing importance of authority in Augustine's thinking, as expressed first in his *Confessions* and developed later in his *City of God*. Because many of his most influential reflections on politics and history emerged in their mature form in his vast *City of God*, and this is the major text on which contemporary students of the history of political thought are asked to reflect, we shall be concentrating on the gradual emergence of these mature observations along with the particular controversies in which he engaged in order to arrive at them.

First we should note that the church had come to accept a strictly limited understanding of 'sacred history' by fixing the canon of scripture so that it comprised what are now the books of the Old and New Testaments. They accepted, thereby, a particular reading

---

36   See G. Bonner, 'Augustine's Doctrine of Man: image of God and sinner', *Augustinianum* 24 (1984), pp. 495–514 for a discussion which takes account of his changing and developing views on many subjects over the years. The classic study is still R. A. Markus, *Saeculum: history and society in the theology of St Augustine* (Cambridge, 1970); also see G. Bonner, *St Augustine of Hippo: life and controversies* (Norwich, 1986).

of the history of the Jews and Jesus and assigned divine authority to this narrative alone, despite contestations from a variety of Christian groups (Gnostics, Manichees) over which books were to be taken as sacred for Christians.[37] Augustine was to alter his originally more optimistic and inclusive reading of history in order, finally, to claim that outside the narrow bounds of church-accepted scripture, no one is authorized to proclaim God's historical and providential intentions. He would also come to establish, contrary to his earlier position, that there was no sacred significance in any historical events that occurred after Christ's Incarnation which could affect the history of salvation. How did he arrive at these views?

If we begin with the *Confessions* we see that the reader is allowed to observe Augustine's reconstruction of his own intellectual and spiritual development, but we need to be reminded that this work, along with all of Augustine's texts that survive for us, are Christian. Nothing survives of his pre-conversion writings.[38] Furthermore, Augustine wrote as a controversialist and his writings grew out of arguments with his earlier self and with views that were current among his contemporaries in North Africa and throughout the wider world of the late Roman Empire.[39] It was from the local and parochial requirements of his pastoral administration of the rank and file of believers in North Africa that many of the great debates of his final years developed, notably his views on history, politics and moral agency. And it is of tremendous importance to realize that North African Christians thought themselves to be guardians of the true faith, often against Christian emperors and popes.[40] Hence, as is the case with all of the political theorists with whom we are concerned, his wide-ranging views cannot be fully appreciated if they are removed from the soil in which they grew.

Belief and Authority: The Limits of Human Certitude

Even before Augustine developed his idea of human dependence on God for the possibility of any moral behaviour, he revealed a tendency to scepticism, probably influenced most directly by Cicero's *Academics,* that led him to discuss his own experiences that confirmed for him the *limits* of human certitude. As a professional student of language and rhetoric he was struck by the comparative failures of men in their attempts to communicate with one another. It was not simply that conventional languages are insufficient to express personal thoughts and intentions, but that humans do not know their own hearts, and their own intentions are not even clear to themselves. Augustine argued that humans dwell in a world of *beliefs* rather than knowledge, inadequately passing on their thoughts, inadequately formulating their thoughts, in thrall to verbal signification that unlocks multiple meanings, all in their attempts to communicate.

Consequently, Augustine would observe that no one can teach anyone else anything at all; only God can teach. We learn what we *will* to learn and if, for instance, we say that we had not heard someone else's statement or question when we are in his presence, Augustine thinks we *did* hear but did not *will* to retain. Even in the most trivial situations, our

37   See E. Pagels, *The Gnostic Gospels* (Harmondsworth, 1979).
38   Rist, *Augustine: ancient thought baptized*, p. 8.
39   Ibid., p. 11.
40   Bonner, *St Augustine*; Markus, *Saeculum*, ch. 5.

willing, conscious attention is the consequence of a deliberate direction of our mind's gaze towards its chosen portion of its field of vision. He later explained how this comes about. He developed the view that we require God's necessary preparation of the will, an inner illumination, to direct our attention in the first place to enable us to be aware of what is there to be heard or seen. Even hearing the preaching of scripture is not sufficient to make a man a Christian with a redirected mental attention; an interior teacher, the anteriority of the knowledge of God in man, somehow stored away in his memory, is the *sine qua non* of the believer. Augustine insists that there is no meaning in scripture for the reader who has no anterior belief. Through the power of introspection humans *can* come to some degree to reach a vision of truth or God within themselves. But if the beginning of understanding is self-awareness, as the Stoics expressed it, then Augustine thinks it possible to be aware of oneself, even of the existence of the vision of truth within oneself, without understanding oneself. Like Socrates, he thinks it is possible to hold beliefs without understanding them. Introspection alone, then, only provides a recognition of the *existence* of the truth within ourselves that is God, but introspection does not provide an understanding either of our own or of the divine nature.

This discovery of God's existence through introspection may fill the philosophical place of the discovery of the formal reality behind appearances in Plato. But for Augustine it subsequently leads to a recognition of unfulfilled desires, a dissatisfaction with the *search* for truth and its replacement with the necessity of the *belief* in one's dependence on an outside, unmerited redirection of willed attention. Augustine's early description of the natural desire for God comes to be replaced by his notion that only the divine gift of grace can provide the effective orientation of the will towards human beatitude: the desire for God seen 'face to face'. Not only is God, like the Platonic Form of the Good, a cause of the real but Augustine finally gives God an additional active function of making the real (forms) knowable to men. If introspection leads to a limited self-knowledge that we exist but cannot establish a clear idea of what we are, then Augustine is sceptical about our unaided capacities to formulate, either in thought or in speech, the nature of our stable and consistent human identity. As a consequence, what we must will and do is equally inaccessible to us if we do not now grasp what we are.[41]

He developed further the Stoic notion that what matters is whether the morally right act is performed for the right reason and intention. But where the Stoics had argued that motives are to be in accord with right reason for them to be considered virtuous, Augustine's mature claim is that to perform the good act in the right spirit requires God's grace. Only acts dependent on grace are salvific and they are of a different quality and kind from those acts that are performed as 'objectively' right acts or duties. This is because a man is good not because of what he knows or does but because of what he loves. Where the Stoics had argued for the individual's *rational* assent to do the right thing, the *honestum*, Augustine thought the assent that was required was with respect to what a man loves, and without God's aid humans now cannot assent to what is truly to be loved. The human love for God must, therefore, be preceded by God's gift of love, which prepares man's will to perform a good act in an undivided way and in the right spirit.

What occurs without this grace is exemplified for him by the evident inconsistency in our behaviour. St Paul had put it thus:

---

41   See Stock, *Augustine the Reader*, 'The Self', pp. 243–78.

For that which I do, I allow not: for what I would, that do I not; but what I hate, that I do. If then I do that which I would not, I consent unto the law that it is good. Now then it is no more I that do it, but sin that dwelleth in me. For I know that in me dwelleth no good thing: for to will is present with me, but how to perform that is good, I find not. For the good that I would, I do not: but the evil which I would not, that I do. . . . I find then a law, that, when I would do good, evil is present with me. (Romans 7:15–21)

Augustine, in the *Confessions* 8, ix, puts it this way. There is some kind of dissonance interior to the human will. When one wills to be continent, and finds that one is not; when one wills not to doubt God, but one finds that one does, it is not simply that the body has not responded to the command of the will. Rather, the mind commands itself to will yet the mind does not do what it commands. The trouble is that the mind does not totally will and therefore it does not totally command. There is, then, a sickness of the soul, in effect, two wills, or a divided will, in fallen man. The source of evil and human suffering is within our will's very structure and its divided desires and loves. In effect, all humans suffer from something even more dire than what Aristotle called *akrasia*, a weakness of will. Humans show themselves to be weak through their consent to their own weaknesses. They struggle and consistently fail to do what they want to do and what they know they ought to do.[42]

Initially, in the *Confessions*, Augustine thought that our condition is one where we try but fail. He would later argue more pessimistically[43] that our condition is such that we do not even try. It is rather that the permanence of our irrational and unintelligible condition is, in modern terms, genetic. Words of praise and blame make no difference to us. We may fail in performing the morally fine act, but we also fail to have the right intentions, the right reasons, the purely moral intention. We do not and cannot conform or even aspire to the Stoic idea of the virtuous self, since it is not only our acts which are inadequate but our wills which are divisive and weak. Our motives, the desires of our will, are always mixed. There are no sages among us. It becomes clear that without some additional assistance, God's, *we cannot perform even a single perfectly good act*. A complete and undivided will cannot arise of its own accord and thinking that it can is, for Augustine, a part of the perverse and pervasive fantasy of self-omnipotence and self-sufficiency. This pride is the original sin. Indeed, when Adam was cast out of the garden of Eden with Eve, his original capacity to reason was weakened. But from now on, the determinant of man's behaviour would be less his weakened reasoning than the set of his will, his multiple and often conflicting loves and hates. He would come to worship himself as a self-sufficient knower, a determiner of his own interests and the means to their fulfilment. Augustine saw this universal scenario replayed in his own life.

Belief, Authority and Language

But if Augustine reached this stage of self-analysis through introspection and self-observation, he did not think the end of the story had been achieved. Instead, he came to see that the results of introspection led to verbal confession of introspection's findings. His theory of what language is and what it is for, takes over. He argues that words do have

---

42 See Connolly, *The Augustinian Imperative*, pp. 52–4.
43 In the *City of God* XIII: *concupiscentia* has nothing to do with trying at all.

a limited use in speech communities which already recognize the specific conventions of communication because there is a shared social context to make them intelligible. On their own, however, words are without intelligibility and they rarely achieve an expression of one's own mind and feelings. The words of Latin or Greek may be conventionally established signs of 'things' but they are only intelligible if we already know the things themselves. Even here, our own experiences of the material world come to be lodged in our mind's imaging and remembering capacities. Where Stoics referred to the memory as a marvellous, even divine, treasure-house of all things, Augustine thinks of his memory as a stomach. Furthermore, he argues that we do not remember the things experienced but rather the images and memories of these experiences. These are mental copies or likenesses, and are open to extraordinary psychological distortions.

Like many of the platonically inspired ancient philosophers, however, he argued that the mind not only perceives through bodily sensual experiences, and 'remembers' these, but also has its own immaterial objects of thought. There are truths that can be known independently of the senses. They include, for instance, mathematical and logical propositions. Augustine argues that they are known by human minds with a superior clarity and certainty than anything 'known' by the body's local experiences. Grammar, mathematics and logic are in the mind somehow as formal, mental furniture.[44] Questions concerning logical categories may be phrased using conventional verbal signs and they pass through the air with a certain noise when spoken. But the things themselves to which they refer are not grasped by a bodily sense.

In the *Confessions* Augustine cannot at first explain how the categorical and logical truths got into our minds, but he says that when he first heard them he recognized them as true, and hence he believes that they must have been there. Indeed, Augustine will later argue that moral and philosophical truths that are divorced from sense experience are the manifestations of God's interior presence in the mind of man. Christ dwells in the human soul as the word of God, illuminated as the intelligible mental word. The immortality and immateriality of the soul require for Augustine, as for Plato and Cicero, that rational knowledge does not enter the mind from outside but is in some way as yet to be explained somehow present to it. But in so far as the human soul is, in this life, the subject of change, sin and repentance, then the soul itself has an empirical history that is never divorced from the vicissitudes of its life. As a consequence, in this life, even that aspect of the soul that is concerned to contemplate moral, philosophical and finally, eternal truths can never do so in a sustained way.[45]

Augustine concentrates on man's condition of individual isolation. He insists that we cannot understand someone else's narrative of his experiences if the things of which he speaks, assuming this is the first time we hear of them, do not correspond to our own memory of having like experiences. If one has never seen a certain colour, tasted a certain taste, heard a certain sound, Augustine says it will be absolutely impossible for a person to represent them in his own mind. If someone relates his past to you, you must have had analogous experiences of your own to understand him. When we listen to

44   Compare Platonic Forms, chapter 3, this volume.
45   Compare Aristotle, *Nicomachean Ethics* book 10. I have discussed aspects of Augustine's epistemology and language theory in Coleman, *Ancient and Medieval Memories*, chs 6 and 7. Also see Markus, 'St Augustine on Signs' and B. D. Jackson, 'The Theory of Signs in St Augustine's *De Doctrina Christiana*', both in R. A. Markus, ed., *Augustine: a collection of critical essays* (Garden City, NY, 1972), pp. 61–91, 92–148.

another's speech we interpret his narrative with our *own* memory as the measure, and we endow the narrative with our own meaning. Only first-hand experience gives a person 'knowledge' and all the rest which we acquire through interpersonal communication is second-hand experience that provides more or less justified *belief*. Quite astonishingly, given what we know of the view of ancient Greek and Latin philosophers, Augustine thinks that the use of language, that is, the conventionally established signs of whatever language we happen to learn, does not demonstrate that humans are related or can relate to one another.[46] Conventional language is merely an artificial and imperfectly useful interpersonal link. Instead, each man is alone in a sea of competing communicative attempts by which he then attempts to understand.

Augustine, the professional teacher of Latin rhetoric, developed a theory of signification which, however, required the verbal sign to be the necessary medium for understanding. For Augustine, there is one set of signs that is not merely conventional, and these are God's signs, given in scripture, which, unlike our mere attempts at communication, are accomplished achievements. Instead of arguing from a natural law written in man's heart and thereby known through a natural self-awareness and introspective reflection on our instincts, Augustine limits himself to arguing that there *are* truths *in* man, the successfully communicated divine word. One of the ways in which the *existence* of these truths is discovered is precisely through our recognition of the inadequacy of human words. Our awareness of the human word's inadequacy points to a truth beyond itself. Words are vehicles of meaning, creating bridges between knower and the objects known. But the realization of inadequate human verbal communication does not lead directly to a *knowledge and certitude* of the meaning of divine, perfect communication. A *belief* in divine, verbal accomplishment must be acquired first. *Credo ut intelligam*, I believe in order that I may understand. His theory of the overwhelming place of belief and authority in human life comes together.

Belief in the Authority of Others Structures Social Life

Augustine insists that men cannot have first-hand experience of, for instance, the historical past or the future. Instead, they must and do follow authorities. They understand on the basis of the testimony of others, but this understanding is a form of *belief* rather than of certain knowledge. Humans are not characterized as certain knowers but as creatures of trust, taking things on trust, and this is what is essential to the conduct of human life. Even their use of conventional language requires a coherent and trusted social context that they believe allows for stable conventions of communication. Belief on the authority of others is a necessary condition of human life in the family and society. Our sources and evidence are judged according to plausibility rather than demonstrated certitude. And this includes evaluations of scriptural authorities, supplemented by the views of the 'wise' who know, that is, church authorities. Trust in the authoritative community is implicit in the very process by which we acquire our habitual behaviour and inclinations. We are habit-forming creatures, just as Aristotle had said, but Augustine thinks we show ourselves to 'assent' far more frequently to habits that are sinful, revealing and reinforcing the competing and disjointed loves and desires that we

---

46   This is the lesson of the Tower of Babel.

are. Where Aristotle had regarded man as indeterminate, Augustine thinks him skewed towards vice.

It is rhetorical plausibility, not demonstrative proof, which actually structures human life as a collective enterprise. Human life in social and political community, is characterized by a search for belief and understanding of such a kind that reinforces our determination to stick with our habits and our 'free choice' to do what we desire. Human life does not show itself to be characterized by a search for indubitable knowing.[47] Although there are things that *are* indubitably known, our own experience of existing, *what* we understand from living and communicating with others resides in the domain of belief. This is what the attempt to communicate by means of conventional language shows us. All political communities understand the centrality of belief, namely the belief in coercive and socializing authorities, which bind people together if only to serve a modicum of peace and stability.

If, however, we are to live in a Christian community, then Augustine believes our central dependence on belief must also be understood by church authorities. If we are what we love, and what we love is the consequence of having established habits that reinforce our perverted desires, then our bad habits must be broken by discipline and corrected in order to promote at least the *conditions* for the performance of good acts done in the right spirit. The 'state', with its institutions and laws, as we shall see, cannot get us to perform good acts done in the right spirit; instead, it maintains through its laws and punitive penalties for non-compliance, no more and no less than a shaky peace. The 'state' cannot improve us. It contains and constrains us. In order to live according to a set of 'traditions' and practices that discipline and correct our habitual desires, Christians must look to practices as defined by Christian authority. Augustine would finally come to believe that Christian traditions and practices are themselves to be coercively applied, if necessary, and for the 'good' of the recipient. And he did not hesitate to say that unbaptized infants were damned; all the ages and classes of humanity had an absolute need of the grace of baptism.

What Distinguishes Christian Authority from Secular, Political Authority?

If what happened in the past is a matter of more or less justified belief – after all, we were not present at a past event to have experienced it – then the plausibility of that belief depends on the belief-worthiness, the credibility of the 'authority' which provides it. When we read competing histories written by historians about the past, which do we choose to believe and why? We may also believe that we are talking about the past and attempt to talk accurately about it, but Augustine thinks we do not succeed if we had not been there. We are left with the task of weighing authorities to settle disputes, and human authorities are themselves prone to distorting their own imaginings and memories of their experiences. The reality is that so long as one lives under some social and political authority – it hardly matters which, so long as it sets up some regularized means of dispute settlement which establishes conventions in which the community has some faith, at least in their utility – the necessity for regularized authority will be granted by all. It will also be granted that none of these systems will achieve infallibility. Again,

---

47   Compare with the views of Aquinas. See *A History of Political Thought* volume 2, chapter 2.

humans operate on trust, faith and belief. Even authoritative biblical history, which is the only history that matters, stands in the uninvestigable realm of the assent of faith; credal statements, such as those concerning particular historical events like the resurrection of Christ, will never be accessible to philosophical reflection since, as particular events, they lie outside the realm of abstract truths. They can only be believed and never known because they are incapable of having been experienced first hand.

But Augustine argues that if the 'factual events' described in scripture can never be experienced first hand and hence known, intelligible and immaterial truths communicated by scripture, not being the subject of change, *can* be known. Augustine had observed that the truths of mathematics and logic are somehow naturally impressed in human minds. Impressed here is also the idea of a kind of universal justice, what Augustine calls a law of conscience against doing to another what one would not bear if done to oneself (*Confessions* I, xviii). In place of Aristotle's indemonstrable set of moral principles which are foundational for humans, arising in each of us from induction, and accepted universally as necessary truths about the way things are, Augustine prefers a Platonist doctrine of indwelling truths impressed in the mind but not as the consequence of sense experience. The rules as principles, themselves unjudgeable, are there in us, but contrary to Aristotle's and Cicero's view, this does not mean that we follow them. God's illumination is required if we are able to use these internally impressed rules. God must will to prepare us to know and then perform according to that knowledge. The inner teacher is not a power within ourselves that introspection alone discovers and activates. Rather, God has to make the indwelling laws of conscience knowable to us. And Augustine insisted that God's decision concerning whose will he unifies from its fallen divisiveness is not only inscrutable to us, but is selective. God's grace is to be understood as a necessary support for our flickering desire for the good that will make us whole, that will enable us to act on the law of conscience, but that grace is limited.[48] It is not offered to all. All Christians are not saved.

On Free Will

Augustine's mature thinking on the nature of the human will (post 411 and as we find it in the *City of God*)[49] establishes that before Adam's Fall through his first disobedience to God's commandment that he not taste the fruit of the tree of knowledge of good and evil,[50] Adam was provided with a capacity to decide between good and evil.[51] He knew the difference and his will had the 'power' to make the right choice. But even in Paradise Adam enjoyed divine grace as a 'help without which' he could not choose the good or avoid evil. Divine grace was the necessary but not sufficient condition for Adam's free

---

48 Rist, *Augustine: ancient thought baptized*, p. 135.
49 Also see *De gratia et libero arbitrio* 20.41, and the even later *De gratia Christi* 18.19–20.21; also see on the later theory of the will J. M. Rist, 'Augustine on Free Will and Predestination', *Journal of Theological Studies* n.s. 20 (1969).
50 See Genesis 2:16–17.
51 On Augustine's earlier discussion of the will as somehow neutral or indifferent, capable of being used either rightly or wrongly, see (*On Free Choice*) *De libero arbitrio* 2.19, 50–3, and Gerard O'Daly, 'Predestination and Freedom in Augustine's Ethics' in Vesey, *The Philosophy in Christianity*, pp. 85–97. This shifts, in *Confessions* 8, viii.19–ix.21 to the view that the will is not an indifferent instrument but is good or evil depending on the value of what is willed.

choice of the good, a grace that did not make him incapable of sin but ensured that he had the means of choosing good.[52] Adam is presented as knowing what is evil and being able to choose it. God, however, is described as incapable of choosing evil. Original Adam had the capacity to choose to be akratic, incontinent. The first freedom of will, given to Adam, was an ability not to sin, combined with the possibility of sinning.[53] God let Adam sin but did not cause him to do so. Augustine regards Adam's choice as permitted rather than caused by God, his sin occurring against, but not apart from, God's will.[54] We are not told why God created what seems to be a less than perfect Adam. But after Adam's Fall, man is no longer able to choose the good, and further, he is now motivated by his desires *certainly* to choose evil. To say that man is created in the image and likeness of God, now means that this likeness is of fallen Adam, and not of the original Adam before the Fall.

Man's 'deformity' is healed through the reception of baptism. This sacrament is received within the church, the Body of Christ, so that the image of God is reformed in man, a renewal that will bring the faithful, only after the end of their lives, to the vision of God in which the image of God in man will have been perfected. Man remains a creature, deified only by God's grace which, on earth, is only a hope rather than a reality.[55]

What is 'free' about fallen man's 'free choice' is that man alone makes the decision, but that decision is already directed by his now corrupted incapacity to be motivated in any of his acts by pure love. God foreknows but does not cause man to sin. God's foreknowledge does not determine events. God's foreknowledge is of the 'fact' that a man will choose to sin. In contrast to Aristotle, for Augustine it is not the power to choose the means to an end which is man's 'virtue', but rather the motivation or loves behind the choosing. In this, he agrees with Plato. There is much here that also conforms with Stoicism, in that the diseases of passion become the basis for the Stoic diagnosis of political disorder. But where Stoics thought of philosophy as a therapy to extirpate the passions and thereby provide a basis for political virtue,[56] Augustine could not accept that any philosophy could 'doctor us' from within. Instead, he argued that man now has a freedom to exercise his choice and to act, but without God's intervention, God's interior teaching, he will now always choose what is wrong because of what he now loves. He insists that the grace which fallen man needs does not take away the freedom of will but restores it, releasing it from its delusion concerning freedom which fallen man takes to be simply doing as he likes. This is because man now holds himself to be of supreme value and he desires not to *be* God but precisely to be autonomously, self-sufficiently, himself.

52   *City of God* XIV, 26.
53   *City of God* XXII, 30.
54   O'Daly, 'Predestination', p. 97, argues that this indeterminist position fits badly with Augustine's determinist account of the operation of grace. A philosophical defence of his notion of the freedom of will is not possible: 'it's a glorious and influential failure'.
55   *De correptione et gratia* 12, 33; *Epistle* (to Honoratus) 140, 4, 10. See Rist, *Augustine: ancient thought baptized*, p. 139; also see G. Ladner, *The Idea of Reform* (Cambridge, MA, 1959), especially p. 154, where he discussed the idea of the reform of man as not a return to Adam's primal state but to a higher condition, a reformation dependent solely on Christ which therefore requires church baptism if men are to be made 'members of Christ'. See also Bonner, 'Augustine's doctrine of man', p. 513.
56   Cicero, *Tusc. Disp.* 3.6.

Plato's 'democratic man' has been transformed into Everyman. But Augustine's 'solution' to democratic man's inconsistency is not Plato's, for whom a rational self-love and self-knowledge could lead to self-mastery and the psychological harmony of justice. For Augustine, those who are redirected in their love through God's grace are restored to an understanding of their *dependence* and to a singular love for God, no longer suffering from mixed and competing loves. Their wills, being what they love, are no longer divided. But in man's fallen state, that mysterious thing, his identity, *what* he is, *is* what he loves, and Augustine, through introspection and by deduction from the observed behaviour of others, is certain that what each man now loves above all else is himself and his own powers. He loves being master of self and over others. This self-love in its corrupted, fallen manifestation is a love which prefers this self and its autonomy to God. The ultimate perversion, the most insidious form of pride and the root of all sin is that of 'privacy', self-enclosure, the isolated self that loves self above everything else, even when living in community.

Grace and Predestination

Augustine insists that the grace which restores man's perverse self-love to a love of God is granted to a limited number of the elect who are predestined to salvation by God. The elect are not being rewarded for something they have done; they cannot be rewarded for something for which they are not responsible. For Augustine, divine grace is simply irresistible in the sense that it is not in a man's power, if predestined, not to consent to it. To many analysts of Augustine's views, it is not clear what remains to be called voluntary in man's 'free' will. Augustine seems to be offering a kind of determinism which he believes to be compatible with human freedom.[57] In addition, those who are not predestined, the rest, are damned and Augustine speaks similarly of their being predestined to damnation in the sense that God permits them to suffer the consequences of Adam's sin.[58] He never explained why it was not God's will that all be elect. This is simply his account of God's inscrutable justice. Nor does he explain his belief that God intervenes to save some and declines to save others.[59] To the question 'Was Christ's sacrifice not sufficient payment for the original sins of Adam and Eve, so that all could be saved?' Augustine answered no, because God's inscrutable justice is beyond justice.[60]

Furthermore, God's inscrutable justice entails that no one can be identified who is saved unless he is explicitly informed by God through revelation. His understanding of moral regeneration and salvation is completely individualized because the gift of grace that redirects man's love, to say nothing of the miraculous, unearned and explicit revelation of salvation, is offered to the individual alone. Augustine is still thinking within the ancient philosophical tradition of 'care for one's soul' and the moral

---

57   A. Kenny, *Will, Freedom and Power* (Oxford, 1975) argues that there is a compatibility of freedom with determinism, but he also notes that to accept Augustine's view makes it difficult to avoid the consequences that God is responsible for sin, that is, for the state of affairs brought about voluntarily, if not intentionally, by God (ibid., pp. 145–61).

58   *In Iohannis evangelius tractatus* CXXIV, 48.4, 6; 107.7; 111.5.

59   Rist, *Augustine: ancient thought baptized*, p. 270 observes that he never argued, as did Calvin, that God intended some or even all to be saved but then was thwarted by man's sin and therefore he punished them with damnation. For Rist's criticism of Augustine's selected election see pp. 279ff.

60   *Sermon* 341.7–9.

individual.[61] But, for Augustine, that individual becomes, only with grace, focused on God rather than on his 'self-sufficient' self. The restored, healthy self is not the ancients' moral self, nor is it Adam's self before the Fall. Augustine describes it as a better self, a likeness of Christ, God's son, with a will that is free from a delight in sin, immovably fixed in a delight in not sinning, and capable only of choosing the good.[62]

Political Outcomes and the *City of God*[63]

If the right motivation, the love of God before self, is no longer an achievement possible to man, then men are now *condemned* to live with and love others, with all the mixed motives that this entails. They are condemned to living the social and political life with its rules and regulations that maintain the peace. Man *is* a social creature and would have been social before the Fall, but the need for *political* organization is a consequence of sin. The natural affection which spurs men to join together as a *populus* precedes any particular political or constitutional regime.[64] The latter will reflect the character of the *populus*, what it loves, but even Rome remained a *populus* when it underwent constitutional transformations from republic to empire. The politics of a *populus,* then, is its *modus vivendi,* not some setting for the achievement of man's true needs, nor the setting for the performance of the morally good act. After all, the very idea of men living in cities reflects their sinfulness, for the city was founded by a fratricide, Cain, whereas Abel, the brother whom he killed, is described in the Bible as a 'sojourner who built no city'. Romulus killed Remus to establish Rome. The political institutions in which men live are not made by God, but are established by men and, in so far as they preserve order, in the last resort by force, are generally sanctioned by God as a necessary evil, given what men now are, that is, what they love. As we shall see, worldly politics is not a good but a necessary evil, an inadequate set of conventionally established authorities backed by coercive force that has utility for instrumental, self-focused selves. Unlike Cicero in his *De officiis*, Augustine cannot see any 'state' as capable of uniting the *utile* and the *honestum*, what is useful with what is right in itself. Every political constitution, whatever its claims to equity and fairness, is underpinned more or less by fallen man's perverse self-love. Politics is a tragic necessity whose foundation is not justice but domination by force or the threat of its use.[65] Consequently, every

---

61   See Rist, *Augustine: ancient thought baptized*, p. 193 on Augustine's argument that by telling an untruth one may save someone else's life but that it is *better*, Augustine believes, to say nothing at all! Each person is responsible for the well-being of his own soul, which Rist argues is a distortion of the Socratic injunction. Furthermore, Augustine defends not only the Socratic position that it is better to suffer evil than to do it, but the stronger view that it is also better for someone else to suffer than that I should do evil (ibid., p. 194).

62   *City of God* XXII, 16 and 30: 'But because human nature sinned when it had the power to sin it is set free by a more abundant gift of grace so that it may be brought to that condition of liberty in which it is incapable of sin. For the first immortality which Adam lost by sinning, was the ability to avoid death; the final immortality will be the inability to die.'

63   The text in translation is readily available as *Augustine, City of God*, ed. D. Knowles, trans. H. Bettenson (Harmondsworth, 1972 and reprints); *Augustine, Political Writings*, trans. M. W. Tkacz and D. Kries (Indianapolis, 1994) (selections); and the excellent R. W. Dyson, ed., *Augustine, The City of God Against the Pagans*, Cambridge Texts in the History of Political Thought (Cambridge, 1998).

64   See J. D. Adams, *The Populus of Augustine and Jerome: a study in the patristic sense of community* (New Haven, CN, 1971).

65   Compare Thrasymachus in Plato's *Republic* book 1.

political system is constituted by some hierarchy of power, ultimately achieving a shaky peace through force when persuasion's success in instilling plausible beliefs proves to be insufficient to achieve the same end.[66] Augustine does not provide a blueprint for the *civitas terrena*, human earthly society, beyond the general framework of political authority as a keeping of order and peace.

Politics, furthermore, provides a tolerable social living precisely because of man's final ignorance of who will be saved and who damned. Christians are to use, not love, the 'state' on their pilgrimage to a hoped-for end: salvation. But Augustine was aware that his explanation of God's predestining some and not others to salvation could lead to the view that since nothing that one does can make any difference to the final salvific outcome, indifference even to the effects of performing evil acts might result, and chaos ensue. Augustine would in the end argue that the church was to use the civil power's coercive command to counter indifference, thereby ensuring obedience to the laws of the imperfect human world. And because he had argued that a *belief* on the authority of others is the necessary condition of human life in the family and society, and men naturally place their trust in the authoritative community whatever its constitution, the political community no less than the spiritual community of Christians, the church, is held together by fallen man's need to believe in authority.[67]

Augustine on Rome

Augustine read a variety of Roman historians, and particularly from Sallust he extracted the criticism that Rome's history showed her to love domination. This *libido dominandi* conditioned the framework of Roman legal authority in the world and enabled Rome to justify her wars of conquest. Rome was a society united by its love of mastery, and pagan Romans were nothing other than exemplars of the condition of fallen man. Rome's civil power, like any state's power, functioned as a necessary evil in a world of political and social instability. Every political history showed secular society to be driven by fear, greed and lust for domination, each of which was regulated and constrained by positive law. But Rome's nature was not divine, and its ultimate purpose, unbeknown to Rome or any other historical polity, was as a means to another end: the furthering of the divine mission, communicated in scripture and as authoritatively interpreted by the church. In establishing peace and order, the state promotes the material conditions in which church authority can thereafter attempt to break fallen man's sinful habits, his self-absorption, and instil in him at least a habitual regard for his proper subordination to God.

Rome as a historical 'state' and its politics were to be understood as an irrelevance in the history of salvation. Rome like any other 'state' without true justice could be considered a gang of criminals. 'What', Augustine asks,

---

66   See *A History of Political Thought* volume 2, chapter 6 on Machiavelli.

67   For a range of interpretations of Augustine's understanding of politics see P. J. Burnell, 'The Status of Politics in St Augustine's *City of God*', *History of Political Thought* 12 (1992), pp. 13–29; Adams, *The Populus*; H. Deane, *The Political and Social Ideas of St Augustine* (New York, 1963); E. L. Fortin, 'Political Idealism and Christianity', in J. B. Benestad, ed., *Classical Christianity and the Political Order: reflections on the theological–political problem* (Lanham, MD, 1996); Markus, *Saeculum*; Markus, *Augustine: a collection of critical essays*, chs 13–15. and the classic J. N. Figgis, *The Political Aspects of St Augustine's City of God* (London, 1921).

are criminal gangs but petty kingdoms? A gang is a group of men under the command of a leader, bound by a compact of association, in which the plunder is divided according to an agreed convention. . . . For it was a witty and a truthful rejoinder which was given by a captured pirate to Alexander the Great. The king asked the fellow, 'What is your idea, in infesting the sea?' And the pirate answered with uninhibited insolence, 'The same as yours, in infesting the earth! But because I do it with a tiny craft, I'm called a pirate: because you have a mighty navy, you're called an emperor'. (*City of God* IV, 4)

Rome and its conversion *did* have a place in God's plan for humankind's history but it was not as the eternal city. Rather, Rome stands for all those aspects of grasping, irrational, uncontrolled man that Augustine saw as part of the necessary contrast between the 'earthly city' and the 'city of God'. Rome had made herself into the new Babylon of scripture. The Christianization of the empire was as accidental to the history of salvation as it was reversible, since, for Augustine, there is nothing definitive about the Christianity of Rome. Augustine argued that the only definitive history is sacred history which ended with the New Testament. Any subsequent human guesswork about the divine purposes in secular history lacks foundation. Man must be sustained only by a belief that God works providentially, albeit inscrutably, through history.

Augustine's approach to Rome's imperial history emphasized how her money economy had collapsed to the point of producing in some areas no more than a barter economy. It showed the Roman middle classes demoralized and impoverished, government corrupt, bribery rampant and the old idealist Ciceronian traditions of honourable and righteous government debased in favour of what Augustine saw as Rome's decline into an imperialism that was no more than a lust to dominate all men over the whole world. Taxation had increased wildly, the slave traffic from North Africa had dried up, and peasants were increasingly tied to the land. Furthermore, large groups of men from the East had moved into Roman territories, gradually pressing on the frontiers of Italy itself. They demanded incorporation into the imperial army and payment in land, power and money in return for peace. These 'barbarians', in the beginning scarcely Romanized, cared little for any of the ideals so greatly admired by Cicero. The old senatorial families were gradually deprived of their command of the armies and professional barbarian soldiers took over. The senatorial order was greatly inflated by new recruits and these indifferent but greedy landowners came to monopolize civilized life. With the crisis in the 380s over the altar of the goddess of Victory, it was evident to Augustine that it was not only Christians who were relatively indifferent to Rome's past, but so too were those who governed her. By 410 the barbarian Alaric moved with his troops on Rome and the eternal city was sacked. Augustine argues that the sack of Rome was merely the latest event in a series brought about by what Rome had become.

His view of Rome, adopted from Sallust, was that she had declined through an excess of ease and plenty, but more importantly, through a decline in her love of liberty and the ancient virtues.[68] Honourable ambition, as described by Cicero, had been replaced by avarice. Rome deserved to decline. Her most serious failure, according to Augustine, was that she lusted after domination and ultimately was dominated by her own passion for domination. Rome had become the type of that 'earthly city' to be contrasted with the 'city of God'. Augustine emphasized that the order of history is of divine institution, but

---

68   Compare Machiavelli in *A History of Political Thought* volume 2, chapter 6.

the events of history are themselves fundamentally of man's own making. If, then, in what Eusebius and his other contemporaries took to be these marvellous Christian times, there is so much tribulation, the world is derelict and Rome is fallen, then it is men who are to blame. Augustine insisted that 'God did not promise permanence to things such as social institutions and political arrangements. Are we to praise God when things go well and blaspheme him in adversity?' Augustine, therefore, repudiated Virgil's myth, taken up by optimistic Christian authors, that Rome was eternal. And he deflated the current Christian theme that contemporary Christian times were to be better. 'Bad times, hard times people keep saying; but let us live well and times shall be good. We are the times. Such as we are, such are the times.' Rome had degenerated and had reaped the consequences.

Beginning his *City of God* on the eve of the sack of Rome, Augustine interprets Alaric's sparing of Christians who had run to Christian shrines as Christ's intervention in inducing the Gothic barbarians to show Christians mercy.[69] He thinks that one cannot read anything more into this event. Instead, if Christians suffered along with pagans, it was to be viewed with the eyes of faith, in the belief that such sufferings tended to their moral improvement. Man is sinful and deserves whatever punishment a neutral history appears to serve out to him. Most importantly, the end of this life must come sooner or later and Alaric's sack of Rome was no more than a moment in the temporal sequence of birth and death. In sum, for Augustine, the Roman Empire had no place in the divine, providential plan of universal history; it had no religious significance.[70]

Church and 'State'

Augustine would come to insist that our knowledge even of the law of conscience, of due number and weight and order, are themselves dependent on authority. And if knowledge *follows* belief, then at least the conditions for belief had to be established by Christian authorities. In a Christian Rome, Augustine came to believe that church authorities were responsible for ensuring that Rome was a properly Christianized society. But if living within the parameters of a Christian community and habitually following its rituals was the necessary condition, it still was insufficient to achieve the required redirection of one's will. There is not a division between the ordinary Christian and the more ascetic, nor is there a division between the ordinary Christian and those who assume church offices, even as bishops. Hidden in God's will is the only division that matters, between the saved and the damned, and this is not revealed before the end. The undivided will to believe must itself be the consequence of God's gift of grace to the individual, and not every member of the historical church is a recipient. Only after the irresistible gift of grace that instils belief can one *know* of the intelligible, indwelling word and live by it. But the grace of adoption on earth is only a hope, not a known reality (*in spe* not *in re*), for it is not yet made manifest what we shall be.[71] Men cannot,

---

69   He never mentions the fact that Alaric and his Visigoths were Christians themselves, although of the heretical Arian kind.

70   Although Augustine's contribution to the debate over the significance of historical states and the church, and their mutual interactions, would help to fuel discussions of their respective jurisdictions in men's lives, his conclusions about the significance of the Christian Roman Empire would not immediately be taken up.

71   *Enarrationes in psalmos* 49, 2 .

self-willed, choose to believe even if they are members of the church. They cannot choose even to follow the laws of conscience: do unto others as you would be done by. Augustine not only extended the domain of belief at the expense of knowledge, but he came to insist that belief itself was not something that men could autonomously and self-sufficiently achieve. Platonists and Stoics could find neither truth nor belief through their unaided introspection. More ordinary, less philosophically inclined Christians could achieve no greater success. The authoritative teaching of the church, once described by Augustine as providing 'Plato for the multitude' was to be replaced by the hoped-for action of God's will. The ordinary Christian was now no further away from grace than the erudite or the ascetic. For both, imperfection is the inescapable condition on earth and in historical time. Humankind, after Adam, is a mass of sin. The gulf between God and man could not be bridged through self-knowledge. It could be mediated only by grace.

The Emergence of Augustine's Mature Spiritual and Political Views Amid Contemporary Conflicts

In the *Confessions* Augustine thought of the soul as managing the body, that somehow the soul which is man 'falls into' the body, and there are remnants in this work of a kind of dualism that pits the soul *against* the body as a tomb. Later, he would argue that man is a mixture of soul and body, where the soul is the better part of man but 'man' names the conjunction of the two. In the *City of God* he speaks of a miraculous combination of the immaterial soul and the material substance which is body. By now it is clear that body is a neutral means of expressing the will's divisions, a tool for expressing divided and often conflicting loves. Evil is not the body *per se*; evil is fallen man's willing choice to do what is wrong. The only way man can will to do what is right is if he loves what is right and this love, directed at its appropriate object of desire, can only come about through God's intervention. God must intervene to redirect man's 'free will', freeing him from his 'freedom' to choose. Augustine thinks God often does this by arranging the circumstances of a man's life, that is, through an external intervention that effects internal changes. How Augustine knows this is unclear. But he frequently refers to Saul's transformation into St Paul on the road to Damascus as an example of this miracle.

The ancient discussion of habitually trained character dispositions, guided by the exercise of the intellectual virtue, reason, which enables man to know his unchosen species-specific end, and prudentially reason about means to that end, is completely jettisoned. Now the chief determinant of our intentions and our behaviour is not described as a matter of reasoning according to principles. Rather, our characters emerge from the peculiar and conflicting wills which are revealed in our multiple loves and hates. Our reasoning is never principled and, if at all operational, it is short term and instrumental. The world is filled with acts, but most are performed for the wrong reasons. We are rarely motivated by a desire for the Platonist good, the beautiful, the ordered, because we have no idea at all what is worth loving. We need both political imposition of order and the spiritual discipline of Christian authority. Political order at least promotes a coerced coherence of wills to provide for a tolerable society. We need both the state and the church, but much more, we need God's grace.

All of these increasingly precise views emerged out of particular, contemporary conflicts with which Augustine was faced as a North African bishop. Most of them were revealed in his *City of God*. The very idea of the two cities, a city of God and the other, earthly, was already discussed by Cicero in his *De legibus* 1.23, by St Paul in his Letter to the Ephesians 2:19 and by the Donatist theologian Tycomius. Augustine had discussed the idea in some of his earlier works, where he promised the large treatise which came to be *The City of God Against the Pagans*.

In his early dispute with the Manichaeans he was concerned to refute a tendency he had observed in his earlier self and in others, to regard the visible and material world as something evil and the flesh as sordid. He came to refute this in order to reject any denials of Christ's incarnation as man. At first he was able to deploy the Neoplatonist argument of a principle of evil, but in Plotinus he found that matter is not so much evil as sterility. He developed this further towards the end of his life, when he came to see that human sexuality was part of man's created nature and was not a result of its corruption through sin. The sin of lust was a sin of the soul rather than of the flesh, a sin of motivation. The wrong and corrupted motivations make men somewhat less 'man'. He came to regard evil as non-being, a nothingness, a diminishing of the good that was created, and evil as a negation was not caused by God. Souls become good or bad in the degree to which they adhere to, or depart from, the source of all goodness, God.

In his North African ministry he also had to contend with a pagan revival. The sack of Rome by Alaric caused numerous educated Romans to make their way with their classical libraries from Italy to a momentarily safer haven in North Africa. Many were recent converts or nominal Christians who still believed in the myth of an eternal Rome and in the sanctity of Roman institutions. Out of this dilemma Augustine sought to prove from historical, philosophical and biblical arguments that the whole range of classical values had been replaced by Christian ones and there was no turning back. But this was because human kingdoms and empires were established by men, sanctioned by divine providence, and not by the goddess Fortuna. Nor were 'states' established by the *merits* of rulers or peoples. He abandoned his earlier view that there might be an enlightened ruler to control society with reason. From this position he would develop his belief that the only *res publica* worth serving was the one which was united in its agreement over the object of its members' love and this must be God instead of earthly values.

Even Scipio's definition of a *res publica* was never achieved in Cicero's Rome. The Roman 'state', at no time in its history, served the true good or true interests of its people. Scipio was correct in saying that a state cannot be maintained without justice and where there is no true justice there can be no right. When there is no true justice there can be no association of men united by a common sense of right. Justice is that virtue which assigns to everyone his due. But in Rome the determination of men's due was a matter of positive law and never included that a man serve God.

> If a soul does not serve God it cannot with any kind of justice command the body, nor can a man's reason control the vicious elements in the soul. And if there is no justice in such a man, there can be no sort of doubt that there is no justice in a gathering which consists of such men. (*City of God* XIX, 21)

The Romans did not serve the true God but rather a range of gods.

> It follows that justice is found where God, the one supreme God, rules an obedient city according to his grace, forbidding sacrifice to any being save himself alone . . . so that just as the individual righteous man lives on the basis of faith which is active in love, so the association or people of righteous men lives on the same basis of faith, active in love, the love with which a man loves God as God ought to be loved, and loves his neighbour as himself. (*City of God* XIX, 23)

Augustine provides his alternative definition of 'a people' and a '*res publica*' to that of Cicero, saying that 'a people is the association of a multitude of rational beings united by a common agreement on the objects of their love'. The Romans were indeed a people and the object of their love was, as their history witnessed, themselves and their own power, even during Cicero's republic. They *were* a united people, but their *res publica*, like all historical states, was devoid of true justice (*City of God* XIX, 24). And true justice is impossible without true religion. Rome's 'virtue' was actually its vice, pride (*City of God* XIX, 25). In this life, even the righteous man who is on pilgrimage in this world needs prayers 'because the reason, though subjected to God, does not have complete command over the vices in this mortal state and in the "corruptible body which weighs heavy on the soul" (*Wisdom* 9, 15)'. Something is all too likely to creep into a man's soul to cause sin (*City of God* XIX, 27). The world and its political constructions, then, are there to be used rather than enjoyed; it is God alone who is to be enjoyed. Good men are those who use this world in order to enjoy God, while evil men are those who try to use God in order to enjoy the world (*City of God* XV, 7). Christians cannot help but be in the world but they need not be of it.

In North Africa Augustine was also confronted with schismatic Donatists with whom there had been a long-running battle throughout the fourth century. Donatists were Christians who so rigorously upheld a notion of a pure church that they refused to accept a return to the fold of those who, during previous persecutions of Christians, had 'betrayed the faith' by handing over copies of scripture to the secular authorities. Nor were those who had been baptized by such 'betrayers' allowed into the church. Donatists argued that true Christians should withdraw from all contact with the corrupt world. Donatism has been described as one of those enthusiastic movements which have broken out in the Christian church throughout its history, commonly characterized by an ascetic hostility to the social order and an urgent expectation of the end of the world.[72] Augustine, in contrast, developed his belief that the corrupt and the sacred, the two cities, could not be separated in time and in history. The separation of the pure and the impure in history was an invisible one. His conflict with Donatists enabled him to establish that the historical church was not a holy huddle of the elect and perfect in history. Rather, the historical church contained the wheat and the chaff. Church officials who may have 'betrayed the church' during persecutions were still to be recognized as ministers of God's sacraments, for it was these and not the state of a minister's soul that mattered to the Christian. He relinquished any notion of the historical church as comprising a spiritual elite set into the world. Nor was Rome simply the city of the damned.

In his later dispute with the British Pelagius, he was concerned to clarify the need for indwelling grace against those who trusted in their own self-perfecting attempts at self-

---

72   G. Bonner, '*Quid imperatori cum ecclesia?* St Augustine on history and society', *Augustinian Studies* 2 (1971), pp. 231–51. This is a discussion of Markus's *Saeculum*.

righteousness. Pelagians tended to see grace in creation, in the natural endowments of man, rather than as Augustine viewed it, as the divine power by which every good act is done. Pelagius had asserted that 'since man must not sin, he therefore must have it in his own power not to sin'. Hence, good deeds and virtuous acts must earn one eternal salvation, so that, in effect, God was forced to reward men who were just in the world. It was in his dispute with the Pelagians that Augustine developed his notion that to have free will is not the same as being free. To regain a full freedom to love and act on that love, a freedom that was corrupted by Adam's sin, the will needed to be restored by grace which liberates man's choice from the prison of his own egoism.[73] In debating with Pelagius whether this trust in grace in effect paralyses effort, Augustine further clarified his view that only those to whom grace is given are able to will in such a way that they carry out what they will.[74] If it is believed that God prepares the will, then it becomes necessary that a man entreats him through prayer that he may will in such a manner, that is, with an intent that would enable him to carry out God's commands. More than this a man cannot do, because men have no final control over their self-determination. Augustine thereby set Christian discourse on the road to salvation by confession, hopeful entreaty and faith alone, *sola fides* and *sola gratia*. A relative perfection in this life is, rather, a progress with the aid of divine grace towards a perseverance in earthly sufferings and temptations, towards a rest in God after terrestrial life. And since the members of the city of God are unknown to men, the will of God predestining some and not others to eternal salvation remains inscrutable.

City of God

Augustine's composition of the twenty-two books of the *City of God against the pagans* spanned the years from 413 to 427. He died as barbarian Vandals battered the walls of the cities of North Africa. *City of God* appeared in instalments during the last fifteen years of his life when he was enmeshed in the ecclesiastical administration and the above-mentioned theological controversies of the times. It is a work with several centres. But certain persistent themes with which we have now become somewhat familiar run throughout the whole. It was begun as an apologetic defence of Christianity, as a re-evaluation of the historical significance of Rome, as a treatise on man's extra-political goal, and as a final statement in that long argument from antiquity to his own times about politics being the means to human fulfilment. It provides a selection of past philosophies, past histories, a contrast between Christian and pagan beliefs, and it opens with a rejection of ideas current in both pagan and Christian circles when Alaric beat down the walls of Rome. Like most of Augustine's writings it can be viewed within the genre of crisis literature, beginning with a specific analysis of Rome's fall in 410 and ending as a repudiation of the classical ideals of politics and historical optimism. Markus has called the work a sustained inner dialogue of a man whose intellectual world had been shaken.[75] He had abandoned the historical notion of a *Christiana tempora*, a Christian age, and its corollary, a positive progress in Roman history through its conversion to

73 *De gratia et libero arbitrio* (426 AD), 14.27.
74 Ibid., 4.7.
75 Markus, *Saeculum*.

Christianity. And he rejected the universal tradition of Christian thinking about the Roman Empire as itself divinely ordained, a last golden age.

Moving as Augustine himself moved in his own thinking from a confrontation with pagan conceptions of history and politics, *City of God* ends with an assertion that true wisdom is only to be found in the Bible and not in the philosophy of men. Reason is placed beneath faith, and man's incapacities as a result of the Fall are ranked before his abilities. The Graeco-Roman political agenda with its concern for peace, order, law and a just society is raised to a higher level where true peace, true order, just law and a just society can only be considered as an achievement after history – and not man's achievement – in heaven with the blessed. Therefore, the work is much more than a political theory tract, although it certainly is a rejection of the classical idealization of the 'state'.

In his biography of Augustine, Peter Brown thought that Augustine's central problem was not so different from that of modern men, in so far as Augustine asked and answered the question: to what extent is it possible to treat man as having a measure of rational control over his political environment?[76] Brown noted that the discovery that the extent of this control is limited has revolutionized political theory. This has resulted in the developments of various determinist systems: one thinks here of Hegel's *Geist*, of Marx's dialectical materialism, of Freud's study of all those unconscious forces which prevent men from being in full rational control of their environments, and of certain contemporary neo-Darwinianisms. Augustine had observed what many today believe to be a truism, that no one is known to another so intimately as he is known to himself, and yet no one is so well known even to himself that he can be sure as to his own conduct on the morrow. If men do not know themselves and even less do they know their neighbours, does it not border on folly to assume that politics and law guided by reason could ever achieve an order which would satisfy the longings of men? Hence, Augustine's contribution to political theorizing about the structure of the perfect state took the form of a pessimistic observation that man is so indeterminate and discontinuous, blind to his own intentions, haphazard and inefficient in his attempts to communicate that he must be determined by some force outside the horizon of his own immediate consciousness. For Augustine, this could only be God. But without God, we have only the absolute state. This is what Hobbes saw in the seventeenth century.

Even within the ancient tradition of ethical discourse, a lack of control regarding one's moral intentions would have to mean the failure of the claim to self-determination in politics. And in a variation on the Stoic focus on internalities, Augustine thought that it was not in our power to reform the underlying evil structures of secular society; we could only vary them fatalistically. Augustine's political thinking, then, gravitates around the problems of human behaviour, so that his concern is less with the larger public institutions, in states or cities themselves, than with the individuals who comprise these collectivities. He concludes that political activity is a symptom not an achievement. It is symptomatic of fallen nature, a utilitarian expression of men's unfulfilled needs. Hence, politics is neither the highest expression of human needs nor the answer to our most central dilemmas and desires.

The Christian does obey the state and its laws, not least because he would not set himself up against the inscrutable ways of God's working in history. Augustine is insistent that there is no *legitimate* resistance to political authority even when it is unjust. He

---

76   Brown, *Augustine of Hippo*.

interpreted the warning in Matthew 26:52 that those who take up the sword shall perish by it, as an injunction against private resistance. It applies only to those who take up arms without the command of a legitimate superior authority. But in spite of the growth in what appeared to be the irresistible institutional structuring of imperial Rome's public life by the fourth century, Augustine was expressing a widely held anxiety that even these institutions could not withstand the onslaught of barbarian invasions. If Rome had not been able to establish a rational control over its political environment, then perhaps politics was not the answer.

Augustine's scepticism about worldly institutions found a resolution in faith rather than in reason. And this leads him to argue in the *City of God* that nature, like governments and historical events, is neutral. There is, none the less, a purpose in history and in the succession of governments. Each neutral institution or natural event can be viewed as either good or bad, but only in terms of their relative usefulness for the Christian, whose ultimate concerns are neither with history nor temporal institutions as such. To grasp something of God's working in human history as presented in the *City of God*, should, Augustine thinks, enable everyone to replace all those pagan Roman histories as well as the more recent optimistic Christian histories with his own work. What all those other histories demonstrated, when viewed against sacred history of scripture, was that history was not the progressively happy story of humankind. If Rome fell to Alaric, then the previously optimistic view that Christianity would enable the extension of the *pax Romana* was shattered. He asks whether we should see it as the fault of the imperial 'state' in having adopted Christianity and abandoning old traditional gods, which brought on this catastrophe. In the first ten books of the *City of God* he answers no, not only because Rome in itself has no sacred significance, but seen from another perspective Rome's own decline as a 'city' with human desires could have been predicted. This enables him to develop his understanding of human history as having its ups and downs with both a beginning and an end, and its movement is linearly progressive, but only in the sense that its destiny is beyond history and time.

Thereafter, Augustine developed his second theme, as a commentary on the historical narrative of the Bible, wherein he explains his influential doctrines of creation, the Fall, redemption and the progress and destiny of the church. This second part some judge to be within the tradition of apocalypse, the best-known Christian example being the Book of Revelation (or Apocalypse) of St John. Here, Augustine surveys the history of the world which is destined to persist through six ages from the creation to the final judgement of Christ. By the time of Christ's birth, five ages had been completed, and the sixth was in progress when Augustine wrote. He describes the end of the sixth age and the Second Coming of Christ in books XX–XXII of the *City of God*, in which the destruction of the earth will be succeeded by a new heaven and a new earth. The saved will be reunited with their incorruptible bodies to enjoy an eternal life of peace with God in the heavenly city. They will not live a life of action so much as of rest and leisure in God's praise. There will be neither idleness nor labour in this final sabbath. The saved soul's disposition is such that there are no enemies without or within (*City of God* XXII, 30) and there will be no penal *imperium*. The order is one of tranquillity. God will not need to keep order among the saints. But it is a 'city' none the less, in that it is a collection of saints in agreement in the object of their love, a collection that is hierarchically arranged and 'administered' in the light of grades of honour and glory appropriate to degrees of merit that have been granted by God to each. There will be inferiors and superiors but without envy. 'And so although one will have a gift inferior to another he will have also the compensatory gift of contentment with what he has' (*City of God* XXII, 30). Furthermore, there will be one and the same freedom of will in all, as well as an individual memory of each soul's past evils as far as intellectual knowledge is concerned. But the saints will have no sensible recollection of past vices, their new freedom consisting in vice being completely erased from their feelings. This wipes out Adam's taste of the forbidden fruit. During this eternal seventh age, the saints will retain only the knowledge of their past misery in order to sing the mercies of God, in harmony.

The first ten books are, then, united with the later twelve through the biblical theme of the two cities. By now it is clear that the 'city of God' is not the historical church. Rather, in historical time it is that *invisible* grouping of men, and it exists in its members individually being on pilgrimage to that transhistorical city of salvation, not knowing if they will achieve it. In contrast, the 'earthly city', the *terrena civitas*, is the new Babylon which Rome typified but which has always existed through its members, whose individual allegiance was to themselves in their own love of self rather than in a higher love and allegiance to God. The two cities are formally defined in terms of the ultimate loyalties of their respective members, which loyalties are themselves the consequence of the members' standing in the sight of God. In historical time, the two cities are intermingled. But after time they will become mutually distinct, coherent and visible. They will be composed respectively of the saints and predestined separated from the unjust and damned. The separation is determined by those who love God to the contempt of self and those who love themselves to the contempt of God. The separation after history is between the elect and the reprobate. The requirements of true justice, order and love can only be met in the city of God and it only takes on the form of a true, cohesive city after its members pass from their pilgrimage in this life to the next.

While on pilgrimage in this life, politics is to be viewed as neutral. In book V Augustine unequivocally states that 'in regard to this mortal life, short and transitory, what does it matter under whose rule a dying man lives (and we are all dying men) so long as those who rule do not compel him to commit impiety or injustice?' This appears to exhort a kind of Christian pacifism. But where some pagan philosophy had also advised abstention from public life, at least for the wise man, Augustine rejected this quietism. In the nineteenth book (*City of God* XIX, 6) he noted that the heavenly city's members, when on earthly pilgrimage, do work for the achievement and maintenance of an earthly peace. They are politically engaged and get their hands dirty if called by their status to do so. But the goal of an earthly peace must not impede the worship of God. The members of the heavenly city on pilgrimage and in history merely use the earthly peace provided by political regimes. Members of the city of God on pilgrimage cherish and desire, as far as they may without compromising their faith and devotion, the orderly coherence of men's wills concerning the things which pertain to the mortal nature of man. The political sphere undoubtedly and necessarily exists, but its significance is relative and restricted. It is a means of order, preventing men from sinning further according to their fallen nature, and it does this by punishing, correcting and holding men at bay. Politics is the domain of the public executioner. This earthly peace does not, because it cannot, provide the setting for human perfection. Human perfectibility and fulfilment are not historically realizable goals. But social arrangements have their due place in an overriding order which embraces men, and hence law is necessary. Order is that which, if we follow it, will lead men to God and for this reason social order must conform to a wider, divinely established order which is itself accomplished in the world by men's reason. But the human condition is now a tragic one, and human reason is of the instrumental variety that helps us to survive in no more than a relative temporal peace. Man, driving ever towards wholeness and perfection, towards a fulfilment of all desires and a lasting peace and order, all the gift of God's grace, cannot find the fulfilment and perfection in human affairs because human society and its very origins are irremediably rooted in a tension-ridden and disordered time and place. Political life, then, lawful and orderly, must serve as a waiting station. Salvation is an escape from history and politics.

Augustine, consequently, rejects creative politics along with the 288 different philosophies of life presented by the encyclopedist Varro. Augustine scorns these traditions. Life must indeed be social but felicity is not to be found in the *polis*. There is no final end, no conceivable good, that is within the range of human achievement. This is why the just man lives not by reason nor by politically virtuous and public activity, but by faith.

Politics is the means to achieve minimum disorder. And it does this through political authority as imposition. Political authority was not natural to original Adam; nor was any form of subject–master relationship between members of the same species. Authority and subordination are the results of man's sinful nature, the results of his misuse of his 'free will'. Man's fallen nature, revealed in the multiplicity of his competing desires, shows obedience to the 'state' and man's dependence on authority to be necessary correctives to man's present delusion of self-determination. Politics is therefore constructed out of the tension between self-determining illusion and authority. Law as it is promulgated by human legislators cannot make men good as Aristotle and Cicero claimed. Civic institutions are not educational. They can only secure public order, property rights and temporal, in fact, temporary, security. Law protects the private self from other private selves. Politics, necessary as it now is and conditioned by human nature, is fundamentally about domination and temporary conflict avoidance. Political hierarchies achieve peace through force. This is not to deny that hierarchies are comprised of men proud of their political ambition and power. Hierarchy is not unnatural to Augustine, and he thinks we can still recognize natural hierarchies in man being subordinated to God, the body to the soul, animals to men. But hierarchies motivated by a love of power pervert a natural relation, intended by God, of authority and subordination. That our politics is driven by the underlying perversion of self-love shows human hierarchies always to have been more or less unjust, and we can expect nothing else. Political history is nothing other than the story of individuals driven by their passions to acquire private goods at the expense of others (*City of God* XVIII, 2ff.). The consequence of men pursuing privatized goals in unrestrained ways is warfare. And therefore Augustine defends rulers and institutional employees such as soldiers and public hangmen as licensed to kill in the name of peace and order. We are condemned to live in a social and political order now that we have disturbed the proper order in which our relationship would be with God. But those concerned with order and peace, give orders because they are concerned for the interests of others, securing their peace as well. He goes further and argues that the soldier who obeys his ruler is not to be regarded as personally, morally responsible for the undoubted harmful act he may commit by obeying orders. He kills 'for others' and on command of an authority. He is the agent of authority and acts only as a sword in authority's hand (*City of God* I, 21 and XIX, 6, 14; on the discipline of slavery as a punishment, XIX, 15). In the public world where we operate within a set of institutions which are not made by God, it is the consequences that matter, and the tragic, overriding necessity is that compromises must be made to keep order. Augustine opposes killing by private individuals, even in self-defence, but his consequentialist position on the necessity of authoritative punishment, his view that the habits of disobedience and self-will can only be broken by suffering at the hands of men, if not God, in order to promote at least the *conditions* for the good will, would have a long and disreputable future history in world politics.[77]

Rist has put this with terrifying simplicity. The function of political systems is to cow the vicious into respect for the law.[78] This prefigures the views of the seventeenth-century Hobbes. Some have also seen Augustinian pessimism having influenced the sixteenth-century Machiavelli. It is the duty of Christians in authority to bring about the short, sharp, shock that will break the spell of vicious habits. In maintaining a shaky peace, the ruler, be he Christian or otherwise, is performing a public obligation of his office. His worldly career is necessary to maintain the structure and the peace in the fallen world, and this necessary maintenance requires risking the deaths of the innocent when necessary, although in terms of original sin, no one is really innocent. Augustine's concern for order proves so intense that he argues that judges who torture even the innocent to get at the 'truth' may regret their severity but can feel no remorse. Even after his condemnation and execution the judge still does not know whether it was a guilty or an innocent person he has executed. Those who pronounce judgement cannot see into the consciences of those on whom they pronounce it. But this is the darkness that attends the life of human society and the judge will not refuse to sit. He will simply be sad that he is required to do what he does, for this is the wretchedness of man's situation. He can only cry out to God: 'Deliver me from my necessities!'(*City of God* XIX, 6). Our natural condition is now a penal one and even the institution of slavery cannot be reformed because if it disappeared from Augustine's world, he is certain it would be replaced by something similar with its name changed. Not only has no one the 'right' to be freed in this life but no one can be freed.

Augustine is famous for having read human history as the momentary establishment of a shaky peace punctuated by the misery of war in repeated, necessary cycles. He is even more famous for having established that there were just wars to be fought. In considering the diversity of human languages separating communities he observes that when men cannot communicate their thoughts with one another simply because of language difference, 'all the similarity of their common human nature is of no avail to unite them in fellowship. So true is this that man would be more cheerful with his dog for company than with a foreigner'. Imperial Rome, of course, tried to overcome this language difference by conquering people and enforcing the Latin language and Roman law on them, but the cost was huge: 'all that slaughter of human beings, all the human blood that was shed!' (*City of God* XIX, 7). The human condition is one of diversity, multiplicity, individually focused selves against selves. The human condition is such that wars are as necessary as the attempts to construct impermanent moments of peace. There are, then, just wars. They are political and religious and are fought under the command of legitimate superior power. Compulsion is required in religion as elsewhere to break

---

77   For another interpretation see P. J. Burnell, 'The Problem of Service to Unjust Regimes in Augustine's *City of God*', *Journal of the History of Ideas* 54 (1993), pp. 177–88.

78   Rist, *Augustine: ancient thought baptized,* p. 225.

the evil habits of men, compelling them to recognize an authoritative truth and bring them into a habituated unity in the first instance. Augustine came to accept that erring sectarian Christians, like the Donatists, should be compelled by 'state' authorities to conform to Catholic Christianity and be coerced into a due respect for God, rather than man. In the political sphere, just wars are also to be fought. He says:

> The wise man will lament the fact that he is faced with the necessity of waging just wars, for if they were not just, he would not have to engage in them, and consequently, there would be no wars for a wise man. For it is the injustice of the opposing side that lays on the wise man the duty of waging wars; and this injustice is assuredly to be deplored by a human being since it is the injustice of human beings, even though no necessity for war should arise from it. (*City of God* XIX, 7)

But if fallen humanity has no clear idea of justice and men's motives are always mixed, then in what sense can any decision of men, even in authority, be seen as 'just'? Again, Augustine's consequentialist thinking is revealed, in that order, however achieved, is the function of authority, and furthermore scripture shows him that God has used men as his agents, legitimating force, as 'the powers that be are ordained by God'. No public authority, simply from his public status, *knows* that he acts in a spirit of love when he imposes punishments and enforces order. But he can see that his public status imposes a necessity on his actions, a necessity that conforms to our now natural penal condition. In this life discipline terrifies into love.

To recover the correct, divinely intended, natural order among men – and Augustine believes such does exist and it is not one where all have equal talents and merits – we must look beyond human institutions and establish, in conjunction with faith, a hope about our eudaimonic destinies. But those destinies, in the last resort, are not within man's control and they are certainly beyond the 'state'.

There is no earthly society that can be modelled on the heavenly. The classical heritage of a politics of perfection is repudiated. All that can and does exist is the members of the city of God moving *in isolated fashion* through history towards a goal which will unify them in a city beyond time. This did not mean, for Augustine, that historically actualized cities were intrinsically bad, but he did not doubt that their constituent elements, their citizens, were. Politics, then, is to be understood as a *necessary* consequence of man's individual psychology. However, man cannot escape himself by ironing out the aberrations of his character in the political forum. The classical categories of ends achieved through reason, where natural man in a natural community seeks a political solution to the question of his purpose, are insufficient for Augustine. Politics as an answer to ultimate goals can only be futile; in fact, human relations of whatever kind cannot bring the kind of stable bliss Augustine says men truly seek without knowing the correct way. The fully satisfying relationship for men is not primarily with other members of their species but with God, and this is known to some only through the grace of faith. It is the love of God that undergirds the love of one's neighbour, so that the love of one's neighbour is not a means by which to achieve the love of God. All virtues, all moral conduct, are enabled by the love of God. To perform the good act in the right spirit takes grace.

Augustine has therefore demoted reason as possessed by men, far below where the ancients had ranked it. He transferred the value placed by the ancients in visible and institutional entities to things invisible. Men are not permanent and therefore their institutions cannot be permanent. The desire for membership in some enduring corporate structure cannot be fully satisfied by men in historical time. Even Cicero's republicanism is challenged by theological arguments based on faith. Men's natural capacities are too limited to allow them to arrive, by the light of their own reason, at universal truths about the workings of providence. If they do not see with the eye of faith then they do not see at all. But if history is read with the eye of faith, then scripture, rather than the products of historians, can show human history to be a universal event in time, a fulfilment of God's will, a process or *procursus* towards a higher and better destiny.

Conclusion

Today one can read a number of intriguing analytical philosophical studies which seek to show Augustine's brilliant inadequacies, especially regarding his engagement with the ancient philosophical tradition and the degree to which he succeeded in reconciling human freedom with divine foreknowledge, and divine foreknowledge with divine causation.[79] It is known that he wrote rapidly, so often 'contra' someone, and under the pressure of events and correspondents. In using a version of the Bible, the *Vetus Latina,* which was diffused in many inaccurate sub-versions (no complete manuscript survives), it is argued that he based some of his literal interpretations on misreadings. He submitted utterly to the authority of a certain body of texts which he believed to be authoritatively interpreted by the contemporary church, even when he agreed that there were obscurities. So much of his preaching is said to have been 'terrific dogma'. But an attempt should be made to understand this 'terrific dogma', in particular on religious coercion and state authority, because it is a perspective that is far more familiar to the Western political tradition than we might at first think or have been led to believe by ahistorical philosophical analyses of his thinking.

When he modified his earlier views on tolerating the Donatists and finally accepted religious coercion against them, it was not that he thought there was no value in alternative views of the church. It was rather that he thought men held views most often through the chains of force of habit. For Augustine it did matter to which 'party' a Christian belonged. He did not hold to there being a plurality of truths. He also thought it important that the church, the Body of Christ, be unified and universal. He held a view, which today we might recognize as the ordinary utility theory, which shows that an infinite harm needs only to be minimally probable in order to be worth avoiding at great cost. Force can be justified in securing assent when the consequences of dissent are grave, and in particular, when its alleged penalty is eternal damnation.[80] It has been argued that he seems to have been oblivious to the theological argument that although it may be easier to change, by threats, someone's allegiance rather than his conviction, it is not more likely that a benevolent God will reward the coerced. If a loving God would spare those whose faith is bought by a policy of oppression, would he not spare them anyway, saving the oppression?[81]

But Augustine seems to have thought of coercion as a necessary paternalism and the

---

79   Notable is C. Kirwan, *Augustine* (London, 1989).
80   Ibid., p. 215.
81   Ibid.

wishes of the sinner need not be decisive.[82] Hence, he thought it permissible to do good to a man against his will. This is not a position altogether unknown in the modern world: the modern state has been characterized as having no serious precedents in its efficient disciplining and punishing of men for their own good and that of the state.[83]

It has been suggested that this was also a dominant perspective to be found in ancient philosophy's insistence that the state, through its laws, should seek to make men good, coercively if need be.[84] But there is a crucial difference which must be observed here. Augustine's understanding of the necessity of coercion is more than, and other than, a mere substitution for the ancients' view of social habituation as a young individual's initially unchosen education to virtuous habits. To the ancients, the habitual discipline of performing virtuous acts was underpinned by these being understood as the means to a knowable and known human good. Rarely did the ancients envisage such acculturation to moral norms to be achieved through pain infliction throughout the whole of one's mature life. Augustine, by contrast, saw pain, psychological and physical, to be an essential and enduring condition of living a fallen, human life. Punishment constrains us to obey the law; it does not re-educate us. We are ineducable without grace which is Christ, the interior teacher. And in this life, should one be granted an indwelling grace, it serves the purpose of helping a man to maintain a fortitude in the face of continuing suffering. There is no ancient who would agree with this so wholeheartedly and without condition. Aristotle's brutish man and the depraved and vicious man, were not universal norms around which ancient ethical and political discourses, or constitutional legislation, were to be constructed. Nor were they the models of the kinds of characters *for* which men constructed their ethical politics. The brutish man and the depraved and vicious man would, however, astonishingly, become the norms for some early-modern political theorists who came to assume that all men are 'knaves'.

Augustine's views, then, are more easily understood as deriving from but crucially breaking with the ancient philosophical tradition. His views and his world mark the beginning of Western Europe's very distinctive trajectory towards its future. If we read Augustine's thought from within the context, social and intellectual, that helped to produce it, we can allow Augustine to be a late fourth, early fifth-century North African Roman, with a standard and unquestioned view about hierarchies of power from the emperor, the army, government, oligarchies, families, masters and servants. Augustine's vision implies a power of ordinary citizens as almost non-existent. Neither Plato, Aristotle nor Cicero had such an empty notion of citizenship, but Augustine's late imperial, North African world was not theirs. He believed without question that women should serve men, children their parents, animals their human owners, because this is just in itself and he read scripture as confirming this. Like any other thinker embedded in a culture who, none the less, seeks to describe norms of behaviour that might transcend that culture, he was perhaps the most outspoken about the degree to which no one escapes, in this world, that kind of verbal and social conditioning to which he is *subjected* by authorities. This observation travelled well beyond his own times.

---

82   See N. Wood, '*Populares* and *Circumcelliones*: the vocabulary of "fallen man" in Cicero and St Augustine', *History of Political Thought* 7 (1986), pp. 33–51.
83   See M. Foucault, *Discipline and Punish: the birth of the prison*, trans. A. Sheridan (Harmondsworth, 1979); French original 1975.
84   See Aristotle, *Nicomachean Ethics* 1103b3–5.

He accepted the Roman conditions of dominance and subservience as the very frame-work of all authority, even if he was also aware of abuses of power. Likewise, in arguing that the church on earth is a mixed community of the predestined saved and the damned, he believed that as an authority, backed by its interpretation of scripture which is never wrong, it still had a certain ability to discern when to take severe measures, even against what might be the innocent. Rist thinks this means his faith in church authority over-came his theory of human nature, where he insisted that no man could reach the truth unaided. But in having said that he would not accept the gospel if the church did not authenticate it,[85] Augustine did not intend to set up two incommensurable theories, of authority on the one hand and of human nature on the other. Rather, his argument is that humans always do and indeed must operate within authority, and authority is nec-essarily of a certain kind in this life precisely because of what human nature now is. The focus on our need to have *faith in authority* is the consequence of his reading of human nature in history.

It may be argued that it was, perhaps, far easier for this to be the view of a late Roman Christian than it could ever be for Western liberals, including those who happen to be religious. But Western history would show that this late Roman Christian's views of human nature and its need for absolute, conventional authority, especially in disruptive times, travelled remarkably well, especially into the early-modern era with its crises of authority. His analysis of the tragedy of our reason as instrumental, operating to secure our conflicting desires, would be revived as a great early-modern insight, but where the trag-edy would be turned into the first positive step in our realization of freedom, leading us to construct the state. His conception of the 'state', defined as that which has the monopoly of coercive force, regardless of any attempts to secure its foundations in moral principle, when revived and given a positive gloss, would also be considered a remarkably modern insight. Many of Augustine's mature views would consciously be revived and redeployed, notably in the Protestant Reformation and the Catholic response to it in the Counter-Reformation, to which the modern state owes so much, theoretically and practically.

In contemporary philosophical terms one may well say that Augustine lacked the conceptual resources to distinguish omnipotence from arbitrariness in God, so that he compromises the workings of the power of God's love, itself a peculiarly Augustinian divine attribute.[86] But Augustine's position was precisely that it was not possible for us to resolve what appears to be an unintelligible limitation of the love of God, with what we do understand of the circumscribed conditions of men who require authority. We sim-ply know that we need the authority to appear arbitrary even if, from some other per-spective, it is not. This was a tension that many later thinkers in the Western tradition thought similarly incapable of resolution. They would sustain the argument that, from the human perspective, God's will *is* arbitrary and his church assumes a similar guise. Later political theories, applying this to the state, and especially to those regimes in which the civil sovereign was also the head of the church, would adopt this notion of absolute sovereign authority, 'the artificial man with an artificial eternity of life', with its unchallenged right to define the terms of justice in order to secure peace, with alacrity.[87]

85   See *Against the letter of the Foundation (Contra epistulam fundamenti)* 5.6. In *Contra Faustum Manichaeum* 25.1.5,6 he said: 'ego vero evangelio non crederem nisi me catholicae ecclesiae commoveret auctoritas'.
86   Rist, *Augustine: ancient thought baptized*, p. 286.
87   See Hobbes, *Leviathan* I, xviii–xix.

Hence, Augustine's views on the irreconcilable nature of God's omnipotence and arbitrariness, and what follows from this, his views on coercion and authority, far from being perverse derivatives of antiquity or a strange, fifth-century 'period piece', were to contribute fundamentally to Europe's future.

When, in later Western European history, religious toleration was to emerge, it did so almost as an unintended by-product of an argument that was much more pervasive: the toleration of different religious beliefs was first to be conditioned by ensuring that such beliefs did not spill out into the public forum to disturb the peace established and maintained by the coercive sovereign authority or the civil magistrate.[88] The later arguments for religious toleration were, for the most part, not based on a notion of plural truths which individuals were entitled to hold both in conscience and in public, but rather on the idea that so long as morality was based on a higher theism, then plural religious beliefs could be shown not to threaten civil peace, and their commercial utility would be evidence of their service to the 'state'.[89]

Augustine insisted that the 'state' is, for religious purposes, neutral. How was he, then, able to approve of the intervention of secular authority in religious controversies so that it could exercise coercion? Markus has argued that Augustine's acceptance of state intervention was of a pragmatic nature. For him, necessary, arbitrary constraints by authority were themselves determined by secular as well as pastoral necessities, as he saw them. Augustine continued to speak of Christian rulers and officials as owing service to God in their public capacity. On this view, when they act in the interest of the church, they do so as Christians who happen to have secular authority rather than as officials of the Christian Roman state. Undoubtedly, he believed that the church uses the 'state' to further Christian interests, as these are interpreted by church authority, in order to establish at least the conditions for the morally good act to be performed upon the reception of grace. But once again, pastoral expediency was part of a larger conviction, based on his understanding of men's need to believe in authority. The need for curbing violence and the sins that men will commit remained paramount.

Hence, Augustine unwittingly erected the signposts to what would emerge as the much later theory of the modern state, despite his intention, in his own times, to liberate the church from its dependence on the secular framework. This liberation would itself lead, much further down the road, to a kind of secularization of history and politics. The civil community, for the Christian, is to be used in its maintenance of peace and order, serving simply to protect men from the invasion of chaos. But on this view, the sphere of politics still belongs irrevocably to the realm infected with sin. It is for this reason that absolute authority alone can constrain the psychology of the state of nature and, even with man's reason somewhat weakened, he can still at least agree to go this far and transfer to an absolute sovereign authority his original free will to do as he wishes. Such a man sees politics as the only reasonable solution to the tragedy of his human condition. Hobbes took over the same insight.

88 See *A History of Political Thought* volume 2, chapter 4 on Marsilius of Padua. The seventeenth-century debate in England on toleration reconfigures the Augustinian position, not least in attempting to distinguish the spheres of jurisdiction of civil government and religious matters. For the Augustinian view see Samuel Parker (1670) *A Discourse on the Ecclesiastical Polity*.

89 H. R. Guggisberg, 'The Secular State of the Reformation Period and the Beginnings of the Debate on Religious Toleration', in J. Coleman, ed., *The Individual in Political Theory and Practice* (Oxford, 1996) and the views of R. Ashcraft in Coleman, *Against the State*, ch. 6. Even for Locke in his *Letter on Toleration* there is no toleration for atheists.

But prior to the seventeenth century, most notably during the twelfth to the early sixteenth centuries, the message of this older Augustine of the *City of God* would be modified, not least by a reading of his more enthusiastically philosophical earlier works, by a range of developing indigenous practices of self-governing communities, and by selective interpretations of alternative ancient and early Christian voices. It is to the varied traditions of medieval political theory and practice that we will turn in volume 2.

Bibliography

In a work of this kind which, in two volumes, treats over two thousand years of political theorizing in different historical contexts, the bibliographies can only be selective. Below I have especially listed works in which a variety of approaches to our subject may be found and which refer to further extensive and more specialist bibliographies.

Achard, G. *Pratique, rhétorique et idéologie politique dans les discours 'optimates' de Cicéron* (Leiden, 1981).

Ackrill, J. L. 'Aristotle on *Eudaimonia*', in A. O. Rorty, ed., *Essays on Aristotle's Ethics* (Berkeley, 1980), pp. 15–33.

Adams, J. D. *The Populus of Augustine and Jerome: a study in the patristic sense of community* (New Haven, CN, 1971).

Adkins, A. W. H. *Moral Values and Political Behaviour in Ancient Greece* (New York, 1972).

Anderson, P. *Passages from Antiquity to Feudalism* (London, 1974).

Andrew, E. 'Equality of Opportunity as the Noble Lie', *History of Political Thought* 10 (1989), pp. 577–95.

Annas, J. 'Plato and Common Morality', *The Classical Quarterly* 28 (1978), pp. 437–51.

Annas, J. *An Introduction to Plato's Republic* (Oxford, 1981).

Annas, J. 'Cicero on Stoic Moral Philosophy and Private Property', in M. Griffin and J. Barnes, eds, *Philosophia Togata* I (Oxford, 1989), pp. 151–73.

Ashcraft, R. *Revolutionary Politics and Locke's Two Treatises of Government* (Princeton, NJ, 1986).

Astin, A. E. *Scipio Aemilianus* (Oxford, 1967).

Austin, M. and P. Vidal-Naquet *Economic and Social History of Ancient Greece* (London, 1977).

Badian, E. *Roman Imperialism in the Late Republic*, 2nd edn (Oxford, 1968).

Baldwin, A. and S. Hutton, eds, *Platonism and the English Imagination* (Cambridge, 1994).

Bambrough, R., ed., *New Essays on Plato and Aristotle* (London, 1965).

Barker, E. *The Political Thought of Plato and Aristotle* (London, 1918).

Barnes, J. *Aristotle's Posterior Analytics* (Oxford, 1975).

Barnes, J. *Aristotle* (Oxford, 1982).

Barnes, J. and M. Griffin, eds, *Philosophia Togata* II (Oxford, 1997).

Barnes, J., M. Schofield and R. Sorabji, eds, *Articles on Aristotle, 1: Science* (London, 1975), 2: *Ethics and Politics* (London, 1977).

Benestad, J. B., ed., *Classical Christianity and the Political Order: reflections on the theological–political problem* (Lanham, MD, 1996).

Benson, H. H., ed., *Essays on the Philosophy of Socrates* (Oxford, 1992).

Berent, M. '*Stasis*, or the Greek Invention of Politics', *History of Political Thought* 19 (1998), pp. 331–62.

Berlin, I. *Four Essays on Liberty* (Oxford, 1969), pp. 118–72.

Bernal, M. *Black Athena, the Afroasiatic Roots of Classical Civilization,* vol. 1 (London, 1987).

Le Blond, J. M. *Logique et méthode chez Aristote* (Paris, 1939).

Bloom, A. *The Closing of the American Mind* (London, 1988).

Bluestone, N. H. *Women and the Ideal Society: Plato's Republic and modern myths of gender* (Oxford, 1987).

Boardman, J., J. Griffin and O. Murray, eds, *The Oxford History of Greece and the Hellenistic World* (Oxford, 1991).

Bodeüs, R. *The Political Dimensions of Aristotle's Ethics,* trans. J. E. Garrett (Albany, NY, 1993).

Boes, J. *La Philosophie et l'action dans la corréspondance de Cicéron* (Nancy, 1990).

Bonner, G. '*Quid imperatori cum ecclesia?* St Augustine on history and society', *Augustinian Studies* 2 (1971), pp. 231–51.

Bonner, G. *St Augustine of Hippo: life and controversies* (Norwich, 1986).

Bonner, G. *God's Decree and Man's Destiny: studies on the thought of Augustine of Hippo* (Variorum, 1987).

Bostock, D. *Plato's Phaedo* (Oxford, 1986).

Bostock, D. *Plato's Theaetetus* (Oxford, 1988).

Boucher, D. *Texts in Context: revisionist methods for studying the history of political thought* (Dordrecht, 1985).

Brickhouse, T. and N. Smith, *Socrates on Trial* (Oxford, 1989).

Brown, P. *Augustine of Hippo: a biography* (London, 1967).

Brown, P. *Religion and Society in the Age of St Augustine* (London, 1972).

Brown, P. *The Body and Society: men, women and sexual renunciation in early Christianity* (London, 1989).

Brunt, P. A. *Social Conflicts in the Roman Republic* (London, 1971).

Brunt, P. A. 'Cicero's *Officium* in the Civil War', *Journal of Roman Studies* 76 (1986).

Brunt, P. A., ed., *The Fall of the Roman Republic and Other Essays* (Oxford, 1988).

Brunt, P. A. 'Philosophy and Roman Religion', in M. Griffin and J. Barnes, eds, *Philosophia Togata I* (Oxford, 1989), pp. 174–98.

Brunt, P. A. *Studies in Greek History and Thought* (Oxford, 1993).

Bryant, J. M. 'Enlightenment Psychology and Political Reaction in Plato's Social Philosophy: an ideological contradiction?', *History of Political Thought* 11 (1990), pp. 377–95.

Bryant, J. M. *Moral Codes and Social Structure in Ancient Greece: a sociology of Greek ethics from Homer to the Epicureans and Stoics* (Albany, NY, 1996).

Burchell, D. 'Civic Personae: MacIntyre, Cicero and Moral Personality', *History of Political Thought* 19 (1998), pp. 101–19.

Burnell, P. J. 'The Status of Politics in St Augustine's *City of God*', *History of Political Thought* 12 (1992), pp. 13–29.

Burnell, P. J. 'The Problem of Service to Unjust Regimes in Augustine's *City of God*', *Journal of the History of Ideas* 54 (1993), pp. 177–88.

Burnet, J. 'The Socratic Doctrine of the Soul', *Proceedings of the British Academy* 7 (1915–16), pp. 235–59.

Burnet, J. *Plato's Phaedo* (Oxford, 1967).

Burns, J. H., ed., *The Cambridge History of Medieval Political Thought c. 350–c. 1450* (Cambridge, 1988).

Burnyeat, M. 'Protagoras and Self-refutation in Plato's *Theaetetus*', in S. Everson, ed., *Companions to Ancient Thought, 1: Epistemology* (Cambridge, 1990), pp. 39–59.

Calvo, F. *Cercare l'uomo: Socrate, Platone, Aristotele* (Genoa, 1989).

Campbell, B. 'Paradigms Lost: classical Athenian politics in modern myth', *History of Political Thought* 10 (1989).

Campbell, B. 'The Epic Hero as Politico', *History of Political Thought* 11 (1990), pp. 189–212.

Carter, L. B. *The Quiet Athenian* (Oxford, 1986).

Cartledge, P. 'Spartan Wives: liberation or licence?', *Classical Quarterly* 31 (1981), pp. 84–105.

Cartledge, P. *Agesilaus and the Crisis of Sparta* (London, 1987).

Cartledge, P. *The Greeks* (Oxford, 1993).

Cartledge, P. 'Comparatively Equal', in J. Ober and C. Hedrick, eds, *Demokratia: a conversation on democracies, ancient and modern* (Princeton, NJ, 1996), pp. 175–85.

Cartledge, P., P. Millett and S. Todd, eds, *Nomos: essays in Athenian law, politics and society* (Cambridge, 1990).

Chadwick, H. *Augustine* (Oxford, 1986).

Charles, D. 'Aristotle on Names and their Signification', in S. Everson, ed., *Companions to Ancient Thought, 3: Language* (Cambridge, 1994), pp. 37–73.

Chroust, H.-H. *Aristotle: new light on his life and on some of his lost works*, 2 vols (London, 1973).

Cohen, D. *Law, Violence and Community in Classical Athens* (Cambridge, 1995).

Coleman, J. *Ancient and Medieval Memories: studies in the reconstruction of the past* (Cambridge, 1992).

Coleman, J. 'The Uses of the Past (14th–16th Centuries): the invention of a collective history and its implications for cultural participation', in A. Rigney and D. Fokkema, eds, *Cultural Participation: trends since the Middle Ages*, Utrecht Publications in General and Comparative Literature 31 (Amsterdam, 1993), pp. 21–37.

Coleman, J. 'The Christian Platonism of St Augustine', in A. Baldwin and S. Hutton, eds, *Platonism and the English Imagination* (Cambridge, 1994).

Coleman, J. *Against the State: studies in sedition and rebellion* (Harmondsworth, [1990] 1995).

Coleman, J. 'St Augustine: Christian political thought at the end of the Roman empire', in B. Redhead, ed., *Plato to Nato: Studies in Political Thought* (Harmondsworth, 1995 [1988]), pp. 45–60.

Colish, M. *The Stoic Tradition from Antiquity to the Early Middle Ages*, 2 vols (Leiden, 1985).

Collingwood, R. G. *The Idea of History* (Oxford, 1946).

Connolly, W. E. *The Augustinian Imperative: a reflection on the politics of morality* (London, 1993).

Coole, D. *Women in Political Theory: from ancient mysogyny to contemporary feminism* (Hemel Hempstead, 1988).

Cornford, F. M. *Plato's Commonwealth* (Cambridge, 1935); reprinted as *The Unwritten Philosophy* (Cambridge, 1950).

Cornford, F. M. *Plato's Theory of Knowledge* (London, 1935).

Cottingham, J. *A Descartes Dictionary* (Oxford, 1993).

Crawford, M. *The Roman Republic* (London, 1978).

Creed, J. 'Aristotle's Middle Constitution', *Polis* 8 (1989), pp. 2–27.

Cumming, R. D. *Human Nature and History: a study of the development of liberal political thought* (Chicago, 1969).

Davies, J. K. *Wealth and Power of Wealth in Classical Athens* (New York, 1981).

Davies, J. K. *Democracy and Classical Greece*, 2nd edn (London, 1993).

Deane, H. *The Political and Social Ideas of St Augustine* (New York, 1963).

Dent, N. J. H. 'Common, Civic and Platonic Justice in the *Republic*', *Polis* 5 (1983), pp. 1–33.

Diels, H. and W. Kranz, *Die Fragmente der Vorsokratiker*, 6th edn (Berlin, 1952).

Dodds, E. R. *The Greeks and the Irrational* (Berkeley, 1951).

Dodds, E. R. *Pagan and Christian in an Age of Anxiety* (Cambridge, 1965).

Douglas, A. E. *Cicero* (Oxford, 1968).

Dover, K. 'Freedom of the Intellectual in Greek Society' (1975), reprinted in K. Dover, *The Greeks and Their Legacy: collected papers* (Oxford, 1988).

Düring, I. *Aristotle in the Ancient Biographical Tradition* (Göteborg, 1957).

Düring, I. *Aristoteles* (Heidelberg, 1966).

Düring, I. and G. E. L. Owen, eds, *Aristotle and Plato in Mid-Fourth Century* (Göteborg, 1960).

Duvernoy, J.-F. *La Pensée de Machiavel* (Paris, 1974).

Duvall, T. and P. Dotson, 'Political Participation and *Eudaimonia* in Aristotle's Politics', *History of*

Political Thought 19 (1998), pp. 21–34.

Elshtain, J. B. *Public Man Private Woman: women in social and political thought* (Princeton, NJ, 1981).

Engberg-Pedersen, T. 'Stoic Philosophy and the Concept of the Person', in C. Gill, ed., *The Person and the Human Mind: issues in ancient and modern philosophy* (Oxford, 1990), pp. 109–135.

Erskine, A. *The Hellenistic Stoa* (Ithaca, NY, 1990).

Euben, P., ed., *Greek Tragedy and Political Theory* (Berkeley, 1986).

Euben, J. P. *The Tragedy of Political Theory: the road not taken* (Princeton, NJ, 1990).

Evans, J. D. G *Aristotle's Concept of Dialectic* (Cambridge, 1977).

Everson, S., ed., *Companions to Ancient Thought, 1: Epistemology* (Cambridge, 1990).

Everson, S., ed., *Companions to Ancient Thought, 2: Psychology* (Cambridge, 1991).

Everson, S., ed., *Companions to Ancient Thought, 3: Language* (Cambridge, 1994).

Ferrary, J.-L. 'Cicéron entre Polybe et Platon', *Journal of Roman Studies* 74 (1984), pp. 87–98.

Figgis, J. N. *The Political Aspects of St Augustine's City of God* (London, 1921).

Fine, G. 'Knowledge and Belief in *Republic* v–vii', in S. Everson, ed., *Companions to Ancient Thought, 1: Epistemology* (Cambridge, 1990), pp. 85–115.

Finley, M. I. *The Ancient Economy* (London, 1973).

Finley, M. I. *Democracy, Ancient and Modern* (London, 1973).

Finley, M. I., ed., *Studies in Roman Property* (Cambridge, 1976).

Finley, M. I. *Ancient Slavery and Modern Ideology* (New York, 1980).

Finley, M. I. *Politics in the Ancient World* (Cambridge, 1983).

Fortenbaugh, W. W. and P. Steinmetz, eds, *Cicero's Knowledge of the Peripatos* (New Brunswick, NJ, 1989).

Fortin, E. L. 'Political Idealism and Christianity', in J. B. Benestad, ed., *Classical Christianity and the Political Order: reflections on the theological–political problem* (Lanham, MD, 1996).

Foucault, M. *Discipline and Punish: the birth of the prison*, trans. A. Sheridan (Harmondsworth, 1979).

Foucault, M. 'The Ethics of the Concern for the Self as a Practice of Freedom', in P. Rabinow, ed., *Michel Foucault: Ethics* (London, 1997), pp. 281–302.

Fox, R. L. *Pagans and Christians in the Mediterranean World: from the second century AD to the conversion of Constantine* (Harmondsworth, 1986).

Frier, B. W. *The Rise of the Roman Jurists* (Princeton, 1985).

Furley, D. *The Greek Cosmologists* (Cambridge, 1987).

Furley, D. and R. E. Allen, eds, *Studies in Presocratic Philosophy*, 2 vols (London, 1970–5).

Gadamer, H.-G. *The Idea of the Good in Platonic–Aristotelian Philosophy*, trans. P. C. Smith (New Haven, CN, 1986).

Gadamer, H.-G. *Truth and Method*, 2nd revd edn, trans. J. Weinsheimer and D. G. Marshall (London, 1989).

Gagarin, M. and P. Woodruff, eds, *Early Greek Political Thought from Homer to the Sophists* (Cambridge, 1995).

Gellner, E. *Reason and Culture: the historical role of rationality and rationalism* (Oxford, 1992).

Gill, C. 'Personhood and Personality: the four *personae* theory in Cicero's *De officiis* I', *Oxford Studies in Ancient Philosophy* 6 (1988), pp. 169–99.

Gill, C. 'The Character–Personality Distinction', in C. Pelling, ed., *Characterization and Individuality in Greek Literature* (Oxford, 1990).

Gill, C., ed., *The Person and the Human Mind: issues in ancient and modern philosophy* (Oxford, 1990).

Gill, C. *Personality in Greek Epic, Tragedy and Philosophy* (Oxford, 1996).

Giorgini, G. *La Città e il Tiranno, il concetto di tirannide nella grecia del vii–iv secolo a.c.* (Milan, 1993).

Gottschalk, H. B. 'Continuity and Change in Aristotelianism', in R. Sorabji, ed., *Aristotle and After* (London, 1997), pp. 109–15.

Grayeff, F. *Aristotle and his School* (London, 1974).

Griffin, M. 'Philosophy, Politics and Politicians at Rome', in M. Griffin and J. Barnes, eds,

Philosophia Togata I (Oxford, 1989), pp. 1–37.

Griffin, M. and J. Barnes, eds, *Philosophia Togata I* (Oxford, 1989).

Guggisberg, H. R. 'The Secular State of the Reformation Period and the Beginnings of the Debate on Religious Toleration', in J. Coleman, ed., *The Individual in Political Theory and Practice* (Oxford, 1996).

Gunnell, J. G. 'Time and Interpretation: understanding concepts and conceptual change', *History of Political Thought* 19 (1998) pp. 641–58.

Guthrie, W. K. C. *A History of Greek Philosophy*, vol.1: *The Earlier Presocratics and the Pythagoreans* (Cambridge,1962); vol. 2: *The Presocratic Tradition from Parmenides to Democritus* (Cambridge, 1965); vol. 3: *The Fifth-century Enlightenment* (Cambridge, 1969); vol. 4: *Plato: the man and his dialogues, earlier period* (Cambridge, 1975); vol. 5: *The Later Plato and the Academy* (Cambridge, 1978); vol. 6: *Aristotle: an encounter* (Cambridge, 1981).

Guthrie, W. K. C. *The Sophists* (Cambridge, 1971).

Haase, W. and M. Reinhold, eds, *The Classical Tradition and the Americas* (Berlin and New York, 1994).

Habicht, C. *Cicero the Politician* (Baltimore, MD, 1990).

Hadot, P. *Philosophy as a Way of Life* (Oxford, 1995).

Hahm, D. E. 'Polybius' Applied Political Theory', in A. Laks and M. Schofield, eds, *Justice and Generosity: studies in Hellenistic social and political philosophy* (Cambridge, 1995), pp. 7–47.

Hansen, M. H. *The Sovereignty of the People's Court in the Fourth Century BC and the Public Action Against Constitutional Proposals* (Odense, 1974).

Hansen, M. H. *Eisangelia* (Odense, 1975).

Hansen, M. H. *The Athenian Assembly in the Age of Demosthenes* (Oxford, 1987)

Hansen, M. H. 'Was Athens a Democracy? Popular rule, liberty and equality in ancient and modern political thought', *Historisk-filosofiske Meddelelser* 59 (Copenhagen, 1989), pp. 3–47.

Hansen, M. H. *Athenian Democracy in the Age of Demosthenes: structure, principles and ideology* (Oxford, 1991).

Hegel, G. W. F. *Lectures on the Philosophy of World History,* trans. H. B. Nisbet, first draft, p. 21 (Cambridge, 1975).

Herrin, J. *The Formation of Christendom* (Oxford, 1987).

Hourani, G. 'Thrasymachus' Definition of Justice in Plato's *Republic*', *Phronesis* 7 (1962), pp. 110–20.

Hussey, E. 'The Beginnings of Epistemology: from Homer to Philolaus', in S. Everson, ed., *Companions to Ancient Thought, 1: Epistemology* (Cambridge, 1990).

Hussey, E. 'Thucydidean History and Democritean Theory', in P. Cartledge and F. D. Harvey, eds, *Crux: essays presented to G. E. M de Ste. Croix on his 75th birthday*; in *History of Political Thought* 6 (1985), pp. 118–38.

Inwood, B. *Ethics and Human Action in Early Stoicism* (Oxford, 1985).

Irwin, T. *Plato's Moral Theory: the early and middle dialogues* (Oxford, 1977).

Irwin, T. *Aristotle's First Principles* (Oxford, 1988).

Irwin, T. *A History of Western Philosophy, 1: Classical Thought* (Oxford, 1989).

Irwin, T. 'Aristotle's Philosophy of Mind', in S. Everson, ed., *Companions to Ancient Thought, 2: Psychology* (Cambridge, 1991), pp. 56–83.

Jaeger, W. *Studien zur Entstehungsgeschichte der Metaphysik des Aristoteles* (Berlin, 1912).

Jaeger, W. *Aristoteles: Grundlegung einer Geschichte seiner Entwicklung* (Berlin, 1923); translated as *Aristotle: fundamentals of the history of his development*, 2nd edn, trans. R. Robinson (Oxford, 1948).

Johnson, C. *Aristotle's Theory of the State* (London, 1990).

Kennedy, E. and S. Mendus, eds, *Women in Western Political Philosophy* (Brighton, 1987).

Kenny, A. *Will, Freedom and Power* (Oxford, 1975).

Kerferd, G. B. 'The Doctrine of Thrasymachus in Plato's *Republic*', *Durham University Journal* 40

(1947), pp.19–27.

Kerferd, G. B. 'Protagoras' Doctrine of Justice and Virtue in the *Protagoras* of Plato', *Journal of Hellenic Studies* 73 (1953), pp. 42–5.

Kerferd, G. B. *The Sophistic Movement* (Cambridge, 1981).

Keyt, D. and F. D. Miller, eds, *A Companion to Aristotle's Politics* (Oxford, 1991).

King, P., ed., *The History of Ideas: an introduction to method* (London, 1983).

Kirk, G. S. and J. E. Raven, *The Presocratic Philosophers* (Cambridge, 1957).

Kirwan, C. *Augustine* (London, 1989).

Klosko, G. 'Provisionality in Plato's Ideal State', *History of Political Thought* 5 (1984), pp.171–93.

Klosko, G. *The Development of Plato's Political Theory* (New York, 1986).

Klosko, G. 'Rational Persuasion in Plato's Political Theory', *History of Political Thought* 7 (1986), pp. 15–31.

Klosko, G. 'The "Straussian" Interpretation of Plato's *Republic*', *History of Political Thought* 7, (1986), pp. 275–93.

Klosko, G. 'Racism in Plato's *Republic*', *History of Political Thought* 12 (1991), pp. 1–13.

Knox, B. *The Oldest Dead White European Males and other reflections on the classics* (London, 1993).

Koselleck, R. *Futures Past: on the semantics of historical time,* trans. K. Tribe (Cambridge, MA, 1985).

Kraut, R. *Socrates and the State* (Princeton, NJ, 1984).

Kraut, R. *Aristotle on the Human Good* (Princeton, NJ, 1989).

Kraut, R., ed., *The Cambridge Companion to Plato* (Cambridge, 1992).

Lacey, W. K. and B. W. J. G. Wilson, *Res Publica: Roman politics and society according to Cicero* (Oxford, 1970).

Ladner, G. *The Idea of Reform* (Cambridge, MA, 1959).

Laks, A. and M. Schofield, eds, *Justice and Generosity: studies in Hellenistic social and political philosophy* (Cambridge, 1995).

Le Glay, M., J.–L. Voisin and Y. Le Bohec, *A History of Rome,* trans. A. Nevill (Oxford, 1996).

Lefkowitch, M. *Heroines and Hysterics* (London, 1981).

Lefkowitch, M. and M. Fant, *Women's Life in Greece and Rome* (London, 1982).

Lehmann, H. and M. Richter, eds, *The Meaning of Historical Terms and Concepts: new studies on Begriffsgeschichte*, German Historical Institute occasional paper, 15 (Washington, DC, 1996).

Lesses, G. 'Virtue and Fortune in Stoic Moral Philosophy', *Oxford Studies in Ancient Philosophy* 7 (1989), pp. 95–128.

Lintott, A. *Violence in Republican Rome* (Oxford, 1968).

Lintott, A. 'Cicero and Milo', *Journal of Roman Studies* 55 (1974), pp. 8–14.

Lintott, A. *Violence, Civil Strife and Revolution in the Classical City* (London, 1982).

Lintott, A. 'The Theory of the Mixed Constitution at Rome', in J. Barnes and M. Griffin, eds, *Philosophia Togata* II (Oxford, 1997), pp. 70–85.

Lloyd, G. *The Man of Reason: 'male' and 'female in western philosophy*, 2nd edn (London, 1993).

Lloyd, G. E. R. *Magic, Reason and Experience: studies in the origins and development of Greek science* (Cambridge, 1979).

Lloyd-Jones, H. *The Justice of Zeus*, 2nd edn (Berkeley, 1983).

Long, A. A. 'Representation and the Self in Stoicism', in S. Everson, ed., *Companions to Ancient Thought 2, Psychology* (Cambridge, 1991), pp. 111–20.

Long, A. A. 'Cicero's Politics in De Officiis', in A. Laks and M. Schofield, eds, *Justice and Generosity* (Cambridge, 1995), pp. 213–40.

Long, A. A. 'Stoic Philosophers on Persons, Property Ownership and Community', in R. Sorabji, ed., *Aristotle and After* (London, 1997), pp. 13–31.

Long, A. A. and D. N. Sedley, *The Hellenistic Philosophers* (Cambridge, 1987).

Loraux, N. *The Invention of Athens: the funeral oration in the classical city* (Cambridge, MA, 1986).

Lord, C. and D. K. O'Connor, eds, *Essays on the Foundations of Aristotelian Political Science* (Berkeley,

1991).

Lovibond, S. 'Plato's Theory of Mind', in S. Everson, ed., *Companions to Ancient Thought, 2: Psychology* (Cambridge, 1991), pp. 35–55.

MacDowell, D. M. *Spartan Law* (Edinburgh, 1986).

McGlew, J. F. *Tyranny and Political Culture in Ancient Greece* (Ithaca, NY, 1993).

MacIntyre, A. 'The Indispensability of Political Theory', in D. Miller and L. Siedentop, eds, *The Nature of Political Theory* (Oxford, 1983).

MacMullen, R. *Christianizing the Roman Empire* (New Haven, CN, 1984).

Markus, R. A. *Saeculum: history and society in the theology of St Augustine* (Cambridge, 1970; revd 1989).

Markus, R. A., ed., *Augustine: a collection of critical essays* (Garden City, NY, 1972).

Markus, R. A. *The End of Ancient Christianity* (Cambridge, 1990).

Meier, C. *Die Rolle des Krieges im klassischen Athen* (Munich, 1991).

Miller, D. et al., eds, *The Blackwell Encyclopaedia of Political Thought* (Oxford, 1987).

Miller, D. and L. Siedentop, eds, *The Nature of Political Theory* (Oxford, 1983).

Miller, F. *Nature, Justice and Rights in Aristotle's Politics* (Oxford, 1995).

Miller, J. 'Aristotle's Paradox of Monarchy and the Biographical Tradition', *History of Political Thought* 19 (1998).

Millett, P. 'Patronage and its Avoidance in Classical Athens', in A. Wallace-Hadrill, ed., *Patronage in Ancient Society* (London, 1989), pp. 15–47.

Mion, M. 'Athenian Democracy: politicization and constitutional restraints', *History of Political Thought* 7 (1986), pp. 219–38.

Mitchell, T. N. *Cicero, the Ascending Years* (New Haven, CN, 1979).

Mitchell, T. N. *Cicero the Senior Statesman* (New Haven, CN, 1991).

Momigliano, A., ed., *The Conflict between Paganism and Christianity in the Fourth Century* (Oxford, 1963).

Momigliano, A. *Alien Wisdom: the limits of Hellenization* (Cambridge, 1975).

Mommsen, T. *History of Rome*, vol. 2, trans. W. Dickson (London, 1868).

Mommsen, T. *Romische Geschichte*, 7th edn, vol. 2 (Leipzig, 1854–6).

Moraux, P. *Les Listes anciennes des ouvrages d'Aristote* (Louvain, 1951).

Morrow, G. *Plato's Epistles: a translation with critical essays and notes* (Indianapolis, 1962).

Mourelatos, A. P. D., ed., *The Pre-Socratics* (New York, 1974).

Mulgan, R. G. *Aristotle's Political Theory: an introduction for students of political theory* (Oxford, 1977).

Mulgan, R. G. 'Liberty in Ancient Greece', in Z. Pelczynski and J. Gray, eds, *Conceptions of Liberty in Political Philosophy* (Oxford, 1984), pp. 7–26.

Mulgan, R. G. 'Aristotle and the Political Role of Women', *History of Political Thought* 15 (1994), pp. 179–202.

Murray, O. *Early Greece* (London, 1980).

Newman, W. L. *The Politics of Aristotle* (New York, 1973 [1887–1902]).

Nicgorski, W. 'Cicero's Focus: from the best regime to the model statesman', *Political Theory* 19 (1991), pp. 230–51.

Nichols, M. *Socrates and the Political Community: an ancient debate* (Albany, NY, 1987).

Nicholson, P. 'Unravelling Thrasymachus' Arguments in the *Republic*', *Phronesis* 19 (1974), pp. 210–32.

Nicholson, P. and G. B. Kerferd, 'Protagoras on Pre-political Man: an exchange', *Polis* 4 (1982), pp. 18–28.

Nicolet, C., ed., *Demokratia et aristokratia* (Paris, 1983).

Nozick, R. *Anarchy, State and Utopia* (New York, 1974).

Nussbaum, M. 'Shame, Separateness and Political Unity: Aristotle's criticism of Plato', in A. O. Rorty, ed., *Essays on Aristotle's Ethics* (Berkeley, 1980), pp. 395–435.

Nussbaum, M. 'Saving Aristotle's Appearances', in M. Schofield and M. Nussbaum, eds, *Language and Logos* (Cambridge, 1982), pp. 267–93.

Nussbaum, M. *The Fragility of Goodness, Luck and Ethics in Greek Tragedy and Philosophy* (Cambridge, 1986).

Nussbaum, M. 'The Discernment of Perception: an Aristotelian conception of private and public rationality', in *Love's Knowledge* (Oxford, 1992), pp. 54–105.

Nussbaum, M. *The Therapy of Desire: theory and practice in Hellenistic ethics* (Princeton, 1994).

Nussbaum, M. and A. O. Rorty, eds, *Essays on Aristotle's De Anima* (Oxford, 1992).

Ober, J. *Mass and Elite in Democratic Athens: rhetoric, ideology and the power of the people* (Princeton, NJ, 1989).

Ober, J. and C. Hedrick, eds, *Demokratia: a conversation on democracies, ancient and modern* (Princeton, NJ, 1996).

Okin, S. M. *Women in Western Political Thought* (Princeton, NJ, 1978).

Osborne, R. *Demos: the discovery of classical Attica* (Cambridge, 1985).

Ostwald, M. *From Popular Sovereignty to the Sovereignty of Law: law, society and politics in fifth-century Athens* (Berkeley, 1986).

Owen, G. E. L. 'Tithenai ta Phainomena', in J. Barnes, M. Schofield and R. Sorabji, eds, *Articles on Aristotle, 1: Science* (London, 1975), pp. 113–26.

Pagden, A., ed., *The Languages of Political Theory in Early-Modern Europe* (Cambridge, 1987).

Pagels, E. *The Gnostic Gospels* (Harmondsworth, 1979).

Pateman, C. *The Sexual Contract* (Cambridge, 1988).

Pelczynski, Z. and J. Gray, eds, *Conceptions of Liberty in Political Philosophy* (Oxford, 1984).

Pelling, C., ed., *Characterization and Individuality in Greek Literature* (Oxford, 1990).

Penner, T. 'Socrates and the Early Dialogues', in R. Kraut, ed., *The Cambridge Companion to Plato* (Cambridge, 1992), pp. 121–69.

Pocock, J. G. A. 'The Concept of Language and the *Métier d'historien*: some considerations on practice', in A. Pagden, ed., *The Languages of Political Theory in Early-Modern Europe* (Cambridge, 1987), pp. 19–40.

Pomeroy, S. *Goddesses, Whores, Wives and Slaves* (New York, 1975).

Popper, K. *The Open Society and its Enemies*, vol. 1: *The Spell of Plato* (London, 1945).

Popper, K. *The Poverty of Historicism* (London, 1957).

Popper, K. *Unended Quest: an intellectual autobiography* (London, 1976).

Popper, K. *Objective Knowledge: an evolutionary approach*, revd edn (Oxford, 1979).

Powell, J. G. F., ed., *Cicero the Philosopher* (Oxford, 1995).

Raaflaub, K. *Dignitatis contentio* (Munich, 1974).

Rahe, P. A. *Republics, Ancient and Modern: classical republicanism and the American Revolution* (Chapel Hill, NC, 1992).

Rankin, H. D. *Plato and the Individual* (London, 1964).

Rawls, J. *A Theory of Justice* (Oxford, 1972).

Rawson, E. 'The Ciceronian Aristocracy and its Properties', in M. I. Finley, ed., *Studies in Roman Property* (Cambridge, 1976), pp. 85–102..

Rawson, E. D. *Cicero: a portrait* (London, 1975 and reprints).

Rawson, E. D. *Intellectual Life in the Late Roman Republic* (London, 1985).

Redhead, B., ed., *Plato to Nato: Studies in Political Thought* (Harmondsworth, 1995).

Reeve, C. D. C. *Practices of Reason: Aristotle's Nicomachean Ethics* (Oxford, 1992).

Reeve, C. D. C. *Socrates in the Apology: an essay on Plato's Apology of Socrates* (Indianapolis, 1996).

Rhodes, P. J., trans. and ed., *Constitution of the Athenians* (Harmondsworth, 1984).

Rhodes, P. J. *The Greek City-States: a source book* (London, 1986).

Rhodes, P. J. *A Commentary on the Aristotelian Athenaion Politeia with Addenda* (Oxford, 1993).

Rice, D. 'Plato on Force: the conflict between his psychology and political temperance in the *Republic*', *History of Political Thought* 10 (1989), pp. 565–76.

Richard, C. J. *The Founders and the Classics:Greece, Rome and the American Enlightenment* (Cambridge, MA, 1994).

Richter, M. 'Reconstructing the History of Political Languages: Pocock, Skinner and the Geschichtliche Grundbegriffe', *History and Theory* 29 (1990), pp. 38–70.

Richter, M. *The History of Political and Social Concepts: a critical introduction* (Oxford, 1995).

Rigney, A. and D. Fokkema, eds, *Cultural Participation: trends since the Middle Ages*, Utrecht Publications in General and Comparative Literature 31 (Amsterdam, 1993).

Rist, J. M. 'Augustine on Free Will and Predestination', *Journal of Theological Studies* n.s. 20 (1969).

Rist, J. M. *Augustine: ancient thought baptized* (Cambridge, 1994).

Roberts, J. T. *Athens on Trial: the antidemocratic tradition in western thought* (Princeton, 1994).

Rorty, A. O., ed., *Essays on Aristotle's Ethics* (Berkeley, 1980).

Rorty, A. O. 'The Pace of Contemplation in Aristotle's *N. Ethics*', in A. O. Rorty, ed., *Essays On Aristotle's Ethics* (Berkeley, 1980), pp. 375–94.

Rorty, R., J. Schneewind and Q. Skinner, eds, *Philosophy in History* (Cambridge, 1984).

Rowbotham, S. *Women, Resistance and Revolution* (Harmondsworth, 1972).

Rowe, C. J. 'Plato on the Sophists as Teachers of Virtue', *History of Political Thought* 4 (1983), pp. 409–27.

de Ste Croix, G. E. M. *The Class Struggle in the Ancient World* (London, 1981).

Salkever, S. G. *Finding the Mean: theory and practice in Aristotle's political philosophy* (Princeton, NJ, 1990).

Salkever, S. G. 'Aristotle's Social Science', in C. Lord and D. K. O'Connor, eds, *Essays on the Foundations of Aristotelian Political Science* (Berkeley, 1991), pp. 11–48.

Sandbach, F. H. *The Stoics*, 2nd edn (London, 1989).

Saxonhouse, A. 'Philosopher and Female in the Political Thought of Plato', *Political Theory* 4 (1976), pp. 195–212.

Saxonhouse, A. *Women in the History of Political Thought: ancient Greece to Machiavelli* (New York, 1985).

Schofield, M. and M. Nussbaum, eds, *Language and Logos* (Cambridge, 1982).

Sellers, M. N. S. *American Republicanism: Roman ideology in the US Constitution* (London, 1994).

Shanley, M. L. and C. Pateman, eds, *Feminist Interpretations and Political Theory* (Oxford, 1991).

Sharples, R. W. 'Cicero's Republic and Greek Political Theory', *Polis* 5 (1986), pp. 30–50.

Shotter, D. *The Fall of the Roman Republic* (London, 1994).

Siemsen, T. 'Thrasymachus' Challenge', *History of Political Thought* 8 (1987), pp.1–19.

Sinclair, R. K. *Democracy and Participation in Athens* (Cambridge, 1988).

Skemp, J. B. 'How Political is the *Republic*?', *History of Political Thought* 1 (1980), pp. 1–7.

Skinner, Q. Parts II and IV in J. Tully, ed., *Meaning and Context: Quentin Skinner and his critics* (Oxford, 1988).

Sorabji, R. 'Body and Soul in Aristotle', *Philosophy* 49 (1974), pp. 63–89.

Sorabji, R. 'Intentionality and Physiological Processes: Aristotle's theory of sense-perception', in M. Nussbaum and A. O. Rorty, eds, *Essays on Aristotle's De Anima* (Oxford, 1992), pp. 195–226.

Sorabji, R., ed., *Aristotle and After* (London, 1997).

Sprague, R. K. *The Older Sophists: a complete translation* (Columbia, SC, 1972).

Springborg, P. 'The Contractual State: reflections on orientalism and despotism', *History of Political Thought* 8 (1987) pp. 395–434.

Springborg, P. *Royal Persons, Patriarchal Monarchy and the Feminine Principle* (London, 1990).

Stalley, R. F. *An Introduction to Plato's Laws* (Oxford, 1983).

Shanley, M. L. and C. Pateman, eds, *Feminist Interpretations and Political Theory* (Oxford, 1991).

Stead, C. 'Augustine's Philosophy of Being', in G. Vesey, ed., *The Philosophy in Christianity* (Cambridge, 1989), pp. 71–84.

Stead, C. *Philosophy in Christian Antiquity* (Cambridge, 1994).

Stein, P. 'Roman Law', in D. Miller et al., eds, *The Blackwell Encyclopaedia of Political Thought* (Oxford, 1987), pp. 446–9.

Stock, B. *Augustine the Reader: meditation, self-knowledge and the ethics of interpretation* (Cambridge, MA, 1996).

Stockton, D. *Cicero, a Political Biography* (Oxford, 1971).

Syme, R. *The Roman Revolution* (Oxford, 1960).

Taplin, O. *Greek Tragedy in Action* (Berkeley, 1978).

Taylor, C. C. W. 'Plato's Totalitarianism', *Polis* 5 (1986), pp. 4–29.

Taylor, C. C. W. 'Aristotle's Epistemology', in S. Everson, ed., *Companions to Ancient Thought, 1: Epistemology* (Cambridge, 1990), pp. 116–42.

Tigerstedt, E. N. *The Legend of Sparta in Classical Antiquity*, 3 vols (Stockholm and Uppsala, 1965–78).

Tigerstedt, E. N. *Interpreting Plato* (Stockholm, 1977).

Treggiari, S. *Roman Freedmen during the Late Republic* (Oxford, 1969).

Tuck, R. 'The Contribution of History', in R. E. Goodin and P. Pettit, eds, *A Companion to Political Philosophy* (Oxford, 1993), pp. 72–89.

Tully, J., ed., *Meaning and Context: Quentin Skinner and his critics* (Oxford, 1988).

Untersteiner, M. *Sofisti, Testimonianze e frammenti* (Florence, 1949–67).

Vernant, J.-P. *Myth and Society in Ancient Greece*, trans. J. Lloyd (London, 1980).

Vernant, J.-P. *Mythe et pensée chez les Grecs, études de psychologie historique*, vol. 1 (Paris, 1981).

Vernant, J.-P. *Mortality and Immortality* (London, 1991).

Vesey, G., ed., *The Philosophy in Christianity* (Cambridge, 1989).

Veyne, P. *Bread and Circuses: historical sociology and political pluralism*, trans. B. Pearce (London, 1990).

Vlastos, G. 'Solonian Justice', *Classical Philology* 41 (1946), pp. 65–83.

Vlastos, G. 'Degrees of Reality in Plato', in R. Bambrough, ed., *New Essays on Plato and Aristotle* (London, 1965), pp. 1–20.

Vlastos, G., ed., *Plato: a collection of critical essays*, 2 vols (New York, 1971).

Vlastos, G. *Socrates: ironist and moral philosopher* (Cambridge, 1991).

Vlastos, G. *Plato's Universe* (Oxford, 1995).

Walbank, F. W. *Polybius* (Berkeley, 1972).

Walbank, F. W. *The Hellenistic World*, 3rd revd edn (London, 1992).

Wallace-Hadrill, A., ed., *Patronage in Ancient Society* (London, 1990).

Wallach, J. R. 'Socratic Citizenship', *History of Political Thought* 9 (1988), pp. 393–414.

Watson, A. *The Roman Private Law around 200 BC* (Edinburgh, 1971).

Weber, M. *Economy and Society* [*Wirtschaft und Gesellschaft*], 2 vols, ed. and trans. G. Roth and C. Wittich (Berkeley, 1978).

West, M. L., ed., *Iambi et elegi graeci*, 2 vols (Oxford, 1971–2).

Whelan, F. G. 'Socrates and the "Meddlesomeness" of the Athenians', *History of Political Thought* 4 (1983), pp. 1–30.

Whittaker, M. *Jews and Christians: Graeco-Roman views*, Cambridge Commentaries on Writings of the Jewish and Christian World 200 BC to AD 200 (Cambridge, 1984).

Whitehead, D. *The Demes of Attica* (Princeton, NJ, 1986).

Wiedemann, T. *Greek and Roman Slavery* (Baltimore, 1981).

Wiedemann, T. *Cicero and the End of the Roman Republic* (London, 1994).

Wilamowitz-Moellendorff, U. von *Platon*, 2 vols (Berlin, 1920).

Wilkinson, L. P. *Letters of Cicero: a selection in translation* (London, 1966).

Williams, B. *Ethics and the Limits of Philosophy* (London, 1985).

Williamson, R. *Jews in the Hellenistic World: Philo*, Cambridge Commentaries on Writings of the Jewish and Christian World 200 BC to AD 200, vol. 1, pt 2 (Cambridge, 1989).

Winspear, A. *The Genesis of Plato's Thought* (New York, 1940).

Wirszubski, C. *Libertas as a Political Idea at Rome During the Late Republic and Early Principate* (Cambridge, 1950).

Wiseman, T. P. *New Men in the Roman Senate 139 BC–AD 14* (Oxford, 1971).

Wiseman, T. P., ed., *Roman Political Life 90 BC–AD 69* (Exeter, 1985).

Wollheim, R. *The Thread of Life* (Cambridge, 1984).

Wood, E. and N. Wood, *Class Ideology and Ancient Political Theory* (Oxford, 1978).

Wood, E. M. *Peasant–Citizen and Slave: the foundations of Athenian democracy* (London, 1988).

Wood, N. '*Populares* and *Circumcelliones*: the vocabulary of "fallen man" in Cicero and St Augustine', *History of Political Thought* 7 (1986), pp. 33–51.

Wood, N. *Cicero's Social and Political Thought* (Berkeley, 1988).

Yack, B. 'A Reinterpretation of Aristotle's Political Teleology', *History of Political Thought* 12 (1991), pp. 15–34.

Zetzel, J. E. G., ed., *Cicero, De re publica, selections*, Cambrige Greek and Latin Classics (Cambridge, 1995).

Index